# ANALYTIC TECHNIQUES IN URBAN AND REGIONAL PLANNING

# ANALYTIC TECHNIQUES IN URBAN AND REGIONAL PLANNING

## With Applications in Public Administration and Affairs

John W. Dickey

Thomas M. Watts

*Division of Environmental and Urban Systems*
*College of Architecture and Urban Studies*
*Virginia Polytechnic Institute and State University*

McGraw-Hill Book Company

New York St. Louis San Francisco Auckland Bogotá Düsseldorf
Johannesburg London Madrid Mexico Montreal New Delhi
Panama Paris São Paulo Singapore Sydney Tokyo Toronto

ANALYTIC TECHNIQUES IN URBAN AND REGIONAL PLANNING



1 2 3 4 5 6 7 8 9 0 D O D O 7 8 3 2 1 0 9 8

This book was set in Times Roman. The editor was Rose Ciofalo and the production supervisor was Milton J. Heiberg.
R. R. Donnelley & Sons Company was printer and binder.

**Library of Congress Cataloging in Publication Data**

Dickey, John W date
Analytic techniques in urban and regional planning.

Includes index.
1. City planning—Mathematical models. 2. Regional planning—Mathematical models. 3. Operations research. 4. System analysis. I. Watts, Thomas M., joint author. II. Title.
HT166.D546 309.2'12'0151 78-4652
ISBN 0-07-016798-2

To Our Students and Secretaries

# CONTENTS

APPENDIX

## A Introductory Mathematics 419



## B Fortran Computer Programming 437



## C APL 460



## D Example Data Sets 487

# PREFACE

Many of the students presently entering urban and regional planning, urban affairs, public administration, and related fields lack the basic systematic tools necessary to cope with the types of problems presented by our modern urban society. Their training often leaves them at best skeptical of such techniques and at times even in the position of rejecting solutions based on analytic methods simply because they do not understand how the corresponding solutions were derived. At the end of their formal training they are loaded with theories of urban and regional growth, urban form, and regional settlement patterns. Yet they lack the necessary skills to test these various theories or to make rational policy choices based on them. As a result the mistakes at times have been costly. City and regional officials faced with critical day-to-day decisions regarding fiscal problems, racial tensions, housing dilemmas, and the like have tended to recognize this lack of training and have turned in increasing numbers to MBAs and systems analysts who in general are well versed in these quantitative skills.

The purpose of this book is to introduce junior, senior, and first-year graduate students in planning, urban studies, public administration, and related fields to basic statistical, operations research, and other systematic intuition-aiding methods which may be used to help forecast, analyze, and solve some of our present urban and regional problems. The book provides a basic introduction to many of the most useful techniques in these areas. The intent of the book is not to make the student an expert in each technique but rather to provide him with both (1) an understanding of the range and potential uses of the various methods which are available as well as (2) a framework for improving rational decision making. By presenting the range of potential uses of these techniques the book also provides the motivation for encouraging students to take additional courses in associated areas.

A few other books are available which touch on similar subject matters. However, in general they tend to be (1) unrelated to urban and regional studies,

(2) much narrower in the breadth of topics covered, and (3) so sophisticated that they simply enhance the students skepticism of the entire area. This book attempts to fill that gap by introducing many of the most recent and advanced techniques within a framework of urban problem solving, emphasizing the purpose and use of the method rather than its mathematical neatness.

The book is organized such that it may be used as a text for either a one semester introductory, survey course or as the major text for a two-semester sequence. If used in a two-semester sequence, it is suggested that the first semester cover Chapters 1 to 11. The first chapter is particularly important because it provides both a systematic framework for the remainder and, in conjunction with Chapter 11, an opportunity for the student to find out how easy it is to develop some fairly complex models of urban and regional systems. The remaining chapters in this group provide an introduction to basic descriptive and inferential statistics, including some discussion of probability, sampling, and hypothesis testing. The student would also be introduced to simple and multiple regression.

The second semester, Chapters 12 to 24, could cover systematic intuition-aiding techniques, such as Delphi, Probe, gaming, and morphological analysis. It could also involve solution formulation techniques such as linear, goal, and dynamic programming (PERT).

For use in a one-semester survey course, the coverage would include chapters 1 to 9 on basic descriptive and inferential statistics. The instructor could then choose from the remaining chapters those techniques which he felt most appropriate for the backgrounds of each particular class.

While the book does build on earlier chapters, particularly the first nine, each chapter constitutes a self-contained unit and may be taught as such for students with an elementary statistical background. Each begins with an introduction to the technique being discussed and then provides an example of its use within an urban and/or regional problem-solving setting. The necessary mathematical basis of the technique is presented briefly and in most instances a second example, based on an actual study, is provided. Problems and references to both theoretical and applied work are provided at the end of each chapter. Almost all of the problems have been tested in our classes over the last six years so that, hopefully, they are as instructive as possible.

The text is structured such that it may be easily integrated with the SPSS (*Statistical Package for the Social Sciences*)† and other computer software‡ for the various techniques taught within the overall framework. Data sets for such application are contained in Appendix D. The last problem in many chapters has been created to enable the student to use some of this "real world" data so that he can develop some facility in understanding and interpreting results that come from each technique. The size of the data set also makes it possible for

† N. H. Nie, et al., "Statistical Package for the Social Sciences" 2d ed., McGraw-Hill, New York, 1975.

‡ See, for example, B. E. Gillett, "Introduction to Operations Research," McGraw-Hill, New York, 1976, for some valuable FORTRAN programs of various operations research techniques.

the instructor to take samples for each student, who then can compare results with others. In addition, Appendix G contains "synthesis" problems—ones that lead to consideration of, and choice between, several techniques. Working with these, the student can start to see comparative advantages and disadvantages of each technique. These problems should be particularly helpful since space limitations have not permitted us to discuss the relative benefits and disbenefits of each technique.

In writing the book we have felt particularly discouraged by the lack of consistent and systematic notation in the various professional fields. So, with some disregard for common (but not consistent) symbology, we have attempted to overcome this problem. While we make no claims about having solved this major dilema, we do feel that we have improved the situation. For instance, random variables (those having an associated probability distribution) all are presented in capital arabic letters. Constants are in lower case letters, population parameters in lower case Greek letters, and so on. While most students probably will not appreciate this effort, we hope the instructor will be better able to draw together the wide variety of techniques presented here into a common package.

As a final technical note, we would like to apologize for using so many examples "close to home." These include those not only related to our nearby geography, but also to our previous publications. Of course, we are victims of our own experience, and certainly would encourage each instructor to develop his own more relevant illustrations.

Naturally a book of this type takes a great variety of efforts and personal considerations. So we find it difficult to face the fact that we cannot give proper thanks to everyone who in some way contributed to this endeavor.

First we wish to mention that Dr. John P. Ross, an economist in our group at Virginia Tech, had intended to help write the book. However, he was drawn away by an attractive offer to work for a year with the Advisory Commission on Intergovernmental Relations. His would have been a valuable contribution.

Particular thanks go to Mike Dove, who ran many of the computer programs needed to produce the results shown in this book. Mike was also one of hundreds of students who "suffered" under various error-filled drafts of chapters and somehow still kept their patience and, in fact, helped us enormously in unearthing and correcting all kinds of mistakes. We think their educational experience was more aggravating but also more instructive.

How can we thank the secretaries? Pat Wade, Christy Seaborn, and Louise Oliver typed incessantly and with very few complaints, despite the fact that many pages required the exasperating process of changing typeballs and correcting over two previous corrections. A special thanks goes to Jacksie Dickerson, who labored over this book almost as much as she did over her two children.

Final thanks go to the reviewers, who gave good constructive criticism. And we certainly owe much to Mrs. Rose Ciofalo, the Editor of Advanced Publishing of McGraw-Hill, who made our joint efforts very pleasant and efficient.

John W. Dickey
Thomas M. Watts

CHAPTER
# ONE
# SYSTEMS AND MODELS

The first step in trying to understand and analyze the people, physical entities, and activities that comprise an urban area or region is to view them as an interrelated set of components or factors. In a broad sense, this means that the important social, political, economic, and artificial and natural environmental elements must be identified along with the relevant physical and behavioral connections between them. It then is possible in many situations to analyze these elements and connections quantitatively to establish more precise relationships and to use these to help determine how to guide the system toward a more desirable state. This approach generally is referred to as *systems analysis*. This initial chapter will focus on some elementary definitions, characteristics, and principles relevant to systems analysis and then indicate how the major types of technique discussed in this book fall within this framework. Given this start, in succeeding chapters we will be able to investigate some of the more detailed methods needed to devise a broad and yet somewhat thorough systems approach to various urban and regional problems.

## 1-1 SYSTEMS

**Definition** A *system* can be defined as an organized or connected group or set of objects, principles, or ideas related by some common function or belief.

Usually we think of a system as a grouping of personnel, practices, and programs that works toward common objectives. In this respect a system represents the real world in the context of the objectives or functions a person or group might have in mind. Urban, economic, nervous, and weapon systems may have some elements in common, but the importance of these to the objectives or the functions of each system differs substantially. Relationships among entities usually are quite large in number, and we shall have to restrict our interest to those that have a relevant effect on the main objectives under study; i.e., from an infinite number of relationships we have to select that set most important to the problem at hand and ignore the trivial and unessential ones.

Any system can be divided into subsystems. The reasons for doing so are mainly simplicity of understanding and ease in manipulation. The idea is to break the system into parts that display a certain richness of intercommunication. This is done to the point where the subsystem elements are clearly identified and their main interactions reduced to a manageable number. For example, in an urban system we may identify various functional subsystems such as transportation, land use, welfare, water supply, and education. The objectives or functions of each of these may differ somewhat, but they do have characteristics in common and they do represent more manageable parts of the entire urban system.

## 1-2 MODELS OF SYSTEMS

Practically all systems are exceedingly complex, especially those social systems of concern to urban and regional analysts. To be able to work with such complicated entities, we must make use of *models*, or abstractions of real-world systems, and treat them as if they were reality. The purpose of a model thus is to simplify a system so that one can comprehend and deal with it. The success of our interventions into the real world consequently depends on the simplicity, adequacy, and validity of the associated model. It is *simple* if one can easily understand and make decisions with it, it is *adequate* if it contains all the important elements, and it is *valid* if the elements are interrelated correctly.

If a model is a poor one, programs based on it are likely to fail. Hence, it is imperative that analysts check the adequacy and validity of their models, be they explicit and mathematical or just implicit. They usually must balance simplicity and adequacy, for these two attributes are often incompatible. Also, since the world is changing so rapidly, models that once were acceptable may no longer be adequate or valid. A frequent problem some people have in dealing with a system is their failure to recognize that their view of it constitutes a mental model, which is in need of frequent reexamination and possible updating. Checking consequently is a continual process.

When a public official develops a program to affect some factor in the environment, he or she does so on the basis of some model of the type and interrelations of the various elements in the corresponding real-world system. While the model may not be well specified in his or her mind, it almost always exists in some form. Consider the simple model in Fig. 1-1 related to housing supply and demand in part of a city. In it there are four elements and six connections between

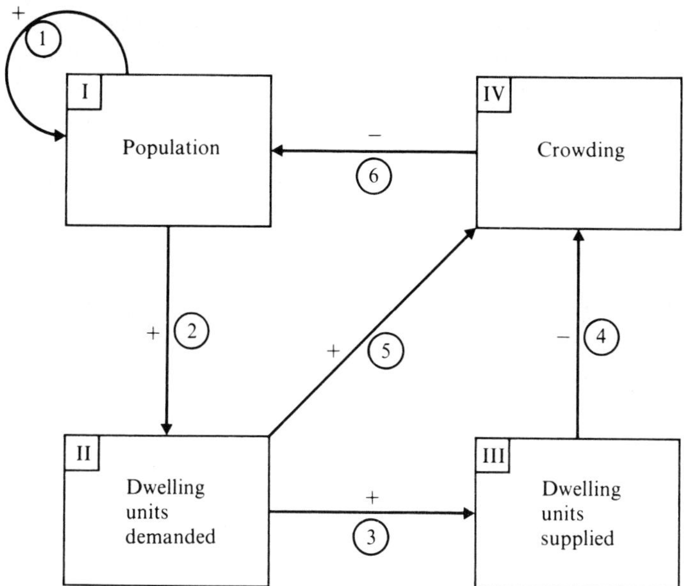


**Figure 1-1** A simple model of housing supply and demand in part of a city.

them, and we might imagine our public official using this model, perhaps subconsciously, for making decisions on, say, a housing renewal program.

The official might know that the population level in the area is affected by two main forces: positively (+ sign) by its own internal growth (from births and deaths, with the former predominating: link 1) and negatively (– sign) by crowding in the existing dwelling units (link 6). Further, any population increase creates a positive demand for housing (link 2), which in turn influences private developers and public agencies to supply more units (link 3). The ratio between demand and supply then determines the amount of crowding that will occur (links 4 and 5). As before, the crowding affects the population level, as people move to other parts of the urban area where dwellings are more readily available.

This simple "head" model is of value because it highlights several important points in gauging the impacts of the proposed housing renewal program. First, it shows that there are factors or forces, beyond the control of any particular agency or group, that could influence the outcome of its decisions. In Fig. 1-1 these factors are exemplified by births and deaths in the population (link 1), which obviously affect the population level and thus the demand for housing as well as the supply, crowding, and again the population. The model thus shows that it is possible that a local initiative in provision of housing could be swamped by a large increase in the natural growth of population.

Second, the model shows that there often are several linkages between factors or elements, each one of which should be considered in an analysis. In Fig. 1-1 the population level is influenced through three linkages: I to I (link 1); I to II to IV to I (links 2, 5, and 6); and I to II to III to IV to I (links 2, 3, 4, and 6). Hence, if more housing is provided by the city (in element III), the immediate impact might be to reduce crowding (link 4), but this may eventually increase population (link 6), which will grow on itself (link 1) and thereby cause a greater demand (link 2) and resultant increased crowding (link 5), and need for more units (link 3). Hence, in the long term, if each set of linkages in Fig. 1-1 is not considered, the unforeseen result from a program to provide more housing units may be increased crowding.

The model further shows, however, that the potential for such a result depends heavily both on the actual strength of relationships between the factors and on their growth (or decline) rates over time. If the birth and death rates represented by link 1 are very small, for instance, population will not grow rapidly on itself, creating a lowered demand for housing (link 2), and therefore less crowding (link 5).

## 1-3 PRINCIPLES OF SYSTEMS

Each of the three points suggested above relate to a major consideration in the modeling and analysis of systems. First, most real-world systems are *open*, i.e., most elements, factors, or events in the real world are connected to a large number and wide variety of other elements, factors, or events. These connections often are so numerous, particularly if they include all the external or *exogenous* forces that could influence a particular factor (e.g., births and deaths on the population, as in link 1 of Fig. 1-1), that it is almost impossible to take them all into account: hence the reason why we need models as abstractions of the important elements and interrelationships in a real-world system.

A model by this definition represents a *closed* system, since it can include only a few of the many factors and connections inherent in the corresponding real-world situation.† But here we might suggest a second common definition of a *closed* system: one in which there are no exogenous factors, i.e., ones *not* influenced by any other factor being considered. The relationships in Fig. 1-1 are an example of a closed system under this second definition. Each factor is affected by at least one other factor. This makes them all *endogenous*. If, however, we were to drop the connection between, say, crowding and population (link 6), the latter factor would become *exogenous:* it would be affecting other elements (in this case the dwelling units demanded) but would not be *affected by* any others. In this book we will adopt the latter definition of a closed system. From a modeler's point of view it is desirable not to have exogenous variables, since these must be forecast separately and externally. On the other hand, it is usually impossible to specify a completely closed system, the world being what it is.

† An electric watch probably is one of the few real-world examples of a closed system, although it also could be influenced by other factors such as heat, vibration, and the like.

A second consideration in systems analysis concerns the likely positive or negative impacts of a set of alternate linkages like those discussed in the previous section. As a *rough* indicator, if there is an odd number of negative signs in a given set of linkages, the impact will be negative. An even number will lead to a positive impact. For example, for the three linkages from the population back to itself in Fig. 1-1 we have the links and corresponding signs:

| | |
|---|---|
| 1 | + |
| 2, 5, 6 | + + − |
| 2, 3, 4, 6 | + + − − |

The first set (of one link) has zero (an even number of) minus signs, so we would expect an overall positive relationship to population. The second set has one minus sign and the third set two, and hence negative and positive influences, respectively, on population.

The third consideration in analyzing a system is identifying the means by which growth or decline can take place, particularly over time. The levels of the various elements, factors, or events in a system generally would change as indicated in Fig. 1-2. Again using the situation modeled in Fig. 1-1 as an illustration, suppose that in 1960 the study area had a population of 5000 contained in 1000 housing units (initial conditions, stage I). These figures also represent the starting levels (or states or conditions) in stage II. Information about them is

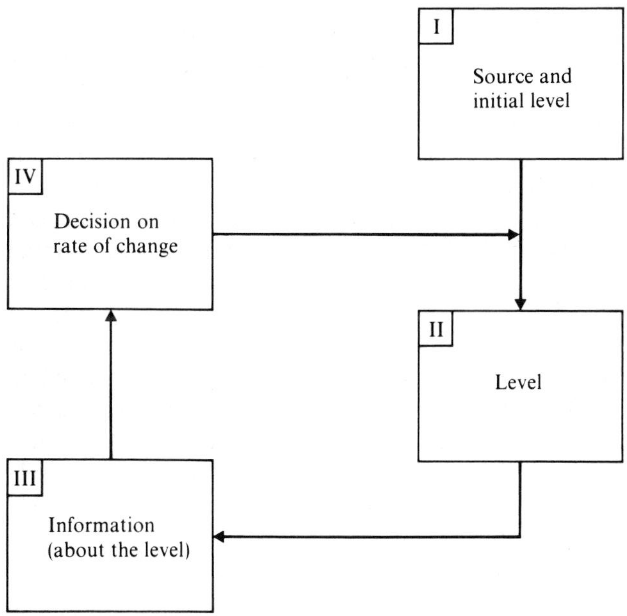


**Figure 1-2** General process of system change.

brought to the attention of the local city council (stage III), which feels that a crowding ratio of 5.0 (5000 people to 1000 units) is too great. They subsequently decide (stage IV) to have more subsidized units built in the area, i.e., to change the *rate* at which dwelling units will be constructed there in, say, the next year. After that year has passed, this decision results in an increase of perhaps 200 units, bringing the total (level) to 1200 (stage II). Assuming that the population has not changed, the crowding ratio now stands at 5000/1200 = 4.17. Many council members, after seeing this information (stage III), still feel the ratio is somewhat too high, but decide (stage IV) to add only, say, 100 units the following year, as financial resources are tight. This brings the new ratio (level) to 5000/1300 = 3.85 (stage II). And so the process continues over time.

Given these three major considerations in systems analysis, we now can proceed to specify a set of principles of systems,† as displayed in Table 1-1. These principles can be illustrated, again using the housing supply and demand model portrayed in Fig. 1-1. First, if we know the levels of the population, demand, supply, and crowding variables, we certainly would know the "condition" of the system. Second, we see that these levels depend on rate changes (actions) made by a variety of decision makers. The population level, for example, depends on (1) the rate at which people are born or die and (2) their decisions to move in or out

**Table 1-1 Principles of systems**

*Levels* (conditions, states)
- Completely describe the condition of the system
- Are the results of decisions, i.e., rate changes
- Can be computed as a function of:
  - (*a*) Previous levels of the same variable
  - (*b*) Other levels
  - (*c*) Rate changes
  - (*d*) Length of the time interval (since the last computation)

*Rates* (decisions, actions, plans, policy statements)
- Completely describe how a "stream" of decisions is generated
- Are based on levels in the system
- Can be computed as a function of:
  - (*a*) Goal (desired) levels
  - (*b*) Actual levels
  - (*c*) The discrepancies between goal and actual levels
  - (*d*) The decisions to be taken based on the above discrepancies

*Initial conditions*
- Are the levels at the point in time or space when the model of the system is "started up"
- Are the coefficients, exponents, and other parameters which are assumed constant in the model

† These are based on the discussion by Forrester in Ref. 1-2.

depending on the level of crowding. The population level thus is a function of (1) the previous year's level, (2) the rate of change in population over the year, and (3) the length of time period being considered—here taken to be one year.

Looking now at the principles concerned with rates, we find that all decisions (and thus rates) are based, either directly or indirectly, on goals. The decision by a couple to increase the population, for instance, might result from either the anticipation of future happiness that a child may bring or the anticipation of the present happiness the production process may bring. In either case, the action taken to increase the rate of production (from 0 to 1 or more per year) depends on the desired goal of additional children, the observed level of a too-small family, the obvious discrepancy between the goal and observed level, and the decision that, given the discrepancy, effort would be made to increase the population level by one (or more). The result of this decision would thus most likely be a rate change of 1 for that time period.

Of course, the changes in levels and rates would have to start from some initial condition (e.g., the 5000 population level in 1960). The changes also would have to be governed by some *parameters*, i.e., factors thought to be constant during the whole process of system change. We might assume, for instance, that for every 1000 people in the area there would be 50 births per year† and that this ratio would hold constant no matter what the age or sex composition of the community.

Often it is desirable to try to find those rate changes which lead to levels (or other rates) that are optimal in some sense. In these situations we need an *objective function*, which shows (1) the *weights of importance* to be attached to each and every variable of concern and (2) the desire to minimize or maximize this function. In addition there may be *constraints* within which such optimization must take place.

Suppose in the previous example we were interested in minimizing crowding, i.e., the number of persons per dwelling unit. This could be done basically in two ways—by increasing the supply of dwelling units, $d_t$, or by decreasing the demand (in terms of population, $p_t$). Assuming that the first option is, say, 50 percent more desirable than the latter, we could specify an objective function for any time, $t$, as

$$\min z = -1.5d_t + 1.0p_t \tag{1-1}$$

where the minus sign in the first term indicates the opposite to minimization (i.e., maximization of dwelling units).

Suppose, further, that there are two constraints operative in our example situation:

† We are defining *rate* here as the *amount* of yearly change rather than in the more common sense as a fraction of some factor. For example, if we had 50 births/1000 people (usually referred to as the "birth rate") for 5000 people, the "rate" under our definition would be (50/1000)(5000) = 250 per year. Items commonly called the "birth rate" or "interest rate" we will denote here as the "birth-rate constant" or "interest-rate constant."

1. Population cannot fall below 4000; otherwise it will be difficult to support the economic and tax base of the community.
2. "Crowding" must remain above 2 persons per dwelling unit; otherwise developers will not be able to maintain a minimal return on investment incentive to further supply dwelling units.

The lines representing these constraints are displayed in Fig. 1-3. The optimum point is where these two intersect at $p_t = 4000$ and $d_t = 2000$. This gives an objective function value of

$$z = -1.5(2000) + 1.0(4000) = 1000$$

Any other feasible point, say $p_t = 8000$ and $d_t = 4000$, would give an undesirably higher value:

$$z = -1.5(4000) + 1.0(8000) = 2000$$

From these results we thus conclude that the community ought to be developing programs to try to stabilize its population at the 4000 lower limit and maintain the "crowding" at 2 persons per dwelling unit (if such is realistically possible).

## 1-4 METHODS IN THIS BOOK

The models and techniques presented in this book can be viewed in the context of systems analysis since they all relate either to the principles which guide the operation of a system or to the means for optimizing its important functions. Not all (in fact, very few) of these methods were originally intended to fit into this context, but the definitions, principles, and optimization procedures in systems

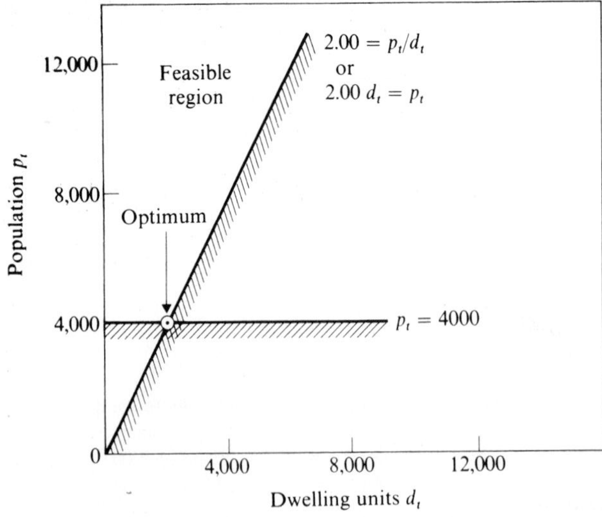


**Figure 1-3** Example of linear programming optimization.

analysis have proven to be so generalizable that with few exceptions it is easy to place each method within that framework.

Since any analysis tool must eventually be judged by the results it produces, this book starts with some of the basic statistical techniques for describing such results (i.e., data). Generally, most variables have a distribution of values and, within that distribution, a central tendency (average) as well as an average deviation from that point.

Because of the expense, in time and money, involved in collecting such data, the usual alternative is to take a *sample* from the overall *population* of values. Thus most of the system parameters (constants, coefficients, etc.) are *estimates* of the population-wide values based on the sample. It is at this point that an hypothesis-testing procedure is needed to help determine if the observed difference between, say, incomes in two areas really exists or whether it arises because the sample selected was somewhat unrepresentative (as it usually is) of the overall population. The second part of the book therefore deals with sampling and hypothesis testing.

In the next part we turn to the development of statistical models. These usually take the form of a regression relationship which, as exemplified in Fig. 1-4, is a curve that fits as closely as possible to a set of data. The resultant function subsequently can be employed to help make estimates of future values of the dependent ($Y$) variable given a certain value of the independent ($X$). Establishing relationships such as that in Fig. 1-4 becomes a complicated procedure when several interrelated dependent and independent variables are involved and when the influence of one or more variables on the others changes over time.

Because of the complexity of these statistical techniques and because they must rely on historical information which often may not be either available or indicative of the future, researchers have developed what we refer to in the next section of the book as *intuition-aiding* techniques. These are perhaps best exemplified by Delphi, a procedure in which members of a committee, unknown to each other, are asked to make a forecast of a particular variable and also provide

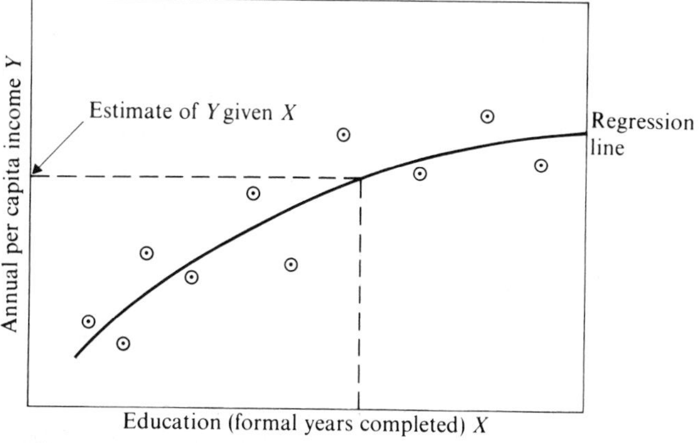


**Figure 1-4** Example regression relationship.

their corresponding rationale. The averages and ranges for all of the forecasts are then fed back to each member along with a summary of the various reasons. A second round of forecasts then is made, and so the process continues until the changes in forecasts become relatively small. Through techniques like this, the experience and judgmental intuition of various experts can be brought to bear on a problem without putting them in a compromising social situation like that usually engendered in the traditional committee.

The final part of the book deals with entirely opposite situations where some of the most powerful mathematical tools can be applied, particularly in the solution-formulation process. In *mathematical programming* (not to be confused with computer programming), the analyst must specify a well-defined objective function along with relevant constraints. Then, as was seen in Fig. 1-3, an optimal solution can be found. This type of technique can be extremely powerful, as demonstrated by several industrial applications where over one million variables and several hundred thousand constraints have been employed. Even in the public sector, where objectives and constraints generally are not as clear-cut, such techniques can be useful in determining optimum levels of those variables that are quantifiable and in making more explicit the trade-offs required to help achieve suggested nonquantifiable benefits.

The context of the overall book is summarized in perhaps its simplest form in Fig. 1-5. Urban and regional analysts and decision makers generally are faced with a "problem" situation, i.e., one in which some goal-related variables are not at the desired level or rate. The crime rate may be too high or income too low, and so on. Their task is to invent policies which, in the face of (or in conjunction with) many factors over which they have no control (e.g., the weather, federal governmental regulations and funding, etc.), will alter the goal-related variables to a more desirable state.

To determine if the policy will have beneficial impacts, the analyst must develop a model of the relevant real-world system and trace the likely influence of the policy changes through this model to gauge the impacts they produce. In some cases statistical models of some sophistication can be employed to simulate the real-world system. In some of these cases it may even be possible to use mathema-

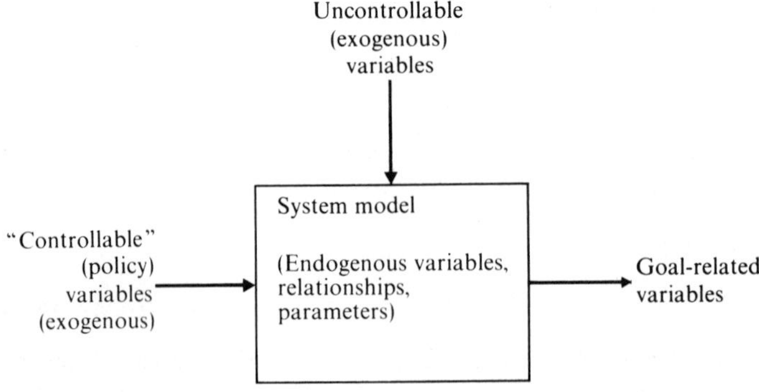


**Figure 1-5** Simplified conceptual framework of systems analysis.

tical programming techniques to find the levels or rates of policy variables that give optimal levels of the goal-related variables. In many other cases, however, it may only be possible to employ a "mental model" of the system and use intuition-aiding techniques to help make the forecast of impacts.

Each chapter in this book describes and gives illustrations of a type of model or technique that has been found useful in various aspects of the model-formulation and/or optimization process.

## PROBLEMS

**1-1** Fill in the blanks with the proper word(s) or number(s).

(*a*) A ________________ is an organized or connected group or set of objects, principles, or ideas related by some common function or belief.

(*b*) A good model is one that is ____________________, ____________________, and ____________________.

(*c*) External factors are also known as ____________________.

(*d*) A ____________________ system (second definition) is one in which there are no external factors.

(*e*) Any factor affected by at least one other factor in a system is called ____________________ ____________________.

(*f*) A ____________________ is a factor held constant during the process of system change.

(*g*) To ____________________ a model, you specify its parameters.

(*h*) In a complicated model, if the number of negative linkages from a variable $x$ to a variable $y$ is even, the impact of $x$ on $y$ is ____________________.

(*i*) When we wish to find an optimal solution, we need to have an ____________________ function along with ____________________ of ____________________ as well as ____________________ within which the optimization takes place.

(*j*) The general set of techniques used for optimization purposes is referred to as ____________________.

(*k*) In collecting data we usually have to take a ____________________ from the whole ____________________. We then make an ____________________, which hopefully is close to the true ____________________ value.

(*l*) Forecasting techniques that call upon the expertise and judgment of individuals or groups are known as ______________________________ techniques.

**1-2** The following verbal descriptions of influences on the average achievement test scores for a school district is an attempt to explain why average test scores in some districts are so much lower than in others. Draw a diagram of this verbal model.

The educational level of the adult population has a positive effect on income level of a school district. Also, higher educational level leads to higher verbal achievement of children because of better verbal atmosphere in homes with well-educated parents. The wealthier the district, the more it can afford to improve school quality. Also, wealthier parents can afford to give their children better verbal enriching experiences such as travel and summer camps. The higher the quality of a school, the higher the verbal achievement of its students. Rapid population growth leads to inadequate school facilities and overcrowded classrooms. Hence a large percentage increase in the population of a district lowers the quality of its schools.

**1-3** The following is a basic pollution model.

Pollution in a region is generated primarily by human activity in and near the region and is absorbed by the environment there. The pollution absorption rate depends upon the amount of pollution present in the environment at any given time. The more the pollution, the more its dissipation by the environment. If there were no pollution generated, the environment eventually would cleanse itself of all existing pollution. The pollution-generation rate is exogenously determined and is constant. Draw a diagram of this model.

**1-4** Go to the library and find an article or book describing a model related to some urban or regional problem of interest. In about 500 words discuss:

(*a*) The problem being studied
(*b*) The general model structure

Then identify:

(*c*) Exogenous and endogenous variables
(*d*) Parameters
(*e*) Rates, levels, and initial conditions
(*f*) Objective functions and constraints (if any)

Then discuss:

(*g*) The simplicity, adequacy, and validity of the model

**1-5** Working with your instructor and using a set of data from App. D as a guide, set up a conceptual model of a particular situation. In so doing, identify those items given in Prob. 1-4(*c*) to (*f*) above.

## REFERENCES

### Theory

1-1. Blalock, Jr., H. M. (Ed.): *Causal Models in the Social Sciences*, Aldine, Chicago, Ill., 1971.
1-2. Forrester, J. W.: *Principles of Systems*, Wright-Allen Press, Cambridge, Mass., 1968.
1-3. Goodman, R.: *Study Notes in System Dynamics*, Wright-Allen Press, Cambridge, Mass., 1974.
1-4. Reif, B.: *Models in Urban and Regional Planning*, Intertext Educational Publishers, Scranton, Pa., 1973.

### Applications

1-5. Ayres, R. U.: *Technological Forecasting and Long-Range Planning*, McGraw-Hill, New York, 1969.
1-6. Berry, B. J. L., and F. E. Horton: *Geographic Perspectives on Urban Systems*, Prentice-Hall, Englewood Cliffs, N.J., 1970.
1-7. Catanese, A. J.: *Scientific Methods of Urban Analysis*, University of Illinois Press, Urbana, Ill., 1972.

1-8. Cooley, W. W., and P. R. Lohnes: *Multivariate Data Analysis*, Wiley, New York, 1971.
1-9. Dickey, J. W. (senior author): *Metropolitan Transportation Planning*, McGraw-Hill, New York, 1975.
1-10. Dickey, J. W.: *Urban Land Use Models*, Council of Planning Librarians Exchange Bibliography 959, Monticello, Ill., January, 1976.
1-11. Guilford, J. P.: *Fundamentals of Statistics in Psychology and Education*, 4th ed., McGraw-Hill, New York, 1965.
1-12. Isard, W.: *Ecologic–Economic Analysis for Regional Development*, The Free Press, New York, 1972.
1-13. Krueckeberg, D. A., and A. L. Silvers: *Urban Planning Analysis*, Wiley, New York, 1974.
1-14. Martino, J. P.: *Technological Forecasting for Decisionmaking*, American-Elsevier, New York, 1972.
1-15. Mathematica, Inc., *A Guide to Models in Governmental Planning and Operations*, NTIS, PB-245 269, Springfield, Va., August, 1974.
1-16. Meyers, Jr., C. R.: *Regional Modeling Abstracts: A Bibliography of Regional Analysis*, vol. 5, Report ORNL-NSF-EP-54, Oak Ridge National Laboratory, Oak Ridge, Tenn., June, 1973.
1-17. Nie, N. H., et al.: *Statistical Package for the Social Sciences*, 2d ed., McGraw-Hill, New York, 1975.
1-18. Shubik, M., G. Brewer, and E. Savage: *The Literature of Gaming, Simulation, and Model Building: Index and Critical Abstracts*, Report R-620-ARPA, The Rand Corp., Santa Monica, Calif., June, 1972.
1-19. Wagner, H. M.: *Principles of Operations Research*, Prentice-Hall, Englewood Cliffs, N. J., 1969.

CHAPTER

# TWO

# MEASUREMENT, CENTRAL TENDENCY, AND DISPERSION

The first step in development and verification of most mathematical models, including the conceptual systems types presented in the preceding chapter, is to note the ways in which variables can be measured. It then is possible with a given set of data to establish the average level of a variable along with its variability. These characteristics are of great importance, for they give us a good description of our data set without overburdening us with large stacks of numbers. This is especially important in urban and regional studies where we may be dealing with literally millions of data items. In addition, the summary numbers generated are useful since they can be employed in various mathematical (i.e., logical) manipulations to help us to establish relationships between variables, find optimum levels of certain factors, and, more generally, determine levels of confidence in our analyses, especially those in which samples are employed. It is with these major advantages in mind that we begin here by discussing measurement, central tendency, and dispersion.

## 2-1 MEASUREMENT

An important point to be noted here initially is that measurement and quantification are not necessarily synonymous. The differences are illustrated by definitions provided by Guilford (Ref. 2-1), which we will adopt throughout this book:

**Definition** *Measurement* is the *assignment of numbers* to objects according to logically accepted rules.

**Definition** *Quantification* is the *ordering* of objects according to quantity or amount.

Since it is possible to assign a number to an object without ordering it (e.g., female = 1, male = 2), we can imagine unquantified measures such as "presence (or lack) of private action on an issue" or "level of government (local, regional, state, federal)." These types of measurement scales obviously are categorical in nature. They are referred to more specifically as *nominal* (or name) scales, being one of four general types:

1. *Nominal.* A set of names, categories, classes, groups, qualities, general responses, or the like
2. *Ordinal.* A set of objects in a particular order or rank
3. *Interval.* A set of numbers having a given, fixed interval size but no absolute zero point
4. *Ratio.* A set of numbers having a given, fixed interval size and an absolute zero point

Examples of ordinal scales are military ranks (1 = private, 2 = corporal, 3 = sergeant, etc.) and priority rankings given to projects (1 = first priority, 2 = second, etc.). Interval scales are not used frequently, but a common example is that of temperature, measured in either °F or °C. In these cases 0° does not represent the coldest possible (absolute zero) point. Hence, while it is correct to say that 5°C is 5°C colder than 10°C, it is not proper to say that 10°C is twice as warm as 5°C. Since absolute zero is −273°C, 10°C is really $(273 + 10)/(273 + 5) = 1.018$ times as warm as 5°C. On an interval scale, then, the ratio between numbers is often misleading.

Ratio-scaled variables, on the other hand, provide definition to multiplication and division by having an absolute zero point. Most physical characteristics are measured on these scales—length (feet, kilometers), time (seconds), weight (pounds, kilograms), and the like. Many economic, social, and political variables—income (dollars), crimes (number), and votes (number)—are also. Note that interval- or ratio-scaled variables may be either *discrete* (integer) or *continuous* in nature. The "number of automobiles passing a given point in a given time period" is a discrete or integer number (there is no such thing as 0.61 autos, except, perhaps, in a junk yard), while the time it takes to get a federal grant (for example, 2.3 years) is continuous (and often long).

Returning to the distinction between measurement and quantification, we see, as Aristotle suggested, that quantification can be thought of as the process of changing qualities into amounts. An interesting example of this is time. Before the advent of the clock many centuries ago, people probably puzzled over the problem of how to keep records on, say, the fastest racers. They were dealing with that mysterious, intangible quality known as "time." Today we have races quantified to the hundredth of a second. The quality, "passage of time," has evolved into the quantity or amount measured on a clock.†

A final differentiation to be made in this section is between *objective* and *subjective* measures. To illustrate: while there is no commonly accepted physical (objective) measure of the "beauty" of, say, a particular scene, we still can obtain people's feelings (subjective) about it. These could be on a scale from $-3$ for "very ugly" to $+3$ for "very beautiful." A 0 rating would indicate "blah," i.e., indifference—neither ugly nor beautiful. The difficulty with subjective measures, of course, is that the "scale" is in people's minds and therefore is inaccessible for calibration to standard readings. Yet in many situations a subjective scale may be the only one available to the analyst.

In many of the sections and chapters to follow, the procedures to be discussed will be divided according to the type of measurement scale. This occurs because different scales generally require somewhat different analysis techniques.

## 2-2 CENTRAL TENDENCY

The initial effort in the statistical analysis of any group of numbers usually is directed toward finding the average or central tendency in that group. This one number often tells us a great deal about the nature of the variable or factor being studied. First, it allows us to see where a particular person or group or geographic area stands in relation to the others. Second, it gives us this information in a very brief, parsimonious manner so that it can be transmitted easily to others (e.g., agency heads or citizen bodies).

There are three major indices of central tendency—the arithmetic *mean* (popularly called the "average"), the median, and the mode. These statistics (indices) are employed in different circumstances, depending mainly on the scale of measurement (nominal, ordinal, interval, or ratio) of the data being analyzed.

The arithmetic mean of a variable is simply the sum of all the observations on that variable divided by the number of observations. In equation form this becomes

$$\bar{X} = \frac{1}{n} \sum_{i=1}^{n} X_i \tag{2-1}$$

where $\bar{X}$ = arithmetic mean of variable $X$

$X_i$ = the value of observation $i$ for variable $X$

$n$ = the number of observations

† Note, however, that even today there are qualitative differences in equal quantities of time. For instance, transit planners know that 5 minutes spent waiting for a bus is much more aggravating to users than 5 minutes actually riding the bus.

**Table 2-1 Example data and statistics on owner-occupied housing unit value** (Census tract 2, Roanoke, Virginia, 1970)

| | Set 1 | | Set 2 | | Set 3 | | Set 4 | | |
|---|---|---|---|---|---|---|---|---|---|
| Index | Census block $i$ | Owner-occupied housing value $X_i$, \$ | Census block $i$ | Owner-occupied housing value $X_i$, \$ | Census block $i$ | Owner-occupied housing value $X_i$, \$ | Census block $i$ | Owner-occupied housing value $X_i$, \$ | For all blocks |
| | 1 | 11,100 | 6 | 15,200 | 11 | 11,900 | 16 | 7,800 | |
| | 2 | 13,900 | 7 | 12,300 | 12 | 12,400 | 17 | 11,300 | |
| | 3 | 11,300 | 8 | 11,100 | 13 | 11,500 | 18 | 12,100 | |
| | 4 | 7,900 | 9 | 11,300 | 14 | 11,300 | 19 | 9,800 | |
| | 5 | 12,400 | 10 | 14,100 | 15 | 11,800 | 20 | 10,300 | |
| Total, \$ | | 56,600 | | 64,000 | | 58,900 | | 51,300 | 230,000 |
| Mean, \$ | | 11,320 | | 12,800 | | 11,780 | | 10,260 | 11,540 |
| Range, \$ | 7900–13,900 (6000) | | 11,100–15,200 (4100) | | 11,300–12,400 (1100) | | 7800–12,100 (4300) | | 7800–15,200 (8400) |
| IQR, \$ | 8700–13,525 (4825) | | 11,150–14,925 (3775) | | 11,350–12,275 (925) | | 8300–11,900 (3600) | | 11,100–12,350 (1250) |
| MAPD, % | 12.93 | | 11.56 | | 2.58 | | 11.38 | | 10.64 |
| Sum of squares | 19,568,000 | | 12,840,000 | | 708,000 | | 10,732,000 | | 60,508,000 |
| Variance | 4,892,000 | | 3,210,000 | | 177,000 | | 2,683,000 | | 3,184,632 |
| Standard deviation, \$ | 2212 | | 1792 | | 421 | | 1638 | | 1785 |

Table 2-1 shows a set of data on value of owner-occupied housing units in each of 20 blocks within Census tract 2 in Roanoke, Virginia, in 1970. If we perform the calculations in Eq. (2-1) for the first five blocks, we obtain:

$$\bar{X} = \frac{11{,}100 + 13{,}900 + 11{,}300 + 7{,}900 + 12{,}400}{5} = \frac{56{,}600}{5} = \$11{,}320$$

Looking further at the table we find that the second set of blocks has the highest mean, being \$2540 more than that for the set with the lowest (set 4). We thus might conclude† that the second set of blocks has the highest valued owner-occupied housing units (among the four sets). The arithmetic mean in this case has been used as a summary statistic to help arrive at this conclusion.

In some situations the data may not come as "raw scores" like those in Table 2-1. Instead they will be grouped into prescribed class intervals. This would be the case if, in the previous example, Census takers had asked each owner-occupier in a block the value class (in Table 2-2) to which his or her housing unit belonged

† Assuming that these data are a 100 percent sample—see Chap. 6.

**Table 2-2 Example group data for owner-occupied housing unit value**
(Census tract 2, Roanoke, Virgina, 1970)

| Class interval $c$ (in \$1000) | Midpoint $X_c$ | Frequency $f_c$ | $f_cX_c$ | Deviation $X_c - \bar{X}$ | Squared deviation $(X_c - \bar{X})^2$ $(\times 10^8)$ | $f_c(X_c - \bar{X})^2$ $(\times 10^8)$ |
|---|---|---|---|---|---|---|
| 7–8 | 7,500 | 2 | 15,000 | −4100 | 0.1681 | 0.3362 |
| 8–9 | 8,500 | 0 | 0 | −3100 | 0.0961 | 0 |
| 9–10 | 9,500 | 1 | 9,500 | −2100 | 0.0441 | 0.0441 |
| 10–11 | 10,500 | 1 | 10,500 | −1100 | 0.0121 | 0.0121 |
| 11–12 | 11,500 | 9 | 103,500 | −100 | 0.0001 | 0.0009 |
| 12–13 | 12,500 | 4 | 50,000 | 900 | 0.0081 | 0.0324 |
| 13–14 | 13,500 | 1 | 13,500 | 1900 | 0.0361 | 0.0361 |
| 14–15 | 14,500 | 1 | 14,500 | 2900 | 0.0841 | 0.0841 |
| 15–16 | 15,500 | 1 | 15,500 | 3900 | 0.1521 | 0.1521 |
| Total | | 20 | 232,000 | | | 0.6980 |
| Mean | | | 11,600 | | | |

(instead of asking the actual value). The mean would be calculated under these circumstances as:

$$\bar{X} = \frac{\sum_{c=1}^{g} f_c X_c}{\sum_{c=1}^{g} f_c} = \frac{1}{n} \sum_{c=1}^{g} f_c X_c \qquad (2\text{-}2)$$

where $f_c$ = the frequency (number) of observations in class interval $c$ and
$X_c$ = midpoint value of $X$ in class interval $c$

The mean for the 20 blocks in Roanoke Census tract 2 calculated from this equation is 232,000/20 = \$11,600. This is slightly more than the \$11,540 found from Eq. (2-1) (see bottom of Table 2-1). Remember, however, that for grouped data we would not know the value for each observation and hence would assume it to fall at the midpoint of its respective class interval.

The second index of central tendency suggested above is the *median*. It is defined as that point on the scale of measurement above which are exactly half the cases and below which are the other half. Note that it is a *point* and not a particular score in the set of observations.

The median for the raw data in Table 2-1 can be found by first arranging them in a continuum from the lowest to highest values. The median would be halfway between the tenth and eleventh lowest (or highest) values. As can be seen in Fig. 2-1, this turns out to be \$11,400, which is the point midway between the tenth observation (\$11,300) and the eleventh (\$11,500).

The median for the grouped data in Table 2-2 is a little more difficult to

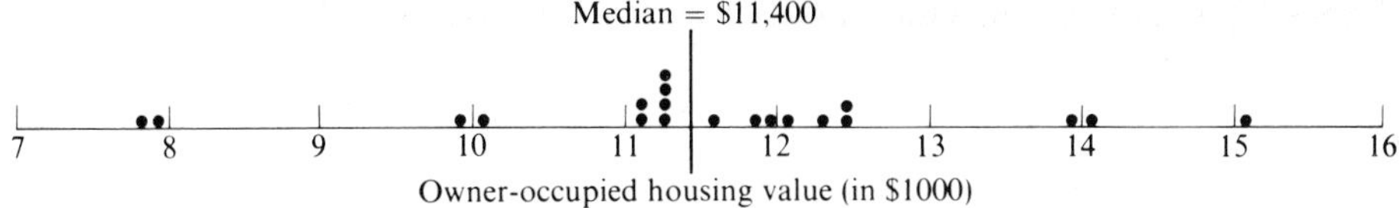


**Figure 2-1** Diagram of owner-occupied housing value scores.

determine. We count down the third column until we reach half the number of observations (frequencies). This lands us somewhere in the \$11,000 to \$12,000 class interval since, for the preceding interval, we have $2 + 0 + 1 + 1 = 4$ and for the \$11,000 to \$12,000 interval we have $2 + 0 + 1 + 1 + 9 = 13$. We then interpolate between the \$11,000 and \$12,000 limits of the latter class, using the assumption that the nine observations falling therein are evenly distributed over that interval. Since we need the first six observations of these nine to give the needed 10, we take six-ninths of the \$1000 interval and add it to the lower limit of \$11,000. This gives a median of $(6/9)(1000) + 11{,}000 = \$11{,}667$. Again, this is different from the previously computed median because we have assumed we were given the values in Table 2-2 in class intervals rather than as raw scores.

In general, the median for grouped data can be found as

$$\text{MD} = l + \frac{(n/2) - f_b}{f_c} s_c \tag{2-3}$$

where MD = median for grouped data
$l$ = exact lower limit of the class interval containing the median
$f_b$ = sum of all frequencies below $l$
$f_c$ = frequency of the class interval containing the median
$n$ = number of cases
$s_c$ = size (or range) of the interval

Hence, for our example,

$$\text{MD} = 11{,}000 + \frac{(20/2) - 4}{9}(1000) = \$11{,}667$$

The third index of central tendency is the *mode*. It is defined as the point (or possibly points) of maximum frequency on the scale of measurement of a variable. For the ungrouped data in Table 2-1 (and Fig. 2-1), the mode is \$11,300. For the grouped values in Table 2-2 it is \$11,500, which is the midpoint of the interval (\$11,000 to \$12,000) with the greatest frequency.

The various central tendency statistics for both grouped and ungrouped example data are summarized in Table 2-3. All the numbers are fairly close, but this is not always the case. Particularly when there are many small values of a variable and just a few large ones (a good example is "employees/establishment"), the mean, median, and mode tend to become widely divergent.

The "owner-occupied housing value" variable employed in the preceding example was measured on a ratio scale, for which we were able to calculate all

**Table 2-3 Summary central tendency indices for owner-occupied housing value ($)**

| | Central tendency indices | | |
|---|---|---|---|
| Data | Mean | Median | Mode |
| Ungrouped | 11,540 | 11,400 | 11,300 |
| Grouped | 11,600 | 11,667 | 11,500 |

three central tendency indices. Similar operations could have been performed for interval-scaled factors, but for variables that are either nominal or ordinal it is not possible to use all three. As an example for ordinal-scaled variables, suppose we asked 50 people to rank the "appearance," along with four other features, of an urban design for a downtown area. The feature thought most significantly beneficial is to be given a rank of 1, the second-most a 2, and so on. Suppose, further, that the outcome of this exercise for the appearance feature is:

| Rank | 1 | 2 | 3 | 4 | 5 | Total |
|---|---|---|---|---|---|---|
| Number of people giving that rank | 5 | 24 | 18 | 2 | 1 | 50 |

Here there is no such entity as a "mean rank," first because ranks are discrete and second because a rank of, say, 4 is not necessarily twice as bad as a rank of 2.† But we can designate a median rank, separating the 50 percent of the people giving the highest rank from the 50 percent giving the lowest. That median rank would be 2, which also happens to be the mode.

When we come to nominal-scaled variables, we really cannot define an index for central tendency since no category or class is any more "central" than another. We can, however, indicate that category (or categories) which occurs most often—the mode. By way of illustration, if we had 100 parcels of land to be classified by use—residential, commercial, manufacturing, and recreational—we might number and arrange the results as:

| Land-use class | Residential | Commercial | Manufacturing | Recreational | Total |
|---|---|---|---|---|---|
| Assigned number | 1 | 2 | 3 | 4 | |
| Number of parcels | 20 | 50 | 12 | 18 | 100 |

† As another illustration, three cities may have 10, 4, and 2 crimes per day, thus ranking 1, 2, and 3, but the number of crimes in the first city is 2.5 times that in the second and 5 times that in the third.

If we tried to establish a "mean land-use class" for these data, it would be 2.20, with a corresponding median of 2. But we could just as well have reassigned the land-use class numbers as:

| Land-use class | Residential | Recreational | Manufacturing | Commercial | Total |
|---|---|---|---|---|---|
| Assigned number | 1 | 2 | 3 | 4 | |
| Number of parcels | 20 | 18 | 12 | 50 | 100 |

This would give a mean of 2.92 and a median of 4. The point is that the mean and median statistics are meaningless for nominal-scaled variables, leaving only the mode as a possibly useful index. In this example (second chart), it has a value of 4 (= commercial).

To summarize: the central tendency of nominal-scaled variables can be measured by the mode, of ordinal-scaled variables by the mode or median, and of ratio- and interval-scaled variables by all three indices.

## 2-3 DISPERSION

Knowing the central tendency of a set of measurements tells us much, but it usually does not give a complete portrayal of the observations. As can be seen in Table 2-1, while the (grand) mean for all twenty blocks is \$11,540, there are none with exactly that figure and there are several which vary from it by as much as \$3000. Hence it also would be beneficial to know the *dispersion* or *variance* about the point of central tendency.

Several types of statistics have been utilized as measures of dispersion. The most obvious one probably is the *range* between the lowest and highest scores. This has been calculated for each set of observations in Table 2-1. Of the five-case sets, the third has the smallest range, being not greater than one-quarter that of the other three sets. Notice, however, that the range for the full 20 observations is much greater than for any of the four smaller sets. This is natural since the chance of getting some extreme values in a set of 20 is much greater than in a set of five. This implies that the range is not a very good index of dispersion if comparisons are made between data sets of different sizes.

As an alternative, we might look at the range covered by some ordered subset of the observations. A commonly employed statistic here is the interquartile range (IQR), defined as the span between the points separating the lower and upper 25 percent, respectively, of the observed values. For the full set of data in Table 2-1 and Fig. 2-1, the lowest quartile (25 percent) would comprise the smallest 20/4 = 5 cases and the highest, the greatest 5 cases. The breakpoints thus would be midway between the fifth and sixth and the fifteenth and sixteenth cases, respectively. In the first situation, cases 5 and 6 both fall at \$11,100, so the lower point is at this value. On the upper side, the division is midway between \$12,300 and \$12,400, which gives \$12,350. The IQR thus is 12,350 − 11,100 = \$1250. We subsequently can use this information to conclude, for instance, that while the overall range is wide (\$8400), the middle 50 percent of the observations lies within a fairly narrow spectrum of \$1250.

Similar calculations would produce the interquartile ranges for the four small data sets in Table 2-1. Equation (2-3) could be employed for this purpose with $n/4$ or $3n/4$ replacing $n/2$ and the phrases "lower quartile point" or "upper quartile point" replacing "median." As can be seen in the table, if the IQR is employed as an index of dispersion rather than the overall range, the full data set turns out to have one of the lowest dispersions.

Still another alternative for measuring dispersion is to take the *mean absolute percentage deviation* (MAPD) of all of the case values from their central point (usually taken as the mean). Of course, we cannot add the deviations directly since, as indicated in the third column of Table 2-4, they would cancel out, thereby giving a MAPD of 0, which certainly is not so. Instead, the procedure is to take the absolute values of the deviations. We then divide each of these by the absolute value of the mean and multiply the corresponding results by 100 (percent). This gives the percentage deviation or difference of every case from the mean. Subsequent addition of these percentages and division by the total number of cases ($n$) leads to the mean absolute percentage deviation. The associated formula is

$$\text{MAPD} = \frac{1}{n} \sum_{i=1}^{n} \frac{|X_i - \bar{X}|}{|\bar{X}|} 100 \qquad (2\text{-}4)$$

Using this equation with the data in Table 2-4 gives a MAPD of 64.66/5 = 12.93 percent. This can be interpreted to indicate that the observations differ from the mean by an average (mean) of 12.93 percent (of the mean). Interestingly, with this

**Table 2-4 Calculations in determining the mean, MAPD, and standard deviation for the first five blocks**

| Census block $i$ | Owner-occupied housing value $X_i$, \$ | Deviation $X_i - \bar{X}$ | Absolute deviation $\lvert X_i - \bar{X}\rvert$ | Absolute percentage deviation $\frac{\lvert X_i - \bar{X}\rvert}{\lvert\bar{X}\rvert} 100$ | Squared deviation $(X_i - \bar{X})^2$ | Squared value $X_i^2$ ($\times 10^8$) |
|---|---|---|---|---|---|---|
| 1 | 11,100 | −220 | 220 | 1.94 | 48,400 | 1.232 |
| 2 | 13,900 | 2580 | 2580 | 22.79 | 6,656,400 | 1.932 |
| 3 | 11,300 | −20 | 20 | 0.18 | 400 | 1.277 |
| 4 | 7,900 | −3420 | 3420 | 30.21 | 11,696,400 | 0.624 |
| 5 | 12,400 | 1080 | 1080 | 9.54 | 1,166,400 | 1.538 |
| Total | 56,600 | 0 | 7320 | 64.66 | 19,568,000 | 6.603 |

index the overall set is seen to have almost as much variation as sets 2 and 4. Yet the IQR had shown a much lower dispersion for the larger set.

The final index of dispersion to be discussed here is the *standard deviation.* It probably is the most widely used. This is due in part to the fact that in earlier days it was easier for statisticians to work with it mathematically than, say, the mean absolute percentage deviation. As a consequence, its use has grown until it is much more common than the MAPD, despite the fact that the latter is easier to understand. In any case, instead of taking the absolute values of the deviations to prevent them from canceling each other out, we square them and later come back and take the square root. The result is summarized in the standard deviation formula:

$$S = \left[\frac{1}{n-1}\sum_{i=1}^{n}(X_i - \bar{X})^2\right]^{1/2} \tag{2-5}$$

Some of the calculations for the first example set of data in Table 2-1 are shown in Table 2-4. In the next to last column each deviation is squared and then added down the column to get a total of 19,568,000. This is divided by $n - 1$ to give 4,892,000. The square root of this is 2212, the standard deviation.

The reason for dividing by $n - 1$ is not immediately evident. But suppose we had only one observation. What would be its standard deviation? A quick response might be "zero," but more logically it should be undefined since an average deviation of a single value really has no meaning. To show this mathematically, we divide by $n - 1$ instead of $n$ to obtain the standard deviation. Thus, if we had one observation, say the first one in Table 2-4, the mean would be 11,400 and the standard deviation would be $[0/(1-1)]^{1/2} = 0/0$, which is undefined mathematically, as desired.†

Another formula of value here is

$$S = \left[\frac{1}{n(n-1)}\right]^{1/2}\left[n\sum_{i=1}^{n}X_i^2 - \left(\sum_{i=1}^{n}X_i\right)^2\right]^{1/2} \tag{2-6}$$

This can be employed when the interest is in obtaining the standard deviation without first calculating the mean, as must be done in Eq. (2-5). Care must be exercised in using Eq. (2-6), however, because the second term might involve subtraction of two very large but nearly equal numbers, in which case it would be necessary to carry six to eight digits in the calculation to get the proper result.

When the data are grouped, as in Table 2-2, Eq. (2-5) translates to

$$S = \left[\frac{1}{n-1}\sum_{c=1}^{g}f_c(X_c - \bar{X})^2\right]^{1/2} \tag{2-7}$$

† Another reason for using $n - 1$ in the standard deviation equation is that the resulting sample estimate of the population standard deviation is unbiased. This is discussed further in Chap. 5.

For the example data, this gives

$$S = \left(\frac{0.698 \times 10^8}{20 - 1}\right)^{1/2} = 1917$$

If it is desired to employ Eq. (2-6) with grouped data, it can be transformed into

$$S = \left[\frac{1}{n(n-1)}\right]^{1/2}\left[n\sum_{c=1}^{g} f_c X_c^2 - \sum_{c=1}^{g}(f_c X_c)^2\right]^{1/2} \tag{2-8}$$

Two definitions of statistics utilized frequently in the rest of the book should be noted here. These are:

**Definition** *Sum of squares* is the sum of the squared deviations of the value of each observation from the mean (SS).

**Definition** *Variance* is the sum of squares divided by $n - 1$ or, equivalently, the square of the standard deviation ($S^2$).

As might be obvious, both of these come from the standard deviation Eq. (2-5). The sum of the squares is the numerator inside the square root while the variance is the whole term inside the square root. Looking back at Table 2-4 we find that the sum of the squares for that data is 19,568,000 (column 5) and the variance is 19,568,000/(5 − 1) = 4,892,000. Table 2-1 shows these two statistics for all five example sets of data.

A review of Table 2-1, particularly of sets 1, 2, and 4, and a study of Fig. 2-2 lead to some interesting comparisons between the four dispersion statistics discussed in this section. Set 1 has a much greater range, IQR, and standard deviation than the other two, but only a slightly higher MAPD. The point is that any conclusions on the relative dispersions of sets of data is dependent on the index of dispersion employed. Hence it is important to consider the characteristics of the indices before employing them in any testing procedure. The standard deviation, for example, weighs a double-sized deviation by a factor of 4.† Consequently, this statistic implicitly assigns greater importance to extreme scores, which may not be desirable to the analyst. Hence he might be better off using, say, the interquartile range as the index of dispersion.

The above discussion has been concerned with ratio-scaled variables. But only one of the four dispersion statistics can be employed in conjunction with all other scales. The MAPD and standard deviation, for example, are limited to ratio and interval scales since they involve division. For ordinal-scaled variables, we thus are left with something similar to the interquartile range. Referring back to our example in Sec. 2-2 on the ranking of appearance in an urban design, we find that we cannot give the exact limits of the middle 50 percent of the observations

† To illustrate: a deviation of 6 is twice as much as 3, but the squared deviation of the first (36) is four times as much as the latter (9).

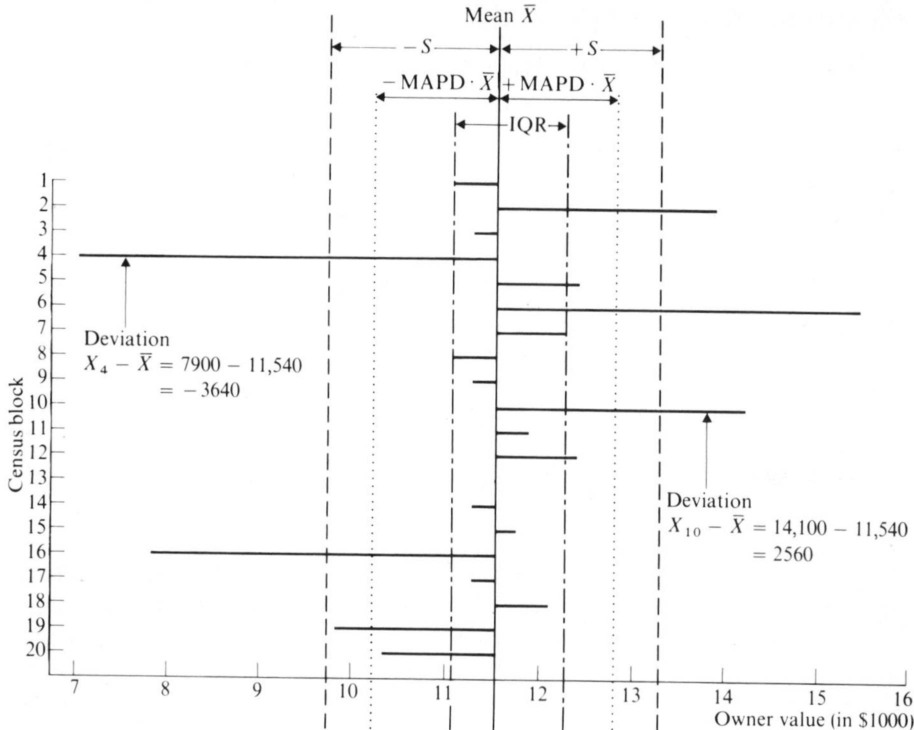


**Figure 2-2** Graphical display of deviations from the mean and three dispersion measures for the data in Table 2-1.

since the ranks are discrete and indivisible. We could say, however, that ranks 2 and 3 comprise the middle 84 percent [(24 + 18)/50] of the cases. By comparison, some other feature (e.g., "cost") might capture only 20 percent of the second and third ranks.

For variables measured on a nominal scale the notion of "dispersion" really is without meaning. A close alternative might be to show the variations in the number of cases in each category *compared to* some other distribution (e.g., an equal number in each category). Yet there is no *a priori* reason to take one distribution or another to use as the base for comparison. For purposes of this book we will not consider a nominal-scaled variable to have any definable dispersion index.

## 2-4 STANDARDIZATION

Knowing the central tendency and dispersion of a variable allows us to determine exactly where each individual or geographic zone or case, etc., stands relative to the others along a particular dimension. They also allow us to compare relative

**Table 2-5 Standardized scores and computations for two variables**

| City | GCP $X_1$ (in $\$10^6$) | Unemployment rate $X_2$, % | $Z_1$ | $Z_2$ |
|---|---|---|---|---|
| 1 | 50 | 3 | +1.265 | −0.632 |
| 2 | 30 | 7 | 0 | +0.632 |
| 3 | 40 | 5 | +0.632 | 0 |
| 4 | 20 | 1 | −0.632 | −1.265 |
| 5 | 10 | 9 | −1.265 | +1.265 |
| Total | 150 | 25 | 0 | 0 |
| Mean | 30 | 5 | 0 | 0 |
| Sum of squares | 1000 | 40 | 4.00 | 4.00 |
| Variance | 250 | 10 | 1.00 | 1.00 |
| Standard deviation | 15.811 | 3.162 | 1.00 | 1.00 |

standings between dimensions. Table 2-5 provides information for an illustration. Suppose we had data on the gross city product† ($X_1$, in \$ million) and the unemployment rate ($X_2$, in percent) for five cities in a given state. If we looked just at city 5 with a GCP of \$10 million we might be impressed, until we saw that this was the least for all of the cities. Hence, for purposes of comparison, we should relate every observation of a variable to its mean (by subtracting the mean). If this tack is taken, city 5 will be at a great disadvantage—with a GCP of \$20 million less than the mean and, to make matters worse, an unemployment rate of 4 percent above the mean.

This comparison is not sufficient, however. A difference (from the mean) of \$10 million in GCP is certainly not as substantial as one of 10 percent in the unemployment rate. If, for instance, city 2 lost \$10 million in GCP, it would still have as much or more as cities 4 and 5. On the other hand, if it added 10 percent to its unemployment, it would have a rate almost twice as much as the worst city. To take this consideration into account, we should compare the difference (deviation) of a given city from the mean to the average deviation for all cities. Since the latter is represented by the standard deviation, the result, called a *standardized score*‡ or *Z score*, is

$$Z_{ij} = \frac{X_{ij} - \bar{X}_j}{S_j}$$

where $Z_{ij}$ = standardized score for observation (case) $i$ for variable $j$
$X_{ij}$ = value of observation $i$ for variable $j$
$\bar{X}_j$ = mean of variable $j$
$S_j$ = standard deviation of variable $j$

† Analogous to the gross national product.
‡ In Ref. 2-3, a standardized score is referred to as a *normalized score*.

Thus, if GCP is considered variable 1 and the unemployment percentage rate variable 2, for city 5 we would have

$$Z_{51} = \frac{10 - 30}{15.81} = -1.265$$

and

$$Z_{52} = \frac{9 - 5}{3.16} = +1.265$$

These figures indicate that city 5 is 1.265 standard deviations below the other cities for GCP and 1.265 above the mean for the unemployment percentage rate.

Several characteristics of a standardized variable should be noted:

1. Sum is 0.
2. Mean is 0.
3. Sum of the squares is $n - 1$.
4. Variance is 1.00.
5. The standard deviation is 1.00.

These characteristics can be verified easily by making the associated computations with either $Z_1$ or $Z_2$ in Table 2-5.

## PROBLEMS

**2-1** Fill in the blanks with the proper word(s) or number(s).

(*a*) Variables measured as categories or classes are called ____________________ -scaled variables.

(*b*) Variables measured on a scale with a given, constant interval but with no absolute zero point are called ____________________ -scaled variables.

(*c*) The other two types of scales are _______________ and ____________________.

(*d*) A ____________________ measure is one in which the scale is "in the brain."

(*e*) The number of trucks passing a given point on a street in 1 hour is an example of a ____________________, not a continuous variable.

(*f*) Another word for "index" used in statistics is ____________________.

(*g*) For ratio- and interval-scaled variables you can use the ______________________ as indices of central tendency.

(*h*) For ratio- and interval-scaled variables you can use the ______________________ as statistics for dispersion.

(*i*) For an ordinal-scaled variable you can use the ______________________ as central

tendency statistics and the ______________________ as a dispersion statistic.

(*j*) The sum of the squared deviations of the value of each observation of a variable from its

mean is called the ______________________.

(*k*) The term suggested in (*j*) above divided by $n - 1$ is called the ____________.

(*l*) To standardize a variable, you ______________________ from each

______________________ of the variable its ______________________ and then

______________________ by the ______________________.

(*m*) The sum of the standardized scores of any variable equals ______________________.

(*n*) The variance of the standardized scores of any variable equals ______________________.

(*o*) The standard deviation of the standardized scores of any variable equals

______________________.

(*p*) The sum of the variances of five standardized variables equals ______________________.

______________________

**2-2** Is each of the following a nominal-, ordinal-, interval-, or ratio-scaled measurement?
(*a*) Technical, political, and social classification of factors in the environment
(*b*) The number of workers in a given industry
(*c*) The number of acres of recreational land in a city over and above the national standard of 5 acres
(*d*) The number of vehicle miles of travel in a metropolitan area

**2-3** Is each of the following discrete or continuous, subjective or objective?
(*a*) The rating on a scale of $-3$ (very bad), $-2$, $-1$, 0 (so-so), $+1$, $+2$, $+3$ (very good) of a new civic center proposal
(*b*) The number of people entering a recreational area in a given day
(*c*) A city mayor's opinion of a proposal to eliminate his position (expressed as "* # # ? ? ! !")
(*d*) The dollar amount by which the bids received on a new water-treatment plant exceed the engineering estimates

**2-4** Give two examples of each of the four types of measurement scale. They should be related to urban or regional situations.

**2-5** The following table lists the number of business establishments within a study area according to a classification code developed for the study.

| Business classification code | Number of establishments | Business classification code | Number of establishments |
|---|---|---|---|
| 001 | 5 | 006 | 2 |
| 002 | 0 | 007 | 9 |
| 003 | 1 | 008 | 5 |
| 004 | 7 | 009 | 1 |
| 005 | 1 | 010 | 3 |

What is the measure of central tendency and its value?

**2-6** A study to determine the number of acres, within the class limits listed below, occupied by one classification of commercial establishments has been undertaken. Determine the mean, median, and mode acreage as well as the range, IQR, MAPD, and standard deviation.

| Acreage | Number of establishments |
|---|---|
| 1.00–1.49 | 0 |
| 1.50–1.99 | 2 |
| 2.00–2.49 | 10 |
| 2.50–2.99 | 9 |
| 3.00–3.49 | 6 |
| 3.50–3.99 | 3 |

**2-7** The data below indicate the number of passenger vehicles passing a given point along a cordon line during a 24-hour period for each of 12 days.

| | | |
|---|---|---|
| 395 | 369 | 374 |
| 376 | 348 | 360 |
| 372 | 337 | 378 |
| 367 | 376 | 380 |

Calculate the mean and median for these data as well as the range, IQR, MAPD, and standard deviation. Calculate the latter using both types of equations.

**2-8** Below are the number of acres of residential land for all parcels in a small town. What is the mean, median, mode, sum of squares, variance, IQR, MAPD, and standard deviation?

| Category, acres | Number of parcels |
|---|---|
| 0–0.3 | 1000 |
| 0.3–0.6 | 2000 |
| 0.6–0.9 | 500 |
| 0.9–1.2 | 1000 |
| 1.2–1.5 | 500 |

**2-9** The town of Strip Mine has six zones. For each zone the following four variables have been measured:

$X_1$ = mean age of residents (years)

$X_2$ = mean travel time to all employment opportunities (min)

$Y_1$ = median annual per capita income (\$$10^4$ per year)

$Y_2$ = mortality rate (deaths per 1000 people per year)

The data are:

| Zone | $X_1$ | $X_2$ | $Y_1$ | $Y_2$ |
|---|---|---|---|---|
| 1 | 25 | 33 | 0.16 | 10 |
| 2 | 24 | 34 | 0.17 | 12 |
| 3 | 40 | 47 | 0.12 | 20 |
| 4 | 42 | 43 | 0.15 | 18 |
| 5 | 29 | 25 | 0.35 | 8 |
| 6 | 32 | 28 | 0.25 | 10 |

(*a*) Find the mean, sum of squares, variance, standard deviation, and standardized scores for each variable. (*Note*. The standardized scores for $Y_1$ and $Y_2$ are designated by $W_1$ and $W_2$, respectively.)
(*b*) Verify these against the figures in App. D.
(*c*) Verify for each standardized variable that its mean is 0, variance is 1.0, and standard deviation is 1.0.

**2-10** Below are the priorities assigned to four goal areas by a panel of 10 citizens in a region. With 1 being the highest priority and 4 being the lowest, what is:
(*a*) The best central tendency statistic?
(*b*) Its value for each goal?
(*c*) The dispersion statistic?
(*d*) Its value for each goal?

| | Priority | | | |
|---|---|---|---|---|
| Goal | 1 | 2 | 3 | 4 |
| Housing | 2 | 6 | 0 | 2 |
| Transportation | 5 | 3 | 1 | 1 |
| Social services | 1 | 0 | 4 | 5 |
| Water, sewer | 2 | 1 | 5 | 2 |

## REFERENCES

### Theory

2-1. Guilford, J. P.: *Fundamental Statistics in Psychology and Education*, 4th ed., McGraw-Hill, New York, 1965.

2-2. Nie, N. H., et al.: *Statistical Package for the Social Sciences*, 2d ed., McGraw-Hill, New York, 1975.

2-3. Ostle, B.: *Statistics in Research*, 2d ed., Iowa University Press, Ames, Iowa, 1963.
2-4. Siegel, S.: *Nonparametric Statistics for the Behavioral Sciences*, McGraw-Hill, New York, 1956.

**Applications**

2-5. Berry, B. J. L., and F. E. Horton: *Geographic Perspectives on Urban Systems*, Prentice-Hall, Englewood Cliffs, N. J., 1970.
2-6. Tanur, J. M. et al. (Eds.): *Statistics: A Guide to the Unknown*, Holden-Day, San Francisco, Calif., 1972.
2-7. Tufe, E. R.: *The Quantitative Analysis of Social Problems*, Addison-Wesley, Reading, Mass., 1970.

CHAPTER

# THREE

## DISTRIBUTIONS

While the calculation of central tendency and dispersion statistics is almost always performed on any set of data, it generally is not the first step. Usually the analyst starts by systematizing the data by grouping them in classes. For nominal- and ordinal-scaled variables, the classes are simply the name or rank categories, respectively, and the systemization consists of counting the number of cases falling into each category. For interval- and ratio-scaled variables it is possible to go a step further by laying out the classes (i.e., intervals) in line. When the cases then are allocated to their associated intervals, the result is a *frequency-distribution* diagram (or, simply, a *distribution*).

After we construct such a diagram, the variations in the data become much more apparent, thereby providing greater meaning to the subsequent central tendency and dispersion statistics. Equally if not more important, the data now can be arranged according to one or more general mathematical distributions, which then can be employed in various logical processes to test hypotheses, deduce various related properties of the data, and so on. The purpose of this chapter is thus to present both the procedure for creating empirical distributions and several theoretical distributions common to many urban and regional studies. Attention will be focused on interval- and ratio-scaled variables since, as noted above, the procedure for variables measured on the other two scales is simply that of counting the number of cases in each category.

## 3-1 FREQUENCY AND PROBABILITY DISTRIBUTIONS

The first step in surveying any data set is to develop a chart portraying each case. If the data are ungrouped, a table like that in Table 2-1 or a diagram such as Fig. 2-1 would be appropriate. If grouped, the data would be charted as in Table 2-2.

The second step in converting empirically derived data into a more usable form is to create a *histogram* or *frequency distribution*, which is a simple graph depicting a set of mutually exclusive and exhaustive classes of a variable on the abscissa ($x$ axis) and the frequency (number of cases) with which the observed values of the variable fall within each class as the ordinate ($y$ axis). Figure 3-1 shows the prescribed transformation of the data like that from Table 2-2. In this case, a larger set of 66 block observations of owner-occupied housing unit values in Census tract 2 has been employed. The next step involves the division of frequencies within each class by the total number of observations to produce the *percentage* of observations falling within each class. This percentage, if divided by 100, also can be considered to be an empirically derived *probability* of an observation belonging to a given class. The equivalent percentages (probabilities) are displayed in Fig. 3-1 on the $y$ axis alongside the frequencies.

In the fourth and final step *cumulative* frequency and probability distributions are formed. This is done by adding the frequency (or probability) in each interval sequentially from left to right and recording the result in the corresponding interval location. To illustrate: the lowest-valued Census block had an owner-occupied housing unit value falling within the \$6000 to \$6999 interval. It would be recorded in Fig. 3-2 as a frequency of 1 (1.5 percent) in that interval. Looking back to

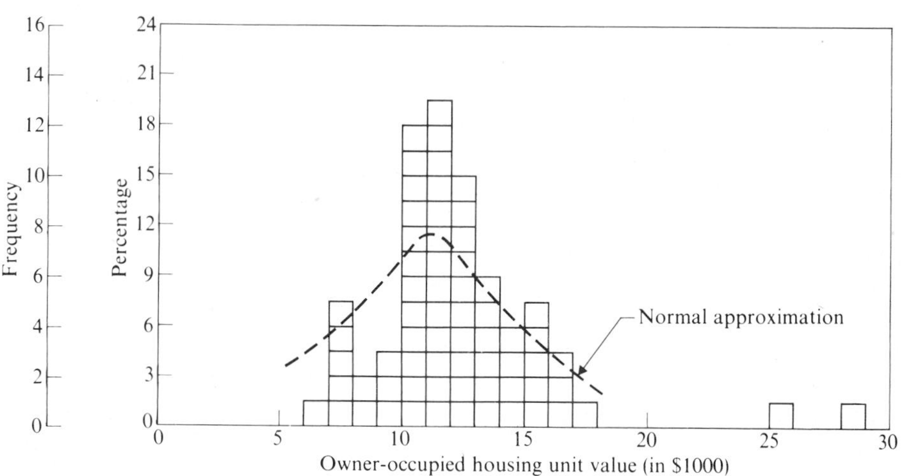


**Figure 3-1** Histogram (frequency distribution) and percentage distribution of owner-occupied housing unit values.

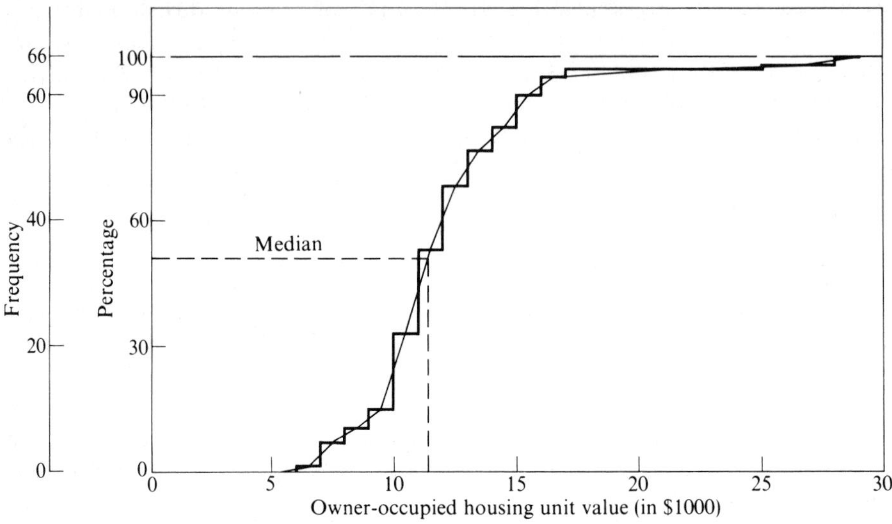


**Figure 3-2** Cumulative frequency and probability distribution of owner-occupied housing unit values.

Fig. 3-1, we see that the next interval ($7000 to $7999) had four cases, so that the *total* or cumulative number of cases up to and including that interval would be 5 (7.5 percent). This number would be recorded for that interval. Proceeding in order, the next interval ($8000 to $8999) contains two cases, bringing the total to this point to 7 (10.5 percent), which would be marked off for that interval. Eventually all 66 cases (100 percent) would be covered (within the $28,000 to $28,999 interval), and those numbers would be recorded above that interval in Fig. 3-2. Finally, if we assume (as has been done in the previous chapter) that the cases in each interval are equally distributed across that interval, we would connect the midpoints of the intervals with a series of straight-line segments, as in Fig. 3-2.

One of the major advantages of the cumulative probability distribution is that it can be readily employed to determine the probability that a given value of a variable is less than or equal to a selected value. For example, in Fig. 3-2 if we desired to know the owner-occupied housing unit value below which 50 percent of all blocks fell (in other words, the median), we would, as shown, go up the *y* axis until hitting 50 percent, proceed horizontally until hitting the cumulative distribution, and then drop vertically to determine the associated housing unit value. This procedure would give a median of roughly $11,300.

## 3-2 THEORETICAL DISTRIBUTIONS

If we consider the fact that any variable can have a distribution associated with it, we quickly realize there are literally millions of possible distributions. To deal with such a large number, we obviously have to generalize so that the possibilities are reduced to a manageable few. There is a trade-off in doing this, of course; not every distribution will match a general type. But then, that is one of the prices we must pay to simplify some of this complex world. In this section we will describe three of the most commonly utilized theoretical (general) distributions in urban and regional studies. We then will present briefly several other types which might prove (and have proven) useful in a variety of related investigations.

## The Binomial Distribution

One of the simplest theoretical distributions is one which relates to situations where there are only two possible choices or outcomes. These outcomes may be "success" or "failure" (defined in some way), "like" or "dislike," "win" or "lose," and so on. The corresponding variable is the number of "successes" or "likes" or "wins" (or the opposites), given a fixed number of repetitions of the situation under study. The distribution employed to find the probability of a given number of "successes" in the repetitions being attempted is called the *binomial* distribution. The equation for this *probability mass function*, as these discrete theoretical distributions are more properly known, is

$$\Pr(x) = \frac{n!}{x!\,(n-x)!}\,p^x q^{n-x} \tag{3-1}$$

where $\Pr(x)$ = probability of exactly $x$ "successes" in $n$ repetitions of a situation
$p$ = probability of any one repetition being successful
$q$ = probability of any one repetition *not* being successful ($= 1 - p$)

Here the factorial (!) indicates that the associated number should be multiplied by successively lower digits until 1 is reached. For example:

$$5! = 5 \cdot 4 \cdot 3 \cdot 2 \cdot 1 = 120$$

The factorial 0! is defined mathematically to be equal to 1.

The binomial probability mass function has been found to resemble empirical distributions when the situations being studied are "independent" of each other. Loosely defined,† this means that the factors which affect one situation or event are not operative in the others. Such may arise when the events are separated by great distances and/or times, political philosophies, cultural conditions, etc.

By way of illustration let us imagine that we are in charge of five experiments in which busing is to be attempted to achieve racial balance in elementary schools. In this example the experiments are to be undertaken in five widely dispersed cities, so that we might assume that what occurs in one place will not influence what happens in the other four.‡ The five situations thus are "independent."

† See Sec. 4-2 for a more precise definition.

‡ In reality, widespread media coverage, similarity in laws, and analogous social-economic conditions might negate this assumption.

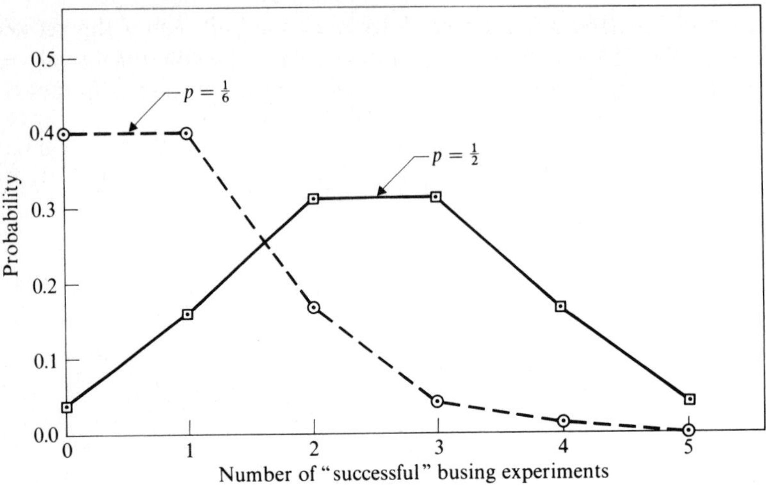


**Figure 3-3** Binomial probability mass functions for successful busing experiments under two conditions.

We will also assume that each experiment can only be classified as a "success" or "failure," with appropriate definitions. For instance, a "success" may be declared when there is no violence for 3 years succeeding the busing and when the ratio of minorities to total students stays constant ($\pm$ 5 percent) each year after busing has been initiated (i.e., there is no significant out-migration of the majority).

Reviewing our past experiences, we may have found from numerous similar experiments that, on the average (mean), only one-sixth of all such experiments are successful. Hence the theoretical probability of, say, 2 successes in our five upcoming experiments is, according to the binomial distribution,

$$\Pr(2) = \frac{5!}{2!(5-2)!}\left(\frac{1}{6}\right)^2\left(\frac{5}{6}\right)^{5-2} = \frac{120}{2(6)}(0.0279)(0.578) = 0.16$$

For 0 successes it would be†

$$\Pr(0) = \frac{5!}{0!(5-0)!}\left(\frac{1}{6}\right)^0\left(\frac{5}{6}\right)^{5-0} = \frac{120}{1(120)}(1)(0.401) = 0.40$$

Through similar calculations we could also find the probabilities for 1, 3, 4, and 5 successes and graph the resulting probability mass function, as has been done with the circled points in Fig. 3-3. Our previous experiences hopefully would closely verify that in 40 percent of the situations in which five school busing experiments were tried there were 0 successes, in another 40 percent there was only 1 success, in another 16 percent only 2 successes, and so on.

† Remember that any number raised to the 0 power is 1.

If the binomial distribution does tend to resemble sufficiently the results found previously, we would then be in a position to make some rather quick calculations of central tendency and dispersion. As examples, the mean† ($\mu$) can be found from

$$\mu = np \tag{3-2}$$

and the standard deviation ($\sigma$) from

$$\sigma = (npq)^{1/2} \tag{3-3}$$

Thus, in our example:

$$\mu = 5\left(\frac{1}{6}\right) = 0.83$$

$$\sigma = \left[5\left(\frac{1}{6}\right)\left(\frac{5}{6}\right)\right]^{1/2} = 0.83$$

In words, the average (mean) number of successes in five experiments, given that the mean for any one is $\frac{1}{6}$, is $\frac{5}{6}$. The corresponding standard deviation is also $\frac{5}{6}$.‡

To push our example a little further, let us now imagine that in recent years there has been a marked increase in the success rate of busing experiments—from, say, $\frac{1}{6}$ to $\frac{1}{2}$. Assuming that the theoretical distribution still holds, we could then calculate the new probabilities of success in five experiments using the binomial probability mass function and thereby save ourselves much time and money expense in data collection and analysis. The result of these calculations would be the second curve (actually series of 6 "squared" points) in Fig. 3-3. While the likelihood of success in any one experiment has increased threefold, the probability of having 0 successes has dropped over 13-fold (from 0.40 to 0.03). Moreover, while the mean has increased to $(5)(\frac{1}{2}) = 2.5$ the standard deviation has also jumped to $[(5)(\frac{1}{2})(\frac{1}{2})]^{1/2} = 1.2$. The binomial distribution thus might help us conclude that if past trends continue, the mean number of successes in five experiments will increase, but we can also expect a lot more variability in successes than had occurred before.

## The Poisson Distribution

Another common distribution involving discrete variables is the Poisson distribution. Like the binomial, it generally is most useful in situations where the events are independent. In addition, they also should be *random*, i.e., with each event having an equal chance of occurrence. Unlike the binomial, however, the number of

† Since we are dealing here with theoretical distributions, thereby involving populations rather than samples, we use the population mean $\mu$ rather than the sample mean $\bar{X}$ and, correspondingly, $\sigma$ rather than $S$.

‡ These happen to be the same in this example, but usually would not be so otherwise.

outcomes of an event can be more than two. The equation for the Poisson probability mass function is

$$\Pr(x) = \frac{e^{-\mu}\mu^x}{x!} \tag{3-4}$$

where $\mu$ is the mean and $e$ is the base of the Naperian logarithms (= 2.71828).

Suppose we were an urban design team concerned with a variety of environmental distractions (loud noise, intense light or darkness, excessive heat or cold, wind drafts, etc.) that would impact the pedestrian as he walked through a downtown mall area. We might assume from previous experience that these distractions (events) occur independently of each other and that there is an equal chance of any type of distribution occurring. Given these two assumptions, we would feel fairly confident that the Poisson distribution would give a close approximation to, say, the percentage of hours in which 0, 1, 2, 3, etc., distractions occurred at a given place in the downtown area.

Suppose now we knew that the mean number of distractions was 3.0 per hour. The distribution of distractions then could be determined as

$$\Pr(0) = \frac{(2.72)^{-3.0}(3.0)^0}{0!} = 0.05$$

$$\Pr(1) = \frac{(2.72)^{-3.0}(3.0)^1}{1!} = 0.15$$

etc.

The resultant distribution would be like that indicated by the "circled" points in Fig. 3-4. As can be seen, it is not symmetrical but somewhat skewed, with the larger portion to the left. This means there is a greater probability of a smaller than a larger number of distractions. The probability of having exactly 3 distractions (equal to the mean) is 0.22, while that for exactly 6 is only 0.06. Viewed in another context, if we were to take films at the given location for, say, 100 hours, we would expect to have 22 hours in which we would detect exactly 3 distractions and 5 hours in which we would find exactly 6. With a mean level of 3, we thus would expect to have 4.4 times as many hours with 3 as opposed to 6 distractions.

The Poisson distribution has the property that the standard deviation $\sigma$ is equal to the mean $\mu$:

$$\sigma = \mu \tag{3-5}$$

This would be helpful to know if, for example, the mean number of distractions were to increase to, say, 5. This could occur for a variety of reasons—new construction projects, increased vehicular traffic, microclimatic changes, and the like. The resultant Poisson probability mass function would be as indicated by the "squared" points in Fig. 3-4. This distribution is more symmetrical than the other in the diagram, but the maximum probability is lower (0.18 versus 0.22) and there is more dispersion ($\sigma$ = 5 versus 3). Thus, in addition to the greater number of distractions, the Poisson distribution shows a greater variability. This may point

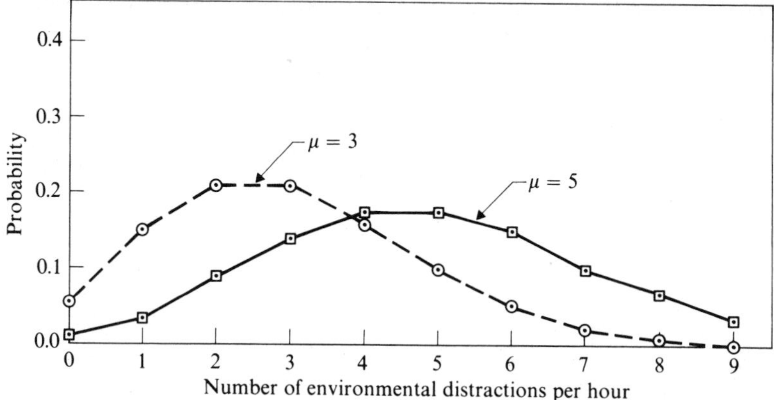


**Figure 3-4** Poisson probability mass function for environmental distributions under two conditions.

to a feature felt undesirable by the urban designers since a person walking in the given location would not know if he would be highly distracted or not distracted at all. He therefore might feel much more uncomfortable than if he knew he would be faced with a more constant (definite) number of distractions.

## The Normal Distribution

Up to this point in this section we have been dealing with discrete-valued variables. For continuous variables the analogies are strong but not complete. The difference lies in the definition of *probability* (or percentage of the cases). If we have an infinite number of points along a continuum and associate a probability of occurrence with each, as was done with the discrete variables, we run into a major problem. When adding these infinite number of probabilities, we obviously get an infinite number. Yet all probabilities (or percentages) in a probability *density* function† are supposed to add to 1 (or 100 percent). It therefore is not meaningful to define the probability at a point—only the probability that an observation will fall into a given interval. A forthcoming example will demonstrate this point.

The normal distribution is undoubtedly the most well known of all continuous probability density functions, being recognized by its bell-shaped curve. If we return to Fig. 3-1, we see that the frequency or probability distribution there could be considered normal (at least in a rough way). This approximation might be justified on the basis of simplicity, rationality, and/or convenience. On the other hand, we might justifiably feel that if we had more observations (perhaps 1000) and if the intervals were made small enough, the set of data would be more nearly normal. Carried to the extreme, we might imagine millions of cases with an

† Distributions of continuous variables are properly known as probability *density* (as opposed to *mass*) functions.

interval of, say, \$1 and hence expect to find a trace of points that highlight a curve very close to normal.

The conclusions to be drawn from this imaginary exercise are twofold. First, no set of data, no matter how large, ever conforms exactly to a normal distribution. We often have to assume normality for some of the reasons suggested above. Second, normal (and all other) probability density functions represent a continuum of *limits* which would be found if the interval sizes were made infinitesimally small and, correspondingly, the number of cases made infinitely large. A point in a continuous distribution thus is a limit rather than a probability. Consequently, it is not meaningful to add these, although it is definitely meaningful to look at the differences between them over a given interval of the continuous variable.

To demonstrate this latter point, which actually is an extension of the discussion two paragraphs previously, let us start with the formula for the standard normal probability density function (with each value of $X$ standardized):

$$f(Z_i) = \frac{1}{(2\pi)^{1/2}} e^{-Z_i^2/2} \tag{3-6}$$

where $Z_i$ = standardized score for case $i$ of variable $X$
$e = 2.718$
$\pi = 3.141$

If we were to use this equation with, say, $X_i = 11{,}300$, $\bar{X} = 11{,}300$, and $S = 3759$, based on the owner-occupied housing unit value data in Fig. 3-1, we would find that $Z_i = 0$ and $f(Z_i) = 0.40$. In other words, at the mean the height of the probability density function is 0.40. Similarly, if we entered with, say, $X_i$ = \$7541, \$9420, \$13,180, and \$15,059, which give $Z_i$ values respectively of $-1.00$, $-0.50$, $+0.50$, and $+1.00$, we would obtain corresponding $f(Z)$ values of 0.24, 0.35, 0.35, and 0.24. Totaling these five $f(Z)$ figures, we get 1.58. We thus can see that if $f(Z)$ were considered a probability, the total of just five selected points on the distribution would add to greater than the allowed 1.00. Moreover, a comparison with the percentages (divided by 100) in Fig. 3-1 would show these five $f(Z)$ values to be much greater than expected. At the point one standard deviation below the mean (\$7541), for instance, the probability from Fig. 3-1 would be 0.08, while as computed from Eq. (3-6) it would be three times as much (0.24). These illustrations show rather clearly that an $f(Z)$ value *cannot* be taken as the probability at a given point.

On the other hand, as indicated previously, it is valid to use the normal probability density function to determine the probability that an observation will fall within a specified *interval*. The easiest way to find such a probability is through the cumulative normal distribution. This is diagramed in Fig. 3-5 along with the cumulative empirical distribution, taken from Fig. 3-2. Again, while the "fit" is not exact, it is close enough for our purposes here. Suppose now that we wanted to find the probability that a block owner-occupied housing unit value fell in the range from, say, \$7000 to \$7999 (containing the $Z = 1.00$ figure from above). Using Fig. 3-5 and following the dashed lines, we would find a difference in

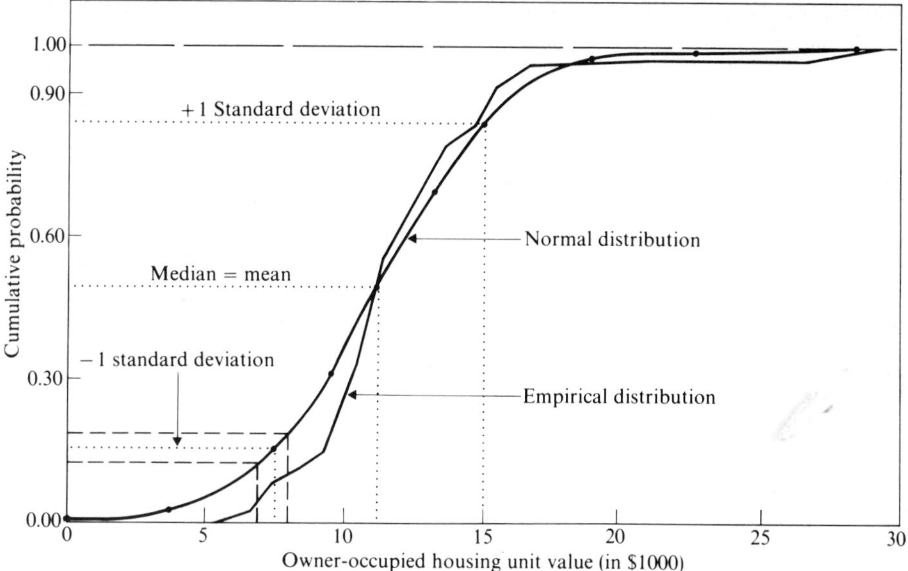


**Figure 3-5** Cumulative normal probability density function and empirical distribution for owner-occupied housing unit values.

cumulative probability of 0.19 − 0.13 = 0.06. A similar difference could have been found by entering the two $Z$ values (for $X$ = \$7000 and \$7999) in Eq. (3-6) and subtracting the results. In any case, a comparison to Fig. 3-1 shows that there actually were five observations (7.5 percent) in the \$7000 to \$7999 interval, while the normal distribution showed 6 percent—a fairly close approximation.

Several properties of the normal distribution should be brought out at this point. First, the interval extending one standard deviation on either side of the mean includes about two-thirds of the cases. Restated, about one-third of the cases fall between the mean (equal to the median in a normal distribution) and $+1\sigma$ and another one-third from the mean (or median) to $-1\sigma$. The actual probability is 0.6826, with 0.3413 on either side. These numbers can be verified in Fig. 3-5. The median of \$11,300 corresponds to a cumulative probability of 0.50 (by definition). The points $\pm 1\sigma$ from the median are 11,300 ± 3759 = \$7541 and \$15,059. Tracing the dotted lines, we find the lower value gives a cumulative probability of 0.16, the higher 0.84. The differences thus are 0.50 − 0.16 = 0.34 and 0.84 − 0.50 = 0.34, which check. The probabilities in the intervals between $\pm 2\sigma$ and $\pm 3\sigma$ are 0.9544 and 0.9974, respectively.

Figure 3-6 shows the probabilities mentioned above in the context of the (noncumulative) normal distribution, with the mean set at 0 for purposes of illustration. From this diagram we can see that the probability of an observation falling in an interval is equivalent to the area under the normal probability density function between the endpoints of that interval. This mathematical fact often

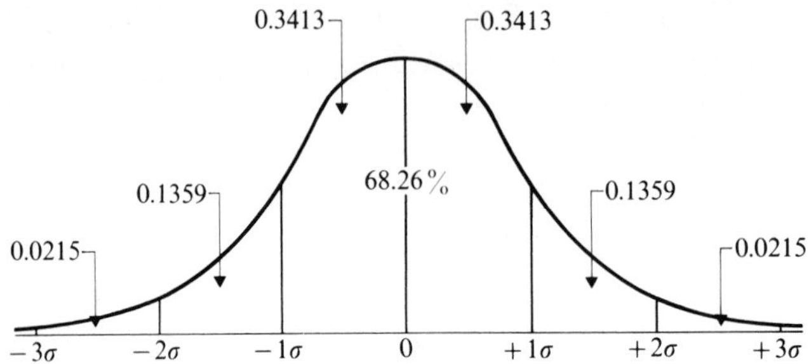


**Figure 3-6** Standard probabilities (areas) under the standard normal probability density function.

is helpful in visualizing the relative probabilities associated with different ranges of $X$.

Figure 3-6 also helps demonstrate the manner in which most tables of normal probabilities (e.g., Table E-1 in App. E) can be employed, instead of a complex formula like Eq. (3-6). If we look at this equation, we see that part of the exponent of $e$ is the standardized score, discussed in Sec. 2-4. Hence all we need to know in Table E-1 is the standardized score for a particular point. We then can find the probability of an observation falling in the interval from 0 (the mean or median) up to that point (the shaded area) and from the point to $+\infty$.

As an example, suppose we had two Census blocks, one with an owner-occupied housing unit value of $5774 and the other with $14,232. What would be the probabilities of an observation falling below and above these points and between these points and the mean? We start by computing the $Z$ scores, which are

$$Z_1 = \frac{5774 - 11{,}300}{3759} = -1.47$$

$$Z_2 = \frac{14{,}232 - 11{,}300}{3759} = +0.78$$

The probability below $Z_1$ (from $-\infty$ to $Z_1$), as deduced from Table E-1† and Fig. 3-7, is 0.0708. In other words, 7.08 percent of the block owner-occupied housing unit values will fall below $5774 in our Census tract area. The corresponding probability for $Z_2$ is 0.5000 (whole area to the left of the mean) $+ 0.2823 = 0.7823$. The likelihood of a block having a value above $Z_1$ or $Z_2$ is, respectively, $0.4292 + 0.5000 = 0.9292$ and 0.2177. Finally, the respective probabilities of falling between the mean (median) and $Z_1$ or $Z_2$ is equal to the associated areas between the intervals under the normal distribution, which in Fig. 3-7 are seen to be 0.4292 and 0.2823.

† Because the normal distribution is symmetrical, the area from $-\infty$ to $Z_1$ $(= -1.47)$ equals that from 1.47 to $+\infty$, which equals 0.50 minus the area from 0 to 1.47 $(=0.4292)$.

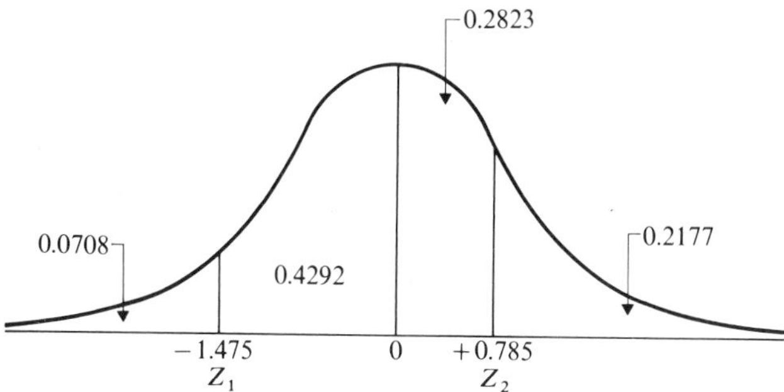


**Figure 3-7** Example calculation of probabilities (areas) for two different levels of owner-occupied housing unit values (standardized).

## Other Theoretical Distributions

In addition to the normal distribution, there are several others for continuous variables that should be mentioned here. They arise primarily in the context of sampling and hypothesis testing (see Chaps. 5 and 6), but certainly can be used independently of these efforts. As might be imagined from the normal distribution, Eq. (3-6), the mathematical formulation of most of these probability density functions can be quite complex, so that most are summarized in Tables E-1 to E-4 (App. E). Moreover, we are by no means restricted to only one variable. If, for instance, we had two variables, each of which were normally distributed and had the same standard deviation, the resulting probability density function would be in three dimensions and look like a real-life bell (see Fig. 3-8*e*). In any case, we will briefly describe four types of cumulative distributions here so that they will be recognizable in future chapters. A comparison will be made to a "smoothed" version of the empirical cumulative distribution for owner-occupied housing unit values, found in Fig. 3-2.

The first distribution is the simplest: it is uniform. As displayed in Fig. 3-8*a*, this distribution is a straight line, in this example running from $X = \$5000$ to $X = \$17,600$, with the same median as the empirical distribution (\$11,300). This uniform distribution surprisingly fits better than the others (although no strong effort was made to find the best-fitting version of the four).

The second distribution, Student's $t$ (or simply $t$), was developed by W. S. Gossett, who published under the name "Student." It bears a close resemblance to the normal distribution, although it would be somewhat flatter and wider if shown as its bell-shaped probability density function (Fig. 3-8*b*). The $t$ score, like the normal, is not necessarily 0 when $X = 0$. Thus a possible inconsistency might arise in comparing a $t$ or normal distribution with some empirical one where the variable (like the owner-occupied housing unit value) could not go below 0.

The third type, shown in Fig. 3-8*c*, is the $\chi^2$ distribution. As will be seen in later chapters, it is used primarily for hypothesis testing related to nominal- or ordinal-scaled variables. The final type, shown in Fig. 3-8*d*, is the $f$ distribution,

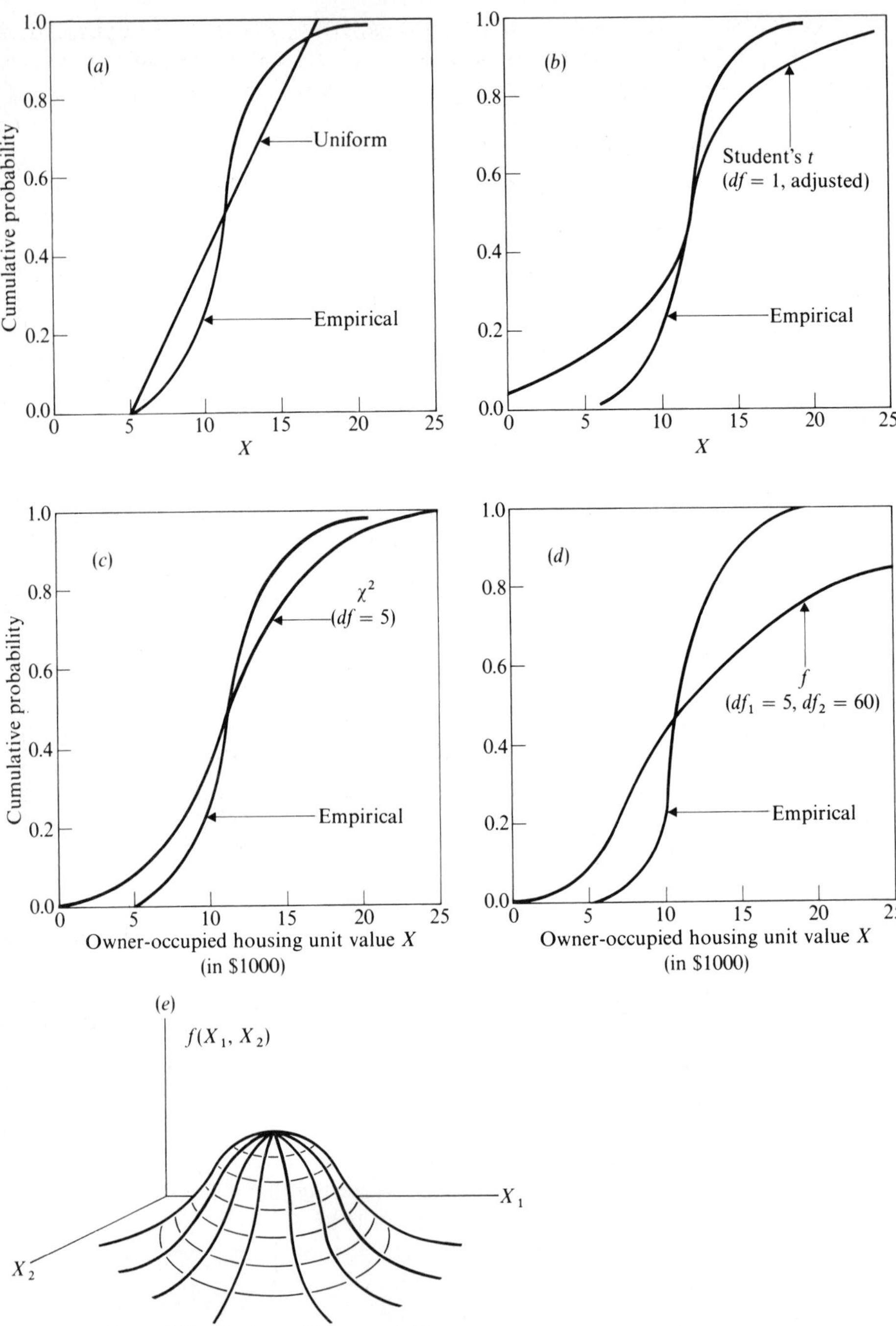


**Figure 3-8** Four different theoretical cumulative distributions compared to an empirical one, and a two-dimensional normal distribution.

named in honor of R. A. Fisher. It does not happen to fit the set of empirical data very well, but this is understandable since it was derived mathematically for the primary purpose of testing the similarity of variances in different distributions.

While none of the four theoretical distributions in Fig. 3-8 closely approximates the empirically derived one, there are many others that might. Usually it is a matter of trial and error to find that distribution which fits best.

## PROBLEMS

**3-1** Fill in the blanks with the proper word(s) or number(s).

(*a*) When a series of interval- or ratio-scaled observations are allocated to their respective class intervals, the resulting diagram is called a ____________________ ____________________.

(*b*) To form a distribution for a nominal- or ordinal-scaled variable, you simply ____________________ the number of ____________________ in each ____________________.

(*c*) A graph depicting a set of mutually exclusive and exhaustive classes of a variable on the $x$ axis (____________________) and the number of cases (____________________) on the $y$ axis (____________________) is called a ____________________ or ____________________ ____________________.

(*d*) The division of the number of cases in each interval, respectively, by the total number gives a ____________________ distribution.

(*e*) If the probabilities in a distribution are added sequentially for each interval, the result is a ____________________ probability distribution.

(*f*) A theoretical distribution in which the variable takes on discrete values is formally called a ____________ ____________ ____________.

(*g*) A theoretical distribution in which the variable takes on continuous values is formally called a ____________ ____________ ____________.

(*h*) In the ____________________ distribution there are only two possible outcomes for each event or situation.

(*i*) The Poisson distribution is closest to reality when the events are both ____________________ and ____________________.

(*j*) In a continuous distribution a probability cannot be specified for a ______________ —only for an ______________.

(*k*) In a normal distribution the probability of a case falling within $\pm 1\sigma$ of the mean is ______________ and within $\pm 2\sigma$ is ______________.

(*l*) The ______________ distribution is similar in form to the normal, only flatter and wider.

**3-2** For the data shown below, plot (to scale):
(*a*) Histogram
(*b*) Probability distribution
(*c*) Cumulative probability distribution

**Urban noise level readings** (decibels)

| Frequency | 2 | 4 | 7 | 10 | 8 | 4 | 3 | 1 |
|---|---|---|---|---|---|---|---|---|
| Noise level | 70–75 | 76–80 | 81–85 | 86–90 | 91–95 | 96–100 | 101–105 | 106–110 |

(*d*) In the above, what is the probability that the decibel noise level will be in the range of 91 to 95 or below?

**3-3** Ten people were asked to give either a negative (N) or positive (P) response to a given building (based on its general utility). It is known that people, in general, are indifferent to the building.
(*a*) What would be the probability that no (0) persons in the sample would respond positively, 1 person, etc., to 10 persons?
(*b*) What would be the mean, standard deviation, and variance of positive responses?

**3-4** It has been found that when a food stamp program was started in any medium-sized city, the average number of new applicants was 2 per hour. Assume that these applicants arrive randomly during the day and that they do not come with other friends or relatives.
(*a*) What is the probability that there will be exactly three applicants arriving in any given hour?
(*b*) What is the standard deviation and variance of arrivals?

**3-5** An average of two vehicles arrives at a local recreation area each 10-minute period on each summer Saturday morning. It has been found that a related group (family) usually comes in one car. What is the probability of three or fewer arrivals during any 10-minute period?

**3-6** A person is being trained to identify substandard housing. There generally is a one-fifth chance of the trainee being incorrect in his evaluation.
(*a*) What is the distribution of the number of incorrect evaluations out of 25 attempts?
(*b*) What is the standard deviation of this distribution?

**3-7** A study is being made of the distribution of floor areas of apartments to determine heating energy needs. The distribution has been found to be close to normal. In terms of standardized scores, what are the points above which the following percentages of the cases fall: 85, 55, 35, 42.3, 9.4?

**3-8** Two-thirds of the residents in a certain neighborhood have incomes less than $10,000 a year. What is the probability that if six different residents from this neighborhood are interviewed, there will be exactly five with incomes under $10,000 per year?

**3-9** The following data were obtained in a housing survey and represent the age of the person termed "head of household."

| | | | | |
|---|---|---|---|---|
| 32 | 26 | 16 | 44 | 28 |
| 40 | 30 | 31 | 17 | 30 |
| 37 | 32 | 42 | 31 | 36 |
| 49 | 35 | 21 | 25 | 40 |
| 27 | 25 | 33 | 34 | 27 |

Assuming these data can be represented by a normal distribution, what is the probability that the age of the head will fall between 40 and 50?

**3-10** Working with your instructor, select a set of data from App. D. For each continuous interval- or ratio-scaled variable:

(*a*) Identify a set of class intervals.
(*b*) Develop a histogram.
(*c*) Develop a probability distribution.
(*d*) Find the cumulative probability distribution.
(*e*) Compare the distribution found in (*d*) to the cumulative normal to see if they are similar.
(*f*) If the normal distribution is not similar, try to find another with a better fit.

For each discrete interval- or ratio-scaled variable:

(*g*) Develop a histogram.
(*h*) Develop a probability distribution.
(*i*) Find the cumulative probability distribution.
(*j*) Compare the distribution found in (*i*) to the cumulative binomial (if appropriate) or Poisson to see how close they fit.
(*k*) If neither seems appropriate, try to find another one with a better fit.

For each nominal- or ordinal-scaled variable:

(*l*) Determine the number of observations falling in each class.
(*m*) Determine the probability of an observation falling in each class.

Use computer programs where available.

## REFERENCES

### Theory

3-1. Guilford, J. P.: *Fundamental Statistics in Psychology and Education*, 4th ed., McGraw-Hill, New York, 1965.
3-2. Krueckeberg, D. A., and A. L. Silvers: *Urban Planning Analysis*, Wiley, New York, 1974.
3-3. Ostle, B.: *Statistics in Research*, Iowa State University Press, Ames, Iowa, 1963.
3-4. Wallis, W. A., and H. V. Roberts: *Statistics: A New Approach*, The Free Press, New York, 1956.

### Applications

3-5. Berry, B. J. L., and F. E. Horton: *Geographic Perspectives on Urban Systems*, Prentice-Hall, Englewood Clifis, N.J., 1970.
3-6. Catanese, A. J.: *Scientific Methods of Urban Analysis*, University of Illinois Press, Urbana, Ill., 1972.
3-7. Tafte, E. R.: *The Quantitative Analysis of Social Problems*, Addison-Wesley, Reading, Mass., 1970.
3-8. Wellman, B.: "Crossing Social Boundaries: Cosmopolitanism Among Black and White Adolescents," *Social Science Quarterly*, vol. 52, no. 3, December, 1971.
3-9. Wohl, M., and B. V. Martin: *Traffic System Analysis for Engineers and Planners*, McGraw-Hill, New York, 1967.

CHAPTER
# FOUR

# PROBABILITY

In Chap. 3 we discussed the concept of frequency distributions and implied ways in which such distributions could be used for hypothesis testing. In the process the concept of probability was briefly introduced. The purpose of this chapter is to develop this concept in greater detail and demonstrate ways in which techniques based on probability theory can be used in policy decision making to reduce the risk of making incorrect decisions.

While we may call it "calculating the odds" or "figuring the chance" or some other name, each of us already uses probability to some extent to aid in our personal decision making. Suppose, for example, that you have just returned from two job interviews, the first for the assistant city manager position in a small town, the second for the assistant budget director post in a major city. While both are acceptable after the interviews, the job of assistant budget director is the more appealing of the two. However, the next day you are offered the assistant city manager's job. Would you accept?

A part of the decision would depend on what you think your chances are of being offered the assistant budget director's job. Assuming there were no other jobs in sight and realizing that working is a necessity, the lower the likelihood of being offered the assistant budget director's job, the more likely you would be to accept the job being offered. You may figure, for instance, that the chance of being offered the preferred job is about one in four. Given these odds you probably would accept the job as assistant city manager. However, if you felt you had about a 75 percent chance of being offered the preferred job, you would probably decide to wait and see.

The point of this little example is that in making this decision you are in effect calculating probabilities and using them in your decision-making process. In this chapter the concept of probability will be formalized and extended to more complicated policy decision-making situations.

## 4-1 THE BASIC CONCEPTS OF PROBABILITY

To understand probability it is necessary to make more explicit some of the terminology used previously or to be employed in succeeding chapters. We usually start any study or experiment with a group of items called a *population* and take a *sample* of them. Each item in the population to be sampled should have an equal chance of being chosen.† Those selected are referred to as *cases*. These may be people or houses or traffic zones or whatever. For each of these cases certain *variables* will be measured. Nominal-scaled variables would be measured in terms of categories or *characteristics*. The observed *value* or *outcome* of a measurement of a variable for a given case is the level or particular characteristic found for that case.

These definitions are illustrated in Table 4-1. We imagine a situation in which 10 people on a particular block in a city are receiving welfare payments. Not all of these recipients are legally entitled to do so. For simplicity, and to avoid some statistical problems, we assume these 10 people comprise both the sample and the total *population*. The *sample* therefore is 100 percent of the population. Each

† Assuming here a random sample. For further elaboration, see Sec. 5-4.

**Table 4-1 Example data on welfare recipients**

| | | Case (person) (recipient) | | | | | | | | | |
|---|---|---|---|---|---|---|---|---|---|---|---|
| Symbol | Variable description | 1 | 2 | 3 | 4 | 5 | 6 | 7 | 8 | 9 | 10 |
| $X_1$ | Receiving legal payments? | L | L | N | N | N | L | L | N | L | N |
| $X_2$ | Age of recipient | M | Y | O | O | O | M | Y | Y | M | M |
| $X_3$ | Race of recipient | B | W | B | W | B | B | B | W | W | B |

| Symbol | Variable description | Characteristic (code) |
|---|---|---|
| $X_1$ | Recipient getting legal payment? | L = receiving legal payment<br>N = not receiving legal payment |
| $X_2$ | Age of recipient | Y = young (under 25 years old)<br>M = middle age (25 to 60 years old)<br>O = old (over 60 years old) |
| $X_3$ | Race of recipient | B = black<br>W = white |

person is a *case*, and we have identified three *variables*, all nominal in scale, for each case. The first variable indicates if the person (case) is legally receiving welfare payments. The *characteristic* L shows he or she is doing so legally, N that he or she is not. As it turns out, person (case) 1 falls in the L category on this variable. Hence he or she receives a *value* (or *outcome*) for this variable of L, as shown in the first row and column in the table.

In our study we will want to refer to situations in which more than one variable is measured for each case. In such studies, often referred to as being *multivariate* (as opposed to *univariate*) in nature, we will call a combination of values or outcomes a *result*. Thus, for example, the result for case 1 is $X_1 = \mathrm{L}$, $X_2 = \mathrm{M}$, and $X_3 = \mathrm{B}$. This definition does not, of course, restrict a result from being only one value or outcome. For instance, we could say that the result for case 1 for variable 1 is L.

We are now in a position to define the *probability* of a particular result. This would be the fraction $n_R/n$, where $n_R$ is the number of cases associated with result $R$ and $n$ is the total number of cases in the sample in the particular study. Thus

$$\Pr(R) = \frac{n_R}{n} \tag{4-1}$$

Note that a probability must range between 0 and 1.

To demonstrate the use of Eq. (4-1), let us define three different results. First, let $R_1$ be the "result" of a recipient being legally entitled to his payment. Since there are five recipients falling in this category ($= n_{R_1}$) and since the total number of cases (people) is 10 ($= n$), we have

$$\Pr(R_1) = \tfrac{5}{10} = 0.5$$

By a similar process, the probability of the result $R_2$ that the recipient is white is $\Pr(R_2) = \frac{4}{10} = 0.4$ and of $R_3$ that the recipient is old is $\Pr(R_3) = \frac{3}{10} = 0.3$. Note here that while a probability is calculated over a set of cases, it is applied to each case in the set.

## 4-2 MUTUALLY EXCLUSIVE AND STATISTICALLY INDEPENDENT RESULTS

Two properties of any pair of results, important from a statistical standpoint, are their mutual exclusiveness and their statistical independence. Two results would be *mutually exclusive* if they had no cases in common. In Table 4-1 the results $R_1$ and $R_3$ have this property. If we lay out the cases for the two relevant variables, we have:

| Case | 1 | 2 | 3 | 4 | 5 | 6 | 7 | 8 | 9 | 10 |
|---|---|---|---|---|---|---|---|---|---|---|
| $X_1$ | (L) | (L) | N | N | N | (L) | (L) | N | (L) | N |
| $X_2$ | M | Y | (O) | (O) | (O) | M | Y | Y | M | M |

Cases 1, 2, 6, 7, and 9 have the L characteristic for $X_1$ (i.e., result $R_1$) but none of these have the O characteristic for $X_2$ (i.e., result $R_3$). In other words, none of the legal recipients are old, and vice versa. On the other hand, some of the youth are legal while others are not, so these two results are not mutually exclusive.

Statistical independence is exemplified by results $R_1$ and $R_2$. Again we lay out the cases for the corresponding variables:

| Case | 1 | 2 | 3 | 4 | 5 | 6 | 7 | 8 | 9 | 10 |
|---|---|---|---|---|---|---|---|---|---|---|
| $X_1$ | L | L | N | N | N | L | L | N | L | N |
| $X_3$ | B | W | B | W | B | B | B | W | W | B |

Pr ($R_1$) is 0.5, as calculated above. Now if we concentrate just on those cases in which the recipient is white, we see that two of the four are legal, or $\frac{2}{4} = 0.5$. Hence the legality of the recipient does not depend on (is statistically independent of) his being white. The same conclusion can be drawn for black recipients since $\frac{3}{6} = 0.5$ of them are "legal." $R_1$ and $R_3$ are not independent, however, since Pr $(R_1) = 0.5$ while none of the legal recipients is old.

## 4-3 RULES OF PROBABILITY

The next step in dealing with probabilities involves combining results. We may want to know, for example, the probability of having either an illegal recipient ($R_4$) or a young recipient ($R_5$) or both. This term would be symbolized as Pr (either $R_4$ or $R_5$ or both) or, for simplicity, Pr ($R_4$ or $R_5$), where it is *understood* that we are also concerned with the situation where *both* $R_4$ and $R_5$ occur. This latter situation is represented by Pr (both $R_4$ and $R_5$), or, for simplicity, Pr ($R_4$ and $R_5$).

Probabilities of combinations like these can be found using the two basic rules of probability. In mathematical form they are

$$\Pr (R_c \text{ or } R_k) = \Pr (R_c) + \Pr (R_k) - \Pr (R_c \text{ and } R_k) \tag{4-2}$$

and

$$\Pr (R_c \text{ and } R_k) = \Pr (R_c) \Pr (R_k \text{ given } R_c) = \Pr (R_k) \Pr (R_c \text{ given } R_k) \tag{4-3}$$

The last term in the second equation is called the *conditional probability*. It is the probability that result $R_c$ will occur or exist on the condition (or given) that $R_k$ has occurred or exists. If a pair of results are independent, it turns out that

$$\Pr (R_k \text{ given } R_c) = \Pr (R_k) \tag{4-4}$$

so that Eq. (4-3) reduces to

$$\Pr (R_c \text{ and } R_k) = \Pr (R_c) \Pr (R_k) \tag{4-5}$$

If a pair of results are mutually exclusive, it turns out that Pr ($R_c$ and $R_k$) = 0, so that the first rule, Eq. (4-2), reduces to

$$\text{Pr}\ (R_c \text{ or } R_k) = \text{Pr}\ (R_c) + \text{Pr}\ (R_k) \qquad (4\text{-}6)$$

These rules can be demonstrated using the information in Table 4-1 to form the cross tabulation in Table 4-2. For instance, 2 of the 10 recipients are both young (Y) and legally receiving payments (L). Hence the number 2 is placed in the corresponding row (one) and column (one) of Table 4-2*a*.

Let us now find the probability of both $R_4$ (illegal recipient) and $R_5$ (young recipient). According to Eq. (4-2), this would be calculated as

$$\text{Pr}\ (R_4 \text{ and } R_5) = \text{Pr}\ (R_4)\ \text{Pr}\ (R_5 \text{ given } R_4) \qquad (4\text{-}7)$$

Since 5 of the 10 people are illegal recipients,

$$\text{Pr}\ (R_4) = \tfrac{5}{10} = 0.5$$

and since 1 of these 5 illegal recipients is young,

$$\text{Pr}\ (R_5 \text{ given } R_4) = \tfrac{1}{5} = 0.2$$

Thus

$$\text{Pr}\ (R_4 \text{ and } R_5) = (0.5)(0.2) = 0.1$$

**Table 4-2 Cross tabulation of data from Table 4-1**

(*a*) Receiving legal payments? versus age of recipient

| | Receiving legal payments? $X_1$ | | |
|---|---|---|---|
| Age of recipient $X_2$ | Yes (L) | No (N) | Total |
| Young (Y) | 2 | 1 | 3 |
| Middle (M) | 3 | 1 | 4 |
| Old (O) | 0 | 3 | 3 |
| Total | 5 | 5 | 10 |

(*b*) Receiving legal payments? versus race of recipient

| | Receiving legal payments? $X_1$ | | |
|---|---|---|---|
| Race of recipient $X_3$ | Yes (L) | No (N) | Total |
| Black (B) | 3 | 3 | 6 |
| White (W) | 2 | 2 | 4 |
| Total | 5 | 5 | 10 |

In this situation $R_4$ and $R_5$ are *not* statistically independent. But we know from previous discussion that $R_1$ (legal recipient) and $R_2$ (white recipient) are. To review, this means that the probability of being a legal recipient is independent of being white or, restated, that the probability of a person being a legal recipient ($\frac{5}{10} = 0.5$) is the same as the probability of being a legal recipient *given that* the person is white ($\frac{2}{4} = 0.5$). So

$$\Pr(R_1 \text{ given } R_2) = \Pr(R_1) = 0.5$$

Hence the probability of being both a legal and white recipient is

$$\begin{aligned} \Pr(R_2 \text{ and } R_1) &= \Pr(R_2)\Pr(R_1 \text{ given } R_2) = \Pr(R_2)\Pr(R_1) \\ &= (0.4)(0.5) = 0.2 \end{aligned} \tag{4-8}$$

Equation (4-5) thus is verified for independent events, although it should be clear from the preceding example that we can use Eq. (4-3) under any circumstances and not really worry about the statistical independence of two results. Note also that the Pr ($R_c$ and $R_k$) can be calculated directly from cross tabulations like in Table 4-2. We simply divide the number in the $c$th row and $k$th column by the total number of cases. Thus Pr ($R_2$ and $R_1$) $= \frac{2}{10} = 0.2$, as computed via the formula.

We are now in a position to find the probability of either $R_4$ or $R_5$ or both, that is, Pr ($R_4$ or $R_5$), using Eq. (4-2):

$$\begin{aligned} \Pr(R_4 \text{ or } R_5) &= \Pr(R_4) + \Pr(R_5) - \Pr(R_4 \text{ and } R_5) \\ &= 0.5 + 0.3 - 0.1 = 0.7 \end{aligned} \tag{4-9}$$

This outcome can be envisioned somewhat intuitively by looking at Table 4-2*a*. We are asking for either illegal recipients, of which the total is 5, or young recipients, of which the total is 3. Together there are 8, but notice that we have counted the 1 young, illegal recipient twice, once for the column total and again for the row total. Hence we should subtract one of these, to give us a total of 7 out of 10, or a probability of 0.7.

If two results are mutually exclusive, by definition there are no overlapping cases and correspondingly the probability of both occurring or existing together is 0. Equation (4-2) subsequently becomes Eq. (4-6). This situation is exemplified by results $R_1$ (legal recipients) and $R_3$ (old recipients) from before. As can be seen in Table 4-2*a*, there are no recipients who are both legal and old; these two results are mutually exclusive. Hence Pr ($R_1$ and $R_3$) $= 0$ and

$$\begin{aligned} \Pr(R_1 \text{ or } R_3) &= \Pr(R_1) + \Pr(R_3) - \Pr(R_1 \text{ and } R_3) \\ &= \Pr(R_1) + \Pr(R_3) - 0 \\ &= 0.5 + 0.3 - 0 = 0.8 \end{aligned} \tag{4-10}$$

Again, it might be noted that we do not have to concern ourselves directly with the question of whether two results are mutually exclusive. Equation (4-2) can be used

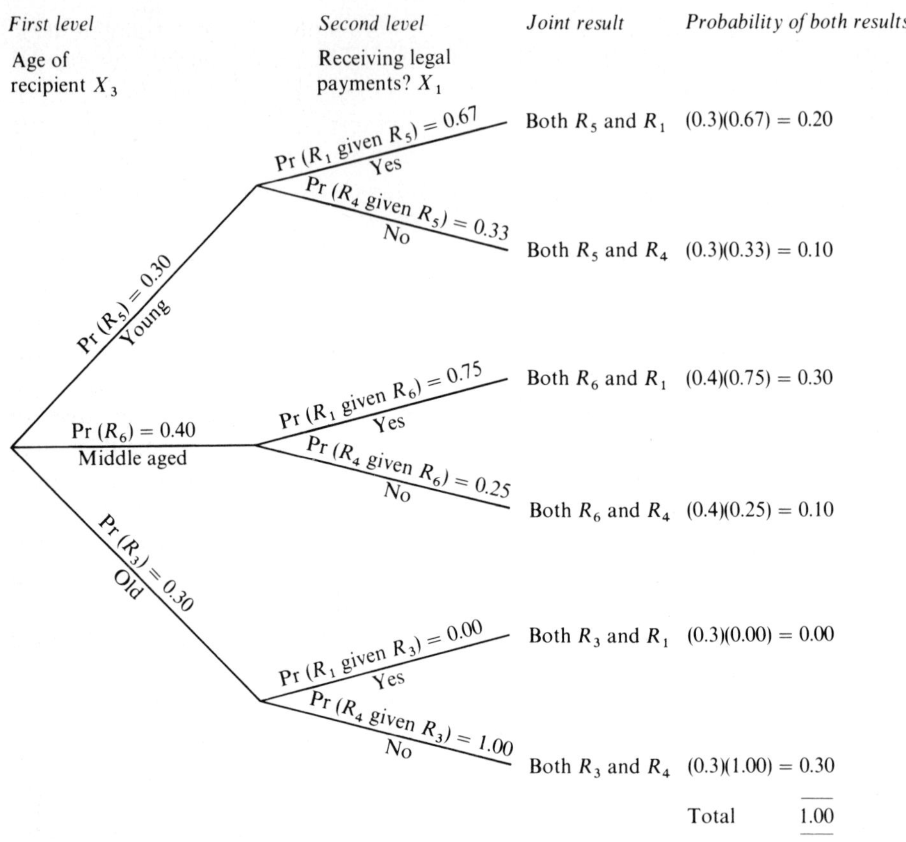


**Figure 4-1** Decision tree for determining probabilities of both of two results.

in any circumstance, with the last term being 0 if the results happen to be mutually exclusive.

While Eqs. (4-2) and (4-3) provide the ultimate approach to calculating probabilities, the use of cross tabulations as in Table 4-2 probably is sufficient for most of the problems the reader of this book will face. In the event a problem is stated in terms of percentages, we would simply imagine the grand total number of cases to be 100 and proceed accordingly from that point.

Another often-useful approach to a probability problem is to consider the characteristics of a variable as branches on a tree, as displayed in Fig. 4-1. We construct such a decision tree (in this case a sideways tree) by letting each of the age characteristics represent a first-level branch. Emanating (or "depending") from each of these are two branches representing the two possible characteristics of payment legality. On each branch on the first level we place the probability for the associated result while on each branch on the second level the relevant conditional probability. To illustrate: in Fig. 4-1 we have defined $R_6$ as the result that a recipient is middle aged. Since 4 of the 10 recipients have this characteristic, Pr $(R_6) = 0.4$ for the middle branch on the first level. Subsequently, if we wanted to find Pr ($R_4$ and $R_6$), we would place the conditional probability Pr ($R_4$ given $R_6$) on the fourth branch down on the second level. Since only one of the four middle-aged people is not receiving legal payments, Pr ($R_4$ given $R_6$) = 0.25, and, multiplying the corresponding branch probabilities, we get $(0.4)(0.25) = 0.10$ for Pr ($R_4$ and $R_6$).

The decision tree can be employed in two additional ways in the process of combining results. First, notice that if a result on a second-level branch is statistically independent of the one on the first level to which it is attached, then according to Eq. (4-5) the conditional probability on the second-level branch becomes simply the probability of the corresponding result. Consequently, if *all* the results with which we are dealing are independent, we can extend the tree out to as many levels as needed and obtain more complex joint probabilities like Pr ($R_c$ and $R_k$ and $R_l$) simply by multiplying the associated individual probabilities together.

Second, if the characteristics (results) for each variable are *mutually exclusive*, the tree can be employed to find the probabilities of combinations of the end results on each branch. This fact can be demonstrated easily if we imagine that the tree in Fig. 4-1 has only the first-level set of branches and we want to find the probability that a recipient was either young or middle aged or both, that is, Pr ($R_5$ or $R_6$). Obviously the recipient cannot have both characteristics, so the results are mutually exclusive and, according to Eq. (4-6), we can simply add the individual probabilities of the two results. This process, of course, would be the same as adding the probabilities on the first two branches of the first level.

To see if we can use one or both of the above procedures, we must establish statistical independence and/or mutual exclusiveness. In many complicated problems these can be determined by answering two questions:

1. *For independence.* Does the occurrence or existence of any result change the probability of any other?
2. *For mutual exclusiveness.* Can any case have two or more characteristics of any variable at the same time?

If the answer to both these questions is "no," the decision-tree approach for finding combinations of probabilities most likely will be useful.

## 4-4 AN EXAMPLE

Suppose it were found from a study of many rural counties across the country that one-quarter had used at least some of their federal revenue sharing money for social programs. The other three-quarters put all their money into other programs, predominately for construction of water and sewer systems, roads, etc. Suppose, further, that we are looking at three other rural counties in an attempt to determine the probability that *at least* two of them will utilize their revenue sharing funds for a social program. Assuming these counties are separated geographically and they are not influenced in their decision by the actions of the other counties, what is the desired probability?

We approach this problem by first identifying the relevant results and probabilities. For example, we might let the result "use of revenue sharing funds by county 1" be designated $R_1$ and the opposite result for county 1 be $R_2$. For county 2 the analogous results would be designated by $R_3$ and $R_4$, and for county 3 by $R_5$ and $R_6$. The probabilities for $R_1$, $R_3$, and $R_5$ are 0.25 and for $R_2$, $R_4$, and $R_6$ are 0.75.

We now try to answer the two questions from the previous section. First, will the occurrence or existence of, say, $R_1$ change the probability of $R_3$, $R_4$, $R_5$, or $R_6$? The answer is "no" since it has been assumed that any one county is uninfluenced by the others. So, for example, county 2 would not change its probability of using the funds for a social program, Pr $(R_3)$, based on the first county's

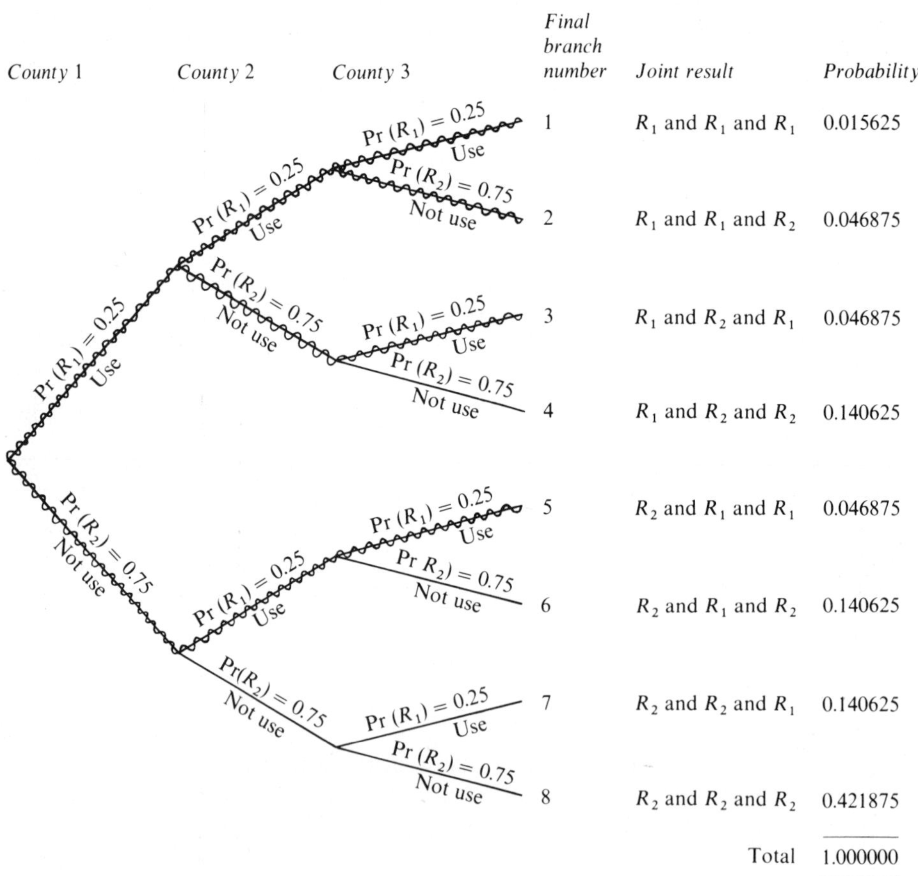


**Figure 4-2** Decision tree for county use of some revenue sharing funds for social programs.

decision. Since this situation pertains to all pairs of results, they are statistically independent and we can use individual instead of conditional probabilities on each branch of our decision tree. As can be seen in the resultant tree in Fig. 4-2, for simplicity we can equate $R_3$ and $R_5$ with $R_1$, and $R_4$ and $R_6$ with $R_2$, since they are, respectively, the same types of result, differing only by county number.

Our response to the second question is also "no." The characteristics (results) for each variable (county) obviously are mutually exclusive since it is impossible for a county to both spend and not spend their funds on social programs. Consequently, we can rightfully add the probabilities at the end of each final branch in Fig. 4-2.

The tree is constructed by starting with county 1 and drawing a branch for each characteristic (use or no use of revenue sharing money for social programs). Similar branches for county 2 are added on to each of those for county 1, and similarly for county 3. Given this construction we subsequently identify those sets of branches which have two *or more* $R_1$ values. Final branches 1, 2, 3, and 5 (hatched) represent the sets that fall into this category. Final branch 1 has three $R_1$ values, the probability of which is $(0.25)(0.25)(0.25) = 0.015625$. Branches 2, 3, and 5 have two $R_1$ values, with a probability for each branch of $(0.25)(0.25)(0.75) = 0.046875$. The total probability for all four sets is $0.015625 + 3(0.046875) = 0.15625$ or, rounded, 0.16. This is the desired probability of two or more counties using some of their revenue sharing funds for social programs.†

## 4-5 ANOTHER EXAMPLE

A second example, with the names changed to protect the innocent, is based on an actual situation where an agency was trying to determine the incidence of venereal disease (VD) in the local population. This example also highlights the use of cross tabulations, instead of equations, to help find desired probabilities.

It was generally known that about 1 in every 1000 people in the locality had VD. A test for the disease had been developed, but it was not absolutely reliable. If a person were known to have VD, the test would show a positive reaction in 99.9 percent of the cases. If a person were known *not* to have VD, the test would give a negative reaction in 99.6 percent of the cases. The agency then wanted to know the probability a person had VD, given that the person had a positive test reaction.

We start by designating results:

$R_1$ = person has VD

$R_2$ = person does not have VD

$R_3$ = person gets positive reaction on test

$R_4$ = person gets negative reaction on test

† Note that this same finding could be obtained using the binomial distribution discussed in Sec. 3-2.

From the problem statement we are given:

$$\Pr(R_1) = 0.001$$

$$\Pr(R_2) = 0.999$$

$$\Pr(R_3 \text{ given } R_1) = 0.999$$

$$\Pr(R_4 \text{ given } R_2) = 0.996$$

and we want to find Pr ($R_1$ given $R_3$).

To solve this problem let us imagine for a moment that a million people have been tested.† This number is placed in the "grand total" (lower right-hand) box of Table 4-3. Since 1 of 1000 people is known to have VD, 1000 of the million will fall into this category, with the remaining 999,000 not having VD (totals on the right-hand side of the table). Further, since 99.9 percent of those having VD (1000 people) will react positively to the test, (0.999)(1000) = 999 will fall under the "positive" column and the "yes" row. The remaining 1 in the row will come under the "negative" column. Of the 999,000 not having VD, 99.6 percent or 995,004 people will react negatively, with the remaining 0.4 percent (3996 people) reacting positively.

Adding down the "positive" column, we see that, of the million people, 4995 react in that manner. The desired probability, that a person who reacts positively to the test has VD, thus can be calculated as 999/4995 = 0.20. This is an astounding outcome. Given the fact that 99.9 percent of those having VD tested positively and 99.6 percent not having VD tested negatively, intuition might lead us to expect the resultant probability to be close to 1.0. Imagine the surprise of health officials and the unneeded anxiety on the part of many of those people being tested when it was anticipated that almost all of those with a positive reaction had VD, but only 20 percent actually did have it.

It is the process for solving this probability problem, however, that is important here. This example shows that it is a relatively easy task to use the cross-tabular approach when there is only a small number (two or three) of variables

† We need a large number here because of some of the small probabilities involved.

**Table 4-3 Cross tabulation of test reactions to incidence of venereal disease**

| Has venereal disease? | Reaction | | Total |
|---|---|---|---|
| | Positive | Negative | |
| Yes | 999 | 1 | 1,000 |
| No | 3996 | 995,004 | 999,000 |
| Total | 4995 | 995,005 | 1,000,000 |

involved. We simply put the available data in their proper place in the table and fill in the remaining boxes. If Eqs. (4-2) to (4-6) had been employed, the resultant algebraic manipulation would have been fairly complex.

## PROBLEMS

**4-1** Fill in the blanks with the appropriate word(s).

(*a*) The entire group of items we consider in a study is called a ____________________.

(*b*) A ____________________ is a subgroup of the items described in (*a*) selected for measurement purposes.

(*c*) Those items selected are referred to individually as ____________________.

(*d*) The entity measured for each selected item is called a ____________________.

(*e*) For a nominal-scaled variable, measurements are made in terms of the variable's

____________________.

(*f*) The observed outcome of any measurement of a variable on an item is called a

____________________.

(*g*) A combination of one or more observed outcomes is called a ____________________.

(*h*) When two or more variables are measured for each case, the study is said to be

____________________ in nature.

(*i*) Two results that have no cases in common are said to be ____________________.

(*j*) If one result has the same probability irrespective of the occurrence or existence of a second

one, the two are said to be ____________________.

(*k*) A ____________________ probability is one in which one result occurs or exists given that another one occurs or exists.

(*l*) A ____________________ shows diagrammatically the different characteristics of a variable in combination with those of another variable (or variables).

(*m*) A ____________________ shows in matrix form the number of cases falling under each combination of characteristics of two variables.

(*n*) A ____________________ can be readily used to find the probabilities of three or more

joint results only when the results are ____________________ and ____________________.

**4-2** What is the probability that a parcel of land is a retail shoe store given that it is a retail commercial property? In a study of urban areas it was found that 10 percent of all parcels were retail commercial and 2 percent of all parcels were retail shoe stores.

**4-3** What is the probability that a criminal will commit either a robbery or injure someone if, from a previous sample of 100 crimes, it was found that 30 were robberies, 20 injuries, and 10 of each of these were a combination of the two.

**4-4** A group of business men consists of 30 percent Democrats and 70 percent Republicans. If 20 percent of the Democrats and 40 percent of the Republicans are in favor of hiring a city planner, what is the probability that a businessman who wants to hire a planner is a Republican?

**4-5** A planner and a developer are involved in 12 conflicts during a period of time. Six are "won" by the planner, four by the developer, and two are standoffs. They are now involved in three other land-use conflicts. Find the probability that:

(*a*) The planner will be successful in all three.
(*b*) Two will be a standoff.
(*c*) The planner and developer will be successful alternately.
(*d*) The developer is successful in at least one conflict resolution.

**4-6** An analysis has been made of the votes by the four members of the planning commission. It has been found that there is an equal chance of an "aye" or "nay" vote on any particular issue. On a future issue, what is the probability of:

(*a*) Four "ayes"
(*b*) Exactly three "nays"
(*c*) Four "ayes" or exactly three "nays"

**4-7** Working with your instructor, develop an exercise to find various individual, joint, and conditional probabilities using the data found in data sets 2 and 6 in App. D. As examples:

(*a*) In data set 2 find the probability of each type of disposal system employed (variable 9), given the selection criteria (variable 10) and/or consideration of a regional approach (variable 16).
(*b*) In data set 2 find the expected cost of collection using the means for each type of collection organization (variables 3 and 8).
(*c*) In data set 6 find the probability that the information helped the client (variable 8), given his or her problem (variable 6).
(*d*) In data set 6 find the probability that a client saw the agency suggested (variable 9), was helped by it or is continuing/pending (variable 11), and was either very or somewhat satisfied (variable 10).

## REFERENCES

### Theory

4-1. Chapman, D., and R. Chaufele: *Elementary Probability Models and Statistical Inference*, Ginn-Blaisdell, Waltham, Mass., 1970.
4-2. Feller, W.: *An Introduction to Probability Theory and Its Applications*, vol. 1, 3d ed., Wiley, New York, 1968.
4-3. Good, I. J.: *The Estimation of Probabilities: An Essay on Modern Bayesian Methods*, MIT Press, Cambridge, Mass., 1965.
4-4. Levinson, H.: *Chance, Luck, and Statistics*, Dover, New York, 1963.
4-5. Ostle, B.: *Statistics in Research*, 2d ed., Iowa State University Press, Ames, Iowa, 1963.
4-6. Raiffa, H.: *Decision Analysis*, Addison-Wesley, Reading, Mass., 1968.

### Applications

4-7. Catanese, A. J.: *Scientific Methods of Urban Analysis*, University of Illinois Press, Urbana, Ill., 1972.
4-8. Dickey, J. W., and R. C. Stuart: "Implementation of Urban Transportation Decisions: A Simultaneous Category Approach," *Highway Research Record 348*, 1971.

4-9. Friend, J. R., and W. N. Jessop: *Local Government and Strategic Choice*, Sage, Beverly Hills, Calif., 1969.
4-10. Krueckeberg, D. A., and A. L. Silvers: *Urban Planning Analysis: Methods and Models*, Wiley, New York, 1974.
4-11. Schneider, J. B.: "Doxiadis' Detroit: Forty Nine Million Alternatives," *Journal of the American Institute of Planners*, vol. 38, September, 1972.

CHAPTER
# FIVE

# SAMPLING

The aim of statistical methods is to find information about a whole population when only a sample is observed. A *population* represents all individuals (objects, elements, processes, etc.) which have a well-defined characteristic, e.g., all households in the Roanoke–Salem SMSA with a member over 60 years of age. Some statistical studies have suffered due to vaguely defined populations. If a population is small, it may be feasible to observe it in total and obtain whatever information is desired. Because populations usually are too large or too scattered, or for other reasons, such a complete survey is not practical and it may even be impossible.

A *sample* consists of those observations of the population that are taken in some well-defined experiment. If the sample is chosen in a suitable manner, it will yield useful information about the whole population. A statistical experiment consists of collecting a sample from a specified population and summarizing and analyzing the sample data, which lead to conclusions about the nature of the population.

## 5-1 ESTIMATING FUNCTIONS

The purpose of the sample is to estimate one or more characteristics of the population, such as median family income, the proportion of housing that is substandard in a region, or the number of deer living in a forest preserve. By using the data taken from a sample of a population, one can compute an estimate of the population characteristic of interest. This estimate, for instance the sample mean or sample variance, is a function of the data; hence, we will call it the *estimating function.*† Each population characteristic has one or more estimating functions. An estimating function is not likely to estimate the population characteristic exactly, but if it is a good function it is highly likely to give a close estimate. In other words, the variance of the function is small and its mean is equal to the population characteristic.

Figure 5-1*a* depicts a distribution of a theoretical function $f$, where its center (the mean of the distribution of the function) equals the population characteristic $\gamma$. The value of $\gamma$ is unknown for, if it were known, there would not be any purpose in estimating it. If the distribution of the estimating function $f$ is normal, then the probability that an estimate from a "good" sample will fall within the dotted lines (one standard deviation above and below the mean) is approximately two-thirds. The estimating function in Fig. 5-1*b* is better than that in Fig. 5-1*a* because its variance is smaller, i.e., the probability an estimate from a sample will be within a specified distance of $\gamma$ is larger for the function which distributes values in the manner shown in Fig. 5-1*b*. The estimating function with the distribution shown in Fig. 5-1*c* overestimates $\gamma$ on the average, while the estimating function in Fig. 5-1*d* underestimates $\gamma$ on the average. We say that an estimating function is *biased* when its mean does not equal the population characteristic it estimates. The function is *unbiased* if its mean equals the population characteristic it estimates. The estimating function in Fig. 5-1*e* is good because it has a small variance in comparison to that in Fig. 5-1*a*, but it is bad because it is biased.

One estimating function of the variance of a population is

$$S^2 = \frac{1}{n} \sum_{i=1}^{n} (X_i - \bar{X})^2 \tag{5-1}$$

However, on the average this function underestimates the population variance by a factor of $(n - 1)/n$, where $n$ is the sample size. Hence, for small samples, Eq. (5-1) is a poor estimating function. The estimate of the population variance given in Chap. 2 is unbiased:

$$S^2 = \frac{1}{n-1} \sum_{i=1}^{n} (X_i - \bar{X})^2 \tag{5-2}$$

## 5-2 SAMPLING ERROR

If one estimates a population characteristic with an unbiased estimating function from a representative sample but the estimate is incorrect (which it will be in almost all cases), the error is called a *sampling error*. This error is not due to the

† Estimating functions are usually called *statistics*. We prefer the name estimating function at this point to emphasize that it is a function and not just a number.

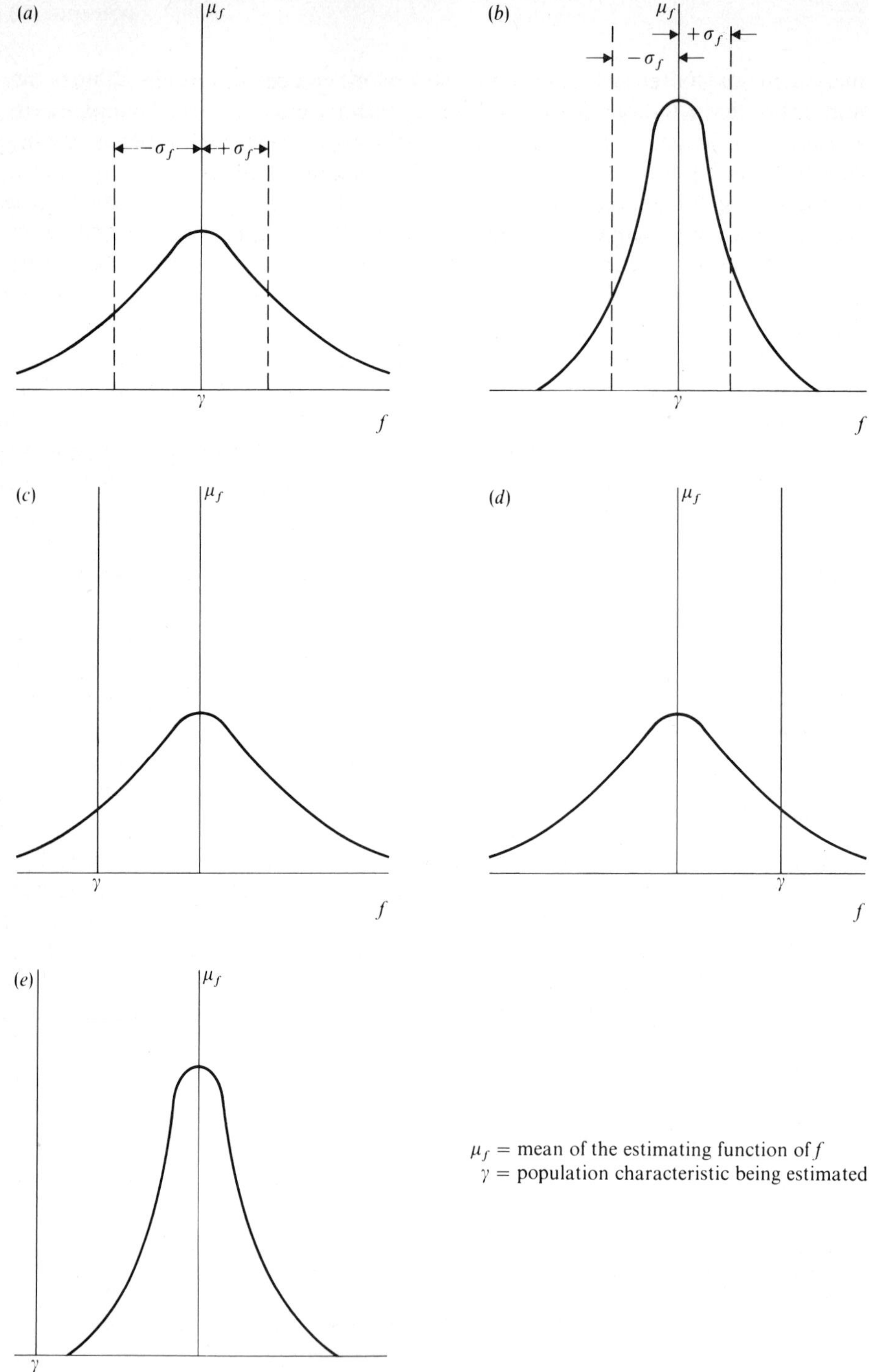


**Figure 5-1** Five different distributions of estimating functions.

incompetence of the researcher but to natural differences in samples. Figure 5-1*a* and *b* show distributions of sampling error with $\mu_f$ and $\gamma$ at zero. To improve the *precision*† of an estimate, one must reduce the standard deviation of the distribution of sampling errors. For practically all estimating functions this can be done by increasing the sample size. To demonstrate the increase in precision from an increase in sample size, we shall explore the distribution of the sample mean.

Let $X$ represent a variable for a given population, e.g., a measure of poverty of a county in the United States such as the percentage of families below the poverty line. We do not know the population mean and variance of the distribution of county poverty in the United States; hence we will refer to them as $\mu_X$ and $\sigma_X^2$, respectively. To estimate $\mu_X$ we will select a sample of size $n$, for we certainly do not want to measure poverty in all of the 3134 counties in the United States, and compute $\bar{X} = (1/n) \sum X_i$. The function $\bar{X}$ is unbiased provided the sample was random and representative. Thus the mean of the sample distribution for $\bar{X}$ is $\mu_{\bar{X}}$:

$$\mu_{\bar{X}} = \mu_X \tag{5-3}$$

The variance of the function is the ratio of the variance of $X$ and sample size $n$:

$$\sigma_{\bar{X}}^2 = \frac{\sigma_X^2}{n} \tag{5-4}$$

The standard deviation, often called the *standard error*, is the square root of Eq. (5-4):

$$\sigma_{\bar{X}} = \left(\frac{\sigma_X^2}{n}\right)^{1/2} \tag{5-5}$$

Figure 5-2 depicts a graph of the standard error versus the sample size. As sample size increases, the standard error decreases but at a decreasing rate. One must consider the diminishing returns when improving precision by increasing sample size. The sample size must be quadrupled to halve the standard error. Later we

† This statistical definition of *precision* is not to be confused with the typical technical (engineering) one of "the number of allowable digits in a measurement."

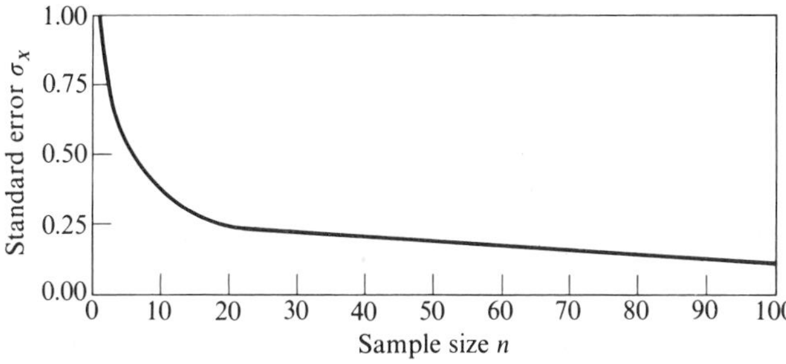


**Figure 5-2** Standard deviation of $\bar{X}$ versus sample size.

will explore other methods of improving precision. When the standard error of an estimating function is inversely proportional to its sample size, we say the function approaches a constant. It also approaches the value of the characteristic being estimated, as $n$ increases, if the function is unbiased. This is known as the "law of large numbers."†

In theory, sampling error can be eliminated if we let the sample be the population. However, in practice, accuracy is lost in attempting to observe the entire population. A sample survey conducted by well-trained interviewers with careful administrative control of the conduct of the survey and the recording and analysis of data give far more accurate results than a massive, poorly controlled population survey. In particular, a mailed population survey that brings returns of 60 percent or less may be far less accurate than a sample survey by personal interview that gets a 100 percent response. An example of how results from samples can be superior to population studies was given by Wallis and Roberts (Ref. 5-11, pp. 32–33):

> During the war, German industrial output and capacity were estimated by British and American statisticians from the manufacturing serial numbers and other marks on captured equipment. According to checks after the war, many of these estimates were quite as good as the estimates by the Germans themselves. They were, moreover, available substantially sooner than the estimates of the Germans, since the Germans waited for complete coverage, whereas the British and Americans were forced to rely on sampling methods. The Germans never did know their total production figures for V-2 missiles, most of which were produced towards the end of the war, while the British and American estimates subsequent to the firing of the first missile, were found by special studies after the war to have been quite accurate.

## 5-3 SAMPLE SIZE

If a planner asks a statistician, "What sample size will I need to survey the proportion of deteriorated houses in a metropolitan area?", he is not likely to get a straight answer, for it depends on many factors, such as the estimating functions that will be used, the variance of the variables being studied, and the precision needed. At this stage of the survey design the planner may not know any of these factors and will not know anything about the variance until after the analysis of the survey results. One way for the statistician to respond to such an unspecific question is to ask, "If your sample gave a proportion of 0.45, how much error could you reasonably accept?" If a difference of amount $\varepsilon$ is the answer, sample size can be computed from the following formula:

$$n = \left(\frac{1}{\varepsilon}\right)^2 \tag{5-6}$$

† There are two laws of large numbers, a "weak" law and a "strong" law. The one referred to above is the "weak law of large numbers." See Ref. 5-4 (pp. 147–149) for an elementary discussion of these laws.

For example, if the planner wants the proportion to be between $0.45 \pm 0.04$, then

$$n = \left(\frac{1}{0.04}\right)^2 = 625$$

Even with this large sample, there exists approximately a 0.05 probability that the absolute error will be greater than 0.04. By using Eq. (5-6) we can only say that there is a 95 percent chance that the true proportion is within the bounds (0.41, 0.49).

Notice that in determining sample size no mention was made of population size. Unless the sample size is large in relation to population size, say one-tenth or more, then population size is not important in determining sample size. A sample of 1500 persons from Nevada's population can give estimates just as precise as a sample of equal size from California's population.

However, the drawback to a small sample from a large population is the difficulty in assuring the representativeness of the sample. A sample such as a Gallup survey of only 1600 persons selected from a population of tens of millions across the United States calls for special procedures to prevent sampling bias. Stratified and cluster sampling are frequently used in such circumstances (Secs. 5-6 and 5-7).

We will now investigate four commonly used probability sampling procedures: simple, systematic, stratified, and cluster random sampling. *Probability sampling* is a selection procedure for which the probability of selecting each member from the population is known. In all of the four procedures some adjustments to the tests described in the following chapter may be needed. These testing procedures assume that a sample was selected by simple random sampling where the sample size is very small in relation to the population size.

## 5-4 SIMPLE RANDOM SAMPLE

A *simple random sample* has the property not only of giving each individual in the population an equal chance of being selected but also of giving each combination (of the same size) of individuals an equal chance of selection. In practice a simple random sample is drawn unit by unit. The units in the population are numbered from 1 to $s$, where $s$ is the population size. A series of random integers between 1 and $s$ is then drawn, either by means of a table of random numbers or by placing the integers 1 through $s$ in a bowl and mixing thoroughly. When a number has been selected, it is not replaced in the bowl or selected again in a random number table, since replacement might allow the same unit to enter the sample more than once. The process is continued until $n$ numbers are selected. The units which bear these numbers constitute the sample of size $n$. Such sampling is described as being *without replacement*. Sampling with replacement is entirely feasible but, except in special circumstances, is seldom used since there seems little point in having the same unit in the sample twice.

It is assumed that there is independence of selection within a sample, i.e., the choice of one individual has no bearing on the choice of another individual to be included in the sample. However, in sampling without replacement, the assumption of independence is not quite met. Whenever the population is large relative to the size of the sample, one can ignore the resulting minor distortion caused by preventing an individual from having a chance to be selected again. If the sample is relatively large as compared with the population, say when the sample size is greater than one-tenth the population size, a correction factor can sometimes be applied to compensate for lack of replacement.

To illustrate: the estimate of the standard error of the estimating function for $\bar{X}$ can be adjusted for the bias caused by sampling without replacement from a finite population:

$$S_{\text{fpe}} = S\left(1 - \frac{n}{s}\right)^{1/2} \tag{5-7}$$

where $s$ is population size. The factor $(1 - n/s)^{1/2}$ is called the *finite population correction factor*. Figure 5-3 shows values of this factor for various sampling fractions, $n/s$.

The failure to give every combination of individuals an equal chance of appearing in the sample may also result in a violation of the independence assumption. For example, to survey the households of a city, a planner may consider this strategy:

1. Separate the city into Census tracks.
2. Randomly select three blocks from each track.
3. Survey two randomly selected households from each block.

If each track has the same number of households, each household has an equal chance of being selected, but not all combinations of households have an equal

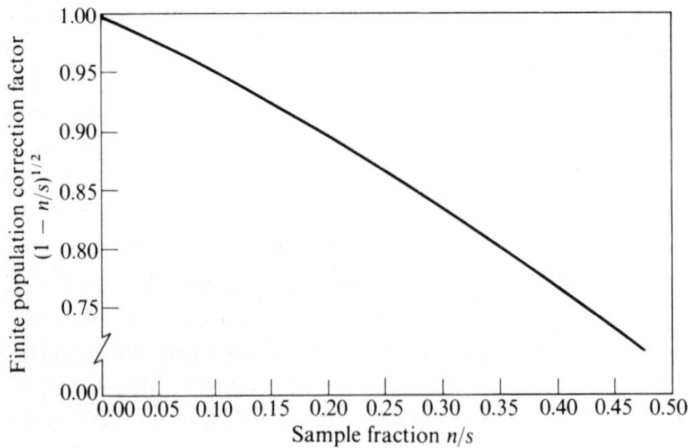


**Figure 5-3** Finite population correction factor versus sampling fraction.

chance of selection. For example, the combination that included three households from the same block has zero chance of selection. Since city blocks are usually relatively homogeneous with respect to characteristics such as the income and education of the head of the household, the result of this type of sampling is to yield less accuracy than a random sample of the same size. If densely populated blocks tend to have the poorer population, then such a sample would be likely to have a smaller proportion of poor households than the proportion in the population. It is possible to get extremely misleading results if, having obtained such a sample, a researcher then used statistical tests that assume a simple random sample.

In conducting a simple random sample, the size of the population and some method to assign a number to each member of the population are needed. Usually a list of the population is necessary; such a list is called a *sampling frame*. Most often in practical research the investigator faces the nearly insolvable problem of the lack of an adequate sampling frame. Frequently the list does not exist. There is no list of all residents of the state of Virginia or all blacks in a city or all households with a member whose age is over 60. Even if a list exists, such as a school roll or a city directory, it usually duplicates many members of the population or does not include important segments of the population, or both. A public school roll may include many duplicates since some families have more than one member in the school. Also, the public school roll may under-represent important segments of the population since many parochial or private school children are not included. City directories may be so out of date by the time they are published as to be highly misleading. Such directories may include many families no longer in the city and exclude new members of the community.

If a list is inadequate or nonexistent, the researcher must consider other sampling schemes or go to the expense of compiling a list or restrict his population to the portion that can be reached. If the purpose of the survey is to determine the need for government service in a region, the researcher may survey only a reachable subpopulation. Then if the analysis of the data indicates a large need in the subpopulation, the researcher may be able to conclude that the total need is not known, but it is known to be large enough to justify the implementation of a program.

## 5-5 SYSTEMATIC SAMPLING

Another type of sampling used quite frequently is *systematic sampling*. It is similar to simple random sampling. Instead of using a random number for each case, we simply go down a list taking every $k$th individual, starting with a randomly selected case among the first $k$ individuals. Our first choice must be determined by some random process such as a selection from a random numbers table. Suppose that we desired a sample of 1000 from a population of 250,000; then $k = 250$. We first select a random number from 1 to 250, say it is 175. The individuals numbered 175, 425, 675, 925, etc., would then be the sample.

Most lists are ordered alphabetically, which usually can be considered random with respect to the variables being measured. If individuals on a list have been ordered according to seniority, age, or by office, then the choice of the starting number may have an inordinate influence on the outcome. Suppose a list were ordered by seniority and that salary was the variable of interest. If the starting number is 2 and the sampling fraction is $\frac{1}{20}$, then the average salary will be larger than a similar sample with a starting number of 18, for, since those with more seniority tend to have larger salaries, $X_{2+20i}$ has more seniority and hence more salary than $X_{18+20i}$ for practically all possible values of $i$.

If the list is ordered according to a periodic characteristic which corresponds to the sampling fraction, then the sample may also be highly biased. For example, in a housing development every eighth dwelling unit may be a corner unit. If it is somewhat larger than the others, its occupants can be expected to differ as well. If the sampling fraction also happens to be $\frac{1}{8}$, one could obtain a sample with either all corner units or no corner units, depending on the random start. To avoid this pitfall, one could change the sampling fraction slightly to $\frac{1}{7}$ or $\frac{1}{9}$ or could make use of several different random starts. After selecting 10 households, one could pick another random number to go to 10 more residences, draw a third number, and so on.

## 5-6 STRATIFIED SAMPLING

In a *stratified sample* we first divide all individuals into groups or categories and then select samples (usually random) within each group or stratum. The strata must be defined in such a way that each individual appears in one and only one stratum. Samples are stratified to obtain more accuracy for a given sample size than with simple random sampling. Another reason is to assure a more representative sample than might be expected from simple random or systematic sampling.

The following notation will be used to discuss stratified random sampling:

$s$ = total population size
$g$ = number of strata into which the population is divided
$s_k$ = population size of stratum $k$; $s = \sum_{k=1}^{g} s_k$
$n_k$ = size of the sample selected from stratum $k$
$n$ = total sample size; $n = \sum_{k=1}^{g} n_k$
$X_{ik}$ = a measure on individual $i$ from stratum $k$
$\bar{X}_k$ = the sample mean of stratum $k$; $\bar{X}_k = (1/n_k) \sum_{i=1}^{n_k} X_{ik}$
$S_k^2$ = the sample variance of stratum $k$; $S_k^2 = [1/(n_k - 1)] \sum_{i=1}^{n_k} (X_{ik} - \bar{X}_k)^2$

If the proportion of individuals in the sample selected from each and every stratum equals the proportion of stratum population size to the total population size, then the sample is called a *proportional stratified sample*. In other words, in proportional stratified sampling:

$$\frac{n_k}{n} = \frac{s_k}{s} \qquad \text{for } k = 1, \ldots, g$$

To gain precision in estimation from such samples, it is important to separate the population into strata that are homogeneous for the variable being investigated. Separating a city into Census tracts may not give homogeneous strata because many of the tracts will include both wealthy and poor neighborhoods.

For proportional stratified samples the estimating function for the population mean is

$$\bar{X} = \frac{1}{n} \sum_{k=1}^{g} \sum_{i=1}^{n_k} X_{ik} \tag{5-8}$$

which is the same as the sample mean ignoring the strata. However, the estimating function for the population variance of the sample mean differs from that given in Eq. (5-4):

$$S_{\bar{X}}^2 = \sum_{k=1}^{g} \left(\frac{S_k}{S}\right)^2 \frac{S_k^2}{n_k} \tag{5-9}$$

If the strata are relatively homogeneous for the variable of interest, then most $\bar{X}_k$ will differ substantially from the population mean and the variance within each stratum, $S_k^2$, will be small relative to the overall sample variance. In other words, the variance between the strata will be relatively large and the variance within the strata will be relatively small.

Further precision can be obtained by disproportionate stratified sampling. If one particular stratum is unusually homogeneous with respect to the variable being studied, it will be unnecessary to select a very large sample from this stratum in order to obtain a given degree of precision. On the other hand, it will be advisable to take a much larger sample from a heterogeneous stratum. The allocation of sample sizes that will maximize efficiency† is the one that minimizes the variance of the estimating function. To obtain this optimum allocation, we need to concentrate on the most heterogeneous stratum, the one with the largest variance. We can obtain such an optimum allocation if we make the sampling fraction for each stratum directly proportional to the standard deviation within the stratum:

$$n_k(\text{optimum}) = \frac{n(s_k \sigma_k)}{\sum_{l=1}^{g} s_l \sigma_l} \tag{5-10}$$

where $s_l$ is the population size and $\sigma_l$ the population standard deviation in stratum $l$ (not necessarily the same one as $k$).

In a study concerned with comparison of means of several subpopulations, such as crime rates among different ethnic groups, some groups may be very small in number relative to the total population. Proportional stratified sampling may produce so few cases in some strata that meaningful comparison will be impossible. Often in such circumstances equal sample sizes are used. To project to the

† See Sec. 5-8 for a definition of the efficiency of a sampling design.

population, we generally adjust each stratum sample mean as will be indicated in Eq. (5-11).

The estimating function for the population mean in the case of disproportionate stratified sampling is

$$\bar{X} = \sum_{k=1}^{g} \frac{s_k}{s} \bar{X}_k \tag{5-11}$$

The variance of this estimating function is the same as for the proportionate case in Eq. (5-9).

Suppose, for example, an estimate of the current average home value in a region that encompasses three counties were wanted. It has been decided to conduct a sample of 500 homes, stratified by county, with optimum allocation of sample sizes. In the last Census a number of years ago the standard deviations of home values in the three counties were 800, 1000, and 2500, and the current population sizes are estimated at 30,000, 20,000, and 50,000 for counties 1, 2, and 3, respectively. "Population" in this problem means the number of single-family residences in a county. Although the standard deviations are no longer correct, it is assumed that their relative sizes have not changed. To determine optimal allocation of sample size for a total size of 500, we compute:

$$\sum_{l=1}^{3} s_l \sigma_l = 30{,}000(800) + 20{,}000(1000) + 50{,}000(2500) = 169{,}000{,}000$$

$$n_1 = (500)\frac{30{,}000(800)}{169{,}000{,}000} = 71$$

$$n_2 = (500)\frac{20{,}000(1000)}{169{,}000{,}000} = 59$$

$$n_3 = (500)\frac{50{,}000(2500)}{169{,}000{,}000} = 370$$

Data for the counties are summarized in Table 5-1. Let us assume that simple random sampling was used within each stratum and the samples were independently drawn. Since sample sizes for the strata are not proportionate, Eqs. (5-11) and (5-9) must be used. Finite population correction factors can be ignored since the ratios of sample sizes to population sizes are very small. The estimated mean and variance are

$$\bar{X} = \frac{30{,}000}{100{,}000}(13{,}000) + \frac{20{,}000}{100{,}000}(11{,}000) + \frac{50{,}000}{100{,}000}(21{,}500)$$

$$= 0.3(13{,}000) + 0.2(11{,}000) + 0.5(21{,}500) = 16{,}850$$

$$S_{\bar{X}}^2 = (0.3)^2\,\frac{(1100)^2}{71} + (0.2)^2\,\frac{(1200)^2}{59} + (0.5)^2\,\frac{(3000)^2}{370} = 8591$$

**Table 5-1 Data for computing estimates from a disproportionate stratified random sample**

| | County | | | |
|---|---|---|---|---|
| | 1 | 2 | 3 | Total |
| Population sizes $s_k$ | 30,000 | 20,000 | 50,000 | 100,000 $(s)$ |
| Sample sizes $n_k$ | 71 | 59 | 370 | 500 $(n)$ |
| Sample means $\bar{X}_k$ | 13,000 | 11,000 | 21,500 | |
| Sample standard deviations $S_k$ | 1,100 | 1,200 | 3,000 | |

One should not expect too much from stratified random sampling. While the best strategy calls for separating the population into homogeneous strata, one cannot sample within the strata nor compute the resulting estimates unless one has a list of the individuals in the strata and knows the population size and variance of each stratum. However, this information frequently is not known. Hence one is forced to create strata for which the information is known or can be easily approximated. But if the strata are heterogeneous for the variables being explored, little is gained by stratification.

A particular stratum may be very homogeneous with respect to one variable being studied and yet heterogeneous with respect to another. Since a research project usually involves a study of more than one variable, it may be extremely difficult to find allocations which are optimal, or nearly optimal, for more than one variable. A design that is very efficient for one variable may be inefficient for another. However, estimates from a stratified random sample are almost always more precise than those from a simple random sample.

## 5-7 CLUSTER SAMPLING

In stratified sampling one divides the population into strata and samples from each stratum. In *cluster sampling* one also divides the population into groups, called *clusters*, selects a sample of clusters, and then samples from the selected clusters. Since in stratified sampling a sample consists of members from each stratum, the best strategy is to divide the population into homogeneous groups. Since each cluster is not represented in cluster sampling, the best strategy is to let each cluster be representative of the population. The aim in cluster sampling is to select clusters as heterogeneous as possible but small enough to reduce costs in conducting the sample.

The simplest cluster sample design is to divide the population into clusters, select $r$ clusters by simple random sampling, and then observe the entire subpopulation within each selected cluster. Such a design is called *single-stage cluster design* since sampling occurs only once in the process. Suppose information about the amount of different types of agricultural land used in a large region is wanted. An example of a single-stage cluster sampling process would be:

> A map of the region is divided into 50 subregions; numbers from 1 to 50 are placed on the subregions; 15 random numbers in the range from 1 to 50 are selected without replacement from a random numbers table; a farm agent is sent to each of the 15 subregions and measures the acreage of each type of agricultural land used in the entire subregion.

In single-stage cluster sampling we have no sampling error within the cluster since each case is observed. The sample error is due to variability between clusters. Hence we reduce the variability between clusters by designing groupings as representative of the population as possible.

A *two-stage cluster design* calls for simple random sampling within the cluster as well. Multistage cluster designs can be very complex, as the following example shows:

> Select a random sample of Census tracts within a city. From the chosen tracts select a simple random sample of blocks. From the chosen blocks select a random sample of dwellings. From the chosen dwellings interview the second oldest adult.

The following notation will be used to discuss cluster sampling:

$g$ = number of clusters in the population
$r$ = number of clusters selected by simple random sampling
$s$ = total population size
$s_k$ = population size of cluster $k$
$n_k$ = size of sample from cluster $k$
$X_{ik}$ = a measure of an individual $i$ from cluster $k$

The sample mean of cluster $k$ is thus

$$\bar{X}_k = \frac{1}{n_k} \sum_{i=1}^{n_k} X_{ik} \tag{5-12}$$

The variance within a cluster is

$$S_k^2 = \frac{1}{n_k - 1} \sum_{i=1}^{n_k} (X_{ik} - \bar{X}_k)^2 \tag{5-13}$$

And the variance between clusters, $S_b^2$, is defined as

$$S_b^2 = \frac{1}{r - 1} \sum_{k=1}^{r} (\bar{X}_k - \bar{X})^2 \tag{5-14}$$

where $\bar{X}$ is the estimating function of the overall (or "grand") population mean through either a one- or two-stage cluster design. Under the former:

$$\bar{X} = \frac{1}{r} \sum_{k=1}^{r} \bar{X}_k \qquad \text{where } n_k = s_k \text{ for all } k \tag{5-15}$$

and under the latter:

$$\bar{X} = \frac{1}{r}\sum_{k=1}^{r}\bar{X}_k \qquad \text{where } n_k \neq s_k \text{ for all } k \tag{5-16}$$

The estimated variance of the single-stage estimating function for $\bar{X}$ is

$$S_{\bar{X}}^2 = \frac{g-r}{g}\,\frac{S_b^2}{r} \tag{5-17}$$

With a two-stage cluster design:

$$S_{\bar{X}}^2 = \frac{g-r}{g}\,\frac{S_b^2}{r} + \frac{1}{r}\sum_{k=1}^{r}\frac{s_k-n_k}{s_k}\,\frac{S_k^2}{n_k} \tag{5-18}$$

Cluster sampling is particularly useful in sampling over a geographical area where a list of the population is not available. If the cost of compiling such a list would be prohibitive, the area can be divided into subregions and a few of these

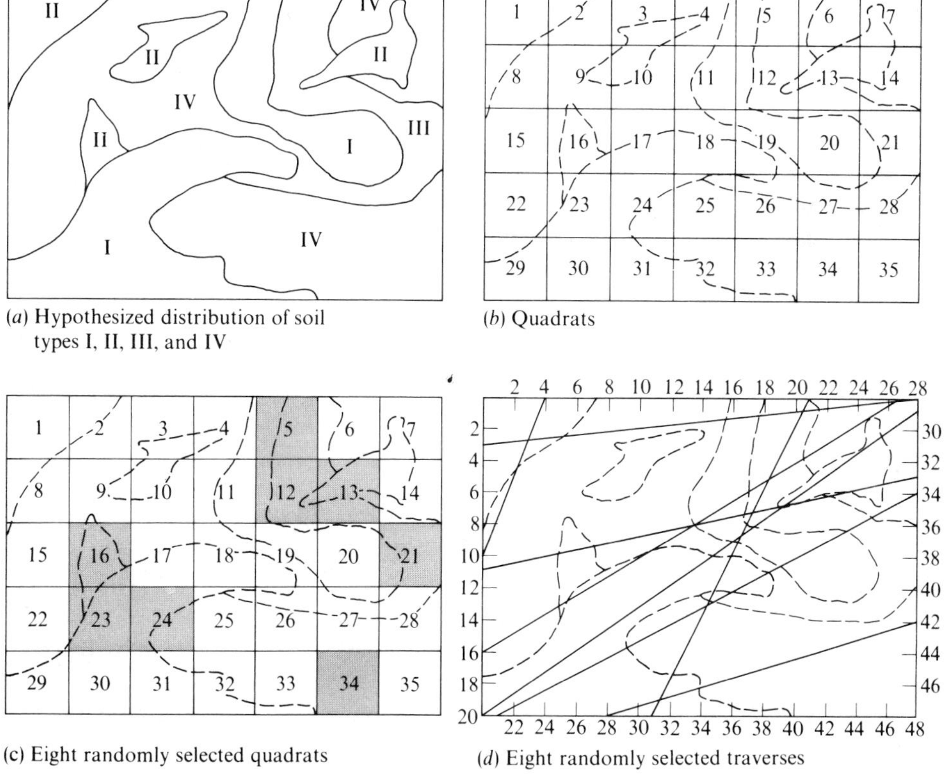


(*a*) Hypothesized distribution of soil types I, II, III, and IV

(*b*) Quadrats

(c) Eight randomly selected quadrats

(*d*) Eight randomly selected traverses

**Figure 5-4** Quadrat and traverse cluster sampling designs for a region with unknown soil-type distribution.

selected by simple random sampling. Instead of compiling a list for each subregion, the researcher visits all individuals in the subregion. We assume that all individuals in a specified subregion can be found.

Suppose we wish to determine soil type of an area. Figure 5-4*a* shows such a region with various types. Figure 5-4*b* indicates the same region divided into quadrats and numbered. Suppose the eight numbers 34, 24, 23, 21, 13, 12, 16, 5 are chosen from a random numbers table; then the shaded quadrats in Fig. 5-4*c* are measured in their entirety for soil types. One problem with the quadrat sample is the tendency of soil types to be homogeneous over small areas. To get more heterogeneous clusters, traverses could be chosen as the clusters. In Fig. 5-4*d* the perimeter of the region is divided and numbered. Pairs of random numbers are chosen. The first number of each pair must fall between 1 and 48, and the second number between 1 and 48. A traverse is drawn between the pairs of numbers. The researcher travels the traverses and records soil types along the way. The proportion of the traverse of one soil type is an estimate of the proportion of that soil type in the area. Traverses tend to cover a variety of soil types; thus they are more likely to be more heterogeneous than quadrats for variables of this type. The traverses in Fig. 5-4*d* are the results of random pairs 20-29, 3-28, 10-4, 31-21, 16-27, 21-34, 11-33, 28-42.

## 5-8 EFFICIENCY OF SAMPLING DESIGN

The efficiency of a sampling design is measured by the ratio of the theoretical variance of the estimating function for the design to the theoretical variance of the function under simple random sampling. For example, consider the function to estimate the population mean. The following formulas indicate conceptually the approximate efficiencies of the estimates under the different designs:

Proportional stratified sampling:

$$\frac{S_{\text{prop}}^2}{S_{\text{ran}}^2} \approx 1 - \frac{\sigma_b^2}{\sigma^2} \tag{5-19}$$

Optimum stratified sampling:

$$\frac{S_{\text{opt}}^2}{S_{\text{ran}}^2} = \frac{1}{g\sigma^2} \sum_{k=1}^{g} (S_k - \bar{S}) - \frac{\sigma_b^2}{\sigma^2} \tag{5-20}$$

where $S_{\text{prop}}^2$ = estimated variance of the sample mean from proportional stratified sampling

$S_{\text{ran}}^2$ = estimated variance of the sample mean from simple random sampling

$\sigma_b^2$ = between-strata variance

$\sigma^2$ = population variance of the sample mean under random sampling

$g$ = number of strata (or clusters)

$S_k$ = sample standard deviation within stratum $k$

Also,

$$\bar{S} = \frac{1}{s} \sum_{k=1}^{g} s_k S_k \tag{5-21}$$

which is a weighted mean overall standard deviation where $s$ is the total population size and $s_k$ the size within stratum $k$.

Cluster sampling:

$$\frac{S^2_{\text{clus}}}{S^2_{\text{ran}}} \approx 1 + \rho(\bar{s} - 1) \tag{5-22}$$

where $\bar{s}$ is the average cluster size and $\rho$ is a number between $-1$ and 1 called the *interclass correlation coefficient.*†

If the clusters are more homogeneous than would be expected by chance, $\rho$ will be positive. The more homogeneous the clusters, the larger the value of $\rho$. In almost all samples $\rho$ will be positive and hence the efficiency ratio will be larger than 1. The larger the efficiency ratio, the less efficient the sampling design. The efficiency of the first two designs will be less than 1 in practically all samples; hence they are usually more efficient than simple random sampling. In the vast majority of samples the estimated variances rank as follows:

$$S^2_{\text{opt}} \leq S^2_{\text{prop}} \leq S^2_{\text{ran}} \leq S^2_{\text{clus}} \tag{5-23}$$

The smaller the variance in this ranking, the more precise the estimate.

## 5-9 CHECKING THE ADEQUACY OF A SAMPLE

When conducting a survey, one or more questions or measures should be included for which population distributions are known. The sample distribution of these variables can be checked with the known distributions. If the sample distributions do not come close to the expected distribution, the sample may be biased. If the sample is biased and important segments of the population are underrepresented, the researcher can consider that his sample is a nonproportional stratified sample. Each case of a variable can be weighted so that its relative importance in the sample equals its importance in the population. For example, suppose a sample of size 100 contains 70 percent males and 30 percent females, but the proportion should be 50 percent males and 50 percent females. Also suppose that one variable is income. The income for males could be weighted by 1 and the income for women could be weighted by $2\frac{1}{3}$ (70/30). This will be equivalent to adding 40 females to the sample, producing a simulated sample of size 140. The mean and variance of the weighted income will be equivalent to the mean and variance under stratified random sampling.

† The correlation coefficient is described in Chap. 9.

## PROBLEMS

**5-1** Fill in the blanks with the appropriate word(s).

(*a*) The aim of statistical methods is to find information about a whole ____________ when only a ____________ is observed.

(*b*) A ____________ consists of those cases in the population that are actually observed in the process of some ____________.

(*c*) A relationship used to find approximations to a population characteristic is called an ____________ or a ____________.

(*d*) An estimating function is ____________ when its ____________ does not equal the population characteristic it estimates.

(*e*) ____________ is that which occurs when an estimate of a population characteristic is incorrect.

(*f*) The standard deviation of an estimating function is often called the ____________.

(*g*) In an estimating function we often have to substitute the ____________ value for the population value to obtain estimates of other population characteristics.

(*h*) ____________ is a sampling procedure for which the probability of selecting each member from the population is known.

(*i*) In ____________ sampling, each individual in the population has an equal chance of being selected, as does each combination (of the same size) of individuals.

(*j*) Sampling can be done with or without ____________.

(*k*) A list of the population is called a ____________.

(*l*) The bias caused by sampling without replacement from a limited population can be corrected through the ____________.

(*m*) Sampling in which every *k*th individual is taken after a random start is called ____________.

(*n*) In a ____________ sample, all individuals are first divided into groups and a random sample then is taken within each group.

(*o*) If the proportion of individuals sampled in each and every stratum equals the proportion of the stratum population to the total population, the sample then is called a ____________.

(*p*) To improve the ____________ of an estimate, one must reduce its standard error.

(q) In ______________________ sampling, the population is divided randomly into groups and then samples taken from selected groups.

(r) The ______________________ of a sampling design is measured by the ______________________ of the theoretical variance of the estimating function for the design to the theoretical variance under simple random sampling.

**5-2** Listed in the table below are the annual household incomes found in a random sample (without replacement) taken from 1000 households in a city.

| Income per year | (in \$1000) |
|---|---|
| 11.8 | 12.0 |
| 11.7 | 11.7 |
| 12.1 | 12.0 |
| 11.9 | 10.8 |
| 12.0 | 12.0 |

(a) Compute the mean of this sample.
(b) Compute the standard deviation.
(c) Compute the standard error of the mean.

**5-3** Suppose that the Office of the Aging wants to survey those over 60 years of age in a city. Census data for the city are available for the 21 Census tracts and for each of the about 100 blocks within the tracts.

(a) The agency wants an estimate of the proportion of women in the elderly population with a 0.95 probability of $a \pm 0.10$ accuracy. What is the minimum sample size needed to get such accuracy?
(b) Design a stratified sampling procedure. Specify in detail how each observation will be made. Point out the weaknesses of the design. Will you need lists of the populations? If you do, suggest where the lists might be found.
(c) Design a cluster sampling procedure and again point out the weaknesses of the design.

**5-4** Results of a survey to determine the amount of crime in an urban area are shown below. The survey was done by a stratified sampling design with equal allocation of 100 cases to each of four strata (police precincts). The key variable was a crime investigation success index, which was a measure of the success of the apprehension and conviction of a criminal weighted by the seriousness of the crime.

| | Precinct | | | | |
|---|---|---|---|---|---|
| | 1 | 2 | 3 | 4 | Total |
| Size of precinct $s_k$ (no. of crimes) | 1500 | 2000 | 1800 | 2200 | 7500 |
| Size of sample $n_k$ | 100 | 100 | 100 | 100 | 400 |
| Sample mean $\bar{X}_k$ | 30 | 25 | 40 | 35 | |
| Sample standard deviation $S_k$ | 5 | 6 | 6 | 7 | 6.093 |

(*a*) Is the sample proportionate or disproportionate?
(*b*) Compute the estimate of the population mean.
(*c*) Compute the estimate of the standard deviation of the estimating function.
(*d*) Assuming, in a somewhat different situation, that we wanted to design an optimum allocation of the total sample of 400 and the above sample standard deviations actually were ones found from a previous study, what are the optimum sample sizes for each precinct?
(*e*) What is the resulting estimate of the standard deviation of the estimating function?
(*f*) What is the efficiency of both types of sampling design?

**5-5** The survey in Prob. 5-4 was repeated, but with a one-stage cluster design. Clusters were Census blocks. Five blocks were chosen from a total of 90 blocks by simple random sampling and all crimes reported in the five blocks were investigated.

| Block | 1 | 2 | 3 | 4 | 5 |
|---|---|---|---|---|---|
| Mean | 33 | 40 | 30 | 35 | 42 |

Compute the following:
(*a*) Estimate of the population mean
(*b*) Estimate of the standard deviation of the estimating function
(*c*) Efficiency of this sampling design if the population variance estimated from the overall sample of 100 were 20.0

**5-6** A traverse sample was employed on the 1970 Census tracts in Roanoke, Virginia (data set 3 in App. D). The traverse along line *AA* crossed tracts 1, 9, 10, 19, 18, 17, and 16. Find for the variable "rent per renter occupied unit" the following:
(*a*) Estimated population mean
(*b*) Standard error of the mean

**5-7** Go go the library and find in some journal or book an application of a (complicated) sampling design. In about 500 words:
(*a*) Describe the sampling design in detail.
(*b*) Discuss possible weaknesses of the design.
(*c*) State any information not given by the author you would need to know if you wished to replicate the design.

**5-8** Working with your instructor, select a set of data from App. D and take a series of samples from it. Find the estimated population mean and standard error for the following:
(*a*) Simple random sample
(*b*) Systematic random sample
(*c*) Proportionate stratified sample
(*d*) Disproportionate stratified sample
(*e*) One-stage cluster sample
(*f*) Two-stage cluster sample
(*g*) Traverse cluster sample (data set 3)
In (*c*), (*d*), and (*f*) also find the within-stratum or cluster population means and standard errors.

## REFERENCES

### Theory

5-1. Cochran, W. G.: *Sampling Techniques*, 2d ed., Wiley, New York, 1963.
5-2. Cochran, W. G., F. Mosteller, and J. W. Tukey: "Principles of Sampling," *Journal of the American Statistical Association*, vol. 49, 1954.
5-3. Kish, L.: *Survey Sampling*, Wiley, New York, 1965.

5-4. Lindgren, B. W., and G. W. McElreth: *Introduction to Probability and Statistics*, 3d ed., Carter Macmillan, London, 1969.
5-5. Yeates, M.: *An Introduction to Quantitative Analyses in Human Geography*, McGraw-Hill, New York, 1974.

**Applications**

5-6. Berry, B. J. L.: "Sampling, Coding and Storing Flood Plain Data," *U.S. Dept. of Agriculture Handbook 237*, U.S.GPO, Washington, D.C., 1962.
5-7. Haggett, P.: "Regional and Local Components in the Distribution of Forested Areas in South East Brazil: A Multivariate Approach," *Geographical Journal*, vol. 130, 1964.
5-8. Haggett, P., and C. Broad: "Rotation and Parallel Traverses in the Rapid Integration of Geographic Areas," *Annals, Association of American Geographers*, vol. 54, 1964.
5-9. Survey Research Center, The University of Michigan: *A Panel Study of Income Dynamics: Study Design, Procedures, Available Data*, vol. I, Ann Arbor, Mich., 1972.
5-10. Tanur, J. M.: *Statistics: A Guide to the Unknown*, Holden-Day, San Francisco, Calif., 1972.
5-11. Wallis, W. A., and H. V. Roberts: *The Nature of Statistics*, Collier Books, New York, 1962.
5-12. Wood, W. F.: "Use of Stratified Random Samples in a Land Use Study," *Annals, Association of American Geographers*, vol. 45, 1955.

CHAPTER

# SIX

# HYPOTHESIS TESTING

In the movie *Twelve Angry Men* a young man was on trial for the murder of his father. The prosecution presented a series of "facts," none of which proved the young man guilty but each of which certainly cast doubt on the major hypothesis required under most justice systems: the accused is innocent. Each "fact" represented a reporting of an event that happened which would be extremely unlikely if the hypothesis were true. So unlikely was the evidence under the assumption of innocence, that eleven of the twelve jurors had rejected the hypothesis even before beginning deliberations.

One piece of evidence was the murder weapon, a knife just like the one once owned by the accused. "A very unusual knife," said the prosecutor, leaving the impression that the coincidence of the murderer and an innocent accused both owning such an unusual knife was extremely unlikely. However, at a dramatic moment in the jury deliberation, the hero, played by Henry Fonda, produced an identical knife he found by accident in a store near the court house during a break in the trial. With this information the event no longer seemed implausible, and the jury no longer was willing to reject the assumption of innocence because of it. However, there were other pieces of evidence, some of which were even more implausible, which convinced many members of the jury to assume the accused was guilty. Piece by piece the plausibility or reliability of the damaging evidence was refuted until no jury member was willing to reject the basic hypothesis of innocence.

This jury, like most juries, had to deal with evidence which was convincing but not conclusive. If a jury finds the accused guilty, it should do so beyond all reasonable doubt. Hence, guilt is not proven, but the conditional probability that the accused is innocent, given that he was declared guilty, should be small:

$$\text{Pr (innocent, given that the accused was found guilty)} = \alpha$$

If the jury finds the accused innocent, it may err in the other direction. Innocence is not proven, but the conditional probability that the accused is guilty, given that he was declared innocent, should also be small:

$$\text{Pr (guilty, given that the accused was found innocent)} = \beta$$

Which is the more important, a small $\alpha$ (the probability of penalizing an innocent person) or a small $\beta$ (the probability of setting free a guilty person)? Those persons who live in a society that places great emphasis on assuring a small $\alpha$ are fortunate. However, there are trade-offs, for reducing $\alpha$ often increases $\beta$. A good justice system is one that assures both a small $\alpha$ and $\beta$ but prefers that $\alpha$ is smaller than $\beta$.

The decision-making process of the jury is in many ways similar to that of the researcher doing hypothesis testing. The point of this discussion and the story that follows is to show that elements of hypothesis testing occur in our daily lives, and it is not a process used only by scientists and those unfortunate students who must take a statistics course. Hypothesis testing is a systematic procedure used to make inferences. We all make inferences about our environment every day of our lives and in so doing use the same elements of hypothesis testing.

## 6-1 PROBLEMS IN THE INFORMAL PROCESS OF MAKING INFERENCES

Suppose there exists a small city that is crossed by two major highways numbered 5 and 220. Highway 220 goes through the poorest section of the city and Highway 5 goes through wealthy neighborhoods and prosperous business sections. A new visitor approaching the city on Highway 220 speculates about what the city will be like. The first hypothesis formed is that it is just another city, like many others seen earlier. However, upon viewing the evidence—block after block of dilapidated neighborhoods—the visitor rejects this notion, and concludes instead that this is an economically depressed city. Another visitor, traveling along Highway 5 through wealthy sections of the city, also rejects the hypothesis that economically the city is average. Instead, the second visitor concludes that it is more prosperous than the average city.

The two visitors meet at a convention and engage in a heated discussion about the economic condition of the city. They leave the convention concluding that their new acquaintances, while intelligent about other matters, are naive about urban affairs.

This story points out problems with the typical day-to-day process of making inferences which formal hypothesis testing attempts to overcome. These problems are:

1. *Observing a biased sample.* Considerable planning is needed to select cases in the population that are to be observed. The above visitors accepted those cases that came to them by accident.
2. *Observing too few cases.* This is often called "jumping to conclusions." Frequently we reject or accept hypotheses based on only one case.
3. *Using an invalid variable.* Determining the economic condition of the occupants of a building by the measurement of its outward appearance may not be valid. The building's appearance may be more a reflection of its age than the economic condition of its occupants. An invalid variable is one that does not measure what the observer intends for it to measure.

   Sometimes we think of a variable as the phenomenon which it is supposed to measure. Other times we think of a variable as data. Neither view is correct in this book. A variable is a scheme for measuring a phenomenon. For example, IQ is neither intelligence nor the IQ scores one finds on a computer output. IQ is the procedure for measuring the phenomenon of intelligence. An invalid variable is one that measures the wrong phenomenon. Is IQ a valid variable?
4. *Using an unreliable variable.* Judgments about the conditions of buildings by observing them from an automobile, called "windshield surveys," are notoriously unreliable. There will be great variation among observers regarding their evaluation of the conditions of the same buildings. Even the same observer will draw one conclusion about the condition of a building one day and a different conclusion about the same building on another day. An unreliable variable is one which may be valid but is not consistent in its measurements of the same event.
5. *Accepting only concurring evidence.* Once a conclusion has been made, either by inference from evaluating a sample or from the testimony of an authority, one tends to ignore new evidence that contradicts the previous conclusion and to accept evidence that supports it. The visitors were not willing to accept the evidence given by each other, but stuck to their original conclusions. In the movie *Twelve Angry Men*, several of the jurors stubbornly resisted the arguments made by their fellow jurors, often rationalizing any contradictory evidence or arguments.
6. *Bias on the part of the observer.* One tends to ignore evidence that is against the conclusion one wishes to make and accepts the evidence that one likes. Often observers are unaware of their bias and steadfastly insist that they are completely objective. Scientists, despite their reputation of objectivity, are not immune from the temptation to manage their experiments to make them come out favorably. One way to do this is to continue measuring an element in the population until the "correct" measurement is obtained. Through this process students in physics laboratories can get estimates of such things as the weight of an electron with uncanny accuracy. Some jurors in *Twelve Angry Men* also

suffered from bias. One juror went into a state of shock when he discovered that his conclusion was based more on a bitter relationship he had with his son than the evidence of the trial.

## 6-2 TESTING THE HYPOTHESIS

To make inferences about reality we must devise a reliable and valid measuring instrument of the phenomenon under question. We must also consider the population to which we wish to limit our inferences. We may be forced to limit our study to a population we can observe.

This *measuring instrument*, which we will call $X$, that is, the rule for measuring elements in the population, will have a distribution with a population mean and variance. Usually these characteristics are not known. We go to great expense to discover their values, for they could tell us a great deal about the phenomenon under question.

For example, let us consider the amount of nitrogen oxides emitted by cars. Let us also restrict the population to new cars of a certain weight category operating under well-specified stop-and-go city traffic conditions. An electronic instrument with a counter is placed over the end of the exhaust pipe to measure the rate of nitrogen oxides emissions. When testing all cars, even of the same make, we find the measurements are not the same. Even if the test were conducted on the same car several times the test results would differ. Hence the amount of emissions will distribute around some population mean with a certain variation. This population mean is often called the *expected value* and is denoted $\mu_X$. The population variance is denoted $\sigma_X^2$. Population parameters of distributions are denoted by Greek letters.

Suppose a manufacturer has come out with a new engine and we wish to determine if the engine emits more or less or the same amount of nitrogen oxides as other engines. Our population under consideration will be new cars with the new engines. We also restrict the population to a certain weight category and certain driving conditions. Not all of these cars will emit the same amount of nitrogen oxides; hence our question is: "Does the average amount of nitrogen oxides emissions from the above population differ from the average amount of emissions for all other new cars?"

We now have three necessary ingredients with which to do hypothesis testing: a research question about a phenomenon, a well-defined population, and a measuring instrument. We will assume the measurement instrument is both reliable and valid. It is now time to formulate a *research hypothesis:* the mean amount of nitrogen oxides emissions from the new engine differs from the mean emissions from other engines. In hypothesis testing we do not test the research hypothesis, but instead we test its opposite, the *null hypothesis.* Based on this test we reject or accept the null hypothesis and hence accept or reject the research hypothesis by contradiction. Thus we try to show that the research hypothesis is true by showing that the null hypothesis is false. The research hypothesis is often called the *alternative hypothesis* and is denoted by $H_1$ or $H_a$. The null hypothesis is denoted $H_0$.

The null and alternative hypotheses must be *mutually exclusive,* i.e., both cannot be true or both false at the same time. The hypotheses must be *exhaustive,* i.e., there must be no other alternative. We can now state the hypotheses in terms of the research question:

$H_0$. There is no difference between the mean nitrogen oxides emission levels of the new engines and mean emission levels of other engines.

(6-1)

$H_1$. The mean nitrogen oxides emission levels of the new engines differ from the mean emission levels of the other engines.

These hypotheses represent the fourth ingredient in the hypothesis-testing process. We need now to restate them in terms of the measuring instrument:

$$\begin{aligned} H_0: &\quad \mu_X = \mu_0 \\ H_1: &\quad \mu_X \neq \mu_0 \end{aligned} \qquad (6\text{-}2)$$

where $X$ is the measurement of emission levels in cars with new engines and $\mu_0$ is the population mean of the distribution of the measurement of emission levels in cars with other engines. We assume a great deal is known about the emission levels of other cars, and hence the exact population mean $\mu_0$ and variance $\sigma^2$ are known. The population mean of emission levels of cars with new engines is not known, of course, for if it were there would be no reason to do hypothesis testing.

Our next step is to devise a model. In this case let us assume the model is

$$X = \mu_0 + \Delta + E \qquad \sigma_E^2 = \sigma_X^2 = \sigma^2 \text{ (known)} \qquad \mu_E = 0 \quad \text{(Model 6-1)}$$

where $\mu_0$ (a constant) is the population mean of emissions from other cars and $E$ (a variable) is the deviation of $X$ from $\mu_0$ and has a mean 0 and standard deviation $\sigma_E$. The model assumes that the variance of the measurement of new engines is the same as the variance of the measurement of other engines. This is an important assumption, as we will see later. The constant, $\Delta$, represents the difference of the mean of the measurement of new engines from the mean of the measurement of other engines, that is, $\Delta = \mu_X - \mu_0$. If $\Delta$ is zero, there is no difference between the means, and hence the null hypothesis is true. If $\Delta$ is positive, then the new engines give off more emissions on the average. If $\Delta$ is negative, then the new engines represent an improvement, i.e., they give off fewer emissions on the average. According to the model the mean of $X$ is $\mu_X = \mu_0 + \Delta$. We now can state the hypotheses in terms of the model:

$$\begin{aligned} H_0: &\quad \Delta = 0 \\ H_1: &\quad \Delta \neq 0 \end{aligned} \qquad (6\text{-}3)$$

We now consider selecting a sample of size $n$ from which evidence will be derived to test the hypotheses. We wish to estimate the population mean from this sample; $\bar{X}$ is a good function for this purpose. As stated in Chap. 5, $\bar{X}$ is unbiased, that is, $\mu_{\bar{X}} = \mu_X = \mu_0 + \Delta$. The variance of $\bar{X}$ depends on the variance of $X$ and sample size $n$: $\sigma_{\bar{X}}^2 = \sigma_X^2/n$.

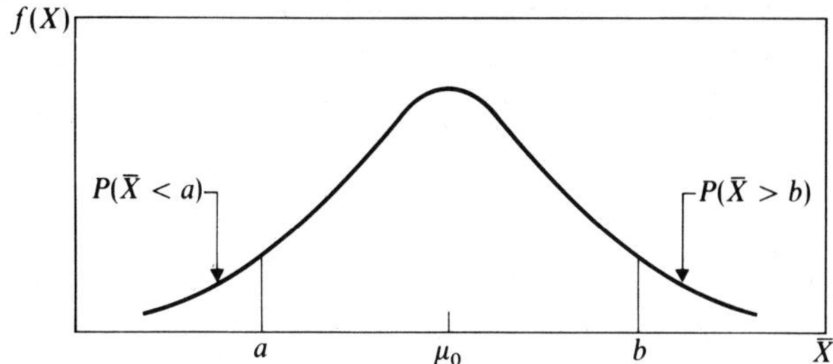


**Figure 6-1** The distribution of $\bar{X}$ when $H_0$ is true.

A *testing function*, sometimes called a *test statistic*, is a function of sample data used to test hypotheses. If $R$ denotes a testing function, the population mean and standard deviation of the distribution of $R$ (called the *sampling distribution*) are denoted by $\mu_R$ and $\sigma_R$.

$\bar{X}$ represents the evidence, the testing function. It does not conclusively tell us if the null hypothesis is true or false. As in the court trial example, the researcher must look at the evidence and decide if it is plausible for a true null hypothesis. If such appears to be implausible, then he rejects that hypothesis and accepts the alternative. We can now state the hypotheses in terms of the testing function:

$$\begin{aligned} H_0&: \quad \mu_{\bar{X}} = \mu_0 \\ H_1&: \quad \mu_{\bar{X}} \neq \mu_0 \end{aligned} \tag{6-4}$$

Sometimes you will find these hypotheses poorly stated, as follows:

$$\begin{aligned} H_0&: \quad \bar{X} = \mu_0 \\ H_1& \quad\;\; \bar{X} \neq \mu_0 \end{aligned} \qquad \text{(Wrong!)} \tag{6-5}$$

These are nonsensical hypotheses, for rarely will $\bar{X} = \mu_0$ under any circumstances. Hypotheses statements (6-1) to (6-4) are equivalent, but hypotheses statement (6-5) is not equivalent to the others.

We must determine when the evidence is plausible or implausible. Precise decision points, called *critical points*, must be established. However, the locations of these critical points depend on the subjective judgment of the researcher. To make this judgment, he or she must know the distribution of the testing function when the null hypothesis is true. Without this knowledge decisions cannot be made.

Suppose the distribution of $\bar{X}$ were known to be as in Fig. 6-1. The sample mean will most likely fall between $a$ and $b$, but it could for some rare samples fall to the right of $b$ or to the left of $a$. Hence we say that $\bar{X} < a$ or $\bar{X} > b$ is possible but implausible for a true null hypothesis. If the researcher chooses $a$ and $b$ as critical points, then he will reject the null hypothesis if the sample mean falls outside the interval $(a, b)$ and accept $H_0$ if it falls within the interval. If the null hypothesis is true, the probability of rejecting the true null hypothesis is $\Pr(\bar{X} < a) + \Pr(\bar{X} > b)$. The rejection of a true null hypothesis is often called a *type I error*, but we will call it a *rejecting error*. The probability of the rejecting error is often denoted by

$$\Pr\,(\mathrm{H}_0 \text{ is true given } \bar{X} < a \text{ or } \bar{X} > b) = \alpha$$

The researcher wishes to select critical points $a$ and $b$ so that $\alpha$ is small, say 0.05 or less. In this case, the chances are less than or equal to 1 in 20 that the rejection of the null hypothesis was in error.

For what reasons will $\bar{X}$ fall outside the interval $(a, b)$? One reason may be that a rare sample was chosen, creating a large sampling error. Another reason may be that the distribution in Fig. 6-1 is not correct, for the null hypothesis is not true. Since the first reason is not likely to occur, we assume the second reason.

How does the researcher pick his critical points? First, one establishes an $\alpha$, Pr (rejecting error), that one is willing to accept. Then from the distribution of Fig. 6-1 one selects $a$ and $b$ so that $\Pr\,(\bar{X} > b) = \Pr\,(\bar{X} < a)$ and $\Pr\,(\bar{X} > b) + \Pr\,(\bar{X} < a) = \alpha$. To do this one must know the distribution of $\bar{X}$.

The acceptance of a false null hypothesis is often called a *type II error*, but we will refer to it as the *accepting error*. The probability of the accepting error is denoted by

$$\Pr\,(\mathrm{H}_0 \text{ is false given } a \le \bar{X} \le b) = \beta$$

In the trial example the rejecting error is the conviction of an innocent person and the accepting error is the declaration of a guilty person to be innocent. As in the trial example, the researcher desires both $\alpha$ and $\beta$ to be small but usually prefers $\alpha$ to be less than $\beta$. There is a trade-off between $\alpha$ and $\beta$; the smaller the $\alpha$, the larger the $\beta$. The probability of the accepting error can be reduced by increasing $\alpha$, by increasing sample size (gathering more evidence), or by improving the validity and reliability of the variable.

A good testing function is one that (1) is unbiased, (2) has a small variance, and (3) has a known distribution for a true $\mathrm{H}_0$. In practice the researcher is rarely so lucky as to have a testing function that meets all three criteria. One must often use a function that (1) is slightly biased, (2) has a variance that is larger than desired, and (3) has a distribution that can only be approximated.

Let us assume that $\bar{X}$ has an approximately normal distribution with a mean of $\mu_0 + \Delta$ and a standard deviation $\sigma/n^{1/2}$. This is a reasonable assumption, the rationale for which will be discussed later. If the null hypothesis is true, $\Delta = 0$, $\mu_{\bar{X}} = \mu_0$, and $X$ will have a distribution similar to curve $\mathrm{H}_0$ in Fig. 6-2. In this case the distribution of $X$ and the distribution of emissions of other engines are identical. Notice that the distributions are not necessarily normal. The shape of the distribution is only speculation, for we do not know its real form.

Superimposed on the distribution of $X$ for a true $\mathrm{H}_0$ is the distribution of $\bar{X}$. Notice that it is nearly normal; this is not speculation. Since $\bar{X}$ is nearly normal we can use the standard normal table to calculate probabilities. To do this, $\bar{X}$ is standardized:

$$Z = \frac{\bar{X} - \mu_{\bar{X}}}{\sigma_{\bar{X}}} = \frac{\bar{X} - \mu_0}{\sigma/(n)^{1/2}} \tag{6-6}$$

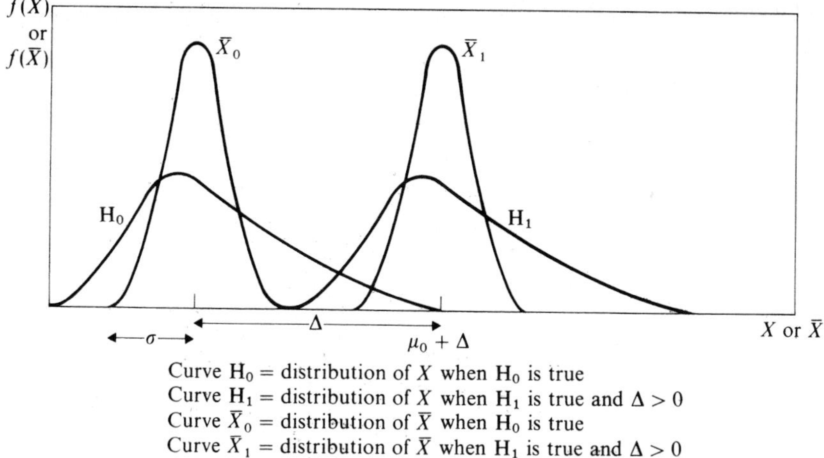


**Figure 6-2** Example distributions of $X$ and $\bar{X}$ if $H_0$ or $H_1$ is true.

We can now state the hypotheses in terms of the standardized testing function:

$$\begin{aligned} H_0&: \quad \mu_Z = 0 \\ H_1&: \quad \mu_Z \neq 0 \end{aligned} \tag{6-7}$$

Suppose the researcher is willing to accept a 0.05 probability of a rejecting error, that is, $\alpha = 0.05$. Then we find $a$ and $b$ from the standard normal tables such that $P(Z > b) + P(Z < a) = 0.05$ and $P(Z < a) = P(Z > b) = 0.025$. Since the standard normal distribution is symmetric about zero, we need only to find $b$. The critical point $a$ will be simply $-b$. Looking in Table E-1 for a $Z$ score corresponding to a probability of $Z > b = 0.025$, we find that $b = 1.96$. The critical points are $-1.96$ and 1.96, which means that if a sample produces a $Z$ score outside the interval $(-1.96, 1.96)$, the researcher would conclude that the null hypothesis is false. In other words, getting a sample that produces such a $Z$ when the null hypothesis is true is highly unlikely—only 1 chance out of 20. If the $Z$ score falls within the interval $(-1.96, 1.96)$, the researcher accepts the null hypothesis, i.e., the evidence was very plausible under the circumstance of a true null hypothesis.

Now that the researcher has come to a conclusion concerning the hypotheses stated in terms of the standardized test statistic in Eq. (6-6), he or she can project that conclusion on all of the equivalent hypotheses. Thus, if one rejects $H_0$ in hypotheses set (6-7), one can now reject $H_0$ in the equivalent sets (6-4), (6-3), (6-2), and (6-1). If one rejects $H_0$, one then determines how the means differ. Is $\Delta$ positive or negative? For either conclusion concerning the hypotheses, one interprets it in the context of the research question and discusses the implications of the results.

Suppose that $\mu_0 = 100$, $\sigma^2 = 25$, $\sigma = 5$, the researcher has chosen $\alpha$ at 0.05, and $n$ is 36. Suppose, further, that the sample of 36 cases gave a sample mean of

**Table 6-1 Steps needed to do hypothesis testing**

1. Establish the research question.
2. Establish the population to be studied.
3. Establish a valid and reliable measurement instrument.
4. State the null and alternative hypotheses.
5. Decide on the model.
6. Decide on the testing function.
7. Decide on the maximum acceptable probability of a rejecting error.
8. Decide on sample size.
9. Find the critical points.
10. Collect a sample and compute the test statistic.
11. Transform the statistic to make it convenient for available tables of probability distributions.
12. Make a conclusion concerning the acceptance or rejection of $H_0$.
13. Interpret the results in the context of the research question and discuss their implications.

101.8; then from Eq. (6-6)

$$Z = \frac{101.8 - 100}{5/(36)^{1/2}} = 2.16$$

Conclusion: reject $H_0$ of set (6-7) since $2.16 > 1.96$.

The general hypotheses-testing procedure suggested in this section is summarized in Table 6-1. This will form the basis for other testing efforts in this chapter and should also be employed in the reader's own hypothesis-testing endeavors.

## 6-3 MODEL FOR UNKNOWN VARIANCE

We now return to the question of the variance $\sigma^2$. In model (6-1) we assumed the variance of $X$ was the same as that of the emission of the other engines. (It may be helpful to review the notation in Table 6-2.) Is this a valid assumption? Since $\bar{X}$ was standardized by using $\sigma$, the assumption can have important consequences. If $\sigma_X^2 > \sigma^2$, then $\sigma_{\bar{X}}^2 > \sigma^2/n$ and our standardized estimating function was too small. This has the effect of increasing the probability of a rejecting error. Hence, instead of an $\alpha$ as small as 0.05 as specified by the researcher, the true $\alpha$ may be as high as 0.10. If $\sigma_X^2 < \sigma^2$, then the true $\alpha$ will be less than 0.05.

If the $\sigma_X^2 \neq \sigma^2$, or the researcher does not know its value, the following model may be used:

$$X = \mu + \Delta + E \qquad \sigma_X^2 = \sigma_E^2(\text{unknown}) \qquad \mu_E = 0 \qquad \text{(Model 6-2)}$$

Since $\sigma_E^2$, which equals $\sigma_X^2$, is unknown, it must be estimated:

$$S_X^2 = \frac{1}{n-1} \sum_{i=1}^{n} (X_i - \bar{X})^2 \qquad (6\text{-}8)$$

**Table 6-2 Definition of main symbols used in hypothesis testing**

$X$ = a variable (rule for measuring a phenomenon)
$\mu_X$ = population mean of $X$
$\sigma_X^2$ = population variance of $X$
$\sigma_X$ = population standard deviation of $X$
$\mu_0$ = a given population mean used in a null hypothesis
$\sigma^2$ = a given population variance
$n$ = sample size
$\bar{X}$ = the sample mean, $(1/n)\sum X_i$, an estimate of $\mu_X$
$SS_X$ = sum of squared deviations, $\sum (X_i - \bar{X})^2$
$S_X^2$ = the sample variance, $1/(n-1)\,(SS_X)$, an estimate of $\sigma_X^2$

Let $R$ be an arbitrary function of the sample $X_1, X_2, \ldots, X_n$.

$\mu_R$ = the population mean of the sampling distribution of $R$
$\sigma_R^2$ = the population variance of the sampling distribution of $R$
$S_R^2$ = an estimate of $\sigma_R^2$

We now standardize $\bar{X}$ by replacing the known standard deviation in Eq. (6-6) with its estimate:

$$T = \frac{\bar{X} - \mu_0}{S_X/(n)^{1/2}} \tag{6-9}$$

We call this new standardized estimating function $T$ because its distribution is close to Student's $t$ distribution described in Chap. 3. The shape of the $t$ distribution is symmetrical about zero, just as in the case of the $z$ distribution, but it is flatter than the $z$ distribution. The amount of deviation of the $t$ from the $z$ distribution depends on the sample size. The larger the size, the closer the distribution is to the standard normal. For a sample size over 40, the two distributions are almost identical.

To find the critical points for the standardized testing function for model (6-2), look at the $t$ table (Table E-3) for a preselected $\alpha$ and degrees of freedom $n - 1$. The degrees of freedom determine the flatness of the $t$ distribution.

Suppose in the previous example the researcher lacks justification in assuming $\sigma_X^2 = 25$. He or she then estimates $\sigma_X^2$ from the sample, computes the $T$ statistic, and finds the critical points in the $t$ table. From this table for 35 degrees of freedom and an $\alpha$ of 0.05, the critical points are $-2.03$ and 2.03. Suppose $S^2 = 33$ ($S = 5.74$), then

$$T = \frac{101.8 - 100}{5.74/(36)^{1/2}} = 1.88$$

Since the $T$ estimate falls between the critical points, $-2.03 < 1.88 < 2.03$, the researcher accepts the null hypothesis.

## 6-4 CENTRAL-LIMIT THEOREM

It was assumed in the previous section that $\bar{X}$ was distributed normally. This assumption was the result of the central-limit theorem.

> **Definition: Central-limit theorem** Let $X_1, X_2, \ldots, X_n$ denote $n$ independent observations, such as a random sample of size $n$, and let $B$ denote the sum and $\bar{X}$ denote the mean of the $n$ observations. The distribution of both $B$ and $\bar{X}$ approach a normal distribution as $n$ gets larger. In addition, if $X_1$ through $X_n$ are identically distributed with mean $\mu$ and variance $\sigma^2$, then the distribution of $\bar{X}$ approaches the normal distribution with mean $\mu$ and variance $\sigma^2/n$.

The theorem does not state how large $n$ must be for the distribution of $\bar{X}$ to be sufficiently close to the normal to use the normal tables. The necessary size of $n$ depends on the underlying distribution of $X$. If it is highly skewed, a large sample is required, but if it is nearly symmetrical, a sample as small as four or five cases may be sufficient to assume a normal distribution of $\bar{X}$.

## 6-5 TESTING FOR THE PROPORTION WITHIN A POPULATION

To determine the proportion of members in a population with a certain characteristic $k$, we randomly select $n$ members from the population and observe how many in the sample possess the characteristic. Let $X = 1$ if the member has characteristic $k$ and $X = 0$ if it does not. The number, $B$, in the sample with characteristic $k$ can be derived by summing all of the ones and zeros, $B = \sum X_i$. For example, suppose a sample of size 14 gave these results:

$$1, 1, 0, 1, 0, 0, 0, 1, 0, 1, 1, 1, 1, 0$$

$$B = 1 + 1 + 0 + 1 + 0 + 0 + 0 + 1 + 0 + 1 + 1 + 1 + 1 + 0 = 8$$

The probability that a case in the sample has characteristic $k$ equals the proportion $\pi$ in the population with characteristic $k$:

$$\Pr(X = 1) = \pi$$

$P$ is the sample proportion, equal to $B/n$, which is an estimating function for $\pi$.

$B$ is a binomial variable since the observations are independent and the probability of "success" (the member has characteristic $k$) is $\pi$. As shown in Chap. 3, $B$ has a mean $n\pi$ and a variance $n\pi(1 - \pi)$. Hence the binomial distribution can be used to choose critical points when testing for the expected number of cases with characteristic $k$ in a sample of size $n$.

Since $B$ is a sum of independent variables, the distribution of $B$ approaches the normal distribution as $n$ gets larger (according to the central-limit theorem; the sample proportion $P$ also approaches the normal distribution as $n$ gets larger). How large should $n$ be to permit us to abandon the bulky binomial tables for the normal tables? The usual rule is if $n\pi > 5$ and $n(1 - \pi) > 5$, then use the normal tables.

Suppose 1 out of every 10 rural houses in a state are substandard according to criteria established by the state's Community Affairs Agency. Officials of a county asked the research question, "Is the proportion of substandard rural housing in their county different from the proportion within the state?" To answer this question the following hypotheses were tested using the sample proportion as the estimating function for a sample of size 64. The probability of rejecting error was set at $\alpha = 0.04$.

$$\text{H}_0: \qquad \mu_P = \tfrac{1}{10} = \pi_0$$

$$\text{H}_1: \qquad \mu_P \neq \tfrac{1}{10} = \pi_0$$

Under the null hypothesis the mean of the testing function $P$ is $\frac{1}{10}$ and the variance of $P$ is $(\frac{1}{10})(\frac{9}{10})/64 = 9/6400 = 0.0014$. Is the distribution of $P$ sufficiently near the normal distribution to use the normal tables? Since $n\pi_0 = 64(0.1) = 6.4 > 5$ and $n(1 - \pi_0) = 64(0.9) > 5$, the answer is "yes." $P$ is now standardized:

$$Z = \frac{P - \mu_P}{\sigma_P} = \frac{P - 0.1}{(0.0014)^{1/2}} \tag{6-10}$$

Critical points for $\alpha = 0.04$ are found in the standard normal tables to be $-2.05$ and 2.05:

$$\text{If } Z < -2.05 \text{ or } Z > 2.05, \text{ then reject H}_0.$$

$$\text{If } -2.05 \leq Z \leq 2.05, \text{ then accept H}_0.$$

Suppose that in the sample of 64 rural houses 11 were found to be substandard:

$$P = \tfrac{11}{64} = 0.172$$

$$Z = \frac{0.172 - 0.100}{0.0375} = 1.92$$

Since $-2.05 \leq 1.92 \leq 2.05$, accept $\text{H}_0$. The evidence does not indicate that the proportion of substandard rural housing in the county is any different than the proportion in the state. The implications are that the county is not atypical in housing, and special programs for rural housing in the county may not be justified.

Steps 1 and 3 for hypothesis testing (see Table 6-1) were not discussed in this example. The researchers need to check the appropriateness of their population and the validity and reliability of their measurement of housing quality. Is the definition of rural housing the same as that used by the Community Affairs Agency? Is the definition of substandard housing the same? Are the surveyors trained to make valid and reliable determinations? The efficacy of the results depends on how well the researcher considers these questions.

## 6-6 STATISTICAL SIGNIFICANCE

In almost all texts about hypothesis testing the rejecting error is called a type I error, and the probability of this rejecting or type I error is called the *significance level.* If a null hypothesis is rejected, then we say that there exists a *statistically significant difference* between the sample estimate and the hypothesized value. Suppose that, upon comparing a sample mean with an hypothesized population mean, the researcher said that the sample mean differed significantly. Is the researcher saying the difference between the population means is substantial? Not necessarily. He or she is only saying that there is enough evidence to suggest the difference is not zero. There is nothing in that statement that suggests the difference is substantial.

## 6-7 ONE-TAILED TEST

In the previous examples the null hypothesis was rejected if the test statistic fell beyond one of the two critical points in the two tails of the sampling distribution. Such tests are called *two-tailed tests.* If the null hypothesis is rejected, the researcher then investigates the *direction* of the difference by observing the sign of the test statistic. In the example of Sec. 6-2, $H_0$ was rejected since $Z = 2.16$ was greater than 1.96. Also, since $Z$ was positive we can conclude that the mean of $X$ exceeds 100.

Occasionally only one direction is of interest. For instance, in an election campaign the research question may be, "If the election were held today, will the candidate win?" Assuming that it takes over 50 percent of the voters to win, there will be little interest in whether $\pi$, the proportion of the voters that will vote for the candidate, is less than 0.50. A *one-tailed test* is called for. The hypotheses for such a test are

$$\begin{aligned} H_0&: \quad \mu_P \le \pi \\ H_1&: \quad \mu_P > \pi \end{aligned} \tag{6-11}$$

For a significance level of $\alpha$, a critical point, $b$, is found such that $\Pr(P > b) = \alpha$ for a special case of a true null hypothesis, when $\mu_P = \pi$. If $Z > b$, reject $H_0$, and if $Z \le b$, accept $H_0$. In the case of the substandard housing problem in the previous section, the critical point of a significance level of 0.04 is 1.75 for a one-tailed test. Since $Z = 1.92$ was greater than this critical point, the null hypothesis would be rejected, an opposite conclusion than that derived for the two-tailed test.

The use of the one-tailed test may reflect prejudice on the part of the researcher. Suppose a planner has implemented a special program to improve a certain situation in an urban area. Since the planner designed and implemented the program, he or she naturally has a special interest in its success. The question is asked: "Does my program improve the situation?" The planner designs a one-tailed test to answer this question, finds the program successful at the 0.05

significance level, and proudly reports that conclusion to the city commission. But was the research design a good one? It is not uncommon that well-intended programs make the situation worse, not better. This other possibility should have been included in the research design. Also, using a 0.05 significance level for a one-tailed test enhances the probability of saying the program was a success. Perhaps a more conservative $\alpha$, such as 0.025, should have been used to overcome the possibility of prejudice on the part of the researcher when conducting a one-tailed test.

## 6-8 DIFFERENCE OF MEANS TEST FOR POPULATIONS WITH EQUAL BUT UNKNOWN VARIANCES

In the nitrogen oxides example the mean of the population of other engines was known. If it were not known, we would have had to estimate the means of both populations and compare the two. We will now consider the model in which the variances are equal, but the values of means and variances of both populations are not known. Let $X_1$ be a measure from population 1 and $X_2$ from population 2. The model can now be expressed as follows:

$$\begin{aligned} X_1 &= \mu_{X_1} + E & \sigma_E^2 &= \sigma_{X_1}^2 = \sigma_{X_2}^2 = \sigma^2(\text{unknown}) \\ X_2 &= \mu_{X_1} + \Delta + E & \mu_E &= 0 \qquad \Delta = \mu_{X_2} - \mu_{X_1} \end{aligned} \qquad \text{(Model 6-3)}$$

The hypotheses are

$$\begin{array}{lll} \text{H}_0\text{:}\ \ \mu_{X_1} = \mu_{X_2} & \text{H}_0\text{:}\ \ \mu_{X_1} - \mu_{X_2} = 0 & \text{H}_0\text{:}\ \ \Delta = 0 \\ \qquad\text{or} & \qquad\qquad\text{or} & \\ \text{H}_1\text{:}\ \ \mu_{X_1} \neq \mu_{X_2} & \text{H}_1\text{:}\ \ \mu_{X_1} - \mu_{X_2} \neq 0 & \text{H}_1\text{:}\ \ \Delta \neq 0 \end{array} \qquad (6\text{-}12)$$

A testing function is $D = \bar{X}_1 - \bar{X}_2$, where $\bar{X}_1$ and $\bar{X}_2$ are the means, and $n_1$ and $n_2$ the sizes of the samples drawn from populations 1 and 2, respectively. If $n_1$ and $n_2$ are sufficiently large, then $D$ is nearly normally distributed with mean zero and standard deviation $\sigma^2/n_1 + \sigma^2/n_2$ when the null hypothesis is true. Since the common variance $\sigma^2$ is unknown, we must estimate it as follows:

$$S^2 = \frac{\sum_{i=1}^{n_1}(X_{i1} - \bar{X}_1)^2 + \sum_{i=1}^{n_2}(X_{i2} - \bar{X}_2)^2}{n_1 + n_2 - 2} \qquad (6\text{-}13)$$

Then

$$S_D^2 = \frac{S^2}{n_1} + \frac{S^2}{n_2} = S^2\left(\frac{1}{n_1} + \frac{1}{n_2}\right) = S^2\left(\frac{n_1 + n_2}{n_1 n_2}\right) \qquad (6\text{-}14)$$

We can now standardize $D$:

$$T = \frac{D - 0}{S[(n_1 + n_2)/n_1 n_2]^{1/2}} \qquad (6\text{-}15)$$

**Table 6-3 Fuel consumption in miles per gallon† of two random samples of automobiles for expressway driving at 55 and 65 mph**

| Automobile | $x_1$ 55 mph (88.5 km/h) | $x_2$ 65 mph (104.6 km/h) |
|---|---|---|
| 1 | 18.1 | 10.9 |
| 2 | 16.3 | 13.3 |
| 3 | 12.5 | 16.8 |
| 4 | 17.4 | 17.1 |
| 5 | 16.5 | 17.9 |
| 6 | 18.4 | 16.1 |
| 7 | 20.7 | 15.1 |
| 8 | 18.4 | 12.7 |
| 9 | 16.7 | 14.5 |
| 10 | 17.1 | 16.4 |
| 11 | 15.2 | 13.6 |
| 12 | 12.1 | |
| Sample size $n_k$ | 12 | 11 |
| Sample mean $\bar{X}_k$ | 16.62 | 14.95 |
| Sum of squares $\sum (X_{ik} - \bar{X}_k)^2$ | 64.2 | 44.9 |

† Multiply by 0.425 to get km/liter.

$T$ has a distribution approximately that of a $t$ distribution with $n_1 + n_2 - 2$ degrees of freedom.

The hypotheses can now be stated in terms of the estimating function $D$ or its standardized form $T$:

$$\begin{aligned} &\mathrm{H}_0\colon\ \mu_D = 0 &&\mathrm{H}_0\colon\ \mu_T = 0 \\ &&\text{or}&& \\ &H_1\colon\ \mu_D \neq 0 &&\mathrm{H}_1\colon\ \mu_T \neq 0 \end{aligned} \tag{6-16}$$

Suppose an experiment were conducted to compare the average miles per gallon consumed by automobiles on expressways at two different speeds, 55 and 65 miles per hour. The results of the experiment are listed in Table 6-3. It was assumed that the variance of the gas mileage was the same for both populations.

The research question is "Is the mean gas consumption for automobiles driven on expressways at 55 mph different from that at 65 mph?" The hypotheses are

$$\mathrm{H}_0\colon\ \mu_{X_1} = \mu_{X_2}$$
$$\mathrm{H}_1\colon\ \mu_{X_1} \neq \mu_{X_2}$$

where $X_1$ represents gas consumption at 55 mph and $X_2$ at 65 mph. The testing function is

$$D = \bar{X}_1 - \bar{X}_2 = 16.62 - 14.95 = 1.67$$

The estimated variance of $D$ from Eqs. (6-13) and (6-14) is

$$S^2 = \frac{64.2 + 44.9}{12 + 11 - 2} = 5.20$$

$$S_D^2 = 5.20\left[\frac{12 + 11}{(12)(11)}\right] = 0.906$$

and the standardized testing function is

$$T = \frac{D - 0}{S_D} = \frac{1.67 - 0}{(0.906)^{1/2}} = 1.75$$

Suppose the probability of the rejecting error were set at 0.05. Looking in the $t$ table (Table E-3) for $\alpha = 0.05$ and degrees of freedom df = 21, we find the critical points $-2.08$ and 2.08. Since $-2.08 < 1.75 < 2.08$, the null hypothesis is accepted. There is no evidence from this experiment that the slower speed leads to better gas mileage.

## 6-9 COMPARISON OF VARIANCES OF TWO POPULATIONS

We assumed in model 6-3 that the two population variances were equal. To test this assumption use the following model:

$$X_1 = \mu_1 + E_1 \qquad \mu_{E_1} = \mu_{E_2} = 0$$
$$X_2 = \mu_2 + E_2 \qquad \text{(Model 6-4)}$$

The hypotheses are

$$\text{H}_0\text{:} \quad \sigma_{X_1}^2 = \sigma_{X_2}^2$$
$$\text{H}_1\text{:} \quad \sigma_{X_1}^2 \neq \sigma_{X_2}^2 \qquad (6\text{-}17)$$

and the testing functions are

$$S_1^2 = \frac{1}{n_1 - 1}\sum_{i=1}^{n_1}(X_{i1} - \bar{X}_1)^2 \qquad (6\text{-}18)$$

$$S_2^2 = \frac{1}{n_2 - 1}\sum_{i=1}^{n_2}(X_{i2} - \bar{X}_2)^2 \qquad (6\text{-}19)$$

$$F = \frac{\text{larger } S_k^2}{\text{smaller } S_k^2} \qquad (6\text{-}20)$$

If the distributions of $X_1$ and $X_2$ are nearly normal, the $F$ ratio will have a nearly $f$ distribution with degrees of freedom $df_1 = n_{num} - 1$ where $n_{num}$ is the size of the sample that produced the larger sample variance (that in the numerator). Similarly, $df_2 = n_{den} - 1$, where $n_{den}$ is the size of the sample that produced the sample variance in the denominator.

An $f$ distribution is shown in Table E-4. If the hypothesis is true, the ratio of the larger sample variance to the smaller will probably be nearly 1. This table gives the probability that $F$ is greater than some given number, $f$, when the null hypothesis is true. There is only one critical point in this test. Like the $t$, the $f$ distribution depends on the degrees of freedom. For the $\alpha$ we have chosen, find the column with $df_1$ and the row with $df_2$. The resulting critical point, $f_\alpha$, is the number such that $P(F > f \text{ given } H_0 \text{ is true}) = \alpha$. If $F \leq f$, accept $H_0$. If $F > f$, reject $H_0$ and conclude that the variance of the population estimated by the sample variance in the numerator has the larger variance.

## 6-10 DIFFERENCE OF MEANS TEST—UNEQUAL POPULATION VARIANCE

In Sec. 6-8 we assumed that the variances of the two populations were equal. If we did not know if this were so, we could test for equality by using the $F$ test in Sec. 6-9. If we concluded from the test that the variances were not equal, then Eq. (6-13) could not be used to compute $S^2$. Consider this model:

$$\begin{aligned} X_1 &= \mu_{X_1} + E_1 & \sigma^2_{E_1} &\neq \sigma^2_{E_2} \text{(unknown)} \\ X_2 &= \mu_{X_1} + \Delta + E_2 & \mu_{E_1} &= \mu_{E_2} = 0 \end{aligned} \qquad \text{(Model 6-5)}$$

In this case the estimated variance of $D = \bar{X}_1 - \bar{X}_2$ is

$$S^2_D = \frac{S^2_1}{n_1} + \frac{S^2_2}{n_2} \qquad (6\text{-}21)$$

where $S^2_1$ and $S^2_2$ are the appropriate sample variances. $D$ can now be standardized:

$$T = \frac{D - 0}{[(S^2_1/n_1) + (S^2_2/n_2)]^{1/2}} \qquad (6\text{-}22)$$

$T$ also has a distribution near the $t$ distribution, but the degrees of freedom are difficult to compute. These can be approximated by

$$\text{df} = \frac{S^4_D}{(S^2_1/n_1)^2[1/(n_1 + 1)] + (S^2_2/n_2)^2[1/(n_2 + 1)]} - 2 \qquad (6\text{-}23)$$

As an illustration of this test, suppose it were questioned whether small cities (less than 25,000) with reform governments spent a greater proportion of their general revenue sharing funds for social programs than towns and cities with nonreform governments. Cities were separated by government types, reform and

**Table 6-4 Proportion of general revenue sharing funds spent on social programs by cities of less than 25,000 population with reform and nonreform governments**

| | Reform government $X_1$ | Nonreform government $X_2$ |
|---|---|---|
| Sample means $\bar{X}_k$ | 0.21 | 0.38 |
| Sample variance $S_k^2$ | 0.07 | 0.13 |
| Sample standard deviation $S_k$ | 0.26 | 0.36 |
| Sample size $n_k$ | 40 | 31 |

nonreform, and a sample from each chosen. The statistics resulting from the sample are listed in Table 6-4.

To compare the means, we must first determine whether the equal or unequal variance model [(6-3) or (6-5)] is appropriate. Hence the equality of variance will be tested to determine the appropriate model, and then the equality of means will be tested to answer the research question. The first hypotheses are

$$\begin{aligned} H_0&: \quad \sigma_{X_1}^2 = \sigma_{X_2}^2 \\ H_1&: \quad \sigma_{X_1}^2 \neq \sigma_{X_2}^2 \end{aligned} \tag{6-24}$$

Suppose an $\alpha = 0.05$ were selected to test these hypotheses. The testing function is

$$F = \frac{\text{larger } S^2}{\text{smaller } S^2} = \frac{0.13}{0.07} = 1.86$$

The degrees of freedom are 30 and 39. The $f$ table for $\alpha = 0.05$ gives a critical value of 1.74. Since $F = 1.86 > 1.74$, reject $H_0$. Hence we reject the equal-variance model (6-3) and accept the separate-variance version (6-5). Now that the question of equality of variance has been settled, we can proceed to test the equality of means.

The second hypotheses are

$$\begin{aligned} H_0&: \quad \mu_{X_1} = \mu_{X_2} \\ H_1&: \quad \mu_{X_1} \neq \mu_{X_2} \end{aligned} \tag{6-25}$$

Let $\alpha$ for these hypotheses also be set at 0.05:

$$D = \bar{X}_1 - \bar{X}_2 = 0.21 - 0.38 = -0.17$$

From Eq. (6-21):

$$S_D^2 = \frac{0.07}{40} + \frac{0.13}{31} = 0.00175 + 0.00419 = 0.00594$$

$$T = \frac{-0.17 - 0}{(0.00594)^{1/2}} = -2.21$$

$$\text{df} = \frac{(0.00594)^2}{(0.00175)^2(1/41) + (0.00419)^2(1/32)} - 2 = 55$$

The critical points for the $t$ distribution with $\alpha = 0.05$ and degrees of freedom of 55 are $-2.00$ and 2.00. Since $T = -2.21 < -2.00$, reject $H_0$. Thus we conclude that small cities with reform governments spent a smaller proportion of their budgets on social programs.

## 6-11 COMPARING MORE THAN TWO MEANS—ANALYSIS OF VARIANCE

In all the previous examples only two populations were compared. Analysis of variance is a technique to test the equality of two or more means using random samples selected from each population. Going back to the example concerning the emissions from automobile engines, let us consider three different emission control devices for an engine. The initial research question is, "Do any of the three devices change the mean emission levels of a certain engine under controlled driving conditions?" Let $X_1$, $X_2$, $X_3$ represent measures of emissions from control devices 1, 2, and 3. The hypotheses can be stated as follows:

$$\begin{aligned} &H_0: \quad \mu_{X_1} = \mu_{X_2} = \mu_{X_3} \\ &H_1: \quad \text{at least one mean does not equal the others} \end{aligned} \tag{6-26}$$

To state the model we will need to consider the population of emissions from all engines with one of the three control devices. We will call the populations for emissions of engines for each control device subpopulations 1, 2, and 3. Let $X$ be a measure of a randomly selected engine from the entire population ignoring the type of control device. Let $\mu$ denote the population mean of the entire population, that is, $\mu_X = \mu$. Also, let $\Delta_k$ represent the difference between the mean of the entire population and from that subpopulation $k$, that is, $\mu_X - \mu_{X_k} = \Delta_k$. The sum of the differences will equal zero, $\sum \Delta_k = 0$. Consider the following model:

$$\begin{aligned} X_1 &= \mu + \Delta_1 + E \qquad && \mu_{X_k} = \mu + \Delta_k,\ k = 1, 2, 3 \\ X_2 &= \mu + \Delta_2 + E && \sigma^2_{X_1} = \sigma^2_{X_2} = \sigma^2_{X_3} = \sigma^2_E \\ X_3 &= \mu + \Delta_3 + E && \mu_E = 0 \end{aligned} \tag{Model 6-6}$$

In terms of the model the hypotheses are

$$\begin{aligned} &H_0: \quad \Delta_1 = \Delta_2 = \Delta_3 \\ &H_1: \quad \text{at least one } \Delta_k \neq 0 \end{aligned} \tag{6-27}$$

The following notation will be used in the discussion of the analysis of variance model:

$X$ = measure of an observation from the entire population
$g$ = number of subpopulations
$X_{ik}$ = measure of observation $i$ from subpopulation $k$
$n_k$ = size of sample from subpopulation $k$
$n$ = total sample size, $n = \sum n_k$

$\bar{X}_k = (1/n_k) \sum_{i=1}^{n_k} X_{ik}$, mean of sample $k$
$\bar{X} = (1/n) \sum_{k=1}^{3} \sum_{i=1}^{n_k} X_{ik}$, mean of the total sample
$\text{SS}_k = \sum_{i=1}^{n_k} (X_{ik} - \bar{X}_k)^2$, sum of squared deviations from sample $k$ mean
$\text{SS} = \sum_{k=1}^{3} \sum_{i=1}^{n_k} (X_{ik} - \bar{X})^2$, sum of squared deviations of the total sample
$S_k^2 = \text{SS}_k/(n_k - 1)$, variance of sample $k$
$S^2 = \text{SS}/(n - 1)$, variance of the total sample

An important assumption in the above model is the equality of variances of each subpopulation, i.e., it assumes that with each subpopulation the variance is the same no matter which hypothesis is true. We can estimate this common (within subpopulation) variance as follows:

$$S_w^2 = \frac{\text{SS}_1 + \text{SS}_2 + \text{SS}_3}{n_1 + n_2 + n_3 - 3} \tag{6-28}$$

This estimation function gives an unbiased estimate of the variance within each subpopulation for a true or a false null hypothesis. The variance *between* subpopulations is due to the variance within the subpopulations and to the $\Delta$ values. We can estimate this as

$$S_b^2 = \frac{n_1(\bar{X}_1 - \bar{X})^2 + n_2(\bar{X}_2 - \bar{X})^2 + n_3(\bar{X}_3 - \bar{X})^2}{3 - 1} \tag{6-29}$$

where $\bar{X}_k - \bar{X}$ is an estimate for $\Delta_k$. The function $S_b^2$ is also an estimate of the common variance $\sigma_E^2$ only if $\text{H}_0$ is true. If $\text{H}_0$ is false, i.e., some or all the $\Delta_k$ values are not zero, $\mu_{S_b^2}$ will exceed $\mu_{S_w^2}$. The statistic for testing the hypotheses is the ratio of $S_b^2$ and $S_w^2$.

In general, for $g$ subpopulations, the hypotheses are

$$\begin{aligned} &\text{H}_0: \quad \mu_{X_1} = \mu_{X_2} = \cdots = \mu_{X_k} = \cdots = \mu_{X_g} \\ &\text{H}_1: \quad \text{at least one } \mu_{X_k} \text{ does not equal the others} \end{aligned} \tag{6-30}$$

For the model below (6-7) the hypotheses are tested by the function in Eq. (6-33):

$$\begin{array}{lll} \bar{X}_k = \mu + \Delta_k + E & \mu_X = \mu & \Delta_k = \mu_X - \mu_{X_k} \\ k = 1, 2, \ldots, g & \sigma_{X_k}^2 = \sigma_E^2 \text{ (unknown)} & \mu_E = 0 \end{array} \qquad \text{(Model 6-7)}$$

$$S_w^2 = \frac{1}{n - g} \sum_{k=1}^{g} \sum_{i=1}^{n_k} (X_{ik} - \bar{X}_k)^2 \tag{6-31}$$

$$S_b^2 = \frac{1}{g - 1} \sum_{k=1}^{g} n_k(\bar{X}_k - \bar{X})^2 \tag{6-32}$$

$$F = \frac{S_b^2}{S_w^2} \tag{6-33}$$

If $X$ is normally distributed, the function $F$ has an $f$ distribution with degrees of freedom $g - 1$ and $n - g$. If $X$ is *nearly* normal or the sample sizes are large, then $F$ has an *approximate* $f$ distribution. For a given $\alpha$, and degrees of freedom

**Table 6-5 Results of a study of three different automobile engine emission control devices†**

| | Devices | | | |
|---|---|---|---|---|
| | 1 | 2 | 3 | Total |
| Sample means $\bar{X}_k$ | 97.2 | 108.1 | 101.2 | $102.6 = \bar{X}$ |
| Sum of squares $SS_k$ | 94.6 | 140.4 | 88.2 | $1116.2 = SS$ |
| Sample sizes $n_k$ | 12 | 14 | 10 | $36.0 = n$ |
| Sample variances $S_k^2$ | 8.6 | 10.8 | 9.8 | $31.9 = S^2$ |

† Measurements were nitrogen oxides emissions from the same engine with different devices operating under controlled driving conditions.

$g - 1$ and $n - g$, a critical point $f_\alpha$ can be found in the $f$ tables (E-4). If $F > f_\alpha$, reject $H_0$, and if $F \leq f_\alpha$, accept $H_0$.

Suppose three different types of emission control device, 1, 2, and 3, were tested, with the results as listed in Table 6-5. Do the results of the test indicate a difference in the ability of the devices to control emissions? To answer this question, the following estimates are computed using Eqs. (6-28), (6-29), and (6-33):

$$S_w^2 = \frac{94.6 + 140.4 + 88.2}{36 - 3} = 9.79$$

$$S_b^2 = \frac{12(97.2 - 102.6)^2 + 14(108.1 - 102.6)^2 + 10(101.2 - 102.6)^2}{3 - 1}$$

$$= \frac{793.0}{2} = 396.5$$

$$F = \frac{396.5}{9.79} = 40.5$$

$$\text{df}_1 = 3 - 1 = 2$$

$$\text{df}_2 = 36 - 3 = 33$$

Suppose $\alpha$ were set at 0.05, then for degrees of freedom 2 and 33, the critical point is 3.28. Since $F$ equals 40.5, which is greater than 3.28, reject $H_0$. In doing so, we can only conclude that at least one device is superior to the others, but we do not learn from the test which is best and which is worst. We see from the table that the sample mean for device 1 is better (smaller) than device 2 and thus conclude that the former represents a superior technology. What about device 3? Is the evidence strong enough to suggest that device 1 is superior to 3 also? This is a new research question needing a new set of hypotheses:

$$\begin{aligned} H_0:&\quad \mu_{X_1} = \mu_{X_3} \\ H_1:&\quad \mu_{X_1} = \mu_{X_3} \end{aligned} \tag{6-34}$$

Since we are dealing with only two subpopulations, these hypotheses can be tested using model (6-3) and Eq. (6-28) to estimate the common variance:

$$T = \frac{(\bar{X}_1 - \bar{X}_3) - 0}{S_w[(n_1 + n_3)/n_1 n_3]^{1/2}} = \frac{(97.2 - 101.2) - 0}{(9.79)^{1/2}[(12 + 10)/(12)(10)]^{1/2}} = -2.99 \tag{6-35}$$

There is no reason to choose the same $\alpha$ that was used in the $F$ test. In fact, $\alpha$ should be lowered because the decision concerning the means to be compared was made after the results were in and not before. Since in any experiment there will always be a smallest sample mean, choosing the subpopulation on such a basis increases the probability of rejecting a true null hypothesis. Hence, let $\alpha = 0.01$. Because the common variance was estimated by all the data (36 cases), the degrees of freedom are $n_1 + n_2 + n_3 - 3$ and not the $n_1 + n_3 - 2$ used in Sec. 6-8. For $\alpha = 0.01$ and 33 degrees of freedom, we can find in the $t$ table the critical points $-2.73$ and $2.73$. Since $T = -2.99$ is less than $-2.73$, reject $H_0$. Hence, we conclude that device 1 is also superior to 3.

## PROBLEMS

**6-1** Fill in the blanks with the proper word(s):

(*a*) A rejecting error is defined as ______________ and is denoted by ______________.

(*b*) An accepting error is defined as ______________ and is denoted by ______________.

(*c*) The six major problems in "unscientific" inference making which the formal hypothesis-testing procedure attempts to overcome are ______________.

(*d*) A variable $X$ is really a ______________ instrument.

(*e*) The two hypotheses in testing are the ______________ and ______________ hypotheses. These must be ______________ and ______________.

(*f*) A ______________ or ______________ is a function of sample data used to test hypotheses.

(*g*) Decision points, known as ______________, are established to determine when to accept or reject the null hypothesis.

(*h*) A statistic usually is ______________ by subtracting its ______________ and dividing by its ______________ to make it convenient for available tables of probability distributions.

(*i*) The ______________ states that the distribution of sample means approaches a ______________ distribution as the sample size increases.

(*j*) The symbol $\alpha$, equal to the probability of a rejecting error, is also known as the ______________.

(*k*) Hypothesis tests can be either ______________ or ______________, depending on our interest in the direction of any difference.

(*l*) The $F$ statistic is the ratio of the ______________ to the ______________ group variance when testing for equality of variance.

For each problem from 6-2 to 6-11 provide the answers to the following steps (based on the hypothesis-testing procedure in Table 6-1):

(*a*) State the model.
(*b*) State the hypotheses.
(*c*) State the significance level.
(*d*) Compute the testing function.
(*e*) Standardize the testing function, if applicable.
(*f*) Find the critical point(s).
(*g*) State the conclusion.
(*h*) Interpret the conclusion in the context of the problem.

**6-2** Past records of a depressed region indicate that the mean level of job skills using a particular scale was 60. A manpower-training program is put into effect at considerable cost. After one year of operation, analysis of the program's effectiveness was carried out. It was decided that a good way to measure the effectiveness of the program was to determine if the mean job skills in the region had changed. A random sample was collected to derive a test statistic, mean job skill. Sample size was $n = 25$, $\bar{X} = 66$, and $S_X = 12.8$. Test the effectiveness of the program.

**6-3** A sample of convicted felons paroled five or more years ago was taken to determine the effectiveness of the parole board in releasing those least likely to return to prison. It is known that 40 percent of paroled prisoners are black. To check on the bias in selecting the sample according to race, test the following question: "Was the population from which the sample was selected the same as the population of all paroled convicted felons, at least as far as race is concerned?"

The proportion of blacks in the sample was computed to estimate the proportion of blacks in the sampled population. The sample consisted of 100 parolees of whom 30 percent were black.

**6-4** A political poll showed that out of a sample of 1600, the candidate of the minority party was preferred by 52.5 percent of those interviewed. (Undecided people were split proportionately between the candidates.)

(*a*) Can you conclude if the election were held at the time of the poll that the minority party will win? (Over 50 percent of the vote is needed to win.)
(*b*) Discuss the appropriateness of a one-tailed test for this problem.

**6-5** The 1970 census data showed that income of families with heads over 50 years of age was $8500 for Backwoods County. Since then incomes have risen 20 percent. A recent survey was conducted to determine the needs of the elderly in the county. Only heads of households over 50 were interviewed. A check was made to see if the sample were biased, for frequently surveyors tend to reach the middle class and avoid the poor. The mean family income was $11,000, with a standard deviation of 4000. Sample size was 100.

(*a*) Discuss whether a one-tailed or a two-tailed test should be employed.
(*b*) Test for bias in the sample.

**6-6** A similar survey (see Prob. 6-5) was conducted by the same team in a neighboring Frontwoods County. The results gave a mean income of \$11,500 and an estimated standard deviation of 3000. Sample size was also 100. Do these counties differ in mean income?

**6-7** An automotive manufacturer claims to get 22.4 miles per gallon for a certain model car. However, the Environmental Protection Agency selected 25 such cars and ran gas mileage tests on them. The results were

$$\bar{X} = 18.2 \qquad \text{and} \qquad S_X = 3.1$$

Test the null hypothesis that the mean gas mileage is 22.4.

**6-8** Two nonadjacent residential areas had homes appraised for tax purposes based on their marketability. The mean values were the same. One year later, area A had changed its composition so that it was now highly integrated, whereas area B was basically all white. Two new random samples of homes, each containing 50 homes, were selected for evaluation. Can we say on the basis of the following data that there is a difference in the mean market value of the home in these two areas?

$$\bar{X}_A = \$18{,}400 \qquad S_A = 4000 \qquad \bar{X}_B = 19{,}600 \qquad S_B = 3000$$

**6-9** A research question under consideration was, "Is the mean educational level of parolees who return to prison within five years different from that of those who do not?" To test this question, the sample was separated into two groups, those who did and those who did not return to prison, and the sample mean of educational level was computed for each group. The sample results were:

| | | | | |
|---|---|---|---|---|
| Returnees: | $\bar{X}_1 = 10.1$ | $SS_1 = 240$ | $S_1^2 = 4.07$ | $n_1 = 60$ |
| Nonreturnees: | $\bar{X}_2 = 11.8$ | $SS_2 = 152$ | $S_2^2 = 3.90$ | $n_2 = 40$ |

What conclusion can be reached concerning the research question?

**6-10** To evaluate planning programs at four different universities, a survey was sent to recent graduates. The survey consisted of a series of questions about the value of the program to the respondents' careers. Ranks 1 to 5 were used: 1 (very poor), 2 (poor), 3 (so-so), 4 (good), 5 (excellent). The average response of each survey is recorded below:

| | University | | | |
|---|---|---|---|---|
| | A | B | C | D |
| Sample responses | 2.1 | 4.1 | 2.5 | 3.8 |
| | 3.6 | 4.8 | 2.8 | 2.1 |
| | 2.2 | 3.6 | 2.5 | 3.5 |
| | 2.5 | 4.8 | 3.8 | 3.8 |
| | 4.4 | 3.1 | 2.2 | 4.0 |
| | 3.1 | | | |

(*a*) Compute the means, $S_b^2$, $S_w^2$, and $F$.

(*b*) Can you conclude that at least one program differs from another in terms of the mean perception of its graduates?

(*c*) If you reject the null hypothesis that all the programs are equally good, compare programs B and C.

**6-11** Four random samples of six cities were each drawn from four regions in the United States. Within each city an index of consumer confidence concerning the government's ability to curb inflation was calculated. The following were the results. Do any of the regions differ in mean consumer confidence?

| | West | North | East | South |
|---|---|---|---|---|
| | 12.3 | 34.8 | 19.2 | 31.9 |
| | 15.9 | 29.3 | 21.8 | 30.5 |
| | 11.7 | 31.4 | 17.5 | 29.6 |
| | 14.8 | 18.4 | 24.3 | 37.1 |
| | 25.7 | 26.3 | 18.7 | 33.3 |
| | 16.2 | 30.5 | 25.3 | 38.8 |
| Means | 16.1 | 28.5 | 21.1 | 33.5 |

$\bar{X} = 24.8 \quad S_w^2 = 20.5 \quad S_b^2 = 357.5$

**6-12** Select a variable from the Central Appalachian Region data set (App. D, data set 4). Compare the mean of that variable between counties that voted for the three primary parties in the 1968 elections. Do a one-way analysis of variance.

**6-13** Go to the library and find in some journal or book an elementary statistical analysis involving hypothesis testing. In about 400 words compare the procedure employed to that suggested in Table 6-1.
(*a*) What steps are left out? Why?
(*b*) Are the proper estimating testing and sampling functions employed?
(*c*) Are the conclusions substantiated?

## REFERENCES


### Theory

6-1. Blalock, H. M.: *Social Statistics*, 2d ed., McGraw-Hill, New York, 1972.
6-2. Chapman, D. G., and R. A. Schaufele: *Elementary Probability Models and Statistical Inference*, Ginn-Blaisdell, Waltham, Mass., 1970.
6-3. Hoel, P. G.: *Introduction to Mathematical Statistics*, 4th ed., Wiley, New York, 1971.
6-4. Hollander, M., and D. Wolfe: *Nonparametric Statistical Methods*, Wiley, New York, 1973.
6-5. Lindgren, B. W., and G. W. McElrath: *Probability and Statistics*, 3d ed., Macmillan, 1969.
6-6. Mendenhall, W., L. Ott, and R. F. Larson: *Statistics: A Tool for the Social Sciences*, Duxbury, North Scituate, Mass., 1974.

### Applications

6-7. Aiken, M., and P. E. Mott (Eds.): *The Structure of Community Power*, Random House, New York, 1970.
6-8. King, L. J.: *Statistical Analysis in Geography*, Prentice-Hall, Englewood Cliffs, N.J., 1969.
6-9. Krueckeberg, D. A., and A. L. Silvers: *Urban Planning Analysis*, Wiley, New York, 1974.
6-10. Phillips, B. S.: *Social Research: Strategy and Tactics*, 2d ed., Macmillan, New York, 1971.
6-11. Tanur, J. M., et al. (Eds.): *Statistics: A Guide to the Unknown*, Holden-Day, San Francisco, Calif., 1972.
6-12. Wallis, W. A., and H. V. Roberts: *The Nature of Statistics*, Collier Books, New York, 1962.
6-13. Wohl, M., and B. V. Martin: *Traffic System Analysis*, McGraw-Hill, New York, 1967.

CHAPTER

# SEVEN

## SURVEY RESEARCH†

As a result of the trend toward administrative decentralization and government responsiveness, public attitudes and opinions have become an important part of urban and regional policy development and implementation. If systematically applied, survey techniques offer an opportunity to obtain citizen feedback which cannot be adequately assessed through traditional channels of citizen communication, such as interest group pressures, complaints, or even voting patterns.

There are multiple applications of survey research. Surveys can be an effective method to determine citizen needs and preferences regarding physical facilities and social services in an urban or rural setting. In addition to establishing priorities in terms of initiating public services, surveys also provide data for empirical evaluation of existing services. In this context, behavioral information concerning the use of services can be related to attitudinal and sociodemographic characteristics of users and nonusers. In the same manner, satisfaction levels regarding the quality of the services being offered can be ascertained. Finally, survey data enable a more comprehensive understanding of the interrelationship between public activities, attitudes, and corresponding sociodemographic characteristics, facilitating the analysis of metropolitan problems and prediction of urban and regional behavior.

† This chapter was written by Dr. Patricia Klobus Edwards of the Division of Environmental and Urban Systems of Virginia Polytechnic Institute and State University.

## 7-1 GENERAL FORMAT OF SURVEY RESEARCH

Development and administration of a survey typically follows a stepwise set of procedures which are shown in the flow chart in Fig. 7-1. First, a problem requiring data collection using survey techniques is identified. Emphasis should be placed on increasing the investigators' knowledge of citizens, their behavior, attitudes, or the quality of their living and social arrangements. After a set of study objectives has been devised, the research problem can be precisely defined and specific data collection needs then identified. The following stage in the survey

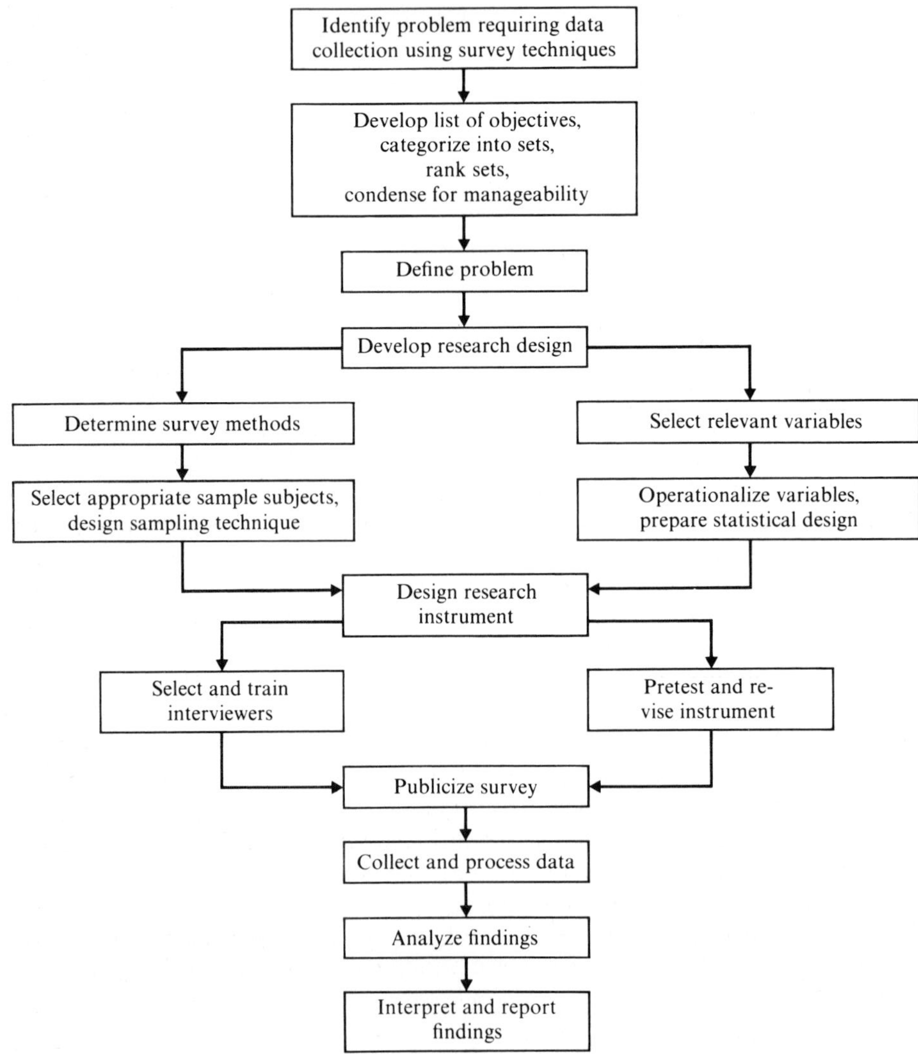


**Figure 7-1** Stages in the development and administration of a survey.

process necessitates development of a research design, identification and operationalization of relevant variables, selection of survey methods and sample subjects, and formulation of a research instrument which will satisfy the project demands.

Implementation of a survey involves selecting and training interviewers, pretest and revision of the survey instrument, and data collection. After data are collected, they must be systematically coded and "cleaned" for recording and processing errors. This is generally accomplished by using computer techniques.

The final stage in the survey research process involves analyzing, interpreting, and reporting the data. A variety of analytical techniques commonly used in survey analysis are discussed throughout this text (see, for example, Chaps. 6 and 8 to 10). The research report, which usually includes a comparison of the findings with previous research as well as suggestions for further study, concludes the survey process.

## 7-2 DEFINING STUDY OBJECTIVES

One of the most vital steps in survey research is the development of a clear set of objectives (see Chap. 20). The importance of this first stage of survey design cannot be overstated, for far too many studies have failed to collect relevant information because designers were not precise in identifying their research goals.

Several procedures may be helpful in establishing the objectives of a study. First, the principal investigators can invite all persons who may be interested or involved in the study to confer, with the purpose of generating a list of goals. Representatives of various segments of the population which are under study may be invited to provide insights regarding the development of appropriate research goals, some of which may not be readily apparent to the research team. The ensuing list of goals should be categorized by the group into sets, and then ranked in terms of their applicability to the problem area. It may be necessary to further reduce the list, considering only goals with top priorities, in order to avoid redundancy and to increase the manageability of the project. At this point the investigators should be able to prepare a clear and concise problem statement which incorporates all pertinent research objectives. The problem statement, if carefully constructed, will also function as a definition of the study parameters.

An additional step in the process of defining survey objectives is the designing of a conceptual model which illustrates the expected relationships of all components in the problem statement. For example, a problem statement concerning the evaluation of a social service program should, if possible, include attitudes and sociodemographic characteristics of nonusers as well as users. The former group may offer invaluable information about citizen needs, accessibility of the service, public image of the administering agency, and factors relating to potential use. Unfortunately, many evaluation studies simply concentrate on user satisfaction which, although undeniably important, does not encompass the criteria for a complete analysis. A model enables the survey investigator to conceptualize, in a more holistic sense, the interdependence of social, economic, and political elements related to the problem statement. This facilitates the selection and operationalization of variables, choice of sample area and subjects, and statistical design. After the model is constructed, it is relatively easy to develop hypotheses concerning the interrelationships of variables for predictive purposes, to design criteria pertaining to the assessment of program costs and benefits, or to identify and evaluate alternative consequences of administrative interventions on various segments of the population.

## 7-3 UTILITY AND COSTS OF FOUR SURVEY METHODS

Four of the most prominently used methods of administering a survey are the mailed questionnaire, group surveys, telephone interviews, and personal interviews. The first two techniques rely on self-administered questionnaires, while the latter forms of survey require that respondents interact with interviewers on a one-to-one basis. Use of self-administered questionnaires proves to be less costly per respondent but is, in fact, disadvantageous because questions cannot be easily clarified, particularly in terms of the mailed questionnaire. Generally speaking, to enhance the response level, self-administered questionnaires must be shorter and achieve less depth in the information gained than the personal interview, though there are exceptions (see Refs. 7-6 and 7-7).

Survey techniques also vary in regard to interviewer bias, the type of information that can be collected, and efficiency in terms of implementation. Table 7-1, which shows the relative attributes of each technique, indicates that the mailed questionnaire and personal interview are diametrically opposed in terms of advantages and disadvantages. It is, therefore, important to determine data specifications before selecting the appropriate method. If the study requires many questions and in-depth responses from a highly representative sample of the total population, the personal interview is the most efficacious choice. If, on the other hand, the information needed is minimal but the geographic area to be sampled is extensive, a mailed questionnaire would be most effective. Choice of an appropriate survey technique, in other words, is a series of trade-offs dependent upon

**Table 7-1 Relative attributes of four survey techniques**

| Attribute | Mailed questionnaire | Group survey | Telephone interview | Personal interview |
|---|---|---|---|---|
| Sampling advantages (e.g., representativeness) | Low | Low | Medium | High |
| Comprehensiveness | Low | Medium | Medium | High |
| Interviewer bias | Low | Medium | Medium | High |
| Response rate | Low | Medium | Medium | High |
| Anonymity | High | Medium | Medium | Low |
| Efficiency in execution | High | High | Medium | Low |
| Cost efficiency | High | High | Medium | Low |

informational requirements, time limitations, and fiscal constraints (Refs. 7-16, 7-18, and 7-19).

The *mailed questionnaire* is particularly useful where costs have to be limited. Mailing lists may be obtained from various civic and social organizations or purchased from advertising concerns. However, the response rate for mailed questionnaires is low, generally ranging from 10 to 70 percent of the survey sample. Several steps may be used to increase the response rate and also ascertain effects of bias due to nonresponse:

1. Enclose a cover letter which legitimates the survey, assures anonymity of responses, urges a prompt reply, and thanks the respondent for his or her cooperation.
2. Include with the mailing a self-addressed, stamped envelope for return of the questionnaire.
3. Send a follow-up mailing to those persons who do not initially respond.
4. Make certain the questionnaire is easy to complete and not ambiguous. Most questions should be of the multiple-choice type, requiring a check for the appropriate answer.
5. Use available sociodemographic data to compare respondents with nonrespondents in order to ascertain possible bias in the data.
6. If funding is sufficient, follow up with a personal interview on a subsample consisting of nonrespondents. This will increase the representativeness of the sample and also make available information regarding the possible bias created by nonresponse.

When the investigator is interested in comparing various groups in terms of attitudes or program needs and impacts, the *group survey* is often an appropriate method. Certainly the sampling procedure is not rigorous, for it is usually not possible to insure either randomness or representativeness. However, this technique, which involves administering questionnaires at group meetings (such as public hearings, church groups, professional organizations, and civic or social clubs), is efficient in regard to both cost and time. The following are suggestions to aid in the implementation of group surveys:

1. When contacting group officers or representatives to request permission for the survey, state your objectives clearly.
2. Prepare a brief outline of the survey goals to present to the group before questionnaires are distributed.
3. Make self-administered questionnaires fairly short and easy to complete. Assure all respondents of confidentiality.
4. Offer to report the results of the survey to the group at a later date.

*Telephone interviews* are a method of reaching a large segment of an urban or regional population but, due to the increasing number of unlisted or multiple-listed numbers, it is impossible to obtain a random sample from the telephone book. However, representativeness, in terms of relevant variables such as age, sex, and voting preference, may be achieved by quota sampling (see Chap. 5 references). When using telephone interviews, care should be taken to have few, if any, sensitive questions such as family income or race. Therefore, the telephone interview is not appropriate for many studies which necessitate collection of sociodemographic information for purposes of control or prediction. It has been found that telephone interviewing is more successful when the questions are concise and do not have an extensive array of categories. A final note about the telephone survey concerns random dialing. This technique generally reduces the error caused by unlisted or multiple-listed telephones, but also can be a problem in that nonresidential listings will be included in the sample.

If study objectives require in-depth information, *personal interviews* are the best source of data. When a random sample of respondents is selected, interviewers are able to make repeated call-backs in order to limit the nonresponse rate. It is expected that some sample subjects will refuse to be interviewed, but if interviewers are properly trained, the nonresponse rate is minimal as compared to other survey modes. Also, random substitutions can be made for nonrespondents to maintain the intended sample size.

Costs of personal interview surveys are dependent upon the length of interview, sample size, and efficiency of interviewers. The National Opinion Research Center (NORC) has engaged in research involving the relative costs of a variety of survey techniques. The resulting monograph (Ref. 7-16) is a valuable guide in assessing the efficiency of quota versus call-back samples; the probability of response rates by age, sex, socioeconomic status, or survey type; and interviewer costs.

Telephone calls can be used in conjunction with the personal interview, e.g., in making advance appointments and screening populations for unique characteristics. The implementation of both personal and telephone surveys necessitates a knowledge of interviewing techniques, a subject which will be reserved for discussion in Sec. 7-9.

## 7-4 SURVEY DESIGN

A research design is the master plan for any survey investigation. It determines the selection of groups to be studied and methods for the analysis of data. Basic designs most commonly used in survey research are experimental, longitudinal, correlational, and panel (Ref. 7-10).

The *experimental design* is one of the most rigorous forms of survey analysis and is used to assess change or evaluate public programs. First, baseline data are collected from each of two groups, which are designated as experimental and control groups. These baseline data are compared to ascertain if any differences exist between the groups ($Y_{1E} - Y_{1C}$).

| | Baseline | Evaluation |
|---|---|---|
| Experimental | $Y_{1E}$ | $Y_{2E}$ |
| Control | $Y_{1C}$ | $Y_{2C}$ |

The experimental group is then exposed to some sort of intervention, e.g., employment training or a public meeting concerning a bond referendum. Following the intervention, both groups are again interviewed and the data are analyzed to ascertain relative changes between the baseline and evaluation surveys ($Y_{2E} - Y_{1E}$; $Y_{2C} - Y_{1C}$) using frequencies, proportions, or means. The control group, which does not receive an intervention, is used as a basis of comparison with the experimental group. If both groups have changed considerably, these changes may be due to external factors rather than the intervention itself. Effectiveness of the intervention is determined by:

$$\text{Effectiveness} = [(Y_{2E} - Y_{1E}) - (Y_{2C} - Y_{1C})] \tag{7-1}$$

Because experimental designs require sampling from two groups at two points in time, the method is costly and time consuming. Also, experimental groups may respond to the effect of being observed rather than simply to the intervention itself, thereby biasing the results of the study. This type of bias, called the *Hawthorne effect*, may occur because the experimental group wishes to perform well or tends to develop a common image of their role in the research project. However, the experimental design is generally advantageous in establishing a time priority of change for use in causal analysis. In addition, it is possible to predict whether change was caused by an intervention or was due to extraneous variables.

*Longitudinal designs* involve observing the same sample at two or more points in time.

| $Y_1$ | $Y_2$ | $Y_3$ | $Y_4$ |
|---|---|---|---|

This type of design is effective in ascertaining the direction of changes within a group over time, but the investigator is unable to determine precisely if the change is solely the consequence of an intervention. Therefore, it is not a rigorous design for program evaluation. Longitudinal analysis, though, is useful when comparing relative changes between sociodemographic variables, attitudes, and behavior. Using multivariate statistical techniques such as regression (Chap. 10), the investigator can compare variation over time, controlling for extraneous variables which may effect the expected relationships.

Longitudinal designs are often used to assess the consequences of stimuli directed at large populations, e.g., those subjected to a health information program. The design can also be used for pilot studies by observing small groups over time in order to develop hypotheses for subsequent research. Studies regarding the perpetuation of poverty are illustrative of this technique.

The longitudinal design, which compares the same set of respondents over time, is often difficult to implement because of the attrition of sample subjects. *Panel designs*, which employ two different samples for two sets of observations, can be used to overcome this problem. These designs are most reliable if employed in cases where both samples can be taken from the same population, or from two populations where the significant variables can be controlled. Generally this latter procedure requires matching relevant characteristics of each group in order to

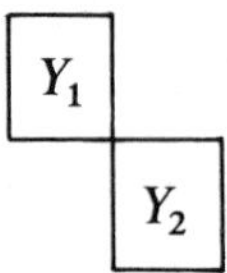


maintain controls. If for some reason it is impossible to match samples and the basic variable characteristics of the populations are known, these variables can be weighted accordingly to simulate a matching. For example, an evaluation of changes in hospital administration cannot review the same patients before and after changes have taken place. However, a baseline study can be taken of patients being serviced at time one. Thereafter, other groups of patients may be interviewed as the administrative changes progress. Each new panel of patients should be matched with the initial group in terms of sex, socioeconomic status, length of stay, severity of illness, type of room, etc. This matching technique, in effect, approximates sampling from the same population. If it is impossible to match panels on all relevant variables, the samples must be large enough to apply statistical controls.

*Correlational designs* require sampling from two groups at the same time.

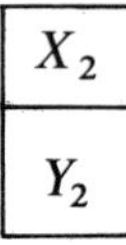


Such designs are static in that the extent and direction of change cannot be measured. In spite of this, correlational designs are effective in relating variables for predictive purposes. To illustrate, a study which concerns predicting the vote on a public transit referendum would need to ascertain and compare the characteristics of a sample of probable voters in relation to their voting preference. This information could then be extrapolated to predict how the entire population of voters would behave.

If historical data are of use in a survey, the correlational design can be used to assess change by employing *recall*. Recall is primarily utilized to measure actual behavior, rather than attitudinal data, in order to minimize error. There is greater reliability in asking respondents how they previously voted as opposed to how they felt about an issue. A design using recall is particularly advantageous when relating prior experiences with current attitudes or preferences. A study which

| $X_1$ | $X_2$ |
|---|---|
| $Y_1$ | $Y_2$ |

focuses, for instance, on the interrelationships of past housing experiences with present housing preferences may utilize recall effectively and with minimal error. In using recall, however, care should be taken to avoid overinterpretation.

Many investigators, due to time and financial constraints, use the *one-shot case study*. A sample $\boxed{Y_2}$ is taken from a population and subsequently subdivided into categories for multivariate analysis. Advantages of this technique are the relative ease of acquiring a representative sample and the avoidance of experimental bias. The one-shot case study is obviously disadvantageous in its limitation for assessing the extent and direction of change.

## 7-5 OPERATIONALIZING VARIABLES

Surveys are generally concerned with the measurement of three classes of data: attitudinal, behavioral, and sociodemographic characteristics of respondents. The selection of indicators which translate these attributes into empirical observations is one of the most important steps in survey research. Unidimensional variables such as age, educational level completed, and frequency of using a service are simply measured by counting and ranking responses. However, many variables are stated in abstract conceptual terms and cannot be measured by a single indicator.

The measurement of organizational involvement, as a case in point, requires a combination of indicators which represent the variety of activities implied when defining the concept: attendance at meetings, holding an office, committee involvement, length of affiliation, and so on. Responses to each of these items may be ranked in terms of their relationship to a high or low level of involvement and then summed to create a total score for individual respondents. If it is felt that some items are more important than others, weights can be assigned to each item before summing.

There are several standardized techniques commonly used to develop scales or indices. *Likert scales* provide a selection of five categories of response for each item: strongly approve, approve, undecided, disapprove, and strongly disapprove. These responses are ranked from 1 to 5, respectively. The ranked items are then summed to obtain an individual score for each item. Likert scales are used to measure attitudes, but variations of the technique may be applied to behavioral measurement by substituting the categories of response as follows: regularly, frequently, sometimes, rarely, or never. The reliability of behavioral measurement is increased, however, if responses are defined in more specific terms, such as: never, once a week, two to three times a week, four or more times a week. These categories of response may vary according to the range of expected answers as well as the form of analysis anticipated by the investigator.

A second scaling technique, the *semantic differential*, is also useful in measuring attitudes. This technique requires the respondent to evaluate an item by means of a scale based on two polar adjectives: good–bad, positive–negative, right–wrong, beautiful–ugly, poor–excellent, and so on. Ratings may be varied, depending on the breadth of response desired, but generally range from 0 to 5, 7, or 10. Low ratings represent negative feelings, while high ones indicate favorable attitudes. The respondent's score is calculated by summing the ratings of all the evaluative items.

*Guttman scalogram analysis* requires a set of items which are expected to be rated in a consistent manner. In other words, all respondents who affirmatively answer an individual item in the set will have higher scores than those who answer the same item negatively. The Guttman technique is useful in transforming nominal into ordinal data if the scale is reliable (see Sec. 7-6).

Robinson, Attianasion, and Head (Ref. 7-11), Bonjean, Hill, and McLemore (Ref. 7-2), Miller (Ref. 7-10), and others have gathered together some excellent collections of scales and indices used in social, political, and economic research. These books provide scale items, scoring techniques, references for previous use of a scale, and reliability estimates. For those interested in learning more about the construction of attitudinal scales, Summers' book (Ref. 7-17) provides an excellent source of information.

## 7-6 MEASUREMENT ERROR IN SURVEYS

When measuring variables through survey techniques, there are two important questions which must be addressed: "Does the survey instrument measure responses consistently?" and "To what degree does the instrument measure the variables under investigation?" The first question refers to the problem of *reliability*—the consistency of ordering respondents relative to other respondents, assuming no changes have taken place. The second question concerns the *validity* of the survey.

Several methods have been developed to assess the reliability of items, particularly when scales are used in the survey design. *Test–retest* compares two sets of responses from the same individuals. The higher the correlation between tests, the greater the reliability of measures. This method of determining reliability is limited, though, because respondents may actually have changed or may score differently due to distraction, fatigue, or misinterpretation of the items. Reliability may be tested by measuring the equivalence of sets of items in a scale. The *split-half method* divides all items measuring the same phenomenon into two groups, either by comparing odd and even items or by comparing the first and second halves of a scale. An estimate of reliability is determined by using the Spearman–Brown formula (Ref. 7-1). Measurement of the internal consistency of a scale also yields an estimation of reliability. This is accomplished by using the Kuder–Richardson formula, which calculates the covariance of all items simultaneously (Ref. 7-1). A fourth technique for measuring reliability is that of *parallel forms of measurement*. Both forms are administered to the same respondents and the degree of correlation between the tests is used as an estimation of reliability.

Validity, the degree to which an item represents the concept to be measured, is more difficult to ascertain. Obviously the measure has to be reliable to attain validity. However, most investigators *assume* validity because it is difficult to measure statistically. Validity, then, is generally based on the observation, logic, and experience of the research team. If possible, their judgments should be confirmed by consulting other experts in the field of inquiry.

Factor analysis may be used to increase the validity of multiple-item measures by determining if all items are measuring the same concept. If an item does not cluster with the other items, it can be discarded in the analysis. In addition, validity can be estimated by correlating attitudinal measures with those of behavior relating to the same concept. Bohrnstedt's chapted entitled "Reliability and Validity Assessment in Attitudinal Measurement" (Ref. 7-1) is an excellent resource for techniques in estimating measurement error.

## 7-7 THE RESEARCH INSTRUMENT

The two basic forms of questionnaires most frequently used in survey research are the *structured* and *moderately structured schedules* (Ref. 7-8). The structured questionnaire is constructed with specific questions which are asked in a fixed order. Usually the respondent is required to select from a set of categories provided in the questionnaire (see Fig. 7-2).

In contrast, the moderately structured questionnaire is defined in terms of purpose, but the sample subject is free to respond in his or her own words. Assume that an investigator wishes to establish interorganizational linkages and conflicts between social service agencies. A moderately structured interview schedule would focus on general questions regarding contacts between social service agencies, the frequency and quality of these contacts, and the problems in dealing with other agencies. For example: Which agencies do you refer clients to most frequently? What are the advantages (or disadvantages) of referring a client to Agency X? Do you find overlap between the functions of your agency and other social service agencies? (If yes) Would you please describe this overlap and identify the agency involved? Moderately structured questionnaires are useful in the collection of qualitative data. Also, they may be instrumental in a pilot study designed to establish questions for a larger investigation.

When developing questions for a structured interview schedule, there are several general considerations which must be taken into account:

1. Make sure all variable categories are mutually exclusive and that, additively, they are inclusive of the range of answers expected.
2. Measure each category consistently, for example:

   *Question.* How far is the nearest university? *Right.* 0 to 2 miles, over 2 to 5 miles, over 5 miles. *Wrong.* 20 minutes, 1 to 2 miles, 2 to 5 miles.

# 1976 SOCIAL SERVICES SURVEY

| | Column number | Code for this response |
|---|---|---|
| INTRODUCTION: | | |
| Hello, my name is ______________________ and I am taking a survey for Montgomery County Community Services. We are interviewing a sample of residents in the County to help Montgomery County administrators plan social service needs. Any information you give us will be entirely confidential. | | |
| Respondent identification number: | 1–3 | 231 |
| Card number: | 4 | 1 |
| Interviewer number: | 5–6 | 09 |
| BY OBSERVATION: | | |
| 1. Sex of respondent: | 7 | 2 |
| Male .................... 1 | | |
| Female .................... ② | | |
| 2. What is the total number of adults living in this household? | 8 | 2 |
| 3. How many years have you lived in Montgomery County? | 9–10 | 08 |
| (*Note.* Record exact number of years using 2 digits. If respondent answers "all my life," ask: "How many years is that?" DK or NA = 99) | | |
| 4. Do you own this home, do you rent it, or is it provided for you by someone else? | 11 | 1 |
| Owns or buying .................... ① | | |
| Renting .................... 2 | | |
| Free housing (from relatives, employer, etc.) .................... 3 | | |
| DK; NA .................... 9 | | |
| I have a list of some social services provided in Montgomery County and would like to ask you some questions about each one. | | |
| SERVICE 1: | | |
| 5. Are you familiar with any child or day care services? | 12 | 1 |
| Yes .................... ① | | |
| No .................... 2 | | |
| NA .................... 9 | | |
| If No or NA, skip to Question 8. | | |
| 6. Have you ever used this type of service? | 13 | 2 |
| Yes .................... 1 | | |
| No .................... ② | | |
| NA .................... 9 | | |
| If No, or NA, skip to Question 8. | | |
| 7. Would you rate this service very satisfactory, unsatisfactory, or very unsatisfactory? | 14 | 9 |
| Very satisfactory .................... 1 | | |
| Satisfactory .................... 2 | | |
| Don't know or indifferent .................... 3 | | |
| Unsatisfactory .................... 4 | | |
| Very unsatisfactory .................... 5 | | |
| NA .................... ⑨ | | |

**Figure 7-2** Format for a structured survey questionnaire.

The wrong list of categories not only combines minutes and miles, but also does not allow a response for a person living closer than 1 mile or farther than 5 miles. In addition, if the respondent lives 2 miles from a university, he or she may check either of two categories.

3. Each variable should have a category for: no response, undecided, don't know or indifferent. These responses may be important in the analysis of data.
4. Do not collapse interval data unless absolutely necessary. The option for restructuring data during analysis is limited when data are collapsed.
5. Avoid long, ambiguous questions.
6. Ask questions which give the most information. For example, ask, "What organizations do you belong to?" rather than "How many organizations do you belong to?" The first question includes the answer to the second.
7. The ordering of questions may often cause a response set. For example, subjects who are asked, "Do you favor a municipal tax increase?" and then, "Do you favor additional recreational facilities in this city?" are most likely to answer each question negatively. In contrast, when the questions are reversed, interviewers are more likely to receive positive answers.
8. The flow of questions is an important item in retaining the respondents' attention. It is helpful to introduce each unique set of questions with a short phrase such as: "Now we would like to ask you a series of questions about your health."
9. Protect the respondent's ego. To illustrate, "Do you *happen* to know the names of your City Council members?" is more tactful than asking, "Who are the members of your City Council?"
10. Sensitive questions such as age and income should be reserved for the end of the questionnaire. If the year of birth is requested rather than actual age there is less likelihood of refusal. Also, responses are more reliable if income is categorized than if an absolute figure is sought.
11. Do not expect respondents to make choices about complex issues for which they have not been sufficiently informed. Respondents generally react more favorably to short-range problems rather than long-term considerations.
12. Open-ended questions such as "What do you like or dislike about the proposed comprehensive land-use plan?" are appropriate, even in a structured interview schedule. They serve to break up monotony and give respondents an opportunity to express opinions which may otherwise be restricted by rigid questions.

## 7-8 CODING THE QUESTIONNAIRE

Precoded questionnaires are the most efficient method of tabulating structured data (see Fig. 7-2). Data cards can be punched directly from the questionnaire, saving the effort of using coding sheets. This procedure also minimizes error because the transference of data requires only one, rather than two, steps.

Each respondent should have a unique identification code which is placed both on the questionnaire and on each computer card. This information is necessary for referral when cleaning the data. In addition, if more than one card per respondent is necessary, each card should be numbered consecutively.

The number of columns necessary to code each question varies according to the number of categories allotted for each question. If there are less than 10 categories, only one column is needed, whereas 10 to 99 categories require two columns. Always *adjust right* when coding, by placing the answer code in the far right column(s) and adding "0" to the blank column(s) on the left. If a respondent has completed 8 years of education, the correct code is "08" because the question requires a two-column answer. The additional column allows coding for respondents having 10 or more years of education.

Be consistent when coding for "nonresponse" (usually "0") or "not appropriate" (usually "9" or "99" if two columns are required). When coding a nonresponse, be sure "0" is not a meaningful category, as it would be if asking a question concerning the number of times a respondent has moved during the past 5 years. In this case, a code other than "0" must be assigned for "no response."

A further suggestion is to code answers consecutively according to rank. Thus, if the categories are: strongly approve, approve, disapprove, strongly disapprove, don't know or indifferent, they should be coded as follows:

| SA | A | DK | D | SD |
|---|---|---|---|---|
| 1 | 2 | 3 | 4 | 5 |

Thus, "don't know" indicates a ranking between approval and disapproval.

If an investigator wishes to quantify an open-ended question such as, "What do you see as the most difficult problems in providing health services in our city?", it is possible to do so by using the following modification of the Delphi technique (Ref. 7-4 and Chap. 13):

1. Write each unique response to a particular question on a small index card.
2. Select a panel of judges to sort the cards for each question so that essentially identical items are placed together.
3. Next the judges must come to an agreement on the items appropriate for each stack and then assign labels to the stacks. These labels will become categories representative of the question.
4. Finally, all responses to a particular question are coded in accordance with the categories determined by the judges.

## 7-9 SELECTING AND TRAINING INTERVIEWERS

There are several factors important in achieving a successful interview. If telephone interviews are used, the interviewer's voice should be pleasant and enthusiastic. Female interviewers have been found to be most successful in conducting telephone surveys (Ref. 7-19). When personal interviews are called for, interviewers are selected for their ability to build rapport with a respondent and should present an inconspicuous appearance. Also, greater rapport is more likely if racial homogeneity between the interviewer and respondent can be maintained.

Project objectives should be carefully presented during the training period in order that interviewers can explain these objectives to prospective respondents. In the training session, the basic techniques of completing a successful interview (Ref. 7-8) must be reviewed. For example, instruct interviewers to keep all information confidential. Expressing personal opinions during an interview or pressuring respondents may invalidate the data. Interviewers should ask questions exactly as worded, but can make clarifications if the objectives of a question are not clearly understood.

The training session is an opportunity to practice interviewing. It is often advisable to have interviewers perform the pretest. Pretests should always be made with a sample analogous to that of the major study. By pretesting, interviewers can flag problems concerning the flow and interpretation of questions and may assist in revising the questionnaire. This experience will also be valuable training in administering the questionnaire to respondents who are characteristic of the actual sample. Finally, familiarize interviewers with coding procedures and explain the purpose of each code. This will allow the interviewer to code all possible ranges of response.

Each interviewer should receive a packet of supplies: interview schedules, instructions for selecting sample subjects, a letter of introduction, and a sheet for recording each completed interview, refusal, and appointments for call-backs. With few exceptions it is customary to publicize the survey during the week prior to its implementation. Interviewers can carry the newspaper clippings along with a letter of introduction to legitimize their request for information.

The final stage of survey research involves processing, analyzing, and interpreting data. Techniques for these steps vary in relation to the type of questions asked, as well as with the intended uses of the information. Various techniques applicable to the analysis and interpretation of survey data are discussed throughout this text. This chapter has been written to address the highlights of survey research methods. Before undertaking the design and implementation of an actual survey, readers should become familiar with the references that follow.

## PROBLEMS

**7-1** Fill in the blanks.

(*a*) The first step in conducting survey research is to ______________________________

______________________________________________________.

(*b*) A ______________________ enables the researcher to conceptualize, in a more holistic way, the elements of a problem.

(*c*) The lowest costs in doing survey research can be achieved by using the

______________________ technique and ______________________ technique.

(*d*) The most comprehensive type of survey is ______________________.
(*e*) The survey technique which is low in response rate but is high in cost efficiency is the

______________________ technique.

(*f*) The ______________________ design is one of the most rigorous forms of survey analysis.

(*g*) ______________________ designs require sampling from two groups simultaneously.
(*h*) Where a respondent is provided with five fixed categories of response for each item, the

technique is called a ______________________ scale.

(*i*) Reliability refers to ______________________.

(*j*) The ______________________ method of assessing reliability divides all items measuring the same phenomenon into two groups.

(*k*) ______________________ may be used to increase validity of multiple-item measures by determining if all items are measuring the same concept.

(*l*) The ______________________ may often cause a response set.

(*m*) The ______________________ questionnaire is constructed with specific questions which are asked in a fixed order.

(*n*) ______________________ refers to the degree to which an item represents the concept to be measured.

(*o*) Using the ______________________ formula one can calculate the covariance of all items simultaneously.

**7-2** List advantages and disadvantages of the mailed survey, group survey, telephone interview, and personal interview.

**7-3** Write an appropriate scenario for *each* of the following survey designs: experimental, longitudinal, panel, and correlation.

**7-4** Go to the library and select a case study involving survey research. Critique the study in terms of the following criteria:
(*a*) The survey method selected.
(*b*) Sampling technique.
(*c*) Research design.
(*d*) Measurement of variables.

**7-5** Prepare the agenda for an interviewer training session. List your objectives and the techniques you plan to cover during these sessions.

**7-6** As an employee of a regional housing administration, you have been asked to implement a survey relating to housing needs for the poor.
(*a*) List the objectives of your study.
(*b*) Develop the rationale for a research design.
(*c*) Choose the method for selecting your sample.
(*d*) Defend your selection of a survey technique.
(*e*) Develop a preliminary questionnaire.

**7-7** In about 400 words criticize the survey employed to obtain the information in data sets 2, 5, or 6 in App. D.

## REFERENCES


### Theory

7-1. Bohrnstedt, G. W.: "Reliability and Validity Assessment in Attitude Measurement," in G. F. Summers (Ed.), *Attitude Measurement*, Rand-McNally, Chicago, Ill., 1970.
7-2. Bonjean, C. M., R. J. Hill, and S. McLemore: *Sociological Measurement: An Inventory of Scales and Indices*, Chandler, San Francisco, Calif., 1967.
7-3. Davis, J. A.: *Elementary Survey Analysis*, Prentice-Hall, Englewood Cliffs, N.J., 1971.
7-4. Delbecq, A. L., A. H. Van de Ven, and D. H. Gustafson: *Group Techniques for Program Planning*, Scott, Foresman, Glenview, Ill., 1975.
7-5. Denzin, N.: *The Research Act*, Aldine, Chicago, Ill., 1970.
7-6. Dillman, D. A.: "Increasing Mail Questionnaire Response in Large Samples of the General Public," *Public Opinion Quarterly*, vol. 36, Summer, 1972.
7-7. Dillman, D. A., et al.: "Increasing Mail Questionnaire Response: A Four State Comparison," *American Sociological Review*, vol. 39, October, 1974.
7-8. Gordon, R. L.: *Interviewing: Strategy, Techniques, and Tactics*, The Dorset Press, Homewood, Ill., 1969.
7-9. Institute for Social Research: *Interviewers Manual*, University of Michigan, Ann Arbor, Mich., 1969.
7-10. Miller, D. C.: *Handbook of Research Design and Social Measurement*, McKay, New York, 1970.
7-11. Robinson, J. P., A. Attianasion, and K. B. Head, *Measures of Occupational Attitudes and Occupational Characteristics*, Survey Research Center, University of Michigan, Ann Arbor, Mich., 1969.
7-12. Robinson, J. P., G. Rusk, and K. B. Head: *Measures of Political Attitudes*, Survey Research Center, University of Michigan, Ann Arbor, Mich., 1968.
7-13. Robinson, I. M. (Ed.): *Decision-Making in Urban Planning*, Sage Publications, Beverly Hills, Calif., 1972.
7-14. Rosenberg, M.: *The Logic of Survey Analysis*, Basic Books, New York, 1968.
7-15. Shaver, P. R., and J. P. Robinson: *Measures of Social Psychological Attitudes*, Survey Research Center, University of Michigan, Ann Arbor, Mich., 1969.
7-16. Sudman, S.: *Reducing the Cost of Surveys*, Aldine, Chicago, Ill., 1967.
7-17. Summers, G. F.: *Attitude Measurement*, Rand-McNally, Chicago, Ill., 1970.
7-18. Webb, K., and H. P. Hatrey: *Obtaining Citizen Feedback: The Application of Citizen Surveys to Local Governments*, The Urban Institute, Washington, D.C., 1973.
7-19. Weiss, C. H., and H. P. Hatrey: *An Introduction to Sample Surveys for Government Managers*, The Urban Institute, Washington, D.C., 1971.

### Applications

7-20. Blair, L. H., and A. I. Schwartz: *How Clean is Our City?*, The Urban Institute, Washington, D.C., 1972.
7-21. Center for Urban and Regional Studies: *Community Profile: Reston, Virginia*, University of North Carolina, Chapel Hill, N.C., 1973.
7-22. Josephson, E.: "Resistance to Community Surveys," *Social Problems*, vol. 16, Summer, 1970.
7-23. National Opinion Research Center: *The NORC General Social Survey: Questions and Answers*, University of Chicago, Chicago, Ill., 1974.
7-24. Serfling, R. E., and I. L. Sherman: "Survey Evaluation of Three Poliomyelitis Immunization Campaigns," in H. C. Schulberg et al. (Eds.), *Program Evaluation in the Health Fields*, Behavioral Publications, New York, 1969.
7-25. Weiss, C. H.: "Validity of Welfare Mothers' Interview Responses," *Public Opinion Quarterly*, vol. 32, Winter, 1969.

CHAPTER

# EIGHT

# REGRESSION BETWEEN TWO VARIABLES

In Chap. 4 we described a situation in which three nominal-scaled variables were observed for each of 10 welfare recipients. Given this information we were able to determine the probability of a given result, e.g., that the recipient was getting the money illegally, given that he or she was old. This method for relating one variable to another can be extended to interval- and ratio-scaled variables through regression, which is a technique for placing a line through a two-dimensional set of points to minimize the squared differences or "errors" between predicted and actual values of the dependent variable. Otherwise known as the *method of least squares*, regression probably is the most used of all the statistical techniques described in this book. When the goodness of fit of such a regression-generated line is gauged with indices like the correlation coefficient (discussed in the next chapter), the usefulness of regression is further enhanced.

## 8-1 ESTABLISHING LINEAR REGRESSION EQUATIONS

Figure 8-1 shows a set of points representing the value of owner-occupied housing units $Y$ and crowding $X$ (fraction of units with 1.01 or more people per room) in the first five blocks of Census tract 2 in Roanoke in 1970. We assume that a linear relationship between owner value and crowding is the most appropriate. Our objective consequently is to find the model of the form:

$$Y = \alpha + \beta X + E \qquad \mu_E = 0 \qquad X \text{ and } E \text{ independent} \qquad \text{(Model 8-1)}$$

which lies closest to all of the points. In this equation $\beta$ and $\alpha$ are the unknown population slope and intercept, respectively, and $E$ is the "error" or difference between the actual and predicted owner value. If the level of crowding and owner value for block $i$ are denoted by $(X_i, Y_i)$ and the corresponding value of $Y$ falling on the regression line directly below $(X_i, Y_i)$ is denoted by $\hat{Y}_i$, then $(Y_i - \hat{Y}_i)$ represents the error which would be made in estimating $Y_i$ when $X = X_i$. In other

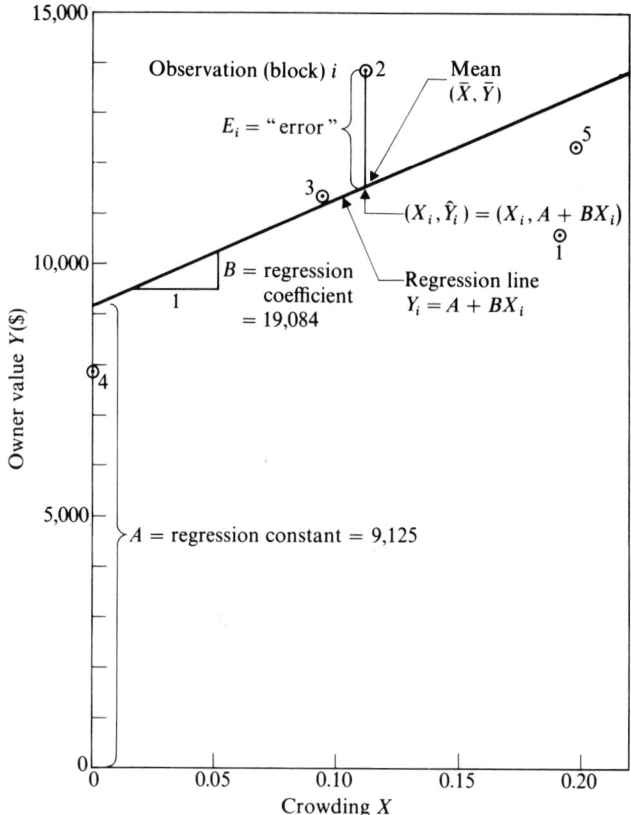


**Figure 8-1** Sample data and regression line for first five blocks of Census tract 2 in Roanoke, Virginia.

words, knowing the amount of crowding, $X_i$, we would estimate that $\hat{Y}_i = A + BX_i$. But from our observations we know that $Y = Y_i$ when $X = X_i$; hence our estimate is in error by the amount $(Y_i - \hat{Y}_i)$. Adding all of the errors from each block would then give the *total error* in estimating $Y$.

One drawback in utilizing the term $(Y_i - \hat{Y}_i)$ as a measure of error is that there may be both positive and negative values for the term and these may (and do) cancel each other out when the addition is made to find the total error. A similar situation arose in regard to the standard deviation, discussed in Sec. 2-3, where the tack taken was that of squaring the deviation term to obtain all positive numbers. Applying the same strategy here we obtain the quantities $(Y_i - \hat{Y}_i)^2$ which, when summed for all blocks, give the *error sum of squares:*†

$$SS_E = \sum_{i=1}^{n} (Y_i - \hat{Y}_i)^2 \tag{8-1}$$

† The reader may find it helpful to review the notation in Table 6-2.

Since $SS_E$ is a measure of the total error, it is desirable to orient the linear regression line in Fig. 8-1, i.e., determine the sample intercept and slope, $A$ and $B$, such that $SS_E$ is a minimum. Thus, from Eq. (8-1)

$$\hat{Y}_i = A + BX_i \tag{8-2}$$

and so

$$SS_E = \sum_{i=1}^{n} (Y_i - A - BX_i)^2 \tag{8-3}$$

and

$$S_E^2 = \frac{SS_E}{n-2} \tag{8-4}$$

is an unbiased estimate of the variance of $E$, $\sigma_E^2$.

Notice that, in contrast to the usual situation, $Y_i$ and $X_i$ are *known* in this equation and we are trying to find the unknown slope ($B$) and intercept ($A$).

Calculus can be employed to determine $A$ and $B$ so as to minimize the error sum of squares. The resulting slope is

$$B = \frac{n\sum_{i=1}^{n} X_i Y_i - \sum_{i=1}^{n} X_i \sum_{i=1}^{n} Y_i}{n\sum_{i=1}^{n} X_i^2 - \left(\sum_{i=1}^{n} X_i\right)^2} \tag{8-5}$$

Knowing the value of $B$, we then can find $A$ from

$$A = \frac{\sum_{i=1}^{n} Y_i - B\sum_{i=1}^{n} X_i}{n} \tag{8-6}$$

Table 8-1 indicates some of the calculations preliminary to the use of Eqs. (8-5) and (8-6). The first of these requires the sum of the cross products $\sum (X_i Y_i)$, as well as the sum of the squared crowding levels $\sum (X_i^2)$, which turn out to be, respectively, 6957 and 0.0896. Inserting these and other relevant figures into Eq. (8-5) subsequently gives

$$B = \frac{5(6957) - (0.575)(56{,}600)}{5(0.0896) - (0.575)^2} = \frac{2240}{0.1174} = 19{,}084$$

and

$$A = \frac{(56{,}600) - (19{,}084)(0.575)}{5} = 9125$$

With these calculations, model (8-1) becomes

$$Y_i = 9125 + 19{,}084X_i + E \tag{8-7}$$

or

$$\hat{Y}_i = 9125 + 19{,}084X_i \tag{8-8}$$

To illustrate the use of these, we find the predicted level $\hat{Y}_i$ of owner value for block 1 as

$$\hat{Y}_1 = 9125 + 19{,}084(0.182) = \$12{,}598$$

**Table 8-1 Example calculations of linear regression between owner value and crowding**

| Block | Actual owner value $Y_i$ | Crowding $X_i$ | $X_i Y_i$ | $X_i^2$ | Predicted owner value $\hat{Y}_i$ | Error $Y_i - \hat{Y}_i$ | Squared error $(Y_i - \hat{Y}_i)^2$ |
|---|---|---|---|---|---|---|---|
| 1 | 11,100 | 0.182 | 2020 | 0.0331 | 12,598 | −1498 | $0.0224 \times 10^8$ |
| 2 | 13,900 | 0.111 | 1543 | 0.0123 | 11,243 | 2656 | 0.0705 |
| 3 | 11,300 | 0.094 | 1062 | 0.0088 | 10,919 | 380 | 0.0014 |
| 4 | 7,900 | 0.000 | 0 | 0 | 9,125 | −1225 | 0.0150 |
| 5 | 12,400 | 0.188 | 2331 | 0.0353 | 12,712 | − 313 | 0.0010 |
| Total | 56,600 | 0.575 | 6957 | 0.0896 | 56,597 | 0 | $0.1104 \times 10^8$ |

The error in this case then is

$$E_1 = (11{,}100 - 12{,}598) = -\$1498$$

If we were to square this error for all five blocks, we would get (Table 8-1, last column) a total of $0.1104 \times 10^8$, which is the lowest $SS_E$ possible for this situation since Eqs. (8-5) and (8-6) were developed explicitly to minimize this quantity.

To help verify some of our computations, we note in Fig. 8-1 that the regression line goes through the mean point for both variables. Since this is true for any regression, the mean values should fit the equation. Thus we ask

$$\frac{56{,}600}{5} = 9125 + 19{,}084\left(\frac{0.575}{5}\right)?$$

Since the answer is "yes," we have a check on our calculation for the slope and the intercept.

## 8-2 HYPOTHESIS TESTING ON A LINEAR RELATIONSHIP

If we were to run a series of regressions on different samples of $Y$ and $X$, we would expect to find different values for the associated slopes and intercepts; these most likely would vary from the slope and intercept for the population as a whole. This point is demonstrated in Table 8-2, which displays the $A$ and $B$ parameters for regressions between 1970 crowding and owner-value variables for four samples of five blocks, one of 20 blocks, and for the overall populations in both 1960 and 1970. The slopes and intercepts vary considerably and, interestingly, the slope for our example in Table 8-1 is positive while that for the 1970 *population* is negative and of a somewhat lower absolute magnitude. This result clearly points to the discrepancies that can arise in using a sample to represent the population as a whole.

**Table 8-2 Slopes and intercepts for various regressions between crowding and owner value**

| Sample | Intercept $A$ | Slope $B$ |
|---|---|---|
| First five blocks | 9,125 | 19,084 |
| Second five blocks | 13,390 | −8,782 |
| Third five blocks | 12,034 | −6,545 |
| Fourth five blocks | 10,966 | −13,418 |
| First 20 blocks | 11,517 | −249 |
| All 52 blocks (1960) | 9,994 | −7,084 |
| All 66 blocks (1970) | 13,576 | −16,642 |

If the population distribution of $E$ in model 8-1 is normal and if the sample is a simple random one† (which that described in Table 8-1 really is *not*, since it consisted of the first five blocks), then the standard deviation (error) of the sampling distribution of the slope $B$ is

$$\sigma_B = \frac{\sigma_Y}{\sigma_X}\left(\frac{1-\rho^2}{n}\right)^{1/2} \tag{8-9}$$

where $\sigma_Y$ = standard deviation of $Y$ in the population
$\sigma_X$ = standard deviation of $X$ in the population
$\rho$ = correlation‡ between $X$ and $Y$ in the population
$n$ = sample size

With substitution of sample for population values and some algebraic manipulation, $\sigma_B$ is estimated by

$$S_B = \left(\frac{\text{SS}_E}{(n-2)\text{SS}_X}\right)^{1/2} \tag{8-10}$$

With the sample data in Table 8-1 we find that the numerator inside the radical is $0.1104 \times 10^8$. The denominator can be calculated as $(5-2)(0.0235) = 0.0705$. Hence the standard error of the slope is 12,530. Since the sampling distribution of the slope for a large sample is normal, the $S_B$ value in this case can be interpreted to mean that the probability is approximately 0.68 that the slope can range from $\pm 12{,}530$ from its actual population level (or, by necessity, the calculated sample slope).

One of the most common hypothesis tests on linear regression equations is that of whether or not the slope is zero. If it is, we could just as well use the mean of $Y$ for forecasting since we would be left with

$$Y = \alpha + (0)X + E = \alpha + E \tag{8-11}$$

† With or without replacement, assuming the sample is small compared to the population.
‡ Discussed in Sec. 9.4.

The hypotheses thus are†

$$\begin{array}{llcll} H_0: & \mu_B = 0 & \text{or} & H_0: & \beta = 0 \\ H_1: & \mu_B \neq 0 & \text{or} & H_1: & \beta \neq 0 \end{array} \tag{8-12}$$

and the standardized $B$ is‡

$$T = \frac{B - \mu_B}{S_B} \tag{8-13}$$

which has a $t$ distribution with $(n - 2)$ degrees of freedom.

Again using the data in our five-block example in Table 8-1, we calculate $T$ as

$$T = \frac{19{,}084 - 0}{12{,}530} = 1.523$$

If our level of significance is 0.05 and we are testing the alternate hypothesis that the population slope $\beta$ is not zero (two tail), then referring to Table E-3 with $5 - 2 = 3$ degrees of freedom, we see that the critical $t$ value is 3.182. Consequently, we conclude that the probability is greater than 0.05 that a sample slope of the magnitude of 19,084 could have come from a population where the actual slope was 0, and we therefore accept the hypothesis that it is 0.

## 8-3 AN EXAMPLE OF LINEAR REGRESSION

Leavitt (Ref. 8-9) has given a simple example of a two-variable regression equation involving valuation of dwelling units. As can be seen in Fig. 8-2, the independent variable is the size of the unit, measured in square feet, and the dependent variable is sales price (in constant dollars for a given year). A sample of nine units was taken from a very large population (those dwellings in Santa Clara County, California). Since it was not mentioned explicitly, we will assume that the sample was random without replacement. The data from the sample and some of the calculations are shown in Table 8-3.

Based on these data, the slope and intercept were calculated as 31.45 and −10,878.65, respectively. The regression equation subsequently became

$$\widehat{\text{SP}} = -10{,}879 + 31.45(\text{SIZE}) \tag{8-14}$$

where SP is the sales price and SIZE the size. The slope is measured in dollars per square foot and therefore represents a kind of average value per square foot of constructed space, a figure often used by architects and building contractors for estimation purposes. The intercept, interestingly, turns out to be *negative*. In fact, any dwelling below about 350 ft$^2$ (32.55 m$^2$) in size would have a negative sales

† The estimating function $B$ is an unbiased estimate of $\beta$, that is, $\mu_B = \beta$.

‡ Another function frequently used (see the SPSS Manual, Ref. 2-2) is $F = T^2$, which has an $f$ distribution with 1 and $(n - 2)$ degrees of freedom.

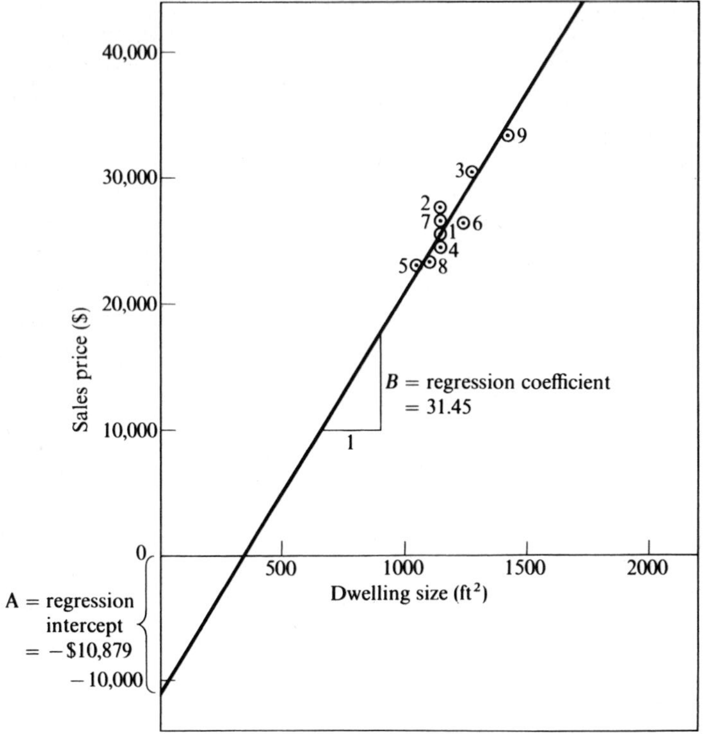


**Figure 8-2** Regression relationship between dwelling size and sales price. (*Adapted from Ref. 8-6, p. 49.*)

## Table 8-3 Sample data for regression between dwelling size and sales price

| Dwelling unit number | Actual selling price, $ | Size, ft$^2$ (0.0929 m$^2$) | Predicted selling price, $ | Error, $ |
|---|---|---|---|---|
| 1 | 26,200 | 1153 | 25,383 | −817 |
| 2 | 27,000 | 1148 | 25,226 | −1774 |
| 3 | 30,500 | 1296 | 29,880 | −620 |
| 4 | 24,700 | 1148 | 25,226 | +526 |
| 5 | 21,500 | 1056 | 22,332 | +832 |
| 6 | 26,400 | 1235 | 27,962 | +1562 |
| 7 | 25,500 | 1150 | 25,289 | −211 |
| 8 | 23,500 | 1102 | 23,779 | +279 |
| 9 | 33,800 | 1426 | 33,969 | +169 |

Adapted from Ref. 8-9, p. 48.

price. While for prediction purposes we really should not consider any points like this outside the range of our original data, we might note that it may be realistic by American standards to have to *pay* a family to live in such a small unit—hence a possible reason for the negative sales price.

The standard error of the slope, as calculated via Eq. (8-10), turns out to be 3.31. This means that there really is not much variation from the sample value of 31.45, a fact verified through a test of the hypothesis that the population slope is zero. A $T$ value of 9.50 is computed from Eq. (8-13). If we assume a level of significance for our two-tailed test of as little as, say, 0.01, then from Table E-3 we find that for $9 - 2 = 7$ degrees of freedom, the critical $t$ value is 3.499. As a consequence, there is almost no chance that the population slope is 0 when our sample slope is 31.45, and subsequently we can work confidently with that value.

## 8-4 STANDARDIZED COEFFICIENT

The size of the slope depends on the units in which $X$ and $Y$ are measured. While $B$ is the estimated expected difference in $Y$ for one unit increase in $X$, a more useful statistic is a standardized slope

$$R = B\frac{S_X}{S_Y} \tag{8-15}$$

The standardized slope, called the correlation for a simple linear regression, is the estimated expected standard deviation change in $Y$ for one standard deviation increase in $X$. If $X$ and $Y$ were standardized,

$$Z_X = \frac{X - \bar{X}}{S_X} \quad \text{and} \quad Z_Y = \frac{Y - \bar{Y}}{S_Y} \tag{8-16}$$

and if $Z_Y$ were regressed against $Z_X$, then the resulting slope would be $R$ and the $Y$ intercept would equal zero:

$$Z_Y = RZ_X \tag{8-17}$$

The range of $R$ is $-1$ to 1. A correlation of 0.25 means that for a standard deviation increase in $X$ one would expect a 0.25 standard deviation larger $Y$. A correlation of $-0.5$ means that for a standard deviation increase in $X$ one would expect a 0.5 standard deviation smaller $Y$.† More will be said about correlation in the next two chapters.

## 8-5 EXPONENTIAL MODELS

In Chap. 11 positive and negative feedback trends are described (see Fig. 11-2). Positive feedback is based on a growth rate of a constant, $\beta$, times the current level and negative feedback on a growth rate of a constant times the difference

† This does not imply $X$ causes $Y$.

between the current level and the limit $\lambda$. Letting $Y_t$ represent the current level, the following equations describe the positive and negative systems:

$$\text{Positive feedback } \textit{rate} \text{ of growth from time } t \text{ to } t+1(\Delta t) = D_{\Delta t} = \beta Y_t \tag{8-18}$$

$$\text{Positive feedback } \textit{level} \text{ at time } t = Y_t = \alpha e^{\beta t} \tag{8-19}$$

$$\text{Negative feedback } \textit{rate} \text{ of growth over } \Delta t = D_{\Delta t} = \beta(\lambda - Y_t) \tag{8-20}$$

$$\text{Negative feedback } \textit{level} \text{ at time } t = Y_t = \lambda - (\lambda - \alpha)e^{\beta t} \tag{8-21}$$

The parameters $\alpha$, $\beta$, and $\lambda$ are constants and $e$ is always the value 2.718 .... When $t = 0$, the value of $Y_t$ equals $\alpha$ for Eqs. (8-19) and (8-21):

$$Y_0 = \alpha e^{\beta 0} = \alpha e^0 = \alpha(1) = \alpha \tag{8-22}$$

$$Y_0 = \lambda - (\lambda - \alpha)e^{\beta 0} = \lambda - (\lambda - \alpha)(1) = \alpha \tag{8-23}$$

As in the linear model, $\alpha$ is the $Y_t$ intercept. For the positive feedback equation, $Y_t$ is increasing for positive $\beta$ and decreasing for a negative $\beta$ (see Fig. 8-3).

In reality, $Y_t$ is rarely determined solely by the rate of growth, $\beta Y_t$. As demonstrated in Chap. 11, a variable may be influenced by many other variables. The exponential growth model can be expressed as follows:

$$Y_t = \alpha e^{\beta t} E \qquad \mu_E = 1 \qquad E \text{ and } t \text{ are independent} \qquad \text{(Model 8-2)}$$

$$Y_t = \lambda - (\lambda - \alpha)e^{\beta t} E \qquad \mu_E = 1 \qquad E \text{ and } t \text{ are independent} \qquad \text{(Model 8-3)}$$

These models are called the *exponential growth* and the *exponential growth to a limit* models. In these models, $E$ represents the other effects on $Y_t$ besides the growth rates $\beta Y_t$ and $\beta(\lambda - Y_t)$. If these other effects are small, $E$ will have a mean of 1 and a small variance.

Suppose one wishes to estimate the value of $\alpha$ and $\beta$. To do this, a sample of observations of $Y_t$ for different times is collected. Of course, the simple linear regression of $Y_t$ versus $t$ will not give good estimates of $\alpha$ and $\beta$. The solution is to transform the exponential equation into a linear equation and then regress the transformed variables. Taking the natural logarithm of both sides of model 8-2 will result in a desired linear model:

$$\ln(Y_t) = \ln(\alpha e^{\beta t} E)$$

$$\ln(Y_t) = \ln(\alpha) + \beta t + \ln(E) \tag{8-24}$$

Our objective is to find functions $A$ and $B$ that estimate $\alpha$ and $\beta$. Let $A'$ and $B'$ represent the estimates from the linear regression of $\ln(Y)$ versus $t$. As shown in Eq. (8-24), $A'$ is an estimate of $\ln(\alpha)$ and $B'$ is an estimate of $\beta$. Hence, estimating functions of $\alpha$ and $\beta$ for model 8-2 are

$$A = e^{A'} \tag{8-25}$$

$$B = B' \tag{8-26}$$

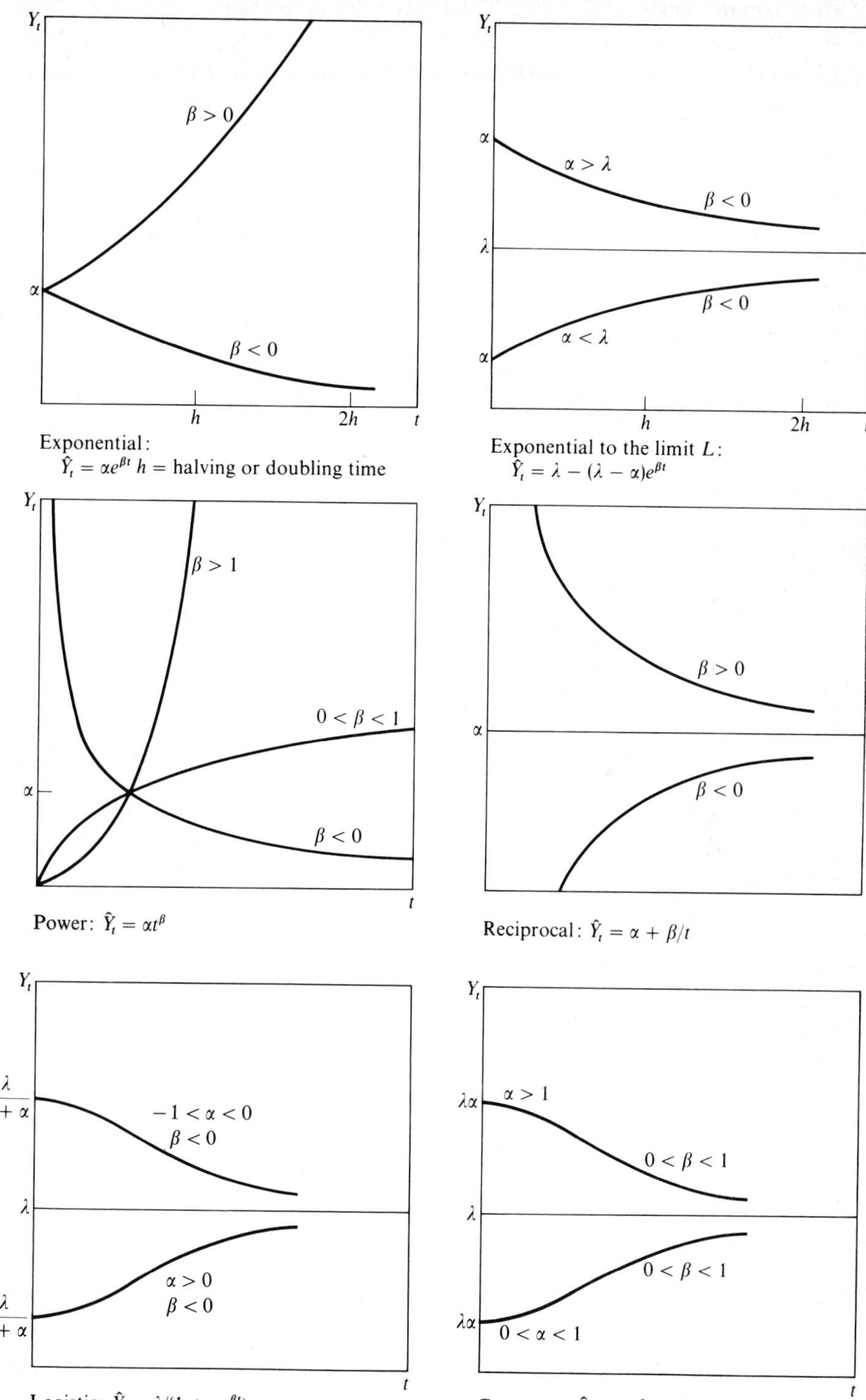


**Figure 8-3** Nonlinear equations.

For model 8-3, the following transformations will produce a linear model:

$$Y_t = \lambda - (\lambda - \alpha)e^{\beta t}E$$

$$Y_t - \lambda = -(\lambda - \alpha)e^{\beta t}E$$

$$\ln (Y_t - \lambda) = \ln [-(\lambda - \alpha)e^{\beta t}E]$$

$$\ln (Y_t - \lambda) = \ln [-(\lambda - \alpha)] + \beta t + \ln (E) \qquad (8\text{-}27)$$

If $\lambda$ is larger than $\alpha$, then $Y_t - \lambda$ will be negative. Since logarithms of negative numbers are not defined, the sign of both sides of the equation must be changed before logarithms are taken. It is assumed that the limit $\lambda$ is known or can be estimated before the transformations. To estimate $\alpha$ and $\beta$, regress $\ln (Y_t - \lambda)$ [or $\ln (\lambda - Y_t)$ if $Y_t - \lambda$ is negative] against $t$. The resulting functions $A'$ and $B'$ estimate $\ln [-(\lambda - \alpha)]$ and $\beta$. Hence, estimates $A$ and $B$ for $\alpha$ and $\beta$ are

$$A = e^{A'} + \lambda \qquad (8\text{-}28)$$

$$B = B' \qquad (8\text{-}29)$$

## 8-6 POWER AND RECIPROCAL MODELS

The power model is characterized by a growth rate of a constant, $\beta$, times the ratio of the current value of $Y_t$ and $t$:

$$D_{\Delta t} = \beta \frac{Y_t}{t} \qquad (8\text{-}30)$$

As with the linear and exponential models, $Y_t$ is an increasing function for positive $\beta$ and a decreasing function for a negative $\beta$. The variable $t$ can never equal zero. The model for such a growth rate is

Power: $Y_t = \alpha t^{\beta} E$ $\quad \mu_E = 1 \quad$ $E$ and $t$ independent (Model 8-4)

Power to a limit: $Y_t = \lambda - (\lambda - \alpha)t^{\beta} E$

$\mu_E = 1 \quad$ $E$ and $t$ independent (Model 8-5)

To transform this model to a linear one, take logarithms (of any base) of both sides of the equation:

$$\log (Y_t) = \log (\alpha t^{\beta} E)$$

$$\log (Y_t) = \log (\alpha) + \beta \log (t) + \log (E) \qquad (8\text{-}31)$$

To estimate $\alpha$ and $\beta$, regress $\log (Y_t)$ against $\log (t)$. Let $A'$ and $B'$ represent the estimates derived from the linear regression. Then $B'$ is an estimate of $\beta$ and $k^{A'}$ is an estimate of $\alpha$ where $k$ is the base of the logarithm.

Another model that represents a growth to a limit is the reciprocal model:

$Y_t = \lambda + \frac{\beta}{t} + E \quad \mu_E = 0 \quad$ $E$ and $t$ independent (Model 8-6)

The power to a limit and the reciprocal models are described in more detail in Table 8-4.

**Table 8-4 Characteristics of linear and nonlinear models**

| Model | 8-1 | 8-2 | 8-3 | 8-4 |
|---|---|---|---|---|
| Name | Linear | Exponential | Exponential to a limit | Power |
| Equation without error term | $Y_t = \alpha + \beta t$ | $Y_t = \alpha e^{\beta t}$ | $Y_t = \lambda - (\lambda - \alpha)e^{\beta t}$ | $Y_t = \alpha t^{\beta}$ |
| Transformation | None | $\ln(Y_t) = \ln(\alpha) + \beta t$ | $\ln(Y - \lambda) = \ln(\alpha - \lambda) + \beta t$ | $\log(Y) = \log(\alpha) + \beta \log(t)$ |
| $Y_t$ intercept | $\alpha$ | $\alpha$ | $\alpha$ | None, $Y_t = \alpha$ at $t = 1$ |
| $Y_t$ increases as $t$ increases if | $\beta > 0$ | $\beta > 0$ | $\alpha < \lambda$ | $\beta > 0$ |
| $Y_t$ decreases as $t$ increases if | $\beta < 0$ | $\beta < 0$ | $\alpha > \lambda$ | $\beta < 0$ |
| Regress | $Y_t$ vs. $t$ | $\ln(Y_t)$ vs. $t$ | $\ln(Y_t - \lambda)$ vs. $t$ | $\log(Y_t)$ vs. $\log(t)$ |
| Required conditions | None | None | $\beta < 0$; take $\ln(\lambda - Y_t)$ if $\alpha < \lambda$ | $t \geq 0$, $t \neq 0$ if $\beta < 0$ |
| Rate of change during $\Delta t$ | $\beta$ | $\beta Y_t$ | $\beta(\lambda - Y_t)$ | $\beta Y_t/t$ |
| Upper or lower limit as $t \to \infty$ | None | None | $\lambda$ | None |
| $Y_t$ increases at what kind of rate? | Constant | Always increasing | Always decreasing | If $\beta > 1$ increasing<br>If $0 < \beta < 1$ decreasing |
| Estimates $A$ and $B$ of $\alpha$ and $\beta$, when $A'$ and $B'$ are linear regression results | $A = A'$<br>$B = B'$ | $A = e^{A'}$<br>$B = B'$ | $A = e^{A'} + \lambda$<br>$B = B'$ | $A = k^{A'}$<br>$B = B'$<br>$k$ is base of log |

[*continued overleaf*

**Table 8-4 (*continued*)**

| Model | 8-5 | 8-6 | 8-7 | 8-8 |
|---|---|---|---|---|
| Name | Power to a limit | Reciprocal | Logistic | Gompertz |
| Equation without error term | $Y_t = \lambda - (\lambda - \alpha)t^{\beta}$ | $Y_t = \lambda + \frac{\beta}{t}$ | $Y_t = \frac{\lambda}{1 + \alpha e^{\beta t}}$ | $Y_t = \lambda\alpha^{\beta^t}$ |
| Transformation | $\log(Y_t - \lambda) = \log(\alpha - \lambda) + \beta \log(t)$ | None | $\ln\left(\frac{\lambda}{Y_t} - 1\right) = \ln(\alpha) + \beta t$ | $\log(\log Y_t - \log \lambda) = \log(\log \alpha) + (\log \beta)t$ |
| $Y_t$ intercept | None, $Y_t = \alpha$ at $t = 1$ | None | $\frac{\lambda}{(1 + \alpha)}$ | $\lambda\alpha$ |
| $Y_t$ increases as $t$ increases if | $\alpha < \lambda$ | $\beta < 0$ | $\alpha > 0$ | $\alpha < 1, \beta < 1$ |
| $Y_t$ decreases as $t$ increases if | $\alpha > \lambda$ | $\beta > 0$ | $-1 < \alpha < 0$ | $\alpha > 1, \beta < 1$ |
| Regress | $\log(Y_t - \lambda)$ vs. $\log(t)$ | $Y_t$ vs. $\frac{1}{t}$ | $\ln\left(\frac{\lambda}{Y_t} - 1\right)$ vs. $t$ | $\log(\log Y_t - \log \lambda)$ vs. $t$ |
| Required conditions | $t \geq 0$; take $\log(\lambda - Y_t)$ if $\alpha > \lambda$ | $t \neq 0$ | Take $\ln(1 - \lambda/Y_t)$ if $\lambda < Y_t$ | Take $\log(\log \lambda - \log Y_t)$ if $\lambda > Y_t, 0 < \beta < 1$ |
| Rate of change during $\Delta t$ | $\beta\frac{(\lambda - Y_t)}{t}$ | $\frac{Y_t - \lambda}{t}$ | $\beta Y_t \frac{\lambda - Y_t}{\lambda}$ | $\beta Y_t\left(\log\frac{\lambda}{Y_t}\right)$ |
| Upper or lower limit as $t \to \infty$ | $\lambda$ | $\lambda$ | $\lambda$ | $\lambda$ |
| $Y_t$ increases at what kind of rate? | Always decreasing | Always decreasing | Increasing then decreasing | Increasing then decreasing |
| Estimates $A$ and $B$ of $\alpha$ and $\beta$, when $A'$ and $B'$ are linear regression results | $A = k^{A'} + \lambda$<br>$B = B'$<br>$k$ is base of log | $\lambda = A'$<br>$B = B'$ | $A = e^{A'}$<br>$B = B'$ | $A = k^{k^{A'}}$<br>$B = k^{B'}$<br>$k$ is base of log |

## 8-7 LOGISTIC MODEL

The exponential model where the growth-rate constant $\beta$ is positive represents an unbounded growth model. Theoretically, world population grows this way. The larger the population, the more offspring are born, resulting in an ever-increasing population. The parameter $\beta$ represents the difference between the average birth rate and the average death rate. Actually, world human population over the past two centuries has been growing faster than exponentially. Such growth is called *superexponential* (Ref. 8-10). Unbounded growth represented by the exponential model is unrealistic over the long run. As demonstrated in Chap. 11, a growth constant of only 0.02 would double the population in 35 years. Hence in 350 years the population would be $2^{10} = 1024$ times as large as it is today if the growth-rate constant remains at 0.02. In time the population growth rate must slow down due to limited resources.

A more realistic model is one where the level $Y_t$ increases at an increasing rate initially. However, as $Y_t$ approaches its limit, growth begins to slow down. Such a growth rate can be represented by $\beta Y_t(\lambda - Y_t)/\lambda$. As $Y_t$ approaches $\lambda$, the factor $(\lambda - Y_t)/\lambda$ approaches zero; hence the growth rate slows down and eventually (when $Y_t$ reaches $\lambda$) all growth stops. Raymond Pearl (1870–1940), the American biologist and demographer, found such a model in his extensive studies of the growth of organisms and of populations. The equation that described their growth quite well is called the logistic curve, the Pearl–Reed curve, or simply the Pearl curve. The equation for this is

$$Y_t = \frac{\lambda}{1 + \alpha e^{\beta t}} \qquad (8\text{-}32)$$

In this equation $\lambda$ is the limit of the growth, and $\alpha$ and $\beta$ are constants. When $t = 0$, then

$$Y_t = \frac{\lambda}{1 + \alpha e^{\beta 0}} = \frac{\lambda}{1 + \alpha} \qquad (8\text{-}33)$$

If $-1 < \alpha < 0$, then $Y_t$ declines to the limit $\lambda$. If $\alpha > 0$, then $Y_t$ increases to the limit $\lambda$ (see Fig. 8-3). Curves as shown in the lower part of that figure are often called "S-shaped curves." The inflection point of the curve occurs at $t = (1/\beta) \ln (\frac{1}{2})$ and $Y = (\frac{1}{2})\lambda$. The curve is symmetrical about this inflection point.

The logistic model can be represented more formally as

$$Y_t = \frac{\lambda}{1 + \alpha e^{\beta t} E} \qquad \mu_E = 1 \qquad E \text{ and } t \text{ independent} \qquad \text{(Model 8-7)}$$

To transform this model to a linear one, the following steps are undertaken:

(*a*) Determine the value of $\lambda$.

(*b*) Find $\dfrac{\lambda}{Y_t} - 1 = \alpha e^{\beta t} E$.

(*c*) Find $\ln \left(\dfrac{\lambda}{Y_t} - 1\right) = \ln (\alpha e^{\beta t} e) = \ln (\alpha) + \beta t + \ln (E)$. (8-34)

If $\lambda$ is less then the values of $Y_t$, then $\lambda/Y_t - 1$ will be negative. This occurs when $Y$ is decreasing toward $\lambda$. In this case the signs of both sides of the equation must be changed before logarithms are taken.

The regression of $\ln(\lambda/Y_t - 1)$, or $\ln(1 - \lambda/Y_t)$ if $\lambda$ is smaller than all $Y_t$, against $t$ produces the estimates $A'$ and $B'$. The corresponding estimates $A$ and $B$ for $\alpha$ and $\beta$ are

$$A = e^{A'} \tag{8-35}$$

$$B = B' \tag{8-36}$$

## 8-8 GOMPERTZ MODEL

Benjamin Gompertz (1779–1865), the English actuary and mathematician, developed an equation which bears his name. It describes growth to a limit that is similar to the logistic curve. The equation for the Gompertz curve is

$$Y_t = \lambda\alpha^{\beta^t} \tag{8-37}$$

The limit is $\lambda$, the parameter $\alpha$ is a positive constant, and $\beta$ is a constant between 0 and 1. When $t = 0$,

$$Y_0 = \lambda\alpha^{\beta^0} = \lambda\alpha \tag{8-38}$$

The Gompertz curve is characterized by a growth rate of $Y_t \log(\lambda/Y_t)$. As $Y$ approaches $\lambda$, $\lambda/Y$ approaches 1, and $\log(\lambda/Y)$ approaches 0. Hence, as in the logistic model, the growth rate slows down as $Y$ approaches $\lambda$. Since $\beta$ is between 0 and 1, $\beta^t$ approaches 0 as $t$ grows larger. When $t = \infty$,

$$Y_\infty = \lambda\alpha^{\beta^\infty} = \lambda\alpha^0 = \lambda \tag{8-39}$$

The inflection point of the curve is $t = \log[\log(\alpha)]/\log(\beta)$ and $Y = \lambda/3$ (see Fig. 8-3). The Gompertz model is

$$Y_t = \lambda\alpha^{(\beta^t)E} \qquad \mu_E = 1 \qquad t \text{ and } E \text{ are independent} \tag{Model 8-8}$$

To transform this into a linear version, the following steps are undertaken:

(*a*) Determine the value of $\lambda$.

(*b*) Find $\dfrac{Y_t}{\lambda} = \alpha^{(\beta^t)E}$.

(*c*) Find $\log\left(\dfrac{Y_t}{\lambda}\right) = \log(\alpha^{(\beta^t)E}) = \beta^t E \log(\alpha)$.

(*d*) Find $\log\left[\log\left(\dfrac{Y_t}{\lambda}\right)\right] = \log[\beta^t E \log(\alpha)]$

$$= \log[\log(\alpha)] + t\log(\beta) + \log(E). \tag{8-40}$$

If $\lambda$ is greater than $Y_t$, $\log(Y_t/\lambda)$ is negative and $\log[\log(Y_t/\lambda)]$ is not defined. In this case the signs of both sides of the equation must be changed after step (c).

The regression of $\log[\log(Y_t/\lambda)]$, or $\log[\log(\lambda/Y_t)]$ if $\lambda > Y_t$, against $t$ produces the estimates $A'$ and $B'$. The corresponding estimates $A$ and $B$ for $\alpha$ and $\beta$ are

$$A = 10^{10^{A'}} \tag{8-41}$$

$$B = B' \tag{8-42}$$

The base of the logarithm used here is 10; however, like the logistics and exponential models, any base could have been used.

The full set of models discussed in this chapter are summarized in Table 8-4.

## 8-9 EXAMPLES OF NONLINEAR REGRESSION

Often in regional transportation air pollution and energy studies it is necessary to know the age distributions of automobiles, since earlier models tend to emit more pollutants and have lower miles-per-gallon efficiencies. To help determine this distribution, we need to know the percentage of autos of different ages which will be scrapped each year. A sample of national data is shown in Fig. 8-4 and Table 8-5.

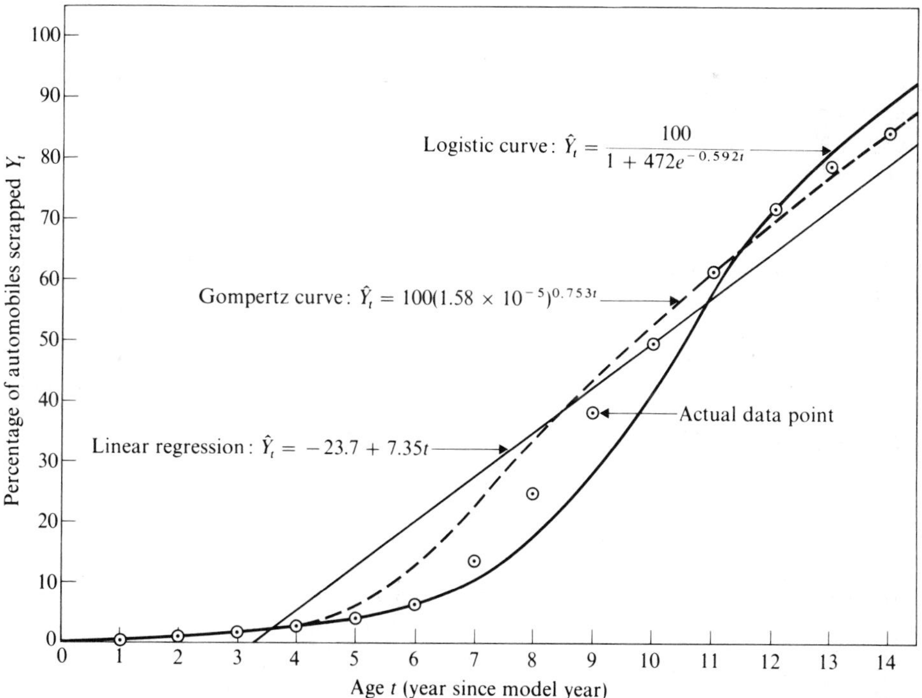


**Figure 8-4** Linear and nonlinear regressions of percentage of automobiles scrapped versus age.

**Table 8-5 Results of regression of auto scrappage against age of automobile under various models**

| Name of model | Linear | Exponential to limit | Logistic | Gompertz |
|---|---|---|---|---|
| Equation without error | $Y_t = \alpha + \beta t$ | $Y_t = 100 - (100 - \alpha)e^{\beta t}$ | $Y_t = \dfrac{100}{1 + \alpha e^{\beta t}}$ | $Y_t = 100\alpha^{\beta^t}$ |
| Transformed equation | None | $\ln(100 - Y_t) = \ln(100 - \alpha) + \beta t$ | $\ln\left(\dfrac{100}{Y_t} - 1\right) = \ln(\alpha) + \beta t$ | $\ln\left(\ln \dfrac{100}{Y_t}\right) = \ln \ln\left(\dfrac{1}{\alpha}\right) + \ln(\beta)t$ |
| Age $t$ | $Y_t$ | $\ln(100 - Y_t)$ | $\ln\left(\dfrac{100}{Y_t} - 1\right)$ | $\ln\left(\ln \dfrac{100}{Y_t}\right)$ |
| 1 | 0.3 | 4.602 | 5.806 | 1.759 |
| 2 | 0.7 | 4.598 | 4.955 | 1.602 |
| 3 | 1.0 | 4.595 | 4.595 | 1.527 |
| 4 | 2.0 | 4.585 | 3.892 | 1.364 |
| 5 | 4.0 | 4.564 | 3.178 | 1.169 |
| 6 | 7.0 | 4.533 | 2.587 | 0.978 |
| 7 | 14.0 | 4.454 | 1.815 | 0.676 |
| 8 | 25.0 | 4.317 | 1.099 | 0.327 |
| 9 | 38.0 | 4.127 | 0.490 | −0.033 |
| 10 | 50.0 | 3.912 | 0.0 | −0.367 |
| 11 | 62.0 | 3.638 | −0.490 | −0.738 |
| 12 | 72.0 | 3.332 | −0.944 | −1.113 |
| 13 | 79.0 | 3.045 | −1.325 | −1.445 |
| 14 | 84.0 | 3.773 | −1.658 | −1.747 |
| $A'$ | −23.7 | 5.123 | 6.16 | 2.403 |
| $B'$ | 7.35 | −0.140 | −0.592 | −0.283 |
| $A$ | −23.7 | $A = 100 - e^{A'} = -68$ | $A = e^{A'} = 472$ | $A = 1/e^{e^{A'}} = 1.58 \times 10^{-5}$ |
| $B$ | 7.35 | $B = B' = -0.140$ | $B = B' = -0.592$ | $B = e^{B'} = 0.753$ |

Data derived from Ref. 8-11, p. 38.

The percentage of automobiles scrapped turns out to be a nonlinear function of age. A graph of the percentage of scrapped automobiles against their age (model year) can be represented by an S-shaped curve with an upper limit of 100 percent (Fig. 8-4). This curve suggests a logistic or Gompertz model. Regressions under linear, exponential to a limit, logistic, and Gompertz models were tried, the results of which are shown in Table 8-5. Given the estimates $A'$ and $B'$ from the linear regressions of the transformed dependent variable against age, the estimates of the parameters $\alpha$ and $\beta$ were calculated as shown in the bottom of

Table 8-5. The following prediction equations were derived for each of the models attempted:

Linear: $\hat{Y}_t = -23.7 + 7.35t$ (8-43)

Exponential to a limit: $\hat{Y}_t = 100 - (100 + 68)e^{-0.140t}$ (8-44)

Logistic: $\hat{Y}_t = \dfrac{100}{1 + 472e^{-0.592t}}$ (8-45)

Gompertz: $\hat{Y}_t = 100(1.58 \times 10^{-5})^{0.753t}$ (8-46)

As can be seen in the figure, some of the models are not appropriate. The linear has negative values for $Y_t$ below $t = 3$, an unrealistic situation. Furthermore, the linear function can grow to be more than 100 percent, also unrealistic. The exponential to a limit model (not plotted) has too low initial values (for example, $-68$ percent at $t = 0$). The logistic and Gompertz models both fit fairly well and are within the proper limits ($0 \leq Y_t \leq 100$ percent). The former, however, gives all low estimates (negative errors or residuals) and the latter all high estimates (positive errors) within the mid range of $t$. The analysis of these residuals as well as the description of other strength-of-association measures for these models will be presented in Sec. 9-6.

## PROBLEMS

**8-1** Fill in the blanks with the appropriate word(s).

(*a*) In regression the objective is to find the __________ and __________ of a line so as to minimize the __________.

(*b*) The deviation or error between an observed and estimated dependent variable is squared because __________.

(*c*) The most common test on the estimated slope coefficient is used to determine if it is significantly different from __________. The estimating function employed is the __________.

(*d*) The standardized coefficient shows the estimated __________ difference in $Y$ for one __________ increase in $X$.

(*e*) The equations for the two types of nonlinear models discussed here which show positive feedback are __________ __________.

(*f*) The equations for the four types of nonlinear models discussed here which show negative feedback are __________ __________ __________ __________.

(*g*) The logistic model is also known as the __________ or __________ model.

**8-2** The data below represent the hundreds of vehicles ($X$) and people ($Y$) passing a given point hourly on a main highway going into the central zone of a small city: $X = 3, 4, 6, 7$ and $Y = 5, 10, 9, 12$.

(*a*) Construct a diagram and determine the least-squares regression equation for estimating $Y$ when $X$ is the independent variable, for $X$ when $Y$ is the independent, and plot the associated regression lines on the scatter diagram.

(*b*) Assuming the data are a random sample from a large population of values for which estimates are to be made, compute the standard error of the slope (for $Y$ as dependent variable) and test to see if the sample is significantly different from 0 ($\alpha = 0.10$).

(*c*) What is the value of $Y$ when $X = 8$?

**8-3** A study yielded the following random sample data for schooling and income:

| Years school completed $Y$ | Income $X$ (in \$1000) | Years school completed $Y$ | Income $X$ (in \$1000) |
|---|---|---|---|
| 10 | 6 | 16 | 7 |
| 7 | 4 | 12 | 10 |
| 12 | 7 | 18 | 15 |
| 12 | 8 | 8 | 5 |
| 9 | 10 | 12 | 6 |

Find:

(*a*) The slope and intercept of the associated linear regression.

(*b*) The standard error of the slope.

(*c*) The critical $t$ value for $\alpha = 0.01$ (one tail).

**8-4** It is thought that poverty and illiteracy are closely related. Data from 16 counties in a multistate region, taken at random from the Census, provide the following information on poverty (percentage of families with an annual income of less than \$3000 per year) and illiteracy (percentage of people 25 years or older with 5 years or less of formal education):

| County | 1 | 2 | 3 | 4 | 5 | 6 | 7 | 8 | 9 | 10 | 11 | 12 | 13 | 14 | 15 | 16 |
|---|---|---|---|---|---|---|---|---|---|---|---|---|---|---|---|---|
| Poverty | 21 | 38 | 51 | 54 | 61 | 58 | 59 | 64 | 59 | 55 | 30 | 29 | 24 | 31 | 53 | 35 |
| Illiteracy | 14 | 15 | 16 | 22 | 18 | 18 | 21 | 23 | 20 | 24 | 11 | 18 | 16 | 18 | 10 | 11 |

Determine:

(*a*) The slope and intercept of the linear regression equation with "poverty" as the dependent variable.

(*b*) The standard error of the slope.

(*c*) If the slope is significantly greater than 0 ($\alpha = 0.10$).

**8-5** A log-log regression has been run relating average monthly rent (AMR) to the number of dwelling units without private baths (or dilapidated) (NB) for a series of Census blocks. The result was

$$\log \widehat{\text{AMR}} = 0.81 \log \text{NB} + 0.39$$

What is the corresponding equation in terms of the initial variables?

**8-6** What are the values of the parameters in the equation $\hat{Y} = AX^B$ where the following observations have been noted?

| $X$ | 1.6 | 1.0 | 4.3 | 2.6 |
|---|---|---|---|---|
| $Y$ | 7.7 | 3.0 | 55.5 | 20.3 |

**8-7** Given below are data on the power generation efficiency (in kilowatt hours per pound of coal) for public utilities across the country in different years:

| Year (19—) | 65 | 60 | 55 | 50 | 45 | 40 | 35 | 30 | 25 | 20 |
|---|---|---|---|---|---|---|---|---|---|---|
| kWh/lb | 1.166 | 1.136 | 1.053 | 0.840 | 0.769 | 0.743 | 0.694 | 0.625 | 0.493 | 0.328 |

Giving an upper limit of 1.30 due to ultimate mechanical and heat losses, find the:
(*a*) Corresponding Gompertz curve
(*b*) Corresponding logistic curve
(*c*) Corresponding power curve
(*d*) Estimated kWh/lb in 1976 for all three relationships

**8-8** Go to the library and find an article, book, or report which describes an application of a particular type of linear or nonlinear regression model (with only one independent variable). Describe in about 400 words:
(*a*) The nature of the problem being addressed
(*b*) The form of the regression equation employed
(*c*) The type of sample taken (if any)
(*d*) The results of any hypothesis-testing efforts
(*e*) Forecasts and other results reached using the regression model
(*f*) Major advantages and disadvantages of regression in this application

**8-9** Working with your instructor, select a sample of data from App. D and run a linear or nonlinear regression on it. Find:
(*a*) Estimates of the appropriate population parameters
(*b*) The significance of these parameters (e.g., are they different from 0?)
(*c*) Any theoretical and/or practical problems in using this type of model for the selected data

# REFERENCES

## Theory

8-1. Acton, F. S.: *Analysis of Straight Line Data*, Wiley, New York, 1959.
8-2. Blalock, Jr., H. M.: *Social Statistics*, 2d ed., McGraw-Hill, New York, 1972.
8-3. Guilford, J. P.: *Fundamental Statistics in Psychology and Education*, 4th ed., McGraw-Hill, New York, 1965.
8-4. Martino, J. P.: *Technological Forecasting for Decisionmaking*, American-Elsevier, New York, 1972.
8-5. Wonnacott, T. H., and R. J. Wonnacott: *Econometrics*, Wiley, New York, 1970.

## Applications

8-6. Berry, B. J. L., and F. E. Horton: *Geographic Perspectives on Urban Systems*, Prentice-Hall, Englewood Cliffs, N.J., 1970.
8-7. U.S. Bureau of the Census, H. S. Shryock, J. S. Siegel, and Associates, *The Methods and Materials of Demography*, 2 vols., U.S.GPO, Washington, D.C., 1973.
8-8. Dickey, J. W. (senior author): *Metropolitan Transportation Planning*, McGraw-Hill, New York, 1975.
8-9. Leavitt, L. D.: "The Appraisal Process Comes of Age," *Valuation*, vol. 21, no. 1, October, 1974.

8-10. Meadows, D., D. Meadows, and J. Behrens: *The Limits of Growth*, 2d ed., Universe Books, New York, 1976.
8-11. Motor Vehicle Manufacturer's Association, *Motor Vehicle Facts and Figures '76*, Detroit, Mich., 1977.
8-12. Quandt, R. E., and W. J. Baumol: *The Demand for Abstract Transport Modes: Theory and Measurement*, D. C. Heath, Lexington, Mass., 1970.

CHAPTER

# NINE

# STRENGTH OF ASSOCIATION

In the previous chapter we described the process by which regression could be employed to develop a least-squares fit to a set of data for two variables, both of which were measured on interval or ratio scales. Nothing was said, however, about how closely the resulting regression line actually fits the data. If the points were completely scattered, a least-squares regression line would provide little improvement in our ability to estimate values of the dependent variable. So we obviously need a measure of the degree to which a regression line fits the corresponding data or, rephrased, a measure of the strength of the association between the two variables.

In this chapter we will present various indices for "strength of association" and also expand our attention to nominal- and ordinal-scaled variables. These were not discussed previously because, as will be seen, for interrelationships on these scales there are no functional analogies to a regression equation. There can only be cross tabulations of raw data. Yet we still can measure the goodness of fit or strength of association between such variables, as will be discussed in the next two sections.

## 9-1 RELATIONSHIPS BETWEEN NOMINAL-SCALED VARIABLES

In relating two nominal-scaled variables, we essentially are trying to estimate the likely category or categories of occurrence of the dependent variable given the category or categories of the independent variable. Consider an oversimplified

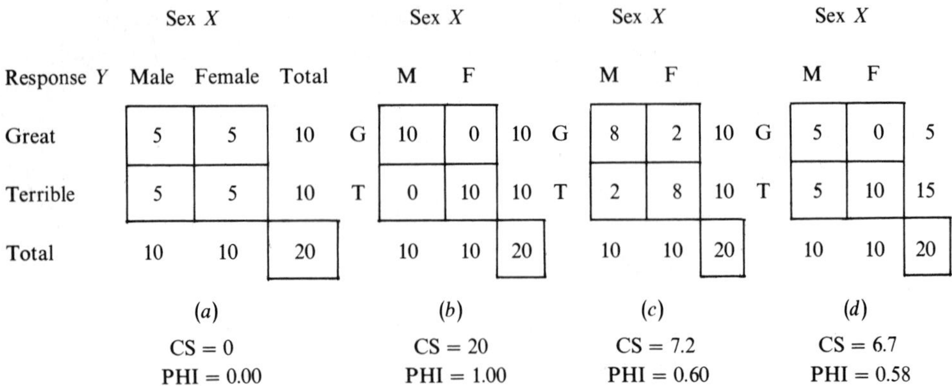


**Figure 9-1** Hypothetical relationships between response to a plan and sex of respondent.

example in Fig. 9-1 in which an urban planner is trying to get citizen feedback on a plan he has developed. The response to the plan can be either "great" (G) or "terrible" (T), and for some reason it is believed that there will be a strong association between the particular response and the sex of the citizen respondent.

Assuming for the moment no error due to sampling, let us say that the planner selects 10 males and 10 females citizens at random and gets their responses, 10 of which happen to fall into the "great" category and the remaining 10 into the "terrible" category. What distributions within the four combinations of G–T and M–F would indicate the lowest strength of association, the highest, and something in between?

The lowest would be that in the first cross tabulation in Fig. 9-1. It would be impossible for the planner to predict a person's response to the plan based on his or her sex since both males and females were equally divided: there is no differentiation. The second cross tabulation, on the other hand, highlights the other extreme. If the respondent is a male, he will say the plan is "great." Every female will say it is "terrible." The planner should have no trouble estimating a response under these circumstances. The third cross tabulation shows a situation intermediate to the two above. Most, but not all, males think it is "great," with the opposite for females. The planner can have some but not complete confidence in predicting the response based on the sex of the citizen.

One index of the strength of the relationship between two nominal-scaled variables is the chi-square (CS) statistic:

$$\mathrm{CS} = \sum_{c=1}^{g} \sum_{k=1}^{r} \frac{(O_{ck} - E_{ck})^2}{E_{ck}} \tag{9-1}$$

where $g$ = number of categories (characteristics) of the dependent (row) variable

$r$ = number of categories (characteristics) of the independent (column) variable

$O_{ck}$ = observed number of cases having characteristic $c$ of the dependent variable and characteristic $k$ of the independent variable

$E_{ck}$ = "expected" number of cases having characteristic $c$ of the dependent variable and characteristic $k$ of the independent variable *if the variables are unrelated*

The expected value is calculated via

$$E_{ck} = \frac{n_c n_k}{n} \tag{9-2}$$

where $n_c$ = total number of cases having row characteristic $c$
$n_k$ = total number of cases having column characteristic $k$
$n$ = grand total number of cases

To illustrate, let us compute the expected value for each box in the first tabulation in Fig. 9-1:

$$E_{11} = \frac{10(10)}{20} = 5$$

which is the same for all four boxes. Thus:

$$\text{CS} = \frac{(5-5)^2}{5} + \frac{(5-5)^2}{5} + \frac{(5-5)^2}{5} + \frac{(5-5)^2}{5} = 0$$

This result shows that when there is no relationship between a pair of nominal-scaled variables, CS = 0, since the expected values (5 for all boxes) are, by definition, those which occur when there is no relationship between the variables.

For the second cross tabulation in Fig. 9-1 we get

$$\text{CS} = \frac{(10-5)^2}{5} + \frac{(0-5)^2}{5} + \frac{(0-5)^2}{5} + \frac{(10-5)^2}{5} = 20$$

This is the greatest CS value obtainable for the given row and column totals. This calculation also highlights the philosophy behind the index. The differences between actual and expected (no association) values are squared so that they do not inadvertently cancel out.† These squared differences are then compared to their associated expected values. Larger differences in large numbers thus are implicitly given as much weight of importance as smaller differences in smaller numbers. The "weighted" differences subsequently are added for all the possible combinations of characteristics of the dependent and independent variables.

## 9-2 HYPOTHESIS TESTING FOR NOMINAL-SCALE VARIABLE RELATIONSHIPS

To explore a research hypothesis concerning the relationship between two nominal-scaled variables, $X$ and $Y$, the following set of hypotheses should be tested:

† This is the same rationale employed in calculating the standard deviation. See Sec. 2-3.

$H_0$: There is *no* association between $X$ and $Y$; in other words, $X$ and $Y$ are independent.

$H_1$: $X$ is associated with $Y$. (9-3)

If the null hypothesis is true, the observed number in category $c$ of $Y$ and $k$ of $X$, $O_{ck}$, is likely to be close to the number expected in these categories. Hence, CS is likely to be nearly zero, depending on the number of categories. If $Y$ is dependent on $X$, that is, the probability of an individual being in category $c$ of $Y$ is dependent on which category the individual is in for $X$, then CS is likely to be large.

The sampling distribution of CS for a true null hypothesis has an approximate $\chi^2$ distribution with $(r - 1)(g - 1)$ degrees of freedom. The distribution of CS will be close to the theoretical $\chi^2$ distribution if the expected values, $E_{ck}$, are not too small. Hence, if none are less than 3 and only a small proportion are less than 5, then the $\chi^2$ table (Table E-2) can be used to find a critical point for determining if CS is unusually large for a true null hypothesis.

When the null hypothesis is true (no association between variables), CS has a mean equal to its degrees of freedom, $(r - 1)(g - 1)$, and variance equal to twice its degrees of freedom. The probability of getting such an uneven distribution or more in the sample of table $c$ in Fig. 9-1 from a population where no association between the variables exists can be approximated by using Table E-2. Suppose we establish a significance level of 0.025; then with degrees of freedom of $(2 - 1)(2 - 1) = 1$ we find the critical point of 5.024. In other words, the probability of getting a CS larger than 5.024 is 0.025 if the null hypothesis is true. Since CS equals 7.2 for this table, we reject $H_0$.

If the null hypothesis is true, CS is independent of sample size. However, when the null hypothesis is false the size of CS is proportional to the sample size. Thus, if sample size is very large, even a very weak relationship can be detected. This is true of practically all statistics used for hypothesis testing (see Sec. 6-6). Thus, CS is useful in testing the existence of a relationship between two nominal variables, but not very useful in expressing the strength of that relationship.

Another possible idea for an index of the strength of association between nominal-scaled variables, and one which is common is statistics, is to arbitrarily assign the lowest strength a value of 0 and the highest 1. In a $2 \times k$ table, the maximum value of CS is $n$, the total sample size. Thus, a CS for $2 \times k$ tables can be scaled between 0 and 1 by dividing by $n$. We might also take the square root of this result to "make up" for the earlier squaring of differences in the CS calculation. The resulting index, known as the *phi coefficient*, becomes

$$\text{PHI} = \left(\frac{\text{CS}}{n}\right)^{1/2} \tag{9-4}$$

For more complex tables PHI can assume a value greater than 1.

Wellman (Ref. 9-13) provides an interesting illustration of hypothesis testing in this context. He explored the often-propounded theory that black ghetto residents are bound in by social as well as physical walls and that, as a result, they would be much less likely to travel outside their home area (in this case taken as a

Census tract) than their white counterparts in other parts of the city. To test this, Wellman questioned black and white ninth-grade students in Pittsburgh about the frequency (rare, few times, often) with which they traveled outside their area. He then cross tabulated these findings with the percentage of black residents in the associated Census tract (neighborhood).

Some of the results of this exercise are presented in Table 9-1. The sample was not taken in a standardized manner, but for our examples we will assume it was random without replacement. The consequent CS values are 15.76 for the black children and 3.21 for the white. With a $3 \times 5$ table for the first group and a $3 \times 4$ for the second, the number of degrees of freedom are, respectively, $(5-1)(3-1) = 8$ and $(4-1)(3-1) = 6$. Referring to Table E-2 in App. E, we find that the first CS value is significant at the 0.05 level while the second is far from being so.

From these results we can conclude that, for blacks, there is a relationship between frequency of movement outside the neighborhood and the percentage of blacks in that neighborhood (Census tract). The same does not hold true for the white children, but just because there is *some* relationship in the former case does not necessarily mean it is very strong. In fact, the calculated PHI coefficient of 0.132 for black children indicates the relationship is very weak. We might conclude that mobility of black children is only slightly influenced by the racial mix of their neighborhood.

The $\chi^2$ test may not be the best test for the above example, for the data really are not nominal in scale. In fact, they are ordinal or perhaps interval and hence

**Table 9-1 Frequency of movement outside of neighborhood by race and tract racial composition†**

| Frequency of movement outside neighborhood | Tract racial composition, % black | | | | | | | | | | |
|---|---|---|---|---|---|---|---|---|---|---|---|
| | Black children | | | | | | White children | | | | |
| | 0–30 | 31–50 | 51–70 | 71–90 | 91–100 | Total | 0–30‡ | 31–50 | 51–70 | 71–90 | Total |
| Rare | 6.0 | 13.0 | 19.8 | 22.3 | 17.9 | | 52.2 | 3.3 | 1.1 | 0.4 | |
| | 3 | 8 | 20 | 21 | 27 | 79 | 54 | 3 | 0 | 0 | 57 |
| Few times | 12.6 | 27.1 | 41.4 | 46.5 | 37.4 | | 177.7 | 11.2 | 3.7 | 1.4 | |
| | 21 | 27 | 39 | 47 | 31 | 165 | 175 | 14 | 3 | 2 | 194 |
| Often | 50.3 | 107.9 | 164.8 | 185.2 | 148.8 | | 531.1 | 33.5 | 11.2 | 4.2 | |
| | 45 | 113 | 167 | 186 | 146 | 657 | 532 | 31 | 13 | 4 | 580 |
| Total | 69 | 148 | 226 | 254 | 204 | 901 | 761 | 48 | 16 | 6 | 831 |
| CS | | 15.76 | | | | | | | 3.21 | | |
| PHI | | 0.132 | | | | | | | 0.0622 | | |

† The top number in each part of the table is the expected value, the bottom number the observed value.

‡ Tract racial composition taken as percentage black for purposes of comparison. Adapted from Wellman, Ref. 9-13, p. 619.

have direction. But CS is always positive or zero and does not show direction. The researcher thus should reanalyze such data to determine direction by comparing the expected and observed numbers. Notice in Table 9-1 that the number of black children from mostly black neighborhoods (91 to 100 percent) who rarely leave the neighborhood is larger than the expected number (27 versus 17.9). This supports the research hypothesis that black children in predominantly black neighborhoods have less mobility than those in other neighborhoods.

Another potential problem in using a $X^2$ test for interval data is the need to choose boundaries when separating the data into categories. This choice can influence the outcome; hence two researchers can get different results using the same data and the same test simply by choosing different category boundaries.

A third potential problem with the above analysis is the small expected number in some of the cells in the table for white children. Three cells have expected numbers less than 3 and six less than 5. For such a table the distribution of CS may not be sufficiently close to the $\chi^2$ distribution to do a $\chi^2$ test as described in this section. A test of association for ordinal data described in the next section and for interval data described in Sec. 9-4 could also be used on these data, which would avoid the potential problems mentioned above.

## 9-3 ASSOCIATIONS BETWEEN ORDINAL-SCALED VARIABLES

In determining associations between ordinal-scaled variables we usually are presented not with a cross tabulation of characteristics but with two lists of rankings or priorities. We are then asked to find the strength of the association based on the similarities between corresponding ranks on the two lists. The index of the strength of association between ordinal-scaled variables will range from $-1$ (ranks are in inverse order) through 0 (no association) to 1 (ranks are in the same order).

The most common index for the strength of association between two ordinal-scaled variables, $X$ and $Y$, is the Spearman rank correlation coefficient, designated by RHO:

$$\text{RHO} = 1 - \frac{6\sum_{i=1}^{n} D_i^2}{n(n^2 - 1)} \tag{9-5}$$

The cases are ranked in ascending order (1 = lowest rank, 2 second lowest, etc.). $D_i$ is the difference in ranks between the two variables for case $i$, and $n$ is the sample size. Equation (9-5) is a simplified formula for the Pearson product moment correlation between the ranks of $X$ and $Y$ see Sec. 9-4).

When $n$ is 10 or larger, hypotheses set (9-3) can be tested for interval data by:

$$T = \frac{\text{RHO} - 0}{[(1 - \text{RHO}^2)/(n - 2)]^{1/2}} \tag{9-6}$$

**Table 9-2 Rank ordering of 10 buildings by two committees**

| Building $i$ | Rank by committee 1 | Rank by committee 2 | $D_i$ | $D_i^2$ |
|---|---|---|---|---|
| 1 | 7 | 5 | 2 | 4 |
| 2 | 4 | 4 | 0 | 0 |
| 3 | 5 | 6 | −1 | 1 |
| 4 | 1 | 2 | −1 | 1 |
| 5 | 2 | 1 | 1 | 1 |
| 6 | 10 | 9 | 1 | 1 |
| 7 | 9 | 8 | 1 | 1 |
| 8 | 8 | 10 | −2 | 4 |
| 9 | 6 | 7 | −1 | 1 |
| 10 | 3 | 3 | 0 | 0 |
| Total | | | | 14 |

For a large $n$, $T$ has an approximate $t$ distribution with $(n - 2)$ degrees of freedom.

As an example of the use of RHO, consider a situation in which two committees are asked to rank 10 prominent buildings in a city according to their appearance. The first committee is made up of art critics, the second of people with relatively little education. Interest centers, of course, on whether these two diverse groups will rank the 10 buildings in the same order.

The results of the endeavor are presented in Table 9-2. As can be seen, the two rank orderings of the buildings turn out to be fairly similar. In fact, the biggest difference in rank for any building is only $\pm 2$. The resulting rank correlation coefficient verifies these findings. With the sum of the $D_i^2$ calculated as 14 in the last column of the table, we find that

$$\text{RHO} = 1 - \frac{6(14)}{10(100 - 1)} = 0.915$$

and

$$T = \frac{0.915(10 - 2)^{1/2}}{(1 - 0.915^2)^{1/2}} = 6.415$$

The critical point for a significance level of 0.02 and 8 degrees of freedom is $\pm 2.90$. Since $T = 6.415 > 2.90$, reject $H_0$. A positive RHO shows that both committees are ranking the buildings similarly. We conclude that there is agreement between the two committees concerning the appearances of prominent buildings in a city.

## 9-4 ASSOCIATION AMONG INTERVAL- OR RATIO-SCALED VARIABLES

The concept of correlation employed in conjunction with ordinal-scaled variables in the preceding section can be extended to those measured on interval and ratio scales. This is done by considering the differences between actual (observed) values for every case and those predicted by means of a regression equation. These differences can then be utilized to find a strength of association by comparing them to those deviations which would arise if we simply utilized the mean of the dependent variable to predict a value for each case.

To understand this concept, let us imagine we need to know the future level of some variable, say the owner-occupied housing value for Census tract 2 in Roanoke, as per our examples in previous chapters. Imagine further that we know nothing about any relationships with other variables. How do we make the prediction? The best answer probably is to use the mean from the previous measurements of the variable.

Yet the use of such a procedure obviously involves errors. If we take data on owner value, $Y$, from the preceding chapter, we see in column (10) of Table 9-3 that there are some fairly large deviations from the mean (which is 56,600/5 = \$11,320). In fact, the mean absolute percentage deviation (MAPD, Chap. 2) is, from column (12), 64.4/5 = 12.9 percent. In other words, if we use the mean we will be in error by 12.9 percent on the average.

Another indicator of the amount of variation inherent in this data set is the total sum of the squared deviations from the mean, denoted by $SS_Y$. As might be remembered from Chap. 2, this is

$$SS_Y = \sum_{i=1}^{n} (Y_i - \bar{Y})^2 \tag{9-7}$$

which, from column (11) of Table 9-3, equals $0.1958 \times 10^8$. A regression equation is developed to reduce this quantity as much as possible.

The regression relationship described in Chap. 8 for these five cases had an equation of

$$\hat{Y}_i = 9125 + 19{,}084X_i \tag{9-8}$$

where $X_i$ was crowding (the fraction of units with 1.01 or more people per unit). If we successively enter the five values for $X_i$ found in column (1) of Table 9-3 into Eq. (9-8), we get the *predicted* owner values, $\hat{Y}_i$, listed in column (6). We now can compare actual and predicted levels to determine the associated differences or *errors*, denoted by $Y_i - \hat{Y}_i$, for each case *i*. Interestingly, for the first case the error of $-1498$ from the predicted regression value exceeds the deviation from the mean of $-220$. Yet over all five cases the average error is less than the average deviation.

One way to demonstrate this point is through the mean absolute percentage error (MAPE), found from

$$\text{MAPE} = \frac{1}{n} \sum_{i=1}^{n} \frac{|Y_i - \hat{Y}_i|}{|\hat{Y}_i|} \times 100 \tag{9-9}$$

This is similar to the mean absolute percentage deviation (MAPD) except that the predicted $Y$ value, $\hat{Y}_i$, takes the place of the mean, $\bar{Y}$. In column (9) of Table 9-3 the numerator of Eq. (9-9) is calculated as 54.9, so that the MAPE is 54.9/5 = 11.0 percent. We thus see that the regression relationship of owner value with crowding has had the effect of reducing the mean deviation or error from 12.9 to 11.0 percent. This decrease, while not substantial, is still of some consequence.

**Table 9-3 Example calculations of linear regression between owner value and crowding**

| Block $i$ | (1) Owner value $Y_i$ | (2) Crowding $X_i$ | (3) $X_i Y_i$ | (4) $X_i^2$ | (5) $Y_i^2$ ($\times 10^8$) | (6) Predicted owner value $\hat{Y}_i$ | (7) Error $Y_i - \hat{Y}_i$ | (8) Squared error $(Y_i - \hat{Y}_i)^2$ ($\times 10^8$) | (9) Absolute percentage error $\frac{\lvert Y_i - \hat{Y}_i \rvert}{\lvert \hat{Y}_i \rvert} \times 100$ | (10) Deviation $Y_i - \bar{Y}$ | (11) Squared deviation $(Y_i - \bar{Y})^2$ ($\times 10^8$) | (12) Absolute percentage deviation $\frac{\lvert Y_i - \bar{Y} \rvert}{\lvert \bar{Y} \rvert} \times 100$ |
|---|---|---|---|---|---|---|---|---|---|---|---|---|
| 1 | 11,100 | 0.182 | 2020 | 0.0331 | 1.232 | 12,598 | −1498 | 0.0224 | 11.9 | −220 | 0.0005 | 1.9 |
| 2 | 13,900 | 0.111 | 1543 | 0.0123 | 1.932 | 11,243 | 2656 | 0.0705 | 23.6 | 2580 | 0.0666 | 22.8 |
| 3 | 11,300 | 0.094 | 1062 | 0.0088 | 1.277 | 10,919 | 380 | 0.0014 | 3.5 | −20 | 0.0000 | 00.0 |
| 4 | 7,900 | 0.000 | 0 | 0.0000 | 0.624 | 9,125 | −1225 | 0.0150 | 13.4 | −3420 | 0.1170 | 30.2 |
| 5 | 12,400 | 0.188 | 2331 | 0.0353 | 1.538 | 12,712 | −313 | 0.0010 | 2.5 | 1080 | 0.0117 | 9.5 |
| Total | 56,600 | 0.575 | 6957 | 0.0896 | 6.603 | | 0 | 0.1104 | 54.9 | 0 | 0.1958 | 64.4 |

Another way to gauge the reduction in error brought about by a regression equation is to compute the squared rather than the absolute error. The total of these squared errors, designated by $SS_E$, is

$$SS_E = \sum_{i=1}^{n} (Y_i - \hat{Y}_i)^2 \tag{9-10}$$

and for our example equals $0.1104 \times 10^8$ [column (8) of Table 9-3]. We now can make another comparison—this time between (1) the amount by which regression has reduced the original squared deviations about the mean ($SS_Y$) minus the squared errors about the regression line ($SS_E$) and (2) the $SS_Y$ with which we started. Since the reduction would be the difference between $SS_Y$ and $SS_E$, the resulting index, called the *coefficient of determination*, is

$$R^2 = \frac{SS_Y - SS_E}{SS_Y} \tag{9-11}$$

For our example we get $R^2 = (0.1952 - 0.1104)/0.1952 = 0.437$. In words, the regression equation has reduced the squared errors by 0.437, or 43.7 percent.

The most common index for the strength of association between interval-scaled variables is the Pearson product moment correlation:

$$R = \frac{\sum_{i=1}^{n} (X_i - \bar{X})(Y_i - \bar{Y})}{(SS_X SS_Y)^{1/2}} = \frac{n\sum_{i=1}^{n} X_i Y_i - \left(\sum_{i=1}^{n} X_i\right)\left(\sum_{i=1}^{n} Y_i\right)}{\left\{\left[n\sum_{i=1}^{n} X_i^2 - \left(\sum_{i=1}^{n} X_i\right)^2\right]\left[n\sum_{i=1}^{n} Y_i^2 - \left(\sum_{i=1}^{n} Y_i\right)^2\right]\right\}^{1/2}} \tag{9-12}$$

Like Spearman RHO, $R$ ranges from $-1$ to 1, with a negative value representing an inverse relationship between $X$ and $Y$, a zero value representing no relationship, and a positive value representing a direct relationship. Using the totals in Table 9-3, we get for our example:

$$R = \frac{5(6957) - (0.575)(56{,}600)}{\{[5(0.0896) - (0.575)^2][5(6.603 \times 10^8) - (56{,}600)^2]\}^{1/2}} = +0.661 \tag{9-13}$$

We have encountered $R$ before, for it is the same as the standardized regression coefficient of simple linear regression [see Eq. (8-15)]. If one knows the correlation between two interval- or ratio-scaled variables, $X$ and $Y$, and their means and standard deviations, then one can easily compute the intercept $A$ and slope $B$ of the linear regression of $Y$ against $X$:

$$B = R\frac{S_Y}{S_X} \tag{9-14}$$

$$A = \bar{Y} - B\bar{X} \tag{9-15}$$

The absolute value of $R$ is also the square root of the coefficient of determination in Eq. (9-11), that is, $|R| = [(SS_Y - SS_E)/SS_Y]^{1/2}$. The maximum

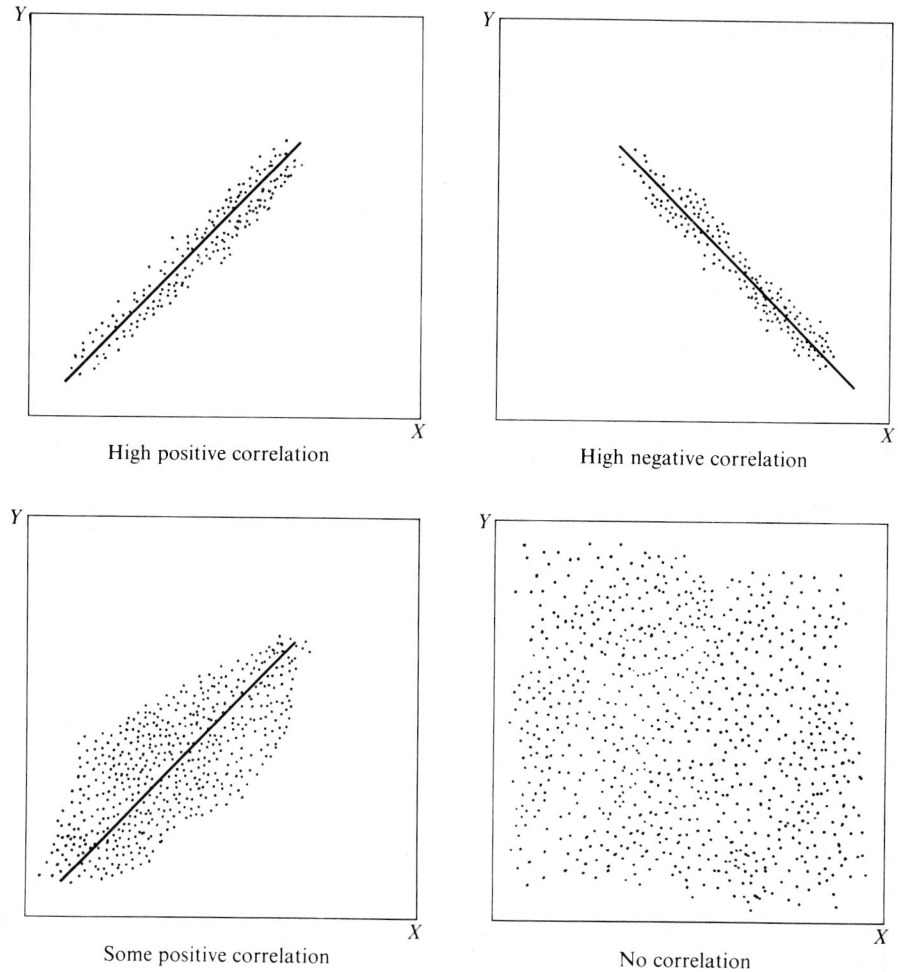


**Figure 9-2** Schematic representation of various degrees of correlation. (*Source: Ref. 9-9, p. 539.*)

value of $R$ is 1 since the least $SS_E$ can be is 0, which gives $[(SS_Y - 0)/SS_Y]^{1/2} = 1.0$. An $R$ of $\pm 1$ thus corresponds to a regression relationship with the greatest strength of association. On the other hand, the worst situation would be when the regression relationship does not reduce the squared deviations from the mean at all. This would imply that $SS_E = SS_Y$ so that $R = [(SS_Y - SS_Y)/SS_Y]^{1/2} = 0$, which is the lowest strength of association.

Figure 9-2 gives some representations of linear relationships having various degrees of correlation. When all the points are on the line (with either a positive or negative slope), the correlation is $\pm 1$, respectively. When there is complete scatter, as in the last case in the figure, the correlation is 0.

Still another measure of the strength of association in regression is the standard error of regression:

$$S_E = \left[\frac{SS_E}{n-2}\right]^{1/2} = \left[\frac{1}{n-2}\sum_{i=1}^{n}(Y_i - \hat{Y}_i)^2\right]^{1/2} \tag{9-16}$$

This is similar to the standard deviation except that the error rather than the total sum of squares is divided by the total number of observations (minus 2) to get an "average" error per observation. The square root of this figure is then taken to balance the previously performed squaring operation. The reason for subtracting 2 in the denominator is similar to that for subtracting 1 in the standard deviation. If we had only two points, a straight line would fit the points exactly. This is an indeterminate situation, having no *degrees for freedom,* since it is impossible to have any errors. The standard error of regression reflects this fact by being undefined, $(0/0)^{1/2}$, when $n$ is 2. In more complex regression equations discussed in the next chapter, the number of degrees of freedom [the denominator of Eq. (9-16)] would be $n - k$, where $k$ is the number of parameters (coefficients, exponents, etc.) in each equation.

In our example, $S_E = [0.1104 \times 10^8/(5-2)]^{1/2} = 1919$. When compared to the standard deviation of 2212 (Table 9-4), we see that the "average error" if the regression equation instead of the mean is employed for prediction purposes is reduced by about 2212 − 1919 = \$293 or 13.2 percent.

A comparison of above three measures of strength of association can be found in Table 9-4, which is an extension of the information on the regressions presented in the previous chapter. Five results are of interest here:

1. In the first sample (first five blocks) the correlation is relatively high compared to that in the other five block samples. Yet the standard error is the highest in this group. This shows that while the corresponding regression relationship has led to a substantial reduction in the squared deviations from the mean (as indicated by the high $R$), the remaining average (standard) error is still great (as indicated by the high $S_E$).

**Table 9-4 Output statistics on various regressions of owner value versus crowding**

| Sample | Mean, \$ | Standard deviation, \$ | Intercept, \$ | Slope, \$ | Correlation | Standard error, \$ | MAPD, % | MAPE, % |
|---|---|---|---|---|---|---|---|---|
| First five blocks | 11,320 | 2212 | 9,125 | 19,084 | 0.661 | 1919 | 12.9 | 11.0 |
| Second five blocks | 12,800 | 1792 | 13,390 | −8,782 | −0.430 | 1867 | 11.6 | 9.5 |
| Third five blocks | 11,780 | 421 | 12,034 | −6,545 | −0.812 | 368 | 2.6 | 1.7 |
| Fourth five blocks | 10,260 | 1638 | 10,966 | −13,418 | −0.483 | 1655 | 11.4 | 12.1 |
| First 20 blocks | 11,540 | 1785 | 11,517 | −249 | −0.009 | 1833 | 10.6 | 10.6 |
| All 52 blocks (1960) | 9,375 | 2189 | 9,994 | −7,084 | −0.292 | 2114 | 17.7 | 16.6 |
| All 66 blocks (1970) | 12,353 | 3552 | 13,576 | −16,642 | −0.348 | 3356 | 18.9 | 17.9 |

2. In the third sample the correlation is high but the MAPD is low. This shows that $R$ is a *relative* rather than absolute index, for while the reduction in the $SS_Y$ was great (signified by the high $R$), the $SS_Y$ really was not very large initially (signified by the low MAPD).
3. In the second sample the standard error is *greater* than the standard deviation. This can happen if the sample size is small and the association not very strong since we are dividing by $n - 2$ in the standard error and by only $n - 1$ in the standard deviation.
4. In the fourth sample the MAPE is *greater* than the MAPD. This occurs because regression is intended to reduce the squared rather than the absolute errors so that the latter in some situations may actually increase.
5. In the last two samples, for all the blocks in 1960 and 1970, respectively, the correlation coefficient increased in absolute terms but so also did the standard error. This result again points to the relative nature of $R$ and the absolute nature of $S_E$.

These findings show that there can be major differences in interpretation of "strength of association" depending on the index or criterion selected as a measure.

## 9-5 TESTS OF SIGNIFICANCE OF CORRELATION

The correlations in Table 9-4 highlight some of the problems which can arise if the sample type and size are not considered carefully. In 1970 the overall (population) correlation was found to be $-0.348$. Yet the correlations from the five samples from this population (the top five rows in Table 9-4) vary quite considerably from this value. In fact, the first one not only is higher but is positive, while that for the 20-block sample essentially is 0. The reasons for this situation are, first, the small sample size in the first four samples and, second, the sampling procedure in which five of 20 blocks were taken *in order* rather than randomly or in some other standard manner.†

To test hypotheses set (Eq. 9-3) with interval-scaled data, the Pearson product moment correlation coefficient is transformed as follows:

$$T = \frac{R - 0}{[(1 - R^2)/(n - 2)]^{1/2}} = \frac{R(n - 2)^{1/2}}{(1 - R^2)^{1/2}} \tag{9-17}$$

The function $T$ has an approximate $t$ distribution with $(n - 2)$ degrees of freedom. If $X$ and $Y$ are two normal variables and together (in two dimensions) have a bivariate normal distribution, then the population parameter $\rho$ is the population

† See Chap. 5 for a discussion of common sampling procedures.

correlation between $X$ and $Y$. The Pearson product moment correlation $R$ is an unbiased estimate of $\rho$. We can restate hypotheses set (9-3) for such variables by:†

$$\text{H}_0: \quad \mu_R = 0$$

$$\text{H}_1: \quad \mu_R \neq 0$$

For our example, $R = 0.661$ and

$$T = \frac{0.661(5-2)^{1/2}}{[1-(0.661)^2]^{1/2}} = 1.526 \tag{9-18}$$

This result is the same as the test of $B$ for this data in Chap. 8. Assuming for our illustration a level of significance $\alpha$ of 0.05 (0.025 in each tail), we find the critical values of $t$ from Table E-3 (with $5 - 2 = 3$ degrees of freedom) to be $\pm 3.182$. We subsequently accept the null hypothesis that the population correlation is 0.

This conclusion is interesting and, incidently, holds for all five (non-100 percent) samples in Table 9-4, even for the third one where the correlation is fairly high ($-0.812$). This result points to the problem with very small samples. We know the actual population correlation is not zero ($-0.348$ in the last row of Table 9-4), yet using a significance level of 0.05, the false null hypothesis was accepted in all five tests. The probability of an acceptance error is very large in this example. This probability can be reduced by increasing either the significance level or the sample size.

## 9-6 STRENGTH OF ASSOCIATION IN NONLINEAR REGRESSION

Determination of the adequacy of a model for linear and nonlinear relations depends on *both* the strength of association (for example, $R^2$) and the nature of the residuals. The latter are the differences between what is actually observed and what is predicted by the regression equation, i.e., the $n$ differences $E_i = Y_i - \hat{Y}_i$, $i = 1, 2, \ldots, n$, where $Y_i$ is an observation and $\hat{Y}_i$ is the corresponding predicted value.

One useful way to study the residuals is to standardize them and the predicted values and plot $Z_E$ against $Z_{\hat{Y}}$:

$$Z_{E_i} = \frac{E_i - \bar{E}}{S_E} = \frac{E_i}{S_E} \qquad \text{since } \bar{E} = 0 \tag{9-19}$$

$$Z_{\hat{Y}_i} = \frac{\hat{Y}_i - \bar{Y}}{S_{\hat{Y}}} \qquad \text{where } S_{\hat{Y}} = \left[\frac{R^2(\text{SS}_Y)}{n-1}\right]^{1/2} \tag{9-20}$$

If $E$ is independent of $X$, then the plot of $Z_{E_i}$ against $Z_{\hat{Y}_i}$ should be a random scatter around the horizontal axis. If $Y_i$ is being predicted with an inadequate

† See Fig. 3-8 and Chap. 5.

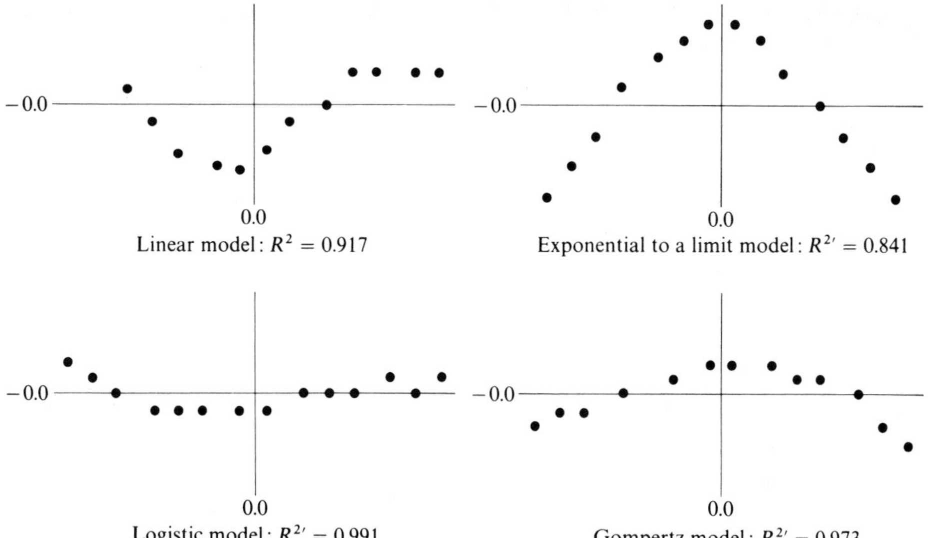


**Figure 9-3** Plot of standardized residuals $Z_{E'}$ (down) by standardized predicted dependent variable $T(\hat{Y})$ (across) for models of auto deterioration.

model, then a pattern in the plot of standardized residuals will be likely to occur. To demonstrate how plots of the residuals can be used to determine inadequacy of models, the residuals from each model employed in the analysis of the auto scrappage example of Sec. 8-9 are shown in Fig. 9-3.† These show that *none* of the models are adequate.

The results of the linear regressions in Sec. 8-9 are based on transformed data. Let $T(Y)$ and $T(\hat{Y})$ represent, respectively, the observed and the predicted *transformed* $Y$ used in the nonlinear regression equations. Also let $E' = T(Y) - T(\hat{Y})$. The graphs in Fig. 9-3 are plots of standardized $E'$ against standardized $T(\hat{Y})$. If the model is correct, the plot should be a random scatter around the horizontal axis. In other words, there should be no section in the range of the variable in which the residuals are all positive or negative, since this would imply that some unincluded variable is consistently influencing $Y_t$. Despite the high values of $R^2$, all models appear to be inadequate; however, the logistic model seems to fit the data best. The value of $R^2$ depends not only on the size of the standard deviation of $E$, $\sigma_E$, but also on the correctness of the model.

The coefficients of determination shown on the graphs in Fig. 9-3 are those from the transformed variables:

$$R^{2\prime} = 1 - \frac{SS_{E'}}{SS_{T(Y)}} \tag{9-21}$$

† Since time $t$ was used as the case or observation unit in these models, the discussion will be in terms of $Y_t$ instead of $Y_i$.

**Table 9-5 Coefficients of determination of auto scrappage models†**

| Model | Linear | Exponential | Logistic | Gompertz |
|---|---|---|---|---|
| $R^2$ transformed | ... | 0.841 | 0.991 | 0.973 |
| $R^2$ untransformed | 0.917 | 0.632 | 0.987 | 0.985 |
| $S_{E'}$ | ... | 0.264 | 0.244 | 0.203 |
| $S_E$ | 9.65 | 20.3 | 3.81 | 4.09 |

† See Table 8-5.

This is not the same as the coefficient based on the untransformed data and $E$:

$$E_t = Y_t - \hat{Y}_t \qquad t = 1, 2, \ldots, n \tag{9-22}$$

where $Y_t$ is computed by the estimated parameters $A$ and $B$ derived from the estimates from the linear regression equation. The coefficients of determination based on the untransformed data were calculated by

$$R^2 = 1 - \frac{\mathrm{SS}_E}{\mathrm{SS}_Y} \tag{9-23}$$

Comparing these from transformed and untransformed data in Table 9-5, one can see that the $R^{2\prime}$ for the transformed data can mislead the researcher into thinking that the independent variable for the model under consideration explains more variance than it really does. For instance, $R^{2\prime}$ for the exponential to a limit model is 0.841 while for the untransformed data it is only 0.632. Also notice that the explanatory power of $t$ under the Gompertz model is essentially the same as it is under the logistic model, a conclusion quite different from that which would be drawn if one compared the coefficients of determination of the transformed data alone.

## PROBLEMS

**9-1** Fill in the blanks with the relevant word(s).

(*a*) Another phrase for "strength of association" is "goodness of ________."

(*b*) Relationships between nominal-scaled variables take the form of ________.

(*c*) The "expected" number of cases is that which would occur on the average if two nominal-scaled variables were ________.

(*d*) If we had a $2 \times 3$ table, the number of ________ of ________ would be 2.

(*e*) A relationship between ordinal-scaled variables takes the form of two

____________________________ of rankings.

(*f*) The RHO index differs from the PHI index in that it can have

____________________________ values.

(*g*) For interval- or ratio-scaled variables, if we did not take into account any relationship with other variables, the best prediction of a value would be the

____________________________.

(*h*) MAPD stands for ________________________ ________________________

________________________ ________________________.

(*i*) MAPE stands for ________________________ ________________________

________________________ ________________________.

(*j*) The total sum of the squared deviations from the mean is desginated by

____________________________.

(*k*) The total sum of the squared deviations from a regression line is designated by

____________________________.

(*l*) The coefficient of determination is the ratio of the ________________________ to the

____________________________.

(*m*) A correlation coefficient is ________________________ if the corresponding regression line has a negative slope.

(*n*) The number of ________________________ of ________________________ is $n - 2$ for the standard error of regression (with one independent variable).

(*o*) The ________________________ is relative rather than absolute in nature.

**9-2** The following data were found for a series of electricity generating plants across the country:

| | Type of area | | |
|---|---|---|---|
| | Rural | Urban | Total |
| Exceed pollution standards | 37 | 49 | 86 |
| Not exceed standards | 340 | 71 | 411 |
| Total | 377 | 120 | 497 |

(*a*) What is the PHI coefficient?

(*b*) Is the corresponding CS value significantly different from 0? Assume a random sample without replacement for a large population of plants ($\alpha = 0.01$).

**9-3** The table below is a random (without replacement) sample from a large number of aye votes registered by three city council members on three policy issues (transportation, subdivision platting, and human resources).

| | Councilmen | | | |
|---|---|---|---|---|
| Policy | A | B | C | Total |
| Transportation | 10 | 6 | 14 | 30 |
| Subdivision platting | 5 | 2 | 2 | 9 |
| Human resources | 5 | 12 | 4 | 21 |
| Total | 20 | 20 | 20 | 60 |

(*a*) What are the expected frequencies for each cell?
(*b*) What is the CS for the data?
(*c*) What is the value of df to be used in interpreting this CS?
(*d*) Is the obtained CS significantly different from 0 at the 0.05 level, at the 0.01 level? Explain.

**9-4** The following is a percentage distribution, by home ownership and income level, from a random sample (without replacement) consisting of 400 families in a city.

| | Income | | |
|---|---|---|---|
| | To $5,000 | $5000 to $10,000 | $10,000 + |
| Home owners | 5% | 35% | 10% |
| Renters | 15% | 25% | 10% |

Test the hypothesis that home ownership is independent of family income level. Use a level of significance of 0.01.

**9-5** What are the correlations between the following ranks given to a set of five goals by three groups of citizens?

| | Group | | |
|---|---|---|---|
| Goal | 1 | 2<br>Rank | 3 |
| Better appearance | 5 | 4 | 5 |
| Increased economy | 2 | 1 | 4 |
| More variety | 4 | 5 | 2 |
| More lives saved | 1 | 2 | 3 |
| Fewer adverse environmental effects | 3 | 3 | 1 |

**9-6** (*a*) Find the correlation coefficient between $X$ and $Y$.

(*b*) Test the hypothesis that the variables $Y$ and $X$ are not related to each other ($\alpha = 0.10$, random sample without replacement).

| Case | $Y$ | $X$ |
|---|---|---|
| 1 | 6 | 4 |
| 2 | 1 | 5 |
| 3 | 2 | 3 |

**9-7** A study yielded the following random sample data for schooling and income:

| Years school completed $X$ | Income $Y$ (in \$1000) | Years school completed $X$ | Income $Y$ (in \$1000) |
|---|---|---|---|
| 10 | 6 | 16 | 7 |
| 7 | 4 | 12 | 10 |
| 12 | 7 | 18 | 15 |
| 12 | 8 | 8 | 5 |
| 9 | 10 | 12 | 6 |

Determine the:
(*a*) MAPD
(*b*) MAPE
(*c*) $SS_Y$
(*d*) $SS_E$
(*e*) $R^2$
(*f*) Standard error of regression
(*g*) Acceptance or rejection of the hypothesis that $\rho = 0$ assuming a very large population from which the data were taken randomly and with replacement ($\alpha = 0.10$).

**9-8** For the town of Strip Mine in App. D, for the relationship between median annual per capita income, $Y_1$, and mean age of residents, $X_1$, find the:
(*a*) Correlation
(*b*) MAPD
(*c*) MAPE
(*d*) Standard error of regression

**9-9** For the example in Prob. (8-6), find the $R^2$, MAPE, and standard error of regression.

**9-10** For the example in Prob. (8-7), find the standard error of regression, $R^2$, and MAPE for each type of relationship. Is the $R^2$ of the power curve the same as that for the log ($Y_t$) versus log ($t$) relationship? If not, why?

**9-11** Go to the library and search for a publication that describes an analysis using simple linear regression. In about 500 words describe:
(*a*) The population(s) and sample type and size
(*b*) The regression equations derived
(*c*) The statistics used to measure strength of relationship
(*d*) The hypothesis tests run on these statistics
(*e*) Your opinion as to the usefulness of regression in this particular application and the validity of the resultant conclusions

**9-12** Working with your instructor, select a set of data from App. D. Using a computer where available, develop relationships between some variables. If the variables are nominal scaled, find:

(*a*) CS

(*b*) PHI

(*c*) If CS is significantly different from 0 (assuming the data are taken randomly with replacement from a much larger population)

If the variables are ordinal scaled, find RHO.

If the variables are interval or ratio scaled, find:

(*a*) MAPD

(*b*) MAPE

(*c*) $SS_Y$

(*d*) $SS_E$

(*e*) $R^2$

(*f*) Standard error of regression

(*g*) If $R$ is significantly different from 0 (*you* should set the level of significance)

# REFERENCES


**Theory**

9-1. Acton, F. S.: *Analysis of Straight Line Data*, Wiley, New York, 1959.

9-2. Blalock, Jr., H. M.: *Social Statistics*, 2d ed., McGraw-Hill, New York, 1972.

9-3. Guilford, J. P.: *Fundamental Statistics in Psychology and Education*, 4th ed., McGraw-Hill, New York, 1965.

9-4. Siegel, S.: *Nonparametric Statistics for the Behavioral Sciences*, McGraw-Hill, New York, 1956.

9-5. Wonnacott, T. H., and R. J. Wonnacott: *Econometrics*, Wiley, New York, 1970.

**Applications**

9-6. Anderson, K. P.: *Residential Energy Use: An Econometric Analysis*, Report R-1297-NSF, The Rand Corporation, Santa Monica, Calif., October, 1973.

9-7. Berry, B. J. L., and F. E. Horton: *Geographic Perspectives on Urban Systems*, Prentice-Hall, Englewood Cliffs, N.J., 1970.

9-8. Bishop, Y. M. A., S. E. Fienberg, and P. W. Holland: *Discrete Multivariate Analysis: Theory and Practice*, The MIT Press, Cambridge, Mass., 1975.

9-9. Dickey, J. W. (senior author): *Metropolitan Transportation Planning*, McGraw-Hill, New York, 1975.

9-10. Glickman, N. J.: "Son of the Specification of Regional Econometric Models," *Journal of Regional Science*, vol. XIV, 1974.

9-11. Liebert, R. J.: "Municipal Functions, Structure and Expenditures: A Reanalysis of Recent Research," *Social Science Quarterly*, vol. 54, no. 4, March, 1974.

9-12. Schivirian, K. P., and A. J. Lagreca: "An Ecological Analysis of Urban Mortality Rates," *Social Science Quarterly*, vol. 52, no. 3, December, 1971.

9-13. Wellman, B.: "Crossing Social Boundaries: Cosmopolitanism Among Black and White Adolescents," *Social Science Quarterly*, vol. 52, no. 3, December, 1971.

CHAPTER

# TEN

# MULTIPLE REGRESSION ANALYSIS

In the simple linear regression model (model 8-1) the independent variable and $E$ are assumed independent, where $E$ represents the accumulation of all other effects on $Y$.† Since this independence assumption is a crucial one, we will explore $E$ in more detail. Let us suppose that $Y$ is a linear combination of the independent variables $X$, $Q_1$, $Q_2$, and $Q_3$. In other words

$$\hat{Y} = \alpha_0 + \alpha_1 X + \theta_1 Q_1 + \theta_2 Q_2 + \theta_3 Q_3 \tag{10-1}$$

where $\alpha_0$, $\alpha_1$, $\theta_1$, $\theta_2$, and $\theta_3$ are constants and no other variables affect $Y$, that is, the variable $E$ does not exist. In the model:

$$Y = \alpha_0 + \alpha_1 X + E_1 \tag{10-2}$$

$E_1$ represents the terms $\theta_1 Q_1$, $\theta_2 Q_2$, and $\theta_3 Q_3$. Two problems may occur with Eq. (10-2):

1. $Q_1$, $Q_2$, and $Q_3$ may have a strong influence on $Y$; hence the variance of $E_1$ is so large that a precise estimate of $\alpha_1$ is difficult to obtain.
2. $X$ may not be independent of $Q_1$, $Q_2$, or $Q_3$, in which case $X$ will not be independent of $E_1$. Thus $\alpha_1$ in Eq. (10-2) will not be the same as $\alpha_1$ in Eq. (10-1).

† Notice the two words "independent" in this sentence. They have entirely different meanings. The independent (or exogenous) variables are usually the ones on the right-hand side of the equation of the model. "Variable $X$ is independent of $F$" means that the distribution of $E$ is the same for any value of $X$.

If our objective is to estimate $\alpha_1$ and problems (1) or (2) or both exists for any of the variables $Q_1$, $Q_2$, or $Q_3$, it is advisable to bring the problem variable(s) into the equation. Suppose $Q_2$ were a problem variable; then we should investigate the model:

$$Y = \alpha_0 + \alpha_1 X + \theta_3 Q_3 + E_2 \tag{10-3}$$

Because $Q_2$ is in the model, $E_2$ has a smaller variance than $E_1$. Although we are not interested in $Q_2$ and its effect on $Y$, we still bring it into the equation to improve our ability to study the effect of $X$ on $Y$. We say that we are "controlling for $Q_2$."

We may want to bring other variables into the equation to see which of the independent variables have the most influence on $Y$. A third reason may be to reduce the variance of $E$ so that more precise estimates of the coefficients can be obtained. For these reasons we will explore the general multiple linear regression model:

$$Y = \alpha_0 + \alpha_1 X_1 + \alpha_2 X_2 + \cdots + \alpha_m X_m + E$$

$$\mu_E = 0 \qquad X_j \text{ and } E \text{ are independent} \qquad j = 1, \ldots, m \qquad \text{(Model 10-1)}$$

$$m = \text{number of independent variables}$$

## 10-1 SOLUTION OF MULTIPLE LINEAR EQUATION

As in Chap. 8, our objective is to estimate the parameters $\alpha_0, \alpha_1, \alpha_2, \ldots, \alpha_m$ from a sample of observations on $n$ cases randomly selected from the population for variables $Y, X_1, X_2, \ldots, X_m$. The derivation of the estimating functions require a great deal of mathematical sophistication. If there are more than two independent variables ($m > 2$), finding a solution may be impractical without a computer. The solution will be described in this section in terms of matrix algebra; it is assumed the reader is familiar with elementary matrix algebra. If not, the reader may wish to study only Eqs. (10-11) through (10-15) and skip the remainder of this section.

If we let $\mathbf{X}$ be a matrix with $n$ rows and $m + 1$ columns where the $j$th row contains the number 1 in column 1 and the $m$ observations on variables $X_1$ through $X_m$ for the $j$th case in columns 2 through $m + 1$. Each row represents a case in the sample:

$$\mathbf{X} = \begin{bmatrix} 1, & X_{11}, & X_{12}, & \ldots, & X_{1m} \\ 1, & X_{21}, & X_{22}, & \ldots, & X_{2m} \\ \vdots & \vdots & \vdots & & \vdots \\ 1, & X_{n1}, & X_{n2}, & \ldots, & X_{nm} \end{bmatrix} \tag{10-4}$$

Let $\mathbf{y}$ be an $n \times 1$ column vector of $n$ observations on the dependent variable, let $\hat{\mathbf{y}}$ be an $n \times 1$ column vector of $n$ predicted values of $Y$ substituting values of the independent variables into the linear equation, and let **e** be the $n \times 1$ column vector of deviations of the predicted from observed values of $Y$:

$$\mathbf{y} = \begin{bmatrix} Y_1 \\ Y_2 \\ \vdots \\ Y_n \end{bmatrix} \qquad \hat{\mathbf{y}} = \begin{bmatrix} \hat{Y}_1 \\ \hat{Y}_2 \\ \vdots \\ \hat{Y}_n \end{bmatrix} \qquad \mathbf{e} = \mathbf{y} - \hat{\mathbf{y}} = \begin{bmatrix} E_1 \\ E_2 \\ \vdots \\ E_n \end{bmatrix} \tag{10-5}$$

We can express the data **y** as a function of the data **X**:

$$\mathbf{y} = \mathbf{Xa} + \mathbf{e} \tag{10-6}$$

where **a** is an $(m + 1) \times 1$ column vector of estimates that provide the "best" linear fit. To establish a criterion for "best," the deviation vector is expressed as the difference between **y** and **Xa**:

$$\mathbf{e} = \mathbf{y} - \mathbf{Xa} \tag{10-7}$$

In matrix notation, the sum of squares, equivalent to Eq. (8-3), is the vector product by its transpose:

$$\mathbf{e}^t\mathbf{e} = (\mathbf{y} - \mathbf{Xa})^t(\mathbf{y} - \mathbf{Xa}) \tag{10-8}$$

Our objective is to find an $m \times 1$ column vector of coefficients

$$\mathbf{a} = \begin{bmatrix} A_0 \\ A_1 \\ A_2 \\ \vdots \\ A_m \end{bmatrix} \tag{10-9}$$

such that $\mathbf{e}^t\mathbf{e}$ is minimum. The solution, if one exists, is

$$\mathbf{a} = (\mathbf{X}^t\mathbf{X})^{-1}\mathbf{X}^t\mathbf{y} \tag{10-10}$$

The predicted dependent variable $\hat{Y}_i$ for a given $\mathbf{x}_i$, the $i$th row of matrix **X**, is $\hat{\mathbf{y}}_i = \mathbf{x}_i\,\mathbf{a}$, or more simply

$$\hat{Y}_i = A_0 + A_1X_{i1} + A_2X_{i2} + \cdots + A_mX_{im} \tag{10-11}$$

The deviation (residuals) of the $i$th observation from the predicted $i$th value is

$$E_i = Y_i - \hat{Y}_i \tag{10-12}$$

As with simple linear regression, the mean residual is 0:

$$\sum_{i=1}^{n} E_i = 0 \qquad \text{and} \qquad \bar{E} = \frac{1}{n}\sum_{i=1}^{n} E_i = 0 \tag{10-13}$$

The sum of squares of residuals and the estimated standard deviation of $E$ are

$$SS_E = \sum_{i=1}^{n} E_i^2 = \sum_{i=1}^{n} (Y_i - \hat{Y}_i)^2 \tag{10-14}$$

$$S_E = \left(\frac{\mathrm{SS}_E}{n - m - 1}\right)^{1/2} \tag{10-15}$$

The estimated standard deviation of the $j$th coefficient is

$$S_{A_j} = S_E[(\mathbf{X}'\mathbf{X})_{jj}^{-1}]^{1/2} \qquad (10\text{-}16)$$

where $(\mathbf{X}'\mathbf{X})_{jj}^{-1}$ is the $j$th element in the main diagonal of the inverse of the matrix product of $\mathbf{X}$ and its transpose.

## 10-2 GOODNESS OF FIT

As shown in Chap. 9, the sum of squares of $Y$:

$$\mathrm{SS}_Y = \sum_{i=1}^{n} (Y_i - \bar{Y})^2 \qquad (10\text{-}17)$$

can be broken down into the sum of squares due to regression and the sum of squares of residuals:

$$\sum_{i=1}^{n} (Y_i - \bar{Y})^2 = \sum_{i=1}^{n} (\hat{Y}_i - \bar{Y})^2 + \sum_{i=1}^{n} (Y_i - \hat{Y}_i)^2 \qquad (10\text{-}18)$$

$$\mathrm{SS}_Y = \mathrm{SS}_{\mathrm{reg}} + \mathrm{SS}_E \qquad (10\text{-}19)$$

If the linear equation fits the data well, then the sum of squares of residuals will be small and the sum of squares due to regression will be relatively large. A measure of goodness of fit is the coefficient of determination:

$$R^2 = \frac{\mathrm{SS}_{\mathrm{reg}}}{\mathrm{SS}_Y} = \frac{\mathrm{SS}_Y - \mathrm{SS}_E}{\mathrm{SS}_Y} \qquad (10\text{-}20)$$

This coefficient can be interpreted as the proportion of the variance of $Y$ "explained" by the independent variables. More precisely, since we assumed that $Y$ is a linear combination of $m$ independent variables, $R^2$ is the proportion of the variance of $Y$ explained by the model.

## 10-3 A SHORT EXAMPLE

In data set 4 of App. D are data from 59 counties that compose the Central Appalachian Region. It can be noted that the death rates vary considerably from county to county. The research question under consideration is:

> Can the variation in average county death rates (DEATHRT) be explained by a linear combination of three other variables, URBAN (percentage of population that is urban), AGED (percentage of population over 65 years of age), and FBPL (percentage of families below the poverty line)?

The model under consideration is

$$\mathrm{DEATHRT} = \alpha_0 + \alpha_1(\mathrm{MEAN}) + \alpha_2(\mathrm{AGED}) + \alpha_3(\mathrm{FBPL}) + E \qquad (10\text{-}21)$$

The result of the multiple linear regression analysis is

$$\text{DEATHRT} = 5.3 + 0.024(\text{URBAN}) + 0.50(\text{AGED}) - 0.014(\text{FBPL}) + E \tag{10-22}$$

The standard deviation of $E$, $S_E$, is 1.18 and the coefficient of determination $R^2$ is 0.50.

The mean death rate in the 59 counties in 1970 is 10.7 per 1000 population and the variance is 2.6. Because $R^2 = 0.50$, we can say that 50 percent of the variance is explained by a linear combination of the three variables, URBAN, AGED, and FBPL. Also, the other 50 percent of the variance is not explained by the linear model. Three possible reasons why so much of the variance is unexplained are:

1. There are many other variables that also explain the variance in death rate.
2. The dependent variables can be explained better by a nonlinear combination of the independent variables.
3. The independent variables are not independent of $E$.

Focusing now on using the multiple regression equation (10-22) in a forecasting mode, we find that, in a given county, for each percentage of the population that lives in urban places 0.024 is added to the death rate; for each percentage of the population that is over 65 years of age 0.50 is added to the death rate; and for each percentage of the families below the poverty line 0.014 is subtracted from the death rate. Suppose now that a county in the Central Appalachian Region were 75 percent urban, had 10 percent of its population over 65 years of age, and 20 percent of its families were below the poverty line; then the expected death rate in that county would be

$$\widehat{\text{DEATHRT}} = 5.3 + 0.024(\text{URBAN}) + 0.50(\text{AGED}) - 0.014(\text{FBPL}) \tag{10-23}$$

or

$$\begin{aligned}\widehat{\text{DEARTHRT}} &= 5.3 + 0.024(75) + 0.50(10) - 0.014(20)\\ &= 53 + 1.8 + 5.0 - 0.3\\ &= 11.3 \text{ deaths per } 1000\end{aligned}$$

## 10-4 HYPOTHESIS TESTING

Let us return to the research question asked in the previous section. Another way of asking this question is, "Is death rate a linear combination of at least some of the three variables URBAN, AGED, and FBPL?" The hypotheses for this question are:

$$\begin{aligned}&\text{H}_0\colon\quad \alpha_1 = \alpha_2 = \alpha_3 = 0 &&\qquad \text{H}_0\colon\ \mu_{A_1} = \mu_{A_2} = \mu_{A_3}\\ &&\text{or}&&\\ &\text{H}_1\colon\ \text{At least one } \alpha_j \neq 0 &&\qquad \text{H}_1\colon\ \text{At least one } \mu_{A_j} \neq 0\end{aligned} \tag{10-24}$$

An estimating function to test these hypotheses is

$$F = \frac{SS_{reg}/m}{SS_E/(n - m - 1)} \tag{10-25}$$

This function has an $f$ distribution with $m$ and $(n - m - 1)$ degrees of freedom, respectively. In our example, the results are

$$SS_{reg} = 74.9 \qquad SS_E = 76$$

$$F = \frac{74.9/3}{76/55} = 18.0 \qquad df = 3;\ 59 - 3 - 1 = 55$$

If these data were a sample, then this $F$ value would be compared to a critical point for some significance level, $\alpha$.† Suppose the probability of the rejecting error were set at 0.05; then the critical point would be 2.73. Since $F = 18.0 > 2.73$, we would reject the null hypothesis. We can now conclude that one or more of the coefficients do not equal zero; however, we do not yet know which one(s). Since the initial $H_0$ was rejected, we can now test to see if a particular coefficient differs from zero.

What does a coefficient in the multiple linear regression model mean? The coefficient $\alpha_j$ for the $j$th variable, $X_j$, represents the expected changes in $Y$ for one unit increase in $X_j$ when holding constant the influence of the other independent variables. For example, in Eq. (10-23) the expected death rate was computed for a county with URBAN = 75 percent, AGED = 10 percent, and FBPL = 20 percent. If URBAN and FBPL were held constant and AGED were increased by one percent to 11 percent, the expected death rate would be 0.5 larger, since $A_2 = 0.5$:

$$\text{Death rate} = 5.3 + 0.024(75) + 0.50(11) - 0.014(20) = 12.3$$

If the data are a sample, then the coefficients are only estimates of the population coefficients. If death rate is independent of AGED when URBAN and FBPL are also in the model, then $\alpha_2 = 0$. Does $\alpha_2$ equal zero? Consider these hypotheses:

$$\begin{aligned} &H_0\colon\ \alpha_2 = 0 && && H_0\colon\ \mu_{A_2} = 0 \\ & && \text{or} && \\ &H_1\colon\ \alpha_2 \neq 0 && && H_1\colon\ \mu_{A_2} \neq 0 \end{aligned} \tag{10-26}$$

The estimating function is

$$T_{A_2} = \frac{A_2 - 0}{S_{A_2}} \tag{10-27}$$

$T_{A_2}$ has a $t$ distribution with $(n - m - 1)$ degrees of freedom.

† This $\alpha$ is not to be confused with any of the regression parameters $\alpha_0, \alpha_1, \alpha_2, \ldots$, etc.

Further results of the analysis are

URBAN: $A_1 = 0.024$ $\quad S_{A_1} = 0.0118$ $\quad T_{A_1} = \dfrac{0.024}{0.0118} = 2.03$

AGED: $A_2 = 0.50$ $\quad S_{A_2} = 0.0755$ $\quad T_{A_2} = \dfrac{0.50}{0.0755} = 6.62$

FBPL: $A_3 = -0.014$ $\quad S_{A_3} = 0.0150$ $\quad T_{A_3} = \dfrac{-0.014}{0.015} = -0.933$

Since there were 59 counties and three independent variables in the analysis, $\text{df} = 59 - 3 - 1 = 55$. If $\alpha$ were set at 0.05, then the critical points would be $-2.00$ and 2.00. Since $T_{A_2} = 6.6 > 2.00$, reject $H_0$. Since $A_2$ is positive and significantly different from zero, we conclude that the greater the proportion of elderly in the population, the greater the death rate in counties with an equivalent percentage of urban and percentage of poverty.

What about the negative coefficient for poverty? Does it mean that in counties with the same proportion of elderly and urban the death rate declines with increased poverty? Since $T_{A_3} = -0.933 > -2.00$, accept the null hypotheses that $\alpha_3 = 0$ and that the death rate is independent of poverty when URBAN and AGED are in the model.

## 10-5 STANDARDIZED REGRESSION COEFFICIENTS AND CORRELATIONS

Consider again the general model (10-1). Notation used in describing this model is listed in Table 10-1. In Chap. 8 we saw that the size of a regression coefficient depended on the units used in the measurements. To compare coefficients one needs first to standardize them. Standardized multiple linear regression coefficients are often called *beta weights* and are computed as follows:

$$B_j = \frac{A_j S_{X_j}}{S_Y} \tag{10-28}$$

The standardized regression coefficient, say $B_2$, when

$$\hat{Y} = A_0 + A_1 X_1 + A_2 X_2 \tag{10-29}$$

stands for the expected number of standard deviations change in $Y$ for 1 standard deviation increase in $X_2$ when $X_1$ is held constant or otherwise controlled. If multiple regression were performed on standardized variables, the resulting coefficients would be the beta weights and the constant term would be zero:

$$\hat{Z}_Y = B_1 Z_{X_1} + B_2 Z_{X_2} \tag{10-30}$$

In simple linear regression the standardized regression coefficient is the same as the correlation. In multiple linear regression, the relationship between beta

**Table 10-1 Multiple linear regression notation for model (10-1)**

$m$ = number of independent variables
$X_{ij}$ = the measure of case $i$ for variable $j$; $i = 1, \ldots, n$; $j = 1, \ldots, m$
$Y_i$ = the measure of case $i$ for the dependent variable
$\alpha_j$ = population coefficient; $j = 1, \ldots, m$
$\alpha_0$ = population constant term
$A_j$ = estimate of $\alpha_j$; $j = 0, 1, \ldots, m$
$A_{Y2 \cdot 1}$ = the estimate of the coefficient for $X_2$ where $Y$ is the dependent variable and $X_1$ is also in the equation; the estimated expected change in $Y$ for 1 unit increase in $X_2$ when controlling for $X_1$
$\hat{Y}$ = predicted (expected) $Y$ for a given vector $[X_1, X_2, \ldots, X_m]$
$\sigma_E$ = population standard deviation of $E$
$SS_E$ = sum of squared errors, $\sum (Y_i - \hat{Y}_i)^2$
$S_E$ = estimate of $\sigma_E$; $[SS_E/(n - m - 1)]^{1/2}$
$SS_Y = \sum (Y_i - \bar{Y})^2$
$SS_j = \sum (X_{ij} - \bar{X}_j)^2$
$S_Y = [SS_Y/(n - 1)]^{1/2}$
$S_j = [SS_j/(n - 1)]^{1/2}$
$R_{Yj}$ = correlation between $Y$ and $X_j$; $\dfrac{\left[\sum_i (Y_i - \bar{Y})(X_{ij} - \bar{X}_j)\right]}{(SS_Y\, SS_j)^{1/2}}$
$R_{Yj \cdot k}$ = partial correlation between $Y$ and $X$ controlling for $X_k$
$R^2_{Y123}$ = coefficient of determination with $X_1$, $X_2$, and $X_3$ in the equation
$SS_{reg}$ = sum of squares due to regression; $SS_Y - SS_E$

weights and correlations can be expressed with the following simultaneous equations:

$$
\begin{aligned}
B_1 \quad\quad + B_2 R_{21} + B_3 R_{31} + \cdots + B_m R_{m1} &= R_{Y1} \\
B_1 R_{12} + B_2 \quad\quad + B_3 R_{32} + \cdots + B_m R_{m2} &= R_{Y2} \\
\vdots \qquad \vdots \qquad\quad \vdots \qquad\qquad \vdots \quad &\quad \vdots \\
B_1 R_{1m} + B_2 R_{2m} + B_3 R_{3m} + \cdots + B_m \quad\quad &= R_{Ym}
\end{aligned}
\tag{10-31}
$$

Thus one could solve for the standardized regression coefficients, given only the matrix of intercorrelations of the variables. If the standard deviations of variables were also known, then the unstandardized coefficients could also be computed by using Eq. (10-28).

## 10-6 PARTIAL CORRELATION

As noted earlier, multiple regression can be used as a means of evaluating the contribution of a particular independent variable with the influence of other independent variables controlled. To appreciate the usefulness of controlling, we will explore some casual models that demonstrate problems with interpreting simple correlations.

When two variables, $X$ and $Y$, are correlated, but $Y$ is not caused by $X$ nor is $X$ caused by $Y$, then we say $X$ and $Y$ have a *spurious correlation*. The following causal diagrams demonstrate such situations:

$$X \xrightarrow{+} Q \xrightarrow{+} Y \quad \text{or} \quad X \xrightarrow{-} Q \xrightarrow{-} Y$$

In the left diagram an increase in $X$ causes an increase in $Q$, but a decrease in $Q$ in the right diagram. A change in $Q$ causes a similar (opposite) change in $Y$. Another example is demonstrated by:

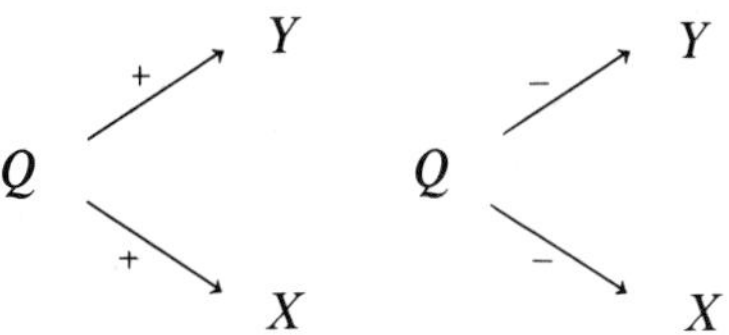


In both cases a comparison of data for $X$ and $Y$ would show a positive but spurious correlation between $X$ and $Y$. If one wishes to explore the direct relationship between $X$ and $Y$, $Q$ must be controlled. This can be done by a function called the partial correlation coefficient:

$$R_{YX \cdot Q} = \frac{R_{YX} - (R_{YQ})(R_{XQ})}{(1 - R_{YQ}^2)^{1/2}(1 - R_{XQ}^2)^{1/2}} \tag{10-32}$$

The partial correlation coefficient computed by Eq. (10-32) represents the correlation between $X$ and $Y$ when controlling for $Q$. The controlling process can be demonstrated by comparing the residuals of the following two equations:

$$Y = \theta_{01} + \theta_{11} Q + E_1 \tag{10-33}$$

$$X = \theta_{02} + \theta_{12} Q + E_2 \tag{10-34}$$

The partial correlation between $X$ and $Y$ when controlling for $Q$ is the simple correlation between the residuals $E_1$ and $E_2$. In the simple regression of $Y$ against $Q$, $R_{YQ}^2$ is the proportion of the variance of $Y$ explained by $Q$ and $1 - R_{YQ}^2$ is the proportion of variance that is unexplained. Thus we can approximate the variance of $E_1$ as follows:†

$$S_{E_1}^2 \approx (1 - R_{YQ}^2) S_Y^2 \tag{10-35}$$

One might ask, "What is the interpretation of the square of the partial correlation, $R_{YX \cdot Q}$?" It is the proportion of the unexplained variance, $S_{E_1}^2$, explained by $X$:

$$R_{YX \cdot Q}^2 = \frac{R_{YQX}^2 - R_{YQ}^2}{1 - R_{YQ}^2} \tag{10-36}$$

† The right-hand side of this equation underestimates $S_E^2$ by a factor $(n - 1)/(n - m - 1)$ where $m$ is the number of independent variables.

$R^2_{YQX}$ denotes the coefficient of determination for the model:

$$Y = \psi_0 + \psi_1 Q + \psi_2 X + E \tag{10-37}$$

In other words, $R^2_{YX \cdot Q}$ represents a proportional reduction of unexplained variance when $X$ is added to Eq. (10-33).

Suppose measures for variables $X$, $Q$, and $Y$ were made for 70 cases and from the analysis of the data the following correlations were derived:

$$R_{YQ} = -0.80 \qquad R_{YX} = -0.60 \qquad R_{QX} = 0.70$$

From this information we can compute the partial correlation between $X$ and $Y$ controlling for $Q$:

$$R_{YX \cdot Q} = \frac{-0.6 - (-0.8)(0.7)}{1 - (-0.8)^2]^{1/2}[1 - (0.7)^2]^{1/2}} = -0.093$$

Since $R_{YQ} = -0.80$, $R^2_{YQ} = 0.64$. Solving for $R^2_{YQX}$ in Eq. (10-36) we get

$$R^2_{YQX} = R^2_{YQ} + R^2_{YQ \cdot X}(1 - R^2_{YQ}) = 0.64 + 0.093(1 - 0.64) = 0.673 \tag{10-38}$$

When controlling for $Q$, we might conclude the simple correlation between $X$ and $Y$ is spurious. However, we do not know from the correlation coefficients alone which of the three correlations is spurious. To reach this type of conclusion, the researcher needs some theoretical understanding of the subject matter.

The relationship between the partial correlation and the standardized regression coefficient is

$$B_{YX \cdot Q} = R_{YX \cdot Q} \frac{(1 - R^2_{YQ})^{1/2}}{(1 - R^2_{XQ})^{1/2}} \tag{10-39}$$

where $B_{YX \cdot Q}$ is the standardized regression coefficient for $X$ in Eq. (10-37):

$$B_{YX \cdot Q} = (-0.093) \frac{[1 - (-0.8)^2]^{1/2}}{[1 - (0.7)^2]^{1/2}} = 0.078$$

When controlling for $Q$, a 1 standard deviation increase in $X$ brings only an expected 0.078 standard deviation increase in $Y$.

Examples of spurious relationships can be found in some genetic explanations often given to certain problems such as low IQ scores. Suppose that members of a society believed that people with red hair were inferior to other people. So deep-seated was the prejudice that red-haired children were only permitted in inferior schools with a curriculum designed for those who were going to engage in unskilled labor. Suppose that performance on IQ tests is influenced by quality of education. The model assumed here is:

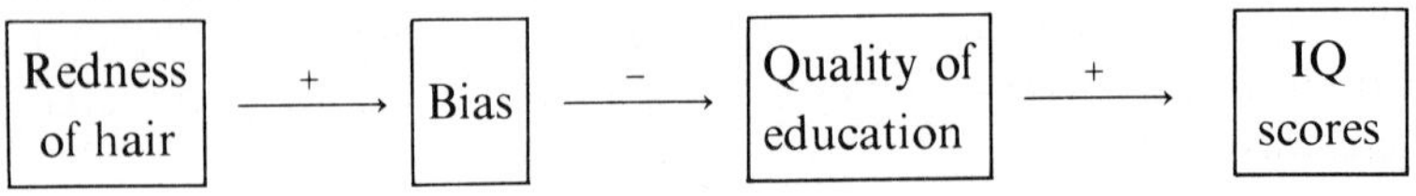

| Redness of hair | $\xrightarrow{+}$ | Bias | $\xrightarrow{-}$ | Quality of education | $\xrightarrow{+}$ | IQ scores |
|---|---|---|---|---|---|---|

Correlation between redness of hair and IQ scores showed a negative relationship. Even after controlling for such environmental influences on IQ scores as income of parents, family size, and so on, a negative relationship persisted. A researcher reported that a certain proportion in variation in IQ is "due to genes." Is hair color the cause of low IQ scores? Perhaps a better explanation is to say that hair color (genes) is the "source" of the low scores, but the "cause" is a lower quality of education available to red-haired children.

Two other situations that lead to a misleading simple correlation between $X$ and $Y$ are:

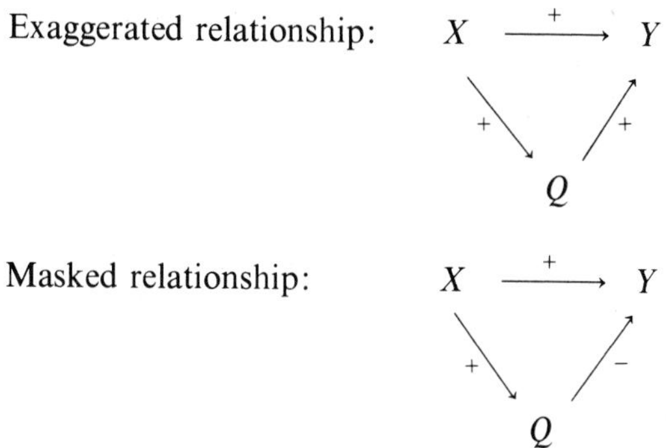


In the first case the correlation between $X$ and $Y$ will be exaggerated. The partial correlation $R_{YX \cdot Q}$ is positive but still smaller than $R_{YX}$. In the second case the negative relationship between $Q$ and $Y$ may mask the positive relationship between $X$ and $Y$. Thus, while the simple correlation between $X$ and $Y$ will be nearly zero, the partial correlation $R_{YX \cdot Q}$ will be positive.

Higher-order partial correlations can be computed. In the case of the three independent variables, $X_1$, $X_2$, $X_3$, the partial correlation of $Y$ to $X_1$ when controlling for $X_2$ and $X_3$ is

$$R_{Y1 \cdot 23} = \frac{R_{Y1 \cdot 2} - (R_{Y3 \cdot 2})(R_{13 \cdot 2})}{(1 - R_{Y3 \cdot 2}^2)^{1/2}(1 - R_{13 \cdot 2}^2)^{1/2}} \tag{10-40}$$

## 10-7 STEPWISE REGRESSION

For some types of research problem it is appropriate to enter independent variables into the regression equation one at a time. The first variable to be entered into the equation is the one most correlated with the dependent variable. The second variable to be included is the one with the highest partial correlation controlling for the first variable already in the equation. Similarly, the third variable chosen is the one with the highest partial correlation controlling for the first two variables. This process is continued until all the independent variables have been included.

**Table 10-2 Selected results from multiple linear regression of average county death rate with seven independent variables**

(*a*) Intercorrelation matrix, means, and standard deviations

| | MIN | URBAN | UNEDU | AGEDBPL | PLUMB | HEALTHEX | AGED | DEATHRT |
|---|---|---|---|---|---|---|---|---|
| MIN | 1.00 | 0.39 | −0.38 | 0.10 | −0.46 | −0.02 | −0.02 | 0.28 |
| URBAN | 0.38 | 1.00 | −0.50 | 0.26 | −0.74 | −0.01 | −0.09 | 0.11 |
| UNEDU | −0.39 | −0.50 | 1.00 | −0.53 | 0.79 | 0.03 | −0.07 | −0.02 |
| AGEDBPL | 0.10 | 0.26 | −0.52 | 1.00 | −0.44 | 0.04 | 0.55 | 0.29 |
| PLUMB | −0.46 | −0.74 | 0.79 | −0.44 | 1.00 | 0.06 | 0.15 | −0.04 |
| HEALTHEX | −0.02 | −0.01 | 0.03 | 0.04 | 0.06 | 1.00 | 0.14 | 0.02 |
| AGED | −0.02 | −0.09 | −0.07 | 0.55 | 0.15 | 0.14 | 1.00 | 0.61 |
| DEATHRT | 0.28 | 0.11 | −0.02 | 0.29 | −0.04 | 0.02 | 0.61 | 1.00 |
| Mean | 2.35 | 15.7 | 16.5 | 16.7 | 38.2 | 3.33 | 11.4 | 10.7 |
| SD | 2.95 | 21.9 | 5.25 | 4.1 | 13.9 | 5.13 | 2.0 | 1.8 |

(*b*) Partial correlations of variables not yet in the equation with DEATHRT controlled by variables within the equation, beta weights of variables in the equation being listed in parentheses

| Step | MIN | URBAN | UNEDU | AGEDBPL | PLUMB | HEALTHEX | AGED |
|---|---|---|---|---|---|---|---|
| 1 | 0.37 | 0.20 | 0.03 | −0.07 | −0.16 | −0.09 | (0.61) |
| 2 | (0.29) | 0.07 | 0.20 | −0.13 | 0.00 | −0.09 | (0.61) |
| 3 | (0.35) | 0.18 | (0.16) | −0.01 | −0.23 | −0.10 | (0.62) |
| 4 | (0.30) | 0.05 | (0.38) | −0.11 | (−0.30) | −0.10 | (0.68) |
| 5 | (0.28) | 0.03 | (0.35) | (−0.13) | (−0.36) | −0.10 | (0.76) |
| 6 | (0.28) | 0.04 | (0.35) | (−0.13) | (−0.36) | (−0.07) | (0.77) |
| 7 | (0.28) | (0.04) | (0.35) | (−0.12) | (−0.32) | (−0.08) | (0.77) |

(*c*) Predictor equations, coefficients of determination, and standard error for each step

| Step | $R^2$ | $S_E$ | Equation |
|---|---|---|---|
| 1 | 0.368 | 1.46 | DEATHRT = 4.4 + 0.55 AGED |
| 2 | 0.453 | 1.37 | DEATHRT = 3.9 + 0.56 AGED + 0.18 MIN |
| 3 | 0.474 | 1.35 | DEATHRT = 2.8 + 0.57 AGED + 0.22 MIN + 0.056 UNEDU |
| 4 | 0.503 | 1.32 | DEATHRT = 2.5 + 0.62 AGED + 0.18 MIN + 0.13 UNEDU − 0.039 PLUMB |
| 5 | 0.509 | 1.32 | |
| 6 | 0.514 | 1.32 | |
| 7 | 0.515 | 1.33 | |

(*d*) *T* scores of each coefficient for each equation

| Step | MIN | URBAN | UNEDU | AGEDBPL | PLUMB | HEALTHEX | AGED |
|---|---|---|---|---|---|---|---|
| 1 | ... | ... | ... | ... | ... | ... | 7.04 |
| 2 | 3.61 | ... | ... | ... | ... | ... | 7.06 |
| 3 | 4.08 | ... | 1.81 | ... | ... | ... | 7.82 |
| 4 | 3.41 | ... | 2.85 | ... | 2.16 | ... | 8.26 |
| 5 | 3.09 | ... | 2.62 | 1.02 | 2.39 | ... | 6.82 |
| 6 | 3.08 | ... | 2.63 | 1.05 | 2.39 | 0.94 | 6.88 |
| 7 | 3.04 | 0.33 | 2.51 | 0.98 | 1.68 | 0.95 | 6.71 |

To demonstrate stepwise regression we will explore an expansion of the death-rate model in the Central Appalachian Region (see Sec. 10-3). The purpose is to determine which of the following variables best explains the variation in death rate. Let:

AGED = % of the population equal to or over 65 years of age

MIN = % of population not Caucasian

URBAN = % of population living in towns over 2500 in population

UNEDU = % of adult population with less than 5 years of education

PLUMB = % of houses without some plumbing

AGEDBPL = % of elderly below the poverty line

HEALTHEX = % of county government expenditures for health care

The initial step in this stepwise regression is to select a variable from among the seven to enter first. The one most correlated with death rate is chosen. The individual correlations with DEATHRT are listed in the eighth row of the intercorrelation matrix in Table 10-2*a*. AGED is the most correlated, 0.61; hence, it is entered first. The resulting equation is

$$\widehat{\text{DEATHRT}} = 4.4 + 0.55(\text{AGED}) \qquad (10\text{-}41)$$

The next step is to select among the remaining six variables the one with the highest partial correlation with DEATHRT when controlling for AGED. These partial correlations can be found in the first row of Table 10-2*b*. Since the highest partial correlation is with MIN, 0.37, it is chosen to enter the equation next:

$$\text{DEATHRT} = 3.9 + 0.56\text{AGED} + 0.18\text{MIN} \qquad (10\text{-}42)$$

The next step is to select among the five remaining variables the one most partially correlated with DEATHRT when controlling for AGED and MIN. This process is continued until all independent variables have entered into the equation. The first four equations are listed in Table 10-2*c*.

Change in partial correlations resulting from step-by-step entrance into the equation can be interesting. Initially, MIN and AGEDBPL along with AGED were highly correlated with death rate. After AGED entered into the regression equation, the 0.29 correlation of AGEDBPL dropped to a partial correlation of −0.07 (see the first row of Table 10-2*b*). However, the 0.28 correlation of MIN increased to a partial correlation of 0.37. These changes suggest that the relationship of poverty to death rate was spurious and the relationship of minority was partially masked by AGED. Thus, counties which have a high proportion of elderly below the poverty line tend to have high proportions of elderly in the population (see the high positive correlation, 0.55, between AGEDBPL and AGED in the intercorrelation matrix in Table 10-2*a*).

Initially there existed a near-zero correlation between death rate and UNEDU, indicating that the proportion of uneducated in a county cannot be used to predict its average death rate. However, there is a negative correlation between MIN and UNEDU. The unsophisticated researcher might conclude from this negative correlation that minorities are better educated than whites. Since our data are aggregated by counties the analysis is about counties and not about individuals living in the counties. The negative correlation indicates that counties in the Central Appalachian Region with high proportions of minorities tend to have small proportions of adults with less than fifth-grade education. Notice the positive correlation between URBAN and MIN, 0.39. Those counties with large proportions of minorities tend to be more urban, and the educational level of the population tends to be higher. The negative correlation between MIN and UNEDU masked the relationship between UNEDU and death rate. After MIN entered the regression equation on the second step, the relationship of UNEDU with death rate, as indicated by the partial correlation, increased from 0.03 to 0.20. UNEDU entered the equation on the third step. The influence of UNEDU becomes even more evident when PLUMB entered the regression equation on the fourth step. Comparing beta weights on the fourth step, we find that UNEDU is the second most-important variable after AGED. When controlling for MIN, AGED, and PLUMB we find that counties with high proportions of uneducated tend to have high average death rates.

After the fourth step there seems little to be gained by adding more variables to the equation. When AGEDBPL enters on the fifth step, the $R^2$ increases by only 0.006 (see Table 10-2*c*). At a significance level of 5 percent, the $T$ score for the AGEDBPL coefficient is not significantly different from 0 (see Table 10-2*d*). HEALTHEX is correlated with no other variables in this analysis and provides essentially no information concerning death rate.

The fourth standardized equation is

$$\hat{Z}_{\text{DEATHRT}} = 0.39Z_{\text{MIN}} + 0.38Z_{\text{URBAN}} - 0.30Z_{\text{PLUMB}} + 0.68Z_{\text{AGED}} \quad (10\text{-}43)$$

Comparing the standardized regression coefficients we find that AGED is the most important in explaining death rate. Suppose two counties, A and B, have the same values for MIN, URBAN, and PLUMB, while AGED for County B is 1 standard deviation larger than it is for County A. Then the estimated expected death rate for County B is 0.68 standard deviations larger than that for County A.

## 10-8 DUMMY VARIABLES

It is assumed all variables in a regression equation are interval scaled. Normally it would be meaningless to enter a nominal variable in a regression equation. Suppose a variable REGION is coded 1 for the Norther Appalachian Region, 2 for the Southern Appalachian Region, and 3 for the Central Appalachian Region. Entering such a variable into the equation may result in a significant but meaningless coefficient, for there is no logic in assuming that the Central Region is one more than the Southern Region which is, in turn, one more than the Northern Region.

The nominal variable with $g$ categories can be entered in the regression equation if a dummy variable is created for all but one of its categories. To demonstrate how this is done, we will regress DEATHRT against AGED and the REGION variable described above. Two dummy variables, which we will arbitrarily call NORTH and SOUTH, will be created. Let NORTH equal 1 for counties in the Northern Region and 0 otherwise. Similarly, SOUTH equals 1 for counties in the Southern Region and 0 otherwise. Notice that $(g - 1)$ dummy variables are needed ($g = 3$ in this example). The regions N, S, and C are represented by the following equations:

$$\text{DEATHRT}_{\text{N}} = \alpha_{\text{N}} + \alpha_1(\text{AGED}_{\text{N}}) + E \tag{10-44}$$

$$\text{DEATHRT}_{\text{S}} = \alpha_{\text{S}} + \alpha_1(\text{AGED}_{\text{S}}) + E \tag{10-45}$$

$$\text{DEATHRT}_{\text{C}} = \alpha_{\text{C}} + \alpha_1(\text{AGED}_{\text{C}}) + E \tag{10-46}$$

It is assumed that $\alpha_1$ is the same for each region. To estimate the intercepts $\alpha_{\text{N}}$, $\alpha_{\text{S}}$, and $\alpha_{\text{C}}$, and the common slope $\alpha_1$, three regressions would be needed. Separating the data into three groups reduces the sample size and decreases the precision of the estimates. A better approach combines the three above models into one:

$$\text{DEATHRT} = \alpha_{\text{C}} + \alpha_2(\text{NORTH}) + \alpha_3(\text{SOUTH}) + \alpha_1(\text{AGED}) + E \tag{Model 10-2}$$

In this equation $\alpha_2 = \alpha_{\text{N}} - \alpha_{\text{C}}$ and $\alpha_3 = \alpha_{\text{S}} - \alpha_{\text{C}}$. The intercept in the combined equation always represents the category for which a dummy variable was not created. The coefficient of a dummy variable represents the mean difference between its category and the one for which a dummy variable was not created when controlling for the other variables in the equation. In this combined equation we can determine if $\alpha_2$ or $\alpha_3$ are significantly different from 0 when controlling for AGED. An analysis of the Appalachian counties is shown in Table 10-3.

The mean death rate in the Northern Region is 0.7 (that is, 11.4 – 10.7) larger than it is in the Central Region; however, this difference may be due to the larger percentage of elderly in the Northern Region. If we control for AGED, is there a difference in death rate between the Northern and the Central Regions? By regressing DEATHRT against AGED, NORTH, and SOUTH we get the coefficients in

**Table 10-3 Regional means of DEATHRT, AGED, and DEATHRT when controlling for AGED**

| Region | Mean DEATHRT | Mean AGED | Coefficients of model (10-2) | $T$ values | Mean DEATHRT controlled for AGED = 0 |
|---|---|---|---|---|---|
| Northern | 11.4 | 11.07 | $A_2 = 0.48$ | 3.08 | $A_C + A_2 = 4.03$ |
| Southern | 10.0 | 10.5 | $A_3 = -0.13$ | 0.84 | $A_C + A_3 = 3.42$ |
| Central | 10.7 | 11.4 | $A_C = 3.55$ | ... | $A_C = 3.55$ |
| Control | | | $A_1 = 0.63$ | 22.5 | $R^2 = 0.61$ |

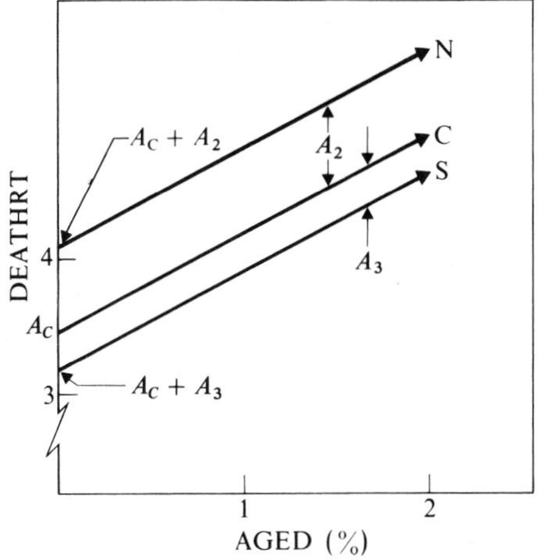


**Figure 10-1** DEATHRT = 3.55 + 0.48NORTH − 0.13SOUTH + 0.63AGED.

Table 10-3. Figure 10-1 shows the relationships drawn with the estimated coefficients from this regression. The vertical difference between the lines for the Northern and Central Regions is $A_2$ and for the Southern and Central Regions is $A_3$. From the coefficients in Table 10-3 we see that the mean difference in death rate between the Northern and Central Regions is 0.48 for a constant AGED. A test of the hypotheses:

$$\begin{aligned} H_0&: \quad \alpha_2 = 0 \\ H_1&: \quad \alpha_2 \neq 0 \end{aligned} \tag{10-47}$$

at a significance level of 0.05 would compare $T_{A_2}$ with a critical point of approximately $-2$ and 2. Since $T = 3.08$ which is greater than 2, reject $H_0$.

## 10-9 NONLINEAR MODELS

Other models to consider for multiple regression are:

$$Y = \alpha_0 + \alpha_1 X + \alpha_2 X^2 + \alpha_3 X^3 + \cdots + \alpha_m X^m + E \qquad \text{(Model 10-3)}$$

$$Y = \alpha_0 X_1^{\alpha_1} X_2^{\alpha_2} X_3^{\alpha_3} \cdots X_m^{\alpha_m} E \qquad \text{(Model 10-4)}$$

$$Y = \alpha_0 + \alpha_1 D + \alpha_2 DX + \alpha_3 (1 - D)X + E \qquad \text{(Model 10-5)}$$

Model (10-3) is an $m$-degree polynomial and is essentially a linear model of multiple powers of $X$ (see Figs. 10-2 and 10-3). Model (10-4) is the product model where the mean of $E$ is assumed to be 1. Taking logs of both sides will transform this model into a linear model:

$$\log(Y) = \log(\alpha_0) + \alpha_1 \log(X_1) + \alpha_2 \log(X_2) + \cdots + \alpha_m \log(X_m) + \log(E) \tag{10-48}$$

The product model is commonly used in economics, and the coefficients can be shown to be the elasticities of the independent variables (see Chap. 11).

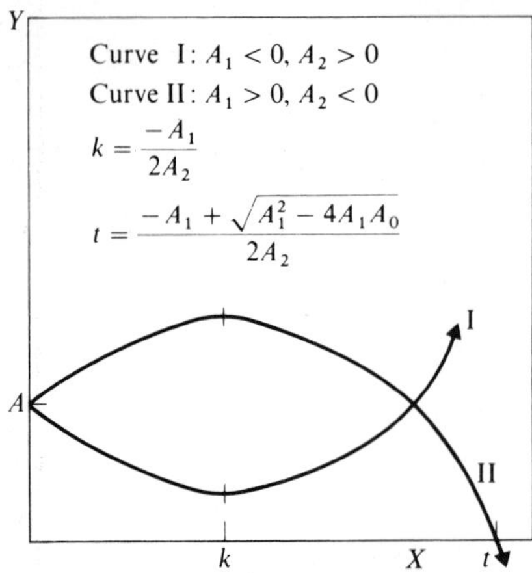


**Figure 10-2** Model (10-3) with $k = 2$: $\hat{Y} = A_0 + A_1X + A_2X^2$.

In model (10-5) $D$ is a dummy variable that equals 1 if a case falls in a specified category and 0 if it does not, and $1 - D$ is the complement of $D$. The product $DX$ equals $X$ if the case falls in the specified category and 0 otherwise, and $(1 - D)X$ is the complement of $DX$. This model represents the situation where not only the $Y$ intercept differs between categories for the equation $Y = \alpha_0 + \alpha_1 X + E$ but so, too, does the slope of $X$ (see Fig. 10-4).

Suppose that it were commonly assumed that the interaction between any two communities, M and N, is directly proportional to the product of the population of M and N and inversely proportional to the square of the shortest travel distance between the two places, $D_{MN}$:

$$I_{\mathrm{MN}} = \alpha_0 \frac{P_{\mathrm{M}} P_{\mathrm{N}}}{D_{\mathrm{MN}}^2} \tag{10-49}$$

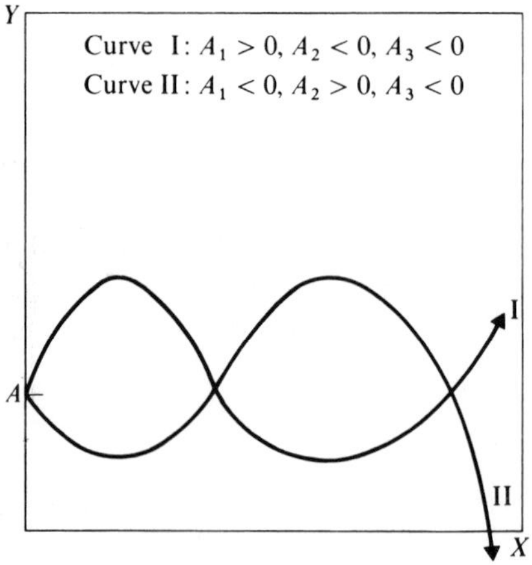


**Figure 10-3** Model (10-3) with $k = 3$: $Y = A_0 + A_1X + A_2X^2 + A_3X^3$.

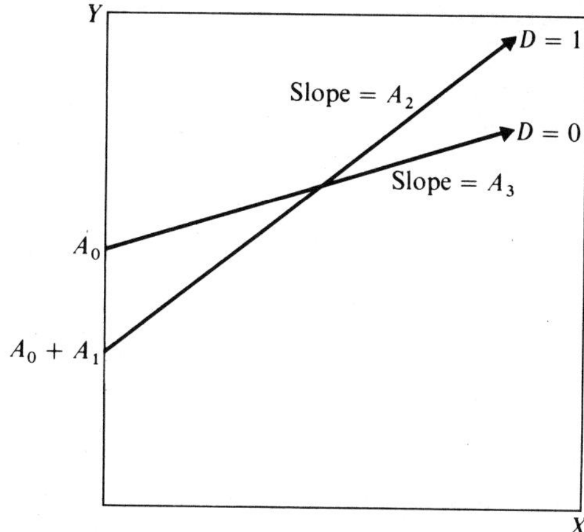


**Figure 10-4** Model (10-4): $\hat{Y} = A_0 + A_1 D + A_2 DX + A_3(1 - D)X$.

This model is known as the *gravity model*, since it is similar to Newton's law of gravitational force. Is there any theoretical justification for the model taking the same form as Newton's law? Let us assume that a researcher gathered data on the interactions between communities. Since the gravity model is a special case of the product model, the researcher regressed the log of $I_{MN}$ against the logs of $P_M$, $P_N$, and $D_{MN}$:

$$I_{MN} = \alpha_0 P_M^{\alpha_1} P_N^{\alpha_2} D_{MN}^{\alpha_3} E \tag{10-50}$$

where it is assumed that $\alpha_1 = \alpha_2 = 1$ and $\alpha_3 = -2$. The following hypotheses were tested:

$H_0$: $\alpha_1 = 1$, $\alpha_2 = 1$, and $\alpha_3 = -2$

$H_1$: At least one of the above is not equal to its assumed value.

The results were $A_1 = 1.56$, $S_{A_1} = 0.24$, $A_2 = 0.89$, $S_{A_2} = 0.15$, $A_3 = -0.6$, $S_{A_3} = 0.89$.

An $F$ test would not be useful for it would test only for all $\alpha$ values equal to zero. The reseracher tested each parameter using a significance level of 0.01. The small significance level was chosen since a series of three tests are required. Using the following general formula:

$$T_{A_i} = \frac{A_i - \alpha_i}{S_{A_i}} \tag{10-51}$$

the $T$ value for each coefficient was computed:

$$T_{A_1} = \frac{1.56 - 1.00}{0.24} = 2.33$$

$$T_{A_2} = \frac{0.89 - 1.00}{0.15} = -0.7333$$

$$T_{A_3} = \frac{-0.60 + 2.00}{0.21} = 6.67$$

There were 43 interactions recorded, which give $(43 - 4) = 39$ degrees of freedom. For a significance level of 0.01 the critical points were $-2.78$ and 2.78. Since $T_{A_3}$ was greater than 2.78, $H_0$ was rejected. In other words, it was concluded that interaction between two communities is not inversely proportional to the square of the distance between them.

## PROBLEMS

**10-1** Fill in the blanks with the appropriate word(s).

(*a*) Two variables are independent of each other if ______________.

(*b*) Input variables (those under our control or obtained from other forecasts) are called ______________.

(*c*) When we bring an additional variable ($Q$) into a regression model, although we are interested in noting the influence on the coefficient of one of the original variables $X$, we say we are ______________ for $Q$.

(*d*) In multiple linear regression, as in regression between two variables, we are interested in finding the ______________ which minimize ______________.

(*e*) In this chapter it is assumed that the data for multiple regression are obtained from a ______________ sample.

(*f*) **X** is a ______________ with the number of columns (minus 1) equal to ______________ and the number of rows equal to ______________.

(*g*) **Y** is a ______________ with the number of rows equal to ______________.

(*h*) **e** is a ______________ with the number of rows equal to ______________.

(*i*) **a** is a ______________ with the number of rows equal to ______________.

(*j*) $SS_Y$ can be divided into ______________ and ______________.

(*k*) The population parameters are designated by ______________ and the sample estimates by ______________.

(*l*) The first hypothesis test for the regression coefficients is that ______________________ ______________.

(*m*) Individual coefficients, then, can be tested using a ______________ estimating function with ______________ degrees of freedom.

(*n*) Standardized coefficients are also known as ______________.

(*o*) The ______________ represents the strength of association between two variables while controlling for a third or more.

(*p*) Correlation that is apparent but not real is called ______________.

(*q*) In ______________ regression, variables are entered one at a time, depending on the ______________ while ______________ for those variables already in the equation.

(*r*) A ______________ -scaled variable can be entered into a regression if a ______________ variable is created for all but one of its ______________.

(*s*) One of the more common types of ______________ regression models shows the independent variables multiplied together, with each being raised to a ______________.

**10-2** Using the data from the town of Strip Mine (App. D) and the procedure suggested in Eq. (10-10), find:
(*a*) The coefficients in the estimated equation $\hat{Y}_1 = A_0 + A_1 X_1 + A_2 X_2$
(*b*) $SS_E$
(*c*) $R^2$
(*d*) If any coefficient is significantly different from 0 ($\alpha = 0.05$)
(*e*) If the coefficient for $X_2$ is significantly different from 0 ($\alpha = 0.05$)

**10-3** Using the Strip Mine data again, find, either by hand or through available computer programs:
(*a*) The coefficients (beta weights) in the estimated equation $W_1 = B_1 Z_1 + B_2 Z_2$
(*b*) The three correlations $R_{YX_1}$, $R_{YX_2}$, $R_{X_1X_2}$
(*c*) The beta weights using Eq. (10-31)

**10-4** For Strip Mine find:
(*a*) The partial correlation between $Y_1$ and $X_1$ holding constant $X_2$
(*b*) The partial correlation between $Y_1$ and $X_2$ holding constant $X_1$

**10-5** For Strip Mine, do a stepwise regression with $Y_1$ as the dependent variable and $Y_2$, $X_1$, and $X_2$ as the independents. Find:
(*a*) The variable which enters first, and the associated equation
(*b*) The variable which enters second, and the new equation including it and the first variable
(*c*) The $R^2$ and standard errors for the equations in (*a*) and (*b*)

**10-6** Again referring to Strip Mine and using $Y_3$ as an *independent* (dummy) variable, find:
(*a*) The coefficients in the equation $\hat{Y}_1 = A_0 + A_1 X_1 + A_2 D$
(*b*) The corresponding $R^2$ and standard error
(*c*) If $A_2$ is significantly different from 0 ($\alpha = 0.05$)

**10-7** Finally, for Strip Mine find:
(*a*) The equation of the form $\hat{Y}_1 = A_0 X_1^{A_1} X_2^{A_2}$
(*b*) The $R^2$ for the transformed equation
(*c*) The $R^2$ for the equation in (*a*)

**10-8** Bingham discusses (Ref. 10-7) the unpopularity of public housing and the difficulty political leaders have in convincing the public to accept federal funding to build subsidized housing. It has been hypothesized that the greater the political stability of a city, the greater the success of public housing. Suppose political stability $P$ and public housing success $H$ were measured for a sample of 101 cities resulting in the following statistics:

$$\bar{P} = 3.6 \qquad S_p = 1.2 \qquad \bar{H} = 3100 \qquad S_H = 600 \qquad R_{HP} = -0.2$$

(*a*) What does a correlation of $-0.2$ between public housing success and political stability mean?
(*b*) Consider the model $H = \alpha_0 + \alpha_1 P + E$. From the information above compute $A_1$, $A_0$, $R^2$, $S_E$, $S_{A_1}$, and $T$.
(*c*) Using a significance level of 0.05 (hence the critical points are $-1.99$ and 1.99), what conclusions can you make concerning your $T$?
(*d*) It was noticed that the type of government ($G = 1$ if the city has a reform type of government and 0 if it does not, that is, $G$ is a dummy variable) was correlated with both political stability $P$ and public housing success $H$:

$$R_{HG} = +0.5 \qquad R_{PG} = -0.8$$

Compute the partial correlation between $H$ and $P$ controlling for $G$, and compare with $R_{HP}$. How and why do they differ?
(*e*) What does the square of this partial correlation mean? What would the $R^2$ be for the model $H = \alpha_0 + \alpha_1 P + \alpha_2 G + E$?
(*f*) Consider the model $H = \alpha_0 + \alpha_1 P + \alpha_2 G + \alpha_3 \text{POVERTY} + \alpha_4 \text{POP} + E$

$$A_1 = 51 \qquad S_{A_1} = 17 \qquad SS_E = 13{,}000{,}000 \qquad SS_{reg} = 23{,}000{,}000$$

Compute $F$, $R^2$, $B_1$, and $T_{A_1}$.
(*g*) Interpret $B_1$.
(*h*) Discuss the difference between the coefficients of $P$ in the model in (*b*) and the model in (*f*).

**10-9** Go to the library and find an application of multiple regression. In about 500 words, describe:
(*a*) The nature of the problem being studied
(*b*) The type and size of sample (if any)
(*c*) The derived regression parameters
(*d*) Any hypotheses tested concerning these parameters
(*e*) The validity of the results and conclusions reached based on the regression relationship
(*f*) The general advantages and disadvantages of regression in this application

**10-10** Working with your instructor and using available computer programs, take a sample of data from App. D:
(*a*) Develop a multiple regression relationship (linear or nonlinear, perhaps involving dummy variables).
(*b*) Compute and interpret the partial correlation coefficients.
(*c*) Test the parameters to see if they are significantly different from 0.
(*d*) Interpret the results of your analysis and draw conclusions.

# REFERENCES

**Theory**

10-1. Bishop, Y. M. M., S. E. Fienberg, and P. W. Holland: *Discrete Multivariate Analysis: Theory and Practice*, The MIT Press, Cambridge, Mass., 1975.

10-2. Ezekiel, M., and K. A. Fox: *Methods of Correlation and Regression Analysis: Linear and Curvilinear*, 3d ed., Wiley, New York, 1959.
10-3. Guilford, J. P.: *Fundamental Statistics in Psychology and Education*, 4th ed., McGraw-Hill, New York, 1965.
10-4. Siegel, S.: *Nonparametric Statistics for the Behavioral Sciences*, McGraw-Hill, New York, 1956.
10-5. Wonnacott, T. H., and R. J. Wonnacott: *Econometrics*, Wiley, New York, 1970.

**Applications**

10-6. Anderson, K. P.: *Residential Energy Use: An Econometric Analysis*, Report R-1297-NSF, The Rand Coporation, Santa Monica, Calif., October, 1973.
10-7. Bingham, R. D.: "On Measuring Local Political Stability," *Urban Affairs Quarterly*, vol. 9, no. 4, June, 1974.
10-8. Correa, H.: "Models and Mathematics in Educational Planning," *World Yearbook of Education*, Harcourt, Brace, Jovanovich, New York, 1967.
10-9. Davidson, G., and T. Dahl: *A Macro-Statistical Model of the Health Sector of the State of Minnesota*, vol. II, Systems Research, Inc., Minneapolis, Minn., February, 1973.
10-10. Martino, J. P.: *Technological Forecasting for Decisionmaking*, Amer.can-Elsevier, New York, 1972.
10-11. Merz, P. H., L. J. Painter, and P. R. Ryason: "Aerometric Data Analysis—Time Series Analysis and Forecast and an Atmospheric Smog Diagram," *Atmospheric Environment*, vol. 6, 1972.
10-12. Quandt, R. E., and W. J. Baumol: *The Demand for Abstract Transport Modes: Theory and Measurement*, D. C. Heath, Lexington, Mass., 1970.
10-13. U.S. Bureau of the Census, H. S. Shryock, J. S. Siegel, and Associates, *The Methods and Materials of Demography*, 2 vols., U.S.GPO, Washington, D.C., 1973.
10-14. Yeates, M.: *An Introduction to Quantitative Analysis in Human Geography*, McGraw-Hill, New York, 1974.

CHAPTER

# ELEVEN

# SYSTEMS DYNAMICS AND DYNAMO PROGRAMMING

*Systems dynamics* is a type of simulation technique developed primarily by Forrester (Ref. 11-1) and applied originally to industrial production situations. In recent years it has been applied to a variety of local to world-wide social, economic, and environmental problems (Refs. 11-4 to 11-10). Associated with the systems dynamics approach is a unique type of FORTRAN-based computer programming technique known as *DYNAMO* (Ref. 11-3). In this chapter we will describe DYNAMO programming and use as an illustration the housing supply and demand model presented in Chap. 1 (see Fig. 11-1). It should also be noted that systems dynamics builds directly on the principals of systems described in Chap. 1, so the interested reader should reread that section before progressing here.

## 11-1 FEEDBACK

An important aspect of any system is *feedback*, which can be either positive or negative. The differentiation is based on the ultimate (or goal) level for each variable in the system. In *positive* feedback the goal level is infinite, in *negative* finite. An example of the former would be income, which many people would like to have as high as possible, with no ceiling. An example of the latter would be room temperature, which most people would like to see as close as possible to the fixed level of 68°F (20°C).

The rationale for these descriptors can be better understood from the graphic illustrations in Fig. 11-2. Suppose that in one case the 1960 population in our

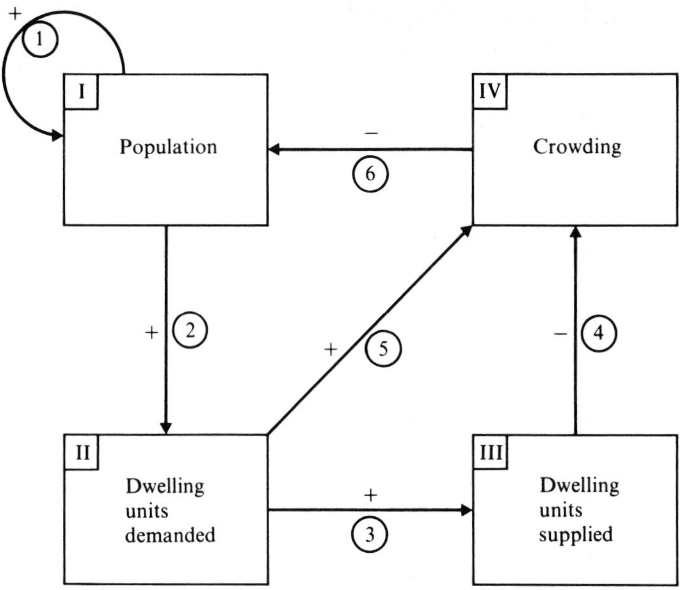


**Figure 11-1** A simple model of housing supply and demand in part of a city.

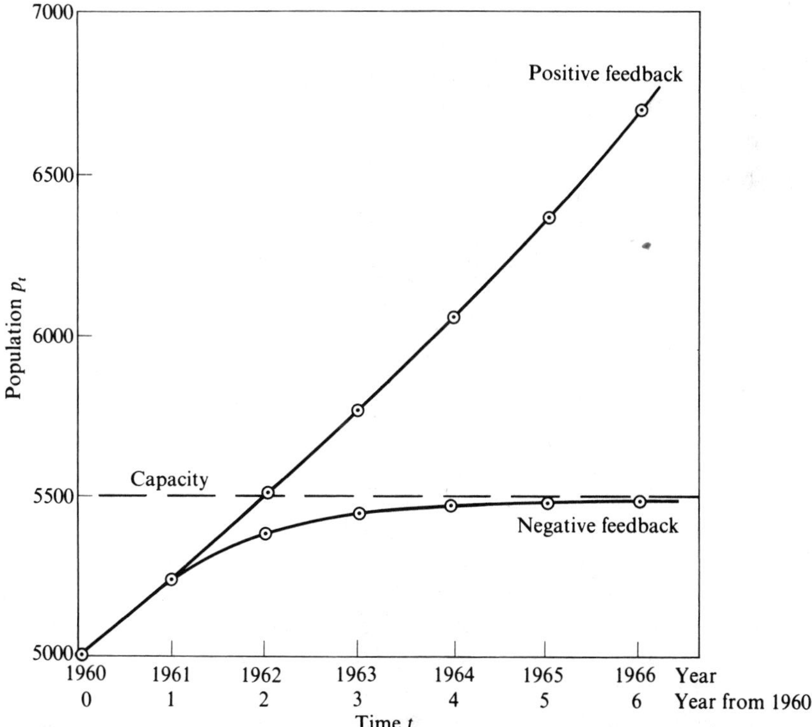


**Figure 11-2** Example of population growth under positive and negative feedback.

**Table 11-1 Population levels with unlimited and limited growth**

| | Case 1: unlimited growth | | Case 2: growth limit of 5500 | | |
|---|---|---|---|---|---|
| Year | Population | Rate | Population | 5500-population | Rate |
| 1960 | 5000 | 250 | 5000 | 500 | 250 |
| 1961 | 5250 | 263 | 5250 | 250 | 125 |
| 1962 | 5513 | 276 | 5375 | 125 | 63 |
| 1963 | 5789 | 289 | 5438 | 62 | 31 |
| 1964 | 6078 | 304 | 5469 | 31 | 16 |
| 1965 | 6382 | 319 | 5485 | 15 | 8 |
| 1966 | 6701 | | 5493 | | |

housing supply and demand illustration in Chap. 1 (and Fig. 11-1) increased with a birth constant of 50 births per 1000 people = 0.05. But in the second case we imagine a housing capacity in the region of 5500 people, with the population increase rate being one-half (0.5) of the *difference* between the fixed capacity and the actual population level. The resulting population levels and rates for the first 6 years for both of these cases are shown in Table 11-1.

In case 1 the initial population ($p_{1960}$) of 5000 is increased by 5000(0.05) = 250 in the first year, which brings the 1961 level ($p_{1961}$) to 5250. In equation form we would have:

$$p_{t+1} = p_t(0.05) + p_t \tag{11-1}$$

or 5250 = 5000(0.05) + 5000. The 1961 level is the same for the other case, but the rate is derived as (5500 − 5000)(0.5) = 250 or, by equation:

$$p_{t+1} = (5500 - p_t)(0.5) + p_t \tag{11-2}$$

or 5250 = (5500 − 5000)(0.5) + 5000. After that, the similarity between the two cases quickly disappears. As can be seen in Fig. 11-2, which is a plot of the population values in Table 11-1, in the first case the population shoots off toward infinity, while in the second case it flattens out to approach the 5500 limit. These results occur because in case 1 the population variable $p_t$ enters the equation with a positive sign and a "goal" of infinity, thus denoting *positive* feedback. In case 2 the sign of $p_t$ is negative and the goal is finite, thus denoting *negative* feedback.

## 11-2 DOUBLING OR HALVING TIME OF A VARIABLE

Another characteristic of interest in most systems dynamic models of the type being demonstrated here is the doubling or halving time of a variable. This is helpful to know for *calibrating* (specifying the parameters of) a model. In the housing demand/supply example we may have found from a previous study that, (due to births, population in the area had doubled between 1950 and 1964 (doubling time = 14 years). This would give a birth-rate constant† of approximately 0.7/14 = 0.05.

† See the footnote in Sec. 1-3 on the definition of a rate constant.

This figure is calculated by assuming a continuous function with time, the equation for which is

$$p_t = p_0 e^{ct} \tag{11-3}$$

where $p_t$ is the population at time $t$, $p_0$ is the initial population, $e$ is the base of the natural logarithms, and $c$ is the birth-rate constant. If we wanted to calculate the rate constant to change from $p_0$ to some multiple, $k$, of $p_0$, we would simply substitute $kp_0$ for $p_t$ in Eq. (11-3) and solve for $c$. Thus:

$$kp_0 = p_0 e^{ct} \tag{11-4}$$

Dividing out the $p_0$ values:

$$k = e^{ct} \tag{11-5}$$

taking the logarithm of both sides:

$$\ln (k) = ct \tag{11-6}$$

and solving for $c$:

$$c = \frac{\ln (k)}{t} \tag{11-7}$$

Now, to get the example birth-rate constant, we let $k = 2$ and $t = 14$ years to get $c$ of approximately $\ln (2)/14 = 0.7/14 = 0.05$. This is an approximate value because $\ln (2)$ is not exactly 0.7 (but this value is easy to remember) and because we have assumed a continuous rather than a discrete time function, as would be used in an actual application of DYNAMO (see Sec. 11-4).

## 11-3 RECALCULATION TIME PERIOD ERRORS

If we recalculate the rates and levels after a fixed time period, a year in our example, an error will be initiated and propagated. Its size will depend on the length of the period, with larger errors for longer periods. This point is demonstrated in Table 11-2, where 1-, 2-, and 3-year recalculation periods are shown for the positive feedback case above. For instance, for the 2-year period, the

**Table 11-2 Population levels for different recalculation time periods**

| | 1-Year period | | 2-Year period | | 3-Year period | | Continuous |
|---|---|---|---|---|---|---|---|
| Year | Population | Rate | Population | Rate | Population | Rate | Population |
| 1960 | 5000 | 250 | 5000 | 500 | 5000 | 750 | 5000 |
| 1961 | 5250 | 263 | | | | | 5256 |
| 1962 | 5513 | 276 | 5500 | 550 | | | 5526 |
| 1963 | 5789 | 289 | | | 5750 | 863 | 5809 |
| 1964 | 6078 | 304 | 6050 | 606 | | | 6107 |
| 1965 | 6382 | 319 | | | | | 6420 |
| 1966 | 6701 | | 6656 | | 6612 | | 6749 |

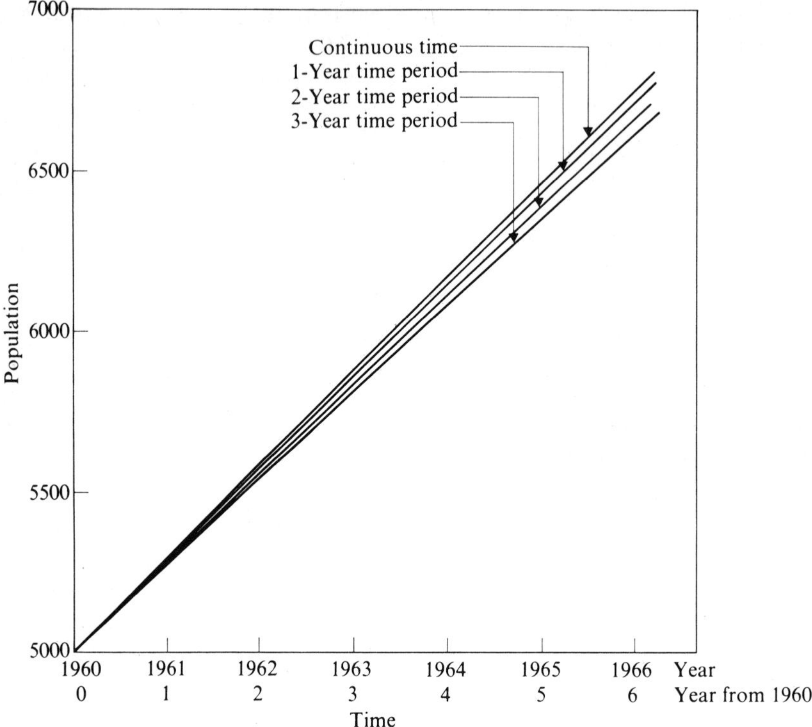


**Figure 11-3** Example of population growth for different calculation periods.

rate (over that 2 years) is 5000(0.05)(2) = 500, where the 0.05 growth-rate constant is specified on an annual basis. This brings the population level in 1962 to 5500, 13 short of the figure calculated on a 1-year basis. This error is caused by considering a continuous growth process as composed of discrete entities of time. If time is treated continuously, as can be done using an exponential function as in Eq. (11-3), the population level in 1962 would be 5526 (see the curve in Fig. 11-3).

## 11-4 DYNAMO PROGRAMMING

Given this brief introduction to systems analysis we are now ready to develop a DYNAMO program to calculate the levels of our four variables (population, demand, supply, and crowding) over time. This can be done by considering the various interrelationships in Fig. 11-1 and using the rules and procedures set out in Table 1-1 and Fig. 1-2, respectively. The logic and computation to be described below will be presented in DYNAMO notation.

We start by considering in order each variable and link in Fig. 11-1. For each variable we will have a level equation (denoted by L) and for each link usually a rate equation (denoted by R). Those level equations not containing rates are defined in DYNAMO as "auxiliaries" and given the special denotation of A. For each variable we will also have an initial level (denoted by N). Furthermore, a level, auxiliary, or rate equation might contain parameters, which are denoted by C (for constant). Finally, DT will stand for the time period to be employed in the calculations (which can be varied at the user's discretion).

Six points to note in DYNAMO programming are:

1. The N,C,L,A, and R letters go in column 1 of the computer card. In addition, the program control statements (discussed below) start in column 1.
2. The actual equations start in column 3 or thereafter. The specifications for the instruction statements start one space after the corresponding instruction commands.
3. Because cards only have one row, subscripts are placed on the same line as the variable and preceded by a period. J is the subscript for the first time interval, K for the second, and L for the third. Variable names are limited to six characters (starting with a letter).
4. Multiplication is indicated by an asterisk (*), so as not to be confused with an x.
5. On the other hand, an asterisk in the first column indicates a comment (not computed).
6. Parentheses can and should be employed to set off terms in an equation (same rules as in FORTRAN, see App. B).

The DYNAMO program for the housing demand and supply model is presented in Table 11-3. It starts with a comment statement indicating the name of this particular run of the program. This step is succeeded by a series of 17 statements portraying levels and rates. For each variable there should be at least one level or auxiliary equation, one initial condition equation, and an equation (usually a rate equation) covering each (or a combination of each) link *into* that variable. These equations can be presented in any order (DYNAMO will sort them out), but for instructional purposes we will start here with the population variable (denoted by POP) and proceed sequentially through Fig. 11-1.

On the first round (1960) we are concerned only with setting the initial conditions and computing rate changes, so we temporarily ignore the level and auxiliary equations. The first equation in Table 11-3 places the initial population at 5000 (in 1960 = J = 0). The first rate equation, corresponding to link 1, shows the number of births (birth rate = BR.KL) expected to occur in the period from 1960 to 1961 (K = 1 to L = 2).† There the birth-rate constant (BRC) is 0.05 and is multiplied by the population level (POP.K). So for the next year the number of births (birth rate) is BR.KL = 0.05(5000) = 250. The other rate in link 1 is for

† For some reason the developers of DYNAMO elected to "move up" the rate equations in time. For example, if J is 1960 = 0, K should be 1961 = 1 and L = 1962 = 2. So, given the 1960 population, we should compute the births from 1960 to 1961 as BR.JK. But the developers used BR.KL instead. As long as we are "consistently inconsistent," however, this alteration should not be a problem.

**Table 11-3 DYNAMO program for housing demand and supply model**

| | | |
|---|---|---|
| * | HOUSING DEMAND/SUPPLY MODEL | Title |
| N | POP = 5000 | Initial Population |
| L | POP.K = POP.J + DT*(BR.JK + DR.JK + MDTC.JK) | |
| Future Population = Present Population + Births + (−) Deaths + (−) Migration Due to Crowding | | |
| R | BR.KL = BRC*POP.K | |
| Births(Rate) = Birth Rate Constant × Population | | |
| C | BRC = 0.05 | Birth Rate Constant |
| R | DR.KL = DRC*POP.K | |
| Deaths(Rate) = Death Rate Constant × Population | | |
| C | DRC = −0.01 | Death Rate Constant |
| N | DEM = 1250 | Initial Housing Demand |
| A | DEM.K = POP.K/APPHC | |
| Demand = Population/Ave. Persons Per Household | | |
| C | APPHC = 4.00 | Ave. Persons/Household Constant (National) |
| N | SUP = 1000 | Initial Housing Supply |
| L | SUP.K = SUP.J + DT*CSDTD.JK | |
| Future Supply = Present Supply + Change Due to Demand | | |
| R | CSDTD.KL = (DEM.K-SUP.K)*SRTDC | |
| Change in Supply Due To Demand = Diff. Between Demand and Supply × Supply Response to Demand | | |
| C | SRTDC = 0.5 | Supply Response to Demand Constant |
| N | CR = 5.00 | Initial Crowding Ratio |
| A | CR.K = DEM.K*APPHC/SUP.K | |
| Crowding Ratio = Population (or Demand × Ave. People Per Housing Unit)/Supply | | |
| R | MDTC.KL = (APPHC-CR.K)*MRTCC*POP.K | |
| Migration Due to Crowding = Diff. Between National Ave. Pers. Per Household and Crowding Ratio × Migration Response to Crowding × Population | | |
| C | MRTCC = 0.03 | |
| PRINT POP,BR,DR,DEM,SUP,CSDTD,CR,MDTC | | |
| PLOT POP = P/SUP = S/CR = C | | |
| SPEC DT = 1/LENGTH = 4/PRTPER = 1/PLTPER = 1 | | |
| RUN | | |

deaths, with the death-rate constant (DRC) being −0.01 and the deaths (death rate) being

$$\text{DR.KL} = -0.01(5000) = -50$$

These calculations, as well as the others from the model up to the year 1964, can be found in Table 11-4.

The next set of three equations after that for the death-rate constant involves the housing-demand variable (DEM). The first of these sets the initial demand of 5000 people at 4 people per unit = 1250 units, with the number 4 (APPHC) being the national average of persons per household (assumed here to represent a

**Table 11-4 Calculations for DYNAMO program for two runs† of the housing demand and supply model**

| Year | Population level POP | Birth rate BR | Death rate DR | Demand level DEM | Supply level SUP | Change in supply rate CSDTD | Crowding ratio level CR | Migration due to crowding rate MDTC |
|---|---|---|---|---|---|---|---|---|
| 1960 | 5000 | | | 1250 | 1000 | | 5.00 | |
| | | 250 | −50 | | | 125 | | −150 |
| 1961 | 5050 | | | 1263 | 1125 | | 4.49 | |
| | | 253 | −51 | | | 69 | | −74 |
| 1962 | 5178 | | | 1295 | 1194 | | 4.34 | |
| | | 259 | −52 | | | 51 | | −52 |
| 1963 | 5333 | | | 1333 | 1244 | | 4.29 | |
| | | 266 | −53 | | | 45 | | −46 |
| 1964 | 5500 | | | 1375 | 1289 | | 4.27 | |
| | | 275 | −55 | | | 43 | | −44 |
| 1960 | 5000 | | | 1250 | 1000 | | 5.00 | |
| | | 250 | −50 | | | 25 | | −50 |
| 1961 | 5150 | | | 1288 | 1025 | | 5.02 | |
| | | 258 | −52 | | | 26 | | −53 |
| 1962 | 5303 | | | 1326 | 1051 | | 5.04 | |
| | | 265 | −53 | | | 27 | | −55 |
| 1963 | 5460 | | | 1365 | 1079 | | 5.06 | |
| | | 273 | −55 | | | 29 | | −55 |
| 1964 | 5620 | | | 1405 | 1107 | | 5.08 | |
| | | 281 | −56 | | | 30 | | −58 |

† Top run: BRC = 0.05 DRC = −0.01 APPHC = 4.0 SRTDC = 0.5 MRTCC = 0.03
Bottom run: BRC = 0.05 DRC = −0.01 APPHC = 4.0 SRTDC = 0.1 MRTCC = 0.01
See Table 11-3 for a definition of each term here.

"no-crowding" situation). On the supply (SUP) side the initial level is 1000 units and the additions to the housing stock from 1960 to 1961 (CSDTD.KL) are computed as

$$\text{CSDTD.KL} = (1250 - 1000)(0.5) = 125$$

Here it is assumed, somewhat simply, that builders can and will provide enough housing in a year to make up exactly half the difference between existing demand and supply.‡

The final set of equations deals with the crowding ratio. The initial level is 5000 people per 1000 units = 5.00. Migration in or out of the area because of crowding (MDTC) subsequently is computed as

$$\text{MDTC.KL} = (4.00 - 5.00)(0.03)(5000) = -150$$

‡ Note that this equation probably would be unrealistic when the demand was less than the supply since CSDTD would be negative, i.e., housing units would be removed from the existing stock.

This figure is based on the theory that for every increase (decrease) of 1.0 in the crowding ratio, 3 percent of the population will want to move out (in) of the area. The first row of Table 11-4 shows the initial conditions and rate calculation results for 1960.

In the next round (1961) we compute both the levels and the rates, doing the relevant former ones first. Starting with the population equation:

$$\text{POP.KL} = 5000 + 1(250 - 50 - 150) = 5050$$

with DT = 1 year, since our calculations are being made every year. The birth and death rates subsequently are

$$\text{BR.KL} = 0.05(5050) = 253$$

and

$$\text{DR.KL} = -0.01(5050) = -51$$

Demand then is

$$\text{DEM.K} = \frac{5050}{4.00} = 1263$$

The remaining calculations for this round are

$$\text{SUP.K} = 1000 + 1(125) = 1125$$

$$\text{CSDTD.KL} = (1263 - 1125)0.5 = 69$$

$$\text{CR.K} = \frac{1263(4.00)}{1125} = 4.49$$

$$\text{MDTC.KL} = (4.00 - 4.49)(0.03)(5050) = -74$$

On the next round (1962), calculations again start with the population level:

$$\text{POP.K} = 5050 + 1(253 - 51 - 74) = 5178$$

and so the computational sequence continues to the end of 1964 (Table 11-4).

The remaining steps in the DYNAMO program involve the instruction statements found at the bottom of Table 11-3. The PRINT statement indicates the factors to be printed in tabular form. The result would be a matrix similar to that at the top of Table 11-4. The PLOT statement shows the variables to be plotted and the single-letter symbols utilized to represent them. The resultant plot, carried out for 14 years, is presented in Fig. 11-4. The time dimensions should be taken as the $x$ (abscissa) axis. The SPEC (or specification) statement indicates that the calculation time period (DT) is 1 year (i.e., one unit), the LENGTH of computation is 4 years, the printer period (PRTPER) is 1 (one line of computations is printed for each year), and the plotter period (PLTPER) also is 1 (one point for each year). Finally, the RUN statement indicates that the program is complete and should be carried out.

Some other options available in DYNAMO programming are displayed in Table 11-5.

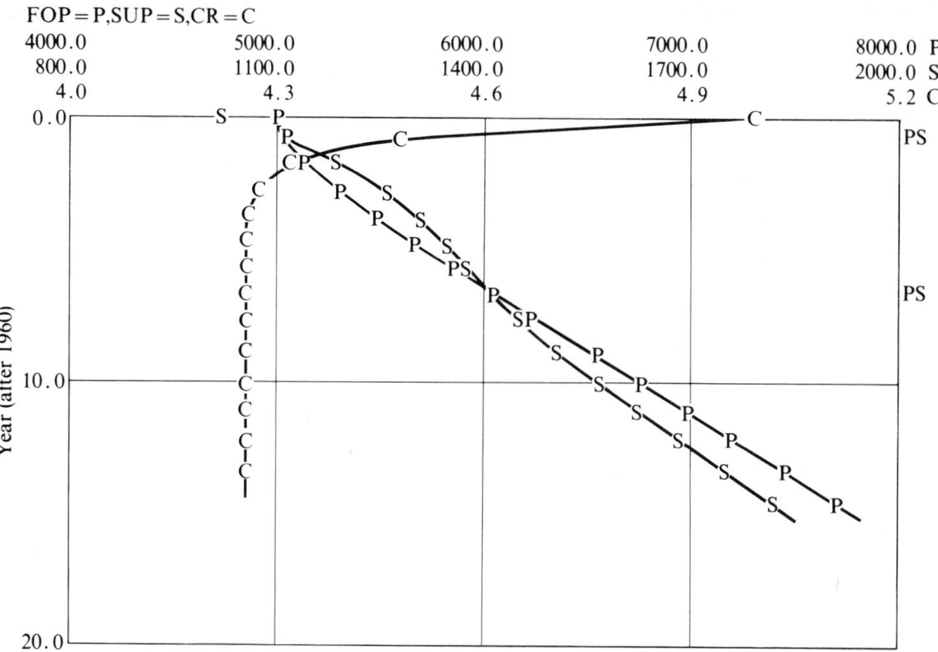


**Figure 11-4** DYNAMO plot of POP, SUP, and CR versus time (year) for time extended to 14 years (1974).

## Table 11-5 Some options available in DYNAMO

*Trigonometric functions*

| *Function* | *DYNAMO equivalent* |
|---|---|
| $e^A$ | EXP(A) |
| ln $(A)$ | LOGN(A) |
| $A^{1/2}$ | SQRT(A) |
| sin $(A)$ | SIN(A) |
| cos $(A)$ | COS(A) |
| $A^B$ | EXP(B*LOGN(A)) |

*RAMP function*

A Y.K = RAMP(SLP, STRT)

Y.K = 0 if TIME $\leq$ STRT

$$Y.K = \sum_{STRT}^{TIME} (SLP)(DT) \text{ if TIME} > \text{STRT}$$

If SLP and STRT are both constants, the graph of Y would be a ramp with slope SLP that starts at time STRT.

**Table 11-5 (continued)**

*SWITCH function*

A Y.K = SWITCH(P,Q,R)
Y.K = P if R = 0
Y.K = Q if R $\neq$ 0

*TABLE function*

A Y.K = TABLE(TAB, X.K,XLOW,XHIGH,XINCR)
T TAB = $n_1/n_2/n_3/\cdots$

TAB designates the values of Y.K for corresponding values of X.K
X.K = independent variable
XLOW = lowest value of range of independent variable recognized for Y
XHIGH = highest value of range of independent variable recognized for Y
XINCR = increment in independent variable

*Maximum and minimum functions*

A Y.K = MAX(P,Q)
Y.K = P if P $\geq$ Q
Y.K = Q if P < Q

A Y.K = MIN(P,Q)
Y.K = P if P < Q
Y.K = Q if P $\geq$ Q

*Clipping or limiting function*

A Y.K = CLIP(P,Q,X.K,S)
Y.K = P if X.K $\geq$ S
Y.K = Q if X.K < S

*Pulse function*

A Y.K = PULSE (HGHT,FRST,INTVL)
HGHT = pulse height (amount of "shock")
FRST = time of first pulse
INTVL = interval between pulses

*Delay function*

A Y.K = DELAY1 (P.K, DEL)
P.K = value of Y.K if there were no delay
DEL = magnitude of the delay (time)

For further information, see Forester (Ref. 11-1) or Pugh (Ref. 11-3).

## 11-5 SENSITIVITY ANALYSIS

One of the major advantages of any quantitative model is that it can be employed for sensitivity analyses. Alternations can be made in initial conditions or parameters from some base case and the resultant changes noted. The sensitivity then can be specified through an elasticity, $e$, which is the proportional change in one factor given a proportional change in another. These proportions are relative to the mean,† thus:

$$e = \frac{y_1 - y_2}{(y_1 + y_2)/2} \bigg/ \frac{x_1 - x_2}{(x_1 + x_2)/2} \tag{11-8}$$

or

$$\frac{(y_1 - y_2)(x_1 + x_2)}{(y_1 + y_2)(x_1 - x_2)} \tag{11-9}$$

where $y_1$ and $x_1$ are the initial values of the factors $x$ and $y$, respectively, and $y_2$ and $x_2$ are the corresponding new values.

The results of one sensitivity study on our example model are displayed at the bottom part of Table 11-4. In this case we have changed SRTDC from 0.5 to 0.1 and MRTCC from 0.03 to 0.01. In words, we have specified that builders can only build 10 percent (instead of 50 percent) of the housing units needed to meet the added demand (above the existing supply) and that only 1 percent (instead of 3 percent) of the people will move if the crowding ratio grows by 1.00. With lowered supply and fewer people moving out because of crowding, we thus would expect to find greater crowding. This is verified in the calculations in Table 11-4, where the crowding ratio actually is shown as creeping up, instead of declining, as was the case in the first run.

The elasticities show, however, that the crowding ratio is not very sensitive to either of the parameter changes. For the SRTDC parameter the elasticity is

$$e = \frac{(4.27 - 5.08)(0.5 + 0.1)}{(4.27 + 5.08)(0.5 - 0.1)} = -0.13$$

This result indicates that crowding decreases with SRTDC, but that the change is slight. The elasticity of CR with respect to MRTCC is a little more (−0.18), but is again low.‡

## PROBLEMS

**11-1** Fill in the blanks with the proper word(s) or number(s).

(*a*) The equation for the continuous positive feedback model is ________________.

(*b*) If the price of an item is increasing at 0.4 percent a year, its price will double in ________________ years.

(*c*) Conversely, if a population is doubling every 20 years, its growth rate constant is ________________.

† Defined as $(y_1 + y_2)/2$ and $(x_1 + x_2)/2$ (see Chap. 2). Note also that the elasticity can be unexpectedly large if the $x$ values are near 0.

‡ Theoretically these elasticities should be calculated holding *all* other influencing variables or parameters constant.

(*d*) is a computer language specifically designed for simulating complicated feedback systems.

(*e*) The five types of equations used in this computer language (denoted by N, C, L, A, and R)

are ____________, ____________, ____________, ____________,

and ____________.

(*f*) Let $y$ be a function of $x$. This means that a change in $x$ will bring a change in $y$. The proportional change in $y$ divided by the proportional change in $x$ is called the

____________.

**11-2** Compute by hand the levels of a population over a 4-year period. Assume population is changing through a simple positive feedback relationship. Let the initial population (at time = 0) equal 10,000.

(*a*) Let the growth-rate constant = 0.2. Compute the population levels three times, once each for DT = $\frac{1}{2}$, 1, and 2.

(*b*) Let the growth-rate constant = 0.3 and DT = 1.

(*c*) Let the growth-rate constant = 0.2, DT = 1, but the growth rate is based on the constant times the difference between the population size and an upper limit of 20,000 (a negative feedback).

**11-3** (*a*) The following data represent population levels of a region:

| | | | | | |
|---|---|---|---|---|---|
| 1950 | 82,300 | 1959 | 159,200 | 1968 | 330,800 |
| 1953 | 103,100 | 1962 | 203,000 | 1971 | 395,100 |
| 1956 | 128,600 | 1965 | 252,500 | 1974 | 496,800 |

Assuming this population to be growing exponentially (graph to check), what is the rate constant?

(*b*) The percentage of corn production in a progressive farm state that comes from a new strain of seed is shown for the years 1955–1963:

| | | | | | |
|---|---|---|---|---|---|
| 1955 | 10 | 1958 | 68 | 1961 | 90 |
| 1956 | 37 | 1959 | 77 | 1962 | 93 |
| 1957 | 56 | 1960 | 85 | 1963 | 95 |

Assuming the trend reflected in the data to be represented by an exponential equation for a negative feedback model, what is the equation?

**11-4** The number of middle-class people in the central city of a metropolitan area has been halving every 5 years. In 1950, they numbered 32,000. Draw a graph of this population from 1950 to 1975. When would it be 8000? What will the middle-class population be in 1895, assuming the past trend will continue in the future?

**11-5** The following is a basic pollution model:

> Pollution in a region is generated primarily by human activity in and near the region and is absorbed by the environment there. The pollution absorption rate depends upon the amount of pollution present in the environment at any given time. The more the pollution, the more its dissipation by the environment. If there were no pollution generated, the environment eventually would cleanse itself of all existing pollution. The pollution generation rate is exogenously determined and is constant.

Assume that pollution = 9 tons at time = 0, the time unit is 1 year, and the pollution generation rate is constant at 10 tons per year. In addition, assume that the environment takes 2 years to dissipate half of the pollution if there were no pollution generation. Design a DYNAMO program to simulate this situation and compute the pollution levels for 4 years with DT = 1.

**11-6** If a DYNAMO compiler is available, set DT = 0.25 and run the DYNAMO program from Prob. 11-5 for 10 years. Find:

(*a*) The pollution levels in each of the 10 years

(*b*) The dissipation rate at the end of each of the 10 years

(*c*) A plot of the pollution levels in (*a*)

**11-7** Suppose in the housing demand supply model (HDSM) in Table 11-3 that it is anticipated that the supply response due to demand constant (SRTDC) may decrease to 0.3 due to difficulties in getting materials and to increased governmental "red tape." For the year 1964, find:
(*a*) The resultant population, demand, and supply levels
(*b*) The elasticities of the factors in (*a*) with respect to SRTDC

*Note.* If you are using a DYNAMO compiler, you can rerun HDSM with SRTDC = 0.3 simply by typing in:

```
C SRTDC = 0.3
RUN
```

after the initial run of the program.

**11-8** In HDSM, use the CLIP, PULSE, and DELAY functions described in Table 11-5. For the CLIP function, suppose that if supply exceeds demand, SRTDC is 0.2 instead of 0.5 otherwise. For the PULSE function, suppose that in the year 1965 population in the study area jumps by 5000 people. Finally, for the DELAY function, suppose that builders delay 2 years (DEL) in supplying new housing. Given these three changes, run the HDSM for a 15-year period (using an available DYNAMO compiler with DT = 0.25) and determine:
(*a*) The yearly population, supply, and demand levels
(*b*) The same factors as in (*a*) with SRTDC = 0.0 and 0.5, respectively
(*c*) Your conclusions as to the ability of the system to absorb shocks

**11-9** Go to the library and find an application of systems dynamics (e.g., references below). For a given application describe in about 1000 words:
(*a*) The problem being studied
(*b*) The general model structure
(*c*) The results
(*d*) Your opinion of the validity of the conclusions based on the results
(*e*) The general advantages/disadvantages of systems dynamics in this study

**11-10** Working with your instructor, set up a systems dynamics model using the information in data set 1 in App. D. You might, for example, try to relate total personal income (TPI) to number of passenger cars registered (NPCR) and to value of mineral production (VOMP) and to relate NPCR in turn to TPI and population (POP).
Run the resultant model from 1960 to 1985, and determine:
(*a*) The "goodness of fit" to actual values in the 1960–1972 time period
(*b*) The predicted values of different variables in 1985
(*c*) Reasons why the predicted values may or may not be correct

## REFERENCES


### Theory

11-1. Forrester, J. W.: *Principles of Systems*, Wright-Allen Press, Cambridge, Mass., 1968.
11-2. Goodman, R.: *Study Notes in Systems Dynamics*, Wright-Allen Press, Cambridge, Mass., 1974.
11-3. Pugh, III, L.: *Dynamo II User's Manual*, 4th ed., The MIT Press, Cambridge, Mass., 1973.

### Applications

11-4. Benesh, F., P. Guldberg, and R. D'Agostino: *Growth Effects of Major Land Use Projects: Vol. I, Specification and Causal Analysis of the Model*, Report EPA-450/3-76-012-a, Contract no. 68-02-2076, U.S. Environmental Protection Agency, Research Triangle Park, N.C., 1976.
11-5. Forrester, J. W.: *World Dynamics*, 2d ed., Wright-Allen Press, Cambridge, Mass., 1973.

11-6. Levin, G., and E. B. Roberts: *The Dynamics of Human Service Delivery*, Ballinger, Cambridge, Mass., 1976.

11-7. Levin, G., E. B. Roberts, and G. B. Hirsch: *The Persistent Poppy, A Computer-Aided Search for Heroin Policy*, Ballinger, Cambridge, Mass., 1975.

11-8. Meadows, D. H., D. L. Meadows, J. Randers, and W. W. Behrens, III: *The Limits to Growth*, 2d ed., Universe Books, New York, 1974.

11-9. Meadows, D. L., et al.: *Dynamics of Growth in a Finite World*, Wright-Allen Press, Cambridge, Mass., 1974.

11-10. Steiss, A. W., J. W. Dickey, B. G. Phelps, and M. W. Harvey: *Dynamic Change and the Urban Ghetto*, D. C. Heath, Lexington, Mass., 1975.

CHAPTER

# TWELVE

# INDIVIDUAL AND COMMITTEE FORECASTING

The statistical procedures discussed in the preceding chapters can be very powerful tools in understanding and making forecasts from a series of recorded past events. Certainly an analyst would be amiss if he did not take advantage of these techniques when relevant, consistent, and accurate data were available. This is not always the case, however. As we deal with new and unique problems, we often find there are no data available, especially for any series of time periods. Even if relevant information can be found, definitions often have changed over time or differ from source to source. Further, the data may be highly subjective, measured very roughly, or simply based on a very small (and perhaps unspecified) sample, all of which would reflect on their accuracy.

The upshot of all these conditions, combined with the fact that data often are expensive and time-consuming to collect and analyze, is that greater use is made of the experience and intuition of experts or groups of experts in a particular field. In this chapter we will highlight a small number of the most basic intuitive means of forecasting, with later chapters devoted to more sophisticated intuition-aiding techniques.

## 12-1 THE INDIVIDUAL "EXPERT"

Perhaps there is nothing more ubiquitous than the "expert." Each of us might claim to be an expert in some field of endeavor (not necessarily scientific). The annals of history are filled with many expert forecasters, from Nostradamus to

Jules Verne, H. G. Wells, Aldous Huxley, George Orwell, Arthur Clarke, and Isaac Asimov. Governments at all levels call on experts to advise them on a wide spectrum of endeavors.

The expert certainly does not represent the antithesis of statistical techniques like those discussed earlier. He may in fact use many of these to aid in his advisory capacity. Still, it is his experience and intuition which differentiate him from the technician.

The beauty and bane of an expert, as any other human being, is his predilection to make forecasts (somewhat facetiously called "genius" forecasts) based on limited or nonexistent data. The beauty is the inexpensiveness and quickness. We do not have to pay for long, exhaustive studies. Nor do we have to wait years to gather data to resolve today's problems. The bane is the low (or zero) sample size, with its obvious problems of generality (see Chap. 5). To illustrate these points: H. G. Wells wrote *Anticipations* in 1902 (Ref. 12-18). He, like other forecasters, made both good and bad predictions. His worst concerned the airplane and the submarine. Regarding the former: "Aeronautics will never come into play as a serious modification of transport and communications" although "Very probably before 1950 a successful aeroplane will have soared and come back home safe and sound" (Ref. 12-18, p. 208). As to the latter, his "imagination refuses to see any sort of submarine doing anything but suffocating its crew and floundering at sea" (Ref. 12-18, p. 217). His forecasts with respect to land travel were somewhat better: he envisaged the advent of motor trucks and buses for heavy traffic transport and privately owned motor carriages with private (i.e., segregated) roads for high-speed motor travel.

Examples of present-day individual forecasts can be found in many books, journals, speeches, and the like. A great many of these have been collected and systematized under the title of Worldcasts® (Ref. 12-14), which are booklets which come out quarterly. Rosen also presents an interesting compilation of possible technological innovations and his forecasts concerning them in *Future Facts* (Ref. 12-15). Samples from his summary in the communications field include:

*Cooperative computer.* "Mr. Computer" is an audio-visual teaching machine developed by Borg-Warner. It has a console unit about 2 feet square, contains a record player, viewing screen, row of buttons, and memory bank. The student can insert a filmstrip and record on a selected topic. He or she hears a question and concurrently sees illustrations that represent possible answers to the questions. Rosen predicts that children will love it since it looks like a television and that its greatest use will be in remedial situations.

*SCAN (silent communication alarm systems).* SCAN is a pen-sized ultrasonic emergency alarm transmitter. It originally was developed for a racially troubled school in California and is now being used in homes for the elderly. Rosen sees them becoming commonplace within a few years, especially for hikers, skiers, and the like.

*Printed speech.* A sound spectrogram machine analyzes spoken words in terms of their timing, frequency, and energy. This analysis can be programmed for computers and thereby produce a printout of the spoken word. Such systems could be employed as automatic translators and could replace secretaries (as we presently know them).

*Three-dimensional television/movies.* In holography, laser beams can be split using mirrors and these divided rays utilized to take a "picture" of different aspects of an object. When recorded on film and "played back," a three-dimensional image will appear in a given space. Rosen sees "teleportation" (the dematerializing of a person, his transmittal across space and time, and his final rematerialization) as a result. It then is possible that future white-collar work can all be done from a distance, with a consequential reduction in need for our present central business districts.

While all of these innovations may or may not materialize, it obviously is difficult to use statistical means to predict such unique, discrete events. The genius forecast thus is much needed under these conditions.

## 12-2 COMMITTEES

Despite the oft-cited metaphor that "a camel is a horse created by a committee," such groups of experts often are extremely valuable in identifying solutions to a problem and/or making forecasts of future events. As is true of individual experts, committees are ubiquitous in almost all public-sector operations, particularly with the recent increase in concern for citizen involvement.

The strength of the committee lies in the accumulation of knowledge from the various members. Hence committee selection is an important factor in its success. Citizen committee structure many times is specified in law or executive regulation. In health planning, for example, the advisory committee must be composed of at least 51 percent *consumers* of health services, with the remainder being providers (e.g., physicians and hospital administrators). This structure is intended to give a majority voice to consumers.

The types of committee approach to urban and regional problem solving and/or forecasting are almost as numerous as the committees themselves. For example, Smith, Stuart, and Hansen (Ref. 12-17) list the following under their approaches to citizen involvement in highway planning and design:

Public meetings/hearings
Mail surveys
Transient field offices
Telephone surveys
Listening posts ("hot lines")
Electronic issue-ballot workshops
Small group meetings
Interviewing key people
Issue ballots in local newspapers
Politician review of news releases

Internal communication at public meetings
Participatory television programs
Nominal group technique
Working session retreats
"Design-ins"
Community seminars
Task forces
Citizen advisory committees
Delphi (Chap. 13)
Games, charettes (Chap. 15)
Brainstorming
"Fishbowl" planning
Third-party mediations
Referendums
Arbitrators

From these it can be seen, for instance, that the members do not necessarily have to interact with each other—nor do they even have to know each other's identity. A committee thus could be simply a sample of unrelated people. In this section we will be able to discuss only a small number of these techniques.

Perhaps one of the simplest and most common forms of committee utilization in a forecasting mode is through the second item on the above list: mail surveys. This approach usually is relatively inexpensive and, with sufficient follow-up, can generate an adequate sample of responses. The usual problem is, however, that since the respondents can decide whether or not to return their questionnaires, the sample almost never will conform to any particular sampling plan (e.g., random or systematic). It therefore is extremely difficult to generalize from the results.

Boucher, Gordon, and Lamson (Ref. 12-10) employed this technique to survey candidate technologies for future technology assessments. As noted in

**Table 12-1 Distribution of invitations and replies to technology assessment questionnaire**

| | Invited | | Responses tabulated | | |
|---|---|---|---|---|---|
| Area | Number | Percentage of total invited | Number | Percentage of total responding | Percentage of category invited |
| Academic | 343 | 53 | 71 | 47 | 21 |
| Industry | 127 | 20 | 37 | 24 | 29 |
| State and local government | 44 | 07 | 13 | 9 | 30 |
| Other | 134 | 20 | 31 | 20 | 23 |
| Total | 648 | 100 | 152 | 100 | 23 |

*Source:* Ref. 12-10, p. 2.

Table 12-1, they sent out 648 questionnaires to academic, industry, state and local government, and other personnel. These questionnaires listed candidate "technologies" (interpreted broadly) in biological, social, and physical areas and asked the respondents to estimate (1) the probability of widespread use by 1983 and (2) the relationships of total positive to total negative impacts. Only 152 of the 648 invited personnel responded, with the percentage in each category varying from 21 to 30 percent (last column of Table 12-1).

This "committee" composition was further confounded (from a statistical standpoint) by asking each respondent if he felt himself an expert on a particular technology. Tabulations then were made for both the full and the "expert" group. Moreover, since everyone did not answer every question, the size and composition of both groups varied for each response. The committee makeup thus differed throughout the survey, a characteristic which, while certainly not unusual for surveys, still should be recognized when trying to draw conclusions from such an effort.

A sample of results is presented in Table 12-2. Here we see the probability of widespread use by 1983 of the ten social "technologies" thought most probable and significant. These were selected from among 62 others in the social area. There were also 60 physical and 66 biological technologies presented to the respondents.

In most cases there was fairly close agreement among all respondents and the subgroup "experts." The all-volunteer armed forces "technology" (index 3.08), for instance, received the highest percentage from the experts under the "virtually certain" category (56.0 percent), matched closely by the 55.1 percent from the total group. This finding might imply that we do not really need an "expert" designation for committee members.

Some of the other conclusions reached by the authors on the basis of this study were:

1. Most of the technologies would have irreversible effects when they reached the level of "widespread use."
2. The technologies could be influenced before the above point was reached.
3. Every technology was seen as having discernable and important negative impacts, although most were outweighed by the positive ones.
4. The area of greatest uncertainty regarding particular technologies is frequently that in which they are supposed to have immediate application.

Again, these conclusions must be considered in the light of the committee composition described above.

Another approach† to committee problem solving and/or forecasting is the nominal group technique (NGT), devised by Delbecq and Van de Ven in 1968. It was developed from social-psychological studies of decision-making conferences, management-science investigation of aggregative group judgments, and social-work studies of problems surrounding citizen involvement in program planning.

† Some of the discussion here is adapted from Delbecq, Van de Ven, and Gustafson (Ref. 12-2).

## Table 12-2 Ten social "technologies" with highest probabilities of widespread use by 1983

| Rank within category | Index number | Candidate technology | Total number of respondents | Estimated probability of widespread use by 1983, % | | | | |
|---|---|---|---|---|---|---|---|---|
| | | | Size of "expert" subgroup | Virtually certain | Very likely | As likely as not | Not very likely | Virtually impossible |
| 1 | 3.17 | A cohesive national energy policy | 71<br>39 | 18.3<br>30.8 | 39.4<br>33.3 | 26.6<br>25.6 | 8.5<br>7.7 | 4.2<br>2.6 |
| 2 | 3.06 | A federal policy designed to achieve zero population growth | 69<br>33 | 4.3<br>9.1 | 20.3<br>24.2 | 15.9<br>21.2 | 46.4<br>45.5 | 13.0<br>0 |
| 3 | 3.02 | Public/private corporations to tackle social issues (e.g., Comsat, New York Urban Redevelopment Corporation) | 54<br>36 | 14.8<br>22.2 | 50.0<br>58.3 | 22.2<br>16.7 | 5.6<br>2.8 | 7.4<br>0 |
| 4 | 3.20 | Guaranteed minimum annual income | 68<br>31 | 8.8<br>9.7 | 41.2<br>41.0 | 35.3<br>29.0 | 11.8<br>16.1 | 2.9<br>3.2 |
| 5 | 3.18 | A cohesive national land-use policy | 70<br>30 | 5.7<br>10.0 | 20.0<br>20.0 | 34.3<br>33.3 | 30.0<br>23.3 | 10.0<br>13.3 |
| 6 | 3.44 | A federal comprehensive health-care plan | 69<br>19 | 13.0<br>26.3 | 46.4<br>52.6 | 27.5<br>21.1 | 13.1<br>0 | 0<br>0 |
| 7 | 3.27 | Automobiles banned from city cores in largest cities in the United States during certain weekday hours | 65<br>33 | 13.8<br>18.2 | 47.7<br>48.5 | 20.0<br>15.2 | 16.9<br>15.2 | 1.5<br>3.0 |
| 8 | 3.10 | Information support systems for most state legislatures, at least equivalent to today's federal system | 71<br>37 | 14.1<br>16.2 | 40.9<br>48.6 | 25.4<br>21.6 | 19.7<br>13.5 | 0<br>0 |
| 9 | 3.08 | All volunteer armed forces | 69<br>25 | 55.1<br>56.0 | 34.8<br>40.0 | 7.2<br>0 | 2.0<br>4.0 | 0<br>0 |
| 10 | 3.36 | Use taxes as an antipollution strategy (e.g., on atmospheric pollution, roads, etc.) | 64<br>26 | 15.6<br>15.4 | 45.3<br>53.8 | 25.0<br>23.1 | 14.1<br>7.7 | 0<br>0 |

*Source:* Ref. 12-10, p. 39.

NGT is a structured committee meeting which proceeds along the following format: imagine a meeting room in which a small number (7 to 10) of individuals is sitting around a table in full view of each other. At the beginning of the meeting they do not speak to each other. Instead each person is writing ideas on a pad of paper in front of him. At the end of 5 to 10 minutes, a structured sharing of ideas takes place. Each person, in round-robin fashion, presents one idea from his or her private list. A recorder writes each idea on a flip chart in full view of other members. There still is no discussion at this point—only the recording of privately narrated ideas. Round-robin listing continues until all members have indicated they have no further ideas to share.

The output of this nominal phase of the meeting is a list of propositional statements usually numbering from 18 to 25. Discussion follows during the next phase of the meeting. This is structured so that each idea receives attention before independent voting. Such is accomplished by asking for clarification, or stating support or nonsupport, for each idea listed on the flip chart. Independent voting subsequently takes place. Each member privately and in writing selects priorities by rank ordering (or rating). The group decision is the mathematically pooled outcome of all individual votes.

The NGT was employed for problem identification and priority setting in Maple Grove, a rural township about 15 miles from Green Bay, Wisconsin (Ref. 12-16).† Community leaders there were concerned about the loss of their local economic base (farming), the potential costs of provision of services to scattered residences, and the health hazards from inadequate residential septic tanks.

An outline of the NGT employed in this situation is presented in Table 12-3. The citizens of Maple Grove were notified of the pending meeting through personal contact and postcard. At the beginning of the meeting, attended by 60 people, they were told that the purpose was to solicit citizen ideas about problems, goals, and objectives but that no attempt would be made to arrive at solutions.

Thereafter each participant was given a sheet of paper or card with the questions to be addressed. These were:

1. In your opinion, what are the development problems requiring attention over the next few years?
2. What suggestions do you have to plan for the future of the township?
3. What should your township look like in 20 years?

The attendees were then divided into subgroups of 6 to 10 people each. Subgroup members were instructed to work individually and silently to compile a key word list of problems facing the community. The participants finishing early were encouraged to review their list for other possibilities.

After each person was given adequate time (20 minutes) to compile his or her

† Much of the discussion here is adapted from Sheffer (Ref. 12-16).

**Table 12-3 Outline of the NGT program planning model for Maple Grove**

I. Notification of client group or citizens
   (Divided according to age, geography, technical application or other appropriate categories)

II. Meeting with citizens to explore problem dimensions
   A. Introduction (10 minutes)
      1. Welcome
      2. Expression of organization(s) interest in citizen's problems
      3. Indication that focus is on problems, not solutions
   B. Directions for small group participation
      1. Assign citizens to small groups of 6 to 9
      2. Instruct them in nominal group format
         *a.* Listing problems on a sheet of paper (20 minutes)
      3. Provide flip chart and recorder for round-robin sharing of individually noted items
         *a.* Items from individual cards
         *b.* New items suggested by process
   C. Fifteen-minute break
   D. Interacting group discussion of items on flip chart for clarification
   E. Nominal group voting on 3 × 5-inch cards for top five priority items
   F. General session discussion of tabulated votes from each small group

*Source:* Ref. 12-16, p. 212.

list of problems, a "recorder" joined each subgroup and asked every individual, in round-robin fashion, for one of his or her statements of community problems. The recorder wrote each citizen's statement verbatim on a flip chart. Debate, rewording, or combining of items was not allowed. The purpose of this phase of the process was to obtain as many ideas as possible listed without the immediate need to provide a defense.

This phase continued until each member in the subgroup had the opportunity to list all his or her concerns. After this tabulation was finished, participants were allowed to mingle (over coffee) and discuss among themselves the issues raised in the various subgroups.

The subgroups then were reformed and clarification of the listed issues was allowed. Throughout, the recorder attempted to minimize "personalities" entering the discussion and keep the focus on issues.

After 10 to 20 minutes for clarification, the participants were asked to vote silently and privately on the five most-important issues before their subgroup. Weights were allocated to the problems listed. The most important was given a weight of 5, the second, 4, etc. The votes were collected, and a tally made for that subgroup. After each had compiled its priorities, the information was reported to the main committee. Following a brief discussion of the results, the town board thanked the attendees for their assistance and indicated it would review their concerns in helping set town policies. No statement of proposed solutions was made at this point, to prevent false expectations of potential courses of action.

The results of this application of the NGT can be found in Table 12-4. Highway improvement, land use, highway safety, water drainage, and rural beautification were the five categories of problems enumerated. The specific items mentioned in these categories highlighted citizen concern for action on problems

**Table 12-4 Community problems as identified by 60 Maple Grove citizens,† through the nominal group technique**

| Problems | Points |
|---|---|
| Highway improvement | |
| General road improvement. Clear brush from ditches and road fence lines. Widen roads. | 197 |
| Land use | |
| Control of urban sprawl. Preserve prime agricultural land. Tax assessed on land use. Designate residential. Develop overall land-use plan. | 168 |
| Highway safety | |
| Sanding of all intersections. Remove bridge wing abutments. Provide visual clearance triangle at all intersections. Improved snow plowing programs. | 115 |
| Water drainage | |
| Promote change of obsolete drainage laws so as to improve agricultural land. | 64 |
| Rural beautification | |
| Clean up junkyards. Promote program of cleanup of home and farm junkyards. | 52 |
| General | |
| Provide numbering system for all homes and farms (fire protection). | 38 |
| Control and prohibit dumping of whey. | 16 |
| Name all town roads. | 16 |
| Town solid waste facilities should be open at more convenient hours. | 10 |
| Restore power and control to local government. | 9 |
| Develop a plan for police protection. | 9 |
| Provide stricter control, supervision, and inspection of private sewage system. | 8 |
| Study and consider possibilities of increasing tax base with industrial development. | 7 |
| Develop and coordinate road plan and zoning with new relocation of Highway 29. | 6 |
| Encourage and promote youth to farm in area. | 6 |
| Build new town hall or improve existing hall. | 5 |
| Allow mobile homes only on limited temporary basis. | 4 |
| Provide sewage and water facilities in high density area. | 3 |
| Plumbing and electrical code inspection (county building code only covers construction). | 2 |
| Control size of driveway culverts to improve drainage. | 1 |
| Prohibit burning of trash on roadways. Provide alternate disposal system. | 1 |

*Source:* Ref. 12-16, p. 213.

† A low number does not necessarily indicate the lack of interest or lack of importance of a problem. Groups were asked to select the five problems they thought were most important and to rate them on a 5 to 1 scale.

of immediate interest. For example, the highway-improvement category included problems with narrow roads and roadside maintenance. The problem of blind intersections appeared under highway safety.

There also was a high degree of concern about land use, urban sprawl, and the protection of agricultural land. Although most citizens were somewhat unsure of how to cope with these problems, their awareness showed they had given them some thought.

Some of the longer-term impacts of this meeting appeared to be:

1. Immediate actions by the town board to correct some of the more visible problems such as the blind highway intersections and narrow bridges.
2. A land-use plan developed by the local planning commission with the aid of informal citizen input. Resultant reactions generally were very favorable.
3. A major amendment incorporated in the county zoning ordinance making the construction of nonfarm residences in an agricultural zone a conditional rather than a permitted use.

Delbecq, Van de Ven, and Gustafson (Ref. 12-2, p. 19) describe NGT and other group processes by means of nine characteristics:

1. *Overall methodology.* The overall structure of the decision-making process (e.g., if members are present together, they are allowed to converse in an unstructured way, etc.).
2. *Role orientation.* The tendency for committees to direct attention toward social roles (e.g., friendship acts or congeniality) or task-oriented roles (e.g., giving ideas or judgment sharing).
3. *Search behavior.* The style used by a committee to generate task-relevant information, and the amount of effort directed to identifying problems.
4. *Normative behavior.* The felt freedom to express ideas in discussions, and the level of conforming behavior in the process.
5. *Equality of participation.* The number of individuals in the committee who contribute to search, evaluation, and choice of the product or output.
6. *Committee composition and size.* The homogeneity or heterogeneity of personnel as well as the number of individuals involved in the committee decision-making process.
7. *Method of conflict resolution.* The procedure used to resolve disagreements and conflicts.
8. *Closure to decision process.* The extent to which the committee arrives at a clear termination point, providing an agreed-upon decision and a sense of accomplishment.
9. *Utilization of resources.* The time, cost, and effort involved for administrators and participants in the process.

These characteristics can be used for comparative purposes, as demonstrated in Table 12-5. There the previously described survey and the NGT are contrasted

**Table 12-5 Comparison of traditional, survey, and NGT committees**

| Dimension | Traditional | Survey | NGT |
|---|---|---|---|
| 1. Overall methodology | Unstructured meeting | Mailed questionnaire | Structured meeting |
| 2. Role orientation | Social-emotional | Task-instrumental | Social-emotional and task-instrumental |
| 3. Search behavior | Relative-short problem focus; task avoidance tendency; new social knowledge | Varied problem focus and avoidance tendency; new task knowledge | Proactive; extended problem focus; high task-centeredness; new social and task knowledge |
| 4. Conforming behavior | High | Very low | Low |
| 5. Equality of participation | Member dominance | Member equality | Member equality |
| 6. Committee size and composition | Small, varied | Large, varied | Small, varied |
| 7. Methods of conflict resolution | Person-centered; smoothing over and withdrawal | Problem-centered; majority rule | Problem-centered; information and problem solving |
| 8. Closure to decisions | Lack of closure; low felt accomplishment | High closure; very low felt accomplishment | High closure; high felt accomplishment |
| 9. Utilization of resources | Low | Low to medium | Low |
| 10. Relative quantity of ideas | Low; focused out effect | High; independent thinking | High; independent thinking |
| 11. Relative quality and specificity of ideas | Low quality; generalization | Varied | High quality; specificity |

Adapted to some extent from Ref. 12-2, p. 32.

with the traditional committee approach to problem solving and forecasting. For example, the traditional approach usually creates a social-emotional setting for each member that can be detrimental if he is hesitant to state his views. The survey approach, however, is strictly instrumented to the task at hand, which may also be detrimental if there is no opportunity for committee interaction for the mutual buildup of ideas. NGT seeks to reach a median between these extremes.

Some of the other major differences between the NGT and the survey and traditional techniques are in search behavior, method of conflict resolution, and closure to decisions. In the NGT it is possible to have proactive, extended problem (or solution) focus so that relatively large amounts of committee time can be directed to the important points. The NGT also allows for useful confrontation in the problem-solving process. Finally, it leads to a relatively high probability of closure to a decision, with high felt levels of accomplishment on the part of committee members. The survey approach is noted by the large number of people who can be incorporated into the "committee" and the very low (if any) conformity on the part of the members (because they would meet only inadvertently). The traditional committee suffers by comparison on most of these dimensions.

## PROBLEMS

**12-1** Fill in the blanks with the appropriate word(s).

(*a*) Predictions by experts are often called ________________ forecasts.

(*b*) NGT stands for ________________________.

(*c*) Nine characteristics useful in assessing different individual or committee forecasting procedures are ________________________.

**12-2** Which of the following items are likely to require expert judgment to determine, and which would be better obtained by some objective means?

(*a*) The likelihood of the Supreme Court declaring the property tax as unconstitutional for financing local schools

(*b*) The probability of a new automotive air-pollution control device, as compared with the device it will replace

(*c*) The likelihood of completely artificial human reproduction being rejected on moral or ethical grounds

(*d*) The willingness of the public to accept a specific alternative to the automobile for personal transportation

(*e*) The federal government's probable response to a new technological advance in lighter-than-air vehicles (e.g., "blimps")

**12-3** You are an official of a private health agency which in the past has supplied funds for a great deal of medical research on a particular class of diseases. Cures or satisfactory preventives for these diseases are expected to be available within the next few years. You need to determine the avenues of medical research to which your organization should shift its support. What kind of committee (or committees) would you select to provide forecasts useful in this situation?

**12-4** The English have had many years' experience with land-value increment taxes (where each year's *increment* in land value over the previous year is taxed rather than the total value). In particular, there is one man there who is thought to be the world's expert on the subject. You want to obtain a forecast of the likelihood, type, and magnitude of such a tax in the metropolitan area for which you are the executive director of the planning commission. Considering the expense of bringing this man here, is it worth it to supplement his judgment by organizing a committee, with him as a member, to prepare the forecast? If "yes," what characteristics would you look for in selecting the other members of the committee?

**12-5** Working with a group of five to seven people, use the NGT to forecast the 1990 population of the locality in which you live.

**12-6** Working with a different group of five to seven people, spend 30 minutes as a traditional committee forecasting the 1990 population of the locality in which you live.
What differences in forecast result, compared to that in Prob. 12-5? To what group dynamic characteristics suggested in Table 12-5 do you attribute this difference?

**12-7** Go to the library and find a book or article in which a mail survey was employed to make a forecast. In about 500 words describe the application, results, and advantages and disadvantages of the approach vis-à-vis that which might be obtained if a traditional committee or NGT were employed.

# REFERENCES


**Theory**

12-1. Cartwright, D., and A. Zander: *Group Dynamics*, 3d ed., Harper and Row, New York, 1968.
12-2. Delbecq, A. L., A. H. Van de Ven, and D. H. Gustafson: *Group Techniques for Program Planning*, Scott, Foresman, and Company, Glenview, Ill., 1975.
12-3. Filley, C.: *Interpersonal Conflict Resolution*, Scott, Foresman, and Company, Glenview, Ill., 1975.
12-4. Harrisberger, L.: *Engineersmanship: A Philosophy of Design*, Brooks/Cole, Belmont, Calif., 1966.
12-5. Martino, J. P.: *Technological Forecasting for Decisionmaking*, American-Elsevier, New York, 1972.
12-6. Massachusetts Institute of Technology, *New Technology for Citizen Involvement*, Report to the Massachusetts Department of Education, Cambridge, Mass., 1974.
12-7. Osborn, A. F.: *Applied Imagination*, Charles Scribner's Sons, New York, 1963.
12-8. Wells, H. A.: *Efficient Use of Groups in the Planning Process*, Unpublished Doctoral Dissertation, Ohio State University, Columbus, Ohio, 1968.

**Applications**

12-9. Ayres, R. U.: *Technological Forecasting and Long Range Planning*, McGraw-Hill, New York, 1969.
12-10. Boucher, W. I., T. J. Gordon, and J. E. Lamson: *Candidates and Priorities for Technology Assessment*, vol. 5, The Futures Group, Glastonbury, Conn., April, 1973.
12-11. Kahn, H., and A. Wiener: *Toward the Year 2000*, Macmillan, New York, 1967.
12-12. King-Hele, D.: *The End of the Twentieth Century?*, St. Martin's Press, New York, 1970.
12-13. Orwell, G.: *1984*, Harcourt, Brace, and World, New York, 1949.
12-14. Predicasts, Inc.: *Worldcasts* ®, Cleveland, Ohio (published quarterly).
12-15. Rosen, S.: *Future Facts*, Simon and Schuster, New York, 1976.
12-16. Sheffer, R. E.: "Citizen Involvement in Land Use Planning: A Tool and an Example," *Journal of Soil and Water Conservation*, September/October, 1975.
12-17. Smith, D. C., R. C. Stuart, and R. Hansen: *Community Involvement in Highway Planning and Design*, Center for Urban and Regional Studies, Virginia Polytechnic Institute and State University, Blacksburg, Va., May, 1975.
12-18. Wells, H. G.: *Anticipations*, Harper and Brothers, New York, 1902.

CHAPTER

# THIRTEEN

# DELPHI

While there are many advantages to using individual experts or groups of experts as consultants in analyzing certain problems and/or making forecasts in a particular area, there are also many disadvantages. A committee often can bring together a wide spectrum of information, but this may turn out to be misinformation. A committee often can get close agreement on future directions, but this may turn out to result from the exertions of strong social pressure on its members to conform with the majority's viewpoints. Reaching an agreement frequently becomes more important than producing a well-thought-out and useful forecast. Sometimes it is the number of comments and arguments for or against a certain position, rather than their validity, which results in a particular forecast being made. Vocal, dominant individuals, not to mention those with vested interests, thus tend to have an undue influence on decisions.

Until recently it was necessary to accept the disadvantages of the individual or committee approach to obtain its advantages. However, a procedure known as Delphi, originally developed by Helmer, Reschner, Gordon, Dalkey, and others (Refs. 13-2 to 13-4) at the Rand Corporation, now makes it possible to obtain many of the advantages of groups while eliminating most of the disadvantages.

## 13-1 A BASIC DESCRIPTION AND EXAMPLE†

The title "Delphi" comes from the ancient Greek Oracle at Delphi, which gave out forecasts based on the analysis of bird entrails and other such devices. The

† Part of the discussion here has been adapted from Martino (Ref. 13-6).

forecasts, however, were such that they could be interpreted in several different, and even contradictory, ways. The founders of the Delphi method at the Rand Corporation obviously had not intended to give all the resultant connotations to their technique, meaning it to be strictly a clever name for a forecasting technique. In any case, the Delphi procedure is characterized by three features which distinguish it from the usual methods of committee interaction. These are: (1) anonymity, (2) iteration with controlled feedback, and (3) statistical response.

1. *Anonymity.* During a Delphi sequence the committee members are not made known to each other. The interaction is handled in a completely anonymous way through the use of questionnaires. This avoids the possibility of identifying a specific opinion with a particular person. The originator of an opinion therefore can change his mind without publicly admitting he has done so (and thereby possibly losing face). It also means that an idea can be considered on its merits, regardless of whether the originator is held in high or low esteem by the other members of the committee.
2. *Iteration with controlled feedback.* The committee interaction is carried out through responses to questionnaires. The individual or agency in charge of the sequence extracts from the questionnaires only those pieces of information relevant to the issue and presents them to the committee. The individual committee member thus is informed only of the current status of the collective opinion of the committee and the arguments for and against each point of view. He is not subjected to harangue or endless restatement of the same old arguments. Both the majority and minority can present their views to the committee, but not in such a way as to overwhelm the opposition simply by weight of repetition. The main effect of this controlled feedback is to prevent the committee from making goals and objectives on its own. It can concentrate on its original purpose without being distracted by self-serving goals such as winning an argument or reaching agreement for its own sake.
3. *Statistical response.* Typically, a committee would produce a forecast containing only a majority viewpoint. It will represent simply that on which most of the committee were able to agree. There could be a minority report if the remainder of the committee felt strongly about the issue. Yet there is unlikely to be any indication of the degree of difference of opinion which may have existed within the committee. The Delphi procedure presents, instead, a statistical response which includes everyone's opinions. On a single question, for instance, the response may be presented in terms either of a median and two quartiles or a mean and a standard deviation. In this way each opinion within the committee is taken into account in the median or mean, and the spread of opinion is shown by the size of the interquartile range (IQR) or standard deviation(s).

In a Delphi sequence each successive submission of a questionnaire is referred to as a "round." The term "questionnaire" is somewhat misleading since it not only has questions but also provides information to the committee members about the degree of consensus, and the arguments presented by the members. The committees of experts used for Delphi sequences are frequently referred to as "panels." There is no commonly accepted, satisfactory term for the person or group collecting the panel responses and preparing the questionnaires. In what follows we will refer to him or her as the "director."

As an example of the Delphi process, we will consider the hypothetical case of a developer wanting to build a $30 million "theme" (amusement) park halfway between San Francisco and Sacramento, 90 miles (155 km) east. In this case the "theme" is "Chinese–American culture," as demonstrated by the biggest attraction in which 3 or 4 people ride downhill together in a fortune-cookie roller coaster and splash into a big tureen of egg-drop soup. The question of concern to the local county government is that of the annual property tax revenues expected to come to the county, and, more specifically, if these are enough to cover the costs of public services needed to support the park.† The elected officials thus have decided to assemble a panel of eight experts for a Delphi exercise to estimate the annual tax revenue 10 years hence. The local planner is made the "director." The exercise proceeds through four rounds as follows:

**Round 1** The first questionnaire is completely unstructured and open-ended. It asks the panelists to make a forecast of revenue and any related events, given preliminary information such as that above about the park and its environs. After the panelists' forecasts are returned to the director, they must be consolidated into a single set. Some panelists may have given their forecast in narrative or scenario form. These must be broken into a set of discrete events. Others may have given a list of events, perhaps arranged chronologically. In any case, the events must be identified, similar events combined, unimportant (for the purposes of the director) events eliminated, and the final list prepared in as precise terms as possible. This list of events then becomes the questionnaire for the second round. The types of events that may evolve in round 1 for the theme park example are displayed in Table 13-1. As can be seen they represent a broad variety of factors, few of which could be considered in any sort of statistical model. The panel is thus serving its main purpose of identifying events that could have a significant effect on revenues. If this process were undertaken without anonymity, it might not have been politically, economically, or socially acceptable to talk about, say, earthquakes or shortages of motels.

**Round 2** The panelists are presented with the combined list of events or factors, as in Table 13-1, and asked to estimate the levels of each in 1985. They are also asked to give reasons why they believe their estimates are correct, i.e., why the levels should not be higher or lower.

After the panelists' forecasts are returned to the director, a statistical summary of the estimates must be prepared, also mentioning the arguments and reasons for

† Note that since there have been no "Chinese" theme parks before (to our knowledge), there are no specific statistical data to use in, say, a regression analysis of costs versus size of "Chinese" theme parks.

**Table 13-1 Hypothetical results from theme park Delphi exercises**

*Round 1 events (and measures)*

$E_1$ = property tax revenue generation in 1985 ($ millions)
$E_2$ = Chinese–American bicentennial brings added interest and visitors (percentage of expected 1985 level)
$E_3$ = California hit by earthquake, which damages park (which is uninsured) and reduces visitors (percentage of expected 1985 level)
$E_4$ = shortage of yearly motel space reduces visitors (percentage of expected 1985 level)

*Round 2 panel forecasts*

| | Panelist | | | | | | | | Statistics | | | |
|---|---|---|---|---|---|---|---|---|---|---|---|---|
| Event | 1 | 2 | 3 | 4 | 5 | 6 | 7 | 8 | MD | $X$ | IQR | $S$ |
| $E_1$, $ million | 5 | 1 | 7 | 6 | 4 | 12 | 10 | 6 | 6 | 6.4 | 4.5–8.5 | 3.4 |
| $E_2$, % | +5 | 0 | 0 | +3 | +1 | +10 | +12 | +5 | 4 | 4.5 | 0.5–7.5 | 4.5 |
| $E_3$, % | −8 | −15 | −2 | −5 | −1 | 0 | +7 | −6 | −3.5 | −3.8 | −7.0–0.5 | 6.5 |
| $E_4$, % | −5 | −20 | −4 | −6 | −15 | −2 | 0 | −10 | −5.5 | −7.8 | −12.5– −3.0 | 6.8 |

*Round 3 and 4 forecasts*

| | | Panelist | | | | | | | | Statistics | | | |
|---|---|---|---|---|---|---|---|---|---|---|---|---|---|
| Round | Event | 1 | 2 | 3 | 4 | 5 | 6 | 7 | 8 | MD | $\bar{X}$ | IQR | $S$ |
| 3 | $E_1$, $ million | 5 | 3 | 7 | 6 | 4 | 8 | 10 | 6 | 6 | 6.1 | 4.5–7.5 | 2.2 |
| 4 | $E_1$, $ million | 5 | 4 | 6 | 7 | 4 | 6 | 10 | 6 | 6 | 6.0 | 4.5–6.5 | 1.9 |

feeling a given event will be of a certain magnitude. The third questionnaire then will consist of the list of events, the panel median and the upper and lower quartile estimates for each event, and the summaries of reasons for the estimates.

The hypothetical forecasts for each of the panel members in round 2 are displayed in the middle of Table 13-1. There we see that the median (MD) and mean ($\bar{X}$) are both near $6 million for the property tax revenue generation. The corresponding interquartile range (IQR) (25 percent on either side of the median) is from $4.5 to $8.5 million, with an associated standard deviation of $3.4 million.

Illustrations of comments which may result from this round are:

Panelist 2 on $E_1$: While there are a lot of Chinese in the San Francisco Bay area, there are not enough nationwide to create a big "draw."

Panelist 6 on $E_1$: Everyone is becoming richer and looking for interesting ways to spend his increased recreational dollars.

Panelist 2 on $E_3$: Severe earthquakes are predicted by the U.S. Geological Survey for California. The park may end up in the ocean.

Panelist 7 on $E_3$: If the earthquake damages the park, the developers will preserve part of that area and call it the "egg foo yung" exhibit.

These comments serve to highlight the extreme positions taken by the panelists, which might influence round 3 and 4 estimates made by the other members.

**Round 3** The panelists are presented with the events or factors, statistical description of panel estimates, and summaries of arguments. They are asked to set a new estimate of the expected level of each factor in 1985. If their estimate falls outside the IQR of the estimates given in round 3 (i.e., more than the upper-middle quartile or less than the lower-middle quartile), they are asked to give reasons to justify their views and to comment upon those in the opposite extreme. Their arguments may include reference to outside factors the other panelists may be neglecting, citing of facts which the others may not be considering, etc.

After the panelists' revised estimates and new arguments are returned to the director, the work is similar to that in the previous round. The director must summarize the results, computing new medians, quartiles, standard deviations, or whatever. The reasons presented on both sides must also be summarized. These are then compiled into a new forecast.

The results of the example round 3, again in Table 13-1,† show that most of the extreme estimates of the property tax revenue generation have been tempered to be closer to the median. This is demonstrated by the smaller IQR (4.5 to 7.5 versus 4.5 to 8.5) and the lower standard deviation (2.2 versus 3.4). Panelist 7, however, is still holding his ground firmly. When questioned about this, he replied that the earthquake probably will not do much, if any, damage because the park is some distance from the fault line. Moreover, he has confidence in local entrepreneurs to overcome quickly any potential motal space shortage. Hence, revenues will be higher than everyone else on the panel expects.

**Round 4** The panelists are again given the list of events, statistical description of the estimates, and arguments on either side. They are to take these into account in the process of making a new forecast. They may or may not be asked to provide new arguments, depending on the needs and desires of the director.

After receiving the forecasts, the director again computes median and quartile levels for each event or factor. Since this is the final round, there probably will be no need to analyze the arguments presented. In some situations, where the panel has not been able to come to any consensus, the director might be interested in the arguments on both sides (because they may have to be presented to his or her own superior, along with the forecast). Therefore the director might ask for reasons and be prepared to analyze them. The final forecast will consist of the list of events, with the associated median, IQR, and other relevant statistics.

As can be seen in the table, the round 4 estimates for our example are not that much different from the previous ones. Panelist 7's comments apparently have swayed panelists 2 and 4 to raise their forecast levels, but the median remains the same as panelists 3 and 6 lower their estimates. The range and standard deviations are reduced slightly, but not enough to warrant another round. The director (local planner) subsequently presents the median forecast of $6 million to the elected officials, telling them that the IQR of the estimates was from $4.5 to $6.5 million.

† For simplicity, only the estimates of $E_1$ are presented for rounds 3 and 4.

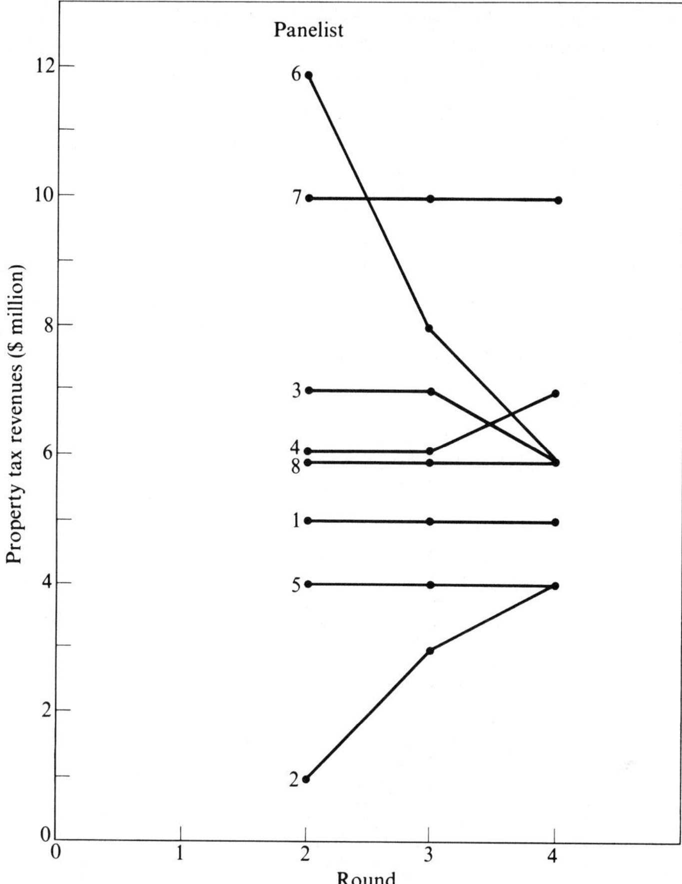


**Figure 13-1** Trace of panelist property tax revenue estimates through each round.

He may also present them with a chart, as in Fig. 13-1, that portrays the round-by-round forecasts graphically.

## 13-2 AN EXAMPLE APPLICATION†

As might have been suspected from the preceding description, the Delphi technique lends itself to a wide variety of applications and adaptations. This is exemplified by the study of Thompson (Ref. 13-14), to be presented in this section. He undertook a pilot study in New York City on the potential use of Delphi for investigation of drug-abuse prevention programs. As a first adaptation, he

† Some of the discussion in this section is adopted from Thompson (Ref. 13-14).

collapsed the procedure to two rounds by providing the list of events beforehand to the panelists so they could proceed directly to two rounds of forecasting. In his second adaptation, he asked the panelists to give a "confidence rating" to their expertise on each question. This was to be on a scale from 0 ("this is a sheer guess") to 3 ("I would be prepared to defend this opinion before a professional audience"). Thompson then weighted the resulting "vote" of each panelist by the 0, 1, 2 or 3 rating, respectively† By doing this he was able to give more credence to the estimates supplied by panelists with such a wide variety of backgrounds and experience (as applied to the wide variety of questions).

The original questionnaire had three parts, only the first two of which will be discussed here. All parts were administered to 19 professionals and nonprofessionals interested in urban problems in New York City (but not directly involved in studies of drug abuse). Eleven of these were professionals, 10 were female, and about 80 percent were between the ages of 23 and 35.

The author found it convenient to distinguish between items essentially descriptive (questions, for example, pertaining to the mechanism through which an individual becomes a drug user) and those primarily evaluative (such as items involving the relative merits of alternative drug-prevention programs). Descriptive questions, in turn, were decomposed into two subcategories: those for which the information sought was inherently numerical ("how many heroin addicts are there in Bedford-Stuyvesant") and those for which it was not. Part I of the questionnaire contained descriptive and nonnumerical multiple-choice items, part II contained those that were "evaluative," and part III contained the descriptive, numerical items.

The question in part I selected for analysis here is shown in Table 13-2, along with the resulting responses, both statistical and verbal, in each round. Each panelist was asked to fill in the blank with one of the four indicated responses. As it turned out, 21 percent of the panelists chose the answers "much less difficult" (response 1), 47 percent "somewhat less difficult" (response 2), and so on. The median for this round was 2.11, with the middle 50 percent falling between 1.58 and 2.71—an interquartile range (IQR) of $2.71 - 1.58 = 1.13$. Verbal feedback from the round was divided into supportive and nonsupportive statements (bottom of Table 13-2), which were presented to all panelists on the second-round questionnaire.

The results in this part of the study show the expected response in a Delphi exercise: the IQR dropped from 1.13 to 0.58 between rounds 1 and 2. An interesting additional finding is that the median confidence rating increased from 1.00 to 1.43 at the end of round 2. This probably is due to the information the panelists received in the verbal feedback from round 1. On the other hand, it is difficult to imagine such an apparent large change coming from the relatively few statistics and opinions emanating from that round.

Part II consisted of evaluative items in the form of "policy objectives" for which respondents were asked to furnish two ratings. The "desirability" rating,

† See Chap. 20, Sec. 20-2 (method 6), for further elaboration of this type of weighting technique.

**Table 13-2 Selected question and responses from part I of the Thompson Delphi exercise**

1-7 [Economic background]
Heroin addicts from middle to high income backgrounds tend to be ______________ to treat in therapy programs than addicts from ghetto areas.

| | | Percentage of respondents | |
|---|---|---|---|
| Number | Response | Round 1† | Round 2 |
| 1 | Much less difficult | 21 | 7‡ |
| 2 | Somewhat less difficult | 47 | 85 |
| 3 | Somewhat more difficult | 32 | 7 |
| 4 | Much more difficult | 0 | 0 |

| | Quartiles of responses† | | | |
|---|---|---|---|---|
| | Low | Medium | High | IQR |
| Round 1 | 1.58 | 2.11 | 2.71 | 1.13 |
| Round 2 | 1.71 | 2.00 | 2.29 | 0.58 |

Median confidence rating:
Round 1 = 1.00
Round 2 = 1.43

*Verbal feedback*

—The notion of therapy is less alien to youngsters from higher economic backgrounds.

—Higher income individuals have more opportunity and hence more motivation than lower income people.

—Lower income individuals have a relatively negative attitude toward health in general.

—Ghetto residents are easier to get through to than higher income people because they are more familiar with addiction and its effects.

—Heroin use on the part of higher income youngsters is apt to be symptomatic of more serious psychic problems.

—Higher income youngsters know exactly what they're doing when they go in for drug use; they are therefore less motivated to kick the habit.

*Source:* Ref. 13-14, p. 31.
† Adjusted to reflect confidence ratings.
‡ Percentages may not add due to rounding.

**Table 13-3 Selected question and responses from part II of the Thompson Delphi exercise**

2-7 [More methadone programs]
POLICY OBJECTIVE: Increase the number of methadone programs in New York City.

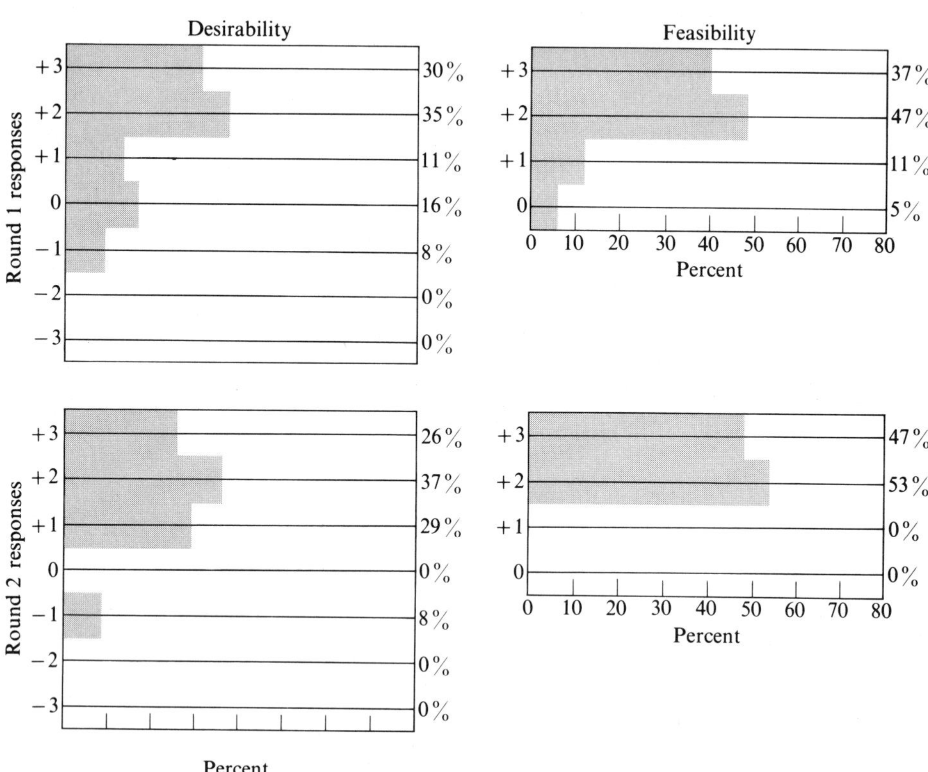


Quartiles of responses†

| | Desirability | | | | Feasibility | | | |
|---|---|---|---|---|---|---|---|---|
| | Low | Med. | High | IQR | Low | Med. | High | IQR |
| Round 1 | +0.56 | +1.92 | +2.66 | 2.10 | 1.69 | 2.22 | 2.82 | 1.13 |
| Round 2 | +1.09 | +1.86 | +2.55 | 1.46 | 1.98 | 2.45 | 2.97 | 0.99 |

Median confidence rating for desirability:

Round 1 = 1.96
Round 2 = 2.00

*Verbal feedback*

—There are long waiting lists for methadone, and it should be made available for anyone who can benefit from it.

—It is better that someone be hooked on something harmless than on something harmful like heroin.

—Methadone programs would reduce the crime associated with heroin addiction.

—Methadone may not solve the problem, but you can treat psychiatric problems later.

—People can return to a somewhat normal life via a methadone program.

—Methadone leaves people with a psychic problem: the need for a needle is still there.

—There will start to be a black market in methadone.

—The side-effects of methadone haven't been sufficiently explored.

—Methadone doesn't create a sense of responsibility in individuals; psychologically they haven't made the transition back into the real world.

—With methadone you end up with an individual who's blocked on heroin but addicted to something else.

---

*Source:* Ref. 13-12, p. 41.
† Adjusted to reflect confidence ratings.

on a scale from $-3$ to $+3$, was a measure of the degree to which the respondent would be pleased or displeased if the objective in question were achieved. The "feasibility" rating, on the other hand, reflected the relative ease with which the objective could be implemented, and was related closely to the likelihood of its coming to pass in the near future; the "feasibility" scale ran from 0 (not feasible) to 3 (very feasible). The objectives which presumably were most promising in the eyes of the evaluators were those with the highest scores on both "desirability" and "feasibility."

An example of one of the evaluative questions is displayed in Table 13-3. The bar charts in the top part show the percentage of the panelists giving various desirability and feasibility ratings in each round. These charts indicate fairly clearly the grouping of responses closer to the medians in the second round. This finding is reinforced by the lowering of the IQR: from 2.10 to 1.46 under "desirability" and from 1.13 to 0.99 under "feasibility." Interestingly, and perhaps more reasonably than in the question in part I, the median confidence rating (for desirability) increased only slightly for this question.

On the basis of these results Thompson could now report that a set of "experts" felt that heroin addicts from middle- to high-income backgrounds tend to be somewhat less difficult to treat and that it was highly desirable and feasible to increase the number of methadone programs in the City. It is interesting to note that on some of the other questions the IQR actually *increased* from the first to the second round, so that similar conclusions would be difficult to make. These results show that a Delphi exercise does not automatically lead to a round-by-round decrease in forecast variability.

## 13-3 A POLICY DELPHI EXAMPLE†

Another type of Delphi exercise, exemplified by questions like those of Thompson's in Table 13-3, focuses on the importance and likelihood of selected policies as opposed to forecasts of future events. This version generally is referred to as a "policy Delphi." Schneider (Ref. 13-13) has followed Turoff's example (Ref. 13-7) on this topic and developed a policy Delphi related to one of the fundamental planning issues facing the residents of the Seattle Metropolitan Area. In its simplest form the question was: "Should the Seattle Central Business District be encouraged to grow substantially during the next 20 to 30 years or should the development of a twin-centered urban structure be encouraged by helping the Bellevue central area emerge as a second major center of office-type employment?" These two areas, separated by a large lake (Lake Washington), are physically located about 7 miles (11.3 km) apart.

The objectives of Schneider's pilot study were (1) to identify several policy statements that related directly to the general issue, (2) to use the policy Delphi technique to determine if there were a consensus on the part of various community leaders on these questions, and (3) to estimate the potential usefulness of this technique for regional planning studies. To accomplish these objectives, the study group first formulated 15 policy statements and circulated them to a panel consisting of 55 local people from Seattle, Bellevue, and the University of Washington. Each panelist was expert in some aspect of the urban development process. The responses to these 15 statements were analyzed and six were selected for a second round of analysis with the same panelist. In the discussion here we will focus only on the first-round findings, highlighting some of the ways in which Delphi results can be analyzed.

The first step in the study was to identify significant policy statements regarding the relative worth of a single-centered versus a twin-centered urban structure in the Puget Sound region. It was felt that a policy statement could be significant if it were judged to be highly important, desirable, probable, and valid by a large number of knowledgeable people.

The study team felt that the "importance" criterion should be included as they wished to deal only with high-priority or relevant questions. If a policy statement were considered unimportant by the panel, it should be dropped from the analysis and not included in the second round. It was felt in addition that all policy questions should have a high "desirability" (effectiveness or benefits) rating, and any statement not given a high rating in this respect in the first round also should be dropped from the analysis. The term "probability" was intended to indicate the likelihood that the event suggested in the statement would occur. No particular expectations were formulated in terms of the desired outcomes for this response. Yet one of the objectives of the study was to determine if there were any highly important and desirable statements given a low probability rating. These situations would be the kind that planners like since they require the invention of

† Some of the discussion in this section is adapted from Schneider (Ref. 13-13).

policies or programs that will increase the probability of desired changes in the environment. The final criterion was "validity" (confidence in the argument or premise). It was determined that any statement not receiving a high validity rating on the first round would be reformulated before being included in the second round.

A relatively simple procedure was employed to combine the four types of response to each statement ("very important," "important," "slightly important," or "unimportant") for each criterion. The responses were first converted to percentages. The percentages in the two upper-level categories were then summed to obtain a rating for each question for each response criterion. For example, suppose 10 persons responded to the "importance" criterion of a statement as follows:

| Response | Number of persons | Percentage of total |
|---|---|---|
| Very important | 5 | 50 } Rating = 70 |
| Important | 2 | 20 } |
| Slightly important | 1 | 10 |
| Unimportant | 2 | 20 |
| | 10 | 100 |

The rating for this question for "importance" would be 70 percent (that is, 50 + 20) on a scale from 0 to 100.

Line *aa′* in Fig. 13-2 illustrates a policy statement rated to be quite satisfactory by the panelist in terms of its importance, desirability, probability, and validity. Line *bb′* designates a policy statement rated as being unsatisfactory in terms of its probability and validity but still somewhat important and desirable. The task of the policy Delphi design team was to try to find a way to move a response pattern like *bb′* up to the satisfactory range (here defined arbitrarily as being a

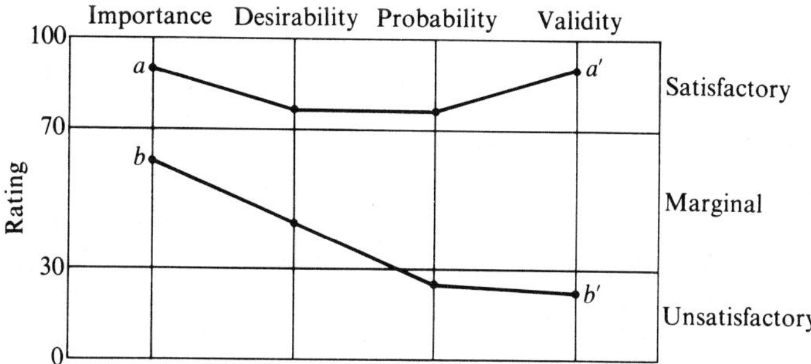


**Figure 13-2** An illustration of ratings of two different policies. (*Source: Ref. 13-13, p. 5.*)

## Table 13-4 First-round statements

1. By 1990, if the great majority of new office jobs locate primarily in the Seattle CBD rather than in other potential office centers such as Bellevue, access to the Seattle CBD will have to be substantially increased. *This will require the addition of at least three new cross-lake bridges.*
2. The addition of 30 to 40 thousand new office jobs to the Seattle CBD would greatly increase peak hour volumes in the main traffic corridors leading to downtown Seattle. *This will increase the need for the development of some form of metropolitan mass rapid transit, requiring large public investment.*
3. With greatly increased employment in Bellevue, the average length of the journey-to-work trip would be substantially reduced both in terms of time and distance. *This will cause an area-wide reduction to occur in traffic congestion, air pollution, and the need for new freeways and other highway facilities.*
4. If the Seattle CBD continues to expand with office and service jobs, the downtown area will become even more congested, inaccessible, and unattractive. *These unfavorable conditions would eventually drive out most retail users, thereby creating a sterile downtown, essentially devoid of people except during working hours.*
5. Public and private investment in the Seattle CBD is large. *Therefore a public policy advocating its continued growth is necessary in order to preserve and enhance this valuable asset and reduce the need for extensive public urban renewal expenditures.*
6. *A large increase in employment in the Seattle CBD can be accommodated only by the construction of additional high-rise office buildings which are needed to mark Seattle as a strong, identifiable, and prestigious regional center.*
7. Under the twin-center concept the great majority of new office and related service-type jobs will be located in Bellevue. *However, with little or no improvement in public transit, these employment opportunities will be of little value for minority and low-income groups living in Seattle.*
8. *The many new jobs associated with continued expansion of the Seattle CBD will be filled largely by suburban commuters.*
9. *Twin-centered growth would tend to suppress land values in the Seattle CBD.*
10. If property values in the Seattle CBD decline as a result of twin-centered growth, the development of open space and many new downtown residential apartments will be stimulated. *This will convert the Seattle downtown area into a viable and attractive 24-hour center.*
11. Increased tax revenues will result from a major expansion of either the Bellevue or Seattle CBD. These revenues will be offset by the added costs of providing the additional public facilities and services required by this expansion. *The costs of these additional facilities and services would be reduced for the region as a whole if most of this expansion takes place in Bellevue.*
12. Bellevue possesses the prestige and desirable amenities such as open space, accessibility, plentiful parking, and nearby quality residential areas which are becoming more important determinants in the choice of new office building locations. *Because of this, Bellevue is very likely to rapidly develop into a major office center, primarily at Seattle's expense.*
13. *If a national or regional firm were to locate a high-rise office building of 25 stories or more in the Bellevue CBD, this would act as the catalyst necessary to stimulate the high rate of office growth required to establish Bellevue as a major office center.*
14. In order to minimize future area-wide public facility expenditures, public policy should be deliberately used to stimulate the expansion of employment opportunities in Bellevue. *This could be done by giving a high priority to public investments such as transit and highway facilities to the Bellevue–Eastside area.*
15. *A strong regional government with extensive land-use controls is required to consciously pursue a twin-centered urban structure.*

*Source:* Ref. 13-13, p. 9.

rating of 70 or more). This was to be done by reformulating the policy statement, clarifying its more troublesome parts, deleting a part of it, or changing it in a variety of other ways.

The 15 policy statements formulated for the first round of the Delphi exercise are presented in Table 13-4. Most of these were intended to be "if–then" type statements with explicit policy implications. Many had two or three parts. The panelists were instructed to take the first part or parts of each question as given and to respond to the "then" or "effect" part of the statement, italicized for emphasis.

## Results of the First Round

The "importance" rating for each of the 15 statements is displayed in Fig. 13-3. As can be seen, all but three of the statements received ratings of 70 percent or more. This means that 70 percent or more of the panelists placed these statements in either the "very important" or "important" categories. The study team had decided that any statement that did not receive an importance rating of 30 percent or more would be eliminated from the analysis, but since there were none in this category, this elimination rule was not employed.

The "desirability" ratings for each of the 15 statements can be found in Fig. 13-3*b*. Four of the 15 statements were rated at less than 30 percent, 6 between 30 and 70 percent, and only the five remaining were above 70 percent. One reason for these low ratings, at least in the case of statements 4 and 7, was that they were formulated in a negative rather than a positive sense (i.e., low desirability ratings were expected), and this might have been confusing to some of the panelists.

The "probability" ratings are illustrated in diagram (*c*). Only one of the 15 statements was rated at 30 percent or less, 10 between 30 and 70 percent, and the other four at more than 70 percent. Statement 15 is an interesting case in this respect. It reads: "A strong regional government with extensive land-use controls is required to consciously pursue a twin-centered urban structure." It was given a 70 percent rating in "importance" and 61 percent in "desirability," but a low probability score. This type of response pattern (highly important and desirable but of low probability) indicates those areas where "policy invention" activity is most likely to be productive (i.e., could have an impact on policy makers and policy making). If, for instance, a political group could show that a policy has high importance and desirability, it could use this finding to exert the kind of pressure needed to convert low into high probability concepts.

Another result of interest relates to statement 8: "The many new jobs associated with continued expansion of the Seattle CBD will be filled largely by suburban commuters." This statement received an importance rating of 90 percent, a desirability rating of 21 percent, and a probability rating of 86 percent (the highest on this criterion). Here is a statement rated important and undesirable but highly probable. Clearly some public intervention policy should be formulated and tested relating to the area covered by this statement.

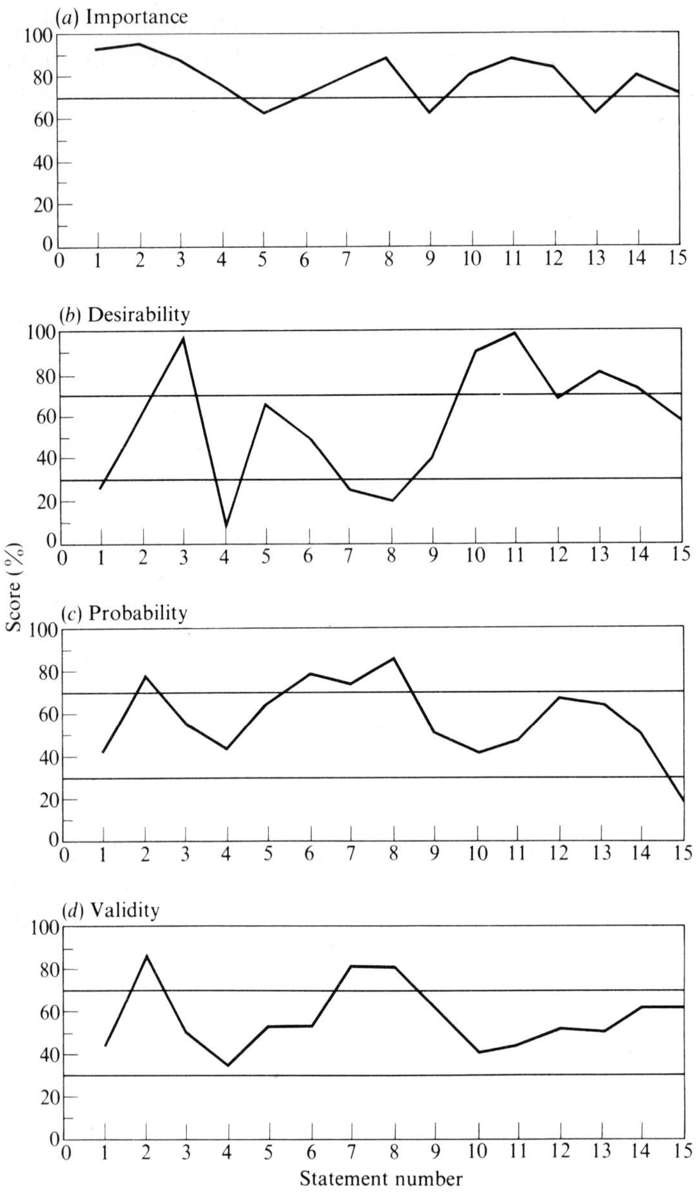


**Figure 13-3** First-round scores for the entire panel. (*Source: Ref. 13-13, p. 16.*)

The validity rating for each of the 15 statements is shown in Fig. 13-3*d*. None of the statements were rated lower than 30 percent, 12 between 30 and 70 percent, and the remaining three above the 70 percent figure. The scores generally were much lower than either desired or anticipated. This may be due to the unclear way in which some of the statements were presented.

## Some Comparisons Between the Response Patterns of the Three Subpanels

As was expected, there were substantial differences between the responses obtained from the Seattle, Bellevue, and University panelists. To get some idea of the size of these differences, a simple *polarization index* (p.i.) was computed for each pair of subpanels. Figure 13-4 illustrates how this difference index is computed. For each criterion it is the sum of the differences in the scores for the three pairs of subpanels (Seattle–Bellevue, Seattle–University, and Bellevue–University). In the figure the p.i. for the importance criterion is $(a + b + c)$. For every question there are 12 such differences (4 response criteria $\times$ 3 differences) and the sum of these 12 is an overall measure of the degree of similarity or diversity among the three subpanels.

For any single criterion the maximum value of p.i. is 200. This value could be obtained, for instance, when two subpanels had a score of 100 and the other 0. This means that for each statement the maximum p.i. is 400 and for all 15 first-round statements the maximum p.i. is 6000.

Table 13-5 shows the p.i. values for the total set of 15 statements. The sum of the p.i. values is 3364, which is about 56 percent of the maximum value of 6000. This means that the subpanels were polarized to about 56 percent of the theoretical maximum values.

The p.i. values in the bottom row of Table 13-5 give a measure of the polarization of the three pairs of subpanels. The larger the index, the more polarized (dissimilar) are the responses of the two subpanels. As can be seen, the most

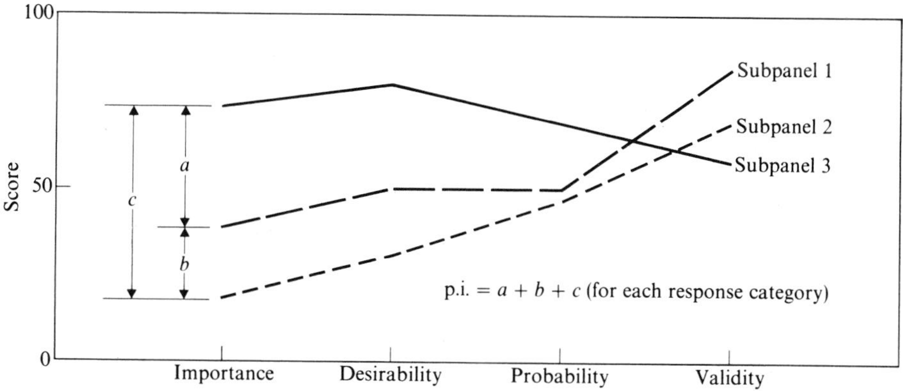


**Figure 13-4** An illustration of the derivation of the polarization index. (*Source: Ref. 13-13, p. 18.*)

**Table 13-5 Polarization indices for all the first-round statements, by subpanel pairs**

| | Subpanel pairs | | | |
|---|---|---|---|---|
| Response categories | Seattle–Bellevue | Seattle–University | Bellevue–University | Total |
| Importance | 294 | 157 | 209 | 660 |
| Desirability | 378 | 400 | 194 | 972 |
| Probability | 259 | 224 | 211 | 694 |
| Validity | 435 | 256 | 347 | 1038 |
| Total | 1366 | 1037 | 961 | 3364 |

*Source:* Ref. 13-8, p. 19.

divergence occurred between the Seattle and Bellevue panels, while the Bellevue and University subpanels were the most alike (closest). The figures in the right-hand column indicate the dissimilarity in the four criteria. They show that the validity and desirability responses were the most diverse.

The polarization index can also be used to determine which statements are most troublesome in terms of response diversity. Considering all four response criteria together, the maximum value of the p.i. for each statement (for three subpanels) is 800. The high p.i. values for statements 12 and 13 stand apart from the others, which indicates that they both should be (and were) included in the second round of the exercise.

## PROBLEMS

**13-1** If you were to conduct a Delphi sequence by mail, would it be better to let the panelists know who their fellow panelists are?

**13-2** What are the relative advantages and disadvantages of asking a Delphi panel to suggest events whose time of occurrence is to be forecast in subsequent rounds?

**13-3** Your regional agency wants a forecast of federal and state policies as well as new technologies that might require significant change in its new comprehensive plan. What are the relative advantages and disadvantages of the following panel types?
(*a*) Experts from outside the region
(*b*) Experts from inside the region
(*c*) A combined panel of each
(*d*) Two separate panels, as in (*a*) and (*b*)

**13-4** Working with a group of five people other than those used in Probs. 12-5 and 12-6, conduct a Delphi experiment to forecast the 1990 population of the locality in which you live. You should go through four rounds and present:
(*a*) The means and standard deviations in each round
(*b*) The lists of reasons in each round
(*c*) The advantages and disadvantages of the Delphi approach to making this forecast
What differences in forecasts do you notice from those in Probs. 12-5 and 12-6? To what group dynamic characteristics do you attribute these differences?

## REFERENCES


**Theory**

13-1. Ayres, R. U.: *Technological Forecasting and Long Range Planning*, McGraw-Hill, New York, 1969.

13-2. Dalkey, N., and O. Helmer: "An Experimental Application of the Delphi Method to the Use of Experts," *Management Science*, vol. 9, no. 3, 1963.

13-3. Gordon, T. J., and O. Helmer: *Report on a Long Range Forecasting Study*, Report P-2982, The Rand Corporation, Santa Monica, Calif., September, 1964.

13-4. Helmer, O., and N. Reschner: "On the Epistemology of the Inexact Sciences." *Management Science*, vol. 6, no. 1, 1959.

13-5. Linestone, H. A., and M. A. Turoff (Eds.): *The Delphi Method: Techniques and Applications*, Addison-Wesley, Reading, Mass., 1975.

13-6. Martino, J. P.: *Technological Forecasting for Decisionmaking*, American-Elsevier, New York, 1972.

13-7. Turoff, M. A.: "The Design of a Policy Delphi," *Technological Forecasting and Social Change*, vol. 2, no. 2, 1970.

**Applications**

13-8. Badger, C. M., W. J. Higgins, and B. D. Ketron: "Population Forecasting in Small Urban Areas: A Delphi Methodology Case Study," *Transportation Research Record* (forthcoming).

13-9. Bell Canada, *Delphi: The Bell Canada Experience*, Montreal, October, 1972.

13-10. Dalkey, N. C., et al.: *Studies in the Quality of Life*, D. C. Heath, Lexington, Mass., 1972.

13-11. Davis, J. M.: *Seventeen County Study Area Delphi Forecast*, Research Report no. 4, Georgia Department of Transportation, Atlanta, Ga., December, 1974.

13-12. Ervin, O. L., and C. R. Meyers, Jr.: *The Utilization of Local Opinion in Land-Use Simulation Modeling: A Delphi Approach*, Memo Report no. 73-8, Oak Ridge National Laboratory, Oak Ridge, Tenn., February, 1973.

13-13. Schneider, J. B.: *Policy Delphi: A Regional Planning Application*, Meeting Preprint 1454, Joint ASCE–ASME Meeting, Seattle, Wash., July, 1971.

13-14. Thompson, L. T.: *A Pilot Application of Delphi Techniques to the Drug Field: Some Experimental Findings*, Report R-1124, The Rand Corporation, Santa Monica, Calif., June, 1973.

CHAPTER

# FOURTEEN

## ANALOGY AND SYNECTICS

The process by which people in a Delphi exercise or in a committee or simply as individuals make forecasts is almost always based on some kind of analogy. In fact most of the scientific process hinges on analogy: it is the basis of both inductive and deductive logic. In regression, for example, we collect a whole series of data on, say, electrical energy consumption versus housing unit floor area and then relate the two mathematically. What we are implying in a sense is that all the data have an underlying pattern of similarity, i.e., the consumption of each unit is analogous to that of the others. The process of forecasting using this relationship also involves analogy. Given the connection between consumption and floor area, we assume through analogy that another housing unit, with a given square footage, will end up utilizing the computed amount of electrical energy. This we assume despite the likelihood that our new unit may not have a floor area equivalent to any of those in the original sample of units.

Analogy also plays a dominant role in everyday public decision making and forecasting. A rural county board of commissioners may be discussing, for example, the merits of a yearly reassessment of property values. One commissioner may have read in the paper about another county where it was tried and found to be more expensive than the increased tax returns. Another commissioner may have spoken to a county manager elsewhere and found his or her experience to be very productive, taxwise. Both these members then might try to determine the analogies with their county (e.g., in population levels, total assessed value, number of commercial enterprises, etc.) to see if the annual reassessment would or would not be beneficial there.

In this chapter we will describe different types and dimensions of analogies. We will then give a large-scale example of one employed in a forecasting mode. The discussion subsequently will turn to the use of analogies in developing creative solutions to problems.

## 14-1 TYPES AND DIMENSIONS OF ANALOGIES

Definition *Webster's New Collegiate Dictionary* defines *analogy* as: "Inference that if two or more things agree with one another in some respects, they will probably agre in others." (Ref. 14-12).

This definition is particularly appropriate in our attempts here to formalize the use of analogies since emphasis will be on the explicit similarity of attributes, circumstances, and effects.

Gordon (Ref. 14-1) has identified and given examples of four major types of analogy differentiated by the approach taken to find such similarities:

1. Personal
2. Direct
3. Symbolic
4. Fantasy

In *personal* analogy an effort is made by the analyst to have an empathetic identification with the subject being studied. In other words, one imagines oneself involved in the working mechanism of the problem. Illustrations of personal analogy abound in urban and regional decision-making situations. City, county, and regional officials often are asked to imagine themselves trying to get an education in a segregated school or attempting to survive as a prisoner or living on welfare. Many of us have been asked to fast for a day to help understand those in hunger or similarly to spend a few hours in a mental institution. All these are examples of attempts to set up personal analogies so that we (hopefully) will become more sympathetic to the plight of a particular group of people.

*Direct analogy* involves the actual, explicit comparison of parallel attributes, circumstances, or effects. As Alexander Graham Bell recalled (Ref. 14-11, pp. 72–73):

> It struck me that the bones of the human ear were very massive, indeed, as compared with the delicate thin membrane that operated them, and the thought occurred that if a membrane so delicate could move bones relatively so massive, why should not a thicker and stouter piece of membrane move my piece of steel. And the telephone was conceived.

A version of direct analogy commonly employed in the past for population forecasting is portrayed in Fig. 14-1. Historical data on population levels for both a study area and its associated state or country are collected for as many years as available. The forecast of population for the area being investigated, in this case

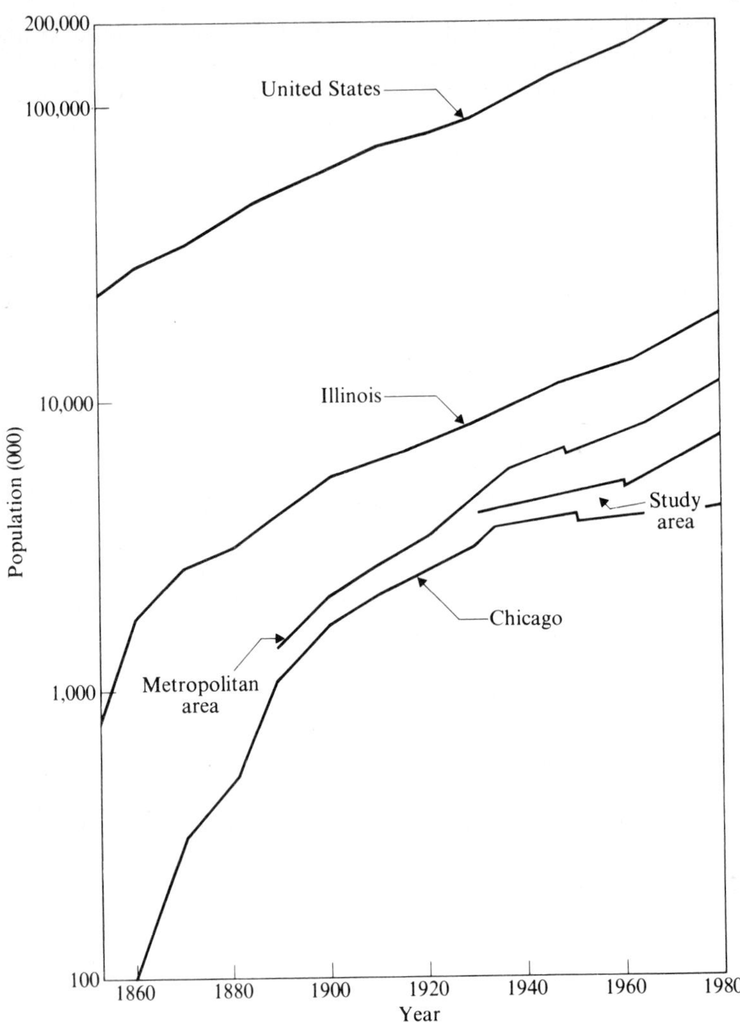


**Figure 14-1** Population growth data and projections, Chicago area. (*Source: Ref. 14-5, p. 7.*)

the Chicago area transportation study region (Ref. 14-5), is then made using an exogenously predicted country population and the assumption (analogy) that the area will grow at the same rate relative to the nation as had been true in the past. This assumption is accepted on the theory that the same factors (political, social, economic, legal, etc.) operate on the study area as on the nation.

*Symbolic analogy* uses objective and impersonal images to describe the similarity in attributes, circumstances, and/or effects. The major differences between symbolic analogies and the others is quantitative. The utilization of regression to find similar patterns, discussed in the early paragraphs of this chapter, is a straightforward illustration of the employment of symbolic analogy. In fact, all of the quantitative techniques discussed in this book exemplify this approach. The relationship in Fig. 14-1 also portrays a symbolic analogy since it could be employed quantitatively. The forecasted Chicago study area population of 7.8 million in 1980 is analogous to that of 259.1 million in the United States in the same year.

The final type, *fantasy analogy*, is based to some extent on Freud's wish fulfillment theory, where the analyst sees similarities by wishing them to be so. In many ways fantasy is the antithesis of direct analogy forecasting, where we see the urban area or region growing in the same way as in the past. In the former the past is almost irrelevant and the analogy is to the future wishes and dreams we have in our mind.

The epitome of a real-world example of a fantasy analogy most likely is Disney World. Almost nothing was fixed at the start of its development, not even major land forms. And from there the things that would be done probably were limited only by imagination, finance, and time. It is highly doubtful that any statistical model ever would have predicted a Disney World-type of development in Florida before Disney Enterprises made its wishes known. Similarly, many of the major civil works projects in the world—the Golden Gate Bridge, the Eiffel Tower, and the damming of the Tennessee River (and others) by the Tennessee Valley Authority—probably would not have been predicted by any mechanism other than a fantasy analogy.

Eventually every type of analogy suggested above must be formalized to make it of value to the analyst of urban and regional problems. Essentially this means that the analogy becomes a direct one (and possible symbolic, too), since he or she must be explicit in comparing every relevant attribute, circumstance, or effect. Martino and O'Conner present nine dimensions which should be considered in developing such formalized analogies (Refs. 14-2 and 14-3). These are listed in Table 14-1 and discussed briefly below:

1. *Technological.* No single technology can exist or grow in complete independence of others. Consideration thus should be given to complimentary as well as competing technologies. This cannot be done unless investigations are made of the support given each technology, as characterized by existing laws and theories on the one hand and trained personnel on the other. Minicomputer and calculator capabilities for small local governments, for example, could not be utilized until, first, the space program enabled miniaturization, and, second, local government personnel were trained to use such equipment.
2. *Economic.* An idea or technology usually is beneficial in the sense that people are willing to pay for it or give up something else of value to use it. The economic dimension consequently entails consideration of costs, finance, income, wealth, and, generally, overall market conditions. To illustrate: an analogy between the utilization of mass transit in European cities versus United States cities often is incomplete because Europeans are, on the average, not as wealthy as Americans. As a result, car ownership is lower and more frequent use is made of transit there.

**Table 14-1 Dimensions of formal analogies**

| | | |
|---|---|---|
| **1. Technological** | | |
| Competing technologies<br>Stage of development<br>Availability of trained people | Complementary technologies<br>Level of understanding of laws, theories, etc.<br>Supporting technologies (energy, transport, production) | |
| **2. Economic** | | |
| Cost of same function to be served<br>General market conditions | Financing<br>Economic climate | |
| **3. Managerial** | | |
| Number of managers<br>Experience<br>Training | Theories, techniques, and management procedures | |
| **4. Political** | | |
| Who benefits?<br>Who loses?<br>parties, groups, individuals<br>Trade-offs for other things of value | Rights, duties, privileges, objections of various groups | |
| **5. Social** | | |
| Population<br>Age distribution<br>Geographic distribution<br>Relative group distributions | Institutional groups<br>church, school, business, family, government | |
| **6. Cultural** | | |
| Values<br>Attitudes | Practices<br>Customs<br>Prohibitions | Exhortations<br>Goals |
| **7. Intellectual** | | |
| Decision makers<br>Spokesmen for prestigious organizations | Opinion leaders | |
| **8. Religious/ethical** | | |
| Standards<br>Doctrines<br>Teachings<br>Answers to man's ultimate destiny | Hierarchy<br>Control<br>Number of institutions | |
| **9. Ecological** | | |
| Pollution (air, water, noise, heat)<br>Tolerable levels | Flora<br>Fauna | |

3. *Managerial.* The introduction of innovation and change usually does not just happen. It must be managed. This dimension therefore involves the number and training of managerial personnel as well as their experience in terms of the size and complexity of tasks previously undertaken. Also involved are the theories, techniques, and administrative procedures researched, developed, demonstrated, and available to management. Many analogies dealing with urban and regional situations will be incomplete on this dimension. The size and complexity of government, especially at the local and substate regional level, has grown to such a scale in recent years that many of the administrative techniques utilized in the past might fail to reach their expected audience.
4. *Political.* This dimension involves primarily the competition between antagonistic interest groups or individuals for power and/or leadership in government or the private sector. The major questions that concern these groups thus are of who benefits and loses, what are the negotiations and trades to be undertaken, and, more basically, what are the rights, duties, and privileges to which each group is rightfully entitled. Analogies developed to help anticipate the likelihood of, say, construction of a new dam or highway would have to have a strong political dimension. For a dam, for instance, environmental groups would be posed against electric power companies and possibly recreationalists, and the "rights" of each might be decided by a variety of executive agencies, elected bodies, and courts.
5. *Social.* The numbers and distributions of different social groups, by age, location, sex, race, religion, etc., always will play an important role in the likely success or failure of all kinds of governmental programs, particularly those of a direct service nature. Most analogies dealing with these kinds of situations therefore should make as explicit as possible the characteristics of the group served and their reactions. A public welfare program, for example, may do well in a location where people are very heterogeneous in ethnic and religious background but may not be popular in those areas where churches and businesses already have their own informal (but perhaps substantial) programs.
6. *Cultural.* Values, attitudes, and customs often play a large role in determining the reactions to various governmental programs. By way of illustration, in many rural areas of the United States land-use controls are equated with communism. While there are some similarities, there obviously are quite a few differences. We might conclude, then, that on the one hand the analogy between communism and land-use controls is incomplete, but that on the other hand cultural values, attitudes, practices, prohibitions, and the like have to be considered if proper analogies related to land-use controls are to be developed for rural areas.
7. *Intellectual.* It often turns out that some of the most influential leaders in community decision making are not elected officials but members of an "intellectual elite." These may be highly educated housewives, presidents of research organizations or universities, medical doctors, and the like. Their word is often taken for granted because of their professional stature. Certainly any analogy dealing with the future, say, of educational programs in a wealthy suburban

county would have to consider the feelings and opinions of the intellectual elite in that community.

8. *Religious/ethical.* The church plays a major role, although sometimes very indirectly, in many decisions made at urban and regional levels. Many clergymen, exemplified by the Rev. Dr. Martin Luther King, have had a significant impact on legislation dealing with a variety of social concerns. Perhaps surprising to some, the survey on access to neighborhood service facilities described in Chap. 20, Sec. 20-2, indicates that distance to a religious building was ranked highest in importance by people in Greensboro, North Carolina. Hence many analogies should take into account the religious, moral, and ethical forces that might be dominant (although implicit) in the situation being compared.
9. *Ecological.* With the increasing recognition that humanity, too, is a biological species and that its continuing survival depends on maintaining a favorable habitat, the ecological dimension has taken on greater importance. Pollution of this habitat is, of course, of greatest concern. Tolerable levels (where known) of air, water, noise, and thermal pollution need to be considered, not only for humanity but also for animals, flora, and fauna. A proper formal analogy, especially one dealing with an environmental issue such as the impact on fish life of a new dam or river levee project, consequently should explore this dimension in some detail.

## 14-2 AN EXAMPLE†

To illustrate the manner in which an analogy focusing on most of the dimensions suggested above might be drawn, we have selected a small case study dealing with health services and cities.

The conquest of epidemic disease by the early twentieth century was one of the greatest triumphs of urban people. Throughout the late eighteenth and nineteenth centuries, epidemics were the scourge of American cities. Disease and urbanization grew together. Beginning with Philadelphia in 1793, yellow fever visited urban areas periodically, carrying off thousands of residents. One observer called the Philadelphia plague the "most appalling collective disaster that had ever overtaken an American city" (Ref. 14-17, p. 68). That epidemic killed nearly 10 percent of the city's population—a figure surpassed by the New Orleans yellow fever epidemic of 1853 and a similar tragedy in Norfolk 2 years later, where almost one-sixth of the city's residents fell victim to the disease.

Besides the personal tragedy brought on by an epidemic, the affected city suffered severe economic distress as business ceased and as other cities placed trade interdicts on the infected metropolis. One physician estimated that the yellow fever and cholera epidemics in New Orleans during the late 1840s cost that

† This section has been written by Dr. David R. Goldfield of the Division of Environmental and Urban Systems of Virginia Tech.

city nearly $45,000,000 in business. Political institutions underwent similar dislocations as councils fled and leaders perished. Finally, the social and cultural life of the city disappeared (Ref. 14-6, p. 261).

The health problems confronting cities today are less spectacular but still of great importance to the personal lives of affected residents. Inadequate health facilities for the poor and elderly, rapidly increasing costs for health services, and research and fiscal emphases in hospitals on "glamorous" diseases have made the delivery of health care to a substantial portion of urban dwellers an obstacle course. Ironically, while life expectancy in the United States was among the highest in the world during the epidemic disease era, at present this country ranks relatively lower.

We now will frame our analogy within the nine dimensions outlined earlier in this chapter.

## Technological

The major technological breakthroughs in the elimination of epidemic disease involved engineering innovations in sewer construction and in water services. Although the specific etiology of epidemic diseases remained unknown for most of the nineteenth century, urban authorities sensed the deleterious impacts of impure water and improper drainage and waste removal. Water-carriage sewerage, where waste was periodically flushed by water, was introduced to urban America from England in the 1850s. The construction of these self-cleansing sewers was so expensive, however, that only a few householders could afford it. Not until the perfection of sanitary sewers—separate sewers attached to homes by small pipes designed to carry household wastes exclusively—did sewerage become widespread (Ref. 14-14).

Health technology is in a similar situation today. Technology to prolong and improve the quality of life exists. The major problem is cost. The sanitary sewer system was in a sense a miniaturization of the more ponderous water-carried system. Miniaturization is an important device in reducing technology costs. The tasks performed by pacemakers, for example, could only be performed in major hospitals at great expense. Scaling down technology enables individuals to play a more active role in their treatment as well.

## Economic

How much does it cost, who will pay it, and by what means, were central questions in improving health services in nineteenth-century cities. Businessmen ran cities a century ago. Planning decisions were based on a rather primitive but still characteristic cost-benefit analysis. Since property taxes were the major sources of revenue, publicly financed services were paid for by businessmen. For a particular service to be implemented, they had to be convinced that the benefits of the service to the city (as defined by the entrepreneurs) outweighed the costs to the urban elite. Even when services were implemented, they often failed to get delivered beyond the business district. Since businessmen found it relatively easy to escape to the country during epidemics, health services were generally neglected by local government. When the situation became serious, as in New Orleans in 1853 and in New York in 1866, the state stepped in to pay for and operate the service. Thus, as cities were unwilling or unable to budget for health services, state governments funded health programs.

Today, health services are not necessarily viewed as a governmental financial responsibility. True, Medicaid is a public financed program, but its private input is heavy. In the nineteenth century, when cities failed to fund health services, the state stepped in. By analogy, local and state governments, unable to foot expensive medical bills, have been aided to a greater extent by the federal government.

## Managerial

Nineteenth-century business leaders were reluctant to relinquish managerial control. It seemed logical to place physicians in charge of implementing and enforcing quarantine, for example. This, however, restricted trade, the lifeblood of the entrepreneurs, and they viewed it dangerous to place nervous doctors in charge of such a service. Instead, as with the implementation of other health services, it became a political appointment. When the state interceded, nonpartisan commissions composed of appointed physicians directed health service activities until the establishment of local boards of health with similarly trained professional personnel. Although this arrangement did not necessarily remove partisanship from health services, the relatively independent and professional physicians performed the necessary tasks designed to protect cities from epidemic diseases: they divided the city into health districts, organized street cleaning operations, imposed quarantines, and set standards for reporting and treating diseases (Ref. 14-15, p. 245).

Local boards of health exist today, but they are minor actors in the delivery of health services. Actually, in contrast to the ninteeenth century, the management of such services is fragmented. All levels of government, professional societies, unions, individual hospitals and nursing homes, and ambulance companies all play a role in modern health services delivery. The fragmented managerial responsibility sometimes means certain segments of the population remain isolated from health services and that coordination in crisis situations may be difficult.

## Political

Health services were weak in early nineteenth-century cities for two reasons: the absence of organized interest groups to demand effective services and the political nature of such services as street cleaning, water supply, and quarantine. By the 1870s, health reform groups were common in American cities, demanding municipal action on health services such as sanitary sewers and water-supply systems. With universal male suffrage and the election of all city officials, the primitive cost-benefit analysis of mercantile leaders was transformed to pay greater attention to organized groups, especially those with financial and intellectual clout. In the end, it also became profitable to institute health services because the loss in lives, revenue, and (equally important) prestige had begun to outweigh the costs of implementation. New Orleans, for example, ravaged by a series of epidemics, dropped from the fifth largest city in 1860 to the fifteenth by 1910. Since growth meant prosperity, epidemic disease was now striking at the heart of the urban economy (Ref. 14-14).

Today, interest groups dominate the political arena with regard to health services. The AMA and their allies are usually arrayed against various consumer and welfare groups with national health insurance legislation a frequent battleground. The political and economic muscle of the AMA has been dominant so far. Analogizing from past experience, it seems that the most appropriate tactic for national health insurance advocates to pursue is to demonstrate that such insurance poses no financial threat to physicians and may even be profitable for them in the long run.

## Social

The rapid influx of large numbers of poor and relatively uneducated immigrants brought the debate on health services to a head. Crowding aggravated skimpy sanitary facilities and epidemic diseases increased in virulence and impact until they spread to the more established sections of the city, as in the 1866 cholera epidemic in New York. It was at this point that churches, physicians, and wealthy citizens launched a health services reform movement.

In the modern city, the poor and the elderly are as equally isolated as the nineteenth-century immigrants. The crisis of health delivery obstacles visited upon these groups rarely touched the lives of other urban residents. The high costs of services, however, like the earlier epidemics, are now spreading to more affluent segments of the population. As these segments begin to feel the inadequacy of the services, the political pressure will mount. Certainly the current positive prospects for national health insurance are due to the increased awareness and alarm of middle-class Americans over the quality and expense of health services.

## Cultural

The attitudes and values of citizens were among the major obstacles in implementing effective health services. Many people looked upon epidemic disease as God's judgment and upon physicians as quacks. Sewers, water-supply systems, and street-cleaning programs were therefore not only useless but blasphemous as well. Not surprisingly, reform advocates came from the wealthy and well educated. Stringent laws were passed requiring innoculation, for example, and even cleansing of individual dwellings became a citywide responsibility (Ref. 14-16).

Our urban society is much more sophisticated today, but there remain values and attitudes that inhibit health reform. Physicians are held in considerably higher regard than politicians, which is one reason why removing the administration of certain health services from private professionals to government is looked upon as a regression by some. There is also the strength of the free-enterprise ideal, which shudders at government involvement in health services, despite historic traditions to the contrary. Finally, since the problem is not necessarily the scarcity of health services but the cost, there is a certain wealth status bias at work as well.

## Intellectual

The reform of health services and the subsequent triumph over epidemic disease was very much the work of an "intellectual elite." The leading actors in health reform, George E. Waring, Jr., an engineer, and Stephen Smith, a prominent New York physician, promoted and implemented the technological and administrative innovations that ensured citizen freedom from attack by epidemic disease. Their work was aided to some degree by the fact that their society was still a deferential one, i.e., decision making was still confined to a relatively small group of well-to-do men (Ref. 14-14).

Decision making is much more complex today, just as health services are more fragmented. The "intellectual elites" are less effectual because they are ranged on both sides of health issues and do not have ready access to the cozy confines of political power as they did a century ago. Indeed, the "intellectual elite" and decision maker often have to be synonymous to accomplish legislation. The emergence of Senator Kennedy as a recognizable leader for national health insurance is a good example of this. The heroic engineer or the battling physician are images of the past in the highly organized interest group era of the present.

## Religious/Ethical

The odyssey of religious institutions from initial opposition or indifference to the implementation of health services to active and vociferous support was a major reason for the success of reform efforts. Religion was a central force, a rock in the often stormy seas of nineteenth-century urban America. Religion was a value-giver and, along with the family, the ethical foundation of urban society. The "social gospel" preached by Protestant churches was an important movement in focusing attention on the poor and their health problems.

Religion and the family are weaker institutions in contemporary urban society. Yet among the poor and the elderly, family, and especially religion, are the only traditions left for succor and comfort. The proliferation of store-front Pentecostal churches in poor black and Hispanic neighborhoods demonstrates the need for these values. In the nineteenth century, Protestant reformers placed settlement houses in immigrant districts to educate the poor in good health practices, among other things. Today, government has taken over the functions once performed by religious and family-oriented organizations. The opening of store-front clinics and the roving presence of medical vans stem from the same desire to reach down into the neighborhood to personalize health services.

## Ecological

Urban leaders in the nineteenth century recognized the link between pollution and disease. The campaigns for sewers and a clean water supply emphasized the dangers of air and water pollution. In fact, medical opinion of the time held that air pollution itself, in the form of bad vapors, was a disease-producing agent. The environment also figured more actively and positively as part of the policy to eradicate epidemic disease. Parks were designed and trees planted to give the city "lungs." Recreational space, shade, and the ventilation of open spaces would not only act as bactericidal agents, but would improve the often-frayed mental condition of the urban inhabitant. The result would be a healthy body less susceptible to disease (Ref. 14-6).

Though couched in more sophisticated terminology, there are efforts underway in many cities to provide recreational areas for poorer neighborhoods. There is, moreover, a correlation between physical exercise, positive mental state, and health. Indeed, part of the problem of servicing the poor's health needs is their greater susceptibility to illness resulting from, in part, the neglect of their physical environment, from housing to parks.

Drawing an analogy from the provision of health services in nineteenth-century urban America, it is possible to forecast the nature of improvements in health delivery for our contemporary cities. Medical technology will miniaturize and personalize its advances. In-home dialysis machines and patrolling cardiac units are already being tested. Small computers fed with physiological readings taken by individuals at home can perform diagnoses of minor ailments or link up with physicians in distant clinics or hospitals, as is the case in the projected plan for Minneapolis' Cedar–Riverside neighborhood.

To finance and manage the new personalized health services—from storefront clinics to pocket computers—greater centralization, probably at the federal level, will occur. Although interest groups like the AMA will undoubtedly oppose such efforts, it can be demonstrated that closer federal monitoring will cut insurance rates, limit malpractice suits, and provide health care for the neglected urban and rural segments of the population.

## 14-3 SYNECTICS

One of the most interesting uses of analogy has been in the process of helping create new solutions to problems. The approach is known as *synectics* and has been developed by W. J. J. Gordon and others (Refs. 14-1, 14-7, and 14-10). It has been employed predominantly in the industrial sector, but could be very useful in the public domain as well. Thus the reason for its presentation here.

The word "synectics" comes from the Greek, meaning "the joining together of different and apparently irrelevant elements." Hence the synectics mechanism focuses on making the familiar different and irrelevant through the four types of analogy suggested in Sec. 14-1 (personal, direct, symbolic, and fantasy). Usually a

**Table 14-2 Excursion steps and examples of the synectics process**

| Excursion steps | Session transcript |
|---|---|
| 1. *Problem as given* (*PAG*). Problem descriptions should contain the central elements and an outline of at least two unsuccessful solution attempts and why they failed. | Fire-fighting apparatus at airports can't reach crashes fast enough to prevent loss of life. Flameout-foam sprinkler systems covering the whole landing field are *impossibly* expensive and awkward to activate. When bunches of fire trucks are spotted in strategic places, they get in the way of takeoff and landing procedures. |
| 2. *Essence analysis* (*EA*). This is the process of identifying the core of the problem. | |
| (*a*) First, the expert sums up the Problem As Given. | (*a*) How to get the fire-fighting apparatus to the spot where it's needed—fast? |
| (*b*) An Essence statement is developed by identifying a unique aspect of the problem. | (*b*) The landing plane is not only on fire, but it is moving. |
| (*c*) The Essence statement is tested to make sure that it does not describe other things or situations. | (*c*) What other things or situations are on fire and moving? . . . A locomotive. |
| (*d*) The discrepancies between the problem situation and a "locomotive" are identified. | (*d*) The locomotive is a controlled fire that is moving. The airplane—it is practically a bomb! |
| (*e*) The Essence statement is refined so that it excludes a "locomotive fire." | (*e*) The landing plane is a moving fire that could explode in an instant. |
| 3. *Problem as understood* (*PAU*). This is a simple statement of the Essence of step 2. | How to get apparatus to appear instantly before a plane explodes like a bomb? |
| 4. *Direct analogy* (*DA*). This metaphorical form is a simple comparison between two things or concepts. Direct Analogy is the primary mechanism for developing new contexts in which to view the Problem As Understood. You should try to make your Direct Analogies distanced from the the idea in your Problem As Understood. | An *evocative question* is a question that forces a metaphorical, rather than an analytical response.<br>*Evocative question for a direct analogy.* What mechanical thing appears instantly?<br>*Direct analogy response.* An umbrella. Whenever you need it you just flip it open. |
| 5. *Personal analogy* (*PA*). This Operational Mechanism is an empathic identification with something living or nonliving. You imagine how it would feel to be that thing. | *Evocative question for a personal analogy.* Imagine you are an umbrella that's just been opened in a driving rainstorm.<br>*Personal analogy response.* I prefer being all wrapped up in nice, floppy pleats with my thin skin protected. But here comes a hard rain and my owner snaps me out into fighting position. I tighten my muscles and my taut skin attacks each raindrop that hits me. |

**Table 14-2 (*continued*)**

| Excursion steps | Session transcript |
| --- | --- |
| 6. *Compressed conflict* (*CC*). This form of metaphor is a poetic, two-word description on a high level of generality. The two words should contradict each other. Make the words in your Compressed Conflicts "fight" each other. | *Evocative question for a compressed conflict.* Take two conflicting roles of the Personal Analogy and put them together into a phrase to describe the umbrella.<br>*Compressed conflict response.* It was both "thin-skinned" and an "attacker." A poetic way of using this conflict to describe the umbrella would be "delicate aggressor." |
| 7. *Final direct analogy.* The purpose of a synectics excursion is to help you get away from your problem. Therefore, your Final Direct Analogy must be more distanced and apparently less relevant to the problem than your first Direct Analogy. | *Evocative question for a final direct analogy.* From the biological world what is an example of "delicate aggressor?"<br>*Final direct analogy response.* A frog's tongue. It is soft and delicate, but it shoots right out and grabs flying insects. |
| 8. *Analysis of the analogue.* You must unearth the underlying Essences and functions of the Final Direct Analogy. This material will be the framework for your new context. Do not limit your analysis to superficial descriptions. It must include Essences of functions. | A frog has a long tongue which is kept curled in his mouth. The tongue "shoots" out like a New Year's Eve noise-maker. But it moves so quickly that you can't see it flip out and back without a special high-speed camera. The tip is broader than the rest of the tongue and it's sticky. An Essence is "faster than the eye." |
| 9. *Algebraic force fit* (*AFF*). The elements of this simple algebraic equation are: the Final Direct Analogy; the Essence of its function; and the essentials of the Problem As Understood. The new context is derived by "solving" for the unknown. Here is a generalized form of the Force Fit equation:<br>$\frac{\text{Analogue}}{\text{Essence of function}} = \frac{\text{Problem As Understood essentials}}{?}$ | What is your particular equation?<br>$\frac{\text{Frog's tongue}}{\text{Faster than the eye}} = \frac{\text{Apparatus appears instantly}}{?}$<br>Now to "solve" for the unknown. If the airport fire-fighting apparatus worked exactly like a frog's tongue, what would replace the question mark?<br>*Response.* There is a huge frog sitting on the control tower. Whenever there is a fire emergency, this frog shoots out a flameout-foam tongue and slaps out the fire with it. "Shoots flameout-foam" completes the equation. |
| 10. *Practical viewpoint.* This is the final step in a synectics problem-solving excursion. Now is the time for the metaphors, the fantasy, and all the apparently irrelevant material to be used to see the problem in a way that is completely different from earlier views. | *Practical viewpoint response.* We could have a gun, set on a tower, that would fire special cartridges containing foam. The whole airport could be divided into grids. The location of a fire could be fed into a computer and the gun would be aimed exactly at the crash site. |

*Source:* Ref. 14-10, pp. 41–45. Please direct all inquiries to Synectics Education Systems, 121 Brattle Street, Cambridge, MA 02138.

formal group is established within a company to undertake this type of analogy generation. For a particular problem the group would go through a process similar to that outlined and described in Table 14-2. We also will use this as our example of the synectics process.

While the type of process suggested above is intended to supplement the creativity of the individuals in developing solutions to problems (or possibly making forecasts), synectics researchers have found that the problem stating–problem solving group should be carefully selected to obtain the best results. The criteria suggested by Gordon are (Ref. 14-1):

1. *Representation.* A small number of people (about five) should be selected to represent a broad variety of technical and nontechnical skills. Experts on a particular problem to be attacked using synectics usually should *not* be part of the group since they have a more difficult time separating themselves from past solutions.
2. *Energy level.* Members should have a high but not frantic energy level. Those not enthusiastic tend to depress ideation.
3. *Age.* Members generally should be in the range from 25 to 40 years of age since this is the age bracket where a person has at least some experience but is not too set in his or her ways.
4. *Administrative potential.* The ability to generalize, basic to synectics, also is present in good administrators. Moreover, since it will be administrators who eventually will implement the synectics ideas, they should be included in the process.
5. *Entrepreneurship.* Each member should be willing to accept the responsibility of success or failure independent of management's sanction. This will prevent the group from being engorged by the agency.
6. *Job background.* The group should be diverse in this characteristic, possibly including several people who did some "job-jumping."
7. *Education.* It is desirable to have those with a record of shifting fields of major interest. This adds more to the potential for identifying analogies.
8. *The "almost" individual.* A person who is tremendously productive but has never quite "made the grade" may be able to liberate the unplumbed potential in a synectics group.

Although some of the above selection and operational procedures may seem strange, the synectics approach apparently has met with some success. According to Gordon (Ref. 14-7), over $100 million has been spent by companies worldwide in organizing and running synectics groups.

## PROBLEMS

**14-1** Develop the ecological dimension of a possible analogy between the introduction of fossil-fueled and of nuclear electric power plants in the United States. Are they analogous on this dimension?

**14-2** Develop the cultural dimension of a possible analogy between the introduction of television and the possible introduction of three-dimensional television.

**14-3** You are working for the Metropolitan Washington Council of Governments, which is exploring the possibility of using new towns as satellite growth nuclei for the year 2000. In about 750 words, develop an analogy based on the English experience with new towns in the London area.

**14-4** Your state is considering a work-release program for prisoners. What can you learn about the potential success of such a program based on analogies with experiences elsewhere?

**14-5** Population forecasts for an urban area sometimes are made on the assumption that growth will be analogous to that of the corresponding state as a whole. Find an example of such an approach in a planning study. List and discuss in two sentences each the advantages and disadvantages of this technique in the particular application.

**14-6** In a synectics exercise, go outside and investigate the habitat of some small animals, birds, or insects. How might their life-style have given early man the idea of living in groups or cities or, conversely, being spread across the countryside?

**14-7** †Working with your instructor, select an urban or regional problem you have been unable to solve so far. Make sure you are sufficiently familiar with it to recognize the usefulness of a new viewpoint. Then:

(*a*) State your problem as given.

(*b*) Analyze the essence of the problem. Have an available expert summarize the problem. Identify unique aspects. Test the statement for uniqueness. Identify differences between problem situations and other similar ones. Refine the statement to exclude other possibilities.

(*c*) Define the problem as understood. Identify the most important needed element in any solution.

(*d*) Develop a direct analogy. Find three analogies whose connections to your problem as understood are *not* obvious. Explain the connections.

(*e*) Develop a personal analogy. Describe your functions. As an analogue, when are you under the most stress? How do your muscles respond under this level of stress?

(*f*) Look for compressed conflicts. What are the two most conflicting statements in your identification? Reword these statements into as poetic and paradoxical phrases as you can.

(*g*) Develop final direct analogies. Fit them to your compressed conflict description. Try some varied activities (e.g., outside your office or house) to find better metaphors.

(*h*) Analyze your best direct analogy. Find general traits and specific qualities which unearth the underlying essences and functions.

(*i*) Do an algebraic force fit. What is the corresponding notion of a solution to your problem as understood? What kind of solution would occur if it functioned exactly as your analogue?

(*j*) Take a practical viewpoint. Describe the practical side implied by your algebraic force fit. What steps might you take to test and implement your practical view?

# REFERENCES

### Theory

14-1. Gordon, W. J. J.: *Syntectics*, Collier-Macmillan, London, 1961.

14-2. Martino, J. P.: *Technological Forecasting for Decisionmaking*, American-Elsevier, New York, 1972.

14-3. O'Conner, T. (Office of Research Analysis, U.S. Air Force): *A Methodology for Analogies*, NTIS, Springfield, Va., June, 1970.

14-4. Stone, P. J., et al.: *The General Inquirer: A Computer Approach to Content Analysis*, The MIT Press, Cambridge, Mass., 1966.

† Adapted from Ref. 14-9.

**Applications and related studies**

14-5. *Chicago Area Transportation Study, Final Report*, vol. II, *Data Projections*, Chicago, July, 1960.
14-6. Goldfield, D. R.: "The Business of Health Planning: Disease Prevention in the Old South," *Journal of Southern History*, November, 1976.
14-7. Gordon, W. J. J.: *Introduction to Synectics Problem-Solving*. Synectics Education Systems, Cambridge, Mass., 1972.
14-8. Gordon, W. J. J.: *Strange and Familiar*, Synectics Education Systems, Cambridge, Mass., 1972.
14-9. Gordon, W. J. J.: *Practice in Synectics Problem-Solving*, Synectics Education Systems, Cambridge, Mass., 1973.
14-10. Gordon, W. J. J., and T. Poze: *The Art of the Possible*, Porpoise Books, Cambridge, Mass., 1976.
14-11. MacKenzie, C.: *Alexander Graham Bell*, Houghton-Mifflin, New York, 1928.
14-12. Mazlich, B.: *The Railroad and the Space Program: An Exploration in Historical Analogy*, The MIT Press, Cambridge, Mass., 1965.
14-13. G. and C. Merriam Company: *Webster's New Collegiate Dictionary*, Springfield, Mass., 1977.
14-14. Peterson, J. A.: *The Impact of Sanitary Reform Upon American Urban Planning, 1840–1890*, Paper presented at the Organization of American Historians' Convention, St. Louis, Mo., April 9, 1976.
14-15. Rosen, G.: *A History of Public Health*, MD Publications, New York, 1958.
14-16. Rosenberg, C. E.: *The Cholera Years*, University of Chicago Press, Chicago, Ill., 1962.
14-17. Still, B.: *Urban America: A History with Documents*, Little, Brown and Company, Boston, 1974.

CHAPTER

# FIFTEEN

# GAMES AND GAMING

Of all the techniques discussed in this book, that of using games as a method both for understanding a situation and for making forecasts probably is the most well known to the student in urban and regional studies. The majority of us have played board games such as *Monopoly* or *Clue* when we were young and know what it is like to become fabulously wealthy or complete beggars, or to have found out who committed the murder, with what instrument, and in which room. And, as a result, we have also known, as the expression goes, "the thrill of victory and the agony of defeat" in the game competition.

In the broadest sense, a *game* might be defined as:

> *Game:* a set of rules for role playing within the context of a given scenario.

Ayres defines the latter as:

> *Scenario:* a logical and plausible (but not necessarily probable) set of events, both serial and simultaneous, with careful attention to timing and correlations (particularly with past and present conditions) (Ref. 15-2, p. 146).

*Gaming*, then, would be the actual playing of the game, although this word has taken on a connotation associated with less-structured (mathematically) games, as will be seen later.

## 15-1 A PRELIMINARY EXAMPLE†

Military and space-related operations, of course, have provided a major setting for games and gaming operations. As an illustration, Boeing, along with Bendix, Minneapolis-Honeywell, and Thiokol, developed a relatively unstructured

† The wording in this section is adapted from Ayres (Ref. 15-2).

gaming procedure referred to as *dynamic contextural analysis* (Ref. 15-2) to explore future military/space requirements and opportunities. A study group was divided into "red" and "blue" teams representing adversaries in a "cold war" situation. Each team prepared (or was given) a political-economic philosophy and a set of basic national goals consistent with it. These were translated into a set of political, economic, and military policies and strategies. A referee or "control team" provided a particular scenario or "world future" to be explored, usually in the form of a brief summary of the events leading up to and the general situation prevailing at the starting point of the game. Each team then chose a series of actions in support of its stated goals and objectives. These were monitored by the "control" team and, if approved, transmitted to the opposing team. Teams moved in turns until their objectives were achieved or "general war" broke out, or until the game was halted by the referee for some reason. Proposed actions by each team were judged by the control team on the basis of relevance, credibility, and feasibility with respect to (1) the team's objectives and policies, (2) the international political situation, (3) the national economy, (4) national security (military posture), and (5) technological feasibility as a function of time.

National policies in the game ranged from peaceful coexistence to world domination. Strategies used to implement these policies included political subversion of uncommitted nations, economic aggression, sponsorship of "wars of national liberation," direct military attack, disarmament and arms-control agreements, cooperative space exploration, military exploitation of lunar space and/or the sun, etc. Many forms of tactics in support of the above strategies were permitted in the game, including subsidy to revolutionary or status quo groups, diversion of resources, military buildup, and implied threat in strategic, "conventional," or new weapons, such as biological or chemical warfare, orbiting bombs, extended antisubmarine (ASW) capability, etc.

In a series of nine exercises carried out by representatives of the four companies many actions were undertaken by "red" and "blue"—either provocative or in response to provocation—with technological implications, but only available technology and fairly straightforward extrapolations of them were allowed. However, possible functional breakthroughs were examined systematically in a special round table session, not for feasibility but for their military and economic implications. The results of this exercise were invariably interesting and, in some cases, contrary to popular notions. For instance, controlled fusion power was found to be an incremental improvement over existing capabilities, while the ability to broadcast power over great distance would offer several order-of-magnitude increases in capabilities for utilizing space, transportation, and weapons (e.g., laser ABM).

From this brief description it can be seen that dynamic contextual analysis highlights the definitions suggested previously. There is a set of rules, first for the conduct of the game (e.g., each team must develop goals and objectives) and second for the way the impacts of the actions are determined (in this case by judgment of the "control" team). The "red" and "blue" teams play roles by creating goals and objectives and by responding to the other team's actions. And there is a scenario on world futures proposed by the "control" team. Moreover, from the standpoint of the definition of a "game," a *competitive* situation is created in which the role players are striving to find strategies for achieving their separate ends through either cooperation or, at the other extreme, war.

## 15-2 GENERATING SCENARIOS

A significant conclusion from the preceding example is that the proper specification of the scenario is extremely important in games and gaming. In some cases the scenario may not be representative or provide sufficient breadth for creative action by the players, or it may "lead" the players in undesired directions.

Basically, any scenario should involve five major elements:

1. A set of actors or actor groups representing different viewpoints
2. A set of actions (past, present, or anticipated future) and/or policies for each actor or actor group
3. Past or anticipated future conflicts and/or agreements between actors, by type and intensity
4. A set of "external" factors that have and/or will help influence the outcome of the game
5. A set of policy alternatives for the analyst (who may be representing one of the actors)

The scenario should touch briefly on each of these elements and their interconnections but should end in an "open" situation, i.e., one in which future conflicts and their resolution can be identified by the players of the game. Certainly no overall answers or conclusions should be provided in the scenario text.

The story in Table 15-1, adapted from *The New York Times* (Ref. 15-12), presents an outstanding (but surely unintended) real-world example of a scenario. A quick reading brings to light several examples under each of the elements listed above. The actors (element 1) are such people or groups as Brownco, Inc., Mayor Fred Hofheinz, the Daughters of the American Revolution (DAR), and the Audubon Society. Each of these have undertaken certain actions or developed certain policies (element 2) that help define their positions and interests insofar as the conflict situation is concerned. Brownco, Inc., for example, has contributed money to the mayor's campaign, obtained permissions for drilling from various groups, and has had environmental impact statements made. The actions taken by members of the Audubon Society, on the other hand, have consisted mainly of complaining to the press, and perhaps also leaving the feeling that they may go to court.

There are several illustrations of conflicts/agreements (element 3). The major conflict, of course, is over drilling in the park. It puts Brownco, Inc., mainly against a variety of as yet uncoordinated environmental groups like the Audubon Society and the Sierra Club. Agreements seem to be imminent between Brownco,

## Table 15-1 Example scenario

Plan to Drill for Oil in a Park in Houston Creates a Dispute

A big oil company has announced plans to drill some wildcat oil wells in a major park in Houston. The setting is the steamy neo-antebellum splendors of Buffalo Bayou, with its mansions, polo ponies and hanging moss. It is an epic story of ambition and suspense. The case includes a rags-to-riches industrialist, the city's oldest family, the Mayor and City Council, various lawyers and academics, and a local character named Bufo Houstonensis, or the Houston toad.

Subscenarios

The main plot is fairly simple. A Houston oil company, Brownco, Inc., wants to drill for oil in Houston's Memorial Park, a 1,500 acre oasis of green serenity in an urban area famous for sprawl. Some people do not want the drilling. Mayor Fred Hofheinz and the City Council must approve the oil lease, and it is fairly certain that they will. But conservationists are fighting.

The sub plots are complicated. As a first question, can Houston, the city that calls itself the "Energy Capital of the World," afford, for the sake of its image, not to drill for oil in its downtown park? Many oil men there say drilling must proceed as an example of the area's people's willingness to do almost anything to help solve the nation's energy crunch.

Brownco's owner certainly does not need the money. He is George R. Brown, the retired founder of Brown and Root, Inc., the giant Houston-based construction contracting company. Mr. Brown, however, is intensely dedicated to both the free enterprise system and energy independence. He was also a prime contributor to Mayor Hofheinz's recent campaign for re-election.

Mr. Brown's main problem was getting permission to drill. He is now one signature away (from the city of Houston) from obtaining a drilling lease. The park was sold to the city in 1924 for $650,147 by the family of James S. Hogg, a former Texas Governor, on the condition that it be used solely as a public park. If put to, say, commercial use, it would revert to the Hogg estate.

Signatures Obtained

To get around that condition, Mr. Brown got written approval for drilling from the Hogg estate trustee of the Hogg estate, also consented. Allan Shivers, chairman of the Board of Regents, signed on philanthropist daughter. She died a month later.

Mr. Brown also obtained the signatures of several other Hogg relatives. The University of Texas, a trustee of the Hogg estate, also consented. Allan Shivers, a chairman of the Board of Regents, signed on the University's behalf.

Margaret Lowery, president of the state chapter of the Daughters of the Republic of Texas, consented. Miss Hogg left to that group her reversionary rights to the park. But the group's Houston chapter wasn't pleased, probably because several of its members live around the park. They oppose the drilling.

So do the Houston chapters of the Audubon Society and the Sierra Club, both of which have understandably felt for years like petunias in the nation's oil patch. They predict Houston's closet environmentalists may come out in the open on this issue. But several prominent, powerful, and nationally-known Houstonians are keeping their opposition to drilling private so that they do not appear hypocritical in keeping their own backyard clean while urging people to drill, for example, off the East and West coasts.

An Important Precedent

"I don't want them drilling in Memorial Park, but that's no big issue in itself," said Robert Deshayes, an architect heading the Audubon chapter there. "More important is the precedent it would set. It would be used as a stepping stone to open up other areas inside cities, across Texas, and around the nation for the same type of exploitation."

However, it's been done before. One Los Angeles city park produces oil and another has been drilled. Oil has been pumped for years from wells directly under the state Capitol in Oklahoma City. Several refuges for wildlife in Texas have been drilled. But that all happened before people became concerned about their environment. Besides, says Mr. Deshayes, Memorial Park is downtown and different.

**Table 15-1 (*continued*)**

Memorial, he said, is a "fantastic urban park"—heavily wooded, mostly with pines and oaks. It has 400 acres of nearly virgin woods disturbed only by foot and horse trails, and it's loaded with animals and birds. It also has a golf course, tennis courts, ballfields, jogging and bike paths, along with parking lots.

Frank W. Calhoun and Charles Sapp, attorneys for Brownco, Inc., say all that would be meticulously protected. They only want to disturb 12 acres, drill only six wells, and restore the well sites afterward. It would mean about $12 million in royalties and taxes for the city, which it could use to build and improve other parks if they so desired.

"It Should Be Drilled"

"It's definitely a good prospect geologically, I'll guarantee you, and it should be drilled," said one independent Houston oil man. Each site would be fenced and hidden during drilling, the Brownco attorneys said. Trucks would move in and out by back trails. If storage tanks were needed, they could be painted green to blend in with the shrubbery. If pipelines became necessary, trenches could be dug quickly and subsequently covered over and sodded. Finally, all this would take place out of public view, in six two-acre sites in remote sections of the park.

"The remote areas of the parks are the most valuable," said Mr. Deshayes. They've had the least human impact. They're the most natural. The logical place to put a well would be in a parking lot, on a ball diamond or some other impacted area."

Brownco paid Don Kennard, a former state Senator, $2,500 for a 36-page ecological survey that states that "oil and gas development in Memorial Park can be undertaken with minimal—and not significant—damage to the park's environment."

Three university professors and a graduate student spent four days surveying and analyzing the park's plants and animals before writing the study. A good study would have taken a year, protested Jerry Akers, head of the local Sierra Club.

"That environmental statement holds no water," said Mr. Deshayes.

Clubs on 2 Sides

Memorial Park has about 1600 acres, about twice the size of New York's Central Park. On one side of it sits the River Oaks Country Club, centerpiece of a bemansioned neighborhood where people like the John Connallys live. On the other side, the Bayou Club, Houston's oldest, hosts weekend polo matches.

Inside the park is Buffalo Bayou, which once held numerous alligators, but today is the home mostly of trash, fish, mosquito larvae, crayfish, and snapping turtles. Birds are everywhere. A few foxes and coyotes are believed on the prowl in the park, and a white-tailed deer or two possibly exist there. In addition, there are many rabbits, raccoons, rats, squirrels, opposums and armadillos, along with the usual number of snakes, salamanders, frogs, and toads.

"The single species of greatest concern within the park is the Houston toad (Bufo Houstonensis), which is an endangered species," said the Brownco's ecological consultants. Except for a few transplants near Austin, the toad has been found only around Houston. Its park population has been reduced to a few hundred, but people here dispute the reasons why.

Antidrilling forces say such actions in the toad's domain will do little for his serenity or for his numbers. Those in support of drilling say that his prime park habitat is already being ruined by water pollution, probably sewage, emanating from the general direction of the Bayou Club.

However, they say, the Houston toad is doing himself in because of his indiscriminate sex life. He is breeding with other toad species.

*Source:* Adapted from Ref. 15-12.

Inc., and the Mayor and City Council. Conflicts do exist, however, even within one actor group, the Daughters of the American Revolution, where local members apparently are disturbed by the signing by the state chapter's president.

External factors (element 4) are those beyond the control of the major actors. A major one here is the sex life of the Houston toad. Irrespective of what the main actors do, the toad may breed himself out of existence. Or, perhaps as another example, because of the environmental study done by Brownco, Inc., greater care may be given to provide an acceptable habitat for the toad, and he then will respond by proliferating wildly. Whatever the outcome, the point is that the sex life of the toad represents an external factor that could have a significant bearing on the impact of future decisions made by the various actors.

In this scenario there is no actor who we, as analysts, might represent. But we could imagine ourselves as working for the Mayor and City Council, providing information for their upcoming decision. In this position we would generate at least two alternative decisions or policies (element 5), namely to approve or disapprove the oil lease. In the gaming exercise we would try each of these alternatives successively, determining the resultant actions of the major actors and finding the impact of these actions. The decision or policy with the most acceptable impacts then would be selected by the Council.

Notice, however, that the scenario does not give any account of the results of the interaction of the analyst's policies with the actions taken by the prime actors and/or with the influence of the external factors. These findings come about from the play of the game, for which the scenario simply (and definitionally) sets the scene.

## 15-3 SIMPLE GAMES†

Some of the simplest games are those whose scenarios call for two "players," a fixed number of strategies for each, and a matrix of "returns" to each player given the choice of strategies by each. Further, the gain of one player is the loss of the other. This general scenario is referred to as a *two-person, zero-sum game*, and it is primarily useful in forecasting the decisions a person or group will make in a competitive situation. The opponent can be either another person (or, say, agency) or "nature," which can be assumed to produce various opportunities or malevolent events (e.g., unusual warm periods, hurricanes, earthquakes, etc.).

By way of a simple example, consider a regional health planning agency which is helping various localities in its jurisdiction to get federal aid. As anyone who has done this knows, "grantsmanship" is certainly a "game," in this case with the "competitor" being the federal government. Whether or not a group gets a grant depends often on the personalities of administrators, yearly vagaries in Congressional actions, court decisions, and so on.

† Some of the discussion in this section is adapted from Baumol (Ref. 15-4).

Now suppose that there are two possible strategies for the regional agency after having prepared and submitted its grant proposal:

1. Ask the local Congressperson to apply pressure on the federal agency to give the grant.
2. Ask the Congressperson to refrain from applying pressure.

Assume in addition that there are three possible events at the federal level:

A. Congress votes large sums for the grant program, all of which go to regional health agencies on a proportional basis.
B. Congress votes large sums for the grant program, to be allocated at the discretion of the responsible federal agency.
C. Congress decides to give only a small amount of "seed" money to the grant program.

Suppose now that the resultant amounts of funds going to the regional agency under these alternatives are as shown in the following *payoff matrix* (with the numbers in $1000):

| | | Federal level events | | | |
|---|---|---|---|---|---|
| | | A | B | C | min |
| Regional agency strategy | 1 | 50 | 2 | (1) | (1) |
| | 2 | 47 | 48 | (0) | 0 |

In this matrix the grants to the regional agency obviously are subsidies to that agency and corresponding deficits to the federal government, so that the game truly is "zero sum."

One decision-making approach by the regional agency would be that of maximizing the minimum grant they would get. This is referred to as the *maximin* criterion. In our example, the agency would look at its first strategy (row 1) and find the return which was least (= 1, which corresponds to the federal event C). Then it would look at its second strategy (row 2) and find the return which was least (= 0, which again corresponds to the federal event C). Finally, it would choose from those two strategies that which gives the maximum return of the minimums. In this case the regional agency would decide to ask the Congressperson to exert pressure (strategy 1) since that approach would give the maximum of the minimum payoffs in terms of grant money (= $1000).

The maximin criterion can be seen to be highly conservative. Even from the point of view of the true conservative, there is much to be said in favor of the second strategy, because its highest and lowest payoffs (in case Congress selects events A or C) are fairly close to those of the first strategy, whereas the second's intermediate payoff (48) is much higher than the corresponding one for strategy 1. Hence strategy 2 appears to offer an excellent hedge against the possibility that neither the best nor worst possible outcome will be realized.

A gambler, on the other hand, might adopt a *maximax* criterion, which considers only the highest prize offered by any strategies and is blind to all other contingencies. In terms of our payoff matrix, the maximax criterion indicates to the decision maker to again employ strategy 1, whose highest payoff, 50, exceeds the 48 first prize of strategy 2.

Two observations are relevant:

1. This example shows that the extremely gambling-oriented maximax rule can sometimes recommend the same course of action as the maximin rule—their advice will coincide when one strategy carries with it the best of both first and last prizes.
2. Like the maximin criterion, the maximax rule ignores all intermediate payoffs and so may suggest to a player that he give up a very great advantage in the less-glittering payoffs for a negligible difference in the highest one.

Still another decision criterion is that of *minimax regret.* The idea is to protect the player against excessive cost of mistakes. From the initial payoff matrix, a second one showing the cost of mistakes (the regret) is calculated by subtracting the payoffs in each column (federal event) from the maximum in that column. The minimax solution then is located.

The regret matrix for our illustration is:

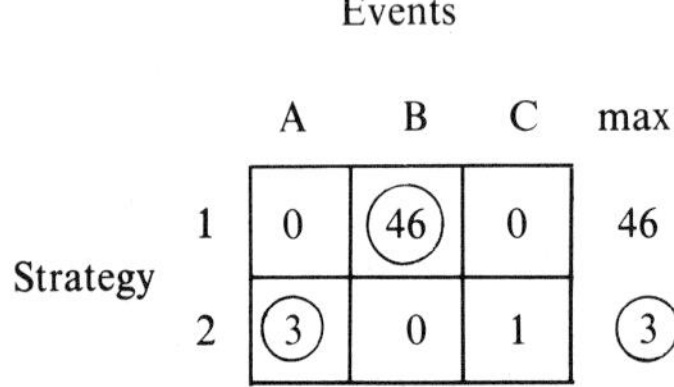

| | | Events A | B | C | max |
|---|---|---|---|---|---|
| Strategy | 1 | 0 | (46) | 0 | 46 |
| | 2 | (3) | 0 | 1 | (3) |

For example, if the regional agency employs strategy 2, it obtains the maximum payoff if the federal event is B and so has nothing to regret. The associated regret figure consequently is 0, which is entered in the matrix in the element corresponding to strategy 2 and event B. But if the regional agency instead had selected strategy 1 and B had occurred, it would have received only 2 (thousand dollars) in grants and "regretted" not getting the additional 46 if it had employed strategy 2. The rest of the regret matrix is computed similarly for the original payoff matrix.

To protect itself against excessive regrets, the regional agency now would apply a minimax criterion (opposite of maximin). For each row the maximum regret is found, and that strategy is chosen which has the smallest of the maximum regrets. In this example it turns out that strategy 2 is most effective in this respect.

Still another decision rule is the *Bayes criterion*. Previously we did not assume anything about the likelihood or probability of any of the federal events occurring. Obviously, if we had such information, perhaps even from a Delphi opinion poll, we would be able to make more informed decisions. At worst we could assume that all the federal events were equally likely (probability $= \frac{1}{3}$) and weigh the payoffs accordingly to get a mean payoff. For strategy 1 this would be:

$$\tfrac{1}{3}(50) + \tfrac{1}{3}(2) + \tfrac{1}{3}(1) = 17\tfrac{2}{3}$$

while for strategy 2 it would be:

$$\tfrac{1}{3}(47) + \tfrac{1}{3}(48) + \tfrac{1}{3}(0) = 31\tfrac{2}{3}$$

The latter strategy would be most desirable under this criterion since the mean or expected value is almost twice as much. In other circumstances it might be possible to get more likely estimates of the probabilities of the federal events and subsequently to refigure the mean values under each strategy.

From these examples it would appear that the use of this type of game theory for decision making and forecasting is limited. In our four cases both strategies were chosen twice—not very discriminating. Of course, the examples were intentionally chosen to highlight these differences. In many situations we may know, for instance, the probabilities of the other player's choices or events. And we would have a good idea of the nature of the decision maker—conservative or gambling. Given these, we would be in a much better position to forecast which strategy the decision maker would be likely to follow.

## 15-4 A LARGE-SCALE GAME

Much effort has been devoted to developing large-scale urban and regional games in which teams of people represent a variety of roles and play many rounds under complicated scenarios. Computers are used to keep track of funds and to make impact forecasts. One such game of this nature is CLUG [the *C*ommunity (Cornell) *L*and-*U*se *G*ame] and its subsequent derivatives—CITY I and the CITY Model (Refs. 15-9 and 15-10). In this section it will be possible to describe the former two of these relatively sophisticated games only in fairly general terms.

### CLUG†

One of the purposes of this game is to illustrate for the player a few of the more fundamental factors affecting land-use decisions in a community and its environs as players attempt to build a city and make money. A second major purpose is to have the model provide a convenient framework upon which more elaborate and realistic models can be built.

† The descriptions here are taken from Ref. (15-6).

Three to five teams begin play with a specified amount of cash with which they are able to purchase land and develop and operate two types of basic (exporting) industries (HI), a nonresidential service industry (BS), a commercial goods business (PG), a commercial service business (PS), and up to four types of residences (*R*). Play begins on a 14 × 14 board on which each parcel represents a square mile of land. Also located on the board is a highway network, a utility plant, and a terminal. The highway network is characterized by low-user cost and high-user cost roads. Since all land uses have travel interactions with the other land uses, parcels alongside the low-cost roads and near other activities have greater advantage. Before parcels can be developed, they must be served by utilities that emanate from the utility plant and run along the edge of parcels. Terminals are a localizing factor, since HI must ship their output to outside system markets via the terminal and pay transportation costs per mile to the terminal.

The major government decisions are made by a majority vote of the teams, and they include setting the local tax rate and expanding utility service. Local revenue is required to pay for annual public expenditures, which include a fixed amount per residence type in the local system, annual operating costs of utility lines, and the capital costs of new utility lines.

The players make all of the employment and commercial matches; i.e., they assign populations, *P*, to work at specific HI, BS, PG, and PS locations, and they sign trade agreements to shop at specific BS, PG, and PS locations. Thus employers may be forced to compete (via better locations) for workers, and commercial establishments may be forced to compete (via lower prices and better locations) for customers.

Money enters the local system through the sale of HI output to national markets at fixed prices. Money leakages occur out of the local system for government expenses, construction costs, land purchases from the bank, transportation charges, and purchases of goods and services from the outside as the result of local insufficiency.

Players may renovate their developments or let them depreciate. Depreciated buildings have a greater chance to be destroyed by the periodic natural disasters that strike the local community.

Taxes are paid on building values (their depreciated value) and on land values. Land values are determined as the average of the value of all owned contiguous land parcels. Thus the price paid for a parcel of land (either for a purchase from the bank or another player) affects the assessed value of that parcel and all adjacent parcels.

## CITY I

This game is an extensive modification of the REGION game that was itself an elaboration upon CLUG. The purpose of CITY I is to provide the user with a decision-making environment that is holistic enough with regard to the economic and governmental sectors that one may see the interrelatedness of decisions across the urban system and over time.

In CITY I, nine teams (one to five members per team) are the decision makers in a partially urbanized county. The playing board is a 25 × 25 grid (comprised of squares each of which represents one square mile). Most of the land is unowned at the beginning of play. These land parcels may be purchased and developed by the teams during the course of the game. There are nine types of private land use which the teams may develop: heavy industry, light industry, business goods, business services, personal goods, personal services, high-income residences, middle-income residences, and low-income residences. Only one private land use per parcel is allowed.

Each of the nine teams is elected or appointed by elected officials to assume the duties of one of nine governmental functions, which are performed simultaneously with the entrepreneurial functions common to all teams. The elected officials must satisfy the electorate (teams have votes in proportion to the number and class of residences they own) in order to stay in office each round. The elected county chairman team appoints other teams to function as the School, Public Works and Safety, Highway, Planning and Zoning, and Finance Departments. The governmental departments build and operate schools, provide utilities, build and upgrade roads and terminals, maintain roads, buy parkland, zone land, and estimate revenues.

Teams set their own objectives for both the public and private actions they undertake. Team decisions are recorded each round (approximately two hours in length) by a computer, which acts as an accountant and indicates the effects of the teams' decisions on one another and on the county itself. The interaction of public and private decisions and their influence over time is illustrated by periodic computer printouts.

The major computer programs in CITY I are for assessments (as in CLUG a new value of a parcel of land has a ripple effect on the values of all other parcels), natural disaster, employment assignments (workers are assigned to jobs in such a way as to maximize salary paid minus transportation to work), routing (travelers are routed along the least-cost path and congestion on given links increases their cost of travel), commercial assignment (customers shop where the prices charged plus travel costs are a minimum), and school assignment (students go to the nearest under-capacity school that meets criteria that vary by income class).

Extensive use is made of computer maps that show changing land uses, land values, transportation congestion, school and government municipal service (MS) districts, zoning, parkland, utility service, and team ownership. Tabular output is also made available to economic teams, governmental departments, and for general use.

## 15-5 ANOTHER LARGE-SCALE GAME†

Another type of game, much more free-form than CLUG or CITY I, was that created by the Institute for the Future for use in forecasting and analyzing different policies for the State of Connecticut (Ref. 15-11). The game had several objectives:

† Part of the description here is taken from Ref. 15-11.

1. Analyzing the effects of external (i.e., world and national) technological and societal developments and of alternative courses of action (policies) on the state.
2. Providing a better understanding of the roles of governmental decision makers and the elements of society affected by their decisions.
3. Generating discussion which would lead to better understanding of the state's future needs and opportunities and wider recognition of the alternative courses of action available to the state.

The participants were divided into three groups. Two of them were called "players," representing legislators, and developed programs of action for the state. The third group, called "evaluators," simulated society at large and (using a voting machine) assessed the status of the indicators before and after each round of play. One team of players was instructed to maximize the per capita GSP (gross state product) and the other to optimize the Connecticut QOL (quality of life). The basic task of the evaluators was to record society's degree of satisfaction with affairs in Connecticut. Each member of the evaluating team represented a certain segment of society: the urban poor, the cultural elite, the middle class, the older citizens, youth, city management, the financial community, and the federal government. Role playing was used to encourage explicit consideration of the interests of these sectors of society.

The procedural flow of the game is shown in Fig. 15-1. The game began with the evaluators discussing their satisfaction with aspects of life in the state in terms of 14 economic and social indicators:

1. Government effectiveness
2. Business climate
3. Housing
4. Transportation
5. Satisfaction with tax structure
6. Employment
7. Standard of living
8. Social climate
9. Control of crime
10. Physical environment
11. Health
12. Education
13. Recreation
14. Personal liberties

Two aggregate indicators, per capita GSP and Connecticut QOL, were also assessed. The scale for each ranged from 20 (situation requiring major reassessment) to 100 (excellent situation), except for the per capita GSP, which was in absolute units.

The players heard (and were permitted to contribute to) the discussion of the current rating of each indicator and so were aware of the criteria used by the evaluating team in its assessment. The evaluators discussed each issue, voted on a preliminary rating, discussed the issue again to seek a consensus, and then cast a final vote. The median of each rating was recorded on the indicator charts. Each round of the simulation represented a 10-year period.

Each team was provided with candidate action cards derived from a previous Delphi study of future issues and opportunities in Connecticut. The cards

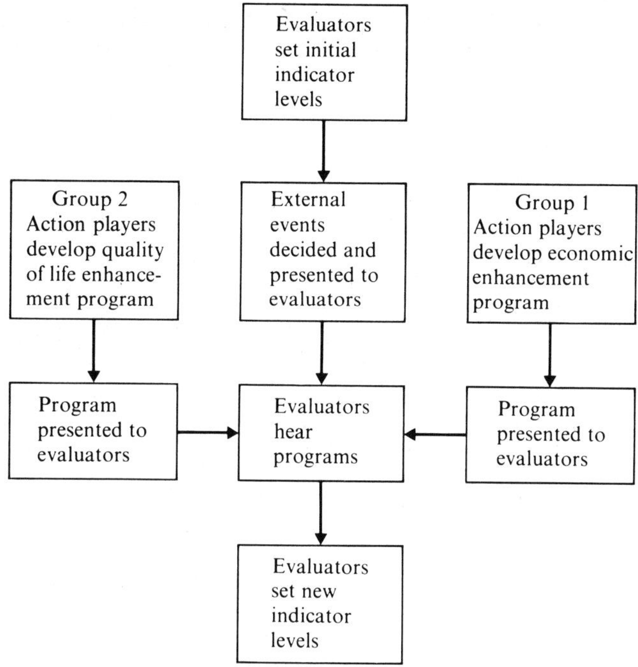


**Figure 15-1** General game flow. (*Source: Ref. 15-11, p. 555.*)

described potential actions and presented short background discussions of the concepts. In addition they indicated a minimum cost and impact of each action on the 14 economic and social indicators. A sample of the candidate actions is displayed in Table 15-2.

The minimum price of an action was taken as an intuitive measure of the combined political effort and monetary cost required to establish a program at a level that would have a noticeable impact on the state. The least expensive actions were assigned a cost of one point.

A pseudoeconomic system was superimposed on the play to force consideration of priorities and limit the number of actions the players could choose. The players had 60 points to spend in the first decade; in the later decades the available budget varied as a function of the action taken and the effect of certain outside events. The two budgetary constraints were that each action had to be allocated at least its minimum price and that total expenditures had to be within the budget.

The players were urged not only to consider the prepared actions but to propose new ones, which were approved and given minimum levels of effort by the evaluators.

Both teams were told that the programs they were preparing were in addition to the normal operation of the state. For example, if no action had been taken in

**Table 15-2 Sample candidate actions**

1. Implement community development programs on a regional basis.
2. Establish an ombudsman's office.
3. Institute a statewide government data management system.
4. Centralize public service and facility districts.
5. Establish statewide regional governments.
6. Subsidize on-the-job retraining.
7. Offer incentives to high-technology industries for migrating to this state.
8. Establish a business climate planning agency.
9. Subsidize moderate-income housing.
10. Subsidize housing for senior citizens.
11. Rezone urban areas to permit greater population density.
12. Make multiple use of highway space.
13. Enact statewide flood controls.
14. Rezone to decentralize urban areas.

*Source:* Ref. 15-11, p. 558.

the area of education, this would not have meant that schools would be closed or even that the normal rate of school construction would be slowed; it meant rather that no innovative improvements would be made in education.

Fifty potential external developments were selected from technological and societal Delphi studies conducted at the Institute for the Future. The events were displayed on cards and in the form of a matrix, which indicated their probability of occurrence, with the expected linkages of interdependencies among events. The outcome of the external events for each simulation period was determined by a probabilistic procedure. Items were chosen at random from the list of 50 external events, and their occurrence in the interval being simulated was "decided" by comparing their probabilities of occurrence as determined from the Delphi study with a random number obtained by casting dice. If an item "happened," the probabilities of the other items were adjusted according to instructions contained in the matrix. The process was continued until every item was decided. Table 15-3 presents a sample list of the titles of the 50 events.

Events determined to have happened were described to the evaluators while the players were choosing their programs. The evaluators were instructed to consider these events later when they assessed new values for the societal indicators.

After the players had selected their actions, the evaluators were briefed on these programs and the indicators were reassessed for 1980. The evaluators considered how the indicators might be affected from the point of view of the societal sector they were simulating. This assessment again involved debate which centered around recognition of pluralistic societal interests and the likely effects of external technological and social change. Once this had been accomplished, the cycle was repeated for the next decade.

**Table 15-3 Sample list of external events**

| Event | Probability | | |
|---|---|---|---|
| | 1970s | 1980s | 1990s |
| 1. Multistate regional authorities | 0.80 | 0.90 | 0.90 |
| 2. Average retirement age: 55 | 0.10 | 0.30 | 0.50 |
| 3. Advanced building codes | 0.60 | 0.80 | 0.90 |
| 4. Nuclear disarmament | 0.20 | 0.40 | 0.40 |
| 5. Biological weapons | 0.30 | 0.30 | 0.30 |
| 6. Wars not directly involving the United States | 0.80 | 0.80 | 0.80 |
| 7. Limited wars directly involving the United States | 0.30 | 0.40 | 0.40 |
| 8. Credit card economy | 0.70 | 0.80 | 0.90 |
| 9. Business recession | 0.20 | 0.20 | 0.20 |
| 10. Continued inflation | 0.60 | 0.60 | 0.60 |
| 11. Educational network | 0.30 | 0.50 | 0.70 |
| 12. Data banks | 0.60 | 0.70 | 0.80 |
| 13. Household robots | 0.20 | 0.30 | 0.40 |
| 14. Thirty-five hours worked per week | 0.30 | 0.50 | 0.60 |
| 15. High IQ computers | 0.30 | 0.60 | 0.70 |

*Source:* Ref. 15-11, p. 562.

## Results of Game Play

In the actual play of the game the teams set about developing their action programs for the 1970–1980 period in accordance with their different policy instructions. In the initial deliberations they decided which indicators needed improvement in view of their goals and the remarks of the evaluators when the indicator values were set. The deliberations were then reviewed in light of the probabilities of the external events and their likely impacts, and as a result, the players formulated an initial action program that included the generation of new actions.

After "pricing" the new actions contemplated by the players, the evaluators were presented with the results of the probabilistic assessments of certain external events occurring during the 1970–1980 period. During this time the player teams pared their action programs down to budget. The review of the external events by the evaluators and the finalization of the action programs were completed at the same time, so that program review and reappraisal of the indicators for 1980 could begin without any group of participants being idle. The results of the appraisal were two possible futures for Connecticut, one for the GSP team and another for the QOL team, both of which would be embedded in the same external environment. These futures represented the two different starting points for the second round, the 1980–1990 period, in which the process just described was repeated.

**Table 15-4 Indicator satisfaction levels**

| | | GSP team | | QOL team | |
|---|---|---|---|---|---|
| Indicator | Initial value (1970) | Changes in 1970s | 1980 value | Changes in 1970s | 1980 value |
| 1. Government effectiveness | 50 | 6 | 56 | 4 | 54 |
| 2. Business climate | 70 | 5 | 75 | 4 | 74 |
| 3. Housing | 50 | 5 | 55 | 2 | 52 |
| 4. Transportation | 45 | 6 | 51 | 4 | 49 |
| 5. Satisfaction with tax structure | 40 | −1 | 39 | −2 | 38 |
| 6. Employment | 70 | 4 | 74 | 2 | 72 |
| 7. Standard of living | 65 | 4 | 69 | 2 | 67 |
| 8. Social climate | 50 | 4 | 54 | 1 | 51 |
| 9. Control of crime | 40 | 2 | 42 | 2 | 42 |
| 10. Physical environment | 65 | 4 | 69 | 2 | 67 |
| 11. Health | 60 | 2 | 62 | 2 | 62 |
| 12. Education | 50 | 6 | 56 | 4 | 54 |
| 13. Recreation | 60 | 1 | 61 | 0 | 60 |
| 14. Personal liberties | 60 | 0 | 60 | 0 | 60 |
| Quality of life | 60 | 6 | 66 | 2 | 62 |
| Gross state product per capita | $5000 | $500 | $5500 | $200 | $5200 |

*Source:* Ref. 15-11, p. 566.

The indicator satisfaction levels, which became the point of departure for the simulation conference, are presented for the 1970–1980 period in Table 15-4. All but the per capita GSP were established by the evaluation team as described above and in accordance with the game rules presented earlier; the GSP indicator started with the projected 1970 value for Connecticut.

Several observations can be made from these values. First, they are low. The actual ratings apparently stemmed from the differences between the achievements of the state and the expectations and aspirations of the evaluators. Second, the QOL indicator is higher than the average of the 14 others, showing that the evaluators considered some indicators more important than others and gave their contribution to the quality of life greater weight. Interestingly, among the indicators rated below average are housing, transportation, and education, all regarded by the earlier Delphi panel as containing the most important issues likely to occur in this state during the remainder of the century.

The actions selected by each team in each of the first rounds are shown in Table 15-5. A sample of the external events and the results of the probabilistic assessments of these events are shown in Table 15-6. The initial probabilities of these events occurring within the 1970–1980 time period are noted in column 2; the events which the analysis concluded had occurred in this decade are in column 3; the new probabilities of these events occurring within the 1980–1990 time

**Table 15-5 Actions selected in the first round (1970–1980) of play**

| No.† GSP team | Action title | Minimum‡ effort |
|---|---|---|
| 1 | Implement community development program on a regional basis. | 3 |
| 7 | Offer incentives to high-technology industry for migrating to Connecticut. | 4 |
| 17 | Reform building codes to accept technological innovation. | 4 |
| 19 | Subsidies for low-income housing. | 7 |
| 22 | Establish new communities in rural areas. | 5 |
| 41 | Provide incentives for urban mass-transportation systems. | 4 |
| 45 | Initiate a state income tax. | 2 |
| 53 | Subsidize new businesses for locating in the ghettos. | 2 |
| 79 | Offer adult educational retraining. | 3 |
| 82 | Institute high school work-study programs. | 3 |
| 89 | Enlarge vocational training programs. | 4 |
| 90 | Offer compensatory payment for scholastic achievement. | 3 |
| 201 | Construct a new airport in eastern Connecticut. | 5 |
| 203 | Provide free post-secondary education for all students. | 5 |
| 209 | Keep schools open evenings and weekends. | 4 |
| 210 | Offer subsidies for the creation of new categories of service employment. | 3 |
| | | 61 |
| QOL team | | |
| 4 | Centralize public service and facility districts. | 3 |
| 5 | Establish statewide regional governments. | 8 |
| 7 | Offer incentives to high-technology industry for migration to Connecticut. | 4 |
| 15 | Place building code control at the state level. | 5 |
| 45 | Initiate a state income tax.§ | 2 |
| 81 | Extend the educational period. | 8 |
| 89 | Enlarge vocational training programs. | 4 |
| 204 | Establish a state new-community development corporation. | 8 |
| 205 | Collect all taxes at the state level. | 3 |
| 210 | Offer subsidies for the creation of new categories of service employment. | 3 |
| 212 | Reconstruct public educational system. | 8 |
| 214 | Enlarge educational opportunities for adults. | 3 |
| | | 61 |

*Source:* Ref. 15-11, p. 567.

† Actions numbered 1–111 were provided in the prepared deck. Actions numbered in the 200s are new actions proposed by the teams in the first period.

‡ Each team had a budget of 60 points for the first decade. Both the "green" and the "buff" programs sum to 61 effort points due to an accounting error which was not discovered until after the programs were evaluated.

§ This is the only action of the entire game which was budgeted at more than minimum cost; it was budgeted at a level of 4.

**Table 15-6 Simulated occurrence of external events**

| (1) External events | (2) Probability of occurrence in the 1970s | (3) Occurred in the 1970s | (4) Probability of occurrence in the 1980s | (5) Occurred in the 1980s |
|---|---|---|---|---|
| 1. Multistate regional authorities | 0.80 | yes | 0.90 | yes |
| 2. Average retirement age: 55 | 0.10 | yes | 1.00 | yes |
| 3. Advanced building codes | 0.60 | | 0.80 | yes |
| 4. Nuclear disarmament | 0.20 | | 0.55 | |
| 5. Biological weapons | 0.30 | | 0.20 | |
| 6. Wars not directly involving the United States | 0.80 | yes | 0.80 | |
| 7. Limited wars directly involving the United States | 0.30 | | 0.35 | |
| 8. Credit card economy | 0.70 | | 0.85 | yes |
| 9. Business recession | 0.20 | | 0.30 | |
| 10. Continued inflation | 0.60 | yes | 0.45 | yes |
| 11. Educational network | 0.30 | | 0.45 | |
| 12. Data banks | 0.60 | | 0.70 | yes |
| 13. Household robots | 0.20 | | 0.40 | |
| 14. Thirty-five hours worked per week | 0.30 | | 0.55 | |
| 15. High IQ computers | 0.30 | yes | 1.00 | □ |

*Source:* Ref. 15-11, p. 570.
Key: "yes" = event occurred in decade shown.
□ = event occurred in the previous decade and had sustained effects.

period are in column 4; and the events deemed to have occurred by 1990 are noted in column 5.

The action programs and the evaluation of these programs in terms of the fourteen indicators provide a very rich source of insight into the goals and methods of the participants. A review of the actions for the 1970–1980 time period shows that four of the actions were common to both teams. Both teams faced the housing issue squarely. The GSP team used the prepared action addressing new communities and the QOL team formulated an even more costly program in this area. Both teams also dealt strongly with the issue of education. The GSP team addressed the transportation issue at the expense of somewhat less ambitious housing and educational programs than were presented by the QOL team.

In total, the 1970–1980 programs for the two teams must be regarded as quite similar, with the QOL team electing to concentrate on fewer areas than the GSP team. This concentration and its attempt at greater thoroughness was not appreciated by the evaluators as much as the broader package offered by the GSP team, which can be seen to have scored higher in almost every indicator, including the QOL indicator itself.

## PROBLEMS

**15-1** Fill in the blanks with the appropriate word(s).

(*a*) ______________ is a set of rules for role playing within the context of a given ______________.

(*b*) ____________ is the actual playing of a game.

(*c*) In the game a ____________________ situation is created in which role players try to achieve their separate ends.

(*d*) The five elements in a scenario are: ____________________.

(*e*) A two-person, zero-sum game is defined as: ____________________.

(*f*) The table of numbers employed in a two-person, zero-sum game is called a ____________________.

(*g*) The four decision rules for two-person, zero-sum games discussed in this chapter are ____________________.

(*h*) CLUG stands for ____________________.

**15-2** Given the following table for two players of a game, what should their strategies be? Player A is out to maximize the returns indicated in the table while player B is out to minimize them.

| | | Player B | | | | |
|---|---|---|---|---|---|---|
| | | 1 | 2 | 3 | 4 | 5 |
| | 1 | 28 | 25 | 15 | 17 | 11 |
| | 2 | 22 | 19 | 13 | 15 | 13 |
| Player A | 3 | 27 | 50 | 16 | 21 | 9 |
| | 4 | 28 | 73 | 18 | 82 | 12 |
| | 5 | 29 | 24 | 106 | 95 | 11 |

**15-3** (*a*) If player A is trying to maximize the maximum returns, what strategy should be followed?
(*b*) What strategy should be followed to try to minimize the maximum "regrets"?
(*c*) What strategy should be followed if player B is equally likely to choose each of the strategies?

**15-4** Go to the library and review a publication dealing with a particular urban or regional game. In about 500 words report on:
(*a*) The type of situation for which the game was developed
(*b*) The type and number of players
(*c*) The nature of the competition in the game
(*d*) Likely strategies of particular players
(*e*) Results from different runs of the game
(*f*) Your opinion of the general usefulness of the game for the situation being investigated

**15-5** War games have always been played by different countries to test military strategies. In the library find a report on such a game and, in about 500 words, describe how you might translate the gaming procedure to an urban or regional situation.

**15-6** Develop a sample scenario in the form suggested in Sec. 15-2. This scenario can be on any urban or regional topic, but must be useful as a first step in a gaming approach similar to Boeing's dynamic contextural analysis.

**15-7** "Play" the scenario generated in Prob. (15-6), perhaps using a procedure analogous to that of Gordon, Enzer, and Rochberg (Ref. 15-11 and Sec. 15-5).

## REFERENCES


### Theory

15-1. Abt, C. C., R. N. Foster, and R. H. Rea: "A Scenario Generating Methodology," in J. F. Bright and M. E. F. Schoeman (Eds.), *A Guide to Practical Technological Forecasting*, Prentice-Hall, Englewood Cliffs, N.J., 1973.

15-2. Ayres, R. U.: *Technological Forecasting and Long Range Planning*, McGraw-Hill, New York, 1969.

15-3. Barton, R. S.: *A Primer on Simulation and Gaming*, Prentice-Hall, Englewood Cliffs, N.J., 1970.

15-4. Baumol, W. J.: *Economic Theory and Operations Analysis*, 2d ed., Prentice-Hall, Englewood Cliffs, N. J., 1965.

15-5. Davis, M. D.: *Game Theory: A Nontechnical Introduction*, Basic Books, New York, 1970.

15-6. Environmetrics. Inc.: *The State-of-the-Art in Urban Gaming Models*, NTIS, PB-201 944, Springfield, Va., July, 1971.

15-7. Shubik, M., G. Brewer, and E. Savage: *The Literature of Gaming, Simulation, and Model-Building*, The Rand Corporation, Report R-620-ARPA, Santa Monica, Calif., June, 1972.

15-8. Stadsklev, R.: *Handbook of Simulation Gaming in Social Education*, 2 parts, Institute of Higher Education Research and Services, The University of Alabama, Tuscaloosa, Ala., 1974.

### Applications

15-9. Environmetrics, Inc.: *City Model Player's Manual*, Technical Analysis Division, National Bureau of Standards, Washington, D.C., 1971.

15-10. Feldt, A. G.: *The Community (Cornell) Land Use Game (CLUG)*, The Free Press, New York, 1972.

15-11. Gordon, T. J., S. Enzer, and R. Rochberg: "Experiment in Simulation Gaming for Social Policy Studies," in J. F. Bright and M. E. F. Schoeman (Eds.), *A Guide to Practial Technological Forecasting*, Prentice-Hall, Englewood Cliffs, N. J., 1973.

15-12. Sterba, J. P.: "Plan to Drill for Oil in Park Creates Dispute in Houston," *The New York Times*, Thursday, January 22, 1976.

15-13. U.S. Environmental Protection Agency: *The River Basin Model*, 14 vols., Water Pollution Control Series 16110 FRU12 71, U.S.GPO, Washington, D.C., 1972.

15-14. U.S. Environmental Protection Agency: *APEX: Air Pollution Exercise*, 21 vols., Office of Air Programs, Washington, D.C., 1972.

CHAPTER

# SIXTEEN

# MORPHOLOGICAL ANALYSIS

Morphological analysis is the study of form (from the Greek word *morphy*). The initial development of the method is attributed to Fritz Zwicky, a famous astrophysicist and jet-engine pioneer, who felt the need for a technique for identifying, indexing, counting, and parameterizing the set of all possible devices to achieve a specific functional capability (Ref. 16-4). The word "analysis" is not entirely descriptive of the technique's usefulness, for it can be employed both in *forecasting* future changes in forms or structures or processes and as a *normative* device for pointing to possible future innovations in such forms.

Perhaps the most obvious applications of morphological analysis are in the investigation of technological opportunities. Apart from the potential for using the technique to anticipate actual inventions, there also is the possibility of characterizing the optimum configuration for a particular mission or task. Even if this cannot be done with complete confidence, we can at least devise a partial ordering of possible inventions in terms of their relative immediacy and importance. This exercise would not produce a forecast per se, but it would be a useful way of organizing ideas, a source of insights, and a starting point for further analyses by other methods.

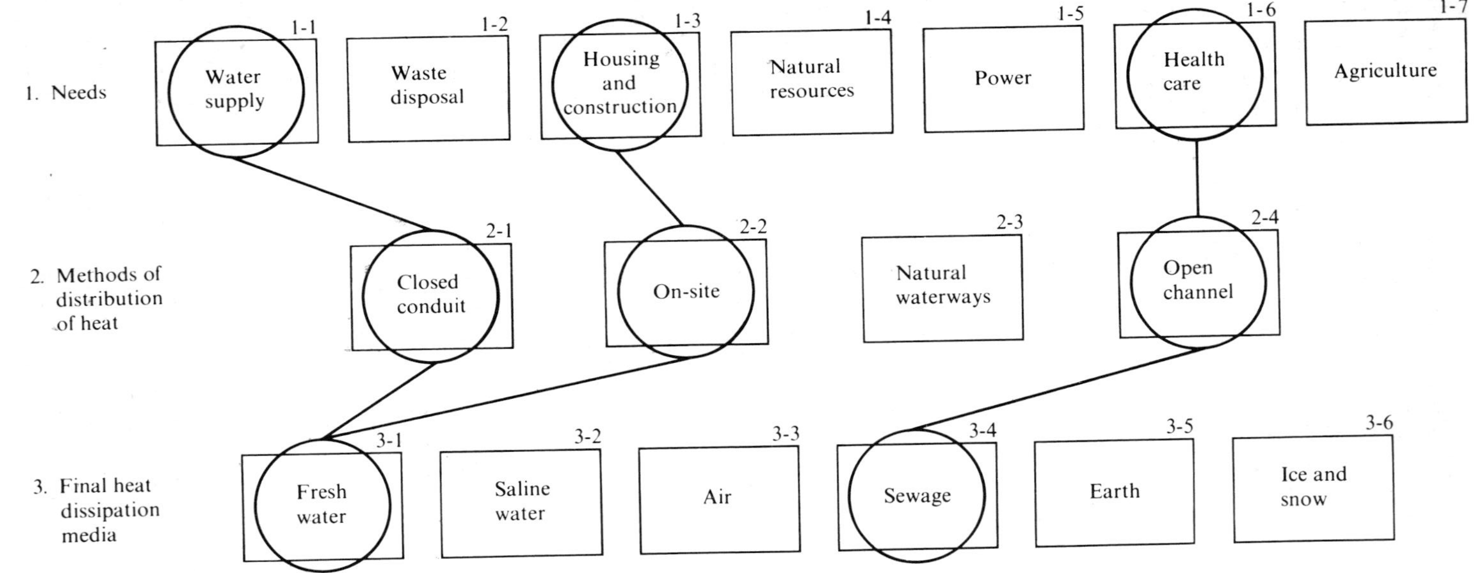


**Figure 16-1** Morphological chart showing potential beneficial uses of thermal plant waste heat. (*Source: Adapted from Ref. 16-6.*)

## 16-1 A SIMPLE EXAMPLE

The basic method and its variations perhaps can be best explained with a specific example. Fields (Ref. 16-6) has done a morphological analysis in the process of discovering and evaluating beneficial applications for waste heat discharged from thermal power plants. Figure 16-1 is a shortened version of his morphological chart. As can be seen, each application satisfied some need, required some method of distributing the waste heat to the areas of eventual use, and utilized some ultimate heat sink or heat dissipation medium. Fields therefore selected the following three dimensions:

1. Needs
2. Methods of distribution of waste heat
3. Final heat dissipation media

These dimensions were subsequently subdivided into their various alternatives. For instance, "needs" included those for water supply, waste disposal, housing and construction, and so on, as displayed at the top of Fig. 16-1.

The morphological analysis was then accomplished by combining one item from each of the three dimensions. By way of illustration, we could take the need for water supply (1-1). The waste heat from the thermal plant could be employed to help create low-grade energy for desalinizing ocean water. But there would have to be some method to transport the heated water to the desalinization plant (assuming the thermal plant is located on a fresh water river). This might be by closed conduit (2-1). The thermal plant water then could be utilized along with the desalinized water to augment existing supplies (3-1).

Other combinations of items in the morphological chart might also be contemplated. Houses, stores, offices, and the like (1-3), particularly those nearby the thermal plant (2-2), could be warmed with the waste heat, with any left over being dissipated in the nearby river (fresh water) (3-1). If either of these or any other combination were evaluated as having great promise, we might then make a *forecast* that such a technology would become prevalent within the foreseeable future.

The morphological chart can be used in a second way. The two technologies cited so far are not unique. In fact, something similar to the latter has been employed in several European countries. If now we wanted to search for some "far-out" technologies in the hope of finding one with significant potential that had yet to be discovered by other researchers, we might try several combinations on the chart. Take, for example, the combination of health care (1-6), open channel (2-4), and sewage (3-4). With a little bit of imagination, we might conceive of the waste heat water being transported in an open channel to the sewage treatment plant where it is used to heat sewage, thereby killing many germs potentially harmful to public health. This combination may seem far-fetched, but with more detailed investigation, it may turn out to be feasible with only slight modifications to existing technologies and to waste treatment facilities in the region under study. In any case, it does point to the usefulness of morphological analysis in normative (solution generation) efforts.

## 16-2 THE THEORY OF MORPHOLOGICAL ANALYSIS†

The rules for morphological analysis, as originally expounded by Zwicky (Ref. 16-4), are as follows:

1. The problem to be solved or the functional capability desired should be stated with as much precision as possible.
2. The characteristic dimensions should be identified. To some extent this process is an automatic consequence of the exact definition of the problem, although the assurance may not be of much practical value to the analyst. There are, for example, no reliable cookbook recipes to determine when the list is *complete*. In Fig. 16-1, for instance, it may be necessary to divide "needs" into several subcategories, as Fields actually has done (Ref. 16-6). As an example, under "water supply" (1-1), he identified subneeds as industrial, agricultural, domestic, and power. He further identified subneeds under domestic as drinking, cooking, sanitation, etc.
3. Each dimension should be subdivided into distinguishable items or "states." Often there is a continuum of values that must be classified into meaningful ranges or regions. Natural resource needs (1-4), for instance, might be viewed in terms of the dollar value added to each unit of product (e.g., coal) through the extraction process. Several ranges of "value added" might then be devised to correspond to different types and levels of "needs."
4. Some "universal" method of evaluating the performance of the various combinations is needed. This obviously is very difficult to find and use since there is such a broad variety of possible combinations. What criteria might be employed to assess water supply, housing and construction, and health care all at the same time? On the other hand, we must realize that one of the major purposes of morphological analysis is simply to eliminate large numbers of combinations that are significantly less beneficial than others. Fields used such evaluation criteria as feasibility and timing, availability, need or value, and capacity to dissipate heat. He thereby was able to reduce the list of candidate technologies substantially.

Two additional points about morphological analysis are that:

5. The number of combinations can become quite large.
6. There are some combinations that can be eliminated since they do not fit together logically.

† Some of the wording in this section is adapted from Ref. 16-1.

To demonstrate point 5, we see that in Fig. 16-1 there are $7 \times 4 \times 6 = 168$ possible combinations. A thoughtful person or group would take many hours to evaluate just these possibilities. On the other hand, if we took all of Field's 17 needs (and not any of his subneeds or subsubneeds), we would have $17 \times 4 \times 6 = 408$ combinations to evaluate. The task would expand to about $2\frac{1}{2}$ times as much as before. And if we included the subneeds and subsubneeds, there would be thousands of choices to assess.

There can be many examples of combinations that do not fit together logically, either because they are strictly illegal, physically impossible, or the like. To illustrate: we could not combine housing and construction (1-3) with on-site distribution of heat (2-2) if for safety reasons it were forbidden to place housing within so many miles of the site (which could be, for example, a nuclear plant).

## 16-3 ANOTHER SIMPLE EXAMPLE

To show that morphological analysis is certainly not restricted to physical systems, let us consider the future of social services systems. Following the rules in the preceding section, we first state the functional capability desired as precisely as possible. In this example we borrow heavily from the goals (or desired functional capabilities) and social service classifications expressed by the United Way of America in their *United Way of America Services Identification System* (UWASIS—Ref. 16-7). They show six major goals, as displayed on the left-hand side of Fig. 16-2.

The second rule is to identify the characteristic dimensions. Here we have elected to use the six goals as the dimensions so that, as suggested in the previous section, this step is an automatic consequence of the preceding definitional phase.

The third rule is to subdivide the dimensions into distinguishable items. This has been done in Fig. 16-2, again conforming to the format in the UWASIS. A close scrutiny of these categories will show that some items which we might consider to be social services are left out. Nothing is mentioned explicitly, for instance, about the material needs (goal 1) for energy for cooking, heating, etc. Hence this item might be added to the end of the second row in the figure.†

To meet the final rule we need to combine and evaluate the various categories under each goal. Suppose for our example that our major interest is in forecasting the likelihood of different social services integration patterns needed to reduce costs and increase the joint benefits of the services. To illustrate, we might take the first item in each row (goal) to form a combination. This would give:

> Employment; food and nutrition; physical health; formal education; individual and family life; and mobilization of people

† Such possibilities are recognized in the UWASIS where an AIN (*a*dd *i*f *n*ecessary) is appended to each list of items.

| Goal (desired functional capability) | Categories | | | | | |
|---|---|---|---|---|---|---|
| 1. Adequate income and economic opportunity | Employment 1-1 | Income maintenance 1-2 | Consumer protection and safety 1-3 | | | |
| 2. Optimal environmental conditions, materials/needs | Food and nutrition 2-1 | Clothing and apparel 2-2 | Housing 2-3 | Transportation 2-4 | Public protection, justice, safety 2-5 | Environmental protection and enrichment 2-6 |
| 3. Optimal health | Physical health maintenance and care 3-1 | Mental health maintenance and care 3-2 | Mental retardation 3-3 | Rehabilitation 3-4 | | |
| 4. Adequate knowledge and skills | Formal education 4-1 | Informal supplementary education 4-2 | | | | |
| 5. Optimal personal and social adjustment and development | Individual and family life 5-1 | Social adjustment, development, and usefulness 5-2 | Cultural and spiritual enrichment and development 5-3 | | | |
| 6. Adequately organized social instrumentalities | Mobilization of people 6-1 | Administration and management capability 6-2 | Equal opportunity 6-3 | | | |

**Figure 16-2** Morphological chart of social services.

Such a combination might bring to mind existing nutrition programs where social welfare personnel (under mobilization of people) are hired (employment) to provide formal education in high schools on proper nutrition and its impact on the physical health of individuals and families.

We subsequently would characterize all other *present* social services in a like fashion. For simplicity, let us imagine that these are covered by all combinations of the first two items in each row. For forecasting, especially short term, we then would assume that any changes would be incremental ones. For example, consumer protection and safety (1-3) might be added to some present combination of items under goals 2 to 6. Of course, we would have to evaluate this incremental change to see if it were more economically beneficial, politically acceptable, physsically feasible, etc., than other incremental changes. In this evaluation we might possibly use a Delphi approach, asking the panel to take into account factors like those just described.

For long-term forecasting the incremental assumption is not as valid, of course, and, in addition, evaluation is more difficult. If we were looking, say, 50 years ahead, we might assume that there will be sufficient time to develop the most beneficial system. We therefore could try all of the different combinations of categories and, finding that one which rated highest, presume that it would be most likely to occur.† Note, too, that we are not really restricted here to taking one item from each row. It is entirely possible to take several from one goal and none from another. The number of combinations of service types thus could get quite large. Some, however, are incompatible. A severely retarded person (3-3), for instance, probably could make little use of standard formal education (4-1) programs, so that any combination involving these two items could be eliminated. Even if this overall procedure did not produce useful forecasts, it might be valuable for identifying desirable and previously not-considered directions for future social service integration efforts.

## 16-4 AN APPLICATION‡

Morphological analysis has been employed by Dickey, Glancy, and Jennelle (Ref. 16-5) to examine the solid waste management program of an urban county (Fairfax County, Virginia). The technique was not employed as much for forecasting as it was simply to describe in a simplified manner the presently complex system and several of the alternatives suggested to improve that system.

The first step was to categorize the types of solid waste that had to be managed by the county. The resultant classification, shown in Table 16-1, was derived from an assessment of other schemes and from existing and forecasted general conditions in Fairfax County.

† Admittedly an overly optimistic viewpoint.

‡ Some of the wording in this section is adapted from Ref. 16-5.

**Table 16-1 Solid waste material classification**

| | | | | |
|---|---|---|---|---|
| m | 1 | Garbage | Wastes from the preparation, cooking, and serving of food<br>Market refuse, waste from the handling, storage, and sale of produce and meats | From households, institutions, and commercial concerns such as: hotels, stores, restaurants, markets, etc. |
| m | 2 | Combustible rubbish (primarily organic) | Paper, cardboard cartons, wood, boxes, excelsior, plastics, rags, cloth, bedding, leather, rubber, grass, leaves, yard trimmings | |
| m | 3 | Noncombustible rubbish | Metals, tin cans, metal foils, dirt, stones, bricks, ceramics, crockery, glass, bottles, other mineral refuse | |
| m | 4 | Ashes | Residue from fires used for cooking and for heating buildings, cinders | |
| m | 5 | Bulky Wastes | Large auto parts, tires<br>Stoves, refrigerators, other large appliances<br>Furniture, large crates<br>Trees, branches, palm fronds, stumps, flotage | From streets, sidewalks, alleys, vacant lots, etc. |
| m | 6 | Street refuse | Street sweepings, dirt<br>Leaves<br>Catch basin dirt<br>Contents of litter receptacles | |
| m | 7 | Dead animals | Small animals: cats, dogs, poultry, etc.<br>Large animals: horses, cows, etc. | |
| m | 8 | Abandoned vehicles | Automobiles, trucks | |
| m | 9 | Construction and demolition wastes | Lumber, roofing, and sheathing scraps<br>Rubble, broken concrete, plaster, etc.<br>Conduit, pipe, wire, insulation, etc. | |
| m | 10 | Industrial refuse | Solid wastes resulting from industrial processes and manufacturing operations such as food-processing wastes, boiler house cinders, wood, plastic, and metal scraps and shavings, etc. | From factories. power plants, etc. |
| m | 11 | Hazardous wastes | Pathological wastes, explosives, radioactive materials | From households, hospitals, institutions |
| m | 12 | Security wastes | Confidential documents, negotiable papers, etc. | From stores, industries, government, etc. |
| m | 13 | Animal and agriculture wastes | Manures, crop residues | From farms, feed lots |
| m | 14 | Sewage treatment residues | Coarse screenings, grit, septic tank sludge, dewatered sludge | From sewage treatment plants, septic tanks |

*Source:* Ref. 16-5, pp. 38, 39.

To keep track of the flow of "goods" both through the solid waste system and "leaking" into the environment, the authors also developed a typology of by-product materials. For example, these included, for an incinerator, particulate matter in the air, wash water, and ashes. The disposal of these by-products determined to some degree the usefulness of the particular alternate technology being studied. The list of by-product materials identified is presented in Table 16-2. Similar types of consideration for identifying and classifying solid waste materials also were involved for the by-product materials.

The authors next developed a morphological representation of the stages and states in the general solid waste handling process. "Stages" were the major phases in the process. "States" were the means by which a stage could be accomplished. For example, incineration is a state in the processing stage of one type of solid waste system. The list of stages and corresponding states is displayed in Table 16-3. This table was intended to be fairly detailed but certainly not exhaustive. As will be shown later, an important benefit of the proposed morphology was the capability to trace the treatment of each waste material and the disposition of all by-product materials, including leakages.

The next step in the study was to do the detailed morphological analysis of the stages and states in the existing Fairfax County solid waste system. This was accomplished through the stages/states transition matrix (Table 16-4), which was employed in place of a morphological chart (like those in Figs. 16-1 and 16-2). As shown in the table, a certain portion of the materials m1 through m4 (garbage, combustible and noncombustible rubbish, and ashes) are all stored temporarily at the production site, mostly in 30-gallon cans (stage I, state g). The rest of these materials are handled privately, and thus were not considered. The nonprivate materials then are collected using manually loaded compacting bodies (trucks) (stage II, state a) and subsequently taken to, and disposed of, at the county landfill (stage VI, state a). The portion handled privately most likely also ended up at the landfill. Bulky wastes (m5) are stored (Ig) and then taken in open trucks (IIf) to the landfill (VIa), as is street refuse (m6) and dead animals (m7). Abandoned vehicles (m8) are hauled to a regional processing plant in Alexandria. Most construction and demolition wastes (m9) are utilized for fill on the construction site, although a portion also is taken to the county landfill by private handlers. Almost

**Table 16-2 Solid waste system by-product classification**

| | | | |
|---|---|---|---|
| b 1 | Paper | b 8 | Protein |
| b 2 | Rubber | b 9 | Animal food |
| b 3 | Glass | b 10 | Meat |
| b 4 | Scrap metal | b 11 | Returnable bottles |
| b 5 | Fly ash | b 12 | Ashes |
| b 6 | Valuable metals | b 13 | Water (L) |
| b 7 | Fertilizer | b 14 | Particulate matter (L) |

*Source:* Ref. 16-5, p. 40.
L = material leaking to the environment

**Table 16-3 Stages and states in the solid waste system**

| System stages | System states |
|---|---|
| Stage I. Source production and processing | a. Grinding<br>b. Baling<br>c. Open burning<br>d. Incineration<br>e. Compaction<br>f. Composting<br>g. Storage |
| Stage II. Collection | a. Manually loaded compacting bodies<br>b. Satellite motor scooter system<br>c. Mechanically loaded bodies<br>d. Vacuum systems<br>e. Side-loaded compacting bodies<br>f. Open-body trucks<br>g. Transfer stations |
| Stage III. Processing | a. Grinding<br>b. Baling<br>c. Liquid waste pulping<br>d. Incineration<br>e. Shredding<br>f. Heating<br>g. Anaerobic digestors<br>h. Open burning<br>i. Aerated lagoons<br>j. Oxidation ditches<br>k. Composting<br>l. Pyrolysis<br>m. Compaction<br>n. Separation |
| Stage IV. Reuse delivery | a. Temporary storing<br>b. Seller delivery<br>c. Purchaser pick-up |
| Stage V. Haul | a. Truck<br>b. Rail<br>c. Barge |
| Stage VI. Disposal | a. Sanitary landfill<br>b. Dump<br>c. Water body |

*Source:* Ref. 16-5, p. 41.

all industrial (m10), hazardous (m11), security (m12), and animal and agricultural (m13) wastes are handled privately, although some security wastes from government offices, after shredding or similar processing, are transferred to the landfill.

The use of the stages/states morphology was further demonstrated through Table 16-5, where the technology (i.e., morphological combination) being

## Table 16-4 Morphology of the existing solid waste system

Technology: Existing
Governance Unit: Fairfax County

| Material | Row | Step A | B | C | D | E | F | From: Row/Step |
|---|---|---|---|---|---|---|---|---|
| m1, m2, m3, m4 | 1 | (Ig) | IIa | VIa | | | | |
| m5 | 2 | Ig | IIf | VIa | | | | |
| m6 | 3 | Ig | IIf | VIa | | | | |
| m7 | 4 | Ig | IIf | VIa | | | | |
| m8 | 5 | Ig | IIf | VIa | | | | |
| m9 | 6 | P | (VIa) | | | | | |
| m10 | 7 | P | (VIa) | | | | | |
| m11 | 8 | P | | | | | | |
| m12 | 9 | P | VIa | | | | | |
| m13 | 10 | P | | | | | | |
| m14 | 11 | Ig | IIf | VIa | | | | |

*Source:* Adapted from Ref. 16-5, p. 63.
P = material handled privately; ( ) = only a certain portion of material is handled publicly; L = leakage to the environment.
For solid waste material classification, see Table 16-1.
For by-product material classification, see Table 16-2.
For state and stage classification, see Table 16-3.

## Table 16-5 Morphology of an adapted solid waste system

Technology: Incineration combined with landfill

Governance Unit: Fairfax County

General description: Only materials m1 to m3 considered here. Incinerator located at landfill site. Separation at incinerator

| Material | Row | Step A | B | C | D | E | F | From: Row/Step |
|---|---|---|---|---|---|---|---|---|
| m1, m2, m3 | 1 | Ig | IIa | IIIn | | | | |
| m1, m2 | 2 | IIId | | | | | | 1C |
| m3 | 3 | VIa | | | | | | 1C |
| b5 | 4 | VIa | | | | | | 2A |
| b12 | 5 | VIa | | | | | | 2A |
| b13 | 6 | VIc | | | | | | 2A |
| b14 | 7 | L | | | | | | 2A |

*Source:* Adapted from Ref. 16-5, p. 78.
L = leakage to the environment.
For solid waste material classification, see Table 16-1.
For by-product material classification, see Table 16-2.
For state and stage classification, see Table 16-3.

explored was incineration combined with landfilling of noncombustible materials and by-products from the incineration process. The only materials considered in this example were m1 to m3 (garbage, combustible and noncombustible rubbage). These go through the following steps in the system:

1. All three materials are stored in 30-gallon cans (Ig), collected in manually loaded compacting trucks (IIa), and separated into combustible and noncombustible materials at the incinerator (IIIn).
2. With the separation process, there are two different types of material to consider (rows 2 and 3). The noncombustible ones (m3), coming from step C of row 1 (1C), are deposited at the sanitary landfill (VIa). The combustible ones (row 2), coming from row 1, step C (1C), are processed for volume reduction by incineration (IIId). Four by-products result from this process: flyash (b5), ashes (b12), waste water (b13), and particulate matter (b14).
3. The flyash and ashes are deposited in the landfill (VIa); the used water is returned to a nearby water body (VIc); and the particulate matter enters the atmosphere (L, leakage to the environment).

Generally, any solid waste or nonleakage by-product material which goes out of the designated system (e.g., through sale or haul) was thought of as "disposed."

The impact analysis and evaluation of the incinerator technology (combination) was carried out using a "technology assessment" approach. This involved:

1. Identifying those individuals or groups who would be affected by the technology
2. Identifying the impact factors of importance to each of these individuals or groups
3. Estimating the peak magnitude of each factor in comparison to an associated standard (which may be subjective in nature)
4. Estimating the likelihood of occurrence of the peak magnitude of the factor
5. Estimating the time ranges (measured from 1970) in which the peak magnitude was likely to occur

An additional feature of this analysis was the delineation of the degree of control county decision makers could exert over a particular factor. This ranged from "no control" to "complete control."

Table 16-6 gives the results of the impact analysis under the conditions where an incinerator technology was inserted into the present Fairfax County system. It was estimated, for instance, that the cost to the waste producer would rise from $37 to $60 per year per household. This was significant since the entire incinerator system was expected to require a capital outlay of $20 million, with an annual operating cost of $2 million. To pay for this, taxes probably would have had to be raised to the equivalent of $8.00 per $1000 of assessed value of property. Other significant disadvantages (compared to the existing system) would appear to be:

**Table 16-6 Impacts of incinerator technology**

| Impact factor | Peak magnitude | Likelihood of occurrence | Timing, years | Controllability |
|---|---|---|---|---|
| Number of regulation changes needed | Slightly increased | 0.90 | 0–4 | None |
| Number of organizational changes needed | Slightly increased | 0.60 | 0–4 | Slight |
| Cost to waste producers | $60 per year per household | 0.85 | 0–10 | Great |
| Tax increase needed for waste producers | $8/$1000 of assessed valuation | 0.50 | 0–10 | Complete |
| Wages to solid waste employees | $3 per hour | 0.60 | 1–10 | Complete |
| Safety of solid waste employees | Accident frequency rate of 60 per year | 0.70 | 0–10 | Complete |
| Dependability of private collection firms | Slightly less than moderate down time | 0.50 | 0–3 | Slight |
| Extent of handling by private collection firms | 2.8 person-minutes per pickup | 0.60 | 2–10 | Great |
| Profits of equipment manufacturers | 5.5% annual return on investment | 0.95 | 0–2 | None |
| Land values of "neighbors" near system | Slightly less than other comparable areas | 0.40 | 2–10 | None |
| Air pollution near "neighbors" | Almost at lowest safety level | 0.90 | 0–10 | Medium |
| Privacy of "neighbors" | Some privacy | 0.70 | 0–10 | Great |
| Cleanliness near "neighbors" | Some litter | 0.70 | 0–10 | Medium |
| Wind scattering near "neighbors" | Some scattering | 0.90 | 0–10 | Great |
| Open-space preservation | Little land taken for system | 0.60 | 4–10 | Great |
| Appearance | Slightly ugly | 0.80 | 0–10 | Great |
| Employment of low-income groups | 0.4% of labor force | 0.70 | 1–10 | Great |
| Profits of end-product consumers | 5.5% annual return on investment | 0.50 | 0–10 | None |

*Source:* Adapted from Ref. 16-5, pp. 73, 74, 88.

1. Increased air pollution
2. Increased organization and regulation for the Fairfax County solid waste agency
3. Less profits for end-product consumers (e.g., waste paper recyclists)

On the positive side would be:

1. Less wind scatteration and increased cleanliness
2. Greater preservation of open space
3. Somewhat increased land values

Generally, it seemed that the real trade-offs to be made in this case were between cost and air pollution on the one hand and greater open-space preservation and overall orderliness on the other.

While this study did not use morphological analysis directly in a forecasting mode, this certainly could have been done. The stages and states in Table 16-3 could have been combined in a manner exemplified in Tables 16-4 and 16-5. It then would be a relatively easy matter to alter the number of steps or rows (while taking into account various physical constraints) to find "new" technologies representing incremental changes from existing ones. An evaluation patterned after that in Table 16-6 subsequently could be performed, and, after several trials, the most likely near-term combination (technology) identified. The forecast thus would be that this technology would be developed because of its inherent usefulness and value.

## PROBLEMS

**16-1** Based simply on your experience, develop a morphological model of the process of extracting food from the sea. For one configuration of your model prepare a forecast of the technologies involved. What are the advantages of your chosen path over those currently in use? When might your path be feasible?

**16-2** Develop a morphological model of alternatives for residential energy supply. Given that you have the responsibility for developing an energy plan for your region, what forecast for 1990 could you make using this model?

## REFERENCES


### Theory

16-1. Ayres, R. U.: *Technological Forecasting and Long Range Planning*, McGraw-Hill, New York, 1969.

16-2. Gilfillan, S. C.: *Sociology of Invention*, Follett, Chicago, Ill., 1935.

16-3. Martino, J. P.: *Technological Forecasting for Decisionmaking*, American-Elsevier, New York, 1972.

16-4. Zwicky, F.: *Discovery, Invention, Research*, Macmillan, New York, 1969.

### Applications and other references

16-5. Dickey, J. W., D. M. Glancy, and E. M. Jennelle: *Technology Assessment for Programs of Local Government*, D. C. Heath, Lexington, Mass., 1975.

16-6. Fields, S. R.: *Technological Forecasting and Morphological Analysis*, Preprint 1475, Joint ASME–ASCE Meeting, Seattle, July, 1971.

16-7. United Way of America: *United Way of America Services Identification System*, Alexandria, Va., January, 1972.

CHAPTER

# SEVENTEEN

# PROBE

The concept of morphological analysis discussed in the previous chapter represents an attempt to dissect a situation by looking at its component parts and their interconnections. It is primarily physical systems that can be viewed in this manner, for they usually seem to be divisible into discrete entities. An extension of this type of analysis using more generic entities called *events* and considering the timing and likelihood of these events might prove more useful in dealing with social as well as physical systems. This is the idea behind Probe, a technique developed by TRW, Inc., to aid in planning their research and development activities as well as in their marketing endeavors (Refs. 17-1 to 17-4). A further advantage of Probe is that, because the timing of events is taken into account, there is a basis for testing and hence clarifying the sequential relations between them and subsequently eliminating many inconsistencies.

Since Probe requires a large-scale effort and has not to our knowledge been employed in urban or regional analysis, we will restrict our attention here to the application described by North and Pyke (Refs. 17-3 and 17-4) and to one small example. The reader hopefully will see further potential applications in his or her field of endeavor.

## 17-1 PROBE I†

The initial attempt by TRW to generate a long-range forecast of the technological future actually was a test of the feasibility of using the Delphi method in an industrial setting. It consisted of an experimental survey, finally completed in

† The description in this and the succeeding sections is adapted from Refs. 17-3 and 17-4.

June, 1966, which led to a 50-page proprietary document titled "A Probe of TRW's Future: the Next 20 Years." This report listed some 401 technical events, grouped into 15 categories, which a single panel of 27 experts specializing in a broad spectrum of technologies felt might occur by 1986 and which they believed would have a significant impact on the company's products, services, and processes. This experiment later was called Probe I. Before launching a second stage, Probe II, the 15 groups of events were refined to focus more closely on TRW's current interests.

A review of research and development (R&D) activities at TRW during the latter half of 1966 revealed that while Probe I had been a useful checklist and a vision-extending exercise for the panelists and others, the main benefit which the company received was a great deal of publicity concerning its foresight. There was no real evidence that it had been used directly in R&D planning.

The creators concluded that many of the final events predicted by the panelists, while interesting, were not events in which the company could participate directly. Some were too formidable to match available R&D resources while others were too far away in time for immediate attention. It was interesting, for instance, to contemplate that "3-D color movies utilizing holographic techniques† will be technically feasible by 1972;" but unless one considers the technological developments which must precede that event, one has no "road map" to use as a basis for planning an R&D program in this or any related technical area. Moreover, a 3-D holographic color movie development project is too big for any one company to contemplate.

## 17-2 PROBE II

Probe II was started in 1967, with the two major rounds completed by 1969. It followed a revised procedure that took advantage of the lessons learned from Probe I. The creators expected the Probe program to undergo continual refinement and to become an increasingly beneficial tool in long-range financial and business planning. Probe II was designed to aid R&D managers in modifying their long-range plans, which would in turn be subjected to the usual executive evaluation to determine how well each meshed with corporate plans and objectives. Hopefully, introducing Probe II in this way would help in deciding to proceed with selected new programs.

In the course of Probe I it was found that the mental exercise involved had appreciably expanded the insight of the 27 experts, and accordingly TRW elected to capitalize on this benefit in Probe II by developing a separate panel for each of the 15 categories and using a larger group of experts drawn from the staff of more than 6000 scientists and engineers employed throughout the company. Table 17-1

† Holography is an optical-projection technique giving the viewer the illusion of true depth perception. Holographic motion pictures would be as much of an improvement over existing motion pictures as stereophonic sound is over monaural sound.

**Table 17-1 The revised categories for Probe II**

| | Automotive | | | | | | | | Electronics | | | | | | Equipment | | | | | | | Systems | | | | | |
|---|---|---|---|---|---|---|---|---|---|---|---|---|---|---|---|---|---|---|---|---|---|---|---|---|---|---|---|
| Probe II categories | Michigan Division | Marlin-Rockwell Division | Ross Gear Division | Valve Division | Replacement Division | Thompson Products Ltd. | Staff | Ramsey Corporation | Electronic Components Division | Semiconductors Inc. | Capacitor Division | United Transformer Company Division | Electro Insulation | Globe Industries Division | Equipment Laboratories | Accessories Division | Jet and Ordnance Division | Metals Division | Magna Corporation | Mark 46 Program Office | Staff | Electronic Systems Division | Power Systems Division | Space Vehicles Division | Systems Engineering and Integration Division | Systems Laboratories | Instruments Division |
| Technologies | | | | | | | | | | | | | | | | | | | | | | | | | | | |
| Electronics and electro-optics | | | | | | | × | | × | × | × | × | | | × | × | | | × | | | × | | × | | × | × |
| Materials (including coatings, fuels and lubricants) | | × | | × | | | | × | × | × | × | × | × | × | × | × | × | × | × | × | | | × | | | × | |
| Mechanics and hydraulics | × | × | × | | × | × | × | × | × | | | | | × | × | × | | | | | | | × | × | | × | × |
| Power sources, conversion, and conditioning | | × | | × | | | × | × | × | × | | × | | × | × | × | | | | × | | × | × | × | | | × |
| Information processing | | | | | | | × | | | × | | | | | | | | | | | × | × | | × | | × | |
| Instrumentation and control | | × | | | | | × | | | × | | | | | × | × | × | | × | × | | | × | × | | × | × |
| Manufacturing processes | × | × | × | × | × | × | × | × | × | × | × | × | × | × | × | × | × | × | × | × | × | × | × | × | × | × | |
| Systems and subsystems | | | | | | | | | | | | | | | | | | | | | | | | | | | |
| Plant automation—production and business | × | × | × | × | × | × | × | × | × | × | × | × | | × | | | | | | | × | × | | | | × | |
| Transportation | × | × | × | × | × | × | × | × | × | × | | | | | × | × | | | | | × | × | × | | × | × | |
| Defense and weapons (exclude missiles) | | × | × | | | | × | | × | × | | | | × | × | × | × | | | | × | × | × | × | × | × | |
| Aerospace (include missiles) | | × | | | | | × | | × | × | × | × | × | × | × | × | × | × | | | × | × | × | × | × | × | |
| Oceans | | | | | | | | | × | × | | | | | × | | | | × | × | × | × | × | | × | × | × |
| Personal and medical | | | | | | | | | × | × | | | | × | | | | | | | × | × | | | × | × | × |
| Urban and international | | | | | | | | | | × | | × | | | | | | | | | × | × | | | × | × | |
| Environmental control | × | × | | | | | × | | | × | | | | × | × | | | | | | | × | × | × | | × | × |

*Source:* Ref. 17-3, p. 71. Key: × indicates the presence of expert opinion in a division for each category.

lists the categories finally selected for investigation in Probe II, and also indicates the method used to identify panel members for each category in the various company divisions. A group captain, appointed by the executive vice president of each of the then-existing divisional groups, was asked to determine which of his divisions were involved in the technologies to be investigated. The crosses in the table reflect combined judgments of all of the group captains.

Each group captain then arranged for one or more experts from each division likely to be affected by events in the 15 categories to participate in Probe II. This procedure led to the selection of 140 panelists. Each panel member was asked to accept the socioeconomic environment assumed in the "long-range corporate business plan." Each was furnished with supplementary publications which elaborated on various aspects of the assumptions made in the plan. A modification of the Delphi procedures for questioning and requestioning the experts was then applied.

**Round 1** In round 1 of the questioning each panelist was asked to use the form shown in Table 17-2 (exhibit I) to list probable technical events in his or her category that could have a significant impact on the company. Each event was to be weighted on the basis on the three factors indicated:

1. *Desirability* was to be considered from the standpoint of the customer, i.e., as reflecting an estimate of potential demand, which indicates the importance of the event from a marketing standpoint.
2. *Feasibility*, on the other hand, was to be considered more from the standpoint of the producer, as reflecting an estimate of both the technical feasibility and the difficulty likely to be encountered in achieving prerequisite developments.
3. *Timing* was intended to reflect (*a*) an estimate of the date by which there was a 50/50 chance that the event would have occurred [Pr $(E_i) = 0.5$] and (*b*) the degree of uncertainty associated with that estimate, i.e., the date by which there is a "reasonable chance" that the event would have occurred [Pr $(E_i) = 0.1$] and the date by which the event is "almost certain" to have occurred [Pr $(E_i) = 0.9$].

The Probe II directors promised anonymity to all participants to stimulate unconventional thinking.

Round 1 produced 2100 predictions. Four critical editings, to eliminate duplicate and trivial or irrelevant forecasts, reduced the list to 1186. In the course of the editing, statements were altered to improve clarity and avoid distortions of intent and meaning.

**Round 2** At the start of round 2, each panelist received a composite list of the edited predictions contributed by his or her panel plus those from other panels

---

**Figure 17-1** A SOON chart showing the steps in the development of 3-D color holographic movies. [*Source: Ref. 17-3* (*insert*).]

PULL OUT TO READ

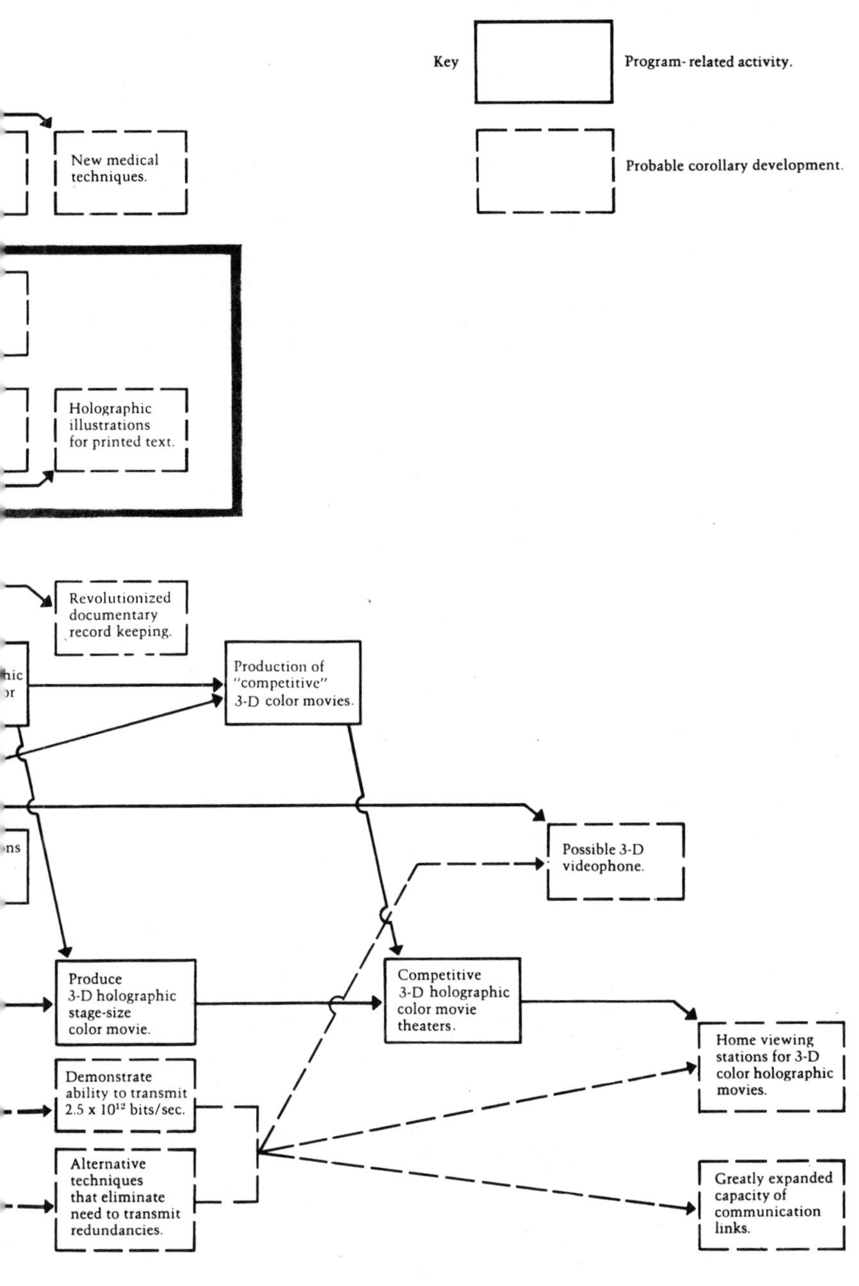

igure 17-1

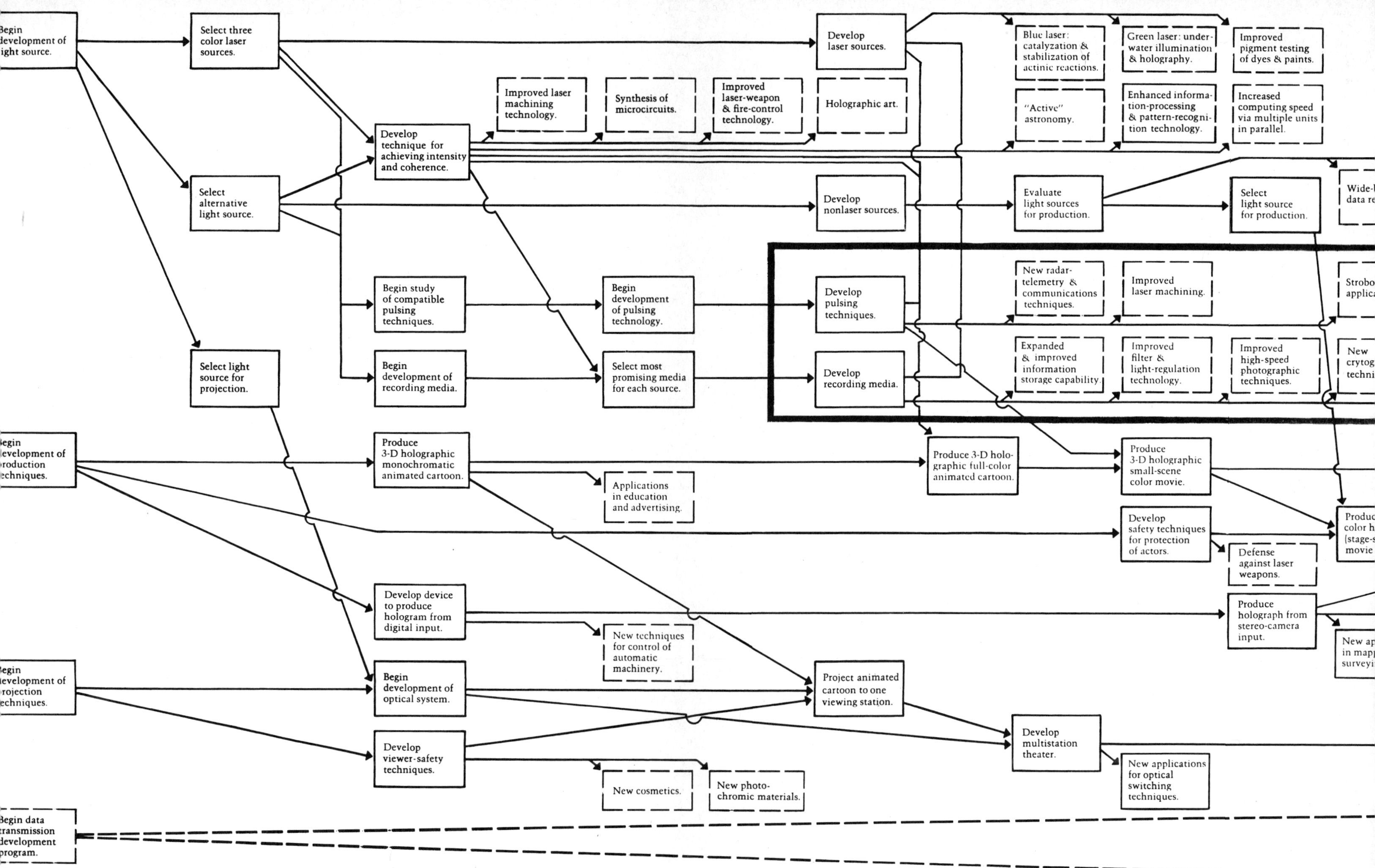

egin development of ight source.
Select three color laser sources.
Develop laser sources.
Blue laser: catalyzation & stabilization of actinic reactions.
Green laser: underwater illumination & holography.
Improved pigment testing of dyes & paints.
Improved laser machining technology.
Synthesis of microcircuits.
Improved laser-weapon & fire-control technology.
Holographic art.
"Active" astronomy.
Enhanced information-processing & pattern-recognition technology.
Increased computing speed via multiple units in parallel.
Develop technique for achieving intensity and coherence.
Select alternative light source.
Develop nonlaser sources.
Evaluate light sources for production.
Select light source for production.
Wide-
data re
Begin study of compatible pulsing techniques.
Begin development of pulsing technology.
Develop pulsing techniques.
New radar-telemetry & communications techniques.
Improved laser machining.
Strobo
applica
Select light source for projection.
Begin development of recording media.
Select most promising media for each source.
Develop recording media.
Expanded & improved information storage capability.
Improved filter & light-regulation technology.
Improved high-speed photographic techniques.
New
crytog
techni
egin evelopment of roduction echniques.
Produce 3-D holographic monochromatic animated cartoon.
Applications in education and advertising.
Produce 3-D holographic full-color animated cartoon.
Produce 3-D holographic small-scene color movie.
Develop safety techniques for protection of actors.
Defense against laser weapons.
Produc
color h
(stage-s
movie
Develop device to produce hologram from digital input.
New techniques for control of automatic machinery.
Produce holograph from stereo-camera input.
New ap
in map
surveyi
egin evelopment of rojection echniques.
Begin development of optical system.
Project animated cartoon to one viewing station.
Develop viewer-safety techniques.
Develop multistation theater.
New applications for optical switching techniques.
New cosmetics.
New photochromic materials.
Begin data transmission development program.

relevant to his or her category. In this round the panelist was asked to evaluate all events according to the same (three) factors considered in round 1: desirability, feasibility, and timing. Each expert was asked specifically to ensure that his or her evaluations and estimates were consistent with each other, especially with regard to the expected date of occurrence. For example, one should not estimate that an event will occur earlier than the date at which one had estimated a prerequisite event would occur.

Exhibit II in Table 17-2 shows a sample question from a round 2 questionnaire, with marks indicating the panelist's responses. Note that each panelist was assigned a code number (here, 304) by which to be identified if further contact concerning his or her evaluations were necessary. The number 201030 references the event statement to a particular source document. The numbers 01, 02, 04, and 09 show that this event would be evaluated by the panels on electronics, materials, power-conditioning, and transportation.

The responses show that the evaluator considers that: (1) he or she is a specialist in a number of the relevant technologies, (2) the occurrence of the event will be sought by a significant segment of the public, (3) substantial technical effort will be needed, (4) the probability is 0.7 that the event will occur, and (5) assuming that the event will occur, it is expected to happen during the period between 1979 (0.1-date) and 1990 (0.9-date), with the most likely date (0.5-date) being 1985.

**Round 3** In an informal third round, TRW hoped to resolve any wide differences of opinion concerning events with estimated dates of occurrence falling outside of the median range (0.1–0.9) by discussing the predictions individually with the panelists involved. At the end of this round, they expect that, on a statistical average, each event will have been evaluated by approximately 40 experts representing three or more different panels.

Exhibit III in Table 17-2 shows how the event of the preceding exhibit might appear in final published form (with a fictitious evaluation, since returns from panels making the evaluation were not yet complete at the time when the original article was written). The composite evaluation by all panelists questioned indicates that:

1. On a scale ranging from +1.0 (desirable) to −1.0 (undesirable), the mean of the evaluations of desirability is +0.7.
2. On a scale ranging from +1.0 (simple) to −1.0 (unlikely), the mean of the evaluations of feasibility is +0.4.
3. The mean of the estimates of the probability that the event will occur sometime is 0.8.
4. If the event occurs, the most likely date for it to happen is 1984 (the median 0.5-date); the period of expectancy ranges from 1977 (the median 0.1-date) to 1987 (the median 0.9-date).

Specially developed computer programs were being employed to process the Probe II data. Although questionnaires could have been typed and copied in a routine fashion, it was obvious that the amount of data generated by the panelists

# Table 17-2 Sample questionnaires and event forms for Probe II

Exhibit I. Questionnaire for round 1

| PROBE CATEGORY PANEL MEMBER | DESIRABILITY | | | TRW DIVISION FEASIBILITY | | | TIMING | | |
|---|---|---|---|---|---|---|---|---|---|
| | NEEDED DESPERATELY | DESIRABLE | UNDESIRABLE BUT POSSIBLE | HIGHLY FEASIBLE | LIKELY | UNLIKELY BUT FEASIBLE | YEAR BY WHICH THE PROBABILITY THAT THE EVENT WILL HAVE OCCURRED | | |
| 1. LIST BELOW ALL ANTICIPATED TECHNICAL EVENTS (INDICATING SOURCE, IF EXTERNAL TO TRW) WHICH WILL HAVE A SIGNIFICANT EFFECT ON TRW IN THE ABOVE CATEGORY<br>2. EVALUATE EACH PREDICTED EVENT WITH RESPECT TO THE THREE FACTORS AT THE RIGHT IN VIEW OF THE ANTICIPATED ENVIRONMENT | | | | | | | Probability = 0.1 | Probability = 0.5 | Probability = 0.9 |

Exhibit II. Excerpt from a round 2 questionnaire

PROBE CATEGORY: no. 9 TRANSPORTATION PANEL MEMBER 304

| EVENT NUMBER | ⊕ EVENT DESCRIPTION | PANELS EVALUATING | FAMILIARITY | DESIRABILITY | FEASIBILITY | PROBABILITY OF EVENT | DATES |
|---|---|---|---|---|---|---|---|
| 201030 | ELECTRIC AUTOMOBILES USING FUEL CELL POWER OR FUEL CELL/BATTERY COMBINATION WILL BE MARKETED COMMERCIALLY | 01, 02, 04, 09 | 1. FAIR<br>2. GOOD<br>3. EXCELLENT | 1. NEEDED<br>2. DESIRABLE<br>3. UNDESIRABLE | 1. SIMPLE<br>2. POSSIBLE<br>3. UNLIKELY | 0.7 | 0.1 1979<br>0.5 1985<br>0.9 1990 |

Exhibit III. Sample of events in final form

| EVENT DESCRIPTION | DESIRABILITY | FEASIBILITY | PROBABILITY | PROBABILITY DATES | | | | | | 2000 AND BEYOND | | |
|---|---|---|---|---|---|---|---|---|---|---|---|---|
| | $\bar{D}$ | $\bar{F}$ | $\bar{P}_r$ | 1970 | 1975 | 1980 | 1985 | 1990 | 1995 | 0.1 | 0.5 | 0.9 |
| ELECTRIC AUTOMOBILES USING FUEL CELL POWER OR FUEL CELL/BATTERY COMBINATION WILL BE MARKETED COMMERCIALLY | +0.7 | +0.4 | 0.8 | | | | | | | | | |

*Source:* Ref. 17-3, p. 73.

would require computer processing. Moreover, the subsequent sampling of data by individuals seeking specific information would be exceedingly difficult without computerization. Thus the entire process was automated, including printing.

## 17-3 USING THE INFORMATION

Most long-range planners and forecasters complain that they experience some difficulty in establishing rapport with the operating executive, whose performance tends to be measured in terms of "this year's profits." From the executive's point of view, the pressures of immediate problems, especially those emergencies threatening the profit picture, leave little time to "dream" about the long-term future. Yet, if the planner is persistent and persuasive, and if the manager realizes that he must look ahead in a fast-moving, technically based industry, the two can combine their energies in an atmosphere of cooperation and mutual appreciation.

Given his understanding, the question of how to communicate effectively with the executive still remained. This led the TRW group to experiment with the preparation of technological "road maps" for the executive. They began with a logic network, shown in the heavy lines in Fig. 17-1. This maps the developments which must precede the technical achievement of holographic color movies. The prerequisite events are merely outlined, but it is evident from the network that many milestones must be passed before the final product can materialize.

The network in that figure shown with light, dotted lines has as components events likely to occur as fallout from the essential subdevelopments. (These are often charted separately as a "sequence of opportunities and negatives." From the acronym, these are known as "SOON" charts.) The portion of this network in the framed area indicates that two of the technical developments essential to achieving competitive 3-D holographic color movies are likely to be accompanied by improvements in radar, telemetry, photographic techniques, communications, and so on.

Charting such a large number of events as in Fig. 17-1 is laborious. It may be too formidable and time-consuming a task for the planners themselves, and fatigue might make them abandon the whole idea. The richness of detail is too valuable to be lost, however, and consequently the creators are considering a computer-based approach for displaying at least a portion of the benefits that would be realized from full SOON charting. This approach would call on TRW scientists and engineers to forecast only the major technical developments required to reach essential milestones, with the dates of achievement projected consistently with the probable date of the final event. A computer-based study of the technologies required for intermediate events could lead a company to strengthen its technical base in those areas it considers will be important to it in the years ahead. As an added advantage, the resulting system could be used (1) to monitor, through time, development of those technologies of importance to TRW and, for that matter, to its competitors and (2) to avoid the necessity for a Probe III by updating the network as required to conform with experience and changes in outlook. The extension of this technique to other variables is, of course, possible.

## 17-4 A SIMPLE EXAMPLE

Because one of the major advantages of Probe is that it can be employed to analyze a large set of events, it obviously is difficult to show its potential for urban and regional studies with anything but a highly oversimplified example. With this in mind we have focused on the events leading to the development of a statewide comprehensive land-use plan, as displayed in Fig. 17-2. We assume that we are dealing with a state that has not already made major strides in this direction (or actually has a plan, like Hawaii).

In Fig. 17-2 we see there are six events leading up to the development of the plan and one event following it (this being a program corollary event). We imagine that we have already gone through a series of questionnaries with those people in the state and elsewhere familiar with its political–economic–social–environmental situation as it relates to land-use planning. This panel has identified the eight events, given the dates at which they expect them to occur, and indicated which are necessary precursors to the remainder. Each event subsequently has been plotted on the SOON chart at the point corresponding to its median expected date. The arrows going into each event come from the precursor events which we assume *must* take place before the succeeding event is realized. Arrows going out from an event indicate that that event is a necessary precursor to another one further along in time.

To illustrate, we have suggested that the first event after the start (in 1975) will be the requirement for a subdivision ordinance in 1976. In the meantime, action is being taken independently on a federal land-use law (event 3), which eventually passes in 1980. This law presumably requires critical environmental area designations from states (event 5), to which our state acquiesces by 1984 (event 5).

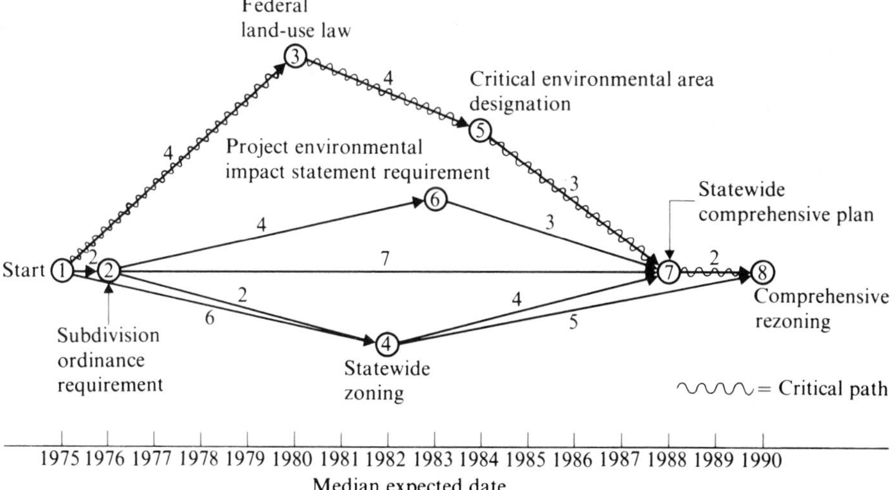


**Figure 17-2** SOON chart leading toward a statewide comprehensive land-use plan.

On another path, the subdivision ordinance requirement (event 2) is a necessary prerequisite to three others:

(*a*) A project environmental impact statement requirement (event 6)
(*b*) Statewide zoning (event 4)
(*c*) The statewide comprehensive plan itself (event 7)

Gathering all this information together, we see that for the plan to become a reality, it must be immediately preceded by events 2, 4, 5, and 6. This consequence is expected to take place about 1988. It is followed two years later by the corollary event (8) of comprehensive rezoning based on the new plan (as happens typically in local government areas, zoning takes place before the plan is complete, so that rezoning is eventually necessitated).

Without going further in the exercise, we can see that the SOON chart already has been of much value. Its primary benefit has been that it allowed us to unscramble a series of events so that we can see more clearly the number and sequence of paths of approach needed to obtain the desired end result. It has also allowed us to identify the nature of potentially beneficial offshoots of the process under study.

The technique can be carried further, however. Suppose we now asked each panel member to estimate the number of years for an event to occur after each precursor event took place. Hypothetical numbers of this nature are shown for our example on each link in Fig. 17-2. We could then use this information both as a check on the accuracy of the expected dates suggested earlier and as a means to find that path (or paths) which are critical (i.e., take the longest) for the accomplishment of the desired end event.

If this procedure is followed in conjunction with our example in Fig. 17-2, we would find that there are five paths to the creation of the statewide comprehensive land-use plan. They and the corresponding times are:

| | |
|---|---|
| 1 to 3 to 5 to 7 | $4 + 4 + 3 = 11$ years |
| 1 to 2 to 6 to 7 | $2 + 4 + 3 = 9$ years |
| 1 to 2 to 7 | $2 + 7 = 9$ years |
| 1 to 2 to 4 to 7 | $2 + 2 + 4 = 8$ years |
| 1 to 4 to 7 | $6 + 4 = 10$ years |

From this display we can draw two major conclusions:

1. At the extreme it will take 11 years from 1975 to achieve a statewide plan. This would occur in 1986, not 1988 as thought earlier.
2. If somehow the process along the first path can be sped up, the comprehensive plan might come even sooner.

We can also see that speeding up the events on the first path will only be useful if the reduction in time is 1 year. At that point the fifth path becomes "binding" or critical, and efforts will have to be made to reduce the times on both sides simultaneously if further reduction in the plan time is needed.

As some readers might have discovered, the Probe technique now has been turned into a PERT (*p*rogram *e*valuation and *r*eview *t*echnique) or CPM (*c*ritical *p*ath *m*ethod) technique. For larger-sized applications, with hundreds of events, an approach involving the automatic determination of critical paths and their sensitivities could be very useful both in identifying events holding back important changes and forecasting likely times of accomplishment if these binds can be released. The reader is hence referred to Chap. 24, where methods for analyzing large-scale networks are described.

## PROBLEMS

**17-1** Based on your experience and intuition, list the events you see that will affect the average fuel efficiency (mpg) of the United States truck fleet in 1990. List also the desirability, feasibility, and timing of each event.

**17-2** Make a SOON chart with the information from Prob. 17-1.

**17-3** Figure 17-3 shows a set of hypothetical events all needed to achieve energy "independence" (a 20 percent reduction in gasoline usage) for urban transportation. Also shown are the expected dates

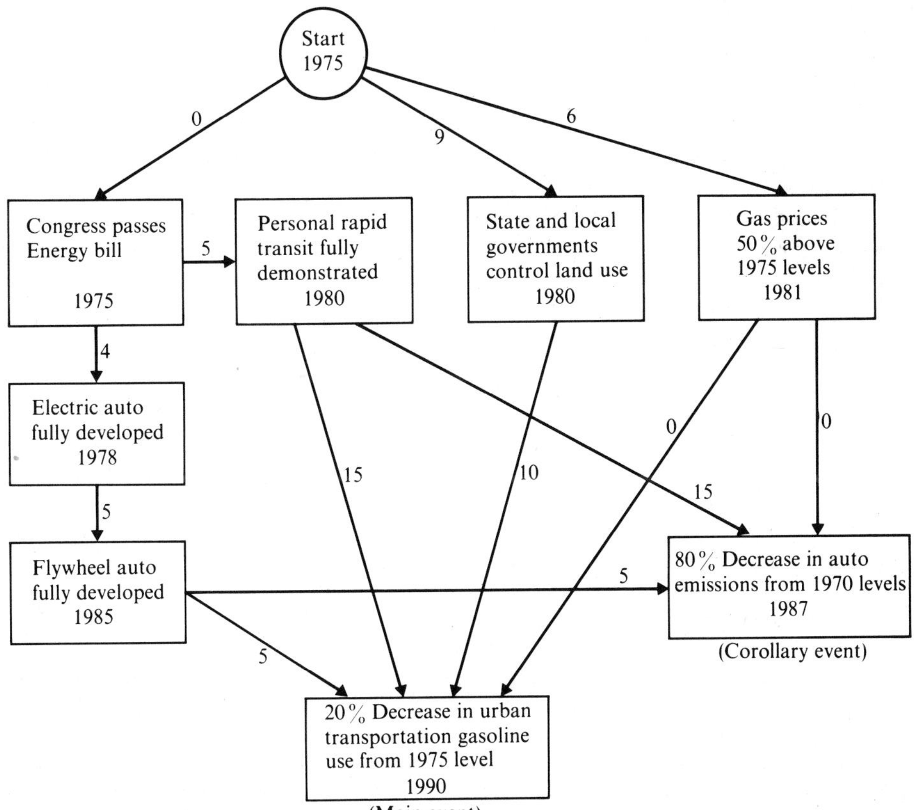


**Figure 17-3** Hypothetical events needed to obtain energy independence for urban transportation.

of the events as well as the times to reach each event from each of its necessary precursors. One corollary event is noted. Find:

(*a*) The critical time path from the start to the main event. List the events and total time on this path.
(*b*) The second longest time path. List the events and total time on this path.
(*c*) The critical path to the corollary event. List the events and total time on this path.
(*d*) The time (year) at which the main event will occur if the full development of the electric auto is sped up by 2 years.
(*e*) The time (year) at which the main event will occur if the full development of the electric auto is retarded by an additional 7 years.

# REFERENCES

**Theory**

17-1. Ayres, R. U.: *Technological Forecasting and Long Range Planning*, McGraw-Hill, New York, 1969.
17-2. North, H. Q., and D. L. Pyke: "Technology, the Chicken—Corporate Goals, The Egg," in J. Bright (Ed.), *First Annual Technology and Management Conference*, Prentice-Hall, Englewood Cliffs, N.J., 1968.
17-3. North, H. Q., and D. L. Pyke: "Probes of the Technological Future," *Harvard Business Review*, May–June, 1969.
17-4. North, H. Q., and D. L. Pyke: "Technological Forecasting to Aid R&D Planning," *Research Management*, vol. 12, no. 4, 1969.

CHAPTER

# EIGHTEEN

# CROSS-IMPACT ANALYSIS

The process of combining a large number of forecasts, as is done in systems dynamics and Probe, usually involves looking at the connections between pairs of influencing factors. If there are any substantial interactions, it may be necessary to trace through several linkages to determine the evental influence on the variable in question. As demonstrated in the discussion of systems dynamics (Chap. 11), two events may not interact directly, but one of them may interact with a third, which in turn relates to the first. Tracing through all of the possible chains of relations can be a very tedious and time-consuming process. In this chapter we will describe cross-impact analysis, which is one systematic approach to examining the interactions among a set of events. It fits within this overall group of chapters on intuition-aiding methods because its primary applications have involved inputs from Delphi and similar opinion-type exercises.

## 18-1 THE BASIC CROSS-IMPACT MATRIX†

Before we can set up a cross-impact matrix we must identify the ways in which a pair of events can interact with each other. Basically an interaction can be described with three characteristics: *mode*, *strength*, and *time lag*.

Looking at the first characteristic: one event can *enhance* or *inhibit* the likelihood of the other, or it can be completely *unrelated*. For the first two cases it is possible to enumerate a number of historical examples. The invention of the steam engine, the availability of economic capital, and the social pressures of the nineteenth century enhanced the start of the Industrial Revolution. Pursuing our

† Some of the discussion in this section is adapted from Refs. 18-3 and 18-5.

**Table 18-1 Examples of enhancing and inhibiting events**

| | Enhancing | | Inhibiting | |
|---|---|---|---|---|
| Examples | Enabling | Provoking | Denigrating | Antagonistic |
| Historical | A political party nomination is a prerequisite for the presidency. | Population increases made development of birth control devices more important. | 1830 railroad development delayed automobile. | Vietnam conflict is antagonistic to reduction of income tax. |
| Future | Advent of a very cheap power source will promote desalination. | Large increases in atmospheric contamination will prompt the development of noncontaminating power sources. | Discovery of pathogenic organisms on Mars will make manned planetary exploration more difficult. | Increasing crime rate may result in anarchy. |

*Source:* Ref. 18-5, p. 104.

Vietnam military enterprises inhibited the expansion of urban programs because of limited funds. These inhibiting and enhancing modes can each be viewed as having two subdivisions, as exemplified in Table 18-1.

The second characteristics, *strength* of interaction, is the influence of one event on the probability of occurrence of a succeeding one. Clearly some events will be strongly linked, i.e., the occurrence of one will produce a large change in the probability of the second happening. Other factors might be weakly linked, however, with the probability of one being only slightly affected by the occurrence of the first.

The *time lag* characteristic refers to the time it takes for the first event to build up its full strength of influence on the second one. Suppose that two events are strongly linked in the enhancing mode. Even though the linkage is substantial, there is little chance that the probability of the affected event will significantly increase immediately after the occurrence of the prior event. Depending on the nature of the events, the time required to realize the higher probability will range from minutes to decades. Project Hindsight data (Ref. 18-8) indicate a time constant of the order of 10 years from scientific discovery to utilization in weapon systems. Edwin Mansfield (Ref. 18-6) has traced the spread of certain ideas from innovation within one company to use by other companies within the same sector. He found that the process of diffusion is generally accelerating in the United States but still may require time intervals of the order of 10 years.

An illustration of a cross-impact matrix is found in Table 18-2. This matrix shows the interactions between three events: $E_1$, $E_2$, and $E_3$, which are the rows of the matrix. These events have probabilities Pr $(E_1)$, Pr $(E_2)$, and Pr $(E_3)$, respectively, that they will happen at all. The events are expected to occur at times (years) $t_1$, $t_2$, and $t_3$, where the events are ordered chronologically from first to last. The events also are represented in the columns of the matrix. Each element of the matrix indicates an interaction between the events. For example, the upper right cell of the matrix indicates an interaction between $E_1$ and $E_3$. The diagonal cells, of course, portray interactions of the events with themselves. These usually are considered meaningless; hence the diagonal elements are ignored. In the matrix shown, the diagonal elements are crossed out. Among the off-diagonal cells, however, there are two possibilities for each interaction. The lower left element indicates an interaction between $E_1$ and $E_3$. Now we assume that the only possible interaction is from the earlier event to the later one, i.e., that a later event does not influence an earlier one, whose outcome has already been decided. Thus we can make use of the duplication of interactions in the matrix in the following way. In the elements above the diagonal, we indicate the interaction which takes place if the row (earlier) event occurs. In the cells below the diagonal we indicate the interaction which takes place if the column (earlier) event does *not* take place. In Table 18-2 the upper right cell shows the impact of $E_3$ if $E_1$ takes place; the lower left cell indicates the impact on $E_3$ if $E_1$ fails to take place.

Now we will examine some of the interactions shown in the cross-impact matrix. The characteristics are shown in the order: mode, strength, time lag. For instance, if $E_1$ occurs, its mode of impact is to enhance the probability of $E_2$ by 10 percent, and the impact is felt immediately, without a time lag. Conversely, if $E_1$ fails to occur, the impact on $E_2$ is to inhibit its likelihood, reducing its probability of occurrence by 20 percent, and the impact is delayed for 5 years. (This implies that if $t_2$ were sooner than 5 years after $t_1$, the detrimental impact of $E_1$ not

**Table 18-2 Illustrative cross-impact matrix**

| | | | Event happens | | |
|---|---|---|---|---|---|
| Event | Date | Probability | $E_1$ | $E_2$ | $E_3$ |
| $E_1$ | $t_1$ | Pr ($E_1$) | ////////<br>///// | Enhance<br>10%<br>immediate | Enhance<br>50%<br>7 years |
| $E_2$ | $t_2$ | Pr ($E_2$) | Inhibit<br>−20%<br>5 years | ////////<br>///// | Enhance<br>0%<br>immediate |
| $E_3$ | $t_3$ | Pr ($E_3$) | Inhibit<br>−10%<br>immediate | Inhibit<br>−70%<br>immediate | ////////<br>///// |
| | | | Event does not happen | | |

*Source:* Adapted from Ref. 18-3, p. 273.

occurring would not have time to take effect; but if $E_2$ were then delayed for some other reason, such as that caused by another event, the detrimental impact from $E_1$ might have time to come into play.)

## 18-2 A SIMPLE EXAMPLE

To provide a concrete illustration of the development as well as utilization of a cross-impact matrix, let us take the simple example portrayed in Table 18-3. Here we imagine we are analyzing the future population growth in the Washington, D.C., metropolitan area, which obviously depends heavily on the federal government for its employment base. In the first event federal jobs are cut by 25 percent in the area by Congress in an economy move. This is expected to happen in 1982, with a probability of 0.4.

Event $E_2$ is a reduction in the metropolitan population growth rate to 2 percent per annum. Given the general nationwide decreases in growth, this event is expected to take place in 1992, with a probability of 0.5. If the job cut happens, however, the indicated probability of reduction in the growth rate will be enhanced by 60 percent and be moved up 1 year in time. On the other hand, if $E_1$ does not happen, $E_2$ would be inhibited immediately by 80 percent.

Let us now evaluate the resultant probabilities. If $E_1$ happens, the probability of $E_2$, currently at 0.5, will be increased by 60 percent. We interpret this to mean that the gap between the existing probability and certainty (probability = 1.00) is closed by 60 percent. Thus:

$$\text{Pr } (E_2 \text{ given } E_1) = 0.50 + 0.60(1.00 - 0.50) = 0.80$$

Moreover, $E_2$ now occurs 1 year earlier in 1991.

If $E_1$ does not happen, the gap between the existing probability and certainty is opened (increased) by 80 percent. Hence:

$$\text{Pr } (E_2 \text{ given no } E_1) = 0.50 - 0.80(1.00 - 0.50) = 0.10$$

$E_2$ still occurs at the same time as before.

**Table 18-3 Example cross-impact matrix**

| | | | | Event happens | |
|---|---|---|---|---|---|
| Event | Description | Date | Probability | $E_1$ | $E_2$ |
| $E_1$ | Federal jobs cut by 25% by Congress (versus staying at present level) | 1982 | 0.4 | ///// | Enhance 60% 1 year |
| $E_2$ | Annual population growth rate reduced to 2% (versus present rate of 6%) | 1992 | 0.5 | Inhibit −80% immediate | ////// |
| | | | | Event does not happen | |

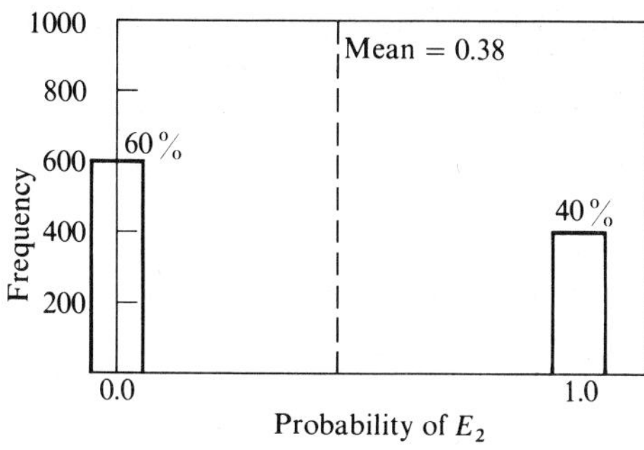


**Figure 18-1** Frequency of various probabilities of $E_2$ in the Monte Carlo routine.

Now if we want to find the overall mean probability that $E_2$ will happen, we need to "weigh" the above two probabilities by the likelihood of $E_1$ happening or not:

$$\text{Pr }(E_2) = \frac{0.8(0.4) + 0.1(0.6)}{0.4 + 0.6} = 0.38$$

Our forecast, then, is that there is a 38 percent chance that the population growth rate will drop to 2 percent by 1992, and if it does drop, it will do so 1 year earlier if the Congressional job-cut takes place.

Another approach to finding the overall probability of $E_2$, and one that is utilized for larger-sized matrices, is the *Monte Carlo routine.* In this procedure we start with a set of random numbers that are employed to determine if $E_1$ does or does not happen. Suppose, for example, that the random numbers between 0.1 and 1.0 are:

0.2, 0.7, 0.5, 0.2, 0.1, 0.2, 0.5, 1.0, 0.6, 0.7, and 0.4

If the selected number is 0.1, 0.2, 0.3, or 0.4, representing $\frac{4}{10}$ of the possibilities (equal to the probability of $E_1$), we then say $E_1$ happens. If not, $E_1$ does not happen.

On the first round the random number (RN) is 0.2, so $E_1$ is assumed to occur. Then, according to the above calculations, Pr ($E_2$ given $E_1$) = 0.8. The second RN is 0.7, so $E_2$ also occurs. The third RN is 0.5, hence $E_1$ does not occur and Pr ($E_2$ given no $E_1$) = 0.1. With the fourth RN being 0.2, $E_2$ subsequently is assumed not to occur. If this procedure is followed for, say, 1000 times, we would end up with a distribution like that in Fig. 18-1. The mean probability would be the same as calculated above.

## 18-3 ADJUSTMENTS FOR LARGE-SIZED MATRICES

As suggested, the direct solution of large-sized cross-impact matrices would be very difficult. This conclusion stems from the mathematics involved, particularly in terms of the changing time lag with the occurrence of certain events. To demonstrate, imagine in the example in Table 18-3 that if $E_1$ happens, $E_2$ is enhanced by

11 years instead of 1. This would put it in 1992–11 = 1981, which is before $E_1$ occurs. This result obviously is inconsistent, but it does point to the need in large-scale matrices to juggle constantly the chronologic order of events to maintain consistency. This can be done much more easily through a Monte Carlo routine.

For computational purposes, Gordon and Haywood (Ref. 18-5) have further simplified the previously described procedures. First, they have eliminated the situation where the prior event cannot be affected by a later one.† Instead, they have allowed all events to be either prior or post in the time domain. Nevertheless, as can be seen in Table 18-4 (a revised version of Table 18-3), there can be a specification of sequence through the second digit in each cell: if the digit is 0, 1, or 2, the predecessor is immaterial, likely, or necessary, respectively. In their procedure the necessary events are considered first, the likely predecessors second, and then the remainder.

A second simplification involved the relations between the initially specified probability, Pr $(E_i)$, for each event, and its revised probability, Pr′ $(E_i)$, when the interactions with the other events are taken into account. Generally, Pr′ $(E_i)$ will depend on Pr $(E_i)$, the mode and strength of interaction with each other event $l$, and the dates at which the event $l$ occurs (the latter three factors are designated by $M_{li}$, $S_{li}$, and $t_l$, respectively), with the latter being relative to the date of the

† This is a particularly important feature for policy analysis since one of the major purposes of such analysis is to *anticipate* future events and try to enhance or inhibit them. Future events thus do affect our current actions.

**Table 18-4 Revised example cross-impact matrix**

| | | | | Change relations | |
|---|---|---|---|---|---|
| Event | Description | Date | Probability | $E_1$ | $E_2$ |
| $E_1$ | Federal jobs cut by 25% by Congress (versus staying at present level) | 1982 | 0.4 | //// | +60 |
| $E_2$ | Annual population growth rate reduced to 2% (versus present rate of 6%) | 1992 | 0.5 | −80 | //// |

*Mode.* + Enhancing
− Inhibiting

*Strength.* First digit (0–9)
0 = unconnected
9 = very strong

*Time lag.* Second digit: predecessor event
0 = immaterial
1 = likely
2 = necessary

horizon year, $t$. We can assume that for both the inhibiting and enhancing modes, when $\Pr(E_i) = 0$, $\Pr'(E_i)$ must equal 0, and when $\Pr(E_i) = 1$, $\Pr'(E_i)$ must equal 1. Therefore, the relation should be something like:

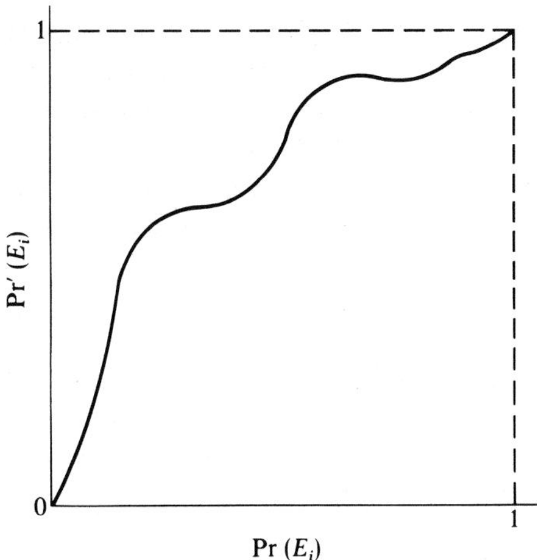


When the influencing event occurs at the horizon year ($t_l = t$), there is no time allowed for the adjustment of the probability of $\Pr(E_i)$ to $\Pr'(E_i)$, so $\Pr'(E_i)$ must equal $\Pr(E_i)$:

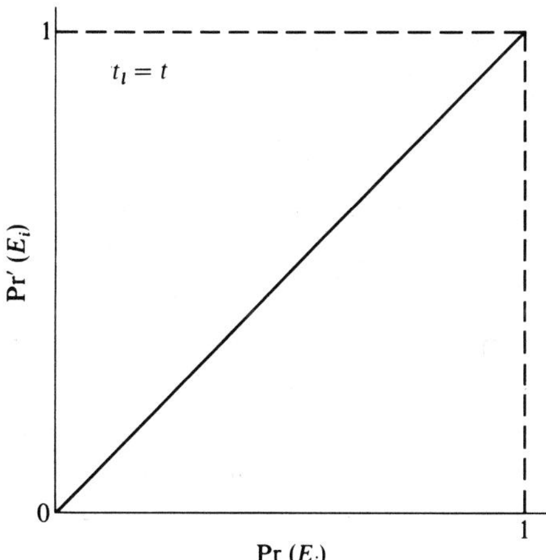


The area above the diagonal contains the enhancing mode and the area below the inhibiting relations, since above the diagonal $\Pr'(E_i) > \Pr(E_i)$ and below $\Pr'(E_i) < \Pr(E_i)$.

The authors assumed as a first approximation that within these regions the relationship between Pr′ $(E_i)$ and Pr $(E_i)$ varies increasingly with time remaining and modal strength; e.g., the greater the time and the higher the strength, then the greater the ratio Pr′ $(E_i)$/Pr $(E_i)$ for enhancing modes. For inhibiting modes: the greater the time and the higher the strength, the lower the ratio Pr′ $(E_i)$/Pr $(E_i)$.

Gordon and Haywood (Ref. 18-5) further assumed the relationship in the first figure to be quadratic:

$$\text{Pr}'\ (E_i) = A[\text{Pr}\ (E_i)]^2 + B\ \text{Pr}\ (E_i) + C \tag{18-1}$$

Then, substituting known end conditions, they obtained:

$$\text{Pr}'\ (E_i) = -A[\text{Pr}\ (E_i)]^2 + (1 + A)\ \text{Pr}\ (E_i) \tag{18-2}$$

For the enhancing case: $$0 < A < 1 \tag{18-3}$$

and for the inhibiting case: $$-1 < A < 0 \tag{18-4}$$

The question still remained as to how $t_1$, $t$, and $S_{li}$ affected $A$. Although greater sophistication was possible, they assumed the relationship was linear:

$$A_{li} = M_{li} S_{li} \frac{t - t_l}{t} \tag{18-5}$$

where $M_{li}$ is $+1$ or $-1$, as determined by the mode; $S_{li}$ is a number between 0 and 0.9† a smaller one representing weaker strength (0 designating an unrelated pair); and $t$ and $t_l$ are as previously defined.

Now substituting back into Eq. (18-2):

$$\text{Pr}'\ (E_i) = -M_{li} S_{li}\left(\frac{t - t_l}{t}\right)[\text{Pr}\ (E_i)]^2 + \left[1 + M_{li} S_{li}\left(\frac{t - t_l}{t}\right)\right] \text{Pr}\ (E_i) \tag{18-6}$$

In words, this equation indicates that the sooner event $l$ starts before the horizon year and the greater the strength of connection between events $i$ and $l$, the greater the change in the revised probability, Pr′ $(E_i)$. The steps in the Gordon–Haywood procedure are displayed in Fig. 18-2. The first step is to classify all *events* according to their predecessor relationship. Necessary events are listed first, then likely, and then immaterial. An *event* is considered "necessary" if it is shown to be necessary in at least one of its interactions with another event. Similar definitions hold for "likely" and "immaterial" events, with each being categorized only once, according to its strongest predecessor relationship.

At the start of the second step an event is chosen at random from the "necessary" category. A random number (RN) is then employed in step 3 to determine if the selected event (called the *affecting* event) occurs. This determination is made by comparing the existing probability of the event with the RN. In steps 4 and 5 the impact of the affecting event on all other events (called *affected* events) is found. If the affecting event has occurred (step 3), the probability of occurrence of the affected one is adjusted using Eq. (18-6). If not, the present probability of the

† Shown as 0 to 9 in tables like Table 18-4.

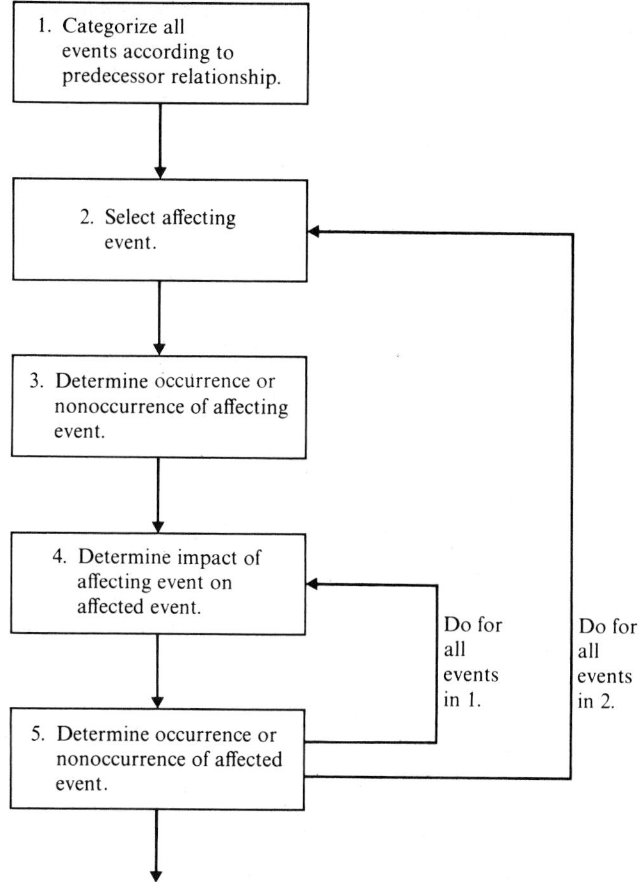


**Figure 18-2** Steps in the Gordon–Haywood procedure for cross-impact matrices.

affected event is maintained. Given the resultant probability of the affected event, a determination is then made of the occurrence or nonoccurrence (step 5) by comparing the probability to a RN.

Steps 2 to 5 are repeated for the remaining necessary events, then the likely, and then the immaterial. The whole process subsequently can be repeated as many times as thought desirable.

An example of the use of this procedure can be developed with the data from Table 18-4. For simplicity we will be dealing with two events, which we assume are the only ones possible in this situation. We also imagine that our horizon year is 2000 and that the current date is 1976. Thus:

$$t = 2000 - 1976 = 24$$

$$t_1 = 1982 - 1976 = 6$$

$$t_2 = 1992 - 1976 = 16$$

Then, utilizing the random numbers in the previous section and example:

Step 1. Event $E_1$ is defined as "necessary" and event $E_2$ as "immaterial."
Step 2. A random selection from the "necessary" events gives $E_1$ (since it is the only one in that category).
Step 3. The first RN is 0.2, which is less than Pr $(E_1) = 0.4$, so $E_1$ is assumed to occur.
Step 4. Since $E_1$ occurred, the impact on event $E_2$ is found from Eq. (18-6).† With $M_{12} = +1$, $S_{12} = \frac{6}{10} = 0.6$, and Pr $(E_2) = 0.5$:

$$\Pr'(E_2) = -(1)(0.6)\left(\frac{24-6}{24}\right)(0.5)^2 + \left[1 + (1)(0.6)\left(\frac{24-6}{24}\right)\right](0.5) = 0.61$$

Under this formulation $E_2$ has 18 years (24 − 6), or 75 percent of the time period under consideration, to be influenced by $E_1$ before the horizon year 2000. Taking into account this effect as well as that of the strength of the interaction (0.6) and the initial probability of $E_2$ (0.5), gives us a revised probability of $E_2$ of 0.61.

Step 5. The second RN is 0.7. Since this is greater than Pr′ $(E_2) = 0.61$, $E_2$ is assumed not to occur.
Step 6. RN = 0.2, which is less than 0.34, so no $E_1$ occurs.

If there were more events, the impact of $E_1$ on their probabilities would be determined (steps 4 and 5) at this point (loop 1), thereby completing round 1. The results can be summarized as in Table 18-5, where a 1 represents the occurrence of an event, a 0 the nonoccurrence.

In the second round we go back to step 2 (loop 2) and select one of the remaining necessary events at random. Since there are none of these, we select a likely one or, continuing, an immaterial one, in this case $E_2$. So:

Step 2. Select $E_2$.
Step 3. RN = 0.5, so $E_2$ occurs since this is less than 0.61, the new probability of $E_2$.

† If $E_1$ had not occurred, $E_2$ would remain at its existing value of 0.5.

**Table 18-5 Tally sheet for the Gordon–Haywood procedure**

| | Round | | | | | | | | | | | |
|---|---|---|---|---|---|---|---|---|---|---|---|---|
| Event | 1 | 2 | 3 | 4 | 5 | 6 | 7 | 8 | 9 | 10 | Total | Probability |
| $E_1$ | 1† | 1 | 0 | 0 | 0 | 1 | 0 | 0 | 0 | 0 | 3 | 0.3 |
| $E_2$ | 0 | 1 | 0 | 1 | 1 | 0 | 1 | 1 | 1 | 0 | 6 | 0.6 |

† 1 = event occurs, 0 = event does not occur.

Step 4. Compute Pr′ $(E_1)$, with $M_{21} = -1$, $S_{21} = \frac{8}{10} = 0.8$, and Pr $(E_1) = 0.4$:

$$\Pr'(E_1) = -(-1)(0.8)\left(\frac{24-16}{24}\right)(0.4)^2 + \left[1 + (-1)(0.8)\left(\frac{24-16}{24}\right)\right](0.4) = 0.34$$

Thus ends the second round, and we could go through several more rounds (steps 2 to 5) again, starting with $E_1$ being the affecting event, then $E_2$, and so on. The probability Pr $(E_i)$ associated with each event would always be the latest one. If continued for 10 rounds, the results might be something like those in Table 18-5. Since $E_1$ occurred in 3 of the 10 rounds, its final probability would be $\frac{3}{10} = 0.3$. The probability of $E_2$ would be $\frac{6}{10} = 0.6$. The interactions between $E_1$ and $E_2$ thus results in a decline in Pr $(E_1)$ from 0.4, its initial value, to 0.3 and an increase in Pr $(E_2)$ from 0.5 to 0.6.

## 18-4 AN EXPANDED EXAMPLE

The procedure described above was employed in a larger-scale example to demonstrate both the types of findings that may result from cross-impact analyses and the sensitivity of these findings to changes in various input values. The illustration focuses on a depressed rural region where the concern is for low population growth and substantial out-migration, especially of young people. The eight events considered are displayed on the left-hand side of Table 18-6. The first event, for instance, is entitled "abortion completely legalized nationwide." It has been assumed that this will happen in 1980, with an overall probability of 0.8. The two events of main concern to the region, $E_7$ (net migration less than zero) and $E_8$ (regional population growth less than zero), are found at the bottom of the table. It is assumed that we are in 1976 looking ahead to the horizon year of 1990.

The interactions between each pair of events have been estimated by us, but in a real-world situation they may be the result of a Delphi process. $E_1$, for example, is thought to have a slight (2) enhancing (+) effect on $E_8$, with the former event being a likely predecessor. In words, completely legalized abortion would decrease the birth rate just about everywhere, including the region under study, and thus would likely be a predecessor in enhancing the probability of less than zero population growth in that region. Note here also that some affecting events may come later in time than the corresponding affected events (for example, $E_6$ or $E_5$). These situations result from actions expected to occur in *anticipation* of future events.

The revised probabilities for each event when the interactions are taken into account are presented in Table 18-7 in the next-to-last column. A comparison with the preceding figures shows that the changes generally are not greater than 0.1. Events $E_4$ and $E_5$ are most highly affected, but, more important to the region, the

**Table 18-6 Sample cross-impact matrix for regional population growth**

| Event | Description | Date | Probability | Change probabilities | | | | | | | |
|---|---|---|---|---|---|---|---|---|---|---|---|
| | | | | $E_1$ | $E_2$ | $E_3$ | $E_4$ | $E_5$ | $E_6$ | $E_7$ | $E_8$ |
| $E_1$ | Abortion completely legalized nationwide | 1980 | 0.8 | | −21 | | +20 | +41 | | | +21 |
| $E_2$ | "Morning after" pill readily available | 1984 | 0.9 | −51 | //// | | +21 | +41 | +21 | | |
| $E_3$ | Medical cures for heart attacks found | 1988 | 0.3 | | | | | +10 | | +21 | −21 |
| $E_4$ | Income tax deductions for child dependents rescinded | 1986 | 0.2 | +10 | | | //// | +30 | | | +10 |
| $E_5$ | Only 50% of couples married | 1979 | 0.6 | +10 | +10 | | +20 | //// | +20 | | +20 |
| $E_6$ | One-day divorce available nationwide | 1983 | 0.3 | | | | | +52 | /// | | +10 |
| $E_7$ | Net migration in the region less than zero | 1985 | 0.5 | | | | | | | //// | +32 |
| $E_8$ | Regional population growth less than zero | 1987 | 0.6 | | | | | | | +20 | //// |

*Mode.* + Enhancing; − Inhibiting

*Strength.* First digit (0–9): 0 = unconnected; 9 = very strong

*Time lag.* Second digit: predecessor event: 0 = immaterial; 1 = likely; 2 = necessary

**Table 18-7 Results of cross-impact analysis of regional population growth**

| Event | Description | Initial probability | Final probability | Sensitivity run probability |
|---|---|---|---|---|
| $E_1$ | Abortion completely legalized nationwide | 0.80 | 0.78 | 0.78 |
| $E_2$ | "Morning after" pill readily available | 0.90 | 0.94 | 0.94 |
| $E_3$ | Medical cure for heart attack found | 0.30 | 0.23 | 0.23 |
| $E_4$ | Income tax deductions for child dependents rescinded | 0.20 | 0.30 | 0.30 |
| $E_5$ | Only 50% of couples married | 0.60 | 0.70 | 0.70 |
| $E_6$ | One-day divorce available nationwide | 0.30 | 0.28 | 0.28 |
| $E_7$ | Net migration in the region less than zero | 0.50 | 0.51 | 0.51 |
| $E_8$ | Regional population growth less than zero | 0.60 | 0.69 | 0.74 |

probability of less-than-zero population growth ($E_8$) has increased from 0.60 to 0.69. While this change is not overwhelming, it does point toward a trend to lowered population levels, due mainly to natural causes (births and deaths) rather than migration (since the migration probability remains almost unchanged). The future of this depressed region thus would seem to be even bleaker.

The results of a sensitivity run on two strength-of-interaction values are shown in the last column of Table 18-7. It was assumed for this experiment that $E_2$ ("morning after" pill availability) would significantly enhance $E_8$, i.e., reduce the population growth in the region, with the strength being 7 and with $E_2$ being a likely predecessor. In addition, we imagined that the impact of $E_7$ on $E_8$ would increase to +72 (enhance; strength of 7; necessary predecessor) from the present status of +32.

The impact of these fairly significant changes on the probability of the regional population growth being less than zero was more substantial than in the previous case. It was raised to 0.74, again in detriment to the apparent goals of the region. None of the other events were affected. This experiment thus highlights some of the interesting results that can evolve from sensitivity tests of cross-impact matrices.

## 18-5 AN APPLICATION†

Gordon and Haywood, in the paper presenting their approach to "solving" large-scale cross-impact matrices (described in Sec. 18-3), also gave an interesting application involving 71 future transportation-related events and developments to occur within the next 20 years (Ref. 18-5). Twenty of these events were related to technological innovations and improvements which might have a significant impact on transportation systems, nine items dealt with new modes which have been proposed, eight items described changing traveler preferences, and the remaining items were associated with changes in society which could have some effect on transportation customs. The authors themselves estimated the dates of occurrence and initial probabilities for each item (simulating the results of Delphi panels) and constructed a cross-impact matrix showing modes of linkage, strength, and predecessor–successor relationships. This matrix was "played" 1000 times and the results evaluated in terms of probability shift and final probability. Table 18-8 illustrates the items which formed the matrix, and their initial and final probabilities.

Some interesting conclusions were drawn from this application:

1. The effect of the judged interactions among the events significantly changed the probabilities associated with the original forecasts. For example, the item relating to increased preference for long-distance commuting (item 69) was initially judged to have a probability of 0.5. The interactions dropped this to 0.179.
2. The probability shifts resulting from this computation indicate that supersonic transport, personal automobiles, air buses, and fast surface and subsurface trains are more likely (greater than 90 percent probability) than initially assessed; while moving sidewalks, mass passenger air-cushion vehicles, StaRCar, and personal rocket belts decreased in probability from their original values.
3. Within the group of items describing future transportation system modes, fast subsurface trains displayed the highest probability gain, suggesting that changing customer preferences, social customs, and technological innovations might favor this mode (item 28 shifted from 0.5 to 0.909).
4. With reference to customer preferences, the judgments interact in a way which suggests that fare is likely to be less important than might have otherwise been estimated (item 30 shifted in the negative direction) and comfort will probably become the most important transportation-mode attribute.
5. Although the items relating to antipollution legislation, automated air-traffic control, and extensive and effective automobile safety devices were originally listed at 0.90 probability, the cross-impact analysis increased each of these to levels of 0.99 or greater; therefore, the interactions indicate that these items should be assessed as virtually certain.

† Much of the wording in this section is adapted from Ref. 18-5.

**Table 18-8 Events (items) and probabilities for transportation study**

| Index | Item | Initial probability | Final probability |
|---|---|---|---|
| 1 | New materials for ultra light-weight construction (the density and cost of aluminum but twice the strength) using, for example, new alloys, composite structures with whiskers or boron filaments, or new plastics | 0.9000 | 0.8990 |
| 2 | Information handling systems which would automatically keep track of all aircraft in flight, warn of impending collision situations and reallocate airspace | 0.9000 | 0.9920 |
| 3 | Automated highways which would track and control the speed and direction of vehicles traveling over them | 0.3000 | 0.9430 |
| 4 | A new large-capacity fixed power source which can produce electricity for cents per kW, using, for example, nuclear power or magneto-hydrodynamic processes | 0.7500 | 0.7690 |
| 5 | A new reliable chemical fuel mobile power source, weighing under 100 pounds which can produce 200 hp for automobiles, etc. | 0.7500 | 0.8790 |
| 6 | A storage battery which can power an automobile at 80 mph, over ranges of 200 miles, weighing less than 200 pounds | 0.9000 | 0.9100 |
| 7 | "Shearing" parallel belts which move slowly at the edges and at higher speeds near the center | 0.5000 | 0.4980 |
| 8 | Nuclear explosives for rapid excavation and tunneling available for use by commercial contractors | 0.5000 | 0.8730 |
| 9 | Electronic circuit techniques which are "self-healing" and maintenance free | 0.6000 | 0.8010 |
| 10 | Relatively inexpensive rocket propellents, capable of being handled and used safely (possible application: inexpensive rocket belts such as Aerojet's rocket man) | 0.3000 | 0.0740 |
| 11 | Room temperature superconducting wire (one use of which might be the construction of magnetic highways over which cars of opposite polarity would float) | 0.2000 | 0.2350 |
| 12 | Mobile highway building machine capable of laying finished road surface at the rate of 2 miles per day and at a cost of $200,000 per mile | 0.7500 | 0.9420 |
| 13 | Antismog device which removes 90% of the pollutants from the exhaust of internal combustion engines at a cost of about 5 cents per 100 miles (may be mechanical or gasoline additive) | 0.3000 | 0.7460 |
| 14 | Fatigue-resistant metals which permit helicopter blades to function 10,000 hours between inspections | 0.6000 | 0.6080 |
| 15 | Linear induction motor of 5000 hp | 0.9000 | 0.8820 |
| 16 | New automobile safety devices which further reduce fatalities by 50% and cost $200 per automobile | 0.9000 | 0.9870 |
| 17 | Beamed power device, perhaps lasers, for transmitting propulsive energy to aircraft | 0.2000 | 0.2990 |
| 18 | Mechanical power pick-up system which permits vehicles to derive electrical energy from fixed sources | 0.9000 | 0.9730 |
| 19 | Nondeflating tires | 0.5000 | 0.8770 |

**Table 18-8** *(continued)*

| Index | Item | Initial probability | Final probability |
|---|---|---|---|
| 20 | Mobile tuneling machine capable of digging a 50-ft diameter hole, 10 miles per day | 0.5000 | 0.8020 |
| 21 | Increased use and performance of the StaRCar—a "mixed" system composed of battery-powered cars which can run free on public roads or on "guideways" which furnish electrical power, at speeds of up to 60 mph | 0.3000 | 0.3310 |
| 22 | Increased use and performance of VTOL/STOL (vertical take-off and landing or short takeoff and landing) aircraft or helicopters, carrying as many as 50 people from suburban centers to downtown metropolitan landing sites | 0.8000 | 0.9460 |
| 23 | Increased use and performance of fast surface trains—commuter trains, running at peak speeds of over 100 mph, using either wheeled or air suspension systems on tracks, above ground | 0.8000 | 0.9270 |
| 24 | Increased use and performance of autos—private automobiles, using internal combustion engines, turbines, electric power, or other propulsive sources; capable of running on public roads | 0.9000 | 0.9620 |
| 25 | Increased use and performance of mass ACVs (air-cushion vehicles) for mass transit, typically carrying 100 passengers or more, over "grassy freeways," water, or roads | 0.6000 | 0.6140 |
| 26 | Increased use and performance of supersonic aircraft transports, carrying 205 passengers at supersonic speeds; optimum operation over 1000-mile trips; terminals in Boston, New York, Philadelphia, and Washington, D.C. | 0.9000 | 0.9770 |
| 27 | Increased use and performance of air bus—a low fare subsonic transport, capable of carrying 500 passengers across the country for $100 each at 500 mph; terminals at almost any commercial airport | 0.9000 | 0.9450 |
| 28 | Increased use and performance of subsurface trains—commuter trains, running at peak speeds of over 100 mph, using pneumatic propulsion, or wheeled or air suspension on tracks, and running through intercity tunnels. | 0.5000 | 0.9090 |
| 29 | Increased use and performance of moving sidewalks—belts used in cities in place of some sidewalks, providing speeds up to 30 mph | 0.5000 | 0.8040 |
| 30 | Increased desire for low fare—the cost to the traveler in terms of dollars per mile | 0.5000 | 0.4740 |
| 31 | Increased desire for reduced travel time—the time to travel from point of origin to destination | 0.7000 | 0.7640 |
| 32 | Increased desire for safety—traveler safety, a measure of which is the number of accidents or fatalities per passenger mile traveled | 0.5000 | 0.6150 |
| 33 | Increased desire for comfort—passenger comfort, in terms of noise, vibration, entertainment, etc. | 0.7000 | 0.9240 |
| 34 | Increased desire for convenience—the accessibility and schedule frequency of the system | 0.7500 | 0.7590 |
| 35 | Increased desire for community safety—the impact of the system on the safety of the community | 0.5000 | 0.5120 |

**Table 18-8** (*continued*)

| Index | Item | Initial probability | Final probability |
|---|---|---|---|
| 36 | Increased desire for favorable environmental factors—the impact of the system on the community in which it is imbedded, such as pollution, noise, etc. | 0.8000 | 0.8760 |
| 37 | Increased desire for improved cargo integrity—the ability of the system to handle cargo smoothly and with minimum breakage | 0.6000 | 0.5920 |
| 38 | Blank | 0.5000 | 0.4800 |
| 39 | GNP per capita grows at 5% per year | 0.5000 | 0.7640 |
| 40 | Society's need for transportation decreases | 0.2000 | 0.5660 |
| 41 | Knowledge of weather conditions, through reliable forecasting, 1 week in advance, for areas as small as 600 square miles | 0.8000 | 0.7970 |
| 42 | Widespread use of nonnarcotic drugs ($\frac{1}{4}$ population on hallucinogenic trips, once per week) | | |
| 43 | Continued automation of office work leading to displacement of 25% of the office workforce | 0.5000 | 0.5320 |
| 44 | Widespread use of automatic decision making at management level displacing 25% of middle management | 0.4000 | 0.4420 |
| 45 | Widespread use of robots service in the home and factories, displacing 25% of the unskilled labor force | 0.6000 | 0.6560 |
| 46 | National urban programme, funded at $3000 million per year, to promote renewal and renovate the physical plant of cities | 0.9000 | 0.9500 |
| 47 | Two years of compulsory post high-school education | 0.5000 | 0.5920 |
| 48 | New high-school curriculum including education for better leisure-time enjoyment | 0.5000 | 0.7290 |
| 49 | Intelligence of most of the population 10 IQ points higher through the use of drugs | 0.3000 | 0.4810 |
| 50 | Improved recreational and agricultural planning through the use of limited weather control (rain falls only on week-nights) | 0.4000 | 0.7350 |
| 51 | High school in the home through the use of teaching machines | 0.9000 | 0.9800 |
| 52 | Four-day work week available to most wage earners | 0.3000 | 0.5240 |
| 53 | Social security benefits available at age 55 for men and women | 0.7000 | 0.8550 |
| 54 | Fifty-year extension in life expectancy; vitality duration extended 25 years through control over ageing process | 0.2000 | 0.2020 |
| 55 | Widespread use of centralized data banks (medical, legal, and general library look-up services), printed-out via facsimile in homes and offices | 0.9000 | 0.9140 |
| 56 | Almost universal use of facsimile mail delivery service | 0.6000 | 0.8210 |
| 57 | Use by low-income families of attractive, prefabricated, very low cost ($1000) buildings for homes | 0.5000 | 0.6150 |
| 58 | Use by half of the population of home computers to "run" households | 0.6500 | 0.8480 |
| 59 | Use by 30% of the population of home communications centers which include conference 3-D television, promoting decentralization of business management | 0.7500 | 0.8970 |
| 60 | Widespread use of 3-D color television receivers with "presence" | 0.5000 | 0.6210 |

**Table 18-8** *(continued)*

| Index | Item | Initial probability | Final probability |
|---|---|---|---|
| 61 | Credit card economy in which direct links are established from stores to banks to check credit, record all transactions, and compute individual taxes automatically | 0.9000 | 0.9740 |
| 62 | High level of urbanization (85% of the population lives in cities over 20,000 by 1980) | 0.9000 | 0.9730 |
| 63 | Full employment (unemployment levels below 3.5%) | 0.5000 | 0.3710 |
| 64 | 50% increase in disposable personal income (by 1980) | 0.5000 | 0.6580 |
| 65 | Availability of more recreational areas (twice as many per capita by 1980) | 0.5000 | 0.9420 |
| 66 | Widespread and extensive federal support for regional transportation programmes | 0.7000 | 0.6940 |
| 67 | Urban crime rates reduced by 50% | 0.2000 | 0.3850 |
| 68 | Antipollution legislation spreads and carries severe penalties | 0.9000 | 0.9970 |
| 69 | Long-distance commuting in the sense that 25% of the workforce travels 50 miles from home to work | 0.5000 | 0.1790 |
| 70 | Regional medical centers | 0.8000 | 0.8880 |
| 71 | Minimum-income law enacted which guarantees subsistence to all citizens | 0.7000 | 0.7210 |
| 72 | Federal mortgage subsidies permit low-income workers to purchase houses | 0.5000 | 0.6270 |

*Source:* Ref. 18-5, pp. 110–113.

The above list of conclusions was not exhaustive but served to illustrate the kinds of inferences which could be drawn from a cross-impact analysis. The authors then proceeded to test the sensitivity of the probability shifts to alterations in the original probability levels. Suppose, for instance, by conscious policy decision or unexpected breakthrough, the world in the next 20 years becomes more highly automated than Table 18-8 suggests. What effect might this alteration have on transportation systems? The sensitivity of the "transportation world" to level of automation was tested by increasing the probability of those items associated with automation:

43. Automation of office work
44. Automation of middle management
45. Automation of unskilled labor
55. Data banks and facsimile
56. Facsimile mail
58. Home computers
61. Credit card economy

Each was increased arbitrarily by 20 percent but in no case was allowed to exceed 95 percent. This new run was then compared with the earlier base case. A number of items shifted in probability as a result of the higher automation levels. The three transportation-relevant items most affected were:

40. Need for transportation decreases
21. Increased use and performance of StaRCars
69. Long-distance commuting (negative change)

The first and last items are intuitively reasonable; if the world were to become more automated, people might travel less, since many of the services and products for which they currently travel would be available to them in their homes. This situation, of course, would make them less likely to be long-distance commuters. The mechanism by which spreading automation enhances the StaRCar is understandable, since the StaRCar system itself is highly automated.

It also was possible to discern the effect of this increased automation on some of the social entries. For example, comparison of the final probabilities of the base case with the more automated world showed that, with more automation, it was increasingly likely we would have (in rank order):

48. Education for leisure
63. Full employment
52. Four-day work week
47. Compulsory post high-school education
39. 5% per year gross regional product growth rate

These results certainly are suggestive of a more automated world.

## PROBLEMS

**18-1** Fill in the blanks with the appropriate word(s).

(*a*) An interaction can be described with three characteristics: its ______________, ______________, and ______________.

(*b*) One event can ______________ or ______________ the likelihood of another or be ______________.

(*c*) A cross-impact matrix starts with the ______________ and initial ______________ of each event.

(*d*) One approach used to find final probabilities in large-sized cross-impact matrices is the ______________ routine.

(*e*) A predecessor relationship can be ______________, ______________, or ______________.

(*f*) Gordon and Haywood assumed that the relationship between Pr′ $(E_i)$ and Pr $(E_i)$ was

________________.

**18-2** The director of institutional planning at your university wants to know what the student body population at the university will be in 1990. You are asked to *set up* a cross-impact matrix to make this forecast. You should list 6 to 8 events, along with their probabilities and years, that might be expected to have a significant influence on the 1990 student population. Then fill out the rest of the matrix. Use genius (you) forecasting for the items in the entire matrix.

**18-3** A dispute has arisen in Utah over the building of a dam. All other things being equal, there is a 30 percent chance it will be built, with 1984 being the most likely year for starting. On the other hand, if Governor Smith is reelected in 1976 (50 percent chance), he has moved to support the project. Astute observers feel that his win will mean that the chances of construction will increase by 50 percent, with the new starting date being 1980. Conversely, if he loses, the chance will be reduced 20 percent and the start delayed 2 years. What is the overall probability of the dam being built, given the election results?

Solve using:

(*a*) Direct mathematical approach
(*b*) Monte Carlo routine with matrix set up like Table 18-2
(*c*) Monte Carlo routine with Eq. (18-6)

**18-4** Use the random numbers in Sec. 18-2 for Prob. 18-3(*b*).

**18-5** Go to the library and find an application of cross-impact matrices. In about 500 words describe:

(*a*) The nature of the problem being attacked
(*b*) The general types of events considered
(*c*) Possibly significant events not considered
(*d*) Your opinion of the validity and reliability of some of the modes and strengths of interactions proposed
(*e*) The validity of the conclusions reached
(*f*) Other advantages and disadvantages of the technique in this application

**18-6** If you have access to a computer program to do cross-impact matrices, use it to find the final probabilities and timing of the events suggested in Prob. 18-2.

## REFERENCES

### Theory

18-1. Boucher, W. I.: *An Annoted Bibliography on Cross-Impact Analysis*, The Futures Group, Report 128-01-14, Glastonbury, Conn., February, 1974.

18-2. Kave, J., I. Vertinsky, and W. Thompson: "KSIM: A Method for Interactive Resource Policy Simulation," *Water Resources Research*, vol. 9, no. 1, February, 1973.

18-3. Martino, J. P.: *Technological Forecasting for Decisionmaking*, American-Elsevier, New York, 1972.

18-4. Turoff, M. A.: "An Alternative Approach to Cross-Impact Analysis," "*Technological Forecasting and Social Change*, vol. 3, no. 3, 1972.

### Applications and other references

18-5. Gordon, T. J., and H. Haywood: "Initial Experiments with the Cross-Impact Matrix Method of Forecasting," *Futures*, vol. 1, no. 2, 1968.

18-6. Mansfield, E.: "Diffusion of Technological Change," in *Reviews of Data and Development*, National Science Foundation, Washington, D.C., October, 1961.

18-7. Schlesinger, B., and D. Daetz: *Development of a Procedure for Forecasting Long-Range Environmental Impacts*, NTIS, PB-244 974, Springfield, Va., August, 1975.

18-8. Sherman, C. W., and R. S. Isenson: "Project Hindsight," *Science*, June 23, 1967.

CHAPTER
# NINETEEN
## EARLY WARNING

While many of the techniques discussed so far in this book are extremely powerful quantitatively and/or take advantage of a wide range of human intuition and experience, it is inevitable that many events will occur that had not been forecasted using such techniques. These events may be in the form of new policies by government at various levels, major changes in private business attitudes, technological breakthroughs, natural disasters, and the like. The list could be quite long, thus indicating the breadth of factors and forces that should, but almost never can, be considered in forecasting. And naturally the number of potentially important impacting events grows larger the further we look into the future.

One way to help reduce uncertainty beyond that already accomplished through statistical models and/or intuition-aiding techniques is through an early-warning system. Such a system requires more than collection of data about what has happened in the past. It also involves the screening and projection of historic trends into the future *and* the evaluation of such projections in terms of their likely implications. The ultimate value is in the appropriate, timely response to these implications by decision makers. A trade-off is inherent: if a trend is seen as developing and the decision maker acts too soon, the anticipated result may not occur, and hence the decision probably will be incorrect. On the other hand, if the decision maker waits too long and the anticipated event does occur, he will not have enough time to react and some negative by-products may result (or some positive by-products missed). The major purpose of an early-warning system therefore is to provide information to help set thresholds at which point uncertainty is as low as possible and yet sufficient time remains for suitable action.

This chapter will focus on the characteristics of early-warning systems. Examples will come from a variety of topical areas (including private business).

But it should be stressed that, to our knowledge, no formal systems of this type have been developed for urban areas or regions (except for defense). The discussion here thus should be understood as somewhat theoretical, lacking the honing experience of practical application.

## 19-1 CHARACTERISTICS OF AN EARLY-WARNING SYSTEM

The four phases of an early-warning system entail:

1. Development of conceptual relationships
2. Collection of data
3. Screening and evaluation of the data
4. Setting of thresholds

A fifth phase might also be included in which checks are made on the fulfillment of short-term projections or trends that seem to be building. Possible procedures for carrying out each of these phases now will be described in turn.

### Conceptual Relationships

Before an early-warning system can be implemented it is necessary to develop some rough limits on the variety of data to be collected. Otherwise the effort will be inundated with irrelevant information. Perhaps the best way to make this delimitation is to create a conceptual model of the factors and interrelationships under study. If the major variables and their connections can be identified, the incoming data can be accepted or screened out according to their relevance to one or more of these factors or interrelationships.

One approach to creating such a conceptual model is to consider the main inputs to one which has already been developed. As an example, Dickey developed a model for estimating statewide gasoline tax revenues in Virginia (Ref. 19-3). The main inputs were the first 14 factors listed in Table 19-1. He then expanded from each factor to take into account the variables that affect it. Figure 19-1, known as a *digraph* (directed digraph), gives an example in terms of the state population level factor. Population is seen as increasing with rises in the birth and in-migration rates (+ sign) and decreasing with rises in the mortality and out-migration rates (− sign). The birth rate, in turn, is affected by the relative employment levels in Virginia (versus the rest of the United States), the average age level, and the level of medical technology. Further expansions could be made on each of these factors if thought desirable by the expert devising the digraph. Eventually, however, he must come to the point where one or more factors are "primary," i.e., stand by themselves, supposedly unaffected by other variables. The "medical technology level" factor (factor 19 in Fig. 19-1) is considered to be in this category. A corresponding designation can then be made in Table 19-1 as to the "type" of factor (next-to-last column). It can be either:

**Table 19-1 Sample list of factors and their characteristics**

| Number | Name of factor | Type | Class |
|---|---|---|---|
| 1 | Yearly state manufacturing investment | 2 | 1 |
| 2 | Service life of manufacturing capital | 2 | 1 |
| 3 | Cumulative yearly household income distribution | 2 | 1 |
| 4 | Overall CPI† | 2 | 1 |
| 5 | Gasoline CPI | 2 | 1 |
| 6 | Parking CPI | 2 | 1 |
| 7 | Labor CPI | 2 | 1 |
| 8 | State population | 2 | 2 |
| 9 | State persons per household | 2 | 2 |
| 10 | Percentage of vehicle miles driven by Virginia residents in state | 2 | 6 |
| 11 | Percentage of vehicle miles driven by non-Virginia households in Virginia for which gasoline was purchased in Virginia | 2 | 6 |
| 12 | Mean auto miles per gallon | 2 | 4 |
| 13 | Mean truck miles per gallon | 2 | 4 |
| 14 | Virginia gasoline tax rate | 2 | 1 |
| 15 | Mean yearly household income | 1 | 1 |
| 16 | Birth rate | 4 | 2 |
| 17 | Mortality rate | 4 | 2 |
| 18 | Average (median) age level | 4 | 2 |
| 19 | Medical technology level | 3 | 4 |
| 20 | In-migration rate | 4 | 2 |
| 21 | Out-migration rate | 4 | 2 |
| 22 | Relative employment level | 4 | 1 |
| 23 | Marriage rate | 4 | 2 |
| 24 | Divorce rate | 4 | 2 |
| 25 | Rate of unrelated persons living together | 4 | 2 |
| 26 | Social acceptance of unrelated persons living together | 4 | 2 |
| 27 | World oil reserves | 3 | 5 |
| 28 | OPEC price levels | 4 | 1 |
| 29 | Oil company price levels | 4 | 1 |
| 30 | Transit usage level | 4 | 6 |
| 31 | Transit service level | 4 | 6 |
| 32 | Mass transit funding | 3 | 1 |
| 33 | Urban driving level | 4 | 6 |
| 34 | Communications technology level | 3 | 4 |
| 35 | Traffic congestion level | 4 | 6 |
| 36 | Speed limit level | 3 | 3 |

*Source:* Ref. 19-6, p. 4.
† *c*onsumer *p*rice *i*ndex.

1. In the model itself
2. A main entry input
3. External—primary
4. External—secondary (affected by another factor)

Note that many of these variables need not be measurable at this point—just recognizable. Also, for simplicity in later endeavors, we should group all factors

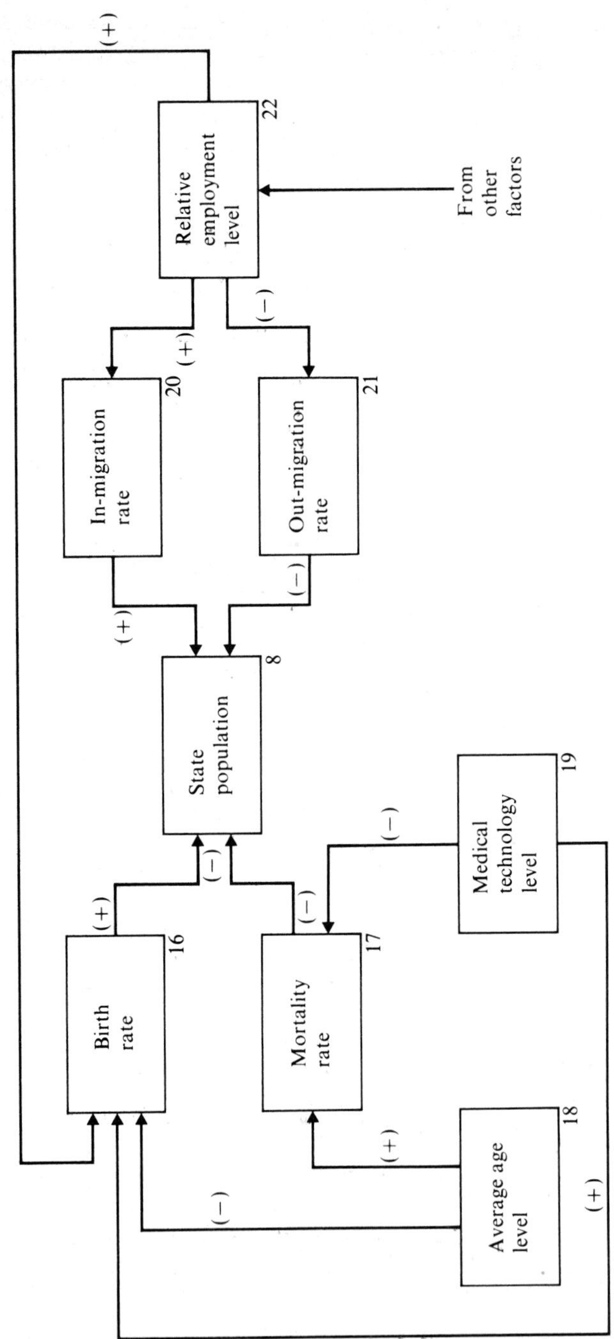


**Figure 19-1** Partial state population digraph. (*Source: Ref. 19-6, p. 5.*)

into a small number of major classes. Dickey (Ref. 19-6) decided that the six major categories in his study would be (last column of Table 19-1):

1. Economic–financial
2. Social–demographic
3. Political–institutional–legal–regulatory
4. Man built–physical–technological
5. Natural environmental
6. Travel behavioral

Given a digraph, it is then possible to identify information sources related to each factor. And as new, relevant factors become known, they can be added to the list, connected into the digraph, and used to indicate other sources of important information.

## Collection of Data

There are three main sources of data relevant to any early-warning system:

1. Discussions with people knowledgeable in particular fields
2. Retrieval from available and continually updated information (data, abstract, etc.) systems
3. Direct search of the literature

Assuming that "good" experts can be found, the first source probably is most useful because the information is as up to date and exhaustive as desired. Studies reported in the literature usually are at least 2 years old and may not describe all the kinds of results and implications of importance to the early-warning system.

**Discussions with knowledgeable people** For the early-warning system proposed by Dickey (Ref. 19-6), contact is made by telephone about once every 2 months with each group listed in Table 19-2. A representative is asked leading questions concerning both recent changes in the area of concern and likely short- and long-term trends. He or she is also asked to suggest implications for future policy decisions. To illustrate: the contact at the Social and Economic Statistics Administration may point out that, while birth rates have been going down steadily, there recently has been an unanticipated upswing. This may be due to childbearing by women in their thirties who in their earlier years had not wanted children. The implications might be that the 1980, 1985, and 1990 population levels in Virginia will be greater than expected. Hence gasoline tax revenues would also be greater.

The form shown in Fig. 19-2 is employed for recording of pertinent information received from any source (verbal or written). This form, known as VINCENT (*V*irginia *i*nformation *n*etwork *c*entered on the *e*valuation of *n*ew *t*ransportation), is a close replica of that used by the Whirlpool Corporation in their monitoring efforts (Ref. 19-4). Most of the form is self-explanatory, except perhaps the

**Table 19-2 Sample list of groups to be contacted**

| Number | Factor of concern | Group (person) |
|---|---|---|
| 1 | State manufacturing investment | Federal Reserve Bank of Richmond<br>Virginia Division of Industrial Development<br>Bureau of Labor Statistics (BLS)<br>Social and Economic Statistics Administration (SESA) |
| 2 | Service life of manufacturing capital | Virginia Department of Taxation<br>SESA |
| 3 | Income distribution | Virginia Department of Taxation<br>SESA<br>BLS |
| 4–7 | Consumer price indices | SESA<br>BLS |
| 8<br>9 | State population<br>State persons per household | Division of State Planning and Community Affairs<br>Tayloe Murphy Institute<br>SESA |
| 10<br>11 | Percentage of vehicle miles by Virginians in-state<br>Percentage of out-of-state vehicle miles in Virginia using gasoline bought in Virginia | Virginia Department of Highways and Transportation<br>Division of Motor Vehicles<br>Federal Highway Administration |
| 12<br>13 | Average auto mpg<br>Average truck mpg | U.S. Department of Transportation<br>U.S. Federal Energy Administration<br>U.S. Environmental Protection Agency<br>Automobile Manufacturers Association |
| 14 | Virginia gasoline tax rates | Legislative Appropriations Committee<br>Division of Motor Vehicles<br>Virginia Department of Highways and Transportation |

*Source:* Ref. 19-6, p. 8.

"class category" and "VINCENT index terms" items. The first refers to the six-part classification of factors presented earlier (Table 19-1). The contents of each contact discussion or reading would be categorized accordingly in item 3 of VINCENT.

The VINCENT INDEX TERMS are key words used for selected information retrieval. Each key word listed by the contact person or author is translated into one of the VINCENT terms. Three major thesauruses have been used as a basis for these INDEX TERMS:

Urbandoc (Refs. 19-8 and 19-9)
TRISNET (Ref. 19-11)
Dickey (see Chap. 20 and Ref. 20-4).

VINCENT SUMMARY

| 1. TITLE (OR CITATION) | 3. †Class category:<br>4. †VINCENT summary no.:<br>5. Division:<br>6. Department:<br>7. Report date: |
|---|---|
| 2. AUTHOR(S) (OR SUBMITTOR) | 8. Report file no.:<br>9. No. of pages: |

| 10. SUMMARY: | | |
|---|---|---|
| 11. SUPPLEMENTARY NOTES:<br><br>12. DISTRIBUTION: | 13. KEY WORDS (Suggested by Author) | 14. †VINCENT INDEX TERMS: |

†*Note.* Items 3, 4, and 14 will be completed by the information center.

**Figure 19-2** VINCENT (*V*irginia *i*nformation *n*etwork *c*entered on the *e*valuation of *n*ew *t*ransportation) form. (*Source: Ref. 19-6, p. 12.*)

In Table 19-3 is displayed an example of the initial set of terms. The first two digits for each term correspond to the letter in the alphabet and the second two to the number of the term within that letter category. As work progresses it may be necessary to add or delete terms—thus the reason for the gaps in the numbers.

**Direct search of literature** The second possibility for collecting data is through readily available information retrieval systems. These may provide regularly updated and transmitted lists of abstracts in a general area of requested searches. A list of those being employed under each heading in the Virginia study is

**Table 19-3 Sample of list of VINCENT index terms**

| Code | Term |
|---|---|
| 01.04 | Acceleration |
| 01.08 | Access |
| 01.12 | Accessories |
| 01.16 | Accounts |
| 01.20 | Acquisition |
| 01.24 | Acreage |
| 01.28 | Aerodynamic |
| 01.32 | Action programs |
| 01.36 | Administration |
| 01.40 | Advertising |
| 01.44 | Agriculture |
| 01.48 | Appearance |
| 01.52 | Age |
| 01.56 | Agencies |
| 01.60 | Air |
| 01.64 | Amortization |
| 01.68 | Appropriations |
| 01.72 | Arterial |
| 01.76 | Associations |
| 01.80 | Automation |
| 01.88 | Automobiles |
| 01.92 | Availability |
| 01.96 | Aviation |
| 02.07 | Bicycling |
| 02.14 | Birth |
| 02.21 | Blue collar class |
| 02.28 | Bonds |
| 02.35 | Boundaries |
| 02.42 | Braking |
| 02.49 | Budget |
| 02.56 | Building industry |
| 02.63 | Building technology |
| 02.70 | Buildings |
| 02.77 | Buses |
| 02.84 | Business |
| 02.91 | Benefits |
| 03.02 | Capacity |
| 03.04 | Capital grants |
| 03.06 | Capital |
| 03.08 | Car pooling |
| 03.10 | Carriers |
| 03.12 | Census |
| 03.14 | Centers |
| 03.16 | Certification |
| 03.18 | Charges |
| 03.20 | Chemicals |
| 03.22 | Cities |
| 03.24 | Citizen participation |
| 03.26 | Climate |
| 03.28 | Coordination |
| 03.30 | Codes |
| 03.32 | Collection |
| 03.34 | Combustion |
| 03.36 | Comfort |
| 03.38 | Commercial activity |
| 03.40 | Communications |
| 03.42 | Communities |
| 03.44 | Commodity |
| 03.46 | Commuting |
| 03.48 | Companies |
| 03.50 | Compensation |
| 03.52 | Competition |
| 03.54 | Compliance |
| 03.56 | Compact |
| 03.58 | Computer |
| 03.60 | Congestion |
| 03.62 | Conservation |
| 03.64 | Consolidation |
| 03.66 | Construction |
| 03.68 | Consumers |
| 03.70 | Containers |
| 03.72 | Contracts |
| 03.74 | Controls |
| 03.76 | Convenience |
| 03.78 | Corporations |
| 03.80 | Cost |
| 03.82 | Counties |
| 03.84 | Courts |
| 03.87 | Credit |
| 03.90 | Crime |
| 03.93 | Cultural activities |
| 04.07 | Data |
| 04.14 | Debt |
| 04.21 | Defense |
| 04.28 | Demand |

*Source:* Ref. 19-6, p. 13.

presented in Table 19-4. The abstracts sent regularly (e.g., *Transportation: Current Literature*) have proven extremely useful, especially in identifying articles in lesser-known journals or newsletters.

**Retrieval from available information systems** A third approach to collecting data is through direct reading of relevant journals, trade magazines, newspapers, and the like. Emphasis would be in two areas:

1. Statistical information on past events
2. Short- and long-term forecasts and implications

This approach requires a fairly exhaustive search in the library. A sample of literature sources employed by Dickey is displayed in Table 19-5. It has generally been found that trade magazines and newsletters are more informative for this purpose than highly "academic" journals. Moreover, many of these are directed specifically to the particular geographic area under study (see the bottom of the table). A review is made of all the number 1 priority items in Table 19-5 at appropriate times (e.g., quarterly for journals, daily for newspapers). During the process of this search it is possible to reduce the number of relevant sources and, when needed, to add new ones focusing on additional significant factors identified through the conceptual modeling (digraph) endeavor discussed earlier.

**Table 19-4 Available information retrieval systems possibilities**

| | |
|---|---|
| *Abstracts* | |
| *National Technical Information Service* (U.S. Department of Commerce) | |
| *Transportation Research Abstracts* (Transportation Research Board) | |
| *Transportation: Current Literature* (U.S. Department of Transportation) | |
| *New Publications* (U.S. Department of Labor) | |
| *Summary of Research in Progress* (Transportation Research Board) | |
| *Requested searches* | |
| NTISearch | (U.S. Department of Commerce) |
| TRISNET | (U.S. Department of Transportation) |
| DIALOG | (Lockheed Missiles and Space Co.) |
| COMPENDEX | |
| SCISEARCH | (Institute for Scientific Information) |
| Social Sciences Citation Index | (Institute for Scientific Information) |
| Domestic Statistics | (Predicasts, Inc.) |
| Smithsonian Science Information Exchange | (Smithsonian Institution) |
| ASI | (Congressional Information Service) |
| CIS | (Congressional Information Service) |
| APILIT | (American Petroleum Institute) |

*Source:* Ref. 19-6, p. 18.

**Table 19-5 Sample list of relevant literature sources**

| Area/Journal | Priority | Relates to factor number | Past data or future |
|---|---|---|---|
| Methodology | | | |
| (*a*) *Futures* | 1 | Many | F |
| (*b*) *The Futurist* | 1 | Many | F |
| (*c*) *Long Range Planning* | 2 | Many | F |
| (*d*) *Technological Forecasting and Social Change* | 2 | Many | F |
| (*e*) *Analyze and Prevision* (*Futuribles*) (French) | 3 | Many | F |
| Demographic—social | | | |
| (*a*) *Population Index* | 2 | 8, 9 | P |
| (*b*) *The Gallup Opinion Index* | 1 | Many | F |
| (*c*) *Daedalus* | 1 | 8, 9 | F |
| (*d*) *New Leader* | 1 | Many | F |
| (*e*) *Monthly Vital Statistics Report* | 2 | 8, 9 | P |
| (*f*) *National Geographic* | 3 | Many | Both |
| (*g*) *Annals of the Academy of Social and Political Science* | 2 | Many | Both |
| Particular to Virginia | | | |
| (*a*) *Business in Virginia* | 1 | | |
| (*b*) *Roanoke Times* | 1 | | |
| (*c*) *Washington Post* | 2 | | |
| (*d*) *Annual Reports* (e.g., Virginia Department of Labor and Industry) | 1 | | |
| (*e*) *Highway Statistics* | 1 | etc. | |
| (*f*) *Average Daily Traffic* | 1 | | |
| (*g*) *Virginia Economic Review* | 1 | | |
| (*h*) *Reports: Tayloe Murphy Institute* | 1 | | |
| (*i*) *Dominion Data* | 1 | | |
| (*j*) *Virginia Business Report* | 1 | | |
| (*k*) *Virginia Economic Indicators* | 1 | | |
| (*l*) *Virginia Trucker* | 1 | | |
| (*m*) *Virginia Energy Review* | 1 | | |

*Source:* Ref. 19-6, p. 19.

## Screening and Evaluation of Data

The second phase in the early-warning system is the screening and evaluation of the collected data. At regular intervals a listing is made of discussions or articles under each functional classification (e.g., economic–financial in VINCENT). Listings also can be made under each index term. The resultant product should be similar to that produced by Whirlpool (Fig. 19-3) in their monitoring efforts. From such a listing it is possible to reclassify or cull out obviously inappropriate items. It is also possible to start to identify trends or patterns in the data through the apparent sequencing of interrelated events.

WIN ALERT 09/09/71

15 RESEARCH, TESTING, METHODS AND EQUIPMENT . . . . . . . . . . PAGE 01
INCLUDES - NEW PRODUCT DEVELOPMENT, LABORATORY PROCEDURES,
STANDARDS AND SPECIFICATIONS.

- - - - - - - - - - - - - - - - - - - - - - - - -

TESTING METHODS AND TECHNIQUES (DOC) BY NASA
15 71 00932 P INFO. CENTER RES

A GUIDE FOR FATIGUE TESTING AND THE STATISTICAL ANALYSIS OF
FATIGUE DATA (DOC) BY ASTM
15 71 00937 P INFO. CENTER RES

PERFORMANCE CURVES OF AN AIR CONDITIONER FOR A COMPUTERIZED
ON-LINE TEST
15 71 00957 U. REMBOLD RES

LABORATORY TEST TO DETERMINE THE FEASIBILITY OF TESTING AIR
CONDITIONERS IN A SHORT PULL DOWN TEST
15 71 00958 U. REMBOLD RES

FEASIBILITY OF 100% ON-LINE TESTING OF WINDOW AIR CONDITIONERS
15 71 00976 P CHEN AND OTHERS RES

ON-LINE AIR CONDITIONER PERFORMANCE TESTING OF SAMPLED UNITS
15 71 00977 P CHEN RES

ON-LINE MEASUREMENT OF WINDOW AIR CONDITIONER CAPACITIES
15 71 00978 P CHEN RES

CONTINUOUS SHORT PULL DOWN TEST TO MEASURE THE PERFORMANCE OF AIR
CONDITIONERS ON THE PRODUCTION LINE
15 71 00993 U REMBOLD P CHEN RES

WIN ALERT

Whirlpool INFORMATION NETWORK

**NOTE:** This *Win Alert* cites all information entering the network during the month in the subject category indicated above. The number in the citation identifies a WIN Summary. Summaries of the above unrestricted citations are available from *WIN Files* located at most divisions, subsidiaries, and from the Information Center. The WIN Program is intended for the exclusive use of authorized personnel of Whirlpool Corp. and its subsidiaries.

**MEDIA CODE:** (Designated after the WIN File number) internal report = no letter; published literature = P; vendor data = V; information alert = A.

INFORMATION CENTER RESEARCH & ENGINEERING CENTER
EXTENSION 7272



**Figure 19-3** Example information retrieval listing from the Whirlpool Corporation system. (*Source: Ref. 19-4, p. 609.*)

The next step in this phase of the process would be to determine the implications of the apparent trends and patterns. One of the best ways to do this is through a regular (e.g., quarterly) newsletter similar to that in Fig. 19-4. The suggested patterns are reported along with the analysts' interpretation of the implications. Naturally the analysts are not in a position to foresee all ramifications, so an important service on their part is to act as a sounding board for reactions to their suggestions (including delineation of other, perhaps more significant, implications).

A final step in this phase is to make short- and long-term projections based on the apparent trends found in the above screening endeavor. If these projections appear to hold up after that period, new strength will be added to the implications; if not, many of the corresponding items in the information system can be eliminated. In any case, the newsletter can also be utilized to report on the results of these experiments.

## Setting of Thresholds

The final phase in an early-warning system is that of setting thresholds. To do this requires studies of the type, timing, and likely fulfillment of relevant decisions, particularly by elected and appointed officials. For example, if it were found in the Virginia study that for a variety of reasons gasoline tax revenues might drop about 40 percent 4 years from now, would that be sufficient notice for any adjustments to be made? The answer depends on the type and magnitude of adjustment (e.g., an increase of 40 percent in the gasoline *tax*) and elected official reaction to such changes. Considering the fact that a 2 cent per gallon increase in the gasoline tax currently is being met in Virginia with some opposition, it is difficult to conceive that a much larger increase could be "sold" in less than 4 years. More advanced notice, therefore, would seem to be needed if the apparent fiscal problem is to be alleviated in time.

Two processes are most useful for threshold setting. The first involves discussions with relevant agency and elected officials. Experts in political science and government also can be questioned. These discussions should provide very rough indications of the response times corresponding to various types of decision that need to be made.

A more useful process, however, involves the previously described newsletter. It is difficult for any decision maker to know the political and institutional hurdles (and the associated response times) until he or she (and everyone else) is faced with an actual decision situation. The newsletter would present one with implications (both the decision maker's and the analysts') and allow one to decide if action were required in the near future. In this way the person in the position to know best can set his own thresholds. Furthermore, if he decides the analysts are not giving enough advanced warning, they can try to respond by making longer-term forecasts (with, of course, more associated uncertainties).

PAGE NO.
PROJECT NO.

**TEXTILE TOPICS**

I. Cotton

1. The Cotton Producers Institute has allocated more than one million dollars in research funds to try to develop Permanent Press cotton. Some of the best known organizations (Stanford Research, Gillette, Battelle, Gagliardi and Southern Research) have been brought into the picture with grants ranging from $7,500 to $120,000.

2. U.S. needs of cotton from the 1969 crop will be down by 700,000 bales from last years usage of 8.9 million.

3. The three big U.S. shirt manufacturers have begun production of a line of pure finish cotton shirts. Prices for these garments will range from $8 to $20 per garment.

**WHAT THESE MEAN TO WHIRLPOOL:**A part of the cotton industry realizes that their market has shrunk and is trying to do something about it. Unfortunately, the projects they are funding are the same projects which have not been successful in the past. The projected usage of 700,000 fewer bales in 1969 reflects the textile industry's attitude toward cotton. The entry of high priced cotton shirts should not be construed as a change in philosophy. There will be few of them made from those people who have been slow in shifting to synthetic/cotton blends.

4. Cotton is witnessing a big intrafamily feud these days. It seems that growers expected high 1967 prices to carry into 1968, so they planted low bearing, high quality varieties. Prices fell and their incomes tumbled. Now they blame textile mills, ginners, Cotton Council, and just about everyone for their troubles. They say they will revert to high yield, lower quality varieties in 1969.

**WHAT THIS MEANS TO WHIRLPOOL:** Just more fuel on the fire that is burning out cotton and promoting synthetics. It seems cotton will remain controlled by individualists and will never become an industry.

II. Synthetics

1. Monsanto announced recently that they will start production soon on a new polyester fiber differing in chemistry from any now on the market. The fiber will be expensive and is not expected to gain mass usage for a number of years. It is a specialty.

**Figure 19-4** Example newsletter from the Whirlpool Corporation system. (*Source: Ref. 19-4, p. 611.*)

## 19-2 ANOTHER EXAMPLE

One of the few examples of a full-time early-warning system (although not called such) in operation is that run by the Institute of Life Insurance (ILI) in its trend analysis program (TAP—Ref. 19-7). While this system has not been fully documented anywhere, a brief description provided by the ILI portrays the process as being divided into input, analysis, and reporting phases.

In the input phase over 100 executives from the ILI's member life insurance companies, as well as a handful of people on the staff, are given a specific publication to monitor. Each "monitor" is assigned one of the following four subject areas:

1. Science and technology
2. Social sciences
3. Business and economics
4. Politics and government

They abstract any article they come across in their subject area which appears in their publication as long as the article meets the following two criteria:

1. It should involve an idea or event indicative of a trend or discontinuity in the environment.
2. The implications to be drawn from it should have some relation to the long-range concerns of our society, and to the insurance business in any of its areas of interest.

In the analysis phase, seven of the ILI staff members, chosen for their diversity of backgrounds and knowledge, meet every other month to discuss the implications of each abstract submitted during the previous 60-day period. A summary of each of these discussions is prepared and forwarded to a Steering Committee—a dozen high-level individuals drawn from member companies and industry trade associations. They read the abstracts, review the summaries of the Abstract Analysis Committee, and meet three times a year to decide the content of the newsletters, known as *Trend Analysis Reports*. They also review the drafts of the reports and help oversee the working of the program.

The *Trend Reports* comprise the reporting phase and are issued approximately three times a year. They contain themes presented in thesis, scenario, and statistical forms. Subjects which have appeared to date include aging, employees, health, social security, inflation, and transportation. Each report (newsletter) generally is divided into five functional areas. These, along with examples from *Trend Report no. 10* (Winter, 1975) on "Science and Health" are:

1. Major technical, political, and similar events and trends.
   Example: Acoustical holograms,† made by using ultrasonic waves and lasers, can produce three-dimensional images of submerged objects; medical researchers believe this is a safe way to get a quick look at hidden body organs.

† See the preceding chapter for a discussion of holography.

2. Social and moral considerations.
   Example: Will the individual's identity get lost in the shuffle as his body is monitored, diagnosed, and prescribed for by a mechanical scanner? In many cases these questions are dwarfed by increased demands society keeps making on our available health services.
3. Questions and implications for life and health insurance company management.
   Example: Where life extension is related to continuous reliance on machines or on doctors and hospitals, a whole new schedule of costs and product offerings in health insurance may come about, and the amount of final medical expenses a life policy is bought to pay for will probably increase.
4. Straws in the wind (usually not related to the overall topic).
   Example: Children's Lib: objectives may be the end of compulsory education, a lowering of the age at which a person can be employed, and the ability of children to enter into financial and contractual agreements independent of their parents.
5. Selected bibliography.
   Example: Lawrence Lessing, "Getting the Whole Picture from Holography," *Fortune*, September, 1971.

Viewed in terms of the characteristics discussed in the previous section, the TAP system places the most emphasis on the data collection and reporting phases. The former is done primarily through literature reviews, but with a great amount of person-to-person contact through the meetings of the ILI staff and the Steering Committee. Each newsletter (*Trend Report*) runs to about 30 pages, and covers the associated topic in some detail. It also provides balancing negative as well as positive impacts and implications.

No specific conceptual model is employed in the TAP effort, but something of this nature may be forthcoming as certain topics are restudied and the relationships over time become more apparent. Finally, the setting of thresholds is left to each reader of the *Trend Reports*, since they go to a large number of insurance and other people across the country. It is obvious, however, that there was a great need felt for such a system within the insurance industry and that consequently there will be strong feedback to the staff and the Steering Committee as to the usefulness of the *Trend Reports* in overall decision making.

## PROBLEMS†

**19-1** Taylor (Ref. 19-10) has forecast the availability of the following capabilities (on the basis of research already completed):

1. Creation of life by entirely artificial means from nonliving substances

† Problems 19-1 and 19-2 are adapted from Martino (Ref. 19-3).

2. Nonsexual human reproduction, including "test-tube babies," parthenogenesis, and "cloning" (production of duplicate individuals starting with a single cell of the duplicated person)
3. Practical development of organ transplantation on a large scale, with establishment of "organ banks" for temporary storage of usable organs
4. Control of aging, and eventual elimination of death from old age
5. Chemical control or modification of intelligence, mood, memory, judgment, and other mental processes
6. "Genetic engineering"—the growing of plants, animals, and humans to meet prescribed specifications on their heredity

For each of these items, answer the following questions:
(*a*) What additional signals would tend to confirm or deny the forecast?
(*b*) What sources should be monitored for these signals?
(*c*) Have any confirming or denying signals appeared since the original forecast was made in 1967?

**19-2** The following items are extracted from Kahn and Wiener's list, "One hundred technical innovations very likely in the last third of the twentieth century":
(*a*) Three-dimensional photography, illustrations, movies, and television
(*b*) Permanent inhabited undersea installations and perhaps even colonies
(*c*) Automated universal (real time) credit, audit, and banking systems
(*d*) Practical large-scale desalinization
What precursor events do you *feel* would tend to confirm or deny each forecast? What sources should be monitored for these precursor events?

**19-3** A small town is worried about the future of its economic base (primarily a university) in relation to the town's long-term (15-year) capital expenditure program. If the university stops growing, there may not be a need for much further spending of this nature. But the opposite may also hold. You have been asked to provide a monitoring system to help in this situation. Describe the major features of your proposed monitoring system and give some specific examples related to each feature (e.g., the sources you would use for each topic monitored).

**19-4** Develop a key word thesaurus to be employed in an early-warning system related to statewide land-use development and control. In what particular topical areas might the system be more detailed than others?

## REFERENCES

### Theory

19-1. Bright, J. R.: "Forecasting by Monitoring Signals of Technological Change," in J. R. Bright and M. E. F. Schoeman (Eds.), *A Guide to Practical Technological Forecasting*, Prentice-Hall, Englewood Cliffs, N. J., 1973.
19-2. Herna, S., and M. J. Vellucci: *Selected Federal Computer-Based Information Systems*, Information Resources Press, Washington, D.C., 1972.
19-3. Marinto, J. P.: *Technological Forecasting for Decisionmaking*, American-Elsevier, New York, 1972.

### Applications and related references

19-4. Davis, R. C.: "Organizing and Conducting Technological Forecasting in a Consumer Goods Firm," in J. R. Bright and M. E. F. Schoeman (Eds.), *A Guide to Practical Technological Forecasting*, Prentice-Hall, Englewood Cliffs, N.J., 1973.
19-5. Dickey, J. W.: *A Model for Forecasting Gasoline Tax Revenue*, Interim Technical Report to the Virginia Division of Motor Vehicles, Virginia Tech, Blacksburg, Va., December, 1975.

19-6. Dickey, J. W.: *A Proposed Early Warning System for the Division of Motor Vehicles*, Interim Technical Report to the Virginia Division of Motor Vehicles, Virginia Tech, Blacksburg, Va., February, 1976.

19-7. Institute of Life Insurance: *Trend Reports* (several numbers), New York (several years).

19-8. Sessions, V. S., and L. W. Sloan: *Urbandoc/A Bibliographic Information System: Technical Supplement 1/General Manual*, Report Urbandoc-71-2, The Graduate Division, The City University of New York, New York, 1971.

19-9. Sessions, V. S., and L. W. Sloan: *Urbandoc/A Bibliographic Information System: Technical Supplemental 2/Operations Manual*, Report Urbandoc-71-3, The Graduate Division, The City University of New York, 1971.

19-10. Taylor, Gordon, R.: *The Biological Time Bomb*, New American Library, Inc., New York, 1968.

19-11. U.S. Department of Commerce, Office of Technology Assessment and Forecast: *Early Warning Report*, NTIS, COM 74-10150. Springfield, Va., December, 1973.

CHAPTER

# TWENTY

# GOALS, OBJECTIVES, CRITERIA, AND STANDARDS

The synectics technique described in Chap. 14 attempts to enhance the creativity in an individual or group so that solutions to pressing problems can be developed. Many other techniques are available with the same purpose, but generally with more formal structures and quantitative foundations. Several of these will be discussed in the chapters to follow, but a requirement of all of them is greater specificity in identification of the goals and objectives for which the particular solutions are being developed. The purpose of this chapter is thus to present a range of approaches to achieve better identification so that the ensuing techniques not only will be more understandable but also more useful.

## 20-1 DEFINITIONS

Before describing various techniques for identifying goals, objectives, and the like, we will first define more precisely the meaning of several of the more important terms. These definitions are by no means universal. In fact, it is for this very reason that we are presenting our versions so that consistency can be maintained throughout this book and, additionally, comparisons with other sources can be facilitated.

To start, all goals and objectives stem from the basic *values* important to people. There are many ways of describing these values. A "good" city is popularly referred to in everyday terms such as "vital," "warm and friendly," "dynamic," "safe," "exciting," "full of opportunity," and "beautiful." A "bad" city is described as "dirty," "ugly," "dangerous," "hostile," "impersonal," "confusing," "overwhelming," "time consuming," "congested," or "wasteful." A more formal listing of abstract values would include terms such as "freedom," "liberty," "dignity," "health and safety," "amenity," "diversity," "economy," "ownership," "mobility," and "affluence."

In most general terms, then, a value can be defined as follows:

> **Definition** *Value* is an element of a shared symbolic system (referred to as a value system), acquired through social learning, which serves as a guide for the selection from among perceived alternatives of orientation.

Indications of the types of values held by individuals in a given society should be of great concern to urban analysts, particularly since these values form the basis for the development of goals for the activities and characteristics of the population and the use of resources in a region. For instance, at the highest and most general level, there should be little disagreement that governmental interest in urban development relates to two major goals:

1. That the quality of life be improved in the whole variety of ways that reflect the common values so often expressed in personal reactions to "the city"
2. That the metropolitan area itself be strengthened in terms of its productive capacity, its democratic institutions, and its ability to allocate and use its natural and human resources to best advantage in each community

As can be seen, these goals rest heavily on inherent values, and this fact serves to emphasize the definition of a goal, which is as follows:

> **Definition** *Goal* is an articulation of values, formulated in the light of identified issues and problems, toward the attainment of which policies and decisions are directed.

Two points regarding this definition need further elaboration. For one, goals are an outgrowth of identified *issues and problems* and usually do not stand on their own. We would not, for example, be concerned about "strengthening democratic institutions" in metropolitan areas, as stated in value 2 above, if we happened to be working for a totalitarian government. But as a second point, we should not *limit* our set of goals to correspond only to problems that presently exist, because in many cases proposed solutions bring about unanticipated new types of problem. As an example, we cannot afford to narrow our consideration of parking in the central business district only to that problem. If we did, we might overlook additional problems such as that of the transfer of large segments of the population between their places of residence and places of business, or that of noise, or air pollution, or congestion near parking facilities, and so forth. The set of goals associated with parking must therefore relate to more than existing problems; otherwise, proposed solutions will bring about new and unexpected difficulties.

Creating an amalgam of values and goals is a complicated process that has by no means been fully developed in the field of urban planning and analysis. Among the complications is the fact that values or goals are not necessarily mutually supporting. Indeed, they are often in polar-like opposition, so that the problem in goal formulation is one of emphasis and balance among values. The process is also complex because points of balance are constantly shifting in time and from place to place. Technological, economic, social, and institutional changes are continually altering the extent to which individual values may be capable of being achieved. This means that the establishment of goals and the determination of relative emphasis to be placed upon various goals is a continuing process that must be applied at many levels and in many places.

Another apparent difficulty in developing goals is that they seem to be hierarchical. Statements of goals usually begin with broad generalizations and are then developed at more detailed levels to guide the various types and stages of planning and design activities. However, we should realize that goals are intended to be broad, extensive statements that form the basis for comprehensive concepts for our undertakings. Thus we should not be quick to give in to the tendency to try to avoid generalizations inherent in goal statements and therefore avoid the accusation of a lack of specificity and "practicality."

To this point little has been said about measurable entities that can be used to give explicit assessment of suggested solutions for urban and regional problems. These more tangible entities are known as *objectives* and contain measurable attributes or quantities known as *criteria*.

**Definition** *Objective* is a specific statement denoting a measurable end to be reached or achieved for a particular group of people, usually in a particular span of time.

**Definition** *Criterion* (measure) is an explicit attribute or characteristic used for the purpose of comparative evaluation.

Associated with each goal should be at least one strongly defined objective and a corresponding criterion (or criteria). In a study done for the Baltimore region (Ref. 20-9), Ockert and Pixton identified a set of goals and associated measures. One goal was to "increase activity access." The criterion suggested was the sum of the following:

1. Number of high-income (> $7500 per year) jobs greater than 5 minutes' driving time from an arterial street and greater than 5 minutes' walking time from a transit stop having less than 30 minute headways
2. Number of low-income (< $3500 per year) jobs greater than 5 minutes' walking time from a transit stop having less than 30 minute headways

The objective was to minimize the total of the two numbers. No particular time period was suggested to accomplish this.

An important point to be made here is that it is not always necessary to have quantifiable criteria—just measurable ones. Guilford (Ref. 20-7) defines these terms as follows:

**Definition** *Measurement* is the assignment of numbers to objects according to logically accepted rules.

**Definition** *Quantification* is the ordering of something according to quantity or amount.

Since it is possible to assign a number to something without ordering it (e.g., male = 1, female = 2), we can employ such criteria as "presence (or lack) of food services in a terminal," "or "operation of vehicle by user required or not required." These criteria are nominal (name or categorical) in scale. While nominal measures are not as precise in nature as the others, they are useful in situations where well-defined and accepted measures are not available. Moreover, because quantification is not a strict necessity in developing criteria, we can feel free to use completely subjective measures derived, for example, from responses of citizens concerned with the appearance of a proposed building. These responses could be measured on a semantic differential scale (Ref. 20-10), which has a range from −3 for "very ugly" to +3 for "very beautiful." A 0 rating would indicate indifference—"neither ugly nor beautiful."

A complete set of definitions must also include *constraints* and *standards*. These two elements are relevant since there often are certain criteria which people would like to minimize or maximize, such as income, while there are others whose values only have to be kept above or below a certain level. A government budget provides a good example. Often a set amount of funds is allocated for, say, water-system improvements. The aim is to go as far as possible toward relevant goals while keeping within the limit of the budget. The budget in this example would be a *constraint*, not a goal or objective.

A *standard* is a *particular desired level* of the criterion which should not be exceeded or undercut (or both), depending on the particular situation. An example of a standard relates to temperature control. Usually it is desirable to have the temperature in a building kept at about 70°F—neither above nor below. Hence an attempt would be made to design the heating and/or air-conditioning systems to achieve this level. Whether in a certain situation one would be dealing with objectives and criteria or constraints and standards is difficult to tell, but seems to depend on how much importance people attach to levels of a criterion beyond its commonly accepted value. If, for example, it were not important as to how much a budget were underspent, then no one would be expected to minimize expenses and the budget should be taken as a constraint to spending, not an objective for it.

## 20-2 TECHNIQUES FOR IDENTIFYING GOALS AND RELATED CHARACTERISTICS

A study by Pardee et al. (Ref. 20-11) has listed eight methods for identifying goals and related characteristics (objectives, standards, constraints, etc.). These will now be discussed and illustrated in turn.

### Method 1. Intuitive Judgment

Probably the most common method, and one that requires comparatively little time and money, is that of intuitive judgment on the part of the analyst and/or decision maker. The advantages in addition to the above two are: ease of application, quick answers, and ability to handle unquantifiable factors or those for which there are no data. Another advantage is that the method allows the political process to work. Often worthwhile trades or deals are made between and among elected and appointed officials and their constituencies. These might involve, for instance, an agreement by one politician to vote for a beneficial project being pushed by another if he reciprocates on some future endeavor. Without such an agreement, an official with sufficient political clout could manage to stifle an otherwise beneficial project (because it may not suit his particular constituency). Method 1 thus allows for useful trade-offs beyond the realm of the particular project in question.

On the disadvantageous side of the ledger we find some severe problems, however. There are always questions about the expertise, broadmindedness, and representativeness of the individuals or groups making the ultimate decision on goals. What if the decision makers do not really understand the meaning of a "decibel" when making choices about noise-abatement plans? What if they have no feeling for or experience with the problems of the poor when setting objectives for a poverty program? What if they are "self-appointed" leaders as opposed to democratically elected? Any of these considerations could severely limit the usefulness and validity of the goals being developed. Moreover, and perhaps of greatest importance from a scientific viewpoint, is the disadvantage that the method is neither explicit nor reproducible, so that hypotheses cannot be stated and tested and no one can replicate the goal-setting "experiment."

### Method 2. Checklist of Goals

The first step in making goals more explicit would be simply to create a set of attributes that might be considered as candidates for goals. To develop such a set is not easy since many important considerations do not present themselves until solutions with characteristics different from the present situation are suggested. Moreover, if adequate thought is given to identification procedures, the resulting list of goals can become quite long, and additional efforts must be devoted to ensure that the items on the list are fairly exclusive and exhaustive and that they are representative of the group of people they are intended to serve.

**Table 20-1 Humanity (and groups)**

| Component I | |
|---|---|
| *Individuals and/or households* | |
| I-1 | By age (including unborn, those that will die, etc.) |
| I-2 | By race, religion, color, ethnic background |
| I-3 | By locality (and future locality) |
| I-4 | By sex |
| I-5 | By employment category |
| I-6 | By political leaning |
| I-7 | By income |
| I-8 | By educational background |
| I-9 | By personality types (including deviants) |
| I-10 | By occupation |
| I-11 | By social status |
| I-12 | By leisure pursuits |
| I-13 | By power/control |
| *Firms and institutions* | |
| I-14 | Firms |
| I-15 | Institutional groups |
| I-16 | Governmental agencies, legislatures, and judiciaries |
| I-17 | Social groups and clubs |
| I-18 | Political groups |
| I-19 | By locality (and future locality) |
| I-20 | Military organizations |
| I-21 | Unions |
| I-22 | Peer groups |

*Source:* Ref. 20-3, p. 83.

Dickey and Broderick (Ref. 20-4) have developed one technique useful for being more exhaustive in identifying goal attributes. Their technique involves a classification into four major components: (1) humanity (and groups), (2) the natural environment, (3) the manmade environment, and (4) activities.

Each of these components are further subdivided, as can be seen in Tables 20-1 to 20-4. These tables also serve as a checklist. By way of illustration, an often-forgotten group in many urban areas and regions are those people who do not at present live in the area being planned or designed. This group would have to be considered, for example, in planning for new towns or new developments involving vacant land within the boundaries of an existing urban area. This group is element I-3 in Table 20-1. Two other groups of possible interest consist of those individuals not yet born or those living now who may not be when actual developments take place in the distant future. These groups are included in the category of "individuals by age" (including unborn, those that will die, etc.), item I-1 in Table 20-1.

**Table 20-2 Elements of the natural environment**

| Component II | |
|---|---|
| II-1 | Earth materials |
| II-2 | Physiographic system (including land surface, etc.) |
| II-3 | Hydrologic system (land-related surface and subsurface waters, etc.) |
| II-4 | Climate (micro and macro) |
| II-5 | Vegetation (forests, flowers, grass, etc.) |
| II-6 | Wildlife (aquatic animals, land animals, insects, etc.) |
| II-7 | Marine and estuarine systems |
| II-8 | Time |
| II-9 | Atmosphere |

*Source:* Ref. 20-3, p. 84.

**Table 20-3 Elements of the manmade environment**

| Component III | |
|---|---|
| III-1 | Food, drink, tobacco, drugs |
| III-2 | Clothing |
| III-3 | Raw materials; intermediate and final goods (including crops, domestic animals, etc.) |
| III-4 | Housing (including institutional) |
| III-5 | Communication facilities (including mail, television, telephone, radio, etc.) |
| III-6 | Transportation facilities (including vehicles, guideways, terminals, and controls) |
| III-7 | Educational and cultural facilities (including schools, museums, libraries) |
| III-8 | Water supply, sewage disposal, solid waste disposal, and drainage facilities |
| III-9 | Health facilities (including hospitals, mental institutions, nursing homes) |
| III-10 | Energy creation and supply facilities (including electric, coal, oil, natural gas, etc.) |
| III-11 | Production facilities (including office buildings, machinery, storage areas, warehouses) |
| III-12 | Sales, administrative, and service facilities (including wholesale and retail) |
| III-13 | Military facilities (including bases, training camps, storage areas, etc.) |
| III-14 | Governmental, police, fire, judicial, and welfare facilities |
| III-15 | Leisure and recreational facilities (including parks, clubs, fraternal organizations, etc.) |
| III-16 | Information |
| III-17 | Monetary capital (stocks, bonds, cash, etc.) |
| III-18 | Laws (including police power, eminent domain, zoning, etc.) |
| III-19 | Energy |

*Source:* Ref. 20-3, p. 84.

**Table 20-4 Activity elements and agents**

| Component IV | | |
|---|---|---|
| | Agent | Activity |
| IV-1 | Individuals and households | Income producing |
| IV-2 | | Child raising and family |
| IV-3 | | Educational and intellectual |
| IV-4 | | Spiritual development |
| IV-5 | | Social |
| IV-6 | | Recreation and relaxation |
| IV-7 | | Clubs |
| IV-8 | | Community service and political |
| IV-9 | | Associated with food, shopping, health, etc. |
| IV-10 | | Travel |
| IV-11 | Firms | Goods producing |
| IV-12 | | Service |
| IV-13 | Institutions | Human development |
| IV-14 | | Basic community service |
| IV-15 | | For welfare and special groups |
| IV-16 | All (long-term) | Migration |
| IV-17 | | Investment |
| IV-18 | | Crime, war |

*Source:* Ref. 20-3, p. 85.

As mentioned, the elements presented in Tables 20-1 to 20-4 serve as a good checklist. Yet it is also important to determine the *characteristics* of interest for each element in these tables. Dickey and Broderick searched the *Thesaurus* (Ref. 20-12) and produced a list of 49 characteristics that could possibly describe each element (see Table 20-5). These characteristics then were cross referenced with each element to produce a matrix of items (possible goals or problems) like that suggested in Table 20-6. As an example of the use of this kind of table, consider element III-6 of Table 20-3, the "transportation system," and characteristic C-3 of Table 20-5, "technical." If we combine these two entities, we might be led to think of those people under 16 years of age, those handicapped, and those too old to be capable (technically) of driving an automobile. One detailed goal for a transportation system, then, may be to reduce the technical requirement for operation (i.e., user operation). In a similar way, a variety of other goals can be identified.

This identification technique has several drawbacks:

1. Not all characteristics in Table 20-5 are descriptive of the elements in Tables 20-1 to 20-4 [e.g., "nicely shaped" (C-34) and "unions" (I-21) do not go together].
2. The elements (and characteristics) are not mutually exclusive [e.g., individuals of certain age classes (I-1) are also of certain races and religions (I-2)].
3. The number of items in Table 20-6 can become quite large.

**Table 20-5 Characteristics to be used in conjunction with elements in Tables 20-1 to 20-4**

| | | | |
|---|---|---|---|
| C-1 | Religious–moral–ethical | C-26 | Beautiful |
| C-2 | Free | C-27 | Quiet |
| C-3 | Technical | C-28 | Healthy |
| C-4 | Stable | C-29 | Safe |
| C-5 | Private | C-30 | Informed |
| C-6 | Cheap | C-31 | Liberal |
| C-7 | Accessible | C-32 | Upper class |
| C-8 | Active | C-33 | Polluted |
| C-9 | Defended (militarily) | C-34 | Nicely shaped |
| C-10 | Large | C-35 | Dark |
| C-11 | Comfortable | C-36 | New |
| C-12 | Wealthy | C-37 | Fragrant |
| C-13 | Just | C-38 | Hot |
| C-14 | Happy | C-39 | Windy |
| C-15 | Parochial | C-40 | Wet |
| C-16 | Natural | C-41 | Flexible |
| C-17 | Numerous | C-42 | Open |
| C-18 | Organized | C-43 | Biased |
| C-19 | Time consuming | C-44 | Hungry |
| C-20 | Law abiding | C-45 | Thirsty |
| C-21 | Tasty | C-46 | Angry |
| C-22 | Exciting | C-47 | Powerful |
| C-23 | Affiliative | C-48 | Fearful |
| C-24 | Symbolic | C-49 | Productive |
| C-25 | Inductive to communication | | |

*Source:* Ref. 20-3, p. 86.

The foregoing technique has several advantages over a strictly intuitive approach, the primary ones being that the goals are more explicit, exhaustive, and exclusive. On the other hand, the technique is time consuming, generally too complex to be understood by the average citizen, and indirectly requires a great many value decisions by the persons or groups filling out the matrix.

## Method 3. Checklist Plus Criteria (Measures)

A direct extension of the preceding method would call for the association of criteria (measures) with each of the identified goals. Table 20-7 presents some example criteria relating to automobile emissions, safety, performance, serviceability, fuel availability, and noise. Also presented for further reference are illustrative standards or limits that should not be exceeded or undercut (or both). Obviously these have to be developed by people with a fairly intimate knowledge of the particular goal under study. On the other hand, the criteria generally should be understandable to average citizens, especially those adversely affected by the projects or programs for which the goals are being suggested.

**Table 20-6 Urban element–performance characteristic items**

| Urban elements | Performance characteristics | | | | |
|---|---|---|---|---|---|
| | C-1 religious–moral–ethical | C-2 Free | C-3 Technical | … | C-49 Productive |
| *Humanity (and groups)* | | | | | |
| I-1 Individuals and/or households by age | | | | | |
| ⋮ | | | | | |
| I-22 Peer groups | | | | | |
| *Natural environment* | | | | | |
| II-1 Earth materials | | | | | |
| ⋮ | | | | | |
| II-9 Atmosphere | | | | | |
| *Manmade environment* | | | Items | | |
| III-1 Food, drink tobacco, drugs | | | | | |
| ⋮ | | | | | |
| III-19 Energy | | | | | |
| *Activities* | | | | | |
| IV-1 Income producing | | | | | |
| ⋮ | | | | | |
| IV-18 Crime, war | | | | | |

*Source:* Ref. 20-3, p. 87.

The experience with airport noise criteria demonstrates the preceding points. In earlier studies measurements were made strictly in terms of decibels (dB—noise pressure levels) at a certain distance (for example, 500 feet) from the runway. This procedure wqs made more sophisticated by considering in more detail the actual pressure on the ear, which led to perceived noise decibels (PNdB). Later it was found that complaints were being received even at supposedly low PNdB levels. The measurement technique was then simplified somewhat to take into account the volume of complaints as a function of the time of flights (e.g., at late evening hours) and the type and number of land uses affected (e.g., elementary schools and churches). The transition was thus made to more and then less sophistication in measurement to help achieve a balance between accuracy and comprehendability.

The major advantages in having criteria associated with goals are twofold: greater explicitness and stronger ties to system design. The disadvantage, of course, is the natural problem of trying to devise measurements for goals that simply may be too vague for proper quantification.

**Table 20-7 Example criteria and standards**

| Criteria | Standard | |
|---|---|---|
| I. *Emissions* (for 4000 miles) | | |
| 1. Hydrocarbons: grams per vehicle mile measured by the 1975 Federal Test Procedure | 0.41 | |
| 2. Carbon monoxide: grams per mile | 3.4 | |
| 3. Oxides of nitrogen: grams per mile | 1.0 | |
| 4. Evaporative hydrocarbons: grams per test | 2.0 | |
| 5. Smoke: percentage capacity during (*a*) acceleration and (*b*) braking | (*a*) 30 | (*b*) 15 |
| II. *Safety* | | |
| 1. Compliance with Federal Motor Vehicle Safety Standards and inherent safety of the vehicle and power plant | | |
| III. *Performance* | | |
| 1. Startup time: seconds at 60°F | 30 | |
| 2. Acceleration: seconds on level surface from 0–60 mph | 16 | |
| 3. Top speed: mph for 1 mile on level surface | 75 | |
| 4. Range: miles at (*a*) 50 mph and (*b*) 65 mph | (*a*) 200 | (*b*) 150 |
| IV. *Serviceability* | | |
| 1. Equivalent to 1972 model year vehicles | ... | |
| V. *Fuel availability* | | |
| 1. Million vehicle-miles per year fuel quantity available (also must be capable of being stored and dispensed by existing methods) | 2.5 | |
| VI. *Noise level* | | |
| 1. Maximum dBA at 50 ft | 80 | |

*Source:* Adapted from *Commerce Business Daily*, Issue No. PSA-5529, March 16, 1972.

## Method 4. Feasible Ranges of Variation on Criteria

The next step in the progression toward greater specification of goals is to set ranges on the criteria within which actual impacts of a project might be restricted. In many cases the limits of the ranges may be standards, as exemplified previously in Table 20-7.

Figure 20-1 gives an illustration of suggested "environmental tolerance zones" for the human body. In terms of temperature (middle right of chart), for instance, we find an upper limit of 75°F and a lower limit of 65°F in the comfort

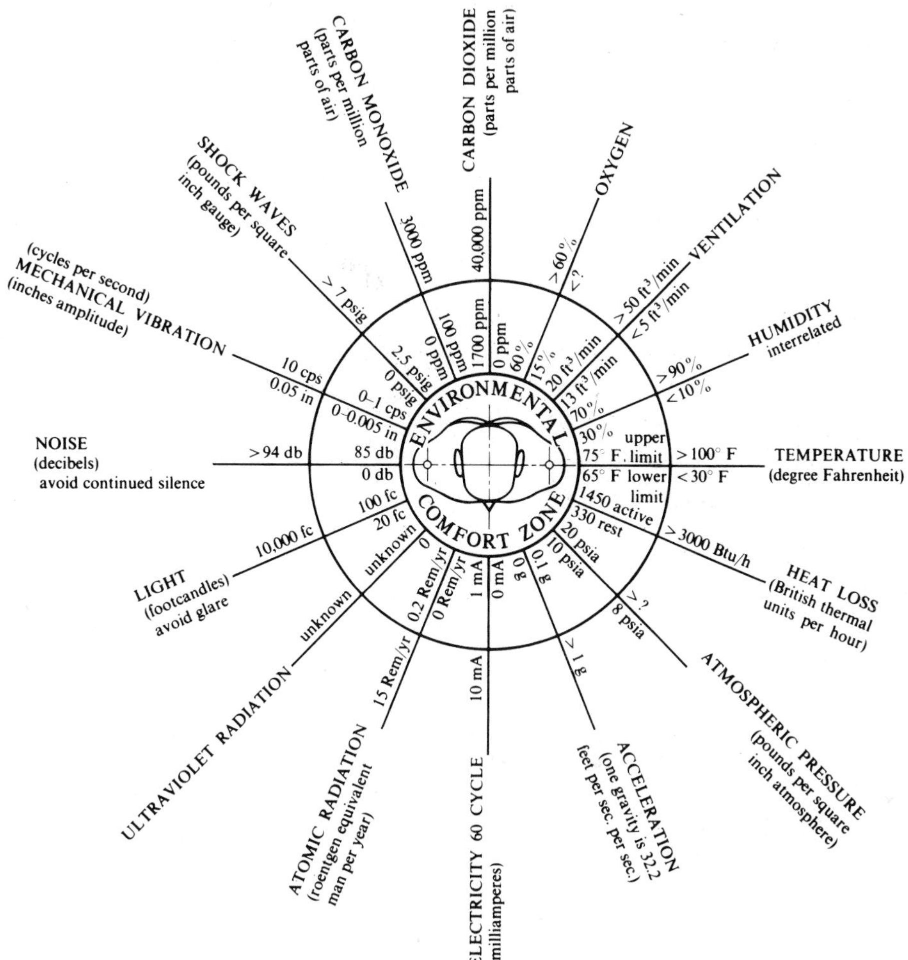


**Figure 20-1** Environmental tolerance zones for the human body. The band between the circles indicates the zone from comfort to the tolerance limit. Outside this limit great discomfort or physiological harm is encountered. (*Source: Ref. 20-5, chart R.*)

zone. The outer limits of tolerance are shown to be 30°F and 100°F. Limits like these could be employed as aids in a variety of urban and regional design situations—for buildings and open spaces, transportation systems, industrial areas, and the like. The identification of such limits is particularly valuable in reducing the amount of information usually required in most design situations. The difficulty, of course, is in treating limits as "hard and fast" when in many cases they are much more flexible.

**Table 20-8 Results of goal-attribute weighting**

| Goal attributes | Mean ranking | Mean rating |
|---|---|---|
| Noise and other human environmental impacts | 0.1332 | 0.1462 |
| Ground access availability | 0.1203 | 0.1274 |
| Natural environment | 0.1218 | 0.1256 |
| Relocation impact (human factors) | 0.1171 | 0.1231 |
| Air space | 0.1110 | 0.1282 |
| Engineering and obstructions | 0.0887 | 0.0897 |
| Economic impact | 0.0923 | 0.0855 |
| Governmental/institutional considerations | 0.0928 | 0.0786 |
| Total project cost | 0.0848 | 0.0786 |
| Utilities | 0.0380 | 0.0171 |
| | 1.0000 | 1.0000 |

*Source:* Ref. 20-2, p. 77.

## Method 5. Ordinal Arrangement of Goals

To this point nothing has been said about the relative importance of goals. The first step in this direction is simply to rank the goals in order of their priority. Table 20-8 gives an example of this method for goal attributes suggested in the evaluation of different sites for a new airport in the Louisville, Kentucky area (Ref. 20-2). A committee comprised of about 30 local citizens and national experts was asked to rank each of the 10 goal attributes, with the most desirable having a rank of 10. A mean ranking† for each attribute $h$, $0_h$, was then established through the equation:

$$\bar{0}_h = \frac{\sum_{i=1}^{n} 0_{ih}}{\sum_{i=1}^{n} \sum_{l=1}^{u} 0_{il}} \tag{20-1}$$

where $0_{ih}$ is the rank given to attribute $h$ (of which there are $u$) by person $i$ (of which there are $n$). For ease of computation the denominator term can be reduced to:

$$\sum_{i=1}^{n} \sum_{l=1}^{u} 0_{il} = \frac{u}{2}(u+1)n \tag{20-2}$$

As the table indicates, noise was felt to be the most important concern and the location of utilities the least. Another interesting finding is that most of the goals are very close in their mean ranking, showing the breadth of concern held by

† In view of the discussion in Chap. 2, ranks (which are ordinal numbers) really should not be treated as ratio-scaled numbers, as is done in Eq. (20-1). This procedure implies that a goal with a rank of 10 is twice as important as one with a rank of 5.

many people (hence requiring an equivalent breadth in analysis and planning endeavors).

The advantage of this method is primarily in its understandability by average citizens. Also, the relevant computations are easy. The disadvantages lie in the difficulties many people face in deciding if some abstract goal is more important than some other abstract goal. A typical response might be: "I can't set priorities until I have a specific situation in mind, and my priorities might differ according to the situation."

## Method 6. Ratio Scaling of Goals

The ranking procedure above can be refined further by assigning a ratio-scaled value to each goal to show its importance. These numbers generally are referred to as *ratings*, or *weights of importance*, or simply *weightings*. The usual approach in this method is to ask people to allocate a fraction or percentage of a fixed constant (for example, 1.00) to each goal attribute, with larger fractions indicating greater importance. If desired, a plus sign can be utilized to show positive interest, a negative to show aversion. School busing for racial integration, for example, would attract pluses from some people and minuses from others.

Table 20-8 shows the mean rating given to the 10 goal attributes for the potential airport sites in the Louisville area. The figures generally are similar to those in the ranking column, which tends to verify the consistency of the importance attached to the different goals.

The derived ratings can be employed to give an indication of the comparative overall utility of a particular project. The process is one of multiplying the rating for each goal attribute by the level of the corresponding criterion and then adding over all the attributes. In mathematical terms this becomes

$$Z_k = \sum_{h=1}^{n} P_{kh} Y_{kh} \tag{20-3}$$

where $Z_k$ = overall utility or objective function value of project $k$
$P_{kh}$ = rating for project $k$ on criterion $h$
$Y_{kh}$ = level of project $k$ on criterion $h$

One difficulty with this formulation is that the variable levels usually are in units varying widely in magnitude. The $Y_{kh}$ values should thus be standardized, as described in Chap. 2.

Suppose by way of illustration there is concern in a city for two variables: income $Y_1$ and fraction of workforce employed $Y_2$. A survey has shown that people rated income as having an importance of 0.75 and employment of 0.25. Thus:

$$Z(\text{objective function value}) = 0.75Y_1 + 0.25Y_2 \tag{20-4}$$

If in one project proposed to help alleviate these concerns, $Y_1 = 10{,}000$ and $Y_2 = 0.96$, then

$$Z_1 = 0.75(10{,}000) + 0.25(0.96) = 7500.24$$

Another project has $Y_1 = 10{,}000$ but $Y_2$ is only half: 0.48. So

$$Z_2 = 0.75(10{,}000) + 0.25(0.48) = 7500.12$$

Note that while employment is half of that in the first project (an obviously severe situation), the $Z$ value is almost the same, since the ratio is almost 1.00:

$$\frac{Z_1}{Z_2} = \frac{7500.12}{7500.24} = 0.999984$$

This obviously is not correct, despite the relatively low rating given to employment. The problem is caused by the size of the respective numbers. Hence, each variable should be standardized, as pointed out above. Suppose now that data on $Y_1$ and $Y_2$ have shown that

$$\bar{Y}_1 = 7000 \qquad S_{Y_1} = 5000 \qquad \bar{Y}_2 = 0.94 \qquad \text{and} \qquad S_{Y_2} = 0.02$$

The equation then becomes:

$$Z = 0.75\frac{Y_1 - \bar{Y}_1}{S_{Y_1}} + 0.25\frac{Y_2 - \bar{Y}_2}{S_{Y_2}} \tag{20-5}$$

Now for the two programs suggested above:

$$Z_1 = 0.75\frac{10{,}000 - 7000}{5000} + 0.25\frac{0.96 - 0.94}{0.02} = 0.70$$

$$Z_2 = 0.75\frac{10{,}000 - 7000}{5000} + 0.25\frac{0.48 - 0.94}{0.02} = -5.30$$

This shows the desired result—that the second program is more severely negative than the first. This is because income is only $(10{,}000 - 7000)/5000 = 0.60$ standard deviations above its mean but $Y_2$ ranges from 1.00 above to 23.00 standard deviations below its mean. Certainly this variation is severe.

To simplify the above objective function further (for purposes of linear programming, to be discussed in Chap. 22), note that we really do not need to know the mean to get the *relative* standing of program 1 versus program 2. Expanding Eq. (20-5) we obtain:

$$Z = 0.75\frac{Y_1}{S_{Y_1}} - 0.75\frac{\bar{Y}_1}{S_{Y_1}} + 0.25\frac{Y_2}{S_{Y_2}} - 0.25\frac{\bar{Y}_2}{S_{Y_2}} \tag{20-6}$$

Since the only factors that will vary from program to program are $Y_1$ and $Y_2$, the second and fourth terms above are constants and can be ignored. Thus, using the numbers from above:

$$Z = 0.75\frac{Y_1}{5000} - 0.75\frac{7000}{5000} + 0.25\frac{Y_2}{0.02} - 0.25\frac{0.94}{0.02} \tag{20-7}$$

or

$$Z = 0.75\frac{Y_1}{5000} + 0.25\frac{Y_2}{0.02} - 12.80 \tag{20-8}$$

or

$$Z' = 0.75\frac{Y_1}{5000} + 0.25\frac{Y_2}{0.02} \tag{20-9}$$

For the respective programs:

$$Z'_1 = 0.75\frac{10{,}000}{5000} + 0.25\frac{0.96}{0.02} = 13.50$$

and

$$Z'_2 = 0.75\frac{10{,}000}{5000} + 0.25\frac{0.48}{0.02} = 7.50$$

Thus the same *differences* in objective function values exist:

$$Z_1 - Z_2 = 0.70 - (-5.30) = 6.00$$

and

$$Z'_1 - Z'_2 = 13.50 - 7.50 = 6.00$$

Two additional points should be made:

1. We can multiply the $Z$ or $Z'$ by a constant without changing the *relative* standing of any program.
2. If a variable is "undesirable," its rating should be preceded by a *minus* sign [assuming we are trying to get the largest (maximum) value for $Z$ or $Z'$].

In general, then:

$$Z_k = \sum_{h=1}^{u} \pm \frac{P_{kh} Y_{kh}}{S_{Y_h}} \tag{20-10}$$

The main advantages of this method are: (1) its high level of precision and (2) its usefulness in very sophisticated and powerful tools for solution formulation such as mathematical programming (Chaps. 22 to 24). But these two characteristics can equally well be disadvantages in certain situations. In particular, if the analyst is working with less-educated or untechnical citizen groups, the method might be viewed as another example of bureaucratic chicanery (in this case, mathematical) to keep the group in question from getting what they feel is their justly deserved project. Then, too, it is amazing how few people can add to 1.00 (or 100).

## Method 7. Indifference Curves and Trade-Offs

Another disadvantage of the preceding method is the implicit assumption that the rating of importance does not vary with the amount of the goal attribute available. This assumption obviously is untenable at the extremes: if you are completely broke, an extra dollar of income is extremely valuable; if you are a billionaire, an extra dollar is hardly worth anything. There should thus be variation in ratings with levels.

One way to achieve this is through the use of *indifference* (or *isopreference*, or *trade-off*) *curves*. Take, for example, a city where decisions have to be made about projects that reflect on $Y_1$ (the mean household income of residents) and $Y_2$ (fraction of the workforce employed). Project 2 from above results in a $Y_1$ of \$10,000 but a $Y_2$ of only 0.48. Suppose we now were to ask, say, the mayor how much of the \$10,000 income for his residents he would be willing to "trade" for an increase in the fraction employed to, say, 0.80. He might answer \$4000, thereby

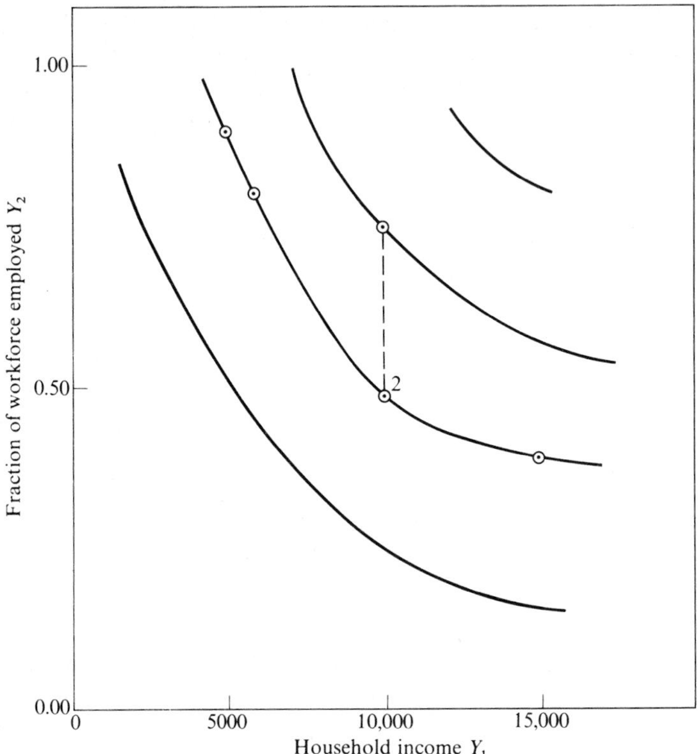


**Figure 20-2** Example curves of indifference between household income and fraction of workforce employed.

leaving \$6000 in income. If we question him further, he may indicate that he would only give up an additional \$1000 to raise the $Y_2$ level to 0.90 and, further, that he would *want* an additional \$5000 (above the \$10,000) if $Y_2$ were to drop to 0.40.

The four points corresponding to these decisions of the mayor are plotted in Fig. 20-2. The resultant curve is called an indifference or isopreference line because the mayor would not care where particular project impacts fell on that line. In other words, all the points are of equal preference. Note, too, that the lines bend toward the middle at the extremes of $Y_1$ and $Y_2$. This indicates a smaller preference (or rating) for an attribute as it becomes overabundant.

The same decision process could be employed to make trade-offs at higher levels of overall preference or utility. For example, we could have started at the point in Fig. 20-2 directly above that for project 2, with $Y_2 = 0.75$ instead of 0.48. This point is obviously preferred over any on the original curve. Then questions could have been asked about the desired fraction employed levels ($Y_2$) if selected changes were made in income ($Y_1$) from that starting point. If this process were continued from several different initial points, the overall result would be a family of indifference curves like those in Fig. 20-2. These could be employed to determine trade-offs between a variety of goal attributes (i.e., criteria).

The process needed to obtain such a family of curves (or "surface") has a major drawback: it would require asking a great many questions, and if several variables were considered at once (instead of just two), the combinations of possibilities would become enormous. Several procedures have been suggested to help circumvent this type of problem. One of the more interesting is that by R. L. Wilson (in Ref. 20-1) in his studies of desirable neighborhood characteristics in Greensboro and Durham, North Carolina.

In his study, Wilson presented to a sample of people in each city a chart or "game" board like that shown in Fig. 20-3. He also gave each respondent a number of "markers" with which to "pay" for lower density development and for "the closeness of neighborhood things to the house." For example, a 60 × 100 ft lot cost 18 markers while a 3-min walk to a grocery store cost 5 markers and a 10-min drive cost only 2 markers. The number of markers associated with each item on the game board was supposed to be in rough proportion to the expenditures needed to provide that item, and the total number of markers given to the respondents was supposed to be in rough proportion to the average income of residents in the particular city: 40 markers in Greensboro and 36 in Durham.

The results of one survey are shown in Table 20-9. It seems that most people in these two cities were desirous of obtaining low-density living (categories 4 and 5), even to the point where they would be willing to "spend" over half their markers for this privilege. This result in itself is of extreme importance to transportation planners since it implies that people generally will spend the travel time gains they achieve from transportation improvements by purchasing homes in lower-density (usually suburban) developments. For the most part, this move to lower density has been what has happened in American cities: a direct outgrowth of the importance attached to the goal of lower-living density.

The rank ordering or choices as to what neighborhood facilities people would like to have nearby also is interesting. In both Greensboro and Durham the religious building is placed at or near the top in importance. This outcome is almost completely unanticipated and should prove to have some interesting ramifications for neighborhood layout and circulation design. Following the religious building in importance are those kinds of facilities visited most frequently—elementary schools, grocery stores, and so forth. Those places not visited often, such as the movie theater, the shoe store, and the library, generally are found at the bottom of the list. These rank orders give the analyst a rough idea of the importance attached to the objectives of connecting places of various types together by means of transportation.

Another interesting conclusion from the Wilson study comes from an inspection of the third column at the bottom of Table 20-9. The group of respondents in Durham were given a second turn at allocating their markers but with no constraint on how many they could spend. The results indicate that, *with unlimited resources*, people in Durham seemed to have an increased desire for access to shopping centers, neighborhood parks, playgrounds, and community centers. When resources are binding, however, these activities are somewhat subjugated to the more mundane matters of getting to the grocery and drug stores. We can

## HOW MUCH BUILDING SHOULD THERE BE ON YOUR BLOCK ?

TYPICAL BLOCK - 200' × 600'

| Nº 1 | Nº 2 | Nº 3 | Nº 4 | Nº 5 |
|---|---|---|---|---|
| 110 FAMILIES PER BLOCK | 40 FAMILIES PER BLOCK | 20 FAMILIES PER BLOCK | 10 FAMILIES PER BLOCK | 2 FAMILIES PER BLOCK |
| A LOT ABOUT 25'×20' FOR EACH FAMILY | A LOT ABOUT 55'×60' FOR EACH FAMILY | A LOT ABOUT 60'×100' FOR EACH FAMILY | A LOT ABOUT 80'×150' FOR EACH FAMILY | A LOT ABOUT 200'×300' FOR EACH FAMILY |
| 6 | 12 | 18 | 24 | 30 |

## NEIGHBORHOOD THINGS--HOW CLOSE TO YOUR HOUSE ?

### SCHOOLS

| | ELEMENTARY SCHOOL GRADES 1 THRU 6 | JUNIOR HIGH SCHOOL GRADES 7-8-9 | A BUILDING FOR RELIGIOUS SERVICES OF YOUR FAITH |
|---|---|---|---|
| A 3 MINUTE WALK (ABOUT 1 BLOCK 600 FEET) | 5 | 5 | 5 |
| B 10 MINUTE WALK (ABOUT 5 BLOCKS 1/2 MILE) | 4 | 4 | 4 |
| C 20 MINUTE WALK OR 3 MINUTE DRIVE (ABOUT 1 MILE) | 3 | 3 | 3 |
| D 10 MINUTE DRIVE (ABOUT 4 MILES) | 2 | 2 | 2 |
| E 25 MINUTE DRIVE (ABOUT 8 MILES) | 1 | 1 | 1 |

| | NURSERY SCHOOL FOR CHILDREN ABOUT 2-4 YRS. OLD | PUBLIC LIBRARY BOOKS FOR LOAN, REFERENCE | PUBLIC MEETING PLACE FOR ORGANIZATIONS "A COMMUNITY CENTER" FOR YOUR NEIGHBORHOOD |
|---|---|---|---|
| A 3 MINUTE WALK (ABOUT 1 BLOCK 600 FEET) | 5 | 5 | 5 |
| B 10 MINUTE WALK (ABOUT 5 BLOCKS 1/2 MILE) | 4 | 4 | 4 |
| C 20 MINUTE WALK OR 3 MINUTE DRIVE (ABOUT 1 MILE) | 3 | 3 | 3 |
| D 10 MINUTE DRIVE (ABOUT 4 MILES) | 2 | 2 | 2 |
| E 25 MINUTE DRIVE (ABOUT 8 MILES) | 1 | 1 | 1 |

### SHOPPING

| | GROCERY STORE | DRUG STORE | BUS STOP TO BOARD BUSSES GOING DOWNTOWN |
|---|---|---|---|
| A 3 MINUTE WALK (ABOUT 1 BLOCK 600 FEET) | 5 | 5 | 5 |
| B 10 MINUTE WALK (ABOUT 5 BLOCKS 1/2 MILE) | 4 | 4 | 4 |
| C 20 MINUTE WALK OR 3 MINUTE DRIVE (ABOUT 1 MILE) | 3 | 3 | 3 |
| D 10 MINUTE DRIVE (ABOUT 4 MILES) | 2 | 2 | 2 |
| E 25 MINUTE DRIVE (ABOUT 8 MILES) | 1 | 1 | 1 |

| | SHOE STORE | SHOPPING CENTER INCLUDING DRUG STORE, SHOE STORE, GROCERY STORE AND OTHERS |
|---|---|---|
| A 3 MINUTE WALK (ABOUT 1 BLOCK 600 FEET) | 5 | 18 |
| B 10 MINUTE WALK (ABOUT 5 BLOCKS 1/2 MILE) | 4 | 15 |
| C 20 MINUTE WALK OR 3 MINUTE DRIVE (ABOUT 1 MILE) | 3 | 12 |
| D 10 MINUTE DRIVE (ABOUT 4 MILES) | 2 | 9 |
| E 25 MINUTE DRIVE (ABOUT 8 MILES) | 1 | 6 |

### RECREATION

| | MOVIE THEATER | PLAYGROUND WITH EQUIPMENT SUCH AS SWINGS, SLIDES, TEETER-BOARDS, ETC. | LARGE PLAYFIELD WITH BASEBALL DIAMOND, FOOTBALL FIELD, TENNIS COURT, ETC. |
|---|---|---|---|
| A 3 MINUTE WALK (ABOUT 1 BLOCK 600 FEET) | 5 | 5 | 5 |
| B 10 MINUTE WALK (ABOUT 5 BLOCKS 1/2 MILE) | 4 | 4 | 4 |
| C 20 MINUTE WALK OR 3 MINUTE DRIVE (ABOUT 1 MILE) | 3 | 3 | 3 |
| D 10 MINUTE DRIVE (ABOUT 4 MILES) | 2 | 2 | 2 |
| E 25 MINUTE DRIVE (ABOUT 8 MILES) | 1 | 1 | 1 |

| | OUTDOOR SWIMMING POOL | SMALL PARK FOR THIS NEIGHBORHOOD ABOUT 1 BLOCK IN SIZE | SPECIAL PLAYSPACE FOR PRE-SCHOOL CHILDREN-UNDER 5 YRS. |
|---|---|---|---|
| A 3 MINUTE WALK (ABOUT 1 BLOCK 600 FEET) | 5 | 5 | 5 |
| B 10 MINUTE WALK (ABOUT 5 BLOCKS 1/2 MILE) | 4 | 4 | 4 |
| C 20 MINUTE WALK OR 3 MINUTE DRIVE (ABOUT 1 MILE) | 3 | 3 | 3 |
| D 10 MINUTE DRIVE (ABOUT 4 MILES) | 2 | 2 | 2 |
| E 25 MINUTE DRIVE (ABOUT 8 MILES) | 1 | 1 | 1 |

**Figure 20-3** Game board used to evaluate aspects of neighborhood density and distance relationships. (The original, 28 × 45 inches, included five photographs of building types typical of the five densities at the top of the board to assist in conveying the concept of relative densities.) (*Source: Ref. 20-1, p. 389.*)

**Table 20-9 Rank order, percentage of respondents who chose neighborhood facilities in Fig. 20-3**

| | Proportion of responses in each density category, % | | | | | Total, % | Total number |
|---|---|---|---|---|---|---|---|
| | 1 | 2 | 3 | 4 | 5 | | |
| Greensboro | 1.1 | 2.7 | 23.2 | 55.7 | 17.3 | 100.0 | 185 |
| Durham | 0 | 1.9 | 24.7 | 35.8 | 37.7 | 100.0 | 162 |

| Greensboro 40 markers | Durham "A" 36 markers | Durham "B" no limit |
|---|---|---|
| 1. Religious building | 1. Bus stop | 1. Religious building |
| 2. Elementary school | 2. Grocery store | 2. Shopping center |
| 3. Grocery store | 3. Religious building | 3. Bus stop |
| 4. Junior high school | 4. Drug store | 4. Neighborhood park |
| 5. Bus stop | 5. Elementary school | 5. Elementary school |
| 6. Shopping center | 6. Shopping center | 6. Junior high school |
| 7. Drug store | 7. Junior high school | 7. Playground |
| 8. Library | 8. Movie theater | 8. Movie theater |
| 9. Community center | 9. Neighborhood park | 9. Community center |
| 10. Swimming pool | 10. Library | 10. Swimming pool |
| 11. Neighborhood park | 11. Playground | 11. Library |
| 12. Playground | 12. Community center | 12. Playfield |
| 13. Movie theater | 13. Swimming pool | 13. Grocery store |
| 14. Playfield | 14. Playfield | 14. Drug store |
| 15. Nursery | 15. Nursery | 15. Preschool play space |
| 16. Preschool play space | 16. Preschool play space | 16. Nursery |
| 17. Shoe store | 17. Shoe store | 17. Shoe store |

*Source:* Ref. 20-1, p. 391.

conclude, therefore, that (1) weight of importance of goals or criteria will change as incomes and total resources increase, and that (2) what people may desire ultimately is somewhat different from what they may desire when forced to stay within the constraints (especially budgetary) of the real world. Both these considerations should play an important role in the analyst's thinking when developing schemes (e.g., zoning) which affect land-use patterns.

While many of Wilson's findings are of interest, they may not apply elsewhere. But it can be seen that the technique has the advantages that it is easy to understand and apply and takes into account constraints as well as trade-offs between preferences.

Another version of the general method being discussed here is to transform all criteria into dollar terms and then add or divide the dollars associated with beneficial attributes by the dollars associated with the disbeneficial ones (usually actual costs of construction, operation, etc.). This process is the basis for the common techniques of benefit-cost and rate of return analyses.† As a simple

† For examples, see Refs. 20-13 and 20-15.

example, suppose a new interstate-standard highway were being considered to take the place of an existing two-lane road. Assume further that each life saved is worth \$50,000 and each hour of travel saved \$5, both in addition to the gasoline cost reductions of \$1 per trip. If these attributes are considered benefits, and if there are 2 lives and 10,000 hours saved in the 100,000 expected yearly trips over the new road, which will have a prorated annual construction and maintenance cost of \$125,000, the benefit cost difference would be

$$\$50{,}000(2) + \$5(10{,}000) + \$1(100{,}000) - \$125{,}000 = \$125{,}000$$

while the ratio would be

$$\frac{\$50{,}000(2) + \$5(10{,}000) + \$1(100{,}000)}{\$125{,}000} = 2.0$$

This technique is extremely useful, particularly in situations where funding is at a premium. But it suffers from the obvious disadvantage of having to determine the proper monetary weights to attach to each goal attribute (e.g., life and time).

### Method 8. Overall Rating and Deduction

This final method to be discussed here does not require that people rate each goal or criterion separately but instead asks for an overall rating for a series of plans or projects. An attempt is then made to correlate the ratings to features (combinations of attributes) that vary between the plans or projects. With a sufficient number of ratings it is possible to determine through deduction the attributes the respondee is implicitly emphasizing.

As a simple example, imagine a group of people shown a three-dimensional model of a small community and asked to place a new elementary school building on one of the available sites. In the process of making this placement they are also asked to rate the sites on a scale of 0 to 10, with the latter representing the best situation. If a large number of people took part, we soon would be able to see the higher ratings corresponding to, say, those sites (1) with sufficient land for recreation or (2) within walking distance of many residences, or a combination of these two. These findings would thus be coming from deductions based on the ratings received.

The strength of this method is in the simplicity for the respondents. Its major weakness is the requirement for a large number of responses to make deductions in complex (but realistic) situations involving, possibly, 70 goal attributes.

## PROBLEMS

**20-1** Write out the definitions for:

| | | |
|---|---|---|
| (*a*) Value | (*f*) Measurement | (*k*) Rate |
| (*b*) Goal | (*g*) Quantification | (*l*) Weight of importance |
| (*c*) Attribute | (*h*) Constraint | (*m*) Weighting |
| (*d*) Objective | (*i*) Standard | (*n*) Indifference |
| (*e*) Criterion | (*j*) Rank | (*o*) Isopreference |

**20-2** Set up a table with each of the eight methods discussed in this chapter as columns and goal attributes for evaluating them as rows. The latter should include cost, time to implement, personnel required, comprehendability by average citizens, precision, accuracy, reliability, usefulness in conjunction with other analysis procedures, ability to handle diverse opinions, etc. Now rank each method in terms of the goal attributes.

**20-3** Locate a comprehensive or transportation plan for a city or an environmental impact statement for a large-scale project. Using the Dickey–Broderick technique, identify goal attributes which are *not* considered (but possibly should be) in the report.

**20-4** Develop and describe 10 goals for the educational program in your department. For each goal give corresponding objective(s), criteria, feasible ranges, and standards.

**20-5** Develop a set of about 10 goals for health services in your locality. Ask five of your friends to:
(*a*) Rank the goals.
(*b*) Rate the goals with a total of 1.00.
Find the *mode* rank and the *mean* rating.

**20-6** Working with your instructor, take a sample from one of the sets of data in App. D. Develop a linear objective function of the form of Eq. (20-10). This will involve:
(*a*) Identifying $Y$ (goal) variables
(*b*) Giving each $Y$ variable a rating
(*c*) Assigning a + or − sign to each $Y$ variable
(*d*) Dividing each $Y$ variable by its standard deviation
Create three hypothetical projects, estimate different $Y$ levels for each, and determine the appropriate objective function values.

**20-7** For the town of Strip Mine (App. D), develop three hypothetical isopreference curves relating $Y_1$ to $Y_2$. Draw to scale on graph paper.

**20-8** Make up a game board similar to that of Wilson's. It should contain six to eight major categories of items; these should concern the relative weight of importance people give to various aspects of the welfare program in your locality. Indicate and discuss how "markers" should be given to each respondent.

## REFERENCES

20-1. Chapin, Jr., F. S., and S. F. Weiss (Eds.): *Urban Growth Dynamics in a Regional Cluster of Cities*, Wiley, New York, 1962.
20-2. CLM/Systems, Inc.: *Airports and Their Environment*, U.S. Department of Transportation, Washington, D.C., 1972.
20-3. Dickey, J. W. (senior author): *Metropolitan Transportation Planning*, McGraw-Hill, New York, 1975.
20-4. Dickey, J. W., and J. P. Broderick: "Toward a Technique for a More Exhaustive Evaluation of Urban Area Performance," *Environment and Planning*, vol. 6, no. 1, March, 1972.
20-5. Dreyfus, H.: *The Measure of Man: Human Factors in Design*, revised and expanded 2d ed., Whitney Library of Design, New York, 1967.
20-6. Goals for Dallas: *Goals for Dallas: Submitted for Consideration by Dallas Citizens*, Graduate Research Center of the Southwest, Dallas, Texas, 1966.
20-7. Guilford, J. P.: *Fundamental Statistics in Psychology and Education*, 4th ed, McGraw-Hill, New York, 1965.
20-8. Mager, R. F.: *Goal Analysis*, Fearon, Belmont, Calif., 1972.
20-9. Ockert, C. W., and C. E. Pixton: *A Strategy for Evaluating a Regional Highway-Transit Network*, Regional Planning Council, Baltimore, Md., 1968.
20-10. Osgood, C. E., G. J. Suci, and P. H. Tannenbaum: *The Measurement of Meaning*, University of Illinois Press, Urbana, Ill., 1957.

20-11. Pardee, F. S., et al.: *Measurement and Evaluation of Transportation System Effectiveness*, Memorandum RM-3869-DOT, The Rand Corporation, Santa Monica, Calif., September, 1969.
20-12. Roget, P. M.: *Thesaurus of English Words and Phrases*, Longmans, Green and Co., Ltd., London, 1936.
20-13. United Nations Industrial Development Organization: *Guidelines for Project Evaluation*, Sales No. E.72.II.B.11, United Nations, New York, 1972.
20-14. U.S. Environmental Protection Agency: *The Quality of Life Concept*, Office of Research and Monitoring, Washington, D.C., March, 1973.
20-15. Winfrey, R.: *Economic Analysis for Highways*, International, Scranton, Pa., 1969.

CHAPTER

# TWENTY-ONE

# RELEVANCE TREES

While much was said in the preceding chapter about such concepts as goals, measurable objectives, and trade-offs, little was mentioned about the obvious hierarchical structure of goals. One reason for this omission is the difficulty inherent in structuring such hierarchies. To date there does not seem to be any commonly accepted, explicit procedure for determining the number of levels in a goal hierarchy, much less the content of each level. Added to this problem is that of the general confusion over the definition of goals and objectives. While we tried to define concepts as tightly as possible in the previous chapter, that certainly is no guarantee that everyone understands and accepts those definitions (and, in reality, there is wide confusion on the subject).

## 21-1 GENERAL DESCRIPTION OF A RELEVANCE TREE†

One of the more innovative attempts to overcome these problems involves structuring of "relevance trees." These are developed by carrying out successive identification of increasingly finer components, at progressively lower levels. An example tree with three levels is diagrammed in Fig. 21-1. Each branch appearing on one level is divided into two branches at the next lower level. The point where each branch is subdivided is known as a *node*. While there must be at least two branches emerging downward ("depending") from a node, there is no higher limit on the number. In addition, there is no requirement that each node in a specific

† Part of the wording in this section is adapted from Ref. 21-2.

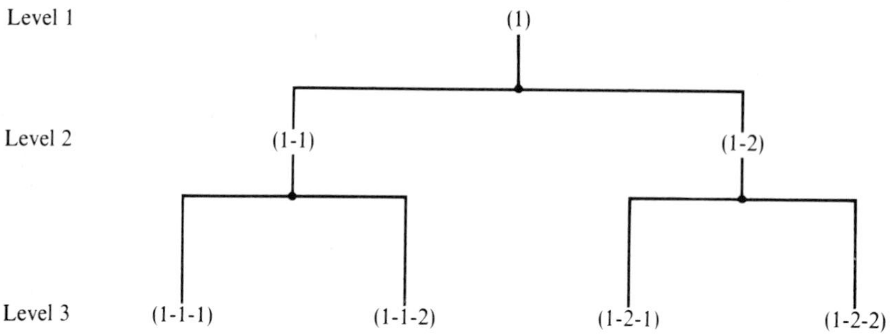


**Figure 21-1** Simple relevance tree.

relevance tree has the same number of branches depending from it. It is a common practice to use a notation such as that in Fig. 21-1 to identify the branches of a relevance tree. The sequence of subscripts should uniquely identify the path from any given branch to the top of the tree.

This figure clearly shows the hierarchical formation of a relevance tree. Several other characteristics of relevance trees, however, are not so apparent in the figure. First, the branches depending from a node must be a closed set. In other words, they must be an exhaustive list of all the possibilities at that node. This closure may come simply from listing all elements that are part of a finite set. In other cases the closure can be made artifically, by agreement that the set of branches includes all those relevant or important. This latter case is more common, but, of course, also more risky. A branch excluded through insufficient care or consideration may actually be more important than some included. As will be seen later, this type of situation may have serious consequences in practical applications of relevance trees.

Second, the branches depending from a node must be mutually exclusive, i.e., there must be no overlap between the elements represented by two distinct branches from the same node. In many cases this lack of overlap arises automatically from the nature of the items, which are unique. But in other cases the items must be carefully defined to avoid overlap and achieve the required exclusiveness.

Finally, a relevance tree used for normative purposes must be viewed as a set of goals and subgoals or objectives. Each node is, in fact, a goal for all those branches depending from it. Each goal is satisfied by the achievement of all branches below it, and in turn derives its validity as a subgoal from the sequence of branches linking it with the top of the tree.

The diagram in Fig. 21-2 shows an example of a goal-related relevance tree based (very loosely) on *Goals for Seattle 2000* (Ref. 21-5). For purposes of clarity and consistency, we have followed Warfield's convention (Ref. 21-3) of stating a goal in the form:

to (action word) (object) (qualifying phrase)

Also, to avoid confusion in defining *goals* and *objectives*, let us refer to this type of statement as an *intent*.

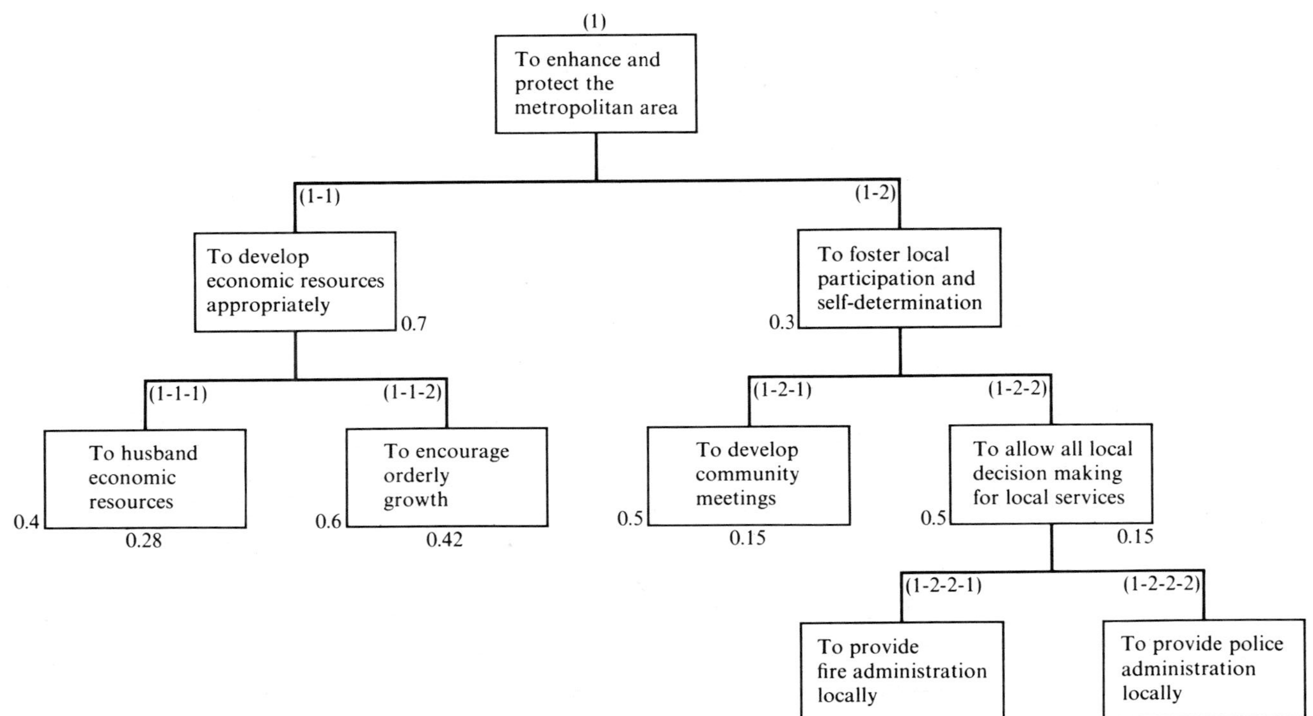


**Figure 21-2** Example relevance tree for a metropolitan area's "intents."

The broadest intent (designated by 1) is "to enhance and protect the metropolitan area." Depending from this are two intent statements which, for simplicity in explanation, are assumed to represent the entire set of intents at this level (actually there are four others). The numbering indicates that the first intent (1-1) is derived from the first (and in this case, the only) intent above it. With this kind of numbering system it is possible to trace the heritage of each lower-level intent all the way to the top of the tree. Depending both from intent (1-1) and (1-2) are two third-level intents, with two more depending from the last intent in this group. Again, for simplicity, we assume that all intents at a given level are exhaustive at that level.

Three additional features of relevance trees make themselves known as we examine Fig. 21-2. We see, first, that the number of branches from top to bottom of the tree may differ for different paths. This is reasonable since different interests can be stated in varying levels of specificity according to the problem under study, the interests of the goal-setting group, and, of course, the nature of the intents themselves. This finding thus points to a second feature: more than one type of relevance tree can be employed to describe an intent structure. This particular tree may be most useful for certain purposes, but it will not be the best for all. Relevance trees therefore are developed on an ad hoc basis, with each tree designed for the particular problem at hand. Consequently, there is no "right" way to set up a relevance tree. In fact, there are a variety of ways in which a relevance tree can be used in a normative manner. It can be utilized in specifying intents for each portion of a system; it can be utilized for specifying intents for alternative solutions to a problem; or it can be utilized for stating the problems which must be solved before an intent can be met. In each of these applications, the relevance tree serves to specify intents at lower and lower levels, representing smaller and smaller elements of some overall problem.

The third and final feature of the tree is that the intents vary from fairly general in nature at the top to what may be almost indistinguishable from action alternatives at the bottom. Thus the question of whether one is dealing with goals, objectives, or action options is unimportant in this context, as it probably should be in any real-world situation.

The general procedure for structuring intents in a relevance tree involves making some basic reasoning about the relationship between them:

1. If intent A necessarily must be accomplished in order to accomplish intent B, A lies below B in the structure.
2. If accomplishment of intent C, either separately or in combination with other intents, represents one alternative way of accomplishing intent D, C lies below D in the structure.

If, in forming an intent structure, one repeatedly asks oneself: "Why do I want to work towards this intent?" one is developing the structure in an upward direction. If one repeatedly asks oneself: "How can this intent be accomplished?" one is developing the structure in a downward direction.

The calculation of relevance numbers is an important part of the relevance tree method. Imagine that in Fig. 21-2 we feel that intent (1-1) has a weight of importance of 0.7 and (1-2) of 0.3, on a total scale of 1.0. These weights become "relevance numbers" at this level. Now further imagine that the intents depending from (1-1) have the weightings of 0.4 and 0.6, respectively, and those from (1-2) both of 0.5. Note that the sum of the relevance numbers depending from each node is always 1.0.

We can now follow all the possible paths from the top of the tree to the bottom, taking the products of the relevance numbers on each branch making up the path. For example, if we follow the path to (1-1-1), we have $0.7 \times 0.4 = 0.28$. The remaining path products are shown below the other intent statements at the same (lowest exhaustive) level in the figure. As a check on the computations, note that the sum of all the products across any level of the tree equals 1.0. If there were another complete level to the tree, with relevance numbers assigned to the branches and standardized to one at each node, we could obtain a new set of products at the bottom level, each involving three relevance numbers. The sum of all these products would equal 1.0.

The products of the relevance numbers indicate the relative importance of moving in the direction of each intent. Working toward (1-1-1) is about twice as important as working toward (1-2-1), which is as important as progressing toward (1-2-2). Had we carried out such a scheme of applying relevance numbers to the fully developed Seattle intent tree, we would have obtained the relative importance of developing projects corresponding to each of the intents. This information, of course, would be of considerable benefit in planning service programs for the Seattle metropolitan area.

## 21-2 A LARGE-SCALE EXAMPLE†

To our knowledge no full-scale development of a relevance tree has been attempted for an urban or regional situation. For this reason, and because we feel that this technique has great potential for such applications, we have elected to present here one of the more significant (and original) endeavors to create a relevance tree for a private sector industry. This was done by Honeywell (Refs. 21-4 and 21-6) in reference to its potential role in various national governmental endeavors, especially defense and space exploration. Their technique comprised a major part of an effort known as PATTERN (*p*lanning *a*ssistance *t*hrough *t*echnical *e*valuation of *r*elevance *n*umbers).

The relevance tree developed by the Honeywell group was basically a structured decision network having eight levels, beginning with national security objectives and progressing through types of conflict, forms of conflict, missions, system concepts, functional subsystems, subsystem configurations, and technology

† Some of the wording in this section is adapted from Ref. 21-4.

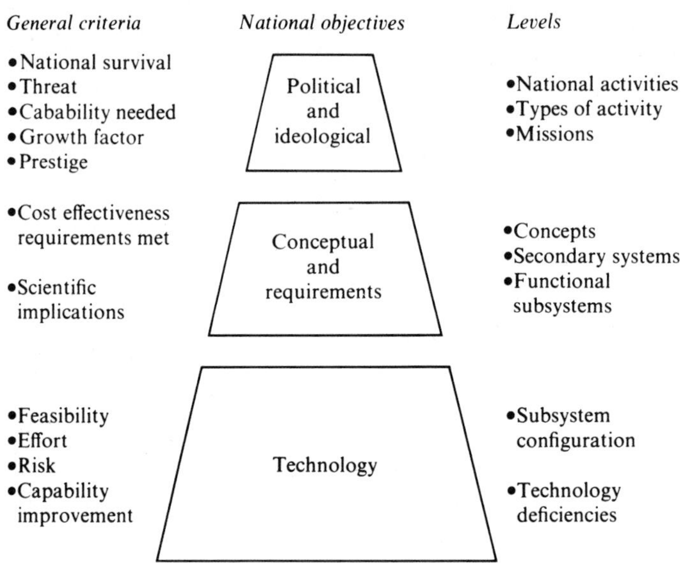


**Figure 21-3** Basic structure of the Honeywell relevance tree. (*Source: Ref. 21-4, p. 151.*)

deficiencies, in a tree-like fashion. Initially they divided the structure into the three major sections shown in Fig. 21-3. At the top, supporting the national objectives, is the political and ideological area, where the President and his advisors make policy-type decisions. The second section, the conceptual and requirements area, is that where the Secretary of Defense, the Administrator of NASA, and the individual Service Chiefs make decisions. The third section, the technology area, is where the individual military and industrial laboratories make technical decisions. This basic three-part structure was then subdivided into the eight levels shown to the right of Fig. 21-3. In order to make value judgments in the horizontal plane at each level of the tree, it is necessary both to apply specific definitions to each item on the tree and to develop a set of ground rules for the "game" situation. The ground rules take the form of criteria. Key words representing the various criteria are shown to the left of Fig. 21-3. In developing the criteria it is necessary to insure that they are both appropriate to the particular level at which the decision is to be made and mutually exclusive to that level insofar as possible.

A more detailed breakdown of the top four levels of the tree to the mission level is presented in Fig. 21-4. At the top is the national objective. Directly below that are the three types of activities identified by Honeywell as producing major challenges that they expected to face in the future. For example, on one side of the cold war is the spectrum of active hostilities and on the other the scientific challenge in peaceful exploration. To meet national security objectives (namely, to control aggression at any point in the world, to win the ensuing conflict if control fails, and to establish scientific preeminence in the field of exploration), the nation must have the technical capability to meet the challenges in all three areas. The

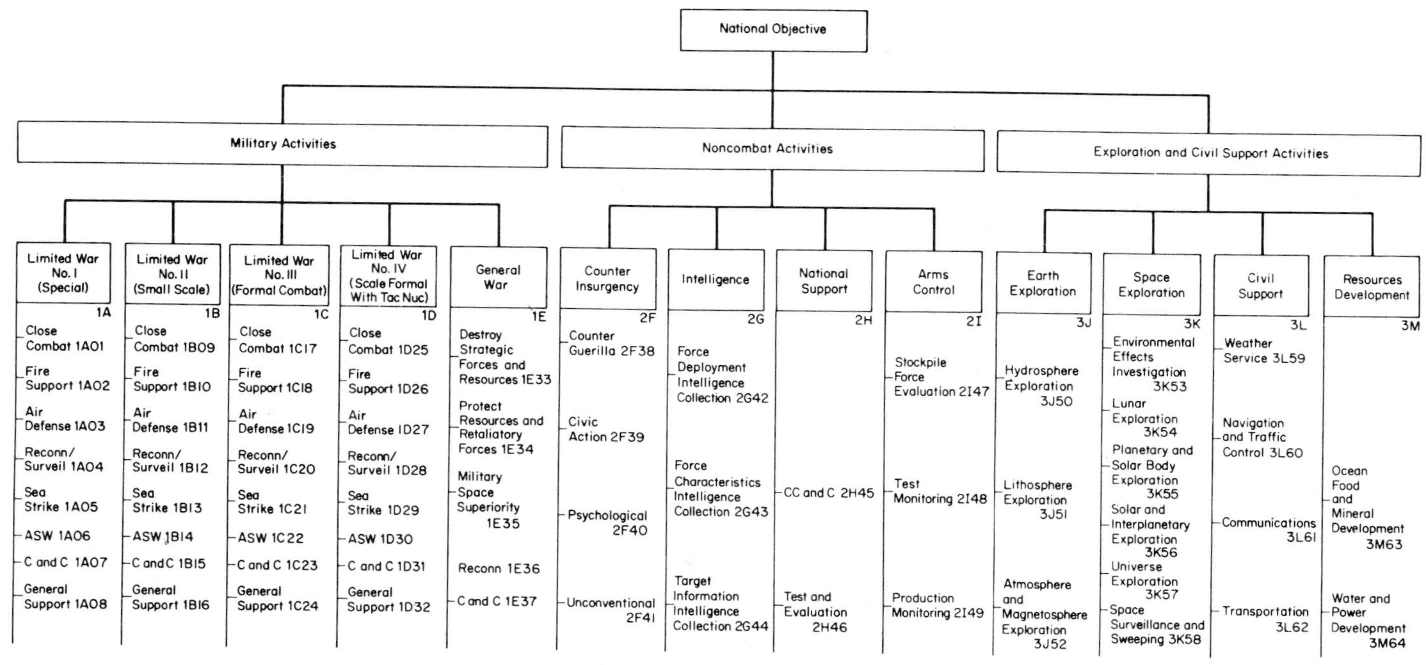


**Figure 21-4** Honeywell relevance tree structure to the mission level. (*Source: Ref. 21-4, p. 153.*)

different ways in which pressures may be brought to bear against the United States, shown at the third level of the relevance tree, are called "forms of activity." For instance, in the military area the country could be pressured into a general strategic global-type conflict or various tactical theater situations of differing intensity. In exploration it could be subjected to pressures principally involving scientific progress in earth-related and space-related activities, and so on.

Under each of these forms of conflict is a spectrum of missions which the country must be capable of carrying out if it hopes to counter the challenge in each specific area of competition. As an example, under Limited War II, if it were able to meet all of the requirements of the eight missions shown in Fig. 21-4, it should be able to engage in that form of conflict with a reasonable expectation of success.

It is very important that each of the areas be defined carefully to determine the type of equipment and the technology upgrading required to achieve the specific intents of each succeedingly higher level of the tree. The advantage of this type of structure is that it divides a large, many-faceted problem into smaller segments, allowing comparisons among smaller numbers of items at any single level. At the same time we retain the capability of looking again at the total package as any entity once the individual value judgments have been made.

Each level of the tree was "closed," i.e., made a complete set by consensus. The Honeywell experts agreed that the items as defined at each level represented a complete capability to accomplish the intents at the next higher level. The basic motivation behind the tree structure, therefore, was to help determine the area to be investigated (universal space) and then subdivide it (into sets and subsets) to a degree that the data could be evaluated in manageable pieces. The Honeywell group attempted to cull out overlapping regions using appropriate definitions, so that they could be handled with straightforward thought process. There was no mathematical constraint that the divisions be mutually exclusive; there were only data insertion and processing constraints. Furthermore, there was no mathematical constraint on the number of sets or their size. Neither was there a requirement that the relevance tree be composed of a specific number of levels, since almost any type of structure could have been used.

As a practical limitation, only those areas judged to need improvement were included on the relevance tree, with existing capability essentially factored out and included in the scenario or technology base. Hence the tree essentially involved upgrading, with the relevance numbers used to measure the marginal utility of the need to improve.

The tree structure therefore was a way of organizing data such that all factors of interest were included, with as little redundancy as possible, through flexibility in the use of stipulative definitions of the scope needed.

Figure 21-5 shows the lower four levels of the tree on a concept worksheet. The postulated concepts represented the fifth level of the tree. At the sixth level, each of the concepts was divided into 17 functional subsystem areas, together with associated requirements needed to meet the concept performance intents. There was no constraint on the number of subsystems used other than that the total would result in a complete set, as defined by consensus. To do this, it was neces-

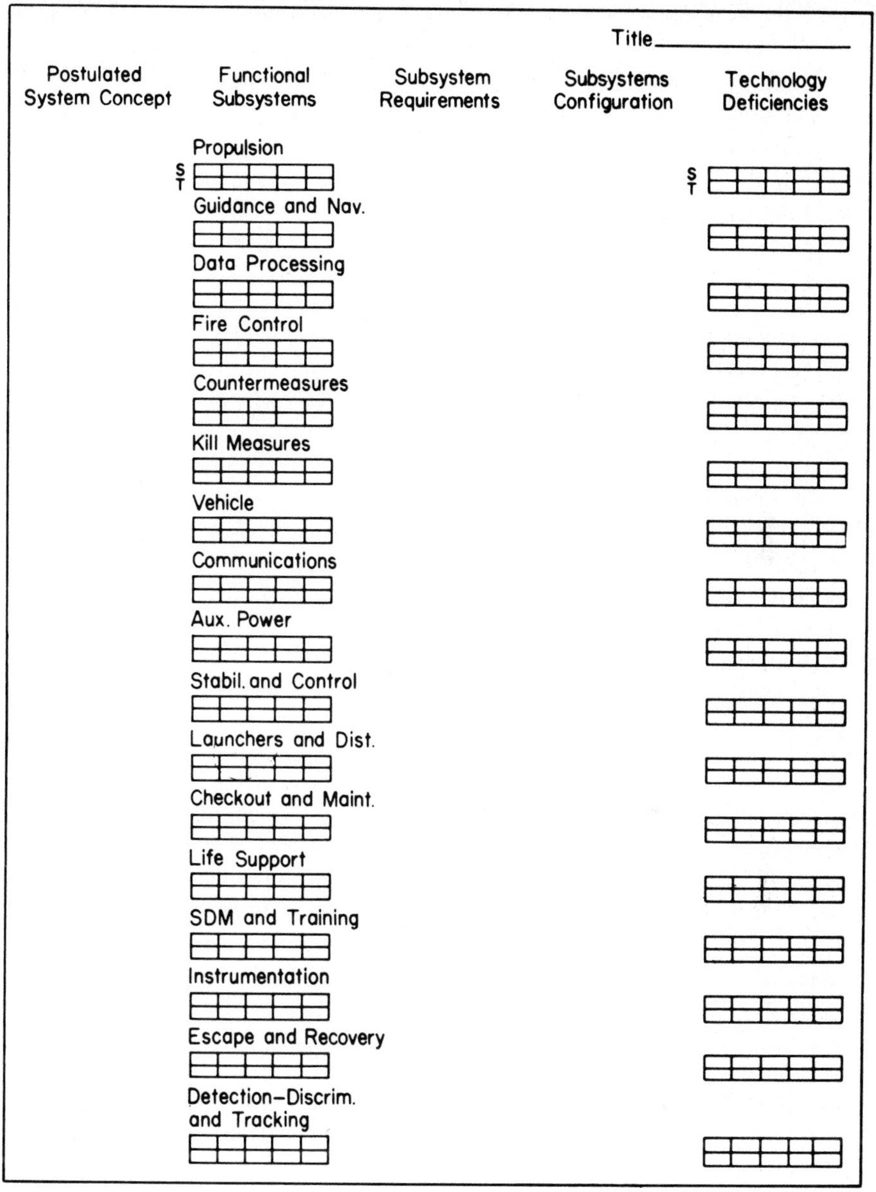

Title
Postulated System Concept
Functional Subsystems
Subsystem Requirements
Subsystems Configuration
Technology Deficiencies
Propulsion
S
T
Guidance and Nav.
Data Processing
Fire Control
Countermeasures
Kill Measures
Vehicle
Communications
Aux. Power
Stabil. and Control
Launchers and Dist.
Checkout and Maint.
Life Support
SDM and Training
Instrumentation
Escape and Recovery
Detection–Discrim. and Tracking

Status $S$ and timing $T$ legend

*Stages*

1. Research
2. Exploratory development
3. Advanced development
4. Product design
5. Available

| | | | | | | |
|---|---|---|---|---|---|---|
| *S* | | X | | | | Present status |
| *T* | | 3 | 2 | 2 | 1 | Years required |
| | 1 | 2 | 3 | 4 | 5 | Stages |

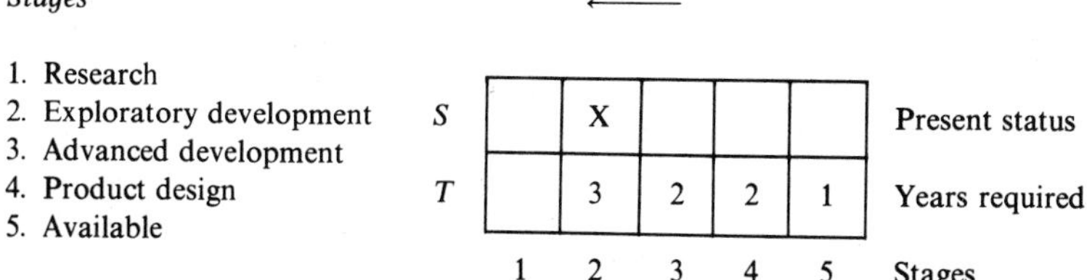

**Figure 21-5** Lower four levels of the Honeywell relevance tree and status $S$ and timing $T$ considerations. (*Source: Ref. 21-4, pp. 155, 159.*)

sary that each item be defined in considerable detail so that every study participant understood precisely what was included in each particular area.

In most cases there were several alternate ways by which the functional subsystem requirements could be met. These alternatives, called subsystem configurations, constituted the seventh level of the tree. Contained within the competing subsystem configurations were the technological deficiencies to be solved. These composed the eighth level of the tree.

Note on this chart that the *status S* and *timing T* of each functional subsystem or technological deficiency are considered, additions which the Honeywell group felt were necessary supplements to the traditional relevance tree. The concepts refer to the progress of a given technology as it moves from research through exploratory development, advanced development, and product design to the available or off-the-shelf category. These categories are very similar to those used by the federal government in defining their development phases. In evaluating a given functional subsystem or deficiency, the Honeywell team placed an "X" in the category where the technology being considered was determined to be in its development cycle. In the example in the lower part of Fig. 21-5, the team felt that the technology being discussed was in the exploratory development phase. They then were asked to determine how long it would take a normally prosecuted program to move the technology from this stage to advanced development. This was felt to be 3 years. Moving from left to right in the chart, 2 more years would be required in advanced development before it was ready to go into product design, and so on. Thus the total time required for the technology to progress from exploratory development to inventory availability in this case was 8 years. These status and timing data therefore basically indicate the capability of the country, time-wise, to meet its military/exploration-type technology needs.

Just as in structuring the tree, the selection of criteria for the assignment of relevance numbers was made on the basis that they be as nearly mutually exclusive as possible at each level (practical constraint) as well as from level to level (logic constraint). The relevance number was to reflect the judgment of the individual as to the degree of improvement needed in the area of interest. All the decisions were made by experts using the same criteria and documented data, and drawing upon their experience. The relevance number was, therefore, no better than the data, criteria, and the judgments of the individuals. Considerable effort was needed in developing a good scenario, which was then read and discussed by the participating team members.

Another change which the Honeywell group incorporated was in the totaling of the relevance numbers. If in the judgment of the evaluation team the number of elements at a given level did not cover a complete set of alternatives necessary in the decision process, adjustment was possible either by modification of the total weightings of the identified elements or by the addition of supplemental (X) elements.

The procedure for assigning relevance numbers is displayed in Fig. 21-6. This shows a typical assignment matrix at the second level of the tree under the exploration and civil support activities area. Here the team was making a judgment

| | Likelihood of technical challenge 0.5 | Capability needed to counter 0.3 | Contribution to international posture 0.2 | Final relevance number |
|---|---|---|---|---|
| Space exploration | 0.50 | 0.45 | 0.22 | 0.43 |
| Earth exploration | 0.30 | 0.30 | 0.55 | 0.35 |
| Civil support | 0.10 | 0.15 | 0.13 | 0.12 |
| Resources deviation | 0.10 | 0.10 | 0.10 | 0.10 |

**Figure 21-6** Relevance number assignment technique. (*Source: Ref. 21-4, p. 156.*)

regarding the technical upgrading required in the four areas shown at the left of the figure using the three criteria shown at the top of the chart. The first task was to give weights to the criteria. The sum of these in a horizontal direction equaled 1.0. Once the relative importance of each criterion was assigned, the team made value judgments among the four items on the left of the chart using the first criterion only. Once this was accomplished, the team made another value judgment using the second criterion. Finally, a third value judgment was made using the third criterion. In each case the values assigned in the vertical direction summed to 1.0 under each criterion used. Once the number assignment was completed, these data were inserted into a computer program where the weights given to the criteria were multiplied by the numbers assigned to each of the items, and the products were then summed across the horizontal axis for each item to give a final relevance number, indicated on the right of the chart. The same relevance number assignment technique was used at each successive node of the tree. In case of arithmetic errors in the assignment of the relevance numbers, they were standardized in such a manner that the sum of the assigned numbers equaled 1.0, and the computation continued.

By way of review, after the structure and criteria data were established, a matrix for the assignment of relevance numbers was generated. The averaged relevance value assigned by each member of the evaluation team was then calculated, as well as the total relevance at each tree node and the relative ranking for each item at the appropriate level of the tree.

A specific example is presented in Fig. 21-7. It shows the process down to the functional subsystem level and the representative numbers that resulted. The various tree levels are shown on the right of the chart and the relevance numbers on the left, along with the associated total rankings of the various situations and configurations. For instance, at the mission level the relevance number was 0.01745 for the Fire Support Mission, and it ranked thirteenth out of a total of 64 missions needing improvement to meet the national objectives. At the secondary system level is shown the necessity for the development of another generation bomb. Note that when used only on this specific airplane, the bomb need ranked relatively low, about in the middle of the total secondary system grouping. The guidance system for this particular bomb, however, had wide utility across so many different applications that it ranked very high (forty-third out of the total of 1610 functional subsystem categories).

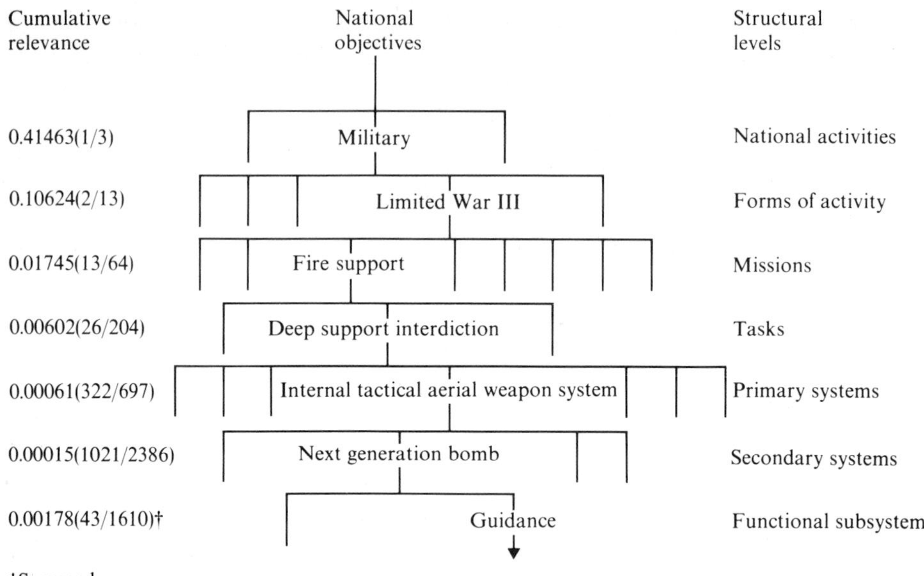


**Figure 21-7** Example computation of relevance numbers. (*Source: Ref. 21-4, p. 158.*)

Once the technological needs had been assessed without particular regard to the nation's ability to perform these functions, it was necessary to get an evaluation of the capability of industry to achieve technical solutions to the identified problems in some time-frame. The basic inputs to this evaluation were the assessments of the current status of each of the technologies being considered as well as the likely rate of improvement in performance of each technological area over time.

These types of inputs were described in Fig. 21-5. They subsequently were employed to determine which technologies had high relevance numbers yet needed considerable development. If these happened to correspond with Honeywell's general capabilities, an obvious area for future effort was established.

Considerable effort has been spent by Honeywell on independent appraisals of the overall technique by analysts from within the company and from the consultant community. These assessments have shown that:

1. The judgments, although subjective in nature, are representative of the type of managerial decisions required in resource allocation, program planning, and so on, where the manager must weigh all factors influencing a decision. The techniques used thus closely parallel and contribute to the managerial function of decision making.
2. When qualified personnel (generally the type which line managers usually seek for advice and opinions) are used in the judgment process, the results are of a high degree of value to managers, are quite specific, and provide very useful data to the ultimate decision.

3. Repeated tests with the data have shown that with similar information and discussion, the results of these judgments are highly repeatable when averaged for a group of at least five experts in the field. They also accurately reflect the consensus of the consulted community.
4. Comparative conclusions from entirely different tree structures have demonstrated that the results are not sensitive to the structure, provided each person understands the specific definitions to each tree decision node.
5. These studies show that the tree can be used to divide and identify specific objectives useful to planning, without fear of reducing the value of the judgment process.

## PROBLEMS

**21-1** Construct a three-level relevance tree of improvements or changes needed in urban public transit. Place relevance numbers on each branch of the tree. (If this problem is worked by a class or group, the Delphi procedure may be used to reach a consensus on the relevance numbers. In this case, the panel estimate should be the mean instead of the median of the individual estimates, to preserve the property that the relevance numbers must sum to 1.0 at each node.)

**21-2** A relevance tree has been developed for a local school board plan for education of the handicapped. At the first level the goals and ratings are:

| | |
|---|---|
| (1) Minimum social "disgrace" to the student | 0.33 |
| (2) Education to be able to "function" unassisted in the real world | 0.67 |

At the second level, under (1) we have the subgoals:

| | |
|---|---|
| (1-1) Keep in regular classroom as much as possible | 0.80 |
| (1-2) Participate in as many extracurricular activities as possible | 0.20 |

And under (1-1) there are three possible programs:

| | |
|---|---|
| (1-1-1) Special classrooms | 0.10 |
| (1-1-2) Part-time work with special instructors | 0.30 |
| (1-1-3) No special help | 0.60 |

What are the relevance number products under the latter three branches?

**21-3** Go to the library and find a study of goals for a particular city or region (e.g., Refs. 21-5 or 20-6). Use this as a basis for defining a relevance tree, with the weights assigned by yourself.

## REFERENCES


### Theory

21-1. Gordon, T. J., and M. J. Raffensberger: "The Relevance Tree Method for Planning Basic Research," in J. R. Bright and M. E. F. Schoeman (Eds.), *A Guide to Practical Technological Forecasting*, Prentice-Hall, Englewood Cliffs, N.J., 1973.

21-2. Martino, J. P.: *Technological Forecasting for Decisionmaking*, American-Elsevier, New York, 1972.

21-3. Warfield, J. N.: "Intent Structures," *IEEE Transactions on Systems, Man, and Cybernetics*, vol. SMC-3, no. 2, March, 1973.

### Applications and other references

21-4. Esch, M. E.: "Honeywell's PATTERN: Planning Assistance Through Technical Evaluation of Relevance Numbers," in J. R. Bright and M. F. Schoeman (Eds.), *A Guide to Practical Technological Forecasting*, Prentice-Hall, Englewood Cliffs, N.J., 1973.

21-5. Seattle 2000 Commission: *Goals for Seattle 2000*, Seattle, 1973.
21-6. Sigford, J. V., and R. H. Parvin: "Project PATTERN: A Methodology for Determining Relevance in Complex Decision-making," *IEEE Transactions on Engineering Management*, vol. EM-12, March, 1965.

CHAPTER

# TWENTY-TWO

# LINEAR PROGRAMMING

It often happens that in the analysis and planning of various urban and regional programs an effort is made to maximize or minimize some goals or, more specifically, an *objective function*. For instance, in the determination of how much money should be spent for different capital expenditure projects in a city, it may be desirable to maximize the ratio of measurable benefits minus costs of the selected project(s). The planning conditions usually are not completely determined, however, when the relevant objective has been specified, for it often turns out that there are certain *constraints* which must be considered. For example, two important constraints which loom heavily over all expenditure considerations are those on the time availability of personnel and the overall budget of the city.

## 22-1 A SMALL EXAMPLE

Consider a social services agency wishing to maximize total benefits (measured in dollars) to its clients by determining the best manpower allocations to each of its two programs: 1 and 2. Let $x_1$ and $x_2$ be the respective number of units of each program undertaken. Two sources of federal funding are available to hire personnel for the programs. One source will permit sufficiently high salaries to hire skilled personnel and the other source will permit only minimum wage salaries with which only unskilled personnel can be hired. Administrative personnel must be paid by the limited funds of the social services agency.

Each unit of output from a program requires a certain number of hours of administration, and skilled and unskilled labor. For instance, we see from Table 22-1 that to produce one unit of output of program 1 requires 2 hours of

**Table 22-1 Data for social services agency example**

| | Personnel hours needed for each unit of program output | | Personnel hours available per month |
|---|---|---|---|
| | Programs | | |
| | 1 | 2 | |
| Administration | 2 | 1 | 80 |
| Skilled | 5 | 5 | 260 |
| Unskilled | 5 | 10 | 480 |
| Benefit per unit of output | $600 | $360 | |

administration, 5 hours of skilled labor, and 5 hours of unskilled labor. This one unit of output has been estimated to be worth $600 to the client. Program 2 looks less favorable than the first one, for it is worth only $360 per unit of output and it requires more unskilled labor. Its sole advantage is the need for only 1 hour of administration per unit of output. There are only 80 hours of administration per month, which constrains the number of units of output. The limitations on skilled and unskilled labor also constrain output.

Another constraint is the need (demand) for each program. However, we will assume that need far exceeds the output permitted by the personnel constraints and it can be ignored. Also, output from the two programs cannot be negative. We can express these constraints with the following linear inequalities:

$$\begin{aligned} 2x_1 + x_2 &\leq 80 \\ 5x_1 + 5x_2 &\leq 260 \\ 5x_1 + 10x_2 &\leq 480 \\ x_1 &\geq 0 \\ x_2 &\geq 0 \end{aligned} \tag{22-1}$$

The variables $x_1$ and $x_2$ are the outputs of programs 1 and 2, respectively. We will assume that they can have fractional values.

The total benefit of the programs per month, $z$, is

$$z = 600x_1 + 360x_2 \tag{22-2}$$

This last equation is the *objective function.* The director of the social services agency needs to determine the amount of output for each program which could be implemented such that the total benefit $z$ is maximum but no constraint is violated. The variables $x_1$ and $x_2$ are called *decision variables.*

This problem is a classic linear programming problem for it meets these conditions:

1. The objective function can be expressed as a linear equation of two or more variables.
2. Values of these variables can be set by a decision maker within certain constraints in order to maximize an objective function.
3. The constraints are linear inequalities such that the left-hand side is less than or equal to the right-hand side.
4. The right-hand side of the inequalities are nonnegative.
5. The decision variables are nonnegative.

What is the best combination of $x_1$ and $x_2$ that will maximize the benefits of the two programs? One's first reaction may be to put all resources into program 1 since its value of output is much larger than that for the second program. To determine the output of program 1, divide the last column in Table 22-1 by the column for program 1:

$$80 \div 2 = 40 \qquad 260 \div 5 = 52 \qquad 480 \div 5 = 95$$

These quotients represent the maximum output of program 1 permitted by each of the constraints. There is sufficient unskilled labor to provide 96 units of output, but because of the shortage of administrators only 40 units can be produced. Under this strategy $x_1 = 40$ and $x_2 = 0$ and

$$z = 600(40) + 360(0) = \$24{,}000$$

What would happen if only program 2 were implemented? Divide the column for program 2 of Table 22-1 into the last column:

$$80 \div 1 = 80 \qquad 260 \div 5 = 52 \qquad 480 \div 10 = 48$$

The most restrictive constraint in this case is the unskilled labor supply. The maximum production of program 2 is 48 units, giving a benefit of

$$z = 600(0) + 360(48) = \$17{,}280$$

This second decision would not be as beneficial as the first. But is \$24,000 the maximum possible benefit? Could the director choose a combination of $x_1$ and $x_2$ that would produce a benefit greater than \$24,000? Since this problem is a simple one involving only two decision variables, it can be solved graphically.

## 22-2 GRAPHICAL SOLUTION OF A LINEAR PROGRAM

A graphical solution requires plotting the constraints. Let $x_1$ be the horizontal axis and $x_2$ be the vertical axis. To plot an inequality, one needs only to plot it in equation form and then shade in that part of the graph which points make the inequality true. In Fig. 22-1*a* a plot of $2x_1 + x_2 = 80$ from Eqs. (22-1) is shown, and all points $x_1 \geq 0$ and $x_2 \geq 0$ that give values less than or equal to 80 are shaded. The same steps are followed for the second and third inequality of Eqs. (22-1) (see Fig. 22-1*b*). The points in the shaded portion of this graph

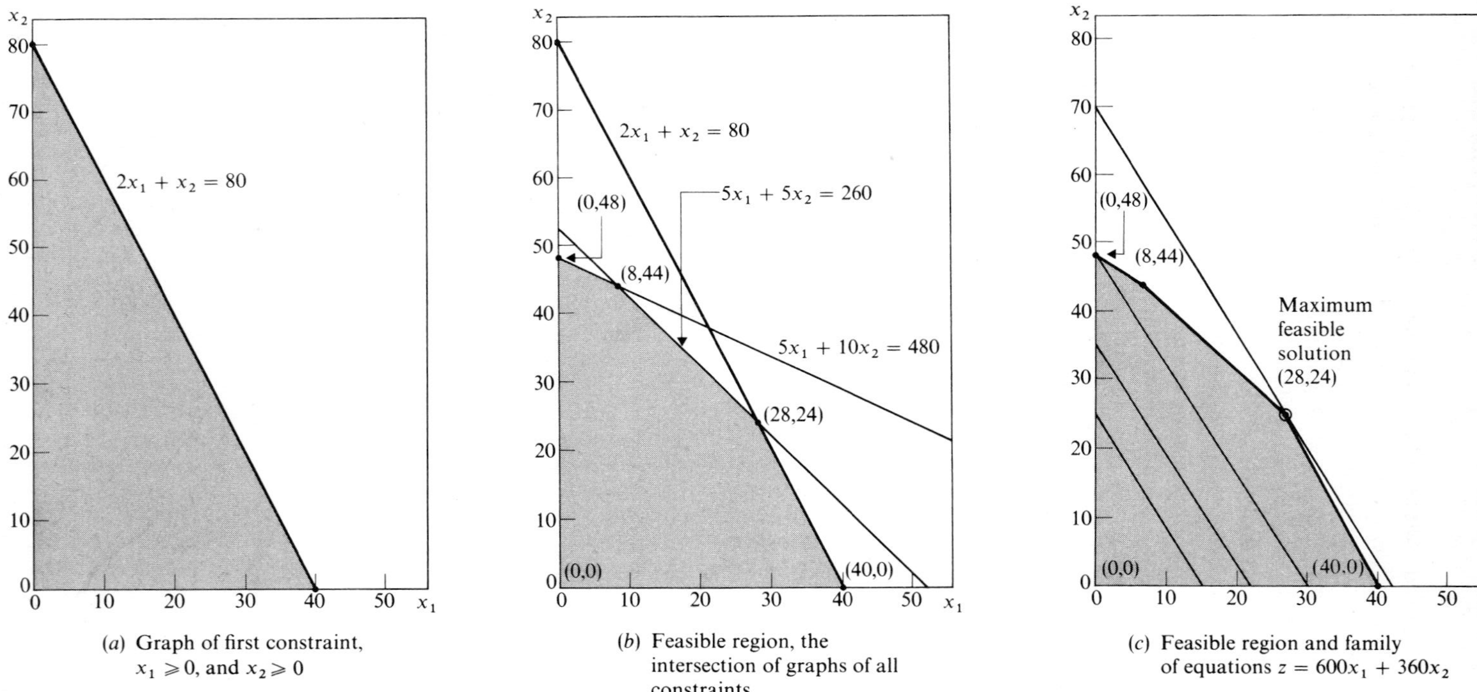


(*a*) Graph of first constraint, $x_1 \geqslant 0$, and $x_2 \geqslant 0$

(*b*) Feasible region, the intersection of graphs of all constraints

(*c*) Feasible region and family of equations $z = 600x_1 + 360x_2$

**Figure 22-1** Graphical solution to hypothetical two-variable linear programming problem.

represent all $(x_1, x_2)$ pairs that satisfy all five inequalities of Eqs. (22-1) simultaneously. Each point in this region is known as a *feasible solution* and the set of all feasible solutions is known as the *feasible region.*

There are an infinite number of feasible solutions; the decision maker must choose one point (or possibly a set of feasible points) that maximizes his objective function. This can be plotted on the graph by solving for $x_2$ and replacing $z$ by arbitrary values:

$$x_2 = \frac{z}{360} - \frac{600}{360}x_1 = \frac{z}{360} - \frac{5}{3}x_1 \tag{22-3}$$

This gives a family of linear equations with slope $-\frac{5}{3}$ and intercept $z/360$, one for each value substituted for $z$ (see Fig. 22-1*c*). The value of $z$ is maximized for the $(x_1, x_2)$ ordered pair that gives the largest intersection, $z/360$, on the $x_2$ axis. Moving the family of equations upward across the feasible region, it is easy to see that the point that maximizes $z$ is the last point that touches the objective function equation line as it moves out of the region. This maximum feasible solution is always a corner point, a fundamental theorem of linear programming. There are only five corner points in the feasible region:

$$(40, 0), (28, 24), (8, 44), (0, 48), (0, 0)$$

It is a simple matter to check these five points to determine the maximum feasible solution:

$$\begin{aligned}
600(40) + 360(0) &= \$24{,}000\\
600(28) + 360(24) &= \$25{,}440\\
600(8) + 360(44) &= \$20{,}640\\
600(0) + 360(48) &= \$17{,}280\\
600(0) + 360(0) &= \$0
\end{aligned}$$

The optimal decision is to produce 28 units of program 1 and 24 units of program 2 for a total benefit of \$25,440.

## 22-3 SOME EXCEPTIONAL CASES†

The examples in the preceding sections illustrate what may be called "properly behaved" linear programming problems. There are, however, certain exceptional cases which must be considered if mistakes in usage are to be avoided. Figure 22-2 shows several such cases. The feasible region is the shaded area. Lines representing the objective function for several values of $z$ are also drawn. Clearly we have encountered some new situations. In Fig. 22-2*a* the line representing the objec-

† The wording in this section is paraphrased from Hadley (Ref. 22-3).

tive function can be moved forever parallel to itself in the direction of increasing $z$ and still have some points in the region of feasible solutions. Hence $z$ can be made arbitrarily large and the problem has no finite maximum value of $z$. In such a case we say that the problem has an "unbounded" solution.

We do not expect a linear programming problem representing some practical situation to have an unbounded solution, since this would imply, for instance, the feasibility of an infinite profit. However, the limitation of resources and the impossibility of making arbitrarily large profits are precisely the reasons for our interest

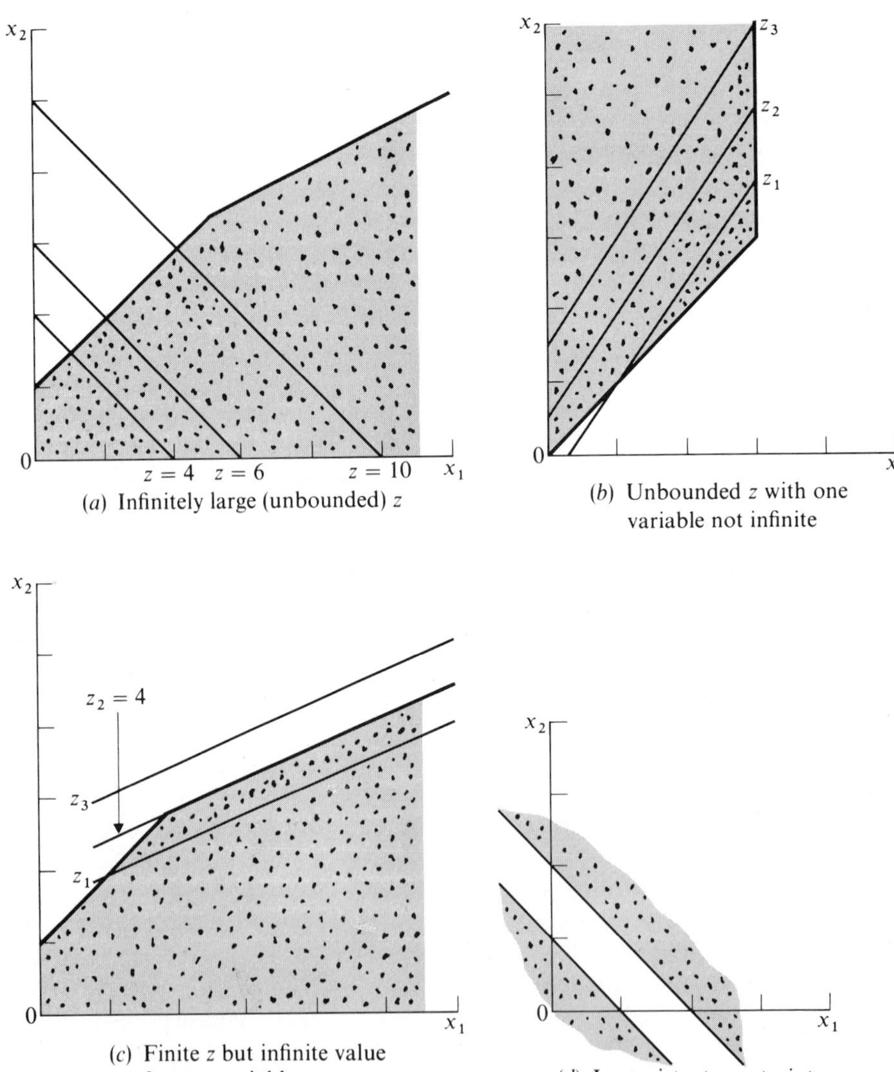


(a) Infinitely large (unbounded) $z$

(b) Unbounded $z$ with one variable not infinite

(c) Finite $z$ but infinite value for one variable

(d) Inconsistent constraints

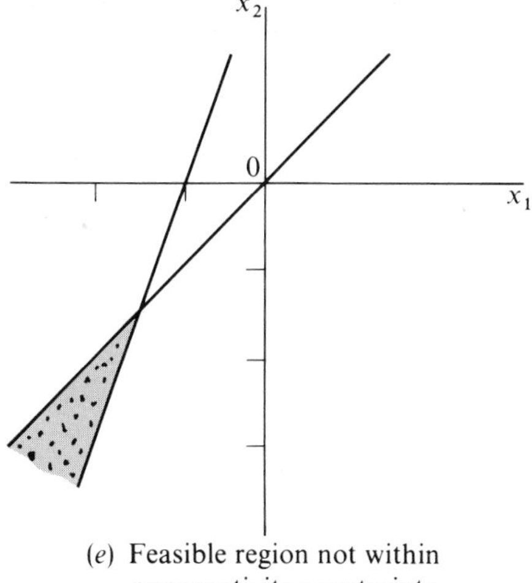


(*e*) Feasible region not within nonnegativity constraints

**Figure 22-2** Example linear programs. (*Adapted from Ref. 22-3, pp. 14-17.*)

in using linear programming. Yet it occasionally happens that a mistake in the formulation of an actual problem leads to an unbounded solution.

In the above example both variables can be made arbitrarily large as $z$ is increased. However, an unbounded solution does not necessarily imply that *all* the variables can be made arbitrarily large as $z$ approaches infinity. This can be seen in the maximization case exemplified in Fig. 22-2*b*. For that program $x_1$ remains at a constant value while $z$ goes to infinity.

We have already noted that the set of variables which maximizes the objective function does not need to be unique. Now it may turn out that although $z$ has a finite maximum value, there are solutions giving this maximum $z$ which have arbitrarily large values of the variables. This is illustrated in Fig. 22-2*c* for another type of maximization situation. This problem is not completely normal since there are solutions with arbitrarily large variables which yield a finite optimal value of $z$. The maximum value of $z$ is 4. Furthermore, any point $(x_1, x_2)$ lying on the edge of the region of feasible solutions, which extends to infinity, yields $z = 4$ and is therefore an optimal solution. This example also shows that if the objective function happens to have the same slope as one of the constraints, there may be an infinite number of solutions to the program (even in a bounded case).

Thus far every example has had a feasible solution. There is no automatic guarantee, however, that all linear programming problems have feasible solutions. The next problem, shown in Fig. 22-2*d*, has no solution because the constraints are inconsistent; i.e., there is no point $(x_1, x_2)$ which satisfies both constraints.

The constraints can be consistent and yet there may be no feasible solution because no point satisfying the constraints also satisfies the nonnegative restrictions. The following problem, illustrated in Fig. 22-2*e*, gives an example of such a case. Any point in the shaded area satisfies the inequality constraints. However, since no solution has $x_1, x_2 \geq 0$, there is no feasible solution.

The reader should not feel that the examples presented in this section are only of hypothetical interest and never occur in the real world. While it is true that we do not expect any properly formulated practical problem to exhibit such characteristics, it is equally true that a problem involving a large number of variables and constraints makes it extremely difficult to be sure that the constraints are indeed consistent, that there is at least one feasible solution, and that there is no unbounded solution. Because of the possibility of making mistakes in the formulation of problems, the exceptional cases discussed in this section can occur in practice.

## 22-4 AN EXPANDED EXAMPLE†

The application to be discussed here refers to a study by Henderson of production and shipment in the coal industry (Ref. 22-11). The problem is to identify for the short run the most efficient pattern of shipments from existing coal deposits in a set of regions to consumers in the same group of regions. First the regions (districts) within the overall system must be specified. The specification (i.e., classification of states into a set of regions) judged most useful from the standpoint of the entire study appears in column 1 of Table 22-2. The regions are numbered from 1 to 14, and of these only the first 11 have capacity to produce coal. Further, because underground and surface mining are quite different technically (as is reflected in the cost data to be presented later), an activity in a region, say region 1, which extracts coal from underground mines and delivers to, say, 2 is different from an activity in 1 which extracts from surface mines and delivers to the same region.

Activities as well as regions must be specified in a precise manner. In this study each activity is defined as combining both the extraction and delivery of coal. Since in any one of the 11 producing regions, say region $i$ ($i = 1, \ldots, 11$), underground coal can be extracted and delivered to any one of the 14 consuming regions, say region $l$ ($l = 1, \ldots, 14$), for each region $i$ there are thus 14 possible activities associated with *underground* coal mining and delivery. Their levels may be designated by $x_{il1}$, where $i$ is the producing region, $l$ is the region to which the coal is delivered, and the subscript 1 refers to underground coal. Similarly, for each region $i$ there are 14 possible activities associated with *surface* coal mining and delivery. Their levels may be designated as $x_{il2}$. The general variable, then, is $x_{ilt}$, where $t$ is the technology involved.

Next the objective function may be set down. Since the goal is to minimize the total cost of producing and delivering coal for the system, the objective function is

$$\min z = \sum_{i=1}^{11} \sum_{l=1}^{14} \sum_{t=1}^{2} c_{ilt} x_{ilt}$$

† The wording in this section is paraphrased from Isard (Ref. 22-12).

**Table 22-2 Unit extraction costs, mining capacities, and demand, by region, 1947**

| | | Unit extraction costs (per $10^{10}$ Btu), $ | | Estimated mining capacities, in $10^{10}$ Btu | | |
|---|---|---|---|---|---|---|
| District | States included (1) | Underground mines (2) | Surface mines (3) | Underground mines (4) | Surface mines (5) | Demand in $10^{10}$ Btu (6) |
| 1 | Pennsylvania, Maryland | 1503 | 828 | 225,598 | 142,982 | 221,400 |
| 2 | West Virginia | 1329 | 893 | 381,733 | 97,282 | 66.276 |
| 3 | Virginia, Kentucky, District of Columbia | 1391 | 655 | 270,831 | 40,506 | 139,708 |
| 4 | Alabama, Tennessee, North and South Carolina, Georgia, Florida, Mississippi, Louisiana | 1891 | 1308 | 49,918 | 7,613 | 107,089 |
| 5 | Ohio | 1414 | 897 | 64,661 | 52,341 | 165,421 |
| 6 | Illinois, Indiana, Michigan | 1238 | 934 | 165,348 | 74,997 | 283,305 |
| 7 | Iowa, Missouri, Kansas, Arkansas, Oklahoma, Texas | 2471 | 1088 | 12,828 | 27,682 | 62,773 |
| 8 | North and South Dakota, Nebraska | 1659 | 1185 | 690 | 3,365 | 15,763 |
| 9 | Montana, Wyoming, Utah, Idaho | 1343 | 761 | 36,690 | 7,382 | 28,548 |
| 10 | Colorado, New Mexico, Arizona, California, Nevada | 1704 | 1220 | 20,424 | 927 | 18,108 |
| 11 | Washington, Oregon | 2855 | 1484 | 1,388 | 609 | 10,522 |
| 12 | Maine, New Hampshire, Vermont, Massachusetts, Connecticut, Rhode Island | ...... | ...... | ...... | ...... | 60,186 |
| 13 | New York, New Jersey, Delaware | ...... | ...... | ...... | ...... | 123,221 |
| 14 | Minnesota, Wisconsin | ...... | ...... | ...... | ...... | 47,005 |
| | Total | | | 1,230,009 | 455,686 | 1,349,325 |

*Source:* Ref. 22-11, pp. 340–342.

where $c_{il1}$ indicates the cost of both extracting and delivering a unit of coal from the underground mine in region $i$ to the consumer in region $l$, and where $c_{il2}$ indicates the same for coal from surface mines. Each $c$ coefficient is assumed to be a constant and given beforehand (on the assumption of constant unit extraction costs at each mine and constant transport rates). To obtain these $c$ values, it is first necessary to estimate unit extraction costs. These costs, for 1947, are listed in columns 2 and 3 of Table 22-2, by region and type of mining.†

To each unit extraction cost must now be added appropriate transport costs to obtain the full value for each $c$. The resulting set of unit delivery (extraction plus transport) costs for 1947 is listed in Table 22-3. Where transport cost data were not available, primarily because such deliveries are not made and are not likely to be made under any reasonable circumstances, the unit transport costs were assumed to be so large as to preclude any shipment. The corresponding cells in Table 22-3 contain the letter N. For example, according to Table 22-3:

$$c_{111} = \$2004$$

$$c_{121} = \$2282$$

$$c_{122} = \$1607$$

$$\vdots$$

and

$$c_{11,14,2} = \text{N}$$

The objective function is subject to two sets of constraints. The first relates to capacities. For any producing region the sum of all underground coal shipments from that region must not exceed the capacity of that region to mine underground coal. Similarly, the sum of all its surface coal shipments must not exceed its capacity to mine surface coal. Since a unit level of any activity thus requires as input one unit of coal (underground or surface), the first constraint for region 1 appears as

$$x_{111} + x_{121} + \cdots + x_{1,14,1} \leq k_{11} \tag{22-4}$$

where $k_{11}$ is total underground-mining capacity (the underground coal resource) of region 1. This set of constraints requires, therefore, that estimates of capacities be made. Such estimates for 1947 are listed in columns 4 and 5 of Table 22-2. For example:

$$k_{11} = 225{,}598$$

The second set of constraints relates to consumption. For any consuming region, the total (in terms of British thermal units) of all coal shipments received, whether underground or surface mined, must be at least as great as the fixed

† Since quality of different types of coal varies, the tonnage unit is not used in favor of the more satisfactory heating value unit, the British thermal unit. (Because of its special properties, coking coal is not included in this study.)

**Table 22-3 Interregional unit delivery (extraction plus transport) costs, 1947** (in dollars per $10^{10}$ Btu)

| From districts | | To district 1 | 2 | 3 | 4 | 5 | 6 | 7 | 8 | 9 | 10 | 11 | 12 | 13 | 14 |
|---|---|---|---|---|---|---|---|---|---|---|---|---|---|---|---|
| 1 | u† | 2004 | 2282 | 2546 | 2952 | 2170 | 2712 | 3529 | 3716 | N | N | N | 3037 | 2539 | 2453 |
| | s | 1329 | 1607 | 1871 | 2277 | 1495 | 2037 | 2854 | 3041 | | | | 2362 | 1864 | 1778 |
| 2 | u | 2313 | 1456 | 2293 | 2556 | 2189 | 2575 | 2887 | 3687 | 6151 | 5123 | N | 2935 | 2469 | 2463 |
| | s | 1877 | 1020 | 1857 | 2120 | 1753 | 2139 | 2451 | 3251 | 5715 | 4687 | | 2499 | 2033 | 2027 |
| 3 | u | 2607 | 1930 | 1895 | 2357 | 2266 | 2551 | 2945 | 2933 | N | N | N | 3146 | 2810 | 2548 |
| | s | 1963 | 1235 | 1197 | 1695 | 1597 | 1903 | 2327 | 2315 | | | | 2544 | 2182 | 1900 |
| 4 | u | 3018 | N | 2620 | 2402 | 2747 | 3120 | 3563 | N | N | N | N | N | N | 3029 |
| | s | 2457 | | 2051 | 1829 | 2180 | 2561 | 3013 | | | | | | | 2468 |
| 5 | u | 2198 | 1988 | 2252 | N | 1899 | 2317 | 3359 | N | N | N | N | 3254 | 2503 | 2191 |
| | s | 1678 | 1471 | 1735 | | 1372 | 1800 | 2842 | | | | | 2747 | 1986 | 1674 |
| 6 | u | N | N | 1959 | 2621 | 2232 | 1804 | 2309 | 3009 | N | N | N | N | N | 2609 |
| | s | | | 1650 | 2308 | 1922 | 1497 | 1999 | 2694 | | | | | | 2298 |
| 7 | u | N | N | 4390 | 3618 | N | 3874 | 3062 | 3793 | 5174 | 4687 | 7706 | N | N | 3903 |
| | s | | | 3044 | 2257 | | 2518 | 1690 | 2435 | 3843 | 3347 | 6423 | | | 2548 |
| 8 | u | N | N | N | N | N | 5792 | 5299 | 2499 | N | N | N | N | N | 3378 |
| | s | | | | | | 5318 | 4825 | 2025 | | | | | | 2905 |
| 9 | u | N | N | N | N | N | N | 3802 | 3055 | 2200 | 3059 | 3506 | N | N | 3442 |
| | s | | | | | | | 3527 | 2686 | 1725 | 2691 | 3194 | | | 3121 |
| 10 | u | N | N | N | N | N | N | 3696 | 3820 | 3225 | 2073 | 4473 | N | N | N |
| | s | | | | | | | 3215 | 3339 | 2743 | 1590 | 3994 | | | |
| 11 | u | N | N | N | N | N | N | N | N | 4300 | N | 3423 | N | N | N |
| | s | | | | | | | | | 2929 | | 2052 | | | |

*Source:* Ref. 22-11, p. 343.

† Underground mines denoted by u, surface mines by s.

demand (in British thermal units) set for it. Thus in symbols this constraint for district 1 appears as (remembering that only the first 11 districts can supply coal)

$$x_{111} + x_{211} + \cdots + x_{11,1,1} + x_{112} + x_{212} + \cdots + x_{11,1,2} \geq d_1 \qquad (22\text{-}5)$$

where $d_1$ is the fixed total demand for region 1. This set of constraints requires the predetermination of a spatial pattern of demand. For the problem under study, the (historical) pattern of system demand in 1947, as recorded in column 6 of Table 22-2, was employed as fixed. For example, $d_{14} = 47{,}005$.

Given the regional demands which must be met, the regional capacities which cannot be exceeded, and unit extraction and transport costs, a computation was

**Table 22-4 An optimal pattern of interregional coal shipments, 1947 (in $10^{10}$ Btu)**

| Region | | Type of | Level of |
|---|---|---|---|
| From | To | mining† | shipment |
| 1 | 1 | u | 78,418 |
| 1 | 1 | s | 142,982 |
| 2 | 2 | s | 66,276 |
| 3 | 3 | u | 99,202 |
| 3 | 3 | s | 40,506 |
| 3 | 4 | u | 99,476 |
| 4 | 4 | s | 7,613 |
| 1 | 5 | u | 48,419 |
| 5 | 5 | u | 64,661 |
| 5 | 5 | s | 52,341 |
| 3 | 6 | u | 42,960 |
| 6 | 6 | u | 165,348 |
| 6 | 6 | s | 74,997 |
| 2 | 7 | u | 35,091 |
| 7 | 7 | s | 27,682 |
| 3 | 8 | u | 11,708 |
| 8 | 8 | u | 690 |
| 8 | 8 | s | 3,365 |
| 9 | 9 | u | 21,166 |
| 9 | 9 | s | 7,382 |
| 10 | 10 | u | 17,181 |
| 10 | 10 | s | 927 |
| 9 | 11 | u | 8,525 |
| 11 | 11 | u | 1,388 |
| 11 | 11 | s | 609 |
| 2 | 12 | u | 29,180 |
| 2 | 12 | s | 31,006 |
| 2 | 13 | u | 123,221 |
| 1 | 14 | u | 47,005 |
| Total demand | | | 1,349,325 |

Unused capacities

| Region | Type of mining | Level |
|---|---|---|
| 1 | u | 51,756 |
| 2 | u | 194,241 |
| 3 | u | 17,485 |
| 4 | u | 49,918 |
| 7 | u | 12,828 |
| 9 | u | 6,999 |
| 10 | u | 3,243 |
| Total | | 336,470 |

*Source:* Ref. 22-11, p. 344.

† Underground mines denoted by u, surface mines by s.

made to derive a solution that minimizes the overall costs of production and transportation for the system.† The optimal solution‡ is recorded in Table 22-4. Twenty-nine shipping activities are run at nonzero levels. (For example, region 1 ships $48{,}419 \times 10^{10}$ Btu of underground-mined coal to region 5, that is, $x_{151} = 48{,}419$.) Underground-mining capacities of seven regions are not fully utilized.

As an aside, this minimum-cost solution is consistent with conditions of both monopoly and perfect competition. From this standpoint the derivation of such a solution is useful. It describes a normative situation in that it suggests an efficient pattern under the given assumptions. A pattern of this sort is valuable for the social and physical planning of "new" regions. Further, through comparison with the actual pattern of shipments and outputs, the solution can point up certain inefficiencies which exist as well as sensitivities. Given certain changes in the data—in demand, capacities, and extraction and transport costs—it can indicate changes in the optimum values for outputs and shipments. In fact, the coal study does spell out in this way the implications of a 10,000-unit increase in the demand of region 9. Obviously, the extent to which such results can be used to project changes in the existing pattern with similar impulses depends on the extent to which the program approximates (or is believed to approximate) reality. Where the approximation is close, clearly this linear program and others can be employed to generate forecasts of changing patterns of shipments and outputs, which in many cases are the prime indicators of economic growth.

## 22-5 THE MATHEMATICS OF LINEAR PROGRAMMING

As stated before, the classic linear programming problem takes the form:

$$\begin{aligned}
&\text{Maximize } z = c_1x_1 + \cdots + c_kx_k \\
&\text{subject to:} \quad a_{11}x_1 + \cdots + a_{1k}x_k \le b_1 \\
&\qquad\qquad\quad \vdots \qquad\qquad\quad \vdots \quad\;\; \vdots \\
&\qquad\qquad\quad a_{m1}x_1 + \cdots + a_{mk}x_k \le b_m \\
&\qquad\qquad\quad x_i \ge 0 \qquad \text{for } i = 1, \ldots, k
\end{aligned} \tag{22-6}$$

where $x_1, \ldots, x_k$ are $k$ decision variables, $c_1, \ldots, c_k$ are their coefficients in the objective function, and $a_{ji}$, $i = 1, \ldots, k$, $j = 1, \ldots, m$, are their coefficients in the $m$ constraints. The parameters $b_1, \ldots, b_m$ are nonnegative limiting values of the

† In this static case the accumulation or depletion of inventories is not permitted.

‡ Strictly speaking, there are an infinite number of minimum-cost solutions in this example. For instance, in Table 22-4 only underground-mining operators in region 1 ship coal to region 4. Yet, without causing total costs to rise, surface-mining operators in region 1 could ship 1, 2, 111, up to 47,005 units of coal to region 14 and that much less to region 1, provided underground-mining operators in region 1 both decreased their shipments to region 14 and increased their shipments to region 1 by the same amount.

constraints. The $m$ constraints determine the feasible region and the point that maximizes the objective function is one of the corner points of the region.

It is not unusual for a linear programming problem to have over 100 variables and constraints. The feasible region for such a problem has thousands of corner points. To evaluate all the corner points would be extremely time consuming. The *simplex method* is a technique to find an optimal solution without finding and evaluating all the corner points. However, even with a small problem, say three decision variables and four constraints, and even using the simplex method, solving a linear programming problem by hand is exceedingly time consuming and prone to careless computational errors. Except for trivial textbook problems, it is not practical to solve such problems except by computer. Because most linear programming canned computer programs do not use the simplex method, but variations of it, we will not present the details of how to solve the linear programming problem in this way. An easy-to-understand description of this method can be found in Ref. 22-1 and a more difficult but still understandable presentation with some good examples can be found in Ref. 22-4. A good theoretical presentation is given in Ref. 22-2. To use most linear programming canned computer programs one needs to know how to set up the data to enter into the computer. This involves converting the inequalities into equations.

The inequality of the constraints can be converted to equations by introducing *slack* variables. The constraints in Eqs. (22-1) can be converted to equations as follows:

$$\begin{aligned} 2x_1 + x_2 + s_1 \phantom{+ s_2 + s_3} &= 80 \\ 5x_1 + 5x_2 + s_2 \phantom{+ s_3} &= 260 \\ 5x_1 + 10x_2 + s_3 &= 480 \end{aligned} \tag{22-7}$$

The slack variables, the $s$ values, represent the amount a solution underutilizes the resources of constraint $j$. For instance, in the first solution evaluated in Sec. 22-1 when $x_1 = 40$ and $x_2 = 0$, utilization of labor was

$$\begin{aligned} 2(40) + 1(0) &= 80 \\ 5(40) + 5(0) &= 200 \\ 5(40) + 10(0) &= 200 \end{aligned}$$

Comparing these results with the right-hand side of Eqs. (22-7), we see that the administration personnel were fully utilized ($s_1 = 0$), but skilled and unskilled labor was not ($s_2 = 60$ and $s_3 = 280$). The optimal solution $x_1 = 28$ and $x_2 = 24$ gives the following labor utilization:

$$\begin{aligned} 2(28) + 1(24) &= 80 \\ 5(28) + 5(24) &= 260 \\ 5(28) + 10(24) &= 380 \end{aligned}$$

Only unskilled labor has a nonzero slack ($s_3 = 100$). Equations (22-7) have five nonnegative unknowns and three equations. A solution at a corner point requires that at least two of the unknowns (5 unknowns − 3 equations) be 0. The optimal solution is $x_1 = 28$, $x_2 = 24$, $s_1 = 0$, $s_2 = 0$, $s_3 = 100$. The objective function can also be expressed in terms of the five unknowns:

$$z = 600x_1 + 360x_2 + 0s_1 + 0s_2 + 0s_3 \tag{22-8}$$

The coefficients for the slack variables are 0.

The classic linear programming problem is restrictive and real problems rarely fit it exactly. However, variations in the type of constraints can be converted so that they will fit the model. Some of these variations and their conversions are discussed below.

If a constraint is an inequality in the wrong direction ($\geq$ instead of $\leq$), one can convert it into an equation by adding a slack variable. For example, suppose the legislation for the unskilled labor program in our example required that the social services agency use 80 hours of unskilled labor per month, i.e., the unskilled labor constraint has a lower as well as an upper bound:

$$\begin{aligned} 5x_1 + 10x_2 &\leq 480 \\ 5x_1 + 10x_2 &\geq \ \ 80 \end{aligned} \tag{22-9}$$

To convert the last inequality into an equation one could easily add a fourth slack variable. But then $s_4$ would be negative, which is not allowed. To overcome this, we need only to subtract a positive number from the left-hand side:

$$5x_1 + 10x_2 - s_4 = 80 \tag{22-10}$$

This causes a new problem. The simplex method requires that at least one variable in each constraint have a coefficient of 1. To overcome this problem an artificial variable is added with such a coefficient:

$$5x_1 + 10x_2 - s_4 + A_1 = 80 \tag{22-11}$$

What is an artificial variable? It is a meaningless variable thrown into the problem to make the simplex method work. The only way the final solution can make sense is to assure that $A_1 = 0$. This can be done by assigning a negative coefficient with a large absolute value to $A_1$ in the objective function:

$$z = 600x_1 + 360x_2 + 0s_1 + 0s_2 + 0s_3 + 0s_4 + MA_1 \tag{22-12}$$

where $M$ is an arbitrarily chosen negative number with a large absolute value. Like the other variables, $A_1$ is never negative, and hence $MA_1$ is never positive. To maximize $z$, the obvious first step is to set $A_1 = 0$.

What should one do if a constraint is an equality in the first place? For example, suppose the legislation required that the number of hours of unskilled labor utilized should equal $1\frac{1}{2}$ times the hours of skilled labor utilized. Looking at Eqs. (22-1), we see that $1\frac{1}{2}$ times the left-hand side of constraint 2 should equal the left-hand side of constraint 3. Simplifying, we get Eq. (22-14):

$$5x_1 + 10x_2 = 1.5(5x_1 + 5x_2) \tag{22-13}$$

$$-x_1 + x_2 = 0 \tag{22-14}$$

Since this constraint is an equation, a slack variable is not needed. However, to overcome the requirement that one variable have a coefficient of 1, an artificial variable is needed:

$$-x_1 + x_2 + A_2 = 0 \tag{22-15}$$

This artificial variable must be zero or this constraint will be violated. Thus, the coefficient $M$ is assigned to $A_2$ in the objective function:

$$z = 600x_1 + 360x_2 + 0s_1 + 0s_2 + 0s_3 + 0s_4 + MA_1 + MA_2 \tag{22-16}$$

It is possible that the legislation is so restrictive that no solution is possible. Such will be the case if the simplex method produces a solution with a nonzero artificial variable.

If the right-hand side of an inequality is negative, simply multiply both sides of the inequality by $-1$. This will change the direction of the inequality. If the objective is to minimize the objective function instead of maximizing it, multiply the function by $-1$ and then maximize. The solution for max $(-z)$ is the same as the solution for min $(z)$. Finally, if a decision variable can be negative, then replace it with the difference of two nonnegative variables, $d^-$ and $d^+$. For any solution, at least one of these variables is zero. For example, let $x_3 = d_3^- - d_3^+$. If $d_3^-$ is zero and $d_3^+$ is 100 for a solution, then $x_3 = d_3^- - d_3^+ = 0 - 100 = -100$.

Consider this problem:

$$\begin{aligned} &\text{Minimize } z = 25x_1 + 10x_2 - 15x_3 \\ &\text{subject to: } x_1 + x_2 \leq 10 \\ &\qquad x_2 + x_3 \geq 2 \\ &\qquad x_1 + x_3 = 5 \end{aligned} \tag{22-17}$$

where $x_1, x_2 \geq 0$, and $x_3$ is unrestricted. This problem can be set up for a simplex solution in the following way:

$$\text{Maximize } z = -25x_1 - 10x_2 + 15d_3^- - 15d_3^+ + 0s_1 + MA_1 + MA_2 - 0s_2 \tag{22-18}$$

$$\begin{aligned} \text{subject to: } & x_1 + x_2 + s_1 = 10 \\ & x_2 + d_3^- - d_3^+ + A_1 - s_2 = 2 \\ & x_1 + d_3^- - d_3^+ + A_2 = 5 \end{aligned}$$

To assure a starting point the simplex method requires a diagonal of variables with coefficients of 1, as seen in the coefficients corresponding to $s_1$, $A_1$, and $A_2$.

## PROBLEMS

**22-1** Fill in the blanks with the appropriate word(s).

(*a*) The function to be optimized in a linear program is called an ______________________.

(*b*) The functions that describe the limits within which the solution must lie are called ______________________.

(*c*) The elements on the right-hand side of the equal (or inequality) signs must be ______________________.

(*d*) These functions must all be ______________________.

(*e*) The set of points that meet all the constraints is called the ______________________.

(*f*) The value of $z$ decreases as the line for the objective function moves ______________________ the origin.

**22-2** Solve the following linear program graphically:

$$\text{Maximize } z = 4x_1 + 2x_2$$
$$\text{subject to: } x_1 + x_2 \leq 7$$
$$x_1 + 4x_2 \leq 16$$
$$3x_1 + x_2 \leq 18$$
$$x_1, x_2 \geq 0$$

What would be the solution if the objective were to minimize $z$?

**22-3** Solve the following linear program graphically.

$$\text{Maximize } z = 3x_1 - 4x_2$$
$$\text{subject to: } 2x_1 + 3x_2 \leq 7$$
$$4x_1 - 2x_2 \geq 2$$
$$3x_1 \leq 9$$
$$x_1, x_2 \geq 0$$

What would be the solution if the objective were to minimize $z$?

**22-4** Solve Probs. 22-2 and 22-3 using a computer program it one is available.

**22-5** Suppose in the application described in Sec. 22-4 there were only five districts (the first five) and only the first two actually produced coal (both surface and underground). Using the corresponding capacity and demand figures from Table 22-2 and the cost figures from Table 22-3, set up a linear programming problem.

**22-6** A private forest owner plans to develop his 5025 acres of land. His land can be subdivided into seven categories:

Hardwood forest (HW), pine forest (P), and bareland (BL)

The two types of forest (HW and P) are subdivided:

Complete understorey (CU), partial understorey (PU), and no understorey (NU)

(Understorey refers to small tree undergrowth.)

The forester can take a combination of five actions:

1. Cut and plant hardwood.
2. Cut and plant pine.
3. Cut and retain understorey.
4. Cut and enrich understorey.
5. Postpone cutting for 10 years.

Due to the cost of getting together a cutting operation, the owner will not cut again until 10 years hence. The values in the table below present profits from the selling of logs and the value (after figuring costs) of the forest 10 years from now.

**Forest types and action taken: area, value, and volume**

| Forest types | HW-CU | HW-PU | HW-NU | P-CU | P-PU | P-NU | BL |
|---|---|---|---|---|---|---|---|
| Area (acres) | 12 | 1897 | 500 | 39 | 170 | 646 | 1761 |
| *Actions* | $ value per acre | | | | | | |
| 1. Cut and plant hardwood. | 287 | 287 | 287 | 187 | 187 | 187 | 87 |
| 2. Cut and plant pine. | 215 | 215 | 215 | 115 | 115 | 115 | 61 |
| 3. Cut and retain understorey. | 228 | ... | ... | 168 | ... | ... | ... |
| 4. Cut and enrich understorey. | ... | 292 | ... | ... | 212 | ... | ... |
| 5. Postpone cutting for 10 years. | 204 | 204 | 204 | 125 | 125 | 125 | 15 |
| Volume of cut, $ft^3$ per acre | 2000 | 2000 | 2000 | 1000 | 1000 | 1000 | ... |

A newly passed state land-use law has restricted how a forester can cut his forest. For this forest the law specifies these restrictions:

1. The volume of hardwood cut cannot exceed 3,000,000 $ft^3$.
2. The volume of pine cut cannot exceed 500,000 $ft^3$.
3. Total area cut cannot exceed 2513 acres.
4. Pine area resulting from the program (including postponed and new pine forest from planting or understorey) cannot exceed 2513 acres.
5. 500 acres at least must be planted in pine.

How many acres must be assigned to each type of action for the seven types of land to maximize value? Set up the constraints and the objective function in the form of Table 22-1. If a linear programming computer program is available, solve the problem accordingly.

**22-7** Go to the library and find a relevant application of linear programming. In about 500 words describe:

(*a*) The general nature of the problem being investigated
(*b*) The nature of the objective function
(*c*) The types of constraints involved
(*d*) The results obtained
(*e*) The general advantages and disadvantages of linear programming in the problem being studied

# REFERENCES


**Theory**

22-1. Frazer, J. R.: *Applied Linear Programming*, Prentice-Hall, Englewood Cliffs, N.J., 1968.
22-2. Gass, S. I.: *Linear Programming, Methods and Applications*, 3d ed., McGraw-Hill, New York, 1969.
22-3. Hadley, G.: *Linear Programming*, Addison-Wesley, Reading, Mass., 1962.
22-4. Hough, L.: *Modern Research for Administrative Decisions*, Prentice-Hall, Englewood Cliffs, N.J., 1970.
22-5. Wagner, H. M.: *Principles of Operations Research*, Prentice-Hall, Englewood Cliffs, N.J., 1969.

**Applications**

22-6. Ben-Sharar, H. A., Mazor, and D. Pines: "Town Planning and Welfare Maximization: A Methodological Approach," *Regional Studies*, vol. 3, 1969.
22-7. Chorley, R. J., and P. Haggett (Eds.): *Integrated Models in Geography*, Metheun, London, 1967.
22-8. Czamanski, S.: "A Model of Urban Land Allocation," *Growth and Change*, June, 1973.
22-9. Dickey, J. W. (senior author): *Metropolitan Transportation Planning*, McGraw-Hill, New York, 1975.
22-10. Hamburg, J. R., et al.: "Linear Programming Test of Journey-to-Work Minimization," *Highway Research Record, 121*, 1965.
22-11. Henderson, J. M.: "A Short Run Model for the Coal Industries," *Review of Economics and Statistics*, vol. 37, November, 1955.
22-12. Isard, W.: *Methods of Regional Analysis*, The MIT Press, Cambridge, Mass., 1960.
22-13. Ochs, J.: "An Application of Linear Programming to Urban Spatial Organization," *Journal of Regional Science*, vol. 9, no. 3, December, 1969.
22-14. Pinnell, C., and G. T. Satterly, Jr.: "Analytic Methods in Transportation: Systems Analysis for Arterial Street Operation," *Journal of the Engineering Mechanics Division*, American Society of Civil Engineers, EM6, December, 1963.
22-15. Tolley, G. S., and F. E. Riggs: *Economics of Watershed Planning*, The Iowa State University Press, Ames, Iowa, 1961.

CHAPTER

# TWENTY-THREE

# GOAL PROGRAMMING

We saw in the last chapter that linear programming is a technique to optimize an objective subject to certain constraints. However, in reality, a decision maker rarely confronts a situation involving only one objective. Particularly in the public sector, one must attempt to attain a set of goals to the fullest extent possible in an environment of conflicting interests, incomplete information, and limited resources. Another approach, and one that might be more useful in planning situations, is to try to come as close as possible to certain preset standards, some or all of which may be unachievable. Charnes and Cooper (Ref. 23-1) initially developed a variant of mathematical programming in which certain constraints were considered to be linear functions with given desired levels, and the objective was altered to that of minimizing the differences between the levels of the constraint functions and their corresponding desired levels. This procedure was called *goal programming.*†

## 23-1 A SHORT EXAMPLE

In the linear programming example of Sec. 22-1 a public service agency attempted to maximize its benefit expressed by the linear function:

$$z = 600x_1 + 360x_2 \tag{23-1}$$

† To be consistent with our definitions in Chap. 20, we should call this technique *standards programming*. But since the term goal programming is in common usage, we shall maintain it here.

subject to these constraints:

$$\begin{aligned} 2x_1 + \phantom{1}x_2 &\le 80 \\ 5x_1 + 5x_2 &\le 260 \\ 5x_1 + 10x_2 &\le 480 \end{aligned} \qquad (23\text{-}2)$$

In goal programming each constraint can be expressed as an equation with a nonzero variable, $d^-$, representing the amount the left-hand side deviates *below* the right-hand side, and another nonzero variable, $d^+$, representing the amount the left-hand side deviates *above* the right-hand side:

$$\begin{aligned} 2x_1 + \phantom{1}x_2 + d_1^- - d_1^+ &= 80 \\ 5x_1 + 5x_2 + d_2^- - d_2^+ &= 260 \\ 5x_1 + 10x_2 + d_3^- - d_3^+ &= 480 \end{aligned} \qquad (23\text{-}3)$$

The left-hand sides of Eqs. (23-2) can deviate above as well as below the limits on the right-hand sides. The mathematics of goal programming will not let both $d^-$ and $d^+$ be nonzero at the same time. For each constraint only one of these variables, called *deviational variables*, can be positive, and neither can be negative.

The objective function can be expressed with deviational variables by setting $z$ to an arbitrarily large and unobtainable value:

$$600x_1 + 360x_2 + d_4^- - d_4^+ = \$100{,}000 \qquad (23\text{-}4)$$

Given the limited resources, the agency cannot come close to providing $100,000 of benefit per month. Thus, $d_4^-$ will be positive and $d_4^+$ will be zero.

This objective function is now a constraint and the new objective function is the minimization of the undesirable deviations in the first three constraints, $d_1^+$, $d_2^+$, and $d_3^+$, and the amount the benefit function is short of $100,000, $d_4^-$.

$$\text{Minimize } z = d_1^+ + d_2^+ + d_3^+ + d_4^- \qquad (23\text{-}5)$$

There are two goals to consider here; one is to meet the personnel constraints and the second is to push the benefit to the largest value possible. In goal programming we can assign priorities to each goal permitting a solution to reflect certain values of the decision maker.

What are the priorities of these two goals? Occasionally, an agency will put the minimization of $d_4^-$ first, i.e., it will provide services to all who request them, resulting in huge cost overruns. This usually brings temporary program termination, forced resignation of some agency personnel, and considerable political controversy. To avoid these results, the first priority, $p_1$, can be placed on the minimization of $d_1^+$, $d_2^+$, and $d_3^+$, that is, the minimization of personnel cost overruns. The objective function is now:

$$\text{Minimize } z = p_1(d_1^+ + d_2^+ + d_3^+) + p_2 d_4^- \qquad (23\text{-}6)$$

Under this arrangement the solution will be the same as that obtained with the original programming problem in Sec. 22-2. So far goal programming has done nothing for us that could not have been done by linear programming; however, we can now consider other goals.

In Sec. 22-5 the constraint that the unskilled labor utilized should be $1\frac{1}{2}$ times that of skilled labor was introduced. It was pointed out that such a program requirement may make a solution impossible or could cause a serious reduction in benefits offered. A more realistic approach would be to reestablish this constraint as a standard with a low priority. To be sure that this standard does not cause a dramatic reduction in services, let us include a standard of total benefit at a level of 90 percent of the average monthly benefit of the previous year. Suppose that figure is \$20,000. This standard can be expressed with the following equation:

$$600x_1 + 360x_2 + d_5^- - d_5^+ = \$20{,}000 \tag{23-7}$$

This standard is given a second-level priority, and that concerning relative levels of labor utilization is given a third-level priority. The constraint is expressed in Eq. (23-8), simplified in Eq. (23-9), and set up as a standard in Eq. (23-10):

$$5x_1 + 10x_2 = 1.5(5x_1 + 5x_2) \tag{23-8}$$

$$-x_1 + x_2 = 0 \tag{23-9}$$

$$-x_1 + x_2 + d_6^- - d_6^+ = 0 \tag{23-10}$$

Under this arrangement the third goal will not interfere with benefits provided until after \$20,000 is assured. The fourth goal will be the attainment of the \$100,000 benefit. The goal programming problem is now:

Minimize $z = p_1(d_1^+ + d_2^+ + d_3^+) + p_2 d_5^- + p_3(d_6^- + d_6^+) + p_4 d_4^-$

subject to:

$$\begin{aligned}
2x_1 + x_2 + d_1^- - d_1^+ &= 80 \\
5x_1 + 5x_2 + d_2^- - d_2^+ &= 260 \\
5x_1 + 10x_2 + d_3^- - d_3^+ &= 480 \\
600x_1 + 360x_2 + d_5^- - d_5^+ &= 20{,}000 \\
-x_1 + x_2 + d_6^- - d_6^+ &= 0 \\
600x_1 + 360x_2 + d_4^- - d_4^+ &= 100{,}000
\end{aligned} \tag{23-11}$$

Two approaches could be used in applying the priorities. One is to substitute numerical values for the $p_i$ such that $p_1 \geq p_2 \geq p_3 \geq p_4$. The problem can then be solved by using a standard linear programming computer program. The other approach is to solve the problem for that part of the objective function containing the first priority:

$$\text{Minimize } z = d_1^+ + d_2^+ + d_3^+ \qquad (23\text{-}12)$$

After this limited objective is satisfied as much as possible, we then consider the remaining priorities one after the other. This second approach has the advantage of not requiring the decision maker to know how to weigh the priorities. Also, standards can be measured with noncommensurate functions. Thus, the objective function can be expressed in dollars, time units, numbers of people, etc.—one type of measure for each standard. Since there are only two decision variables, the solution of the problem through a hierarchy of standards can be obtained graphically.

## 23-2 GRAPHICAL INTERPRETATION

Each constraint of Eqs. (23-11) is drawn on the graph in Fig. 23-1*a*. This graph is the same as that in Fig. 22-1*b* except that three more equations have been added to reflect the three additional standards of Eqs. (23-4), (23-7), and (23-10). Deviations are shown as arrows pointing from the equation lines. Only those deviation variables in the objective function are shown, for only these are to be minimized. The first step is to minimize $d_1^+$, $d_2^+$, and $d_3^+$, which can be reduced to 0, giving the feasible region *ABDE*0 in Fig. 23-1*b*. The next step is to minimize $d_5^-$, which can be made to be 0, reducing the feasible region to *ABDG* (see Fig. 23-1*c*). Any point in this region will satisfy the first four constraints in Eqs. (23-11).

The third step is to minimize both $d_6^-$ and $d_6^+$. These can be made to be 0, reducing the feasible region to all points on the line segment *FC* (see the heavy line in Fig. 23-1*d*). The reader may wonder under what circumstances a deviation variable cannot be reduced to zero. This will occur when an equation line does not intersect a feasible region obtained from standards of higher priority. If this happens, the shortest line segment between the region and the line equation will be the minimum deviation. The equation of the last constraint in Eqs. (23-11) is such an equation, for it passes far above the feasible regions shown in Fig. 23-1*b*,*c*, and *d*. The shortest distance to that line is the line segment *CH*. Hence, our final solution for the decision variables is the point *C*, that is, $x_1 = 26$ and $x_2 = 26$, the deviation variables $d_1^+, d_2^+, d_3^+, d_5^-, d_6^-, d_6^+$ are all zero and $d_4^-$ is the distance of line segment *CH*.

The careful reader has probably noticed that the same result could have been obtained in the linear programming problem of Eqs. (22-1) by simply adding the constraint $-x_1 + x_2 = 0$. However, the communality between linear and goal programming in this example was coincidental, for the latter can give results quite

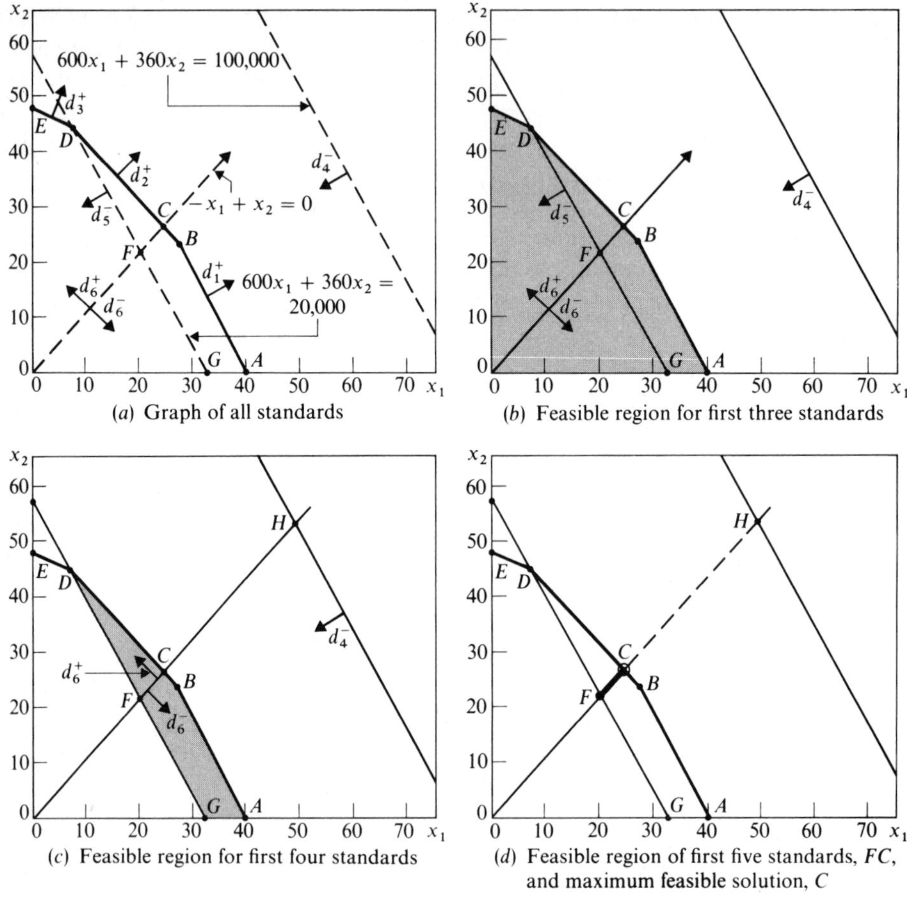


**Figure 23-1** Feasible region and point of intersection of standards.

different from the former. Unlike linear programming, goal programming permits nonattainment of a standard even at high priority levels, as will be shown in the following example.

## 23-3 AN EXPANDED EXAMPLE

Lee and Sevebeck have developed a goal program for municipal economic planning (Ref. 23-5). They employed empirical data from the town of Blacksburg, Virginia, to help make capital budgeting decisions. The full funding of each item on a list of specific capital projects comprised the standards in their program. The decision variables ($x$ values) in most cases were the amounts of the General Fund and the Sewer and Water Funds allocated to each project in each budget year.

By way of background, Blacksburg is responsible for public rights-of-way, municipal planning and zoning, enforcement of traffic regulations, control of public utilities, and related operations. Municipal tax and public utility rates are also set by the town. The town council provides funds for town beautification, recreational areas and equipment, as well as public land and institutions.

Blacksburg is a rapidly growing university town. The natural population increase, the growth of the university, and the expansion of existing industries clearly indicate the need for new business areas and additional services to be provided by the local government in the not-too-distant future. But in many cases the immediate satisfaction of these needs will not be possible by the time that they make themselves obvious. This type of municipal responsibility also entails long-range planning and the efficient allocation of financial resources to ensure that future needs are satisfactorily met on time.

A capital improvement budget for the town is prepared on an annual basis. There is no formal long-term program which includes those projects that cannot be financed during the fiscal year but can be undertaken sometime within the next 5 years. For illustrative purposes a 3-year planning period will be used. The town's budgeting process takes place through essentially two funds: (1) General Fund and (2) Water and Sewer Fund. In the event that bond financing is used for some series of projects, a Bond Fund is also maintained. However, in the program the activity pertaining to bond financing will be assumed in the General Fund. Provisions for transfers to the Water and Sewer Fund will be made.

If the town is to provide an environment attractive to new industry and business and also be capable of meeting the needs of a growing population, it must consider the types of capital improvement which will contribute to achieving these goals and their relative priorities. It must also take into consideration costs and revenue requirements and the need for additional financing.

The General Fund and the Water and Sewer Fund were broken down into variable and fixed revenues and expenditures. Included under variable expenditures were the amounts of money spent in a year for each capital improvement project. Each set of variables (General Fund and Water and Sewer Fund) were given different designations for each year. There were six basic subgoals for the 3-year planning periods, these being to remain solvent in each fund at the end of each fiscal year. In addition to the subgoals, each variable was constrained according to what were believed to be the objectives of the town. The list of revenue variables, revenue variable coefficients, expenditure variables, expenditure variable coefficients, fixed revenues, fixed expenditures, beginning balances, and ending balances is given in Table 23-1.

## Constraints and the Objective Function

To summarize the long-range goals of the town: there is a serious need to increase the number of businesses and industries to create a broader economic base, so that

**Table 23-1 Revenue and expenditure variables**

(*a*) Revenue

| Fund | Current, $ | Year 1 | Year 2 | Year 3 |
|---|---|---|---|---|
| *General Fund* | | | | |
| Amount of 1-year bank loan ($1000) | 0 | $x_1$ | $x_{12}$ | $x_{21}$ |
| Assumed credit limits ($1000) | | 100.00 | 100.00 | 100.00 |
| Amount of new bond issue ($1000) | 0 | $x_2$ | $x_{13}$ | $x_{22}$ |
| Assumed upper limits of issue ($1000 | | 0 | 200.00 | 250.00 |
| Property tax rate per $1000 of assessed value | 20.00 | $b_1$ | $b_5$ | $b_9$ |
| Assumed upper limits | | 20.00 | 25.00 | 25.00 |
| Effective business license tax rate per $1000 of receipts | 2.10 | $b_2$ | $b_6$ | $b_{10}$ |
| Assumed upper limits | | 2.30 | 2.50 | 2.50 |
| Average garbage collection charge per collection | 2.50 | $b_3$ | $b_7$ | $b_{11}$ |
| Assumed upper limits | | 2.50 | 2.75 | 3.00 |
| Real property valuation base ($1000) | 8,503.05 | $a_1$ | $a_1$ | $a_1$ |
| Gross business receipts ($1000) | 20,134.00 | $a_2$ | $a_2$ | $a_2$ |
| Total garbage collections | 29,800.00 | $a_3$ | $a_3$ | $a_3$ |
| *Water and Sewer Fund* | | | | |
| Transfer from General Fund | 0 | $x_5$ | $x_{16}$ | $x_{25}$ |
| Assumed lower limits | | 0 | 0 | 0 |
| Water and sewer service rate per 10,000 gal | 7.00 | $b_4$ | $b_8$ | $b_{12}$ |
| Assumed upper limits | | 7.00 | 7.50 | 8.00 |
| Water and sewer service charge base | 47,616.00 | $a_6$ | $a_6$ | $a_6$ |
| *Fixed revenues* | | | | |
| General Fund | — | $a_{12}$ | $a_{14}$ | $a_{16}$ |
| Value used | | 240,493.00 | 240,493.00 | 240,493.00 |
| Water and Sewer Fund | — | $a_{19}$ | $a_{20}$ | $a_{21}$ |
| Value used | | 16,459.00 | 16,459.00 | 16,459.00 |

(*b*) Expenditure

| Fund | Value | Year 1 | Year 2 | Year 3 |
|---|---|---|---|---|
| *General Fund* | | | | |
| Percentage of completion of Main St. (Clay to Roanoke) | — | $x_3$ | $x_{14}$ | $x_{23}$ |
| Percentage of completion of Main St. (Faculty to north corporate limits) | — | $x_4$ | $x_{15}$ | $x_{24}$ |
| Transfer to Water and Sewer Fund | — | $x_5$ | $x_{16}$ | $x_{25}$ |
| Repayment of prior year's loan ($1000) | — | | $x_1$ | $x_{12}$ |
| Amount of principal due on first-year bonds | — | | $a_9x_2$ | $a_9x_2$ |
| Amount of principal due on second-year bonds | — | | | $a_9x_{13}$ |
| Prevailing interest rate on new bond issue | 0.05 | $a_{18}$ | $a_{18}$ | $a_{18}$ |
| Prevailing interest rate on bank loan | 0.06 | $a_{11}$ | $a_{11}$ | $a_{11}$ |
| Main St. improvement cost (Clay to Roanoke) ($1000) | $87.4 | $a_4$ | $a_4$ | $a_4$ |

**Table 23-1** (*continued*)

(*b*) Expenditure

| Fund | Value | Year 1 | Year 2 | Year 3 |
|---|---|---|---|---|
| Main St. improvement cost (Faculty to north corporate limits) | \$1018.9 | $a_5$ | $a_5$ | $a_5$ |
| Percentage of new bond issue to be returned each year (\$1000) | 10.0 | $a_9$ | $a_9$ | $a_9$ |
| *Water and Sewer Fund* | | | | |
| Percentage of completion of water tank A | — | $x_9$ | $x_{18}$ | $x_{27}$ |
| Percentage of completion of water tank B | — | $x_{10}$ | $x_{19}$ | $x_{28}$ |
| Cost of water tank A (\$1000) | 70.0 | $a_7$ | $a_7$ | $a_7$ |
| Cost of water tank B (\$1000) | 70.0 | $a_8$ | $a_8$ | $a_8$ |
| *Fixed expenditures* | | | | |
| General Fund | — | $a_{13}$ | $a_{15}$ | $a_{17}$ |
| Value used | | \$637,516 | 655,816 | 653,586 |
| Water and Sewer Fund | — | $a_{22}$ | $a_{23}$ | $a_{24}$ |
| Value used | | \$374,161 | 374,161 | 374,161 |

(*c*) Beginning and ending balances

| | | Year 1 | Year 2 | Year 3 |
|---|---|---|---|---|
| *Beginning balances* | | | | |
| General Fund | | $x_6$ | | |
| Water and Sewer Fund | | $x_8$ | | |
| *Ending balances* | | | | |
| General Fund | | $x_7$ | $x_{17}$ | $x_{26}$ |
| Water and Sewer Fund | | $x_{11}$ | $x_{20}$ | $x_{29}$ |

the town may become economically less dependent on population as such. At the same time, however, the physical needs of a rapidly expanding population must be adequately met. The financial resources of the town are limited and must be efficiently allocated not only to meet the present needs but also to provide for future ones. According to the Blacksburg Planning Commission, the most viable area for new business development is along Main St. from Faculty St. north. In addition, Main St. must be widened and improved from Clay St. to Roanoke St. It is desirable that both of these stretches should be completed within the next 3 years. Also, it is essential to improve water storage capacity within this period, which will require two new water tanks. These may be constructed concurrently.

The goal program thus developed contained 29 decision variables, 44 slack or deviational variables, and 35 constraints. The most general equations, in both descriptive and algebraic forms, are presented below. These are simply accounting balance equations, showing the standard of a zero difference between revenues and expenditures in each fund in each year (i.e., no deficits).

*General Fund, year 1*

(Short-term bank loan + amount of new bond issue + property tax revenue + business license taxes + garbage collection charges) + (fixed revenue) −

[(amount spent on Main St., Clay to Roanoke) + (amount spent on Main St., Faculty to north corporate limits) + (interest due on new bonds)] – (fixed expenditures) – (transfer to Water and Sewer Fund) + (beginning balance) – (ending balance) = 0

$$1000x_1 + 1000x_2 + a_1b_1 + a_2b_2 + a_3b_3 + a_{12} - a_4x_3 - a_5x_4 - a_{18}x_2 - a_{13} - x_5 + x_6 - x_7 + s_1 = 0 \qquad (23\text{-}13)$$

*Water and Sewer Fund, year 1*

(Water and sewer service charges) – (amount spent on water tank A) – (amount spent on water tank B) + (transfer from General Fund) – (ending balance) = 0

$$a_6b_4 + a_{19} - a_7x_9 - a_8x_{10} - a_{22} + x_5 + x_8 - x_{11} + s_2 = 0 \qquad (23\text{-}14)$$

*General Fund, year 2*

(Short-term bank loan + amount of new bond issue + property taxes + business license taxes + garbage collection charges) + (fixed revenue) – [(amount spent on Main St., Clay to Roanoke, year 2) + (amount spent on Main St., Faculty to north corporate limits, year 2) + (interest due on year 1 bonds) + (principal due on year 1 bonds) + (interest due on year 2 bonds) + (repayment of year 1 bank loan) + (interest due on year 1 bank loan)] – (fixed expenditures) – (transfer to Water and Sewer Fund) + (beginning balance) – (ending balance) = 0

$$1000x_{12} + 1000x_{13} + a_1b_5 + a_2b_6 + a_3b_7 + a_{14} - a_4(x_{14} - x_3) - a_5(x_{15} - x_4) - a_{18}(x_2 - a_9x_2/1000) - a_9x_2 - a_{18}x_{13} - 1000x_1 - a_{11}x_1 - a_{15} - x_{16} + x_7 - x_{17} + s_3 = 0 \qquad (23\text{-}15)$$

*Water and Sewer Fund, year 2*

(Water and sewer service charges) – (amount spent on water tank A, year 2) – (amount spent on water tank B, year 2) + (transfer from General Fund) + (beginning balance) – (ending balance) = 0

$$a_6b_8 + a_{20} - a_7(x_{18} - x_9) - a_8(x_{19} - x_{10}) - a_{23} + x_{16} + x_{11} - x_{20} + s_4 = 0 \qquad (23\text{-}16)$$

*General Fund, year 3*

(Short-term bank loan + amount of new bond issue + property taxes + business license taxes + garbage collection charges) + (fixed revenue) – [(amount spent on Main St., Faculty to north corporate limits, year 3) + (amount spent on Main St., Clay to Roanoke, year 3) + (interest due on year 1 bonds) + (principal due on year 1 bonds) + (interest due on year 2 bonds) + (principal due on year 2 bonds) + (interest due on year 3 bonds) + (principal due on year 3 bonds) + (repayment of year 2 bank loan) + (interest due on year 2 bank loan)] – (fixed expenditures) – (transfer to Water and Sewer Fund) + (beginning balance) – (ending balance) = 0

$$1000x_{21} + 1000x_{22} + a_1 b_9 + a_2 b_{10} + a_3 b_{11} + a_{16} - a_4(x_{23} - x_{14})$$
$$+ a_5(x_{24} - x_{15}) - a_{18}(x_2 - 2a_9 x_2/1000) - a_9 x_2$$
$$- a_{18}(x_{13} - a_9 x_{13}/1000) - a_9 x_{13} - a_{18} x_{22} - 1000x_{12} - a_{11} x_{12}$$
$$- a_{17} - x_{25} + x_{17} - x_{26} + s_5 = 0 \qquad (23\text{-}17)$$

*Water and Sewer Fund, year 3*

(Water and sewer service charges) – (amount spent on water tank A, year 3) – (amount spent on water tank B, year 3) + (transfer from General Fund) + (beginning balance) – (ending balance) = 0

$$a_6 b_{12} + a_{21} - a_7(x_{17} - x_{18}) - a_8(x_{28} - x_{19})$$
$$- a_{24} + x_{25} + x_{20} - x_{29} + s_6 = 0 \qquad (23\text{-}18)$$

The category "variable revenue" (bank loans, bonds, property taxes, business license taxes, and garbage collection charges) provides for two common forms of external financing, as well as three of the most significant sources of revenue in the town budget. In addition to the above revenue sources the Water and Sewer Fund utilizes the combined water and sewer service charges. The bank loans and bonds were left as unknown in the program, since it was desired to solve only for the amount of financing needed and no more. However, these external sources of funds were constrained by establishing upper limits of borrowing for each year. Thus if external funds were required, they could only be appropriated up to the amounts set by the credit limits. As for the internal sources of revenue, these were precalculated before insertion into the program. They therefore were treated as constraints in the final version. The values used for each of these rates were assumed to be the permissible upper limits for each year as determined by the existing financial policies of the town. These rates, multiplied by their respective computation bases, yielded the maximum amounts of revenue expected in each year from these sources. This is the type of procedure which would normally be used in budget planning. The "fixed revenue" terms in the above equation consisted of budget items which, although variable to some extent, were not considered to contribute significantly to revenue individually; nor were they related to the planned capital expenditures.

As may be noted from the above relationships, the primary financial activity takes place through the General Fund (a procedure common to many municipalities). With respect to major capital expenditures, the General Fund has been utilized for all new road construction or street improvements. The Water and Sewer Fund has been used for construction of new water tanks. Although it is possible for needed extra funds to come into the Water and Sewer Fund from the

General Fund if they are available, it was felt that any revenues accruing from water or sewer sources should be applied only to water and sewer expenditures. Also, the General Fund has access to external financing, but the Water and Sewer Fund does not. Whereas the equations allow for transfers into the Water and Sewer Fund, there were no transfers permitted out of it into the General Fund. It was also necessary to assume for purposes of the program that all capital expenditures would be on a "pay-as-you-go" basis since construction can conceivably take place in all years of the planning period. Furthermore, many of the variables which were developed had to be simplified for inclusion. For instance, the business license tax actually consists of a schedule rather than one flat rate. However, this does not detract from the usefulness of the method for budget programming. The technique will pinpoint the expected degree of completion of projects based on the expected values of various revenues, not rates in particular.

Although the general program can be adapted to changing environmental conditions by forecasting the expected values of the revenue and expenditure coefficients for each year in the planning period, for the purpose of clarity this was not done in this paper. Instead it was assumed that for the 3-year period under consideration, factors such as gross business receipts, water consumption, etc., remained constant.

By substituting the various coefficients, constants, and variables into the balance equations and rearranging, the appropriate constraints were written as shown in Table 23-2.

## Solution

The goal programming solution is based primarily upon the priority structure of the established goals. In other words, the program dictates the solution according to the policy of the administration. As it turns out, the administration has no explicit priorities for the suggested standards. The following were obtained from the mayor and town manager:

$p_1$ Because the town issued $50,000 in bonds in 1968, there is no desire to have further bonded indebtedness in the first year. The first priority then is (*a*) to reduce bond issues in that year and further (*b*) to eliminate any deficits in the budget in any year.

$p_2$ Since it often is desirable to obtain external financing before attempting to start any projects, the second priority, $p_2$, is assigned to achieving credit limits for bank loans and bonds.

$p_3$ The third priority is to complete the improvement of the two Main St. sections. The completion of a short section between Clay St. and Roanoke St. is assumed to be twice as urgent as one between Faculty St. and the north corporate limits.

**Table 23-2 Program constraints**

*General Fund, year 1*

$$1000x_1 + 950x_2 - 87.4x_3 - 1018.9x_4 - x_5 + x_6 - x_7 + s_1 = 47{,}305$$

*Water and Sewer Fund, year 1*

$$-x_5 - x_8 + 70x_9 + 70x_{10} + x_{11} + s_2 = 3129$$

*General Fund, year 2*

$$-1060x_1 - 145x_2 + 87.4x_3 + 1018.9x_4 + x_7 + 1000x_{12} + 950x_{13} - 87.4x_{14}$$
$$-1018.9x_{15} - x_{16} - x_{17} + s_3 = 1614$$

*Water and Sewer Fund, year 2*

$$70x_9 + 70x_{10} + x_{11} + x_{16} - 70x_{18} - 70x_{19} - x_{20} + s_4 = 582$$

*General Fund, year 3*

$$-140x_2 - 1060x_{12} - 145x_{13} + 87.4x_{14} + 1018.9x_{15} + x_{17} + 1000x_{21} + 950x_{22}$$
$$-87.4x_{23} - 1018.9x_{24} - x_{25} - x_{26} + s_5 = 1934$$

*Water and Sewer Fund, year 3*

$$-70x_{18} - 70x_{19} - x_{20} - x_{25} + 70x_{27} + 70x_{28} + x_{29} + s_6 = 23{,}226$$

| | |
|---|---|
| $x_1 + d_7^- = 100$ | $x_{16} - d_{25}^+ + s_{26} = 0$ |
| $x_2 + s_8 = 0$ | $x_{17} - d_{27}^+ + s_{28} = 0$ |
| $x_3 + d_9^- = 100$ | $x_{18} + d_{29}^- = 100$ |
| $x_4 + d_{10}^- = 100$ | $x_{19} + d_{30}^- = 100$ |
| $x_5 - d_{11}^+ + s_{12} = 0$ | $x_{20} - d_{31}^+ + s_{32} = 0$ |
| $x_6 + s_{13} = 0$ | $x_{21} + d_{33}^- = 100$ |
| $x_7 - d_{14}^+ + s_{15} = 0$ | $x_{22} + d_{34}^- = 250$ |
| $x_8 + s_{16} = 0$ | $x_{23} + d_{35}^- = 100$ |
| $x_9 + d_{17}^- = 100$ | $x_{24} + d_{36}^- = 100$ |
| $x_{10} + d_{18}^- = 100$ | $x_{25} - d_{37}^+ + s_{38} = 0$ |
| $x_{11} - d_{19}^+ + s_{20} = 0$ | $x_{26} - d_{39}^+ + s_{40} = 0$ |
| $x_{12} + d_{21}^- = 100$ | $x_{27} + d_{41}^- = 100$ |
| $x_{13} + d_{22}^- = 200$ | $x_{28} + d_{42}^- = 100$ |
| $x_{14} + d_{23}^- = 100$ | $x_{29} - d_{43}^+ + s_{44} = 0$ |
| $x_{15} + d_{24}^- = 100$ | |

$p_4$ The fourth priority is to complete the construction of two water tanks. It is desired to complete tank A before tank B is considered. Therefore, twice the weight is assigned to the completion of tank A.

$p_5$ While any surpluses resulting in the General Fund should be transferred to the Water and Sewer Fund, the fifth priority is to minimize any such transfers since they represent "unearned" subsidies to the receiving fund.

$p_6$ The last priority is the minimization of ending balances in the General and Water and Sewer Funds.

The objective function then becomes:

$$\begin{aligned}\text{Minimize } z = {} & p_1(s_1 + s_2 + s_3 + s_4 + s_5 + s_6) + p_1(s_8 + s_{12} + s_{13} \\ & + s_{15} + s_{16} + s_{20} + s_{22} + s_{26} + s_{28} \\ & + s_{32} + s_{34} + s_{38} + s_{40} + s_{44}) \\ & + p_2(d_7^+ + d_{21}^+ + d_{33}^+) + 2p_3(d_9^- + d_{23}^- \\ & + d_{35}^-) + p_3(d_{10}^- + d_{24}^- + d_{36}^-) \\ & + 2p_4(d_{17}^- + d_{29}^- + d_{41}^-) + p_4(d_{18}^- + d_{30}^- + d_{42}^-) \\ & + p_5(d_{11}^+ + d_{25}^+ + d_{37}^+) \\ & + p_6(d_{14}^+ + d_{19}^+ + d_{27}^- + d_{31}^- + d_{39}^- + d_{43}^-) \end{aligned} \tag{23-19}$$

subject to the constraints set forth in Table 23-2.

The results of the computer solution are presented in Table 23-3. With the output variables shown in the table, the following achievement of standards related to each priority resulted:

$p_1$ Achieved. No bonds were issued in year 1.

$p_2$ Achieved. The full borrowing limits were utilized for bank loans and bonds.

**Table 23-3 Solution results**

| | Computed value | | |
|---|---|---|---|
| | Year 1 | Year 2 | Year 3 |
| (*a*) Revenue variables | | | |
| *General Fund* | | | |
| Amount of 1-year bank loan (in \$1000) | 100.00 | 100.00 | 100.00 |
| Amount of new bond issue (in \$1000) | 0 | 200.00 | 250.00 |
| *Water and Sewer Fund* | | | |
| Transfers from General Fund | 0 | 0 | 0 |
| (*b*) Expenditure variables | | | |
| *General Fund* | | | |
| Percentage of completion of Main St. (Clay St. to Roanoke St.) | 60.29 | 100.00 | 100.00 |
| Percentage of completion of Main St. (Faculty St. to north corporate limits) | — | 14.49 | 24.36 |
| Ending balances | 0 | 0 | 0 |
| *Water and Sewer Fund* | | | |
| Percentage of completion of water tank A | 4.47 | 8.11 | 36.82 |
| Percentage of completion of water tank B | — | — | — |
| Ending balances | 0 | 0 | 0 |

$p_3$ Not achieved. Clay St. to Roanoke St. section is completed in year 2, but Faculty St. to north corporate limits is completed by only 24 percent in year 3.

$p_4$ Not achieved. Water tank A is completed by only 37 percent at the end of year 3 and tank B is not even considered.

$p_5$ Achieved. Road improvements exhausted funds in the General Fund and there were none to be transferred to the Water and Sewer Fund.

$p_6$ Achieved. All funds were exhausted and there were no ending balances.

This example has shown that, within the existing limitations of financing, tax schedules, and service charges, as well as the priority structure, it was not possible to achieve full completion of all projects. However, the most important standards were met consistent with the assigned priorities. This type of situation is quite common in municipal planning.

## 23-4 THE MATHEMATICS OF GOAL PROGRAMMING

As mentioned earlier, goal programming is just another version of mathematical programming and can be solved accordingly. If, for instance, the objective function includes weights for priority levels, the standard linear programming simplex method process can be utilized to find a solution. If the priorities are to be solved in steps, then the first step is solved using the simplex method for only that part of the objective function reflecting the first priority. The objective function is then replaced by the second priority part, and the search for an optimal solution continues. This process continues until an optimal solution is found for the last priority. The resulting values of the decision variables will then be the optimal solution according to the hierarchy of priorities used.

## PROBLEMS

**23-1** Fill in the blanks with the appropriate word(s).

(*a*) Goal programming is similar to linear programming except that some or all of the constraints are expressed as goal equations with differences of two ____________ variables, denoted ________ and ________.

(*b*) The objective of goal programming is to ____________ a selective set of these ____________ variables.

(*c*) For each constraint the two ______________ variables can never assume ______________ values and only one can assume a ______________ value at the same time.

(*d*) The variable $d^-$ represents ______________________________ and the variable $d^+$ represents ______________________________.

**23-2** Find a solution to the following goal programming problem by using the graphical technique:

$$\text{Minimize } z = p_1 d_1^- + p_2 d_4^+ + 5p_3 d_2^- + 3p_4 d_3^- + p_4 d_1^+$$

subject to:

$$\begin{aligned} x_1 + x_2 + d_1^- \qquad\qquad\qquad - d_1^+ \qquad &= 80 \\ x_1 + \qquad + d_2^- \qquad\qquad\qquad &= 70 \\ x_2 \qquad + d_3^- \qquad\qquad &= 45 \\ x_1 + x_2 \qquad\qquad + d_4^- \qquad - d_4^+ &= 90 \end{aligned}$$

**23-3** Set up and find the solution by the graphical technique for the following standards:

$$3x_1 + 2x_2 \le 12\} \quad \text{priority 2}$$

$$\left.\begin{aligned} -x_1 + x_2 &\ge 4 \\ x_1 + x_2 &\ge 8 \end{aligned}\right\} \quad \text{priority 1}$$

**23-4** Go to the library and find a relevant application of goal programming. In about 500 words describe:

(*a*) The general nature of the problem being investigated
(*b*) The standards set for relevant variables
(*c*) The rankings or ratings attached to each standard
(*d*) The nature of the constraints (other than those directly involving the standards)
(*e*) The results obtained
(*f*) The general advantages and disadvantages of goal programming in the problem being investigated

**23-5** Working with your instructor, take a sample from one of the data sets presented in App. D and set up a goal program. This should involve, first, constraints:

(*a*) Regression relationships between the identified *y* and *x* variables (one relationship for each *y* variable)
(*b*) Possible upper and lower limits on any variable
(*c*) Set values for any variables beyond the control of the assumed decision maker
(*d*) Levels of standards

as well as an objective function with deviational variables "standardized" by their standard deviations.

Run the program using available linear programming codes in your computing center.

Alter the priorities (or weights of importance) attached to the deviational variables and rerun the program to determine corresponding sensitivities.

## REFERENCES

### Theory

23-1. Charnes, A. B., and W. W. Cooper: *Management Models and Industrial Application of Linear Programming*, 2 vols., Wiley, New York, 1961.

23-2. Ijiri, Y.: *Management Goals and Accounting for Control*, North-Holland, Amsterdam, 1965.

**Applications**

23-3. Dickey, J. W.: "Minimizing Economic Segregation Through Transit System Changes: A Goal Programming Approach," in G. F. Newell (Ed.), *Proceedings of the Fifth International Symposium on the Theory of Traffic Flow and Transportation*, American-Elsevier, New York, 1972.

23-4. Dickey, J. W., and A. W. Steiss: "Optimizing the Distribution of Housing in Large Scale Developments," *Journal of the Town Planning Institute*, vol. 56, no. 3, March, 1970.

23-5. Lee, S. M., and W. R. Sevebeck: "An Aggregate Model for Municipal Economic Planning," *Policy Sciences*, vol. 2, 1971.

CHAPTER

# TWENTY-FOUR

# PERT

The success of any large-scale program can be very much dependent upon the quality of the planning, scheduling, and control of the various projects in the program. Unless some type of planning and coordination tool is used, the number of projects does not need to be very large before management becomes difficult. One such tool used on large-scale projects to help management in expediting and controlling the utilization of personnel, materials, facilities, and time is the program evaluation and review technique (PERT). This technique is employed to pinpoint critical areas in a program so that necessary adjustments can be made to meet the scheduled completion date.

PERT was developed in 1958–1959 as a research and development tool for the U.S. Navy Polaris Missile Program. Through its use, the Polaris program was completed 18 to 24 months ahead of its originally scheduled completion date. Since 1959, PERT has been utilized successfully in almost every type of large-scale industry. Many federally sponsored projects even require its use through specification of work programs highlighting interrelated work elements. The critical-path method (CPM) is a similar planning and coordinating tool.

## 24-1 PERT NETWORKS†

The first step in any PERT analysis is to identify the projects or tasks which must be accomplished before the overall program is completed. Each task, called an *activity*, requires time and resources, and represents work that must be done. Resources might be personnel, money, materials, facilities, and/or space. It should

† Part of the discussion in Secs. 24-1 to 24-3 is adapted from Gillett, Ref. 24-1.

be clear that not all activities can be accomplished at the same time. Some cannot be started until others have been finished.

The relationship between all activities in a project can be represented by a network involving nodes and arrows. The arrows represent the various activities, and the nodes the start and completion of these activities. Specifically, the tail of each arrow in Fig. 24-1 represents the start of an activity and the head the completion of that activity. The circles or nodes are called *events*. They indicate the completion of all activities coming into the node and the beginning of all those leaving the node. Events do not require time or resources; they are simply milestones, or points in time, signifying the completion of some activities and the beginning of others. An event is said to be *accomplished* when *all* activities leading into that event are finished. Activities leading from a given event cannot begin until the event is accomplished. An activity that begins at event $i$ and ends at event $j$ will be referred to as *activity* $(i, j)$.

Event 1 in Fig. 24-1 indicates the start of the program and event 7 represents its completion. Event 4 is not accomplished until activities (1, 4) and (3, 4) are both completed. Also, activity (4, 7) cannot begin until event 4 is accomplished. The final event, 7, is accomplished when activities (5, 7), (6, 7), and (4, 7) are all completed.

The guidelines and rules for constructing a network to represent the interrelationship of activities are:

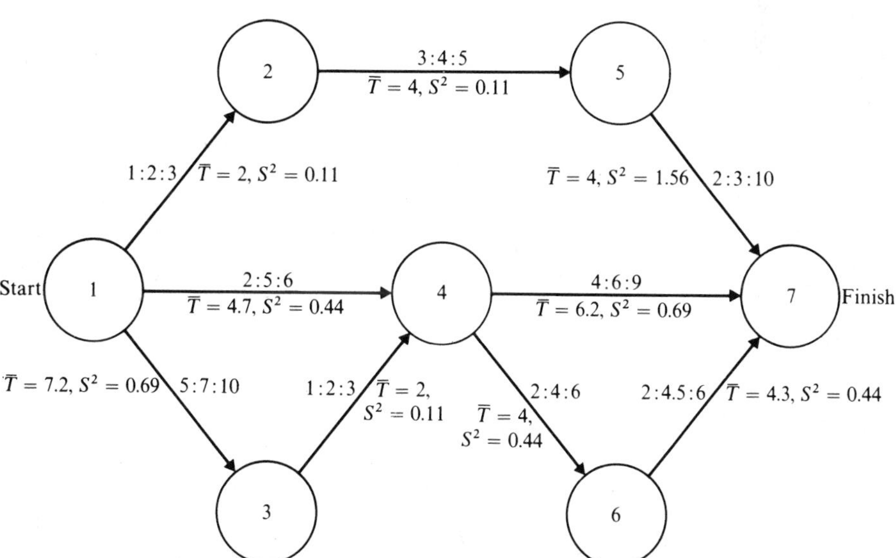


**Figure 24-1** Example PERT network for setting up a social services information and referral system. (*Source: Adapted from Ref. 24-1, p. 439.*)

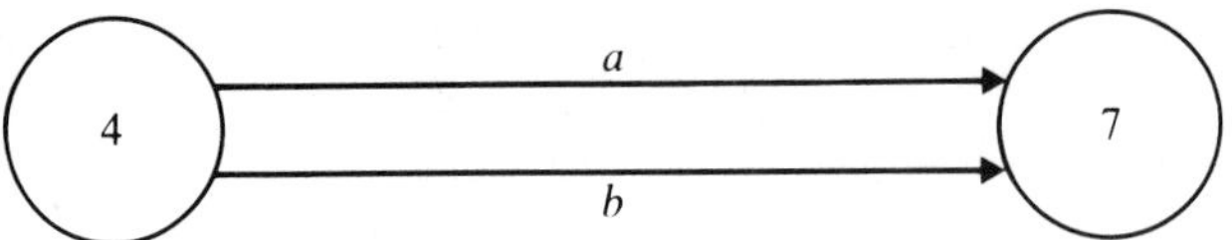


**Figure 24-2** Two activities from event 4 to event 7.

1. Event 1 is the start of the project. All activities not preceded by other activities emanate from event 1.
2. Event $M$ denotes the completion of the program, where $M$ is the maximum number of events.
3. Activity $(i, j)$ starts at event $i$ and ends at event $j$.
4. For each activity $(i, j)$, $i < j$.
5. For each $j$, all activities of the form $(i, j)$ must be completed before event $j$ is considered accomplished.
6. Each activity $(i, j)$ must be unique.

Consider the implications of the last rule. If two or more activities need to start at event $i$ and go to event $j$, dummy events and dummy activities with zero time are set up. For instance, suppose two different activities, $a$ and $b$, need to start at event 4 and end at event 7. This situation could *not* be represented as shown in Fig. 24-2. Instead, a dummy event, 8, and a dummy activity (8, 7) are introduced. This is illustrated in Fig. 24-3. The dashed line from event 8 to event 7 represents the dummy activity. The dummy event 8 indicates the completion of activity $a$, while event 7 represents the completion of both activities $a$ and $b$.

As another example use of rule 6, suppose $a$, $b$, $c$, and $d$ are four activities that must be accomplished. Activities $a$ and $b$ must precede $c$, but only $b$ needs to come before $d$. This is attained by adding a dummy activity, as shown by the dashed line in Fig. 24-4.

Time estimates for each activity in a PERT network must be supplied before the network is a useful planning and management tool. In some cases a single best-possible time estimate of each activity is utilized. But, to highlight the uncertainty in such figures, three estimates normally are employed:

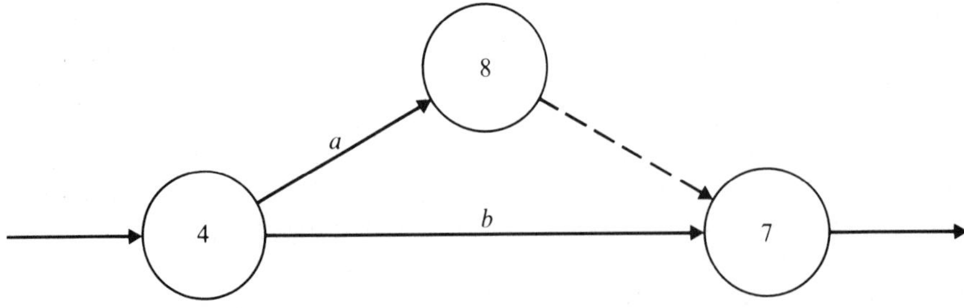


**Figure 24-3** Revised PERT network of Fig. 24-2 with dummy event and activity.

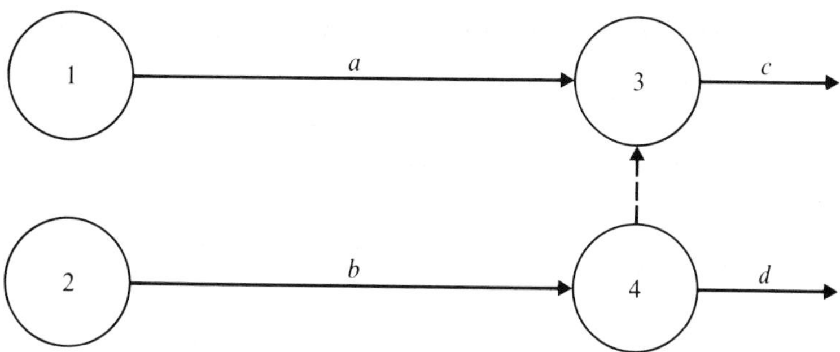


**Figure 24-4** PERT network with dummy activity (4, 3).

$A$ = optimistic time—the expected time if everything proceeds without delays
$M$ = most likely time—the expected time if the activity proceeds in the usual fashion
$B$ = pessimistic time—the expected time if just about everything goes wrong

Based on these estimates, the mean completion time for each activity is estimated to be

$$\bar{T} = \frac{A + 4M + B}{6} \tag{24-1}$$

The variance of the completion time of each activity has then been found to be

$$S^2 = \left(\frac{B - A}{6}\right)^2 \tag{24-2}$$

## 24-2 A SIMPLE EXAMPLE

As a first illustration, suppose we are trying to set up a social services information and referral (I&R) system in a region and our concern is to get it operating as soon as possible. Unfortunately, some preliminary projects must be started and completed before this can be done. Looking at Table 24-1 and back at Fig. 24-1, we find, for example, that we first must develop an application [activity (1, 3)] for funding to collect the necessary data (e.g., on each service, its types and times of operation, etc.). We then must send in the application and wait for approval [activity (3, 4)]. The next step would be to collect the data and carry out the prototype experiment [activity (4, 6)], and subsequently to develop a study report, operating manual, and the like [activity (6, 7)]. These are but a few links in the overall network of subprojects that must be completed before the I&R system is ready for operation.

**Table 24-1 Activities needed to set up the example information and referral system**

| From node | To node | | Optimistic time, months | Most likely time, months | Pessimistic time, months |
|---|---|---|---|---|---|
| 1 | 2 | Develop application for personnel funds from federal health agency | 1 | 2 | 3 |
| 1 | 3 | Develop application for data collection funds from state welfare agency | 5 | 7 | 10 |
| 1 | 4 | Use available funds to design I&R system and prototype experiment | 2 | 5 | 6 |
| 2 | 5 | Apply for personnel funds | 3 | 4 | 5 |
| 3 | 4 | Apply for data collection funds | 1 | 2 | 3 |
| 4 | 6 | Undertake data collection and prototype experiment | 2 | 4 | 6 |
| 4 | 7 | Purchase equipment and material needed for full-scale I&R system | 4 | 6 | 9 |
| 5 | 7 | Hire personnel | 2 | 3 | 10 |
| 6 | 7 | Develop study report, operating manuals, etc. | 2 | 4.5 | 6 |

The optimistic, likely, and pessimistic completion times for each activity listed in Table 24-1 are shown separated by colons on the top of the corresponding link in Fig. 24-1. The corresponding means and variances, calculated from Eqs. (24-1) and (24-2), are then shown below the activity links. To illustrate: from Table 24-1 the activity (1, 2) has times of 1, 2, and 3 months, thereby giving a mean of

$$\bar{T} = \frac{1 + 4(2) + 3}{6} = 2.0$$

and a variance of

$$S^2 = \left(\frac{3 - 1}{6}\right)^2 = \frac{1}{9} = 0.11$$

## 24-3 OPTIMAL COMPLETION TIMES AND CRITICAL PATHS

Given that we want to minimize the time to become operational and that each preliminary activity *must* be done (and in the order shown), we first try to locate that path through the network which would give the longest time we will have to wait to finish. Specifically, the activity times are summed for each possible path leading from the starting to the final event, and the largest sum is the earliest expected completion time. Fortunately it is not necessary to sum the activity times over each possible path for each event. Instead we define:

$\bar{T}_{ij}$ = expected completion time of *activity* $(i, j)$

$E_j$ = earliest expected completion time of *event* $j$

Then, for a fixed value of $j$, say $j^*$, $E_{j^*}$ is given by

$$E_{j*} = \max_{i} [E_i + \bar{T}_{ij*}] \tag{24-3}$$

where $i$ ranges over all activities in the category $(i, j^*)$. For the events in Fig. 24-1:

$$E_1 = 0$$

$$E_2 = E_1 + \bar{T}_{12} = 0 + 2 = 2$$

$$E_3 = E_1 + \bar{T}_{13} = 0 + 7.2 = 7.2$$

$$E_4 = \max_{i=1,3} [(E_1 + \bar{T}_{14}), (E_3 + \bar{T}_{34})]$$

$$= \max_{i=1,3} [(0 + 4.7), (7.2 + 2)]$$

$$= 9.2, \text{ with } i = 3$$

$$E_5 = \max_{i=2} [E_2 + \bar{T}_{25}] = 2 + 4 = 6$$

$$E_6 = \max_{i=4} [E_4 + \bar{T}_{46}] = 9.2 + 4 = 13.2$$

$$E_7 = \max_{i=4,5,6} [(E_4 + \bar{T}_{47}), (E_5 + \bar{T}_{57}), (E_6 + \bar{T}_{67})]$$

$$= \max_{i=4,5,6} [(9.2 + 6.2), (6 + 4), (13.2 + 4.3)]$$

$$= 17.5, \text{ with } i = 6$$

These $E$ values are shown in Fig. 24-5. The $E$ time for each event indicates the earliest time the event can be accomplished if each activity $j$ on every path leading to the given event is completed in exactly $E_j$ units of time. The path followed to compute the $E$ value for the *sink* or *final event* is called the *critical path of the network*. The sum of the activity times for the critical path is greater than the sum of the activity times for *any other path* through the network. In terms of our example, then, we cannot expect to get our I&R system operational for at least 17.5 months.

Another measure often associated with each event in a PERT network is the *latest allowable event completion time*, $L_i$. It is the longest time an event can take without delaying the scheduled completion date of the program if all succeeding events are completed as anticipated.

To calculate $L_i$ for a given event, $i$, the activity times are cumulatively subtracted from the scheduled project completion time along the various paths between the given event and the final event. The smallest result is the $L_i$ for that event. Suppose we define

$$L_i = \text{latest allowable event completion time for event } i$$

Then for a fixed value of $i$, say $i^*$, $L_{i*}$ is given by

$$L_{i*} = \min_{j} [L_j - \bar{T}_{i*j}] \tag{24-4}$$

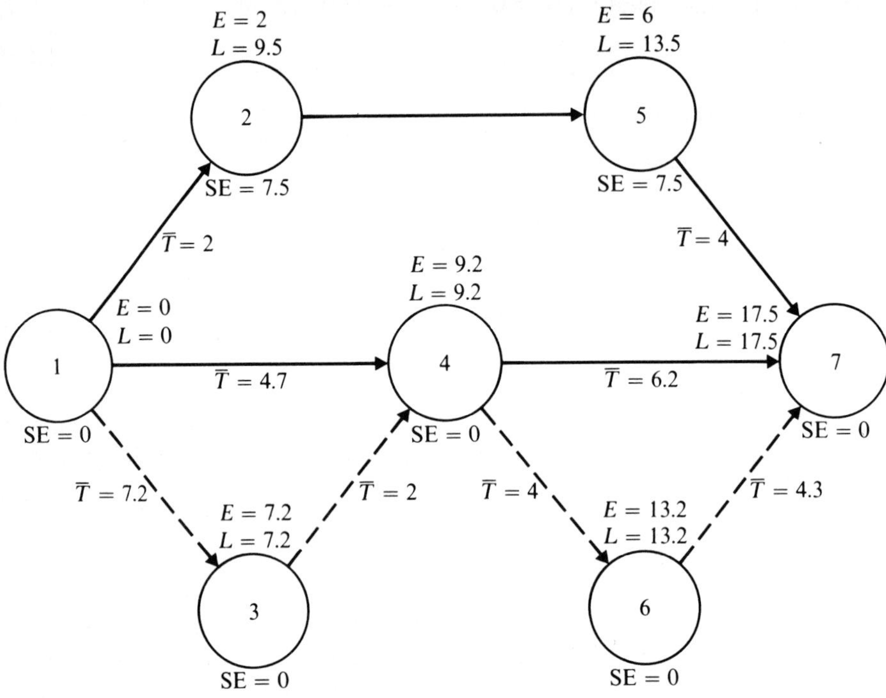


**Figure 24-5** PERT network with $\bar{T}$, $L$, and SE for each event. (*Source: Adopted from Ref. 24-1, p. 441.*)

where $j$ is defined for all activities in the category $(i^*, j)$. Hence, for $m$ events, Eq. (24-4) is employed in backward (*recursive*) order, starting with the last event, $m$, and continuing to the first. In Fig. 24-5 the latest allowable completion time for event 7, $L_7$, is taken to be the same as the earliest expected completion time: $E_7 = 17.5$ months. The $L$ for the final event, however, is generally taken as the scheduled completion time for the *whole* program and thus may or may not be the same as the $E$ for that event.

The $L$ values in Fig. 24-5 are calculated from Eq. (24-4) as follows:

$$L_7 = E_7 = 17.5$$

$$L_6 = \min_{j=7} [L_7 - \bar{T}_{67}] = 17.5 - 4.3 = 13.2$$

$$L_5 = \min_{j=7} [L_7 - \bar{T}_{57}] = 17.5 - 4.0 = 13.5$$

$$\begin{aligned} L_4 &= \min_{j=7,\,6} [(L_7 - \bar{T}_{47}), (L_6 - \bar{T}_{46})] \\ &= \min_{j=7,\,6} [(17.5 - 6.2), (13.2 - 4.0)] \\ &= 9.2, \text{ with } j = 6 \end{aligned}$$

$$L_3 = \min_{j=4} [L_4 - \bar{T}_{34}] = 9.2 - 2.0 = 7.2$$

$$L_2 = \min_{j=5} [L_5 - \bar{T}_{25}] = 13.5 - 4.0 = 9.5$$

$$L_1 = \min_{j=4,3,2} [(L_4 - \bar{T}_{14}), (L_3 - \bar{T}_{13}), (L_2 - \bar{T}_{12})]$$

$$= \min_{j=4,3,2} [(9.2 - 4.7), (7.2 - 7.2), (9.5 - 2.0)]$$

$$= 0, \text{ with } j = 3$$

With respect to our I&R system, we might conclude, for instance, that we can absorb a delay in getting funds for personnel (event 5) up to 13.5 months after the start of the program.

An event slack time, SE, can now be defined. For each event it is the amount of time the event can be delayed without affecting the scheduled completion time for the project. In equation form this becomes

$$\mathrm{SE}_j = L_j - E_j \tag{24-5}$$

Events that have "small" slack times are considered to be "critical" and should be watched very closely. To facilitate events with small slack times, resources can be shifted from activities leading to the events with larger slack times to activities that affect the $E$ events with the smaller slack times. For example, in Fig. 24-5, events 2 and 5 have rather large slack times, so we might want to consider shifting some resources from activities (1, 2), (2, 5), and/or (5, 7) to activities on the critical path (dashed line). This would tend to speed up the activities on the critical path and to slow down those between events 2, 5, and 7. This transfer should decrease the earliest expected completion time for the program.

Returning to our information and referral system illustration, we find, for example, that development of the application for personnel funds (event 2) can be held off 7.5 months without lengthening the critical path. Hence we initially may want to divert some existing staff time to, say, the application for data collection funds. If this can be developed sooner, the total program of 17.5 months might be reduced.

As noted, the critical path is designated by a dashed line in Fig. 24-5. In our illustration we can see that all the events on the line have 0 slack times. But this is also true for the events on the path 1 to 4 to 7. This is not a critical path, however. To be on the critical path, an activity $(i, j)$ must satisfy three conditions:

$$(a) \quad L_i - E_i = \mathrm{SE}_m \tag{24-6}$$

$$(b) \quad L_j - E_j = \mathrm{SE}_m \tag{24-7}$$

$$(c) \quad E_j - E_i = L_j - L_i = \bar{T}_{ij} \tag{24-8}$$

where $\mathrm{SE}_m$ is the slack time for the final event. All activities on the path 1 to 3 to 4 to 6 to 7 in Fig. 24-5 satisfy these conditions, so that is the critical path.

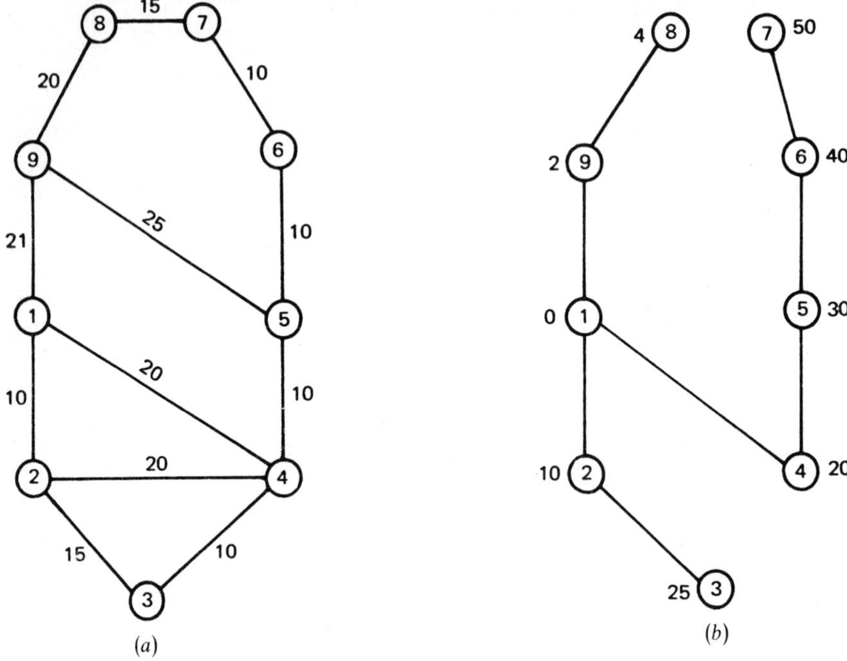


**Figure 24-6** Simplified representation of (*a*) the highway network and (*b*) a minimum time path tree in the San Francisco Bay area. (*Source: Ref. 24-5, p. 554.*)

In summary, one of the main objectives of a PERT analysis is to pinpoint the critical path so that resources from outside the system or from activities on noncritical paths can be supplied to activities on the critical path if needed. In connection with this, when the actual work begins on a project, the PERT network should be updated either weekly, monthly, or as needed, with all of the latest available information. This information might include scheduled dates, available resources, activity time estimates, actual activity completion times, etc.

## 24-4 MINIMUM TRAVEL TIME PATHS†

A common use of PERT-type analyses is in transportation planning, where interest often centers on finding the minimum time path over a street network between a pair of points (centroids of areal zones) in a city or region. The corresponding times are needed as inputs to most of the land-use and travel models employed in the planning process. Note, however, that the process to be utilized here is similar to but opposite to that demonstrated in the preceding sections: we want the *minimum*, not maximum time path. A "min" should thus be substituted for the

† Some of the discussion in this section is adapted from Ref. 24-5.

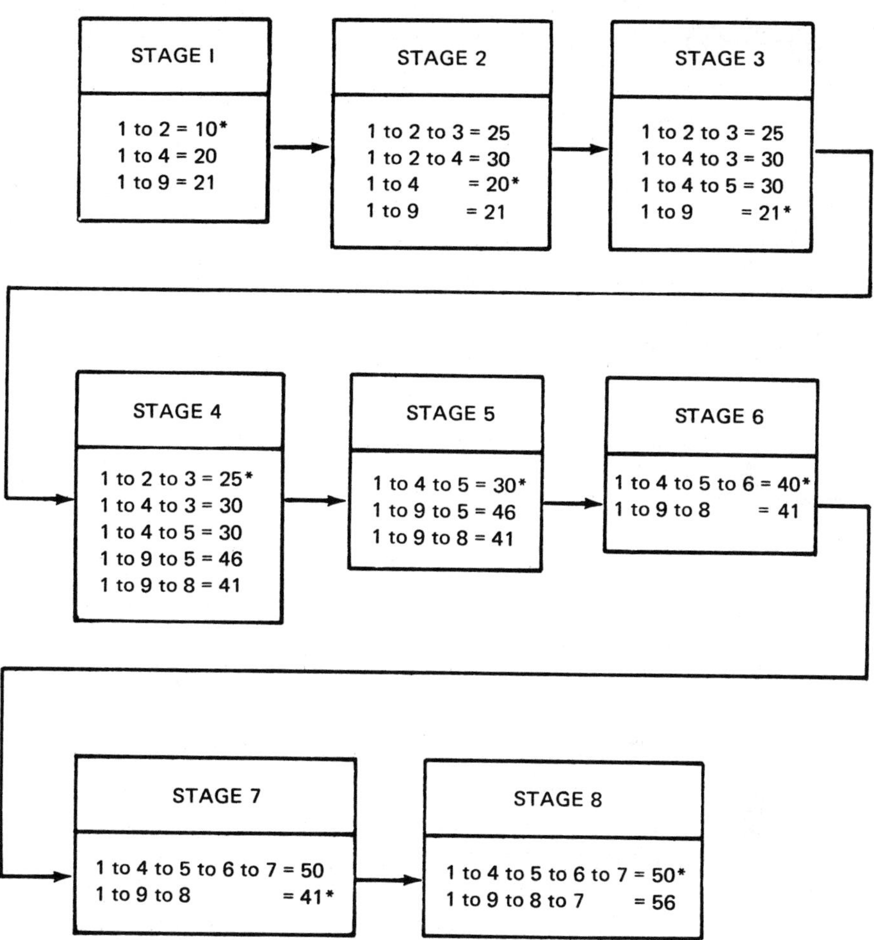


**Figure 24-7** Complete set of calculations to obtain minimum time path "tree" from the network in Fig. 24-6 (asterisks indicate minimum time at each stage). (*Source: Ref. 24-5, p. 555.*)

"max" in Eq. (24-3). Also, most transportation analyses concentrate on the peak time on a link, so that no means or variances are calculated as in Eqs. (24-1) and (24-2).

As an example of the approach we will take the overly simplified network in Fig. 24-6 representing the highway system in the nine counties of the San Francisco Bay area. Travel times are marked on the links, and our interest is centered on finding the minimum time route between centroid 1 and centroid 7. We start by determining the minimum path from centroid 1 over all links connecting to it. Thus, min $(21, 20, 10) = 10$ on the link from 1 to 2. In the second stage, we find the minimum total (from 1) time path from centroids 1 and 2 to all centroids directly connected to 1 or 2. So, min $(10 + 15, 10 + 20, 20, 21) = 20$, which corresponds to the 1-to-4 path. Continuing in a similar manner, we take the minimum total time from 1 to 2 to all connecting centroids except 4, from 1 to 4 to all connecting centroids except 2, and from 1 to all connecting centroids except 2 and 4. This gives min $(10 + 15, 20 + 10, 20 + 10, 21) = 21$, which is the time on the link from 1 to 9. The remaining calculations along with those shown above are presented in detail in Fig. 24-7, with the resulting minimum time paths shown together in Fig. 24-6. An interesting outcome of this procedure is that in finding the minimum time path to the farthest centroid, we also find the minimum time paths to all other centroids.

The output of the algorithm therefore is a set of minimum travel time paths known as a *minimum path tree*, emanating from one centroid. Figure 24-6*b* displays the tree for the first centroid in the network in Fig. 24-6*a*. It should be noted that this tree was developed for only one centroid. A complete analysis would require the building of trees from all centroids.

## PROBLEMS

**24-1** Fill in the blanks with the appropriate word(s).

(*a*) PERT stands for __________ __________ and __________ __________.

(*b*) CPM stands for __________ __________ __________.

(*c*) Each task in a PERT network is called a ____________________.

(*d*) A ____________________ represents the completion of all activities coming into a node.

(*e*) An event is said to be ____________ when ____________ activities leading into that event are ____________.

(*f*) If two or more activities need to start at one event and end up at a second but same event, then ____________ events and activities with ____________ times are set up.

(*g*) The three times usually associated with an activity are the ________________, ________________, and ________________.

(*h*) The path through the PERT network which gives the maximum time to the ____________ event is called the ____________ path.

(*i*) The path suggested in (*h*) also gives the ____________ ____________ completion time.

(*j*) The longest time an event can take without delaying the scheduled completion date of the overall program is called the ________________.

(*k*) Equations employed "backward" are known as ________________________.

(*l*) The difference between the latest allowable and earliest expected event completion time is called the ________________________.

(*m*) A ________________________ shows the ________________________ between a zonal centroid and all other centroids.

**24-2** Set up a PERT network for the tasks shown on the following chart. Simply show each activity letter as a link leading into each event (numbered).

**House construction activities**

| | Activities | Preceding activities | Times *A* | *M* | *B* |
|---|---|---|---|---|---|
| *a* | Start project | | 0.5 | 1.0 | 1.5 |
| *b* | Select building site | *a* | 0.6 | 1.0 | 2.0 |
| *c* | Dig basement and foundation | *b* | 0.2 | 0.6 | 1.0 |
| *d* | Purchase carpet | *a* | 0.2 | 0.4 | 0.6 |
| *e* | Purchase basic precut house | *a* | 0.5 | 0.7 | 0.9 |
| *f* | Construct basic precut house | *e, t* | 1.4 | 2.0 | 2.6 |
| *g* | Lay carpet | *d, p* | 0.2 | 0.4 | 0.5 |
| *h* | Complete plumbing | *i* | 1.5 | 2.0 | 2.6 |
| *i* | Lay flooring | *j, l* | 0.6 | 1.5 | 2.3 |
| *j* | Put on roof | *f* | 0.8 | 1.0 | 1.4 |
| *k* | Pour basement and foundation | *q* | 0.3 | 0.5 | 0.7 |
| *l* | Put in stairs to basement | *f* | 0.2 | 0.4 | 0.6 |
| *m* | Put up guttering | *n* | 0.2 | 0.4 | 0.6 |
| *n* | Paint outside of house | *j* | 1.0 | 1.5 | 2.0 |
| *p* | Paint inside of house | *w* | 2.2 | 2.5 | 2.8 |
| *q* | Rough-in plumbing | *c* | 0.8 | 1.1 | 1.4 |
| *r* | Wire house for intercom and radio | *i* | 0.1 | 0.1 | 0.1 |
| *s* | Wire house for electricity | *i* | 0.8 | 1.2 | 1.6 |
| *t* | Finish preparation for house construction | *k* | 0.2 | 0.4 | 0.6 |
| *u* | Grade and landscape | *m* | 1.5 | 2.0 | 2.5 |
| *v* | Hang pictures | *p* | 0.1 | 0.2 | 0.3 |
| *w* | Finish walls and ceiling | *h, r, s* | 0.4 | 0.5 | 0.6 |
| *x* | Finish project | *g* | 0.2 | 0.3 | 0.4 |

*Source:* Adapted from Ref. 24-1.

**24-3** For the PERT network set up in Prob. 24-2 find:
(*a*) The critical path events and corresponding maximum time
(*b*) The earliest expected completion time for each event
(*c*) The latest allowable completion time for each event
(*d*) The slack time for each event

**24-4** Assume that Fig. 24-6*a* is a PERT network and that the numbers are the mean times. Find the same elements as in Prob. 24-3. (Some thought will indicate the direction in which the arrows *must* point in the network.)

**24-5** Assume that Fig. 24-1 is a highway network and that the link means are travel times. Find the minimum time path tree and corresponding times for the first centroid.

**24-6** Go to the library and find a relevant application of PERT. In about 500 words describe:
(*a*) The general nature of the program being planned
(*b*) The results obtained
(*c*) The general advantages and disadvantages of PERT in the situation being studied

**24-7** If you have access to a relevant PERT or CPM computer program, work with your instructor to set up and solve the SOON chart developed in Prob. 17-2. You should show:
(*a*) The maximum time at which the latest forecasted event is expected to occur.
(*b*) The events lying on the critical path found in (*a*).
(*c*) The sensitivity of the maximum time, and changes in the critical path events if the time to achieve each of the existing events on the critical path is sped up by 15 percent.

## REFERENCES

### Theory

24-1. Gillett, B. E.: *Introduction to Operations Research*, McGraw-Hill, New York, 1976.
24-2. Moder, J. J., and C. R. Phillips: *Project Management with CPM and PERT*, 2d ed., Van Nostrand, New York, 1970.
24-3. Wiest, I. D., and F. K. Levy: *A Management Guide to PERT/CPM*, Prentice-Hall, Englewood Cliffs, N.J., 1969.

### Applications

24-4. Archibald, R. D., and R. L. Villoria: *Network-Based Management Systems (PERT/CPM)*, Wiley, New York, 1966.
24-5. Dickey, J. W. (senior author): *Metropolitan Transportation Planning*, McGraw-Hill, New York, 1975.
24-6. Levin, R., and C. A. Kirkpatrick: *Planning and Control with PERT/CPM*, McGraw-Hill, New York, 1966.
24-7. U.S. Department of Transportation, Federal Highway Administration: *Traffic Assignment and Peripheral Programs*, U.S. GPO, Washington, D.C., 1969.

APPENDIX

# A

# INTRODUCTORY MATHEMATICS

Since mathematical detail tends to escape our memories from disuse, a brief review of some of the basic algebraic operations may be helpful. To use this book the reader should have a firm grasp of the following operations, rules, and facts. Reviewing the pages of this appendix and doing the problems at the end, although time consuming, may save the reader time in the long run.

## A-1 ABSOLUTE VALUES

By the absolute value of a number or variable is meant the number with a positive sign. Absolute value is indicated by two vertical lines surrounding the number.

$$|X| = X \text{ if } X \geq 0$$

$$= -X \text{ if } X < 0$$

$$|X - Y| = |Y - X|$$

$$|XY| = |X||Y|$$

## A-2 FACTORIALS, PERMUTATIONS, AND COMBINATIONS

The $n$ factorial is the product of all whole numbers from 1 to $n$ and is denoted by $n!$

$$n! = n(n-1)(n-2)(n-3)\cdots 3 \times 2 \times 1$$

$$6! = 6 \times 5 \times 4 \times 3 \times 2 \times 1 = 720$$

$$2! = 2 \times 1$$

$$1! = 1$$

$$0! = 1$$

$$\frac{8!}{5!} = \frac{8 \times 7 \times 6 \times (5!)}{5!} = 8 \times 7 \times 6 = 336$$

The permutation of $n$ things, $r$ at a time, is an arrangement of $r$ objects taken from a set of $n$ objects. The total number of such permutations is denoted by ${}_nP_r$, where $r \leq n$:

$${}_nP_r = \frac{n!}{(n-r)!} = n(n-1)(n-2)\cdots(n-r+1)$$

$${}_8P_3 = \frac{8!}{(8-3)!} = 8 \times 7 \times 6 = 336$$

A combination of $n$ objects taken $r$ at a time is a subset of $r$ objects selected without regard to their order from a set of $n$ different objects. The total number of such combinations is denoted by ${}_nC_r$ or by $\binom{n}{r}$, where $r \leq n$:

$$\binom{n}{r} = \frac{n!}{r!\,(n-r)!} = \frac{{}_nP_r}{r!}$$

The following rules may help in computing combinations:

$$\binom{n}{n-r} = \binom{n}{r}$$

$$\binom{n+1}{r} = \binom{n}{r-1} + \binom{n}{r} \qquad \text{for } 1 \leq r \leq n \text{ (Pascal's rule)}$$

## A-3 SPECIAL SYMBOLS

The constant $e$, sometimes referred to as the natural number, is used frequently in mathematical formulas. It is the number 2.7183 ....

Pi, denoted by $\pi$, also appears in many mathematical formulas, even in cases that have nothing to do with circles. Pi is the ratio of the circumference of a circle to the length of its diameter, which is 3.14 ... for all circles.

Infinity, denoted $\infty$, is not a number but a concept about unboundedness. To say "as $n$ approaches infinity" is synonomous with "$n$ gets larger and larger" or "$n$ increases without bound." If $n$ approaches negative infinity, denoted $-\infty$, then $n$ is decreasing without bound.

## A-4 FRACTIONS

$$\frac{a+b}{c} = \frac{a}{c} + \frac{b}{c} \quad \text{but} \quad \frac{c}{a+b} \neq \frac{c}{a} + \frac{c}{b}$$

$$\frac{a/b}{c/d} = \frac{a}{b}\frac{d}{c} = \frac{ad}{bc}$$

$$\frac{a}{b} + \frac{c}{d} = \frac{ad+cb}{bd}$$

$$\frac{ab}{ac} = \frac{b}{c}$$

## A-5 REMOVING OR ADDING PARENTHESES

$$b(X+Y) = bX + bY$$

$$aW + aY + bW + bY = a(W+Y) + b(W+Y) = (a+b)(W+Y)$$

A negative sign before a parenthesis means that each term within the parentheses must have its sign changed if the parentheses are removed:

$$-(a-b) = b-a$$

$$-aX + aY - aZ = -a(X - Y + Z)$$
$$= a(Y - X - Z)$$

## A-6 POWERS

1. *Expanding a squared sum or difference*

$$(a+b)^2 = a^2 + 2ab + b^2$$
$$(a-b)^2 = a^2 - 2ab + b^2$$

2. *Negative and zero exponents.* A number raised to a negative power may be written as the reciprocal of that number raised to the absolute value of that power:

$$X^{-2} = \frac{1}{X^2} \qquad (X \text{ may not equal } 0)$$

$$\frac{1}{X^{-3}} = X^3$$

$$X^{-a} = \frac{1}{X^a} \qquad (\text{for any } a \text{ and for any nonzero } X)$$

$$X^0 = 1 \qquad (\text{for any nonzero } X)$$

$$X = X^1$$

3. *Multiplication and division of powers.* If a number is raised to the power $b$ and the same number is raised to the power $c$, then their product can be obtained by adding exponents and their quotient can be obtained by subtracting exponents:

$$X^b X^c = X^{b+c}$$

$$\frac{X^b}{X^c} = X^{b-c}$$

$$\frac{R^a R^b}{R^c} = R^{a+b-c}$$

$$\frac{Z^4 Z^{-2}}{Z} = Z^{4-2-1} = Z^1 = Z$$

4. *Power of products and quotients*

$$(X^a)^b = X^{ab}$$

$$(XY)^b = X^b Y^b$$

$$\left(\frac{X}{Y}\right)^b = \frac{X^b}{Y^b}$$

$$X^2 Y^4 Z^2 = (XY^2Z)^2$$

5. *Fractional exponents*

$$X^{1/2} = \sqrt[2]{X} = \sqrt{X} \qquad (\text{the square root of } X; X \text{ must be nonnegative})$$

$$X^{1/n} = \sqrt[n]{X} \qquad (\text{the } n\text{th root of } X \text{ where } n \text{ is an integer; if } n \text{ is even, then } X \text{ must be nonnegative})$$

$$9^{1/2} = \sqrt{9} = 3$$

$$8^{1/3} = \sqrt[3]{8} = 2$$

$$(-8)^{1/3} = \sqrt[3]{-8} = -2$$

Since taking the square root of a number is the same as raising that number to the one-half power, the rules for exponential notation apply to square roots.

$$\sqrt{XY} = \sqrt{X}\sqrt{Y}$$

$$\sqrt{\frac{X}{Y}} = \frac{\sqrt{X}}{\sqrt{Y}}$$

$$\sqrt{X+Y} \neq \sqrt{X} + \sqrt{Y} \qquad \text{(cannot be simplified)}$$

$$\sqrt{X^a} = X^{a/2}$$

$$\sqrt{X}\sqrt{X} = X^{1/2+1/2} = X$$

$$\sqrt[4]{X}\sqrt{X} = X^{1/4+1/2} = X^{3/4} = \sqrt[4]{X^3}$$

$$\sqrt{X^4 Y} = \sqrt{X^4}\sqrt{Y} = X^{4 \times 1/2}\sqrt{Y} = X^2\sqrt{Y}$$

6. *Scientific notation.* Any number can be expressed in the form $a \times 10^b$, where $a$ and $b$ are unique for each number. For example, 843.5 can be expressed as $8.435 \times 10^2$. This kind of notation is called scientific notation, where the decimal point is positioned between the two most-left digits, and the power of 10 represents the number of places the decimal point was moved. Frequently in computer output the decimal point is placed before the most-left digit and the base 10 is replaced by the letter "E." For example, 843.5 = 0.8435E3.

   Scientific notation is very useful when dealing with very large numbers or numbers near 0:

$$3{,}214{,}000{,}000{,}000 = 3.214 \times 10^{12}$$

(decimal point moved 12 places to the left)

$$0.00000000214 = 2.14 \times 10^{-9}$$

(decimal point moved 9 places to the right)

$$\frac{8{,}140{,}000{,}000 \times 0.000000617}{446{,}000{,}000} = \frac{8.14 \times 10^9 \times 6.17 \times 10^{-7}}{4.46 \times 10^8}$$

$$= \frac{8.14 \times 6.17}{4.46} \times 10^{-6}$$

$$= 11.3 \times 10^{-6} = 1.13 \times 10^{-5}$$

## A-7 LOGARITHMS

Any number can be expressed as a power of a constant, such as a power of 10:

$$2000 = 10^{3.30103}$$

$$120 = 10^{2.07918}$$

The exponents in exponential notation when the base is 10 are called *common logarithms* and are denoted by log ( ):

$$\log(2000) = 3.30103$$

$$\log(120) = 2.07918$$

The exponents in exponentials notation when the base is $e$ are called *natural logarithms* and are denoted by ln ( ):

$$\ln(2000) = 7.6009$$

$$\ln(120) = 4.7875$$

Hence, we say:

$$\log(X) = k \text{ if } 10^k = X \qquad \text{where } X \text{ must be positive}$$

$$\ln(X) = c \text{ of } e^c = X \qquad \text{where } X \text{ must be positive}$$

The following results can be useful when working with logarithms:

1. If $X > Y$, then $\log(X) > \log(Y)$
2. If $0 < X < 1$, then $\log(X) < 0$ and $\ln(X) < 0$
3. $\log(1) = \ln(1) = 0$
4. $\log(AB) = \log(A) + \log(B)$
5. $\log(A/B) = \log(A) - \log(B)$
6. $\log(A^b) = b\log(A)$
7. $\log(10^b) = b$ and $\ln(e^b) = b$
8. $\ln(10) = 2.303$
9. $\log(X) = \ln(X)/2.303$
10. $\ln(X) = 2.303\log(X)$
11. If $Y = ae^{bX}$, then $\ln(Y) = \ln(ae^{bX}) = \ln(a) + bX$
12. $\log(A + B)$ cannot be simplified

*Antilogarithms*, denoted by anti log ( ) or anti ln ( ), are the opposite of logarithms. It is the number, $X$, which results when 10 (or some other base) is raised to a given power. Therefore:

$$\text{anti log}(k) = X \text{ if } 10^k = X \qquad \text{where } X \text{ must be positive}$$

$$\text{anti ln}(c) = X \text{ if } e^c = X \qquad \text{where } X \text{ must be positive}$$

So, for examples:

$$\text{anti log}(3) = 10^3 = 1000$$

$$\text{anti ln}(3) = e^3 = 20.086$$

$$\text{anti log}(-2.14) = 10^{-2.14} = 1/10^{2.14} = 0.00724$$

## A-8 TRIGONOMETRIC FUNCTIONS

*Trigonometric functions* deal with the relationships between the length of sides and the size of angles in triangles. For a triangle with a right angle:

1. $\sin \theta = a/c$
2. $\cos \theta = b/c$
3. $\tan \theta = a/b$
4. $\cot \theta = b/a$

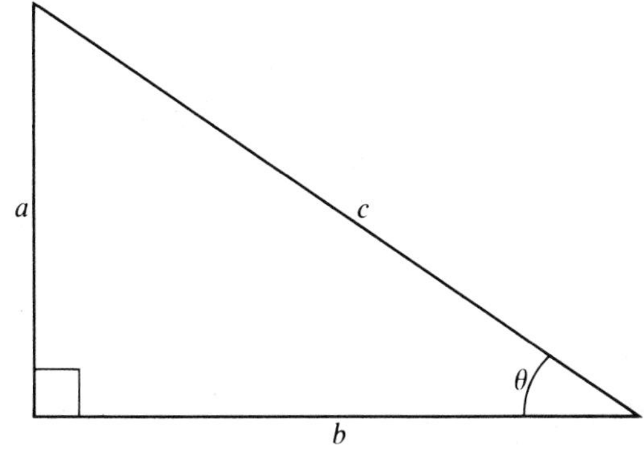


To illustrate:

$$\cos 30^\circ = 0.866 \qquad \sin 30^\circ = 0.5$$

$$\tan 30^\circ = 0.577 \qquad \cot 30^\circ = 1.732$$

Angles can also be measured in *radians*, where $360^\circ = 2\pi$ radians or 1 radian = $360^\circ/2\pi = 57.3^\circ$. So:

$$30^\circ = 30/57.3 = 0.524 \text{ radians}$$

$$\cos 0.524 \text{ radians} = 0.866$$

It is possible to represent angles greater than 90° in terms of angles under that level. This enables us to take the sines and cosines of angles of any size. Those for $0^\circ \leq \theta \leq 360^\circ$ are shown in Fig. A-1. There it can be seen, for instance, that:

$$\sin(265^\circ) = -\sin(85^\circ) = -0.996$$

$$\cos(325^\circ) = \cos(35^\circ) = 0.819$$

## A-9 INDEXING VARIABLES

In statistics it is frequently necessary to discuss several values of a variable. For instance, one may wish to describe $n$ observations from a sample. We denote these observations as $X_1, X_2, X_3, \ldots, X_n$ where $X_1$ is the first observation, $X_2$ the second observation, and so on. The subscript is the index of the variable.

To represent more than one observation of several variables, it is convenient to use double subscripts, such as $X_{ij}$, where $i$ = observations 1, 2, ..., $n$ and $j$ = variables $1, 2, \ldots, m$. Thus, there are $m$ variables, each with $n$ observations. $X_{34}$ represents the third observation of the fourth variable. If the sample size of each

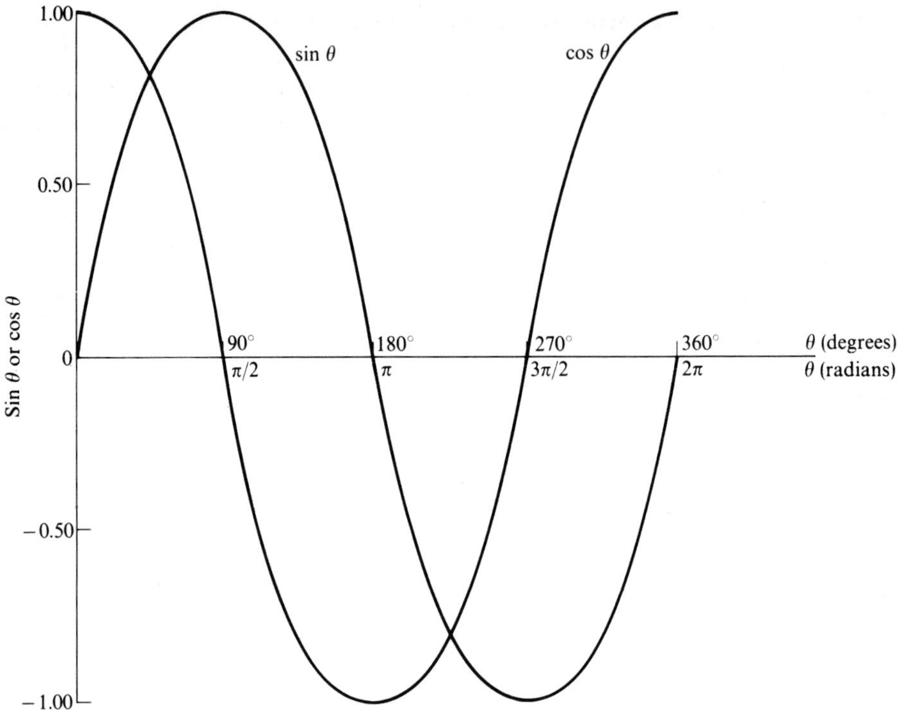


**Figure A-1** Sin $\theta$ and cos $\theta$ between 0° and 360°.

**Table A-1 Percentage of families below the poverty line, from samples taken from the Coastal, Piedmont, and Mountainous Regions of the Eastern States**

| | Regions | | | |
|---|---|---|---|---|
| Counties | Coastal | Piedmont | Mountainous | Total |
| 1 | 3 | 8 | 13 | 24 |
| 2 | 12 | 4 | 10 | 26 |
| 3 | 10 | 5 | 11 | 26 |
| 4 | 8 | 4 | 15 | 27 |
| 5 | 5 | 6 | 9 | 20 |
| 6 | 14 | 8 | 10 | 32 |
| Total | 52 | 35 | 68 | 155 |

variable differs, then we denote the various sample sizes as $n_j$. The variable is now defined $X_{ij}$, where $i$ = observations $1, 2, \ldots, n_j$ and $j$ = variables $1, 2, \ldots, m$. While the symbols $X$, $i$, $j$, $n$, and $m$ and the subscript order (observations first and variables second) are commonly used by authors, they are arbitrary choices. One could say $Y_{ab}$, where $a$ = variables 1, 2, ..., $s$ and $b$ = observations 1, 2, ..., $t$.

Consider samples of counties taken from the Coastal, Piedmont, and Mountainous Regions of the Eastern States of the United States. The data represent the percentage of families in a county that are below the poverty line (see Table A-1):

$X_{ij}$ = percentage families in the $i$th county of region $j$ below the poverty line
$X_{23}$ = 10 percent, the second observed county of the sample from the Mountainous Region
$X_{32}$ = 5 percent, the third observed county of the sample from the Piedmont Region

## A-10 SUMMATIONS

We often wish to indicate the sum of several observations. It is convenient to be able to express such sums in compact form. The Greek letter $\sum$ (capital sigma) is used for the purpose of denoting "summation of."

Suppose that $X_i$ = county tax revenue, $i$ = observations 1, 2, ..., $n$, where $i$ represents the counties in a region of $n$ counties. The sum of the $n$ revenue figures could be represented by

$$X_1 + X_2 + \cdots + X_n$$

Another way of representing the same sum, using the summation symbol $\sum$, is

$$\sum_{i=1}^{n} X_i \qquad \text{(A-1)}$$

We read expression (A-1) as follows: "summation of $X$-sub-$i$ for $i$ equals 1 through $n$."

In general, the summation notation

$$\sum_{i=l}^{n} X_i \qquad \text{where } l < n$$

means the sum of the numbers $X_l, X_{l+1}, \ldots, X_n$. The lower limit of the summation is $l$, the upper limit is $n$. While the symbols $X$, $i$, $n$, and $l$ are frequently used, any convenient symbol can be employed. We sometimes omit the limits and write simply $\sum X_i$. This notation means that the summation is to extend over all values of $X_i$ under discussion, unless something is said to the contrary. For instance, if the only values in a particular discussion are $X_1$, $X_2$, $X_3$, $X_4$, then $\sum X_i$ means $X_1 + X_2 + X_3 + X_4$.

For example, let $X_1 = 2$, $X_2 = -5$, $X_3 = 10$, $X_4 = 6$. Then:

$$\sum_{i=1}^{4} X_i = 2 + -5 + 10 + 6 = 13$$

$$\sum_{i=2}^{3} X_i = -5 + 10 = 5$$

$$\sum 2X_i = 2 \times 2 + 2 \times -5 + 2 \times 10 + 2 \times 6 = 2(2 + -5 + 10 + 6) = 26$$

$$\sum X_i^2 = 4 + 25 + 100 + 36 = 165$$

*General summation rules*

1. $\sum_{i=1}^{n} X_i^2 = X_1^2 + X_2^2 + \cdots + X_n^2$

2. $\sum_{i=1}^{n} X_i Y_i = X_1 Y_1 + X_2 Y_2 + \cdots + X_n Y_n$

3. $\sum_{i=1}^{n} (X_i + Y_i) = (X_1 + Y_1) + (X_2 + Y_2) + \cdots + (X_n + Y_n)$

$$= (X_1 + X_2 + \cdots + X_n) + (Y_1 + Y_2 + \cdots + Y_n)$$

$$= \sum_{i=1}^{n} X_i + \sum_{i=1}^{n} Y_i$$

4. $\sum_{i=1}^{n} (X_i - Y_i) = \sum_{i=1}^{n} X_i - \sum_{i=1}^{n} Y_i$

5. $\sum_{i=1}^{n} CX_i = CX_1 + CX_2 + \cdots + CX_n = C(X_1 + X_2 + \cdots + X_n) = C\sum_{i=1}^{n} X_i$

6. $\sum_{i=1}^{n} C = C + C + \cdots + C(n \text{ times}) = nC$

7. $\sum_{i=1}^{n} (X_i + Y_i)^2 = \sum_{i=1}^{n} (X_i^2 + 2X_i Y_i + Y_i^2) = \sum_{i=1}^{n} X_i^2 + 2\sum_{i=1}^{n} X_i Y_i + \sum_{i=1}^{n} Y_i^2$

   Hence, $\sum_{i=1}^{n} (X_i + Y_i)^2$ does *not* equal $\sum_{i=1}^{n} X_i^2 + \sum_{i=1}^{n} Y_i^2$.

8. $\left(\sum_{i=1}^{n} X_i\right)^2 = (X_1 + X_2 + \cdots + X_n)^2$

$$= X_1^2 + X_2^2 + \cdots + X_n^2 + 2X_1X_2 + 2X_1X_3 + \cdots + 2X_{n-1}X_n$$

   Hence, $\sum X_i^2$ does *not* equal $(\sum X_i)^2$.

9. $\sum_{i=1}^{n} i = 1 + 2 + \cdots + n = (\frac{1}{2})n(n + 1)$

We may also find it convenient to express a sum in terms of a double summation over two indices $i$ and $j$. The quantity

$$\sum_{i=1}^{n}\sum_{j=1}^{m} X_{ij}$$

means that we first sum the second subscript $j$ from 1 to $m$ and, then, working outwards, we sum $i$ from 1 to $n$. Thus

$$\begin{aligned}\sum_{i=1}^{n}\sum_{j=1}^{m} X_{ij} &= \sum_{i=1}^{n}(X_{i1} + X_{i2} + \cdots + X_{im})\\ &= (X_{11} + X_{12} + \cdots + X_{1m}) + (X_{21} + X_{22} + \cdots + X_{2m})\\ &\quad + \cdots + (X_{n1} + X_{n2} + \cdots + X_{nm})\end{aligned}$$

Using data in Table A-1, the following summations can be evaluated:

$$\sum_{i=1}^{6} X_{i2} = 35$$

$$\begin{aligned}\bar{X}_{\cdot 2} &= \frac{1}{6}\sum_{i=1}^{6} X_{i2} = \frac{35}{6}\\ &= 5.833 \qquad \text{(average "poverty" in the Piedmont Region)}\end{aligned}$$

$$\begin{aligned}\sum_{j=1}^{3}\sum_{i=1}^{6} X_{ij} &= 52 + 35 + 68 = \sum_{i=1}^{6}\sum_{j=1}^{3} X_{ij}\\ &= 24 + 26 + 26 + 27 + 20 + 32 = 155\end{aligned}$$

## A-11 FUNCTIONS AND GRAPHS

A *variable* is a symbol which may assume any one of a set of values during a discussion. A *constant* is a symbol which stands for only one particular value during the discussion. A variable $y$ is said to be a function of a variable $x$ if there exists a relation between $y$ and $x$ such that for each value which $x$ may assume there corresponds one or more values of $y$. The functional notation $y = f(x)$, read "$y$ equals $f$ of $x$," is often used to designate that $y$ is a function of $x$. With this notation $f(2)$ represents the value of the dependent variable $y$ when $x = 2$.

Consider the function $y = f(x) = 3 + 2x$. Then $f(2) = 3 + 2 \times 2 = 7$ and $f(-2) = 3 + 2 \times -2 = -1$, that is, $y = 7$ when $x = 2$ and $y = -1$ when $x = -2$. $y$ is called the *dependent* variable and $x$ is called the *independent* variable. Any letter can be used in the functional notation, such as $s = f(t)$. In this case $s$ is the dependent variable and $t$ is the independent variable.

A rectangular coordinate system is used to give a picture of the functional relationship between two variables. Figure A-2 shows such a system, where two mutually perpendicular lines $X'X$ and $Y'Y$ intersect at the point 0. The line $X'X$,

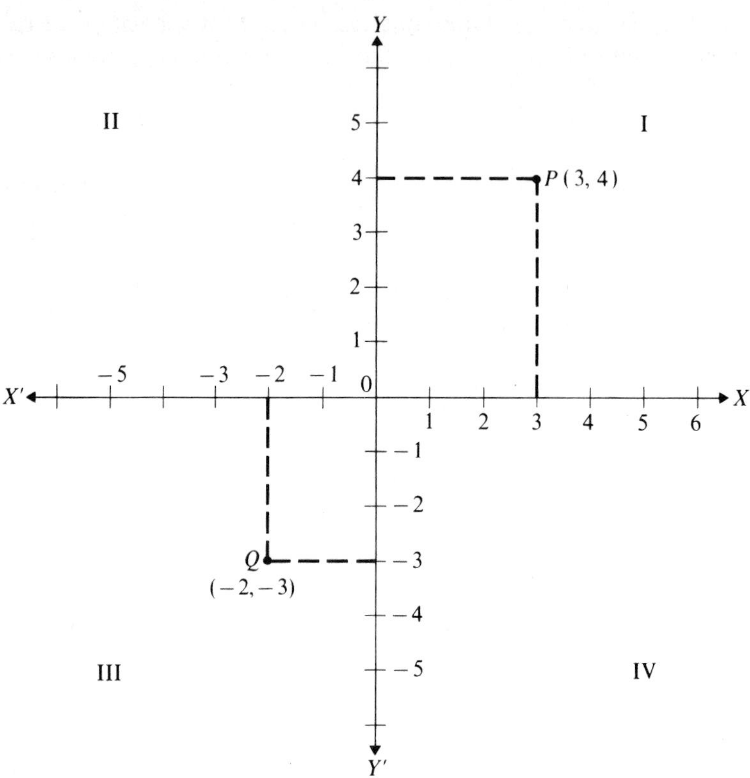


**Figure A-2** Rectangular coordinate system.

called the $x$ *axis*, or *abscissa*, represents the values of the independent variable. The line $Y'Y$, called the $y$ *axis*, or *ordinate*, represents the values of the dependent variable. The point 0 is called the *origin*.

To construct the coordinate system, lay off points, using a convenient unit of length, on the $x$ axis at successive multiple units to the right and left of the origin 0. In Fig. A-2 the unit 1 was utilized. The positive direction is to the right of the origin and the negative direction is to the left. Do the same on the $y$ axis, letting the positive direction be above the origin.

The $x$ and $y$ axes divide the plane into four parts known as quadrants, which are labeled I, II, III, IV in the figure. Given a point $P$ in this $xy$ plane, drop perpendiculars from $P$ to the $x$ and $y$ axes. The values of $x$ and $y$ at the points where these perpendiculars meet the $x$ and $y$ axes determine, respectively, the $x$ coordinate and the $y$ coordinate of the point $P$. These coordinates are indicated by the symbol $(x, y)$. Conversely, given the coordinates of a point, we may locate or plot the point in the $xy$ plane. For example, the point $P$ in the figure has coordinates (3, 4); the point $Q$ has coordinates $(-2, -3)$.

The graph of a function $y = f(x)$ is the locus of all points $(x, y)$ satisfied by the equation $y = f(x)$. Given a set of points one can estimate other values of the function by drawing lines or curves between the points. Consider the point set $A$ and $B$ and their graphs in Fig. A-3.

A linear function is one of the form $y = a + bx$, where $a$ and $b$ are constants. This function defines a straight line, i.e., for any line there exists an $a$ and $b$ such that $y = a + bx$. In curve $A$ in Fig. A-3, the straight line is defined by $a = 1$ and $b = 2$, that is, $y = 1 + 2x$. Substituting the values of $x = 3, -1, 2$, and 0 into the equation gives the values for $y = 7, -1, 5$, and 1, agreeing with point set $A$ where a line crosses the $y$ axis at the point where $x = 0$; the intersecting point is called the *y intercept*. In a linear equation, $a$ is always the $y$ intercept, and the slope of the line is $b$. Hence $b$ represents the change in $y$ for 1 unit change in $x$. To compute $b$, one needs only to take the ratio:

$$b = \frac{y_2 - y_1}{x_2 - x_1}$$

where $x_2 > x_1$ and $(x_1, y_1)$ and $(x_2, y_2)$ are two points on the graph. In point set $A$, the coefficient $b$ can be computed from any pairs of points. For example,

$$\frac{7 - (-1)}{3 - (-1)} = \frac{8}{4} = 2 \quad \text{and} \quad \frac{5 - 1}{2 - 0} = \frac{4}{2} = 2$$

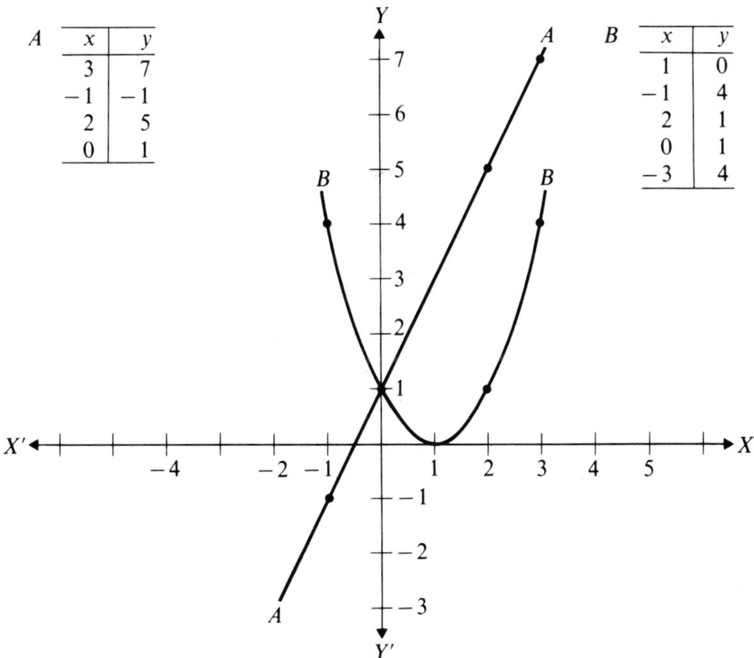


A

| x | y |
|---|---|
| 3 | 7 |
| −1 | −1 |
| 2 | 5 |
| 0 | 1 |

B

| x | y |
|---|---|
| 1 | 0 |
| −1 | 4 |
| 2 | 1 |
| 0 | 1 |
| −3 | 4 |

**Figure A-3** Projected graphs of point sets $A$ and $B$.

Some other functions that are discussed in this text are

1. $y = a + bx + cx^2$ (quadratic)
2. $y = ae^{bx}$ (exponential)
3. $y = ax^b$ (power)
4. $y = \dfrac{c}{1 + ae^{bx}}$ (logistic)

In these functions *a*, *b*, and *c* are arbitrary constants, and *e* is always the constant 2.718 ....

## A-12 LOGIC

To classify cases we need to be able to state the rules of the classification in precise terms. This can be done with relational, logical, and conditional action statements.

An *operation* is a well-defined rule that determines an outcome for a given input. In the case of a relational operation, the inputs are pairs of numbers and output can only be one of two values—true or false. For example,

$$X \text{ equals } Y$$

is a relational statement. Inputs are the values of $X$ and $Y$, and if $X$ does equal $Y$ then the output is true—otherwise, it is false. Some relational operators and their symbols used in various computer languages are listed in Table A-2.

A logical operator input is a pair of relational values, true (T) or false (F), and its output is either true or false. The three primary logical relations are AND, OR, and NOT. In the operation $X$ AND $Y$, the inputs $X$ and $Y$ must be the results of

**Table A-2 Some relational operators and their symbols in FORTRAN, SPSS, and APL computer languages**

| | Symbols | | |
|---|---|---|---|
| Name of operator | FORTRAN | SPSS | APL |
| Equal to | .EQ. | EQ | = |
| Greater than | .GT. | GT | > |
| Greater than or equal to | .GE. | GE | ≥ |
| Less than | .LT. | LT | < |
| Less than or equal to | .LE. | LE | ≤ |
| Not equal to | .NE. | NE | ≠ |

**Table A-3 Definitions of the logical operators AND, OR, and NOT**

| Input | | Output | | | |
|---|---|---|---|---|---|
| $X$ | $Y$ | $X$ AND $Y$ | $X$ OR $Y$ | NOT $X$ | NOT $Y$ |
| F | F | F | F | T | T |
| F | T | F | T | T | F |
| T | F | F | T | F | T |
| T | T | T | T | F | F |

relational operations. If $X$ and $Y$ are both true, the result is also true. If $X$ or $Y$ or both are false, then the result is false (see Table A-3).

The outcome of the operation $X$ OR $Y$ is true if $x$ or $y$ or both are true. It is false only if both $x$ and $y$ are false. The operator NOT has only one input and simply changes the true or false value of that input. The definitions of relational operations are listed in Table A-3. See Table A-4 for examples.

The conditional action statement specifies a change if its input is true and no change if its input is false. The form of the statement is:

IF $X$ THEN action $Y$

If $X$ is true, then action $Y$ is to be taken. For example, suppose one wanted to assign the value of 0 to $W$ only if the current value of $X$ were between and including the numbers 10 and 14. This can be stated by the following conditional action statement:

IF $X \geq 10$ AND $X \leq 14$ THEN $W = 0$

For example, let $X$ and $W$ represent the data in Table A-4. $W$ is to be changed to 0 only if $X$ meets the condition of the above statement. The results of the statement applied to each of the six values are listed in Table A-5.

**Table A-4 Examples of relational and logical operators**

| Variables | | | Relations | | | | Logical | | |
|---|---|---|---|---|---|---|---|---|---|
| $W$ | $X$ | $Y$ | $W = 3$ | $X \geq 10$ | $X \leq 14$ | $Y > 0$ | NOT ($X \geq 10$) | $X \geq 10$ AND $X \leq 14$ | $W = 3$ OR $Y > 0$ |
| 1 | 10 | −4 | F | T | T | F | F | T | F |
| 2 | 8 | 3 | F | F | T | T | T | F | T |
| 2 | 14 | −1 | F | T | T | F | F | T | F |
| 8 | 10 | 0 | F | T | T | F | F | T | F |
| 4 | 6 | 2 | F | F | T | T | T | F | T |
| 3 | 16 | −4 | T | T | F | F | F | F | T |

**Table A-5 Reclassification of $W$ of Table A-4 when $X$ is between and including 10 and 14, that is, IF $X \geq 10$ AND $X \leq 14$ THEN $W = 0$**

| Old $W$ | $X$ | $X \geq 10$ | $X \leq 14$ | $X \geq 10$ AND $X \leq 14$ | New $W$ |
|---|---|---|---|---|---|
| 1 | 10 | T | T | T | 0 |
| 2 | 8 | F | T | F | 2 |
| 2 | 14 | T | T | T | 0 |
| 8 | 10 | T | T | T | 0 |
| 4 | 6 | F | T | F | 4 |
| 3 | 16 | T | F | F | 3 |

## PROBLEMS

**A-1** Simplify these mathematical expressions.

(*a*) $|3 - 10| =$
(*b*) $-|3 - 2| \times |5 - 7| =$
(*c*) $4! =$
(*d*) ${}_4P_2 =$
(*e*) $\binom{4}{2} =$
(*f*) $\dfrac{3/4}{2/5} =$
(*g*) $\dfrac{1}{5} + \dfrac{5}{6} =$
(*h*) $5^3 =$
(*i*) $4^{-2} =$
(*j*) $8^0 =$
(*k*) $6^1 =$
(*l*) $9^{1/2} =$
(*m*) $27^{1/3} =$

**A-2** Simplify and answer the following in scientific notation:

$$\frac{420{,}000{,}000 \times 0.000002}{0.000021}$$

**A-3** Simplify.

(*a*) $X^4X^2 =$
(*b*) $X^5X^2X^{-3} =$
(*c*) $\dfrac{XX^{-5}}{X^2} =$
(*d*) $\sqrt[3]{X^2}\sqrt[2]{X} =$
(*e*) $\sqrt{X^4} =$

**A-4** Given log (8) = 0.90 and log (2) = 0.30, approximately, compute approximately the following logarithms and antilogarithms without a calculator. Use the rules of Sec. A-7.

(*a*) log (16) = *Note:* $16 = 8 \cdot 2$
(*b*) log (4) = *Note:* $4 = 8/2$
(*c*) log (512) = *Note:* $512 = 8^3$
(*d*) $\log (8^{3 \cdot 4}) =$
(*e*) ln (2) =
(*f*) $\log (\frac{1}{8}) =$ *Note:* $\frac{1}{8} = 8^{-1}$
(*g*) anti log (0.9) =
(*h*) anti log (1.2) =
(*i*) anti log (2.7) =
(*j*) anti log (6) =
(*k*) anti ln (1) =

**A-5** Let $X_1 = 2$, $X_2 = 3$, $X_3 = 4$.
Let $Y_1 = 4$, $Y_2 = 1$, $Y_3 = 5$.
Evaluate the following expressions. Use the rules of Sec. A-9 for shortcuts.
(*a*) $\sum X_i$
(*b*) $\sum Y_i$
(*c*) $\sum (X_i + Y_i)$
(*d*) $\sum 3.7X_i$
(*e*) $\sum X_i Y_i$
(*f*) $\sum X_i^2$
(*g*) $\sum (X_i + Y_i)^2$
(*h*) $\sum \sum X_{ij}$, assuming the $X_{i1}$'s are the $X_i$'s above and the $X_{i2}$'s are the $Y_i$'s
(*i*) $\sum \sum X_{ij}^2 - (\sum \sum X_{ij})^2$, assuming as in (*h*)

**A-6** (*a*) Plot the function $Y = -2 + 3X$ on a rectangular coordinate system.
(*b*) Plot these points on the same coordinate. Is it linear? If it is linear determine the function.
$X_1 = 2$, $Y_1 = 2$; $X_2 = 1$, $Y_2 = 4$; $X_3 = -1$, $Y_3 = 8$
(*c*) Let $a = 2$, $b = \frac{1}{2}$, and $c = 4$. Plot the graphs of quadratic, exponential, power, and logistic functions for values if $X = 0, 2, -1$, and 6.

**A-7** Fill in the following table with T or F or an appropriate value:

| $X$ | $Y$ | $X < 0$ | NOT ($X < 0$) | $X < 0$ AND $Y > 2$ | $X < 0$ OR $Y > 2$ | IF ($X < 0$) THEN $X = 0$ |
|---|---|---|---|---|---|---|
| 2 | 8 | | | | | $X =$ |
| −3 | 1 | | | | | $X =$ |
| 0 | 7 | | | | | $X =$ |
| −1 | 3 | | | | | $X =$ |

**A-8** A city council has the following members: Adams, Baker, Campbell, Daniels, and Edwards.
(*a*) How many three-member committees can be formed from this council?
(*b*) How many three-member committees can be formed if Adams and Baker refuse to sit on the same committee?

**A-9** A law requires that a nine-member housing committee has at least five homeowners. How many five-member subcommittees can be formed if the overall committee is split 5 to 4 (homeowners/nonhomeowners).
(*a*) If no restrictions are placed on the composition of the subcommittees.
(*b*) If the subcommittees must contain exactly two nonhomeowners.

**A-10** In how many ways can seven parcels of land be arranged in seven places in an urban area if (*a*) any arrangement is possible, (*b*) the first three parcels must be arranged in the first three places, (*c*) the first two parcels must be at the first two places, respectively?

**A-11** Out of a group of five planners and six environmental systems people, a committee (for design) composed of three planners and two systems people is to be formed. How many different (i.e., with completely unique memberships) committees can be formed if (*a*) no restrictions are imposed, (*b*) two particular planners must be on the committee, (*c*) one particular systems person must be on the committee?

**A-12** Find the following:
(*a*) cos 60°
(*b*) sin 45°
(*c*) tan 90°
(*d*) cos 350°
(*e*) sin 720°
(*f*) sin $3\pi/2$
(*g*) tan $\pi/2$
(*h*) $y = (3 \sin 25°)/\cos 40°$
(*i*) $y = 3 \sin (25°/\cos 40°)$

## REFERENCES

A-1. Bryant, S.: *College Algebra and Trigonometry*, Goodyear, Pacific Palisades, Calif., 1974.
A-2. Kemeny, J. G., et al.: *Finite Mathematics with Business Applications*, Prentice-Hall, Englewood Cliffs, N.J., 1962.
A-3. Nielson, K. L.: *College Mathematics*, College Outline Series, Barnes and Noble, New York, 1958.
A-4. Spiegel, M. R.: *Theory and Problems of College Algebra*, Schaum's Outline Series, Schaum Publishing Co., New York, 1956.
A-5. Thomas, Jr., G. B.: *Calculus and Analytic Geometry*, Addison-Wesley, Reading, Mass., 1953.

APPENDIX

# B

# FORTRAN COMPUTER PROGRAMMING

The type of computer programming utilized by many scientists is called FORTRAN (FORmula TRANslation). This appendix provides a quick introduction to FORTRAN using as an example the calculation of descriptive statistics for a small set of data.

## B-1 STATEMENTS

A FORTRAN program consists of a sequence of four types of statements.

1. *Arithmetic assignment.* This performs an arithmetical computation, derives a single value result, and stores this result in a specific location in the computer memory.
2. *Control.* This enables the creator of the FORTRAN program to exercise control over the order in which statements are performed.
3. *Input/output.* This transfers data from or to the computer memory to or from a computer's peripheral storage medium: cards, printed page, magnetic tape, or disk.
4. *Specification.* This specifies for the duration of the computations the size, type, and usage of variable names.

A statement must be punched on 80-column cards, starting at column 7 and ending at column 72. Statements are referenced by positive integers placed in columns 2 through 5. The program performs in sequential order from one statement to the next as they are encountered in the program. This flow of operations may be interrupted by the appearance of control statements, which send control to statements referenced by positive integers in columns 2 through 5. Below is displayed an arithmetic statement on a computer card. Although no spaces appear in the example, spaces are permitted:

```
1 0           A = 4 . 1 + 2 .
1 2 3 4 5 6 7 8 9 0 1 2 3 4 5 6 7 8 9 0 1 2 3 4 5 6 7 8 9 0...
```

(card column number)

## B-2 CONSTANTS

There are three types of constants in FORTRAN: integer (sometimes called fixed point), real (floating point), and exponential (also called floating point).

*Format for integer constants*

1. An integer of one or more digits is preceded by a negative sign if the number is negative.
2. No commas or decimals are permitted.

**Examples**

| Correct form | Incorrect form | |
|---|---|---|
| −2 | −2. | (decimal point not allowed) |
| 1322140 | 1,322,140 | (commas not allowed) |

*Format for real constants*

1. A number of one or more digits with a decimal point and a negative sign if the number is negative. The maximum number of digits allowed is determined by the type of computer being used.
2. No commas are permitted, but a decimal point is required.

**Examples**

| Correct form | Incorrect form | |
|---|---|---|
| −2. or −2.0 | −2 | (must have a decimal point) |
| 3281.4 | 3.281.4 | (comma not permitted) |

An alternative form for designating real constants employs a notation that is similar to scientific notation. It is frequently used when designating very large or nearly zero numbers.

**Examples**

| Real | Scientific notation | One of many exponential forms |
|---|---|---|
| 26000000. | $2.6 \times 10^7$ | 26.0E6 |
| −1800000 | $-1.8 \times 10^6$ | −0.18E7 |
| 0.00004 | $4.0 \times 10^{-5}$ | 4.0E − 5 |

*Format for real constants in exponential forms*

1. "E" designates "$\times$ 10".
2. Real part precedes "E". It contains a decimal point but no commas.
3. Exponent part follows "E". It contains only two digits and a negative sign if appropriate, but no decimal point.
4. The size of the absolute values of the number and, hence, the exponent is limited depending on the type of computer being used.

**Examples**

| Correct form | Incorrect form | |
|---|---|---|
| 3162.1E4 | 3,162.2E4 | (comma not permitted) |
| 1.0E9 | 1E9 | (decimal required in real part) |
| 2.1E − 4 | 2.1E − 4. | (decimal point not permitted in exponent) |
| −5.6E − 11 | −5.6E − 011 | (too many digits in exponent) |

## B-3 VARIABLES

Mathematical quantities which are the result of computation or which may vary from problem to problem are called variables. The FORTRAN language provides the capacity for referencing variables by means of symbolic names consisting of alphabetic and numeric characters. A variable must also take one of two forms, i.e., either integer or real.

### Integer Variables

The integer variable name must follow these rules:

1. It may consist of one to six alphanumeric characters.
2. The first character must be I, J, K, L, M, or N.
3. The other characters may be any alphabetic letter or number.
4. Special characters such as .$ / − ()* or blanks are not permitted.

### Examples

| Correct form | Incorrect form | |
|---|---|---|
| IX | XI | (begins with letter X) |
| KBC | I.X | (special character not permitted) |
| ISUM | ISUMATION | (more than six characters) |
| N1 | N 1 | (embedded blanks not allowed) |

The type of computer used will determine the absolute magnitude an integer variable may assume. This absolute maximum for most IBM computers is $10^{10}$.

### Real Variables

The real variable name must follow the same rules as integer variables except the first character must be alphabetic but not I, J, K, L, M, or N.

### Examples

| Correct form | Incorrect form | |
|---|---|---|
| RI | IR | (begins with the letter I) |
| XA | X.A | (special character not permitted) |
| SUM | SUMATION | (more than six characters) |
| Z1 | Z 1 | (embedded blanks not allowed) |

## B-4 EXPRESSIONS

A FORTRAN expression is any sequence of constants, variables, and functions separated by operation symbols, commas, and parentheses.

In arithmetic-type expressions, the following operation symbols are used:

| Symbol | Operation | Algebraic example | FORTRAN example |
|---|---|---|---|
| + | Addition | $a + b$ | A + B |
| − | Subtraction | $a - b$ | A − B |
| * | Multiplication | $a \cdot b$ or $a \times b$ | A*B |
| / | Division | $a/b$ or $a \div b$ | A/B |
| ** | Exponentiation | $a^2$ | A**2 |

## Rules for Constructing Expressions

1. Just as constants, variables, and functions (to be defined later) may be either integer or real, so expressions may be composed of constants, variables, and functions written in either integer or real form, but not in both. The only exception to this rule is that an integer quantity or expression may appear as an exponent in a real expression.
2. Variables are of the same mode (either integer or real) as the name of the variable. For example, the integer variable name JOB must represent an integer value.
3. Functions (to be defined later) are of the same mode as the function name.
4. Exponentiation does not affect the mode of the expression; however, an integer variable may not be given a real exponent.
5. Parentheses may, and should, be used to clarify the meaning of complex arithmetic-type expressions. Excessive and unnecessary use of parentheses is usually avoided by good programmers. Ambiguous expressions such as A**B**C are not permitted. This expression must be coded as A** (B**C) or (A**B)**C, whichever is intended.
6. No two operation symbols may appear in sequence. The expression Z+ −B is not valid and must be coded as A+(−B) or −B + A.
7. When the hierarchy of operations in an expression is not explicitly specified by the use of parentheses, it is understood that the order of operation will be as follows:

| Order | Symbol | Operation |
|---|---|---|
| First | ** | Exponentiation |
| Second | * and / | Multiplication and division |
| Third | + and − | Addition and subtraction |

8. If parentheses have been omitted from a sequence of consecutive operations of the same order or for a sequence of such operations within a set of parentheses, the operations are understood to be grouped from left to right.

   Note that there is no preference for addition over subtraction or for multiplication over division. Within a given order each operation has the same rank (usually left to right).

## Parentheses

Parentheses take precedence over these hierarchical rules. The order of operation is from the innermost to the outermost set of parentheses. Within each inner set of parentheses the usual hierarchical rules prevail.

For example, the algebraic expression

$$\frac{A + B^2}{C - D}$$

must be coded as follows:

(A + B**2)/(C – D)

This expression will be computed in four steps. To demonstrate, the variable names are replaced by arbitrarily chosen numbers that may be in the memory location that these names represent. Say that $A = 6$, $B = 3$, $C = 8$, and $D = 2$. The computation the computer performs are:

| Step | Computation |
|---|---|
| 1 | (6 + 9)/(8 – 2) |
| 2 | 15/(8 – 2) |
| 3 | 15/6 |
| 4 | 2.5 |

## B-5 ARITHMETIC ASSIGNMENT STATEMENT

The general form of an arithmetic assignment statement is

$X$ = arithmetical expression

A number is computed according to the arithmetical statement and stored in the computer memory location addressed by $X$. This value can be referenced by $X$ in preceding statements until the value is changed by another arithmetic statement where $X$ appears again on the left of the = sign.

**Examples**

| Correct form | Incorrect form | |
|---|---|---|
| A = B | A + B = C + D | (quantity on left side of = sign not a single variable) |
| ABC = A*B*C | AIC = A*I*C | (mixed mode) |
| MC = 2 + I*IC | 2 + I*IC | (no variable and = sign to store the result) |

An example of a program to compute the mean, variance, and standard deviation of the numbers 23, 17, 7, 4 is shown in Fig. B-1. This example is written on a FORTRAN coding sheet.

Program EXAMPLE
Coded by TMW
Checked by JD

FORTRAN CODING FORM

Identification 73–80

Date April 1, 1976
Page 1 of 1

| C FOR COMMENT / STATEMENT NUMBER (1–5) | Cont. (6) | FORTRAN STATEMENT (7–72) |
|---|---|---|
| C | | PROGRAM TO COMPUTE:A MEAN, VARIANCE, AND STANDARD DEVIATION |
| | | XN=4. |
| | | X1=23. |
| | | X2=17. |
| | | X3=7. |
| | | X4=4. |
| | | XMEAN=(X1,+ X2 + X3 + X4)/XN |
| | | SUMX2=X1*X1 + X2*X2 + X3*X3 + X4*X4 |
| | | XVAR=(SUMX2 – XN*XMEAN**)/(XN–1.) |
| | | XSD=XVAR**.5 |

**Figure B-1** Simplified program to compute a mean, variance, and standard deviation.

**Table B-1 Some common FORTRAN real functions**

| Description | Name | Restrictions |
|---|---|---|
| Exponential, $e^x$ | EXP(X) | |
| Natural logarithm | ALOG(X) | Argument must be positive |
| Logarithm to base 10 | ALOG10(X) | Argument must be positive |
| Square root | SQRT(X) | Argument must be nonnegative |
| Trigonometric sine | SIN(X) | Argument in radians |
| Trigonometric cosine | COS(X) | Argument in radians |
| Trigonometric arctangent | ATAN(X) | |
| Absolute value | ABS(X) | |

*Note:* X stands for an arithmetical expression.

## B-6 FUNCTIONS

Some mathematical functions are encountered so often that they are "built into" the FORTRAN language. The number and permissible arguments (input into the functions) vary for different versions of FORTRAN, but some functions that come with virtually all computers and compilers using FORTRAN are shown in Table B-1.

Most FORTRAN compilers will not permit function names to be used as variable names. The argument of the function can be any expression, with some limitations listed above, and may include other functions.

### Examples

| Correct form | Incorrect form | |
|---|---|---|
| SQRT(ABS(A – B)) | SQRT A – B | (argument not in parentheses) |
| ABS(X/Y) – SQRT(V) | ALOG(I) | (incorrect mode) |
| SIN(Y)**2 | SIN**2(Y) | (left parenthesis must follow the function name) |

## B-7 COMMENT STATEMENTS

Comments should be placed in the program to describe what parts of the program are supposed to do. These comments aid others to read the program or help the programmer remember how the program works when he reviews it months after it was written. Comment statements start with the letter C in column 1 and a space in column 2. What follows is the comment and is printed when the program is printed, but it will have no effect on the execution of the program. The comment card can be placed anywhere within the program. See Fig. B-2 for an example.

Program Example 2
Coded by TMW
Checked by JD

FORTRAN CODING FORM

Identification 73–80

Date April 30, 1976
Page 1 of 1

C FOR COMMENT — STATEMENT NUMBER (1–5) | Cont. (6) | FORTRAN STATEMENT (7–72)

```
C  PROGRAM TO COMPUTE:A MEAN, VARIANCE, AND STANDARD DEVIATION
      READ, XN, X1, X2, X3, X4
      XMEAN = (X1 + X2 + X2 + X4)/ XN
      SUMX2 = X1 * X1 + X2 * X2 + X3 * X3 + X4 * X4
      XVAR= (SUMX2-XN* XMEAN ** 2)/ (XN - 1.)
      XSD = XVAR ** 0.5
      PRINT = XMEAN, XVAR, XSD
      STOP
      END
4 , 2 3 . , 1 7 . , 7 . , 4 .
```

**Figure B-2** More general program to compute a mean, variance, and standard deviation.

## B-8 CONTROL STATEMENTS

These statements permit the programmer to control the flow of his program.

### GO TO Statement

The general form of the GO TO statement is

GO TO $n$

where $n$ is a positive integer constant that indicates the statement number that is to be executed next. The program then continues sequentially from statement $n$.

#### Examples

| Correct form | Incorrect form | |
|---|---|---|
| GO TO 10 | GO TO J | (Statement number must be an integer constant) |
| GO TO 2 | GO TO −2 | (statement number cannot be negative) |

### Arithmetic IF Statement

The arithmetic IF statement provides a means of branching to one of three statements by examining an arithmetical expression. The general form of the statement is

$$\text{IF (arithmetical expression) } n_1, n_2, n_3$$

where $n_1$, $n_2$, and $n_3$ are statement numbers (not variables). The program will branch to:

1. Statement number $n_1$ if the expression is negative
2. Statement number $n_2$ if the expression is zero
3. Statement number $n_3$ if the expression is positive

All three statement numbers must be listed in the program, even if one is never to be used. The numbers may all be different, or any two may be the same.

#### Examples

| Correct form | Incorrect form | |
|---|---|---|
| IF(A − B)5,3,10 | IF(A − I)5,3,10 | (mixed mode) |
| IF(X)2,10,10 | IF X 2,10,10 | (X must be in parentheses) |
| IF(A)2,2,5 | IF(A),2,2,5 | (too many commas) |
| IF(B*B − 4*A*C)3,1,4 | IF(I)N1,N2,N3 | (statement numbers must be integer constants) |

## Logical IF Statement

The logical IF statement has the general form:

IF (logical expression) arithmetical or control expression

If the logical expression is true, then the arithmetical or control statement is executed. If the logical expression is false, then the arithmetical or control statement is ignored and the program continues with the next statement.

The logical expression is usually of the form:

$$(X \text{ relational operator } Y)$$

where $X$ and $Y$ are two variable names of the same type and the relational operator is one of the following:

| Relational operator | Meaning |
|---|---|
| .LT. | Less than |
| .LE. | Less than or equal to |
| .EQ. | Equal to |
| .NE. | Not equal to |
| .GT. | Greater than |
| .GE. | Greater than or equal to |

The "periods" in these relational operators are essential and are inserted to differentiate relational operators from variables which may be inadvertently chosen by the programmer.

### Examples

| Correct form | Incorrect form | |
|---|---|---|
| IF(A .EQ. B)GO TO 10 | IF(A EQ B)GO TO 10 | (periods are missing) |
| IF(X .GT. 10.)X = 10. | IF(X .GT. I)X = I | (mixed mode) |

The combination of logical operations with relational operations greatly extends the usefulness of the logical IF statement. The following logical operators are permitted in the logical expression:

| Logical operator | Expression | Meaning |
|---|---|---|
| .AND. | $S_1$ and $S_2$ | If both $S_1$ and $S_2$ are true, then the expression is true; otherwise it is false. |
| .OR. | $S_1$ or $S_2$ | If either $S_1$, or $S_2$, or both are true, then the expression is true; otherwise, it is false. |
| .NOT. | Not $S_1$ | The expression is opposite $S_1$. |

**Examples**

IF(X .GT. 4. .AND. X .LT. 8.)GO TO 10

If $X$ is greater than 4 and also $X$ is less than 8 (in other words, if $X$ is between 4 and 8) then the program branches to line 10. Otherwise, the program continues to the next statement:

IF(A .GT. B .OR. .NOT.(X .LT. S))A = S

If either $A$ is greater than $B$ or if $X$ is not less than $S$, then $A$ is assigned the value of $S$. Otherwise, no assignment takes place and the next statement is executed.

### STOP Statement

This statement causes a halt to further execution of the program. It must be in the program and may appear in more than one place in the program. It also may be the included in the logical IF statement.

**Examples**

IF(I .EQ. 11)STOP

STOP

Also see the example in Fig. B-2.

### END Statement

This statement differs from the previous control statements in that it does not affect the flow of control in the program. The END statement must be the last statement in the program. See the example in Fig. B-2.

## B-9 INPUT/OUTPUT STATEMENTS

In the example in Fig. B-1 the variables were assigned values with assignment statements. To compute descriptive statistics with new data several lines of the program must be rewritten. To prevent rewriting, the program data could be read in from cards with an input statement. Also, to observe the results of the program, the mean, variance, and standard deviation must be sent to a printer. This is done with the output statement PRINT or WRITE. The simplest input/output statements are the free field type.

### Free Field Input/Output Statements

The general form of free field input and output statements are

READ, variable list

PRINT, variable list

1. A comma must separate the input/output command and the first variable in the list.
2. Variable names must be separated by commas.

### Examples

| Correct form | Incorrect form | |
|---|---|---|
| READ,X1,X2,X3,X4 | READ X1,X2,X3,X4 | (no comma between READ and X1) |
| PRINT,XMEAN,XSD,SVAR | PRINT XMEAN SD XVAR | (missing commas) |
| PRINT,A,B | PRINT,A,B,A + B | (list cannot include an arithmetical expression) |

The PRINT statement causes three variables to be printed on a page in the specified order and in the mode of the variable name. The READ statement will read four numbers listed on a data card separated from the program by a control card. The format of the control is dependent on the computer and FORTRAN compiler being used. A WATFIV version of FORTRAN on an IBM machine uses this control card: "//DATA" starting in the first column.

The data that will be read by the program using a free field READ statement must appear on a card separated by spaces or commas. The data must have the same mode as the variable name; hence, real numbers should include decimal points and fixed point numbers must not have decimal points. See Fig. B-2 for an example.

### Fixed Field Input/Output Statements

Although more difficult to use, fixed field input/output statements allow more flexibility. Also, many "canned" computer programs require the use of fixed field formats.

### WRITE Statement

The general form of the WRITE statement is

WRITE $(n_1, n_2)$ variable list

$n_1$ is an integer constant that specifies a disk unit number, and with almost all installations $n_1 = 6$ means "to write on printer." $n_2$ specifies the statement number of the FORMAT statement. This FORMAT statement specifies where the numbers are to be printed on the output page.

### Fixed Field READ Statement

The general form of the READ statement is

READ $(n_1, n_2)$ variable list

$n_1$ is an integer constant that specifies a disk unit number, and with almost all installations $n_1 = 5$ means "to read from cards." $n_2$ specifies the statement number of the FORMAT statement. This FORMAT statement specifies the location of the numbers on the data cards.

## FORMAT Statement

Fixed field input/output statements require that numbers be read from or written on records at specified locations. The location and the type of variable is specified by the FORMAT statement. In this example, the value to be placed in memory location $N$ is an integer—located in the first six columns of a data card:

```
      READ (5,100) N
100   FORMAT (I6)
```

If several numbers of the same type are read or printed with the same specifications, then a repeat digit can be used. In general:

rFw.d

means to read or print $r$ real numbers each with field length of $w$ columns and with $d$ decimal places.

**Example**

```
      READ (5,75) I1,I2,I3, X1,X2,X3,X4
75    FORMAT (3I4,4F6.1)
//DATA
  10  12   8  41    14.8  8.21    .3114
```

Notice that $X1$ will be read as 4.1 and the decimal place specification for $X3$ and $X4$ are overridden since decimal points appear in the numbers.

Words can be printed by their inclusion in FORMAT statements within quotes:

```
      WRITE (6,10) XMEAN,XSD
10    FORMAT (' MEAN = ',F8.2,' STANDARD DEVIATION = ',F10.2)
```

The carriage on the high-speed output printer can be controlled in much the same fashion as the carriage on a typewriter. Practically all computing systems have adopted the convention of using the first column in each line of output for this purpose. This character is never printed, and causes paper spacing as follows:

a blank—single space

a zero—double space

a one—skip to the next page

The carriage control can be integrated with other field specifications. For example, the output from the statement:

```
FORMAT (5X,F8.2)
```

is four blank columns followed by the real variable. The first blank from the *X* field causes the printer to single-space. As a further illustration, consider the following statements:

```
    WRITE (6,100)
100 FORMAT ('1NEXT PAGE')
```

The words NEXT PAGE are printed at the top of the next page as directed by the 1 in the first column. The '1' is not printed.

A frequently used option is the (/) within the FORMAT statement, such as:

```
   WRITE (6,60) X,Y,I
60 FORMAT (1X,F10.2/1X,F10.2/1X,I10)
```

The slash causes one record line to be terminated and another to be begun. In the above case, the value of *X* appears on the first line, the value of *Y* on the second line, and the value of *I* on the third line of the output. Note that the carriage control is required for each line of output, and thus the 1*X* for carriage control following the slash in the aforementioned example. Slashes on input are treated similarly. Consecutive slashes simply cause consecutive record lines to be terminated.

**Example**

```
  READ (5,1) X,Y
1 FORMAT (F8.2//F8.2)
```

The value for *X* is read from the first card, the second card is skipped, and the value for *Y* is read from the third card.

## B-10 ARRAYS

Variable names can represent arrays, provided the dimension of the array is defined at the beginning of the program with a DIMENSION statement.

### DIMENSION Statement

A vector of *n* elements and a matrix of *r* rows and *c* columns can be defined with the following general statement:

DIMENSION *V*(*n*), *M*(*r*,*c*)

where $V$ and $M$ are real or integer variable names and $n$, $r$, and $c$ are integer constants. The purpose of the DIMENSION statement is to provide blocks of memory storage for the arrays before the program begins execution. The size of these blocks may be larger than needed; however, they can never be smaller.

### Subscripting

An element of an array such as $V_i$, the $i$th element of the vector $V$, or $M_{ij}$, the $i$th row and $j$th column of the matrix $M$, can be represented with this general form:

$$V(i) \quad M(i,j)$$

where $i$ and $j$ may be integer constants, integer variables, or a restricted arithmetical expression. Depending on the FORTRAN compiler, the permitted subscript expressions are usually limited to these general forms:

$$c,\ v,\ (v + c),\ (c^*v),\ (c^*v \pm k)$$

where $c$ and $k$ are integer constants and $v$ is an integer variable.

### Examples

| Correct form | Incorrect form | |
|---|---|---|
| ARRAY(3,4) | ARRAY(3.*R,4.) | (subscripts must be integers) |
| M(I,2*J) | M(I,J*2) | (second subscript argument in wrong order) |
| X(3*K − 4) | X(L(2)) | (subscript may not be a subscripted variable) |
| R = ARRAY(I,J)*VEC(N + 4) | | |

## B-11 PROGRAM LOOPING

The subscripted variable can be very useful when doing repeated operations with program loops. For example, say that $X$ is a vector of $N$ real numbers and the mean of these numbers is to be computed. This program loop will compute the mean:

```
      DIMENSION X(100)
         ⋮
      I = 1
      SUMX = 0.0
10    SUMX = SUMX + X(I)
      I = I + 1
      IF(I .LE. N) GO TO 10
      XMEAN = SUMX/N
```

Notice that *I* and SUMX must be initialized before starting the loop. SUMX accumulates the values of *X* until I is larger than *N*. At this point the looping stops and the XMEAN is computed. Notice also that the division in the last statement is performed on mixed variable types. This is permissible in some cases and is discussed later.

## B-12 DO STATEMENT

The DO statement can be used to replace some of the statements in a loop. The general form of the statement is

$$\text{DO } n\ i = b,e \qquad \text{or DO } n\ i = b,e,s$$

where *n* is a statement number for the last statement in the loop, *i* is a nonsubscripted integer variable, *b* is the beginning value of *i* in the loop, *e* is the last value of *i*, and *s* is the increments *i* assumes in each step of the loop. If *s* is missing, it is assumed to be 1. The variables *b,e*, and *s* must be nonsubscripted integer variables or constants.

**Examples**

```
DO  100 J = 1,5
DO  50  L = 1,K,2
```

In the first example the last statement in the loop is statement number 100, the initial value of *J* is 1, and the last value is 5. *J* increases by one in each loop; hence, five loops are made.

In the second example the initial value of *L* is 1; it increases two for each loop and its last value within the loop is *K* or *K* − 1 depending on whether *K* is odd or even. When the value of *J* exceeds 5 in the first example or when *L* exceeds *K* in the second, the loop stops.

The statement computing the mean of *X* can now be written as follows:

```
      DIMENSION X(100)
         ⋮
      SUMX = 0,0
      DO 10 I = 1,N
10    SUMX = SUMX + X(I)
      XMEAN = SUMX/N
```

The DO statement replaces the need to initialize and increment *I* and to branch to line 10 when *I* does not exceed *N*.

Any statement is permitted within the DO loop except one that changes the value of the index. An IF statement can branch out of the loop before the index exceeds its last permissible value. However, a control statement outside the range of the loop may not branch to a statement within the loop. The loop must start with the DO statement. A DO loop may also contain another DO loop provided the inner loop terminates within the outer loop. The last statement of the DO loop may not be a transfer statement such as IF or GO TO or with another DO statement.

The FORTRAN language provides a dummy statement which may be used at the end of DO loops which would otherwise end with one of the above types of statements. This statement is coded simply CONTINUE. CONTINUE is a dummy statement which results in no instructions in the program.

**Example**

```
          DIMENSION M(100,100)
              .
              .
              .
          DO 20 I = 1,100
          DO 20 J = 1,100
          IF (M(I,J) .EQ. K) GO TO 40
 20       CONTINUE
              .
              .
              .
 40       . . . . . .
```

This program compares each element of the integer matrix *M* with the value of *K*. If at least one element in *M* equals *K*, the program branches to the statement number 40, which is outside the loop. There is a loop "nested" within another, both ending at the CONTINUE statement.

## Reading and Writing Arrays

An array of *N* elements can be read and printed with one READ or WRITE statement as shown by the following example:

```
          READ (5,501) (X(I),I = 1,N)
 501      FORMAT (10F8.2)
          READ(5,501) ((Y(I,J),J = 1,NC),I = 1,NR)
          WRITE(6,601) (X(I),I = 1,N)
 601      FORMAT(1X,10F8.2)
```

*N* is the number of elements read and assigned to the array *X*. NR is the number of rows and NC is the number of columns in the matrix *Y*. All elements of *X* are on a single data card and the same is true for each row of *Y*. The READ statement for *Y* specifies that the index of the inside parentheses (in this case, *J*) is incremented first. Hence, the rows of the matrix are read one at a time. The rules for these implied DO input/output statements are the same as that for the DO statements.

## B-13 MIXED MODE

In some cases mixing modes can be useful. In FORTRAN the quotient of two integers, such as 5/2, is an integer since the decimal part is truncated. Thus, the quotient is 2, not 2.5. If one or both of the numbers are real, then the result is not truncated: 5./2, 5/2., and 5./2. are all equal to 2.5.

If the variable name on the left of the = sign is an integer and the expression on the right is real, the result is first computed in the real mode and then truncated and converted to an integer before it is stored as the new value of the variable.

**Examples**

| | |
|---|---|
| X = Y | Store the value of *Y* in the location reserved for *X*. The value of *Y* remains unchanged. |
| I = Y | Truncate the value of *Y* to an integer and store in *I*. |
| Y = I | Convert the value of *I* to real and store in *Y*. |
| Y = X/N | Mixed expression. Convert the value of *N* to real, divide the value of *X* by real *N*, and store in *Y*. |
| I = X**2 | Multiply the value of *X* by itself in the real mode, truncate the result to an integer value, and store in *I*. |
| Y = X**2. | Multiply the log of the value of *X* by 2.0, extract the antilog of the product, and store in *Y*. |

A final example is the separation of the integer and decimal parts of a real number. This can be done with the following statements:

```
R = 3.21
INT = R
DEC = R - INT
```

The value of INT is 3 and the value of DEC is 0.21.

The original program to compute the mean, variance, and standard deviation of a set of numbers is rewritten in Fig. B-3 using the techniques described above. The program is now more general, for it will compute the statistics for almost any set of numbers without changing the program. The first data card must contain the number of elements in *X* and the following data cards contain the numbers to be computed. The program is limited by the DIMENSION statement which permits *X* to have no more than 100 elements and by the FORMAT statement number 502 which requires the numbers to fit in fields of eight columns.

Program ______________ FORTRAN CODING FORM Date ______

Coded by ______________ Identification (73–80) Page ___ of ___

Checked by ______________

C FOR COMMENT

| STATEMENT NUMBER (1–5) | Cont. (6) | FORTRAN STATEMENT (7–72) |
|---|---|---|
| C | | PROGRAM TO COMPUTE:A MEAN, VARIANCE, AND STANDARD DEVIATION |
| | | DIMENSION X(100) |
| | | READ (5.501) N |
| 501 | | FORMAT (15) |
| | | READ (6,502) (X(I), I=1,N) |
| 502 | | FORMAT (10F8.1) |
| | | SUMX=0 |
| | | SUMX2=0 |
| | | DO 10 I=1.N |
| | | SUMX = SUMX + X(I) |
| 10 | | SUMX 2=SUMX2+X(I) *X(I) |
| | | XMEAN=SUMX/N |
| | | XVAR = (SUMX2 − N*XMEAN*2)/(N − 1) |
| | | XSD=SORT(XVAR) |
| | | WRITE (6,601)XMEAN,XVAR,XSD |
| 601 | | FORMAT ('1XMEAN=',F10. 2,' XVAR=',F10.1 ' XSD='F10.2) |
| | | STOP |
| | | END |
| //DATA 4 | | |
| 2 | 3 | . 0 17.0 7.0 4.0 |

**Figure B-3** Most general program to compute a mean, variance, and standard deviation.

## PROBLEMS

**B-1** Fill in the blanks with the appropriate word(s).

(*a*) All FORTRAN statements must start in column ________________ or thereafter.

(*b*) All FORTRAN statement addresses must be contained in columns ____________ to ________________.

(*c*) Using an implied DO loop, READ(5,2) X1(1),X1(2) can be rewritten as: ________________________________.

**B-2** Identify possible problems in each of the following FORTRAN statements. (If none, write "none." Assume all characters are in the proper columns. The symbol "Ø" stands for the letter "o."

(*a*) READ (17,2000) X ________________________

(*b*) RA = X5B/IW7 ________________________

(c) QQ = BLAB**2 ________________________

(*d*) GØ TØ X ________________________

(*e*) DIMENSIØN X(I) ________________________

(*f*) IF (XME) 1, 2, 3 ________________________

(*g*) WRITE (6,3) (L(J), J = 1.5)
3 FØRMAT (5F7.2) ________________________

(*h*) HIGH(JJ) = ((BL(J)*A(JJ)) ________________________

(*i*) DØ 30 X = 1, 17
17 HELP = REST(X) ________________________

(*j*) IBLIMPX = AIRS(JM321) ________________________

**B-3** Determine if each of the following FORTRAN statements is acceptable or not. (If it is, write "yes" next to it. If not, write "no.") The symbol "Ø" stands for the letter "o."

(*a*) READ (8, 1000) X(I)
(*b*) I = 2I + 3
(*c*) B = C*MNA**2.
(*d*) GØ TØ K
(*e*) READ, AA, Q (I), J5, BUM
(*f*) IF (A – BQØD) 7, 10, 25
(*g*) B123(II,PQ) = 1000.
(*h*) DIMENSIØN X(I, J), Y(K, L)
(*i*) DIMENSIØN Q, P, R, S

(*j*) WRITE (6, 202), ESTIM
(*k*) ITEMIZE = J + 53
(*l*) DELTA(I, KK3) = PRØB
(*m*) Y3/X = Q228*22.
(*n*) AA = 3* BB
(*o*) Q3R = (718. * X ** 2. * 5. Y5)
(*p*) J = 10* 6 * 5/8*3
(*q*) DØ KK, I = 1, N
(*r*) FORMAT (5X, 3F7.0, 10I20)
(*s*) IF (((Q3 – 21.) *8.)/X(8)) 18,200,63
(*t*) E = E(Q + K)

**B-4** If it were desired to read the data below into a computer, what columns on a computer card would each *digit* of each number be under if the following formats were used?
(*a*) (8X, 4F4.1)
(*b*) (6X, 2F4.2, 2X, 2F4.0)
(*c*) (12X, F3.1, 12X, F3.2, 6X, 2F3.0)

| $x_1$ | $x_2$ | $y_1$ | $y_2$ |
|---|---|---|---|
| 14 | 7 | 0.7 | 102 |
| 10 | 8 | 1.5 | 20 |
| 1 | 15 | 0.9 | 5 |
| 7 | 4 | 3.7 | 3 |

**B-5** Spearman's RHO, as you remember from Chap. 9, is:

$$\text{RHO} = 1 - \frac{6 \sum D^2}{n(n^2 - 1)}$$

where $n$ is the number of factors being ranked and $D$ is the difference in rank for each factor. Develop and present a FORTRAN program to compute RHO for five factors. Describe each variable used in a separate glossary. Use DO loops.

## REFERENCES

### Theory

B-1. Golden, J. T.: *FORTRAN IV, Programming and Computing*, Prentice-Hall, Englewood Cliffs, N.J., 1965.
B-2. Heterick, Jr., R. C., and J. H. Sword: *An Introduction to Computers and Elementary FORTRAN*, William C. Brown, Dubuque, Iowa, 1969.
B-3. Kennedy, M., and M. B. Solomon: *Ten Statement FORTRAN Plus FORTRAN IV*, 2d ed., Prentice-Hall, Englewood Cliffs, N.J., 1975.
B-4. McCracken, D. D.: *A Guide to FORTRAN Programming*, Wiley, New York, 1961.
B-5. Murrill, P. W., and C. L. Smith: *FORTRAN IV Programming for Engineers and Scientists*, International, Scranton, Pa., 1968.
B-6. Sterling, T. D., and S. V. Pollack: *Introduction to Statistical Data Processing*, Prentice-Hall, Englewood Cliffs, N.J., 1968.

**Programs**

B-7. Cooley, W. W., and P. H. Lohnes: *Multivariate Data Analysis*, Wiley, New York, 1971.
B-8. Gillett, B. E.: *Introduction to Operations Research: A Computer Oriented Algorithmic Approach*, McGraw-Hill, New York, 1976.

APPENDIX

# C

# APL

APL (*a* *p*rogramming *l*anguage) is a powerful time-sharing computer language. This power comes in part from a large operation set and vector and matrix capability. Not only is APL an easy-to-use programming language but it also permits the user to operate a computer terminal as a calculator. In this mode the user can do highly sophisticated calculations, even on vectors and matrices, without writing a program.

APL is designed for use through a terminal. After the user has signed onto the computer and has indicated a wish to use APL, he or she is ready to go to work. For example, to multiply 19 by 12.5, just type:

19 × 12.5 (spaces may be left between numbers and operators)

Push RETURN. The computer does not receive what is typed on one line until the RETURN button is pushed. After receiving the entire message and the RETURN signal, it will compute the answer and print it out on the next line, but indented six spaces to the left of the user's type. It will look like this:

```
      19 × 12.5
237.5
```

The computer starts typing at a different point from the operator to make it possible to tell who typed what on the printout.

## C-1 VARIABLES

A number or the result of a calculation may be put in a storage location in the computer. A stored item of data is called a *variable* and every variable has a *name* and a *value*. The name can be one letter or a group of letters and numbers.

The variable name must follow these rules:

1. The first character must be any alphabetic letter.
2. The other characters may be any alphabetic letter or number.
3. Special characters such as + − /( ) or blanks are not permitted.

**Examples**

| Correct form | Incorrect form | |
|---|---|---|
| X3 | 3X | (begins with a number) |
| I2 | I 2 | (embedded blanks not allowed) |
| XYZ | X−Y−Z | (special characters not permitted) |

To assign a value to a storage location, use the left-pointing arrow. If you type the instruction:

X←184.5  (do not forget to push RETURN)

the computer will store the value 184.5 in a storage location called *X*. In our example:

RESULT←19 × 12.5

the computer will calculate 19 × 12.5 and store the answer into a storage location called RESULT. It will not print out the result as it did in the example given previously. To find out what is stored in RESULT, just type RESULT and push RETURN. Forthcoming on the printout sheet will be all of the following:

```
      X←184.5
      RESULT←19 × 12.5
      RESULT
237.5
```

To continue the example, add 10 to *X* and put that result in another storage location (let us call it XPLUSTEN):

```
      XPLUSTEN←X + 10
      XPLUSTEN
194.5
```

Multiply *X* times RESULT:

```
      X × RESULT
43818.75
```

Store this result:

```
        Y←X × RESULT
        Y
  43818.75
```

The value of $X$ can also be changed:

```
        X←X × RESULT
        X
  43818.75
```

This operation takes the value stored in $X$ (184.5) and multiplies it times the number stored in RESULT (237.5). The product (43,818.75) is stored in the location $X$ and the old value there is wiped out.

A variable name (except on the left-hand side of the specification arrow) cannot be used until a value has been assigned to it:

More

```
        A←2
        B←4
        A + B
  6
        B − A
  2
        B ÷ A
  2
        A ÷ 4
  0.5
        C←A + 1
        C
  3
```

You can do more than one operation on a line

```
        C × A × B
  24
```

## C-2 OPERATIONS

The definition of an *operation* is slightly different in APL than those in textbooks. But this should not be a problem, for various textbooks do not agree on the definition of an operation either.

An operation is a rule which is applied to one or two elements from certain sets of elements giving us another element that is unique. The word *unique* means that if you use the same rule on the same elements, you will always get the same result, i.e., the operation must be consistent. Notice the word 'element' is used here instead of 'number,' for there are four types of elements used with operators in APL. They are:

1. Scalars (these are what most people call numbers)
2. Vectors (a row of scalars)
3. Matrices (rows and columns of scalars)
4. Literals (letters and other characters)

If the negation symbol is put between two arguments it will be used as subtraction, a binary operation:

```
      4 − 3
1
      5 − 8
¯3
      ¯4 − ¯2
¯2
```

The ¯ symbol next to the result is different from the operation symbol next to the argument. The operation symbol is lower and longer.

The most common operations are addition, subtraction, multiplication, division, and exponentiation. But in APL there are over 20 operation symbols and most of these are used with two rules, one as a binary operation and one as a monary operation. Some examples of operation symbols used in two ways are

+ − × ÷ * ⌊ ⌈ | ! ⍟ ?

It will be necessary to learn the double meanings of these operation symbols. Definitions of these operations can be found in Table C-1.

Since an operation symbol has two meanings, how does the computer know which is intended? If there are two arguments around an operation symbol, the computer will assume a binary operation meaning. If there is only one argument

**Table C-1 Definition of 21 monary and binary operators**

| Monary form | | Operator | Binary form | |
|---|---|---|---|---|
| +B | $0 + B$ | + | A + B | *A* plus *B* |
| −B | $0 - B$ | − | A − B | *A* minus *B* |
| ×B | $-1$ if $B < 0$, 0 if $B = 0$, 1 if $B > 0$ | × | A × B | *A* times *B* |
| ÷B | $1 \div B$ | ÷ | A ÷ B | *A* divided by *B* |
| ∗B | *e* to the *B* power ($e = 2.71828 \ldots$) | ∗ | A ∗ B | *A* to the *B*th power |
| ⌈B | next integer $\geq B$ | ⌈ | A ⌈ B | larger of *A* and *B* |
| ⌊B | next integer $\leq B$ | ⌊ | A ⌊ B | smaller of *A* and *B* |
| \|B | absolute value of *B* | \| | A\|B | *A* modulo *B* |
| ⊛B | natural logarithm of *B* | ⊛ | A ⊛ B | logarithm of *B* to base *A* |
| !B | factorial of *B* or the gamma function of $B + 1$ | ! | A ! B | combinations of *B* things taken *A* at a time |
| ○B | $B \times 3.14159 \ldots$ | ○ | A ○ B | trigometric functions (see insert at left) |
| | | < | A < B | 1 if *A* is less than *B* |
| | | ≤ | A ≤ B | 1 if *A* is not greater than *B* |
| | | = | A = B | 1 if *A* equals *B* |
| | | ≥ | A ≥ B | 1 if *A* is not less than *B* |
| | | > | A > B | 1 if *A* is greater than *B* |
| | | ≠ | A ≠ B | 1 if *A* is not equal to *B*, otherwise six above = 0 |
| | | ∧ | A ∧ B | and |
| | | ∨ | A ∨ B | or |
| | | ⍲ | A ⍲ B | nand |
| | | ⍱ | A ⍱ B | nor |

Trigometric binary operations

| (−A) ○ B | A | A ○ B |
|---|---|---|
| $\sqrt{1 - B^2}$ | 0 | $\sqrt{1 - B^2}$ |
| arcsin *B* | 1 | sine *B* |
| arccos *B* | 2 | cosine *B* |
| arctan *B* | 3 | tangent *B* |
| $\sqrt{-1 + B^2}$ | 4 | $\sqrt{1 + B^2}$ |
| arcsinh *B* | 5 | sinh *B* |
| arccosh *B* | 6 | cosh *B* |
| arctanh *B* | 7 | tanh *B* |

| *A* | *B* | *A* ∧ *B* | *A* ∨ *B* | A ⍲ B | A ⍱ B |
|---|---|---|---|---|---|
| 0 | 0 | 0 | 0 | 1 | 1 |
| 0 | 1 | 0 | 1 | 1 | 0 |
| 1 | 0 | 0 | 1 | 1 | 0 |
| 1 | 1 | 1 | 1 | 0 | 0 |

next to the operation symbol, the computer assumes the monary operation meaning. For example, let us use the ⌈ symbols (see Table C-1 for the definition of ⌈):

```
      3 ⌈ 4.2
4.2
      ⌈ 4.2
5
```

**Binary operation** A binary operation is a rule that is applied to two elements from two sets which gives a third element. (A binary operation is sometimes called a *dyadic function.*) The result must be unique. Addition is an obvious example of binary operation:

```
      4 + 2
6
```

Two numbers are used to get a third number. The number 4 and 2 always equals 6, so the answer is unique.

To use a binary operation, there must be an operation symbol (+ in the above example), an element on the left of the symbol, and another element on its right. The elements used with the rule are called *arguments.* The binary operation always has two arguments, a left and a right. The set of elements from which the left argument comes is called the *left domain* and the set of elements for the right argument is called the *right domain.* The result is an element from a set called the *range.*

**Monary operation** An operation with only one argument is called a *monary* operation. In some APL literature the monary operation is called a *monadic function.* In APL the argument of the monary operation always appears on the right of the operation sign. An example of a monary operation is negation. The rule of negation is to change the sign of the argument (with the exception of zero which has no sign and is not changed):

```
      −4    (monary operation sign and argument)
¯4    (result)
```

## C-3 ARGUMENTS

So far all the examples have used only scalar arguments. But other types can be used, too.

**Vector** A vector is a row of elements. Here are some examples:

```
3  4
2  4.1   ¯3  6  7
6
1  2  3  4  5  6  7  8  9  10
```

The elements of a vector are called *components* and are separated by spaces. A vector may have almost any number of components, or even no components. The vector which has no components is called an *empty* vector. Empty vectors are very useful in APL, and you will use them extensively in writing programs. The maximum number of components allowed depends on the computer installation. Some permit as many as 10,000.

Vectors can be used as arguments for many binary operations such as +, ×, =, and ÷:

```
      2  3 + 4  5
6  8
```

The operation in the above example has only two arguments, where each *argument* is a two-component vector. Addition of vectors is done with component-by-component addition. If the arguments of the operations are vectors, the vectors must have the same number of components. For instance, if we type

```
      1  3  4 + 2  3
```

then the computer will respond with

```
LENGTH ERROR
```

The above vectors cannot be added because they do not have the same length or dimension, i.e., they do not have the same number of components. The left and right domains can be vectors, but they must be of the same length. The *range* will be the set of all vectors of the same length as the vectors of the domains.

The right and left domain do not have to contain the same type of elements. For instance, the left domain could be the set of scalars and the right domain could be vectors of any length. APL assumes a single number is a scalar and not a one-element vector:

```
      4 × 2  1  6  7
8  4  24  28
```

The above operation multiplies the scalar (4) by each component of the vector (2 1 6 7).

Here are some more examples with division:

```
      4  8  2 ÷ 2  4  1
2  2  2
```

```
      2 ÷ 4 8 2
.5  .25  1
      4 8 2 ÷ 2
2 4 1
```

**Matrix** Matrices consist of rows and columns of numbers. They are two-dimensional arrays. Here are four examples of matrices:

```
2  4      3  8      2  6      4
6  1      2  1
          4  6
```

Arrays can have 3, 4, or even more dimensions in APL.

The first matrix above is a "two by two," for it has two rows and two columns. Rows are the horizontal lists of numbers and columns the vertical lists. The second example is a three-by-two matrix (three rows and two columns). The third example is a one-by-two matrix, and the last example is a "one by one." Matrices can also be empty.

Matrices are said to be *conformable* if they have the same number of rows and columns, respectively. No two of the matrices listed above are conformable because no two of them have the same number of rows and columns:

```
      2  4  1     1  3  2
               +
      1  0  2     6  7  2
3  7  3
7  7  4
         8  7
               -  4
        ¯1  2
    4  3
   ¯5 ¯2
```

## C-4 ORDER OF OPERATIONS

When a mathematical statement has more than one operation, the order in which the operations will be performed must be considered. For instance, in the statement:

$$4 - 3 \times 5 + 2$$

what should be done first, $4 - 3$, or $3 \times 5$, or $5 + 2$? Normally one would multiply $3 \times 5$ first because of the hierarchy of multiplication over addition. Then, proceeding from left to right, would come subtraction and addition. There is an hierarchy of operations in conventional notation because there are only about five operations to consider. But APL uses well over 30 operations and the user can design his or her own operations by writing a program. (This will be discussed later.) A hierarchical rule to determine which of these many operations should be done first would be very complicated.

APL solves this problem by abolishing the hierarchy of operations altogether. In APL the order of operations is from *right to left*. This may seem rather clumsy at first because we are used to working from left to right. Using APL the computer will solve $4 - 3 \times 5 + 2$ in this way:

$$4 - 3 \times (5 + 2) = 4 - 3 \times 7 = 4 - (3 \times 7) = 4 - 21 = {}^{-}17$$

Parentheses are still used in the traditional way. For example:

$$5 + (2 - 6) \times 3$$

The left argument of the multiplication is the value within the parentheses $(2 - 6)$ or $^{-}4$. Thus this statement is computed as follows:

$$5 + {}^{-}4 \times 3 = 5 + ({}^{-}4 \times 3) = 5 + {}^{-}12 = {}^{-}7$$

The right-to-left rule does not mean that the computer reads the line backwards, but that it executes the rightmost operation in a statement first, the next rightmost second, and so on. In:

$$8 \div 4 \div 2, \text{ the 4 is divided by 2 first}$$

$$8 \div (4 \div 2) = 8 \div 2 = 4$$

Here are some more examples (see Table C-2 for a definition of $\iota$).

| Examples | Computer's executions | Answers |
|---|---|---|
| $\iota 4 \times 2$ | $\iota(4 \times 2) = \iota 8$ | 1 2 3 4 5 6 7 8 |
| $(\iota 4) \times 2$ | 1 2 3 4 × 2 | 2 4 6 8 |
| $\iota 2 * 4 - 2$ | $\iota 2 * (4 - 2) = \iota 2 * 2 = \iota 4$ | 1 2 3 4 |
| $(4 + 12) * \div 6 \div 3$ | $(4 + 12) * \div 2 = (4 + 12) * 0.5 = 16 * 0.5$ | 4 |

## C-5 SOME SPECIAL OPERATORS

**Dimension (size): using ρ as a monary operation** The result is a vector describing the dimension of the argument. If the right argument is a vector, the result is a one-component vector representing the number of components in the right argument:

$\rho V$

13 (*V* is a vector with 13 components)

```
        ρR
1               (R is a one-component vector)
        ρC
                (an empty vector result means that C is a scalar)
        ρA
3  4            (A is a matrix with three rows and four columns)
        ρB
0               (B is an empty vector)
```

As a binary operation, $\rho$ will create a matrix from the right argument according to the left argument:

```
        2  3 ρ 1  2  3  4  5  6
1  2  3
4  5  6
```

To create a constant matrix, use a scalar as the right argument:

```
        2  4  ρ 0
0  0  0  0
0  0  0  0
```

To create a vector, use a scalar as the left argument:

```
        8  ρ  1
1  1  1  1  1  1  1  1
```

**Reduction** In conventional algebraic notation:

$$\sum_{i=1}^{n} A_i$$

means that $A$ is a vector and all its elements are summed. The $i$ next to the $A$ refers to its index.

In APL the same result is obtained by typing +/A. The / symbol means that the operation on its left is applied to all the elements of the vector.

If $A$ is the vector $A \leftarrow 1\ 2\ 3\ 4\ 5\ 6\ 7\ 8$, then +/A is executed by the computer as follows:

```
        1 + 2 + 3 + 4 + 5 + 6 + 7 + 8
36
        + /A
36
```

The / sign is called *reduction*, and in general it means that certain binary operations on its left are applied in right-to-left order to the vector on the right of the / sign.

If $B$ is the vector (1 2 3 4), then ×/B means 1 × 2 × 3 × 4:

```
        B←1  2  3  4
        ×/B
24
```

If $M$ is an $m$ by $n$ matrix, then +/M will sum each row and +/[1]M will sum each column:

```
        M←2  3 ρ 3  4  1  6  ¯2  7
        M
3   4   1
6  ¯2   7
        +/M
8   11
        +/[1]M
9   2   8
        +/+M     (sum of all elements in M)
19
```

**Relational operations** There are six relational operators in APL: <, ≤, =, ≥, >, ≠. They have the usual mathematical meanings. They give the truth or falsity of the relationship between two quantities. These operation symbols are used as binary operators only, and their domains and range are of standard scalar binary form. The result consists of only two numbers, 0 or 1. If the relationship is true, the result is 1; if false, 0:

```
        4 < 10
1
        10 < 4
0
        5 = ¯5
0
        3 ≤ 1  2  3  4  5
0  0  1  1  1
```

```
      1  2  3  4 = 1  2  3  4
1  1  1  1
      A←4
      B←5
      X←3 × A = B
      X
0
      X←3 × B > A
      X
3
      X←¯1  2  ¯3  8  6  0  ¯2
      X < 0
1  0  1  0  0  0  1
```

A vector of only ones and zeros is called a *logical* vector. Using a relational operation on *X* will always give us a logical vector. The logical vector above indicates which elements in *X* are negative. To find the number of negative elements in *X* we can count the ones or add all the elements in the logical vector:

```
      +/X < 0
3
```

**Catenation: using , as a binary operator** The comma is used in APL as an operator with domains of scalars, vectors, or literals (more about literals later). The *catenation* operation is used to chain together two vectors to make a single vector. It will also attach a scalar to a vector or make a vector of two or more scalars:

```
      A←2
      B←3
      C←5
```

The numbers 2 3 5 can be typed with spaces between them to obtain a vector, but if A B C are typed with spaces, an error message will result. To make a vector out of A, B, and C, one must type:

```
      A,B,C
2  3  5
```

Compatible matrices can be catenated by rows or by columns:

```
        M1←2 3 ρ 1 2 3 4 5 6
        M2←2 3 ρ 7 8 9 10 11 12
        M1, M2
 1 2 3   7   8   9
 4 5 6  10  11  12
        M1,[1]M2
  1   2   3
  4   5   6
  7   8   9
 10  11  12
```

## C-6 PROGRAMS

Figure B-3 shows a FORTRAN program to compute the mean, variance, and standard deviation of a vector of *N* numbers. Below are the steps needed in APL to compute the same statistics for the vector 23 17 7 4 without writing a program:

| | |
|---|---|
| X←23 17 7 4 | (assign the data to *X*) |
| MEAN←(+/X) ÷ 4 | (compute $\sum X/4$ and assign to MEAN) |
| DSQ←(X − MEAN)*2 | (square the deviations of all numbers from the mean and assign them to DSQ) |
| SS← +/DSQ | (sum the squared deviations and assign the sum to SS) |
| VAR←SS ÷ N − 1 | (compute the variance; notice that parentheses are not needed around $N - 1$) |
| SD←VAR * .5 | (compute the square root of the variance) |
| MEAN, VAR, SD | (print out the three numbers) |

It would be convenient to store these instructions so that every time they need to be repeated, they could simply be called from storage.

The computer has the ability to store a set of instructions as well as a set of numbers. The latter can be stored by assignment to a variable name such as $X \leftarrow 2\ 3\ 5$, and a set of instructions can be stored by defining a program under a program name. The program name has the same characteristics as a variable name.

1. Program names can contain letters and numbers, but a letter must start the word.
2. No spaces are allowed.
3. There is no limit on the size of the name.

The numbers stored under variable names can be used by typing the variable name, and stored instructions can be executed by typing the program name.

## Starting the Program Definition

To define a program under a certain program name, the symbol ∇ (called *del*) is typed along with the program name. When the RETURN is pushed the computer will print [1]. Next to this 1 in square brackets the user types his first line of instructions. After the RETURN button is pushed and the [2] is typed, the second line is inserted. In this way all the lines of instructions are submitted. At the end ∇ is typed again to indicate to the computer that the definition is finished.

As an example, let us program the steps to compute the mean, variance, and standard deviation of a set of numbers. Let us call the program DSTAT.

First, ∇ and the program name must be typed:

```
      ∇ DSTAT
[1]   N←ρ X
[2]   MEAN←(+/X)÷N
[3]   DSQ←(X − MEAN) *2
[4]   SS←+/DSQ
[5]   VAR←SS ÷ N − 1
[6]   SD←VAR * 0.5
[7]   MEAN, VAR, SD
[8]   ∇                    (closes the definition)
```

To run the program, first assign a vector to $X$ and then type the program name. The desired information will be printed out automatically:

```
   X←23  17  7  4
   DSTAT
12.75    77.58    8.808
```

If a vector is not assigned to $X$ before typing the program name, the computer notes this error:

VALUE ERROR (type of error)

DSTAT [1] N←ρX (location of error in program)

Value error means that a variable name was used before it had been assigned a value. The program run has been suspended on line 1 waiting for the operator to find the error and correct it. So assign a vector to $X$:

X←10 4 5 6 15

To restart the program where it stopped, type, an arrow pointing to line 1:

→1

1 6.4 9

Now the run is completed. To start from the beginning, type →0, and then type the program name:

→0

DSTAT

1 6.4 9

Not typing →0 before running the program will probably cause no harm. However, the suspended run will be stored in the active workspace. It is advisable to always unsuspend an unfinished program run to avoid possible difficulties.

## C-7 CONTROLLING THE ORDER OF EXECUTION OF A PROGRAM

Inside each workspace there is a line counter which tells the computer which line of the program to execute next. Normally, when a program name is typed, the line counter starts out as one and increases by one as each new line is executed. If a program has seven lines, then after the computer executes line 7, it sets its line counter to 8 and looks for line 8. If there is no line 8, it concludes that it has reached the end of the program. However, the normal execution of the line counter can be interfered with by using the branch arrow →.

The statement →2 tells a program to branch to line 2. The statement →0 tells a program to branch out of the program, i.e., to quit. A branch to an empty vector means to branch to nowhere, but to continue the program in sequence.

**Compression: using / as a binary operator** The left domain must be the set of logical vectors or scalars and the right domain the set of vectors or scalars of any number or literals. However, the right and left arguments must be compatible.

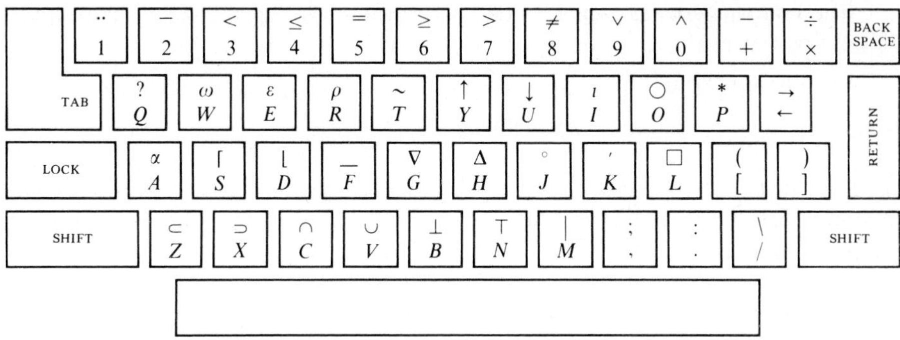


**Figure C-1** APL keyboard.

## Table C-2 The APL character set

<table>
<tr><td>¨</td><td>dieresis</td><td>⍺</td><td>alpha</td><td>⍱</td><td>nor</td><td>~</td><td>∨</td></tr>
<tr><td>¯</td><td>overbar</td><td>⌈</td><td>upstile</td><td>⍲</td><td>nand</td><td>~</td><td>∧</td></tr>
<tr><td><</td><td>less</td><td>⌊</td><td>downstile</td><td>⍒</td><td>del stile</td><td>∇</td><td>|</td></tr>
<tr><td>≤</td><td>not greater</td><td>_</td><td>underbar</td><td>⍋</td><td>delta stile</td><td>∆</td><td>|</td></tr>
<tr><td>=</td><td>equal</td><td>∇</td><td>del</td><td>⌽</td><td>circle stile</td><td>○</td><td>|</td></tr>
<tr><td>≥</td><td>not less</td><td>∆</td><td>delta</td><td>⍉</td><td>circle slope</td><td>○</td><td>\</td></tr>
<tr><td>></td><td>greater</td><td>∘</td><td>null</td><td>⊖</td><td>circle bar</td><td>○</td><td>−</td></tr>
<tr><td>≠</td><td>not equal</td><td>'</td><td>quote</td><td>⍟</td><td>log</td><td>○</td><td>*</td></tr>
<tr><td>∨</td><td>or</td><td>⎕</td><td>quad</td><td>⌶</td><td>I-beam</td><td>⊥</td><td>⊤</td></tr>
<tr><td></td><td></td><td></td><td></td><td></td><td></td><td></td><td></td></tr>
<tr><td>∧</td><td>and</td><td>(</td><td>open paren</td><td>⍫</td><td>del tilde</td><td>∇</td><td>~</td></tr>
<tr><td>−</td><td>bar</td><td>)</td><td>close paren</td><td>⍎</td><td>base null</td><td>⊥</td><td>∘</td></tr>
<tr><td>÷</td><td>divide</td><td>[</td><td>open bracket</td><td>⍕</td><td>top null</td><td>⊤</td><td>∘</td></tr>
<tr><td>+</td><td>plus</td><td>]</td><td>close bracket</td><td>⍀</td><td>slope bar</td><td>\</td><td>−</td></tr>
<tr><td>×</td><td>times</td><td>⊂</td><td>open shoe</td><td>⌿</td><td>slash bar</td><td>/</td><td>−</td></tr>
<tr><td>?</td><td>query</td><td>⊃</td><td>close shoe</td><td>⍝</td><td>cap null</td><td>∩</td><td>∘</td></tr>
<tr><td>⍵</td><td>omega</td><td>∩</td><td>cap</td><td>⍞</td><td>quote quad</td><td>'</td><td>⎕</td></tr>
<tr><td>∊</td><td>epsilon</td><td>∪</td><td>cup</td><td>!</td><td>quote dot</td><td>'</td><td>.</td></tr>
<tr><td>⍴</td><td>rho</td><td>⊥</td><td>base</td><td>⌹</td><td>domino</td><td>⎕</td><td>÷</td></tr>
<tr><td>~</td><td>tilde</td><td>⊤</td><td>top</td><td></td><td></td><td></td><td></td></tr>
<tr><td>↑</td><td>up (arrow)</td><td>|</td><td>stile</td><td></td><td></td><td></td><td></td></tr>
<tr><td>↓</td><td>down (arrow)</td><td>;</td><td>semicolon</td><td></td><td></td><td></td><td></td></tr>
<tr><td>⍳</td><td>iota</td><td>:</td><td>colon</td><td></td><td></td><td></td><td></td></tr>
<tr><td>○</td><td>circle</td><td>,</td><td>comma</td><td></td><td></td><td></td><td></td></tr>
<tr><td>*</td><td>star</td><td>.</td><td>dot</td><td></td><td></td><td></td><td></td></tr>
<tr><td>→</td><td>right (arrow)</td><td>\</td><td>slope</td><td></td><td></td><td></td><td></td></tr>
<tr><td>←</td><td>left (arrow)</td><td>/</td><td>slash</td><td></td><td></td><td></td><td></td></tr>
<tr><td></td><td></td><td></td><td>space</td><td></td><td></td><td></td><td></td></tr>
</table>

The left argument compresses the right argument depending on the position of the zeros in the logical vector:

```
        1 0 1 / 2 −8 4   (the middle zero compresses out the middle
                          element of 2 −8 4)
  2 4
        0 0 1 0 0 1 / 1 2 3 4 5 6
  3 6
```

Only the third and the sixth elements are retained in the result because the other positions contained zeros in the logical vector:

```
        1/10
  10
        0/10
                (an empty vector)
```

The left argument of / can be computed by a relational operator:

```
        (X = 2)/4
```

If $X = 2$ is true, then the result is 4. If $X = 2$ is false, then the result is an empty vector. Using this in a branch statement:

```
        → (X = 2)/4
```

the program will branch to line 4 only when $X$ equals 2, otherwise it will continue to the next line.

For example, suppose one wished $Y$ to be the square root of $X$ if $X$ is positive, and to equal 0 if $X$ is not positive.

```
[1] → (X ≤ 0)/4     (go to line 4 if X ≤ 0)
[2] Y←X*.5          (Y is assigned √X)
[3] → 5             (go to line 5)
[4] X←0
[5]
```

## C-8 PROGRAM LOOPING

Some programs need to repeat a sequence of instructions $N$ number of times. To do this a counter is needed to count the number of repeats of a sequence of instructions (program loops) and a conditional branch statement is needed to terminate the looping. The following lines of a program are the necessary instructions to make the program loop $N$ times. $I$ is the counter:

```
[1]  I←1
[2]                   (lines 2 through 4 do the required computation)
[5]  I←I+1            (increment I by 1)
[6]  →(I≤N)/2         (branch to line 2 or proceed to line 7)
[7]
```

### Branching To Line Label

The instruction $\rightarrow X$ will cause the program to branch to the line number having the value of $X$. Thus $X$ must be assigned a nonnegative integer.

A line label is a variable that is automatically assigned the value of the line that it is in. This must be done in a special way.

```
[1]  I←1              (beginning line 2 with B1 followed by a
[2]  B1:              colon automatically gives B1 the value
                      of 2)
[5]  I←I+1
[6]  →(I≤N)/B1
```

Line labels permit changes in line numbers without the inconvenience of changing the branch statement. Changing line numbers is such a common occurrence that one should always use line labels in one's branch statements when designing a program.

## C-9 OUTPUT CONTROL

Alphabetic characters (literals) may be assigned to variables if the character string is surrounded by quotes:

```
      L←'MEAN ='
      ρL
5                        (the character string has five characters)
```

Blanks are characters also:

```
      L←' MEAN  ='
      ρL
7
```

To convert numbers to literal characters one needs to surround them by quotes. However, to convert a numeric value of a variable to a literal string one must use the format operator "top null," ⍕, which is the overstrike of null, ∘, and top, ⊤. As a monadic operator, ⍕ converts the value of the right argument to a literal string in a format determined automatically by APL. If the user wishes to specify the format to be printed, he does so by a two-element left argument:

```
      X←5.0
      X
5                 (the number 5 is printed with APL determined format)
      ⍕X³
5                 (literal 5 is printed with APL determined format)
      5 2⍕X       (literal output in five spaces and rounded to two
 5.00              decimal places)
```

The first element of the left argument determines the number of spaces used to print the number and the second element determines the number of decimal places. The last line of the program in Sec. C-6 can now be printed as follows:

```
[7]  'MEAN = ',(8 2⍕MEAN),' VAR = ',(8 0⍕VAR),' SD = ',(8 2⍕SD)
```

Calling the program by typing its name, prints out the results as specified by the above formats:

```
      X←23  17  7  4
      DESC
MEAN =      12.75  VAR =       78  SD =      8.81
```

## C-10 SOME SPECIAL MATRIX OPERATORS

The matrix product is a special case of the inner product operator denoted by +.×:

```
      M1←2  2ρ3  4  1  7
      M1
3    4
1    7
```

```
        M2←2  2ρ8  1  2  3
        M2
  8   1
  2   3

        M1 + . × M2
  32   15
  22   22

        B←2  1
        M1 + . × B
  10   9
```

(APL does not distinguish between row and column vectors)

The Domino operator, denoted ⌹ (the overstrike of the quad, □, and divide, ÷), computes the generalized inverse of a matrix when used as a monary operator. If the right argument is a square matrix, then it will find the inverse of that matrix if one exists:

```
        ⌹M1
  0.4118      0.2353
  0.05822     0.1765
```

To find the solution to the system of equations $(M1)X = B$, one needs only to "divide" $B$ by $M1$:

```
        X ← B⌹M1
        X
  0.5882     0.0588
```

Thus, B⌹M1 is equivalent to (⌹M1) + . × B.

If $X$ and $Y$ are vectors of equal length, then $Y$⌹$X$ finds the least-squares solution $b$ to the equation $Y = bX$, the line of best fit through the origin:

```
        X←1  2  3  4
        Y←3.1  4.5  12.3  14
        X⌹Y
  3.5
```

**Transpose** The transpose of a matrix can be obtained by using ⍉ (overstrike of circle, o, and slope, \) as monary operator:

```
        ⍉M1
3    1
4    7

        X←1  1  1  1,X
        X
1  1  1  1  1  2  3  4

        X←2  4⍴X
        X
1  1  1  1
1  2  3  4

        X←⍉X
        X
1  1
1  2
1  3
1  4

        Y⌹X
−1.65  4.05
```

After changing $X$ into a matrix with ones in the first column, the operation $Y$⌹$X$ finds the least-squares solution of the equation $Y = a + bX$. To find the least-squares solution to the equation $Y = a + bX + cZ$ where $Z$ is the vector [0.5 −0.3 0.1 −1.2], the following steps are needed:

```
        Z←.5 ¯.3 .1 ¯1.2
        X←1 2 3 4
        X←⍉3 4⍴1 1 1 1,X,Z
        X
1  1   0.5        (this step is not needed but is
1  2  ¯0.3         included to check to see
1  3   0.1         if X is in the desired form)
1  4  ¯1.2
```

```
      Y⌹X
¯5.14    5.77   3.67      (a = ¯5.14, b = 5.77, and c = 3.67)
```

## C-11 EDITING A PROGRAM

In the program EXAMPLE displayed below, the word MISPELLED is mispelled on line 2, and line 5 is a duplicate of line 4. To correct the program it must be opened by typing ∇ and the program name. The response will be the line number of the line following the last line in the program. To display the function, type quad in brackets, [□].

```
        ∇EXAMPLE
[6]     [□]
        ∇EXAMPLE
[1]     'THIS PROGRAM WAS CREATED'
[2]     'WITH A MIPELKED WORD'
[3]     'TO DEMONSTRATE EDITING'
[4]     'CAPABILITY OF APL.'
[5]     'CAPABILITY OF APL.'
[6]
```

The system is waiting for input of more instructions on line 6. The programmer can now add more lines to the program, go to another line for editing, or close the program without change by typing ∇. To correct line 2 the programmer types [2□*n*] where *n* is an arbitrary positive integer. Line 2 will be displayed and the terminal will space *n* spaces. The programmer then spaces or backspaces until the typeball is at the point of correction. To put a space between I and P in MIPELKED and delete K and leave one space, a 1 is typed under P, a / is typed under K, and a 1 is typed under E. When the carriage is returned, the statement is redisplayed. Each character understruck by a / is deleted, each character understruck by a digit *k* is preceded by *k* added spaces, and each character understruck by a letter is preceded by 5 × *R* spaces, where *R* is the rank of the letter in the alphabet:

```
[6]     [2□10]
[2]     'WITH A MIPELKED WORD'
                  1   /1
[2]     'WITH A MI PEL ED WORD'
```

The carriage now returns automatically to the first space for input into the space. The programmer types S between I and P and L between L and E. To delete line 5, the programmer types [Δ5]. Editing commands are listed below:

| | |
|---|---|
| ∇EXAMPLE | (opens program EXAMPLE) |
| [□] | (displays entire program) |
| ∇EXAMPLE[□] | (opens program EXAMPLE and displays entire program |
| ∇EXAMPLE[□]∇ | (opens, displays, and closes the program EXAMPLE) |
| [n□] | (displays line number *n*) |
| [□n] | (displays line *n* and all following lines) |
| [Δn] | (deletes line *n*) |

∇EXAMPLE[2.5] 'AND DUPLICATED LINE'∇

(opens program EXAMPLE, adds a line between lines 2 and 3, and closes the program; the program lines will now be renumbered from 1 to 6)

| | |
|---|---|
| [n□k] | (displays line *n*, spaces *k* spaces, and awaits editing instructions) |
| [0□k] | (to edit line 0, the header of the program) |

## C-12 MORE PROGRAMMING DETAILS

### Creating Operations

A program can be defined in such a way that it can be used as a monary or binary operator. Suppose, for example, that the program DESC of Sect. C-6 were written as a monary operation where the right argument is a vector and the output is a three-element vector for the mean, variance, and standard deviation of the right argument. To do this the header and line 7 are changed as follows:

```
        DESC[0]
[0]     D←DESC X;N,MEAN,DSQ,SS,VAR,SD
[7]     D←MEAN,VAR,SD∇
```

The variables following the semicolon are now local, i.e., the values assumed by the variables as the result of the program are temporary during the execution of the program. They resume their old values, if any, after the execution of the program. The variables *D* and *X* are also local to the function. DESC is now a monary operator and behaves as any other such operator:

```
      DESC  23    17    7    4
 12.75  77.58     8.808
```

```
      Y←23    17    7    4
      R←DESC Y
      R
12.75  77.58   8.808
      2 × DESC Y
25.5   155.2   17.62
```

## Table C-3 Advanced APL operators

| Operation | Definition and example |
|---|---|
| A?B | *A* random integers from 1 to *B* without duplication |
| ?B | random equiprobable integer from 1 to *B*; ?10 10 ≡ 3 7 |
| ~ B | not *B*(logical arguments only); ~0 1 0 ≡ 1 0 1 |
| AρB | reshape *B* to have dimension *A* |
| ρB | dimension of *B*; ρ3 2 1 3 ≡ 4 |
| A[B] | the elements of *A* at locations *B* |
| AιB | first location of *B* within *A* or 1 + ρ*A*; 2 3 1 3ι3 ≡ 2 |
| ιB | the first *B* consecutive integers; ι4 ≡ 1 2 3 4 |
| A ∊ B | which elements of *A* are members of *B*(logical result); 4 ∊ 2 3 1 3 ≡ 0 |
| A ⊤ B | representation of *B* in base *A*; 24 60 60⊤ 2723 ≡ 1 2 3 |
| A ⊥ B | value of *B* in base *A*; 10⊥1 7 7 6 ≡ 1776 |
| A⌽B | rotation of *B* according to *A*; 3⌽ι4 ≡ 2 3 4 1; ¯3⌽ι4 ≡ 4 1 2 3 |
| ⌽B | reversal of *B*; ⌽1 2 3 4 ≡ 4 3 2 1 |
| A⍉B | transpose by *A* of *B* |
| ⍉B | tranpose of *B* |
| ,B | ravel of *B*(make *B* a vector) |
| A,B | *B* catenated to *A* |
| A↑B | take the first *A*(or last *A* if *A* < 0) elements of *B*; 2↑ι5 ≡ 1 2 |
| A↓B | drop the first *A*(or last *A* if *A* > 0) elements of *B*; 2↓ι5 ≡ 3 4 5 |
| ⍋B | indexes of elements of *B* in ascending order; ⍋ 2 3 1 3 ≡ 3 1 2 4 |
| B[⍒B] | reorders *B* into ascending order |
| ⍒B | indexes of elements of *B* in descending order; ⍒2 3 1 3 ≡ 2 4 1 3 |
| B[↓B] | reorders *B* into descending order |
| A⌹B | division of matrix *A* by matrix or vector *B*; A⌹B ≡ (A⌹) + . × B |
| ⌹B | generalized inverse of *B* |
| ⍎ B | execute the character vector *B* as an APL expression |
| ⍕B | convert numeric value of *B* to characters |
| A⍕B | format *B* using *A* to determine the field width and precision |
| A/B | *A*(logical) compression of *B*; 1 0 1 0/2 3 1 3 ≡ 2 1 |
| A\B | *A*(logical) expansion of *B*; 1 0 1\1 2 ≡ 1 0 2 |
| f/B | reduction of *B* by the operator *f*; *B*[1]f*B*[2]f*B*[3]f... for all elements of B; +/ι4 ≡ 10 |
| f\B | scan of *B* by the operator *f*; R←f\B ≡ R[1]←B[1], R[2]←f/B[1 2], R[3]←f/B[1 2 3], ...; +\ι3 ≡ 1 3 6 |
| A∘.fB | outer product by operator *f*; R ← A°. fB ≡ R[I;J] ← A[I]fB[J] for all I,J |
| Af.gB | inner product by operators *f* and *g*; R ← Af.gB ≡ R[1;J] ← g/A[I;]fB[;J] |

**Table C-4 APL system commands**

| Command | Definition |
|---|---|
| )OFF | End work session |
| )OFF HOLD | End APL work session but hold connection |
| )LOAD wsname | Activate a copy of a stored workspace named wsname |
| )COPY[lib]wsname | Copy all variables, programs, and groups from workspace wsname in library lib |
| )COPY[lib]wsname obj1,obj2,... | Copy one or more variables, programs, or groups from workspace wsname in library lib |
| )PCOPY | Same as above, but will not copy items already named in current workspace |
| )GROUP gpname [objects] | Gather variables and programs into a group |
| )ERASE object(s) | Erase one or more variables, programs, or groups |
| )SAVE | Save a copy of the active workspace using its current identification |
| )SAVE wsname | Save a copy of the active workspace with new identifier wsname |
| )FNS | List names of programs |
| )VARS | List names of variables |
| )GRPS | List names of groups |
| )GRP gpname | List names of variables and programs within gpname |
| )LIB [lib] | List names of workspaces in library lib |
| )MSG userid[text] | Address text to designated user and lock keyboard |
| )OPR[text] | Address text to system operator and lock keyboard |

## Program Input

A program can be temporarily suspended to wait input as demonstrated by the following program:

```
      ∇PRIN; C,I,P
[1]   'ENTER CAPITAL AMOUNT IN DOLLARS'
[2]   C←⎕
[3]   'ENTER RATE OF INTEREST IN PERCENT'
[4]   I←⎕
[5]   'ENTER PERIOD IN YEARS'
[6]   P←⎕
[7]   'PRINCIPAL AFTER ', ⍕P,' YEARS IS',10 2⍕C × (1 + .01 × I)*P
      ∇
```

A summary of advanced APL operations is presented in Table C-3. Other possibly necessary system commands can be found in Table C-4.

## PROBLEMS

**C-1** Fill in the blanks with the appropriate word(s).

(*a*) A rule which performs on one or two elements to produce a unique result is called a(n) ______________________.

(*b*) A(n) ______________________ operation has one ______________________, and a(n) ______________________ operation has two ______________________.

(*c*) Four types of elements used with operators in APL are ______________________, ______________________, ______________________, and ______________________.

(*d*) An operator is defined for certain sets of elements. These sets are called ______________________; for example, the left ______________________ of the binary operator $\rho$ is the set of positive integers or set of vectors of positive integers.

(*e*) The APL symbols for the algebraic expression $R = \sum X_i$ where $X$ is a vector are ______________________.

(*f*) The APL symbols for the algebraic expression for the maximum of two numbers $X$ and $Y$, $R = \max(X, Y)$, are ______________________.

(*g*) The APL symbols for a program statement to branch to line 2 if $X$ is less than 10 are ______________________.

**C-2** Write a program to compute the mean, standard deviation, mean deviation, and range of a vector $X$. Use ⌈/X and ⌊/X to find the largest and smallest numbers in $X$.

**C-3** Write a program that creates a vector of standardized scores from a vector of data. The program must compute the mean and standard deviation. (See the program in Sec. C-6.)

**C-4** Do Prob. 8-3(*a*) and (*b*) on an APL terminal.

**C-5** Write a program to compute the Spearman rank correlation coefficient [see Eq. (9-5)].

**C-6** Do Prob. 9-7 on an APL terminal.

## REFERENCES

### Theory

C-1. Gilman, L., and A. J. Rose: *APL: An Interactive Approach*, 2d ed., Wiley, New York, 1974.

C-2. Gray, L. D.: *A Course in APL/360 with Applications*, Addison-Wesley, Reading, Mass., 1973.

C-3. Iverson, K. E.: *A Programming Language*, Wiley, New York, 1962.

C-4. Mock, T. J., and M. A. Vasarhelyi: *APL for Management*, Wiley-Becker and Hayes, New York, 1972.

C-5. Polivka, R. P., and S. Pakin: *APL: The Language and Its Usage*, Prentice-Hall, Englewood Cliffs, N.J., 1975.

### Applications

C-6. Gazis, D. C.: *A Computer Model for the Financial Analysis of Urban Projects*, Report No. RC-2850, IBM Research Center, Yorktown Heights, N.Y.

C-7. Kvaternik, R.: *An APL Terminal Approach to Computer Mapping*, Technical Report CSRG-21, Toronto University, Toronto, December, 1972.

C-8. Loken, S. A.: "An Interactive Long Range Planning Model Written in APL," in P. Gjerlov, H. J. Helms, and J. Nielsen (Eds.), *APL Congress 73*, American-Elsevier, New York, 1973.

C-9. Petersen, T. I.: *The Ecology Decision Game: Introduction*, Report No. G320-2073, IBM Cambridge Scientific Center, Cambridge, Mass., September, 1971.

C-10. Smart, J. S.: *An APL Version of JABOWA, the Northeastern Forest Growth Simulation*, Report No. RC-3985, IBM Research Center, Yorktown Heights, N.Y., August, 1972.

C-11. Thygesen, S., and N. C. Mortensen: "APL in Local Government Economical and Physical Planning," in P. Gjerlov, H. J. Helms, and J. Nielsen (Eds.), *APL Congress 73*, American-Elsevier, New York, 1973.

C-12. Wahi, P. N., and T. I. Petersen: *The Ecology Decision Game: Management Science and Gaming*, Report No. G320-2076, IBM Cambridge Scientific Center, Cambridge, Mass., October, 1971.

APPENDIX

# D

# EXAMPLE DATA SETS

## DATA SET 1. ECONOMIC TIME SERIES

The following data are taken from *Fifth District Figures*, put out every year by the Federal Reserve Bank of Richmond.† They are totals of various economic indicators for those jurisdictions in the region covered by the fifth district of the Bank (Maryland, District of Columbia, Virginia, West Virginia, North Carolina, and South Carolina). The variables are as follows:

| Variable number | Description |
|---|---|
| 1 | Year |
| 2 | Population |
| 3 | Employment in nonagricultural establishments (1000) |
| 4 | Total personal income (millions of current dollars) |
| 5 | National consumer price index for all goods (1967 = 100.0) |
| 6 | State and local government employees |
| 7 | Federal government civilian employees |
| 8 | Land in farms (1000 acres) |
| 9 | Value of mineral production (millions of current dollars) |
| 10 | Value added by manufacturing (millions of current dollars) |
| 11 | New passenger cars registered (1000) |
| 12 | New trucks registered (1000) |
| 13 | Value of new private residential construction (millions of current dollars) |
| 14 | Sale of electric energy (billions of kilowatt hours) |
| 15 | Total investment of all banks (millions of current dollars) |
| 16 | Total revenues of state governments (millions of current dollars) |

† The consumer price index data are taken from the *Economic Report of the President*, U.S. Government Printing Office, Washington, D.C., 1975.

| Variable number | | | | | | | | | | | | | | | |
|---|---|---|---|---|---|---|---|---|---|---|---|---|---|---|---|
| 1 | 2 | 3 | 4 | 5 | 6 | 7 | 8 | 9 | 10 | 11 | 12 | 13 | 14 | 15 | 16 |
| 1960 | 16,631 | 4676 | 30,353 | 88.7 | 464,838 | 410,650 | 51,850 | 1055 | 12,262 | 507 | 75 | 681 | 60.4 | 5,022 | 2628 |
| 1961 | 16,925 | 4712 | 32,041 | 89.6 | 489,525 | 423,124 | 51,100 | 1052 | 12,478 | 468 | 79 | 777 | 64.8 | 5,440 | 2744 |
| 1962 | 17,218 | 4899 | 34,370 | 90.6 | 501,710 | 443,705 | 50,550 | 1093 | 13,768 | 568 | 93 | 921 | 69.8 | 5,718 | 3015 |
| 1963 | 17,530 | 5056 | 36,403 | 91.7 | 529,278 | 453,939 | 49,900 | 1149 | 14,872 | 643 | 113 | 1081 | 75.1 | 5,768 | 3271 |
| 1964 | 17,805 | 5219 | 39,462 | 92.9 | 556,300 | 457,001 | 49,250 | 1229 | 15,945 | 685 | 118 | 1170 | 82.6 | 6,010 | 3537 |
| 1965 | 18,056 | 5461 | 42,720 | 94.5 | 590,963 | 475,408 | 48,800 | 1307 | 17,612 | 786 | 124 | 1354 | 86.7 | 6,211 | 3921 |
| 1966 | 18,133 | 5788 | 47,141 | 97.2 | 641,375 | 513,218 | 47,300 | 1359 | 19,009 | 783 | 136 | 1067 | 94.6 | 6,276 | 4438 |
| 1967 | 18,310 | 6020 | 51,064 | 100.0 | 671,100 | 550,784 | 45,800 | 1420 | 19,988 | 702 | 125 | 1353 | 102.1 | 7,539 | 4904 |
| 1968 | 18,477 | 6210 | 56,105 | 104.2 | 709,800 | 571,699 | 45,100 | 1420 | 22,233 | 797 | 147 | 1555 | 114.5 | 8,265 | 5491 |
| 1969 | 18,591 | 6463 | 61,468 | 109.8 | 730,300 | 570,209 | 44,600 | 1494 | 23,507 | 832 | 161 | 1592 | 126.2 | 7,583 | 6245 |
| 1970 | 18,744 | 6588 | 67,266 | 116.3 | 757,800 | 547,964 | 43,200 | 1903 | 24,518 | 736 | 155 | 1796 | 135.0 | 8,974 | 7154 |
| 1971 | 19,039 | 6676 | 72,712 | 121.3 | 796,700 | 563,575 | 42,400 | 1935 | 26,279 | 873 | 177 | 2630 | 143.5 | 10,488 | 8189 |
| 1972 | 19,269 | 6910 | 80,446 | 125.3 | 843,500 | 522,659 | 41,700 | 2213 | 29,289 | 905 | 216 | 3472 | 153.7 | 11,272 | 9053 |
| 1973 | 19,420 | | | 133.1 | | | 41,100 | | | | | | | | |
| 1974 | | | | 147.7 | | | 40,700 | | | | | | | | |
| 1975 | | | | | | | | | | | | | | | |

# DATA SET 2. SURVEY OF SOLID WASTE HANDLING

These data were obtained in a 1971 mail survey of local governments.† Of those cities with a population greater than 150,000 people, 34 responded to the questionnaire. The variables included were:

| Variable number | Description | Code | Definition |
|---|---|---|---|
| 1 | Population (in thousands) | . | .... |
| 2 | Type of home storage of solid wastes | 1 | Plastic bags |
| | | 2 | Metal or plastic cans |
| | | 3 | Both |
| 3 | Type of collection organization | 1 | Municipal owned and operated |
| | | 2 | Contracted to private collections |
| | | 3 | Private, with homeowner paying collector |
| | | 4 | Both 1 and 2 |
| | | 5 | Both 1 and 3 |
| 4 | Location of collection | 1 | Backyard |
| | | 2 | Curb |
| | | 3 | Alley |
| | | 4 | Both 1 and 2 |
| | | 5 | Both 1 and 3 |
| | | 6 | Both 2 and 3 |
| | | 7 | All three |
| 5 | Mean haul distance to point of disposal | – | Miles |
| 6 | Control over private collectors? | 1 | Yes |
| | | 2 | No |
| 7 | Transfer operations employed in transport of solid waste? | 1 | Yes |
| | | 2 | No |
| 8 | Estimated cost of collection per home | – | $ per year (1971) |
| 9 | Type of disposal system employed | 1 | Sanitary landfill |
| | | 2 | Incineration |
| | | 3 | Both |
| 10 | Criteria used to select the disposal method being employed | 1 | Capital cost |
| | | 2 | Operating cost |
| | | 3 | Haul distance |
| | | 4 | Both capital and operating costs |
| | | 5 | All of these |
| | | 6 | None of these |
| 11 | Is the disposal site being employed the first priority location? | 1 | Yes |
| | | 2 | No |
| | | 3 | Not applicable |

† Dickey, J. W., D. M. Glancy, and E. M. Jennelle, *Technology Assessment for Programs of Local Government*, Lexington Books, Lexington, Mass., 1973.

| Variable number | Description | Code | Definition |
|---|---|---|---|
| 12 | Should a municipal government become involved in salvaging and receiving solid waste | 1 | Yes |
| | | 2 | No |
| | | 3 | No response |
| 13 | Does your city currently have a program to salvage marketable items from solid waste? | 1 | Yes |
| | | 2 | No |
| | | 3 | No response |
| 14–17 | If 13 is "yes," for which items? | 0 | On any variable = not that item |
| | | 1 | On variable 14 = paper |
| | | 1 | On variable 15 = glass |
| | | 1 | On variable 16 = cans |
| | | 1 | On variable 17 = large metal items |
| 18 | Do you use or have you considered a regional approach (at least countywide) for disposal operations? | 1 | Have considered |
| | | 2 | Have not considered |
| | | 3 | Use a regional approach |
| | | 4 | Do not use a regional approach |
| | | 5 | Have considered and do not use a regional approach |
| | | 6 | No response |

Variable number

| City number | 1 | 2 | 3 | 4 | 5 | 6 | 7 | 8 | 9 | 10 | 11 | 12 | 13 | 14 | 15 | 16 | 17 | 18 |
|---|---|---|---|---|---|---|---|---|---|---|---|---|---|---|---|---|---|---|
| 1 | 155 | 2 | 1 | 6 | 3 | 2 | 2 | 15.60 | 1 | 5 | 2 | 1 | 1 | 1 | 0 | 0 | 0 | 1 |
| 2 | 155 | 3 | 1 | 1 | 5 | 1 | 2 | | 3 | 3 | 1 | 1 | 1 | 1 | 1 | 0 | 1 | 3 |
| 3 | 165 | 3 | 2 | 6 | 11 | 1 | 1 | 15.60 | 1 | 6 | 3 | 1 | 2 | 0 | 0 | 0 | 0 | 6 |
| 4 | 165 | 2 | 1 | 2 | 6 | | 2 | | 1 | 2 | 1 | 2 | 2 | 0 | 0 | 0 | 0 | 3 |
| 5 | 178 | 2 | 2 | 6 | 6 | 2 | 2 | | 1 | 4 | 2 | 2 | 2 | 0 | 0 | 0 | 0 | 2 |
| 6 | 190 | 2 | 1 | 2 | 10 | 2 | 2 | 15.00 | 1 | 2 | 1 | 2 | 1 | 1 | 0 | 0 | 0 | 4 |
| 7 | 216 | 3 | 1 | 6 | 8 | 1 | 1 | 23.00 | 1 | 4 | 1 | 2 | 2 | 0 | 0 | 0 | 0 | 3 |
| 8 | 220 | 2 | 3 | 1 | | 1 | 2 | 28.00 | 1 | 4 | 1 | 1 | 2 | 0 | 0 | 0 | 0 | 3 |
| 9 | 250 | 3 | 1 | 5 | 2.5 | 2 | 2 | | 1 | 6 | 3 | 2 | 2 | 0 | 0 | 0 | 0 | 5 |
| 10 | 250 | 3 | 1 | 7 | 4 | 1 | 1 | | 3 | 5 | 2 | 2 | 2 | 0 | 0 | 0 | 0 | 5 |
| 11 | 260 | 2 | 1 | 4 | 20 | 2 | 2 | 26.00 | 1 | 4 | 1 | 1 | 2 | 0 | 0 | 0 | 0 | 4 |
| 12 | 273 | 3 | 1 | 6 | 8 | 1 | 2 | 50.00 | 1 | 4 | 1 | 2 | 1 | 1 | 0 | 0 | 0 | 3 |
| 13 | 300 | 2 | 1 | 1 | 5 | 1 | 2 | 36.00 | 3 | 4 | 2 | 1 | 1 | 0 | 0 | 1 | 1 | 1 |
| 14 | 303 | 3 | 1 | 2 | 6 | 1 | 2 | | 1 | 2 | 2 | 2 | 2 | 0 | 0 | 0 | 0 | 1 |
| 15 | 335 | 2 | 1 | 1 | 4 | 1 | 2 | | 2 | 6 | 3 | 2 | 2 | 0 | 0 | 0 | 0 | 5 |
| 16 | 360 | 3 | 2 | 5 | 9 | 1 | 1 | 30.00 | 1 | 5 | 2 | 1 | 2 | 0 | 0 | 0 | 0 | 1 |
| 17 | 390 | 2 | 1 | 2 | 11 | 2 | 2 | | 3 | 6 | 2 | 2 | 1 | 1 | 0 | 1 | 0 | 1 |
| 18 | 395 | 1 | 1 | 7 | 6 | 2 | 2 | 18.00 | 1 | 2 | 1 | 1 | 2 | 0 | 0 | 0 | 0 | 1 |
| 19 | 400 | 3 | 1 | 6 | 6 | 2 | 2 | | 1 | 5 | 2 | 2 | 1 | 0 | 0 | 0 | 1 | 1 |
| 20 | 500 | 3 | 1 | 7 | 7 | 2 | 2 | 19.00 | 3 | 2 | 1 | 3 | 2 | 0 | 0 | 0 | 0 | 1 |
| 21 | 500 | 3 | 3 | 1 | 6 | 2 | 2 | 33.00 | 1 | 6 | 1 | 2 | 2 | 0 | 0 | 0 | 0 | 5 |
| 22 | 500 | 2 | 5 | 7 | 3.5 | 1 | 1 | 25.00 | 1 | 4 | 1 | 2 | 2 | 0 | 0 | 0 | 0 | 3 |
| 23 | 500 | 3 | 1 | 2 | 12 | 2 | 2 | | 3 | 5 | 1 | 1 | 1 | 0 | 0 | 0 | 1 | 3 |
| 24 | 509 | 1 | 4 | 7 | | 1 | 2 | | 1 | 5 | 1 | 1 | 2 | 0 | 0 | 0 | 0 | 1 |

| City number | Variable number 1 | 2 | 3 | 4 | 5 | 6 | 7 | 8 | 9 | 10 | 11 | 12 | 13 | 14 | 15 | 16 | 17 | 18 |
|---|---|---|---|---|---|---|---|---|---|---|---|---|---|---|---|---|---|---|
| 25 | 517 | 3 | 4 | 6 | 10 | 1 | 2 | 32.00 | 1 | 5 | 2 | 1 | 2 | 0 | 0 | 0 | 0 | 5 |
| 26 | 531 | 2 | 2 | 1 | 2.5 | 1 | 1 | | 1 | 5 | 1 | 1 | 1 | 1 | 1 | 1 | 1 | 3 |
| 27 | 550 | 2 | 1 | 1 | 5 | 1 | 2 | | 3 | 3 | 1 | 1 | 1 | 0 | 0 | 1 | 0 | 1 |
| 28 | 625 | 2 | 1 | 6 | 5 | 2 | 2 | 16.00 | 2 | 6 | 3 | 1 | 1 | 0 | 0 | 0 | 1 | 6 |
| 29 | 641 | 3 | 2 | 6 | | 1 | 1 | 24.00 | 3 | 6 | 1 | 2 | 2 | 0 | 0 | 0 | 0 | 1 |
| 30 | 680 | 2 | 1 | 5 | 6 | 1 | 2 | 36.00 | 1 | 5 | 2 | 1 | 1 | 1 | 1 | 1 | 0 | 1 |
| 31 | 700 | 2 | 3 | 1 | 5 | 1 | 1 | 28.80 | 1 | 5 | 2 | 1 | 1 | 1 | 0 | 1 | 0 | 1 |
| 32 | 910 | 2 | 1 | 6 | 3 | 2 | 2 | 11.00 | 3 | 6 | 3 | 1 | 1 | 1 | 1 | 1 | 1 | 1 |
| 33 | 2800 | 3 | 1 | 6 | 12 | 2 | 2 | 15.00 | 1 | 2 | 1 | 3 | 3 | 0 | 0 | 0 | 0 | 3 |
| 34 | 7890 | 3 | 5 | 2 | | 1 | 1 | 50.00 | 3 | 5 | 1 | 2 | 1 | 1 | 1 | 0 | 0 | 2 |

## DATA SET 3. HOUSING AND TRAVEL

The data below come from the 1960 and 1970 *Census of Population and Housing* for the City of Roanoke, Virginia, and from the *Roanoke Valley Area Thoroughfare Plan, Roanoke, Virginia.*† The former is based on a complete (100 percent) sample of households. The latter is based on a $12\frac{1}{2}$ percent systematic sample of households in 1965. All data have been aggregated to fit the boundaries of the 1970 Census tracts (see Fig. D-1). The Census tract variables for both 1960 and 1970 are, except for total population and housing units, means of block values. The variables are as follows:

| Variable number | Description |
|---|---|
| 1 | Total population |
| 2 | Percentage of units lacking some or all plumbing |
| 3 | Percentage of units owner-occupied |
| 4 | Percentage of units with 1.01 or more persons per room |
| 5 | Number of rooms per owner-occupied housing unit |
| 6 | Number of rooms per renter-occupied housing unit |
| 7 | Value per owner-occupied housing unit |
| 8 | Rent per renter-occupied housing unit |
| 9 | Total housing units |

† Metropolitan Transportation Planning Division, Virginia Department of Highways, Richmond, Va., 1969.

## Census tract population and housing data

| Census tract number | 1960 variable number | | | | | | | | | 1970 variable number | | | | | | | | |
|---|---|---|---|---|---|---|---|---|---|---|---|---|---|---|---|---|---|---|
| | 1 | 2 | 3 | 4 | 5 | 6 | 7 | 8 | 9 | 1 | 2 | 3 | 4 | 5 | 6 | 7 | 8 | 9 |
| 1 | 4,498 | 15 | 1097 | 96 | 5.55 | 4.58 | 11,018 | 62.30 | 1389 | 4541 | 12 | 1130 | 92 | 5.6 | 4.8 | 14,100 | 81 | 1480 |
| 2 | 3,819 | 20 | 890 | 81 | 5.83 | 4.72 | 9,375 | 65.50 | 1110 | 4813 | 7 | 1048 | 119 | 5.9 | 5.0 | 12,600 | 74 | 1407 |
| 3 | 5,584 | 14 | 1333 | 68 | 5.66 | 4.40 | 12,566 | 69.30 | 1799 | 5099 | 22 | 1248 | 46 | 5.7 | 4.3 | 16,200 | 94 | 1944 |
| 4 | 4,709 | 0 | 1215 | 73 | 5.41 | 4.54 | 12,759 | 70.10 | 1431 | 6052 | 8 | 1596 | 70 | 5.8 | 4.2 | 17,200 | 104 | 1993 |
| 5 | 6,141 | 21 | 1273 | 168 | 5.52 | 4.30 | 9,986 | 61.60 | 1969 | 5826 | 49 | 1266 | 84 | 5.4 | 4.4 | 12,800 | 87 | 2168 |
| 6 | 10,307 | 108 | 663 | 179 | 5.32 | 4.71 | 5,821 | 36.20 | 1260 | 2537 | 73 | 586 | 72 | 5.3 | 4.7 | 9,100 | 59 | 855 |
| 7 | 7,595 | 162 | 1150 | 208 | 6.19 | 4.53 | 6,500 | 39.90 | 2256 | 6365 | 156 | 967 | 216 | 6.0 | 4.7 | 8,300 | 51 | 2184 |
| 8 | 5,061 | 147 | 798 | 186 | 6.24 | 4.69 | 7,108 | 50.40 | 2044 | 4681 | 33 | 741 | 148 | 6.5 | 5.2 | 8,500 | 56 | 1281 |
| 9 | 3,517 | 16 | 525 | 151 | 5.20 | 4.52 | 9,154 | 48.10 | 991 | 2006 | 20 | 270 | 60 | 5.5 | 4.3 | 13,000 | 55 | 665 |
| 10 | 5,550 | 189 | 580 | 268 | 6.53 | 4.12 | 7,743 | 45.08 | 1884 | 6889 | 175 | 1062 | 195 | 6.1 | 4.3 | 12,400 | 62 | 2363 |
| 11 | 2,150 | 283 | 170 | 78 | 6.7 | 2.96 | 6,750 | 40.75 | 951 | 1160 | 83 | 78 | 28 | 6.6 | 3.6 | 9,100 | 62 | 496 |
| 12 | 6,142 | 140 | 725 | 121 | 8.05 | 3.77 | 10,093 | 25.25 | 2793 | 5503 | 111 | 525 | 114 | 6.5 | 3.6 | 12,300 | 76 | 2693 |
| 13 | 6,953 | 339 | 1231 | 235 | 5.80 | 4.00 | 5,928 | 42.20 | 2371 | 5817 | 168 | 1102 | 156 | 6.0 | 4.4 | 6,800 | 57 | 2174 |
| 14 | 4,135 | 133 | 920 | 104 | 5.77 | 4.62 | 6,115 | 45.80 | 1390 | 3697 | 97 | 992 | 65 | 5.7 | 4.5 | 8,500 | 61 | 1378 |
| 15 | 3,469 | 44 | 743 | 114 | 4.93 | 4.29 | 6,526 | 47.40 | 998 | 3257 | 50 | 817 | 61 | 5.3 | 4.7 | 10,700 | 62 | 1044 |
| 16 | 5,249 | 19 | 1278 | 30 | 7.35 | 4.54 | 20,647 | 66.25 | 1871 | 5804 | 86 | 1528 | 23 | 7.5 | 4.6 | 32,400 | 96 | 2243 |
| 17 | 1,974 | 5 | 466 | 30 | 5.83 | 4.58 | 16,688 | 69.33 | 626 | 2301 | 5 | 569 | 19 | 6.5 | 3.5 | 27,700 | 106 | 914 |
| 18 | 4,586 | 34 | 1086 | 30 | 6.31 | 4.58 | 13,052 | 65.61 | 1873 | 4650 | 20 | 1112 | 36 | 6.3 | 4.3 | 15,800 | 86 | 1981 |
| 19 | 5,744 | 20 | 1274 | 83 | 6.01 | 4.60 | 11,242 | 68.77 | 2047 | 5700 | 48 | 1301 | 54 | 6.1 | 4.1 | 14,200 | 93 | 2366 |
| 20 | 5,473 | 9 | 1425 | 20 | 6.23 | 4.74 | 16,468 | 75.92 | 1748 | 5417 | 6 | 1526 | 22 | 6.4 | 4.7 | 20,700 | 109 | 1999 |

## Census tract to Census tract trip table (1965 daily vehicle trips/10)

| From Census tract | To Census tract 1 | 2 | 3 | 4 | 5 | 6 | 7 | 8 | 9 | 10 | 11 | 12 | 13 | 14 | 15 | 16 | 17 | 18 | 19 | 20 | Outside of area | Total |
|---|---|---|---|---|---|---|---|---|---|---|---|---|---|---|---|---|---|---|---|---|---|---|
| 1 | 37 | 31 | 26 | 16 | 14 | 21 | 31 | 17 | 37 | 32 | 16 | 20 | 11 | 3 | 1 | 5 | 3 | 5 | 8 | 4 | 203 | |
| 2 | 31 | 35 | 16 | 14 | 15 | 25 | 30 | 34 | 28 | 64 | 17 | 24 | 14 | 5 | 1 | 7 | 4 | 10 | 13 | 10 | 138 | |
| 3 | 26 | 16 | 86 | 69 | 54 | 42 | 52 | 17 | 9 | 19 | 22 | 21 | 18 | 8 | 2 | 6 | 4 | 5 | 4 | 3 | 154 | |
| 4 | 16 | 14 | 69 | 109 | 81 | 74 | 74 | 25 | 10 | 21 | 29 | 28 | 33 | 12 | 4 | 9 | 6 | 8 | 7 | 5 | 147 | |
| 5 | 14 | 15 | 54 | 81 | 164 | 124 | 129 | 25 | 11 | 22 | 44 | 33 | 56 | 22 | 11 | 18 | 10 | 12 | 8 | 7 | 184 | |
| 6 | 21 | 25 | 42 | 74 | 124 | 168 | 159 | 40 | 23 | 39 | 97 | 51 | 113 | 45 | 27 | 34 | 20 | 22 | 20 | 18 | 387 | |
| 7 | 31 | 30 | 52 | 74 | 129 | 159 | 223 | 51 | 28 | 55 | 92 | 61 | 64 | 34 | 16 | 39 | 22 | 25 | 26 | 18 | 353 | |
| 8 | 17 | 34 | 17 | 25 | 25 | 40 | 51 | 48 | 17 | 43 | 30 | 36 | 22 | 9 | 4 | 13 | 7 | 18 | 14 | 11 | 131 | |
| 9 | 37 | 28 | 9 | 10 | 11 | 23 | 28 | 17 | 69 | 39 | 26 | 19 | 10 | 4 | 3 | 8 | 5 | 9 | 11 | 10 | 308 | |
| 10 | 32 | 64 | 19 | 21 | 22 | 39 | 55 | 43 | 39 | 55 | 43 | 39 | 163 | 49 | 67 | 20 | 7 | 7 | 23 | 13 | 255 | |
| 11 | 16 | 17 | 22 | 29 | 44 | 97 | 92 | 30 | 26 | 49 | 129 | 88 | 53 | 22 | 19 | 45 | 29 | 35 | 23 | 18 | 303 | |
| 12 | 20 | 24 | 21 | 28 | 33 | 51 | 61 | 36 | 19 | 67 | 88 | 182 | 47 | 21 | 34 | 106 | 51 | 94 | 34 | 36 | 226 | |
| 13 | 11 | 14 | 18 | 33 | 56 | 113 | 64 | 22 | 10 | 20 | 52 | 47 | 92 | 67 | 33 | 28 | 14 | 19 | 8 | 7 | 205 | |
| 14 | 3 | 5 | 8 | 12 | 22 | 45 | 34 | 9 | 4 | 7 | 22 | 21 | 67 | 46 | 27 | 10 | 5 | 7 | 2 | 2 | 85 | |
| 15 | 1 | 1 | 2 | 4 | 11 | 16 | 4 | 3 | 7 | 19 | 34 | 33 | 27 | 56 | 19 | 11 | 8 | 2 | 3 | 1 | 109 | |
| 16 | 5 | 7 | 6 | 9 | 18 | 34 | 39 | 13 | 8 | 23 | 45 | 106 | 28 | 10 | 19 | 95 | 67 | 36 | 25 | 25 | 124 | |
| 17 | 3 | 4 | 4 | 6 | 10 | 20 | 22 | 7 | 5 | 13 | 29 | 51 | 14 | 5 | 11 | 67 | 34 | 33 | 14 | 19 | 105 | |
| 18 | 5 | 10 | 5 | 8 | 12 | 22 | 25 | 18 | 9 | 33 | 35 | 94 | 19 | 7 | 8 | 36 | 33 | 63 | 30 | 31 | 90 | |
| 19 | 8 | 13 | 4 | 7 | 8 | 20 | 26 | 14 | 11 | 43 | 23 | 34 | 8 | 2 | 2 | 24 | 14 | 30 | 94 | 96 | 143 | |
| 20 | 4 | 10 | 3 | 5 | 7 | 18 | 18 | 11 | 10 | 35 | 18 | 36 | 7 | 2 | 3 | 26 | 19 | 7 | 2 | 3 | 170 | |
| Outside of area | 203 | 139 | 237 | 184 | 186 | 375 | 351 | 128 | 312 | 222 | 280 | 270 | 205 | 82 | 83 | 152 | 105 | 112 | 450 | 315 | | 244,840 |

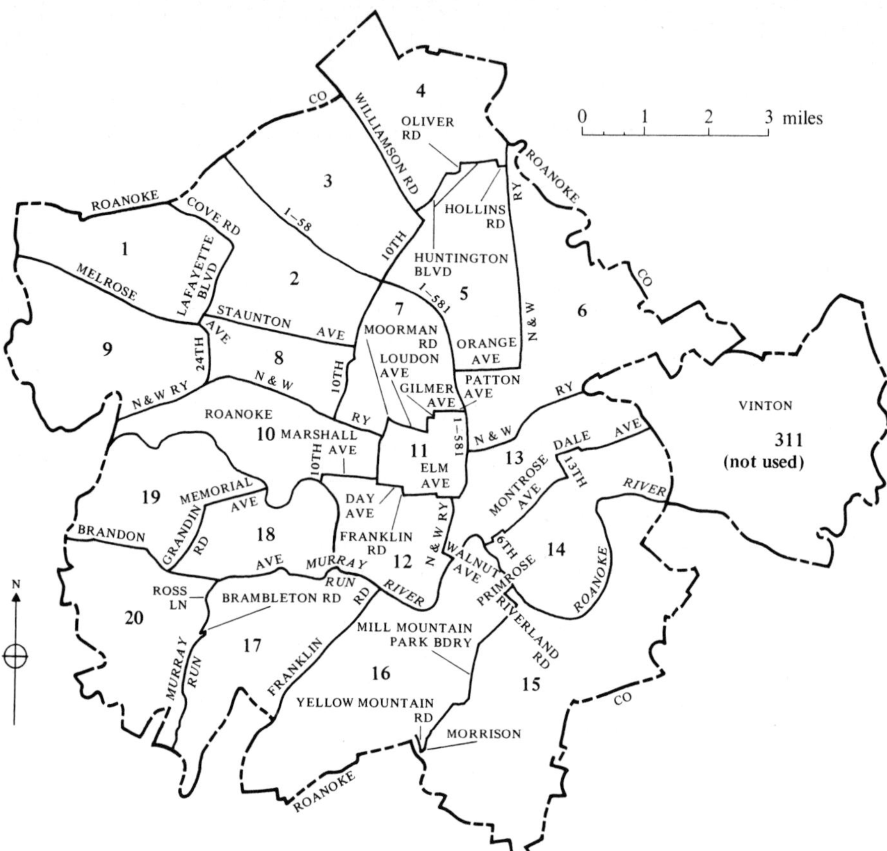


**Figure D-1** Census tracts in the Roanoke, Virginia, standard metropolitan statistical area. (*Source: 1970 Census of Population and Housing, Final Report PHC(1)-174.*)

## DATA SET 4. CENTRAL APPALACHIAN REGION CHARACTERISTICS

The following data are taken from the Census Bureau's *1972 City County Data Book* for the 59 counties of the Central Appalachian Region. The date is 1970 unless otherwise noted. The variables are as follows:

| Variable number | Description |
|---|---|
| 1 | Population |
| 2 | Percentage population change 1960 to 1970 |
| 3 | Percentage population noncaucasian |
| 4 | Percentage population 18 years old and over |
| 5 | Percentage population 65 years old and over |
| 6 | Births per 1000 in 1968 |
| 7 | Deaths per 1000 in 1968 |
| 8 | Percentage population over 24 with less than 5 years of school |
| 9 | Percentage families that are female headed |
| 10 | Percentage families that are below the poverty line |
| 11 | Percentage elderly ($\geq 65$) who are below the poverty line |
| 12 | Median number of rooms per housing unit |
| 13 | Median rent |
| 14 | Percentage housing units lacking some plumbing |
| 15 | Per capita expenditures by county government |
| 16 | Percentage expenditures for education |
| 17 | Percentage expenditures for roads |
| 18 | Percentage expenditures for welfare |
| 19 | Percentage expenditures for health |
| 20 | Percentage adults who voted for the President in 1968 |
| 21 | Leading party in presidential election: (1) American Independent, (2) Democratic, (3) Republican |
| 22 | Average size of farms in acres |

| | | Variable number | | | | | | | | |
|---|---|---|---|---|---|---|---|---|---|---|
| County | State | 1 | 2 | 3 | 4 | 5 | 6 | 7 | 8 | 9 |
| BELL | KY | 31087 | −11.9 | 3.6 | 63.4 | 12.0 | 19.5 | 13.0 | 22.9 | 15.3 |
| BREATHITT | KY | 14221 | −8.2 | 0.2 | 58.5 | 10.1 | 17.7 | 10.2 | 24.2 | 14.0 |
| CLAY | KY | 18481 | −10.9 | 1.8 | 57.0 | 9.1 | 23.4 | 8.7 | 26.5 | 11.0 |
| CLINTON | KY | 8174 | 8.0 | 0.5 | 67.5 | 13.1 | 15.5 | 10.2 | 16.0 | 12.0 |
| FLOYD | KY | 35889 | −13.8 | 0.5 | 63.1 | 9.8 | 18.1 | 9.0 | 18.9 | 11.7 |
| HARLAN | KY | 37370 | −26.9 | 6.1 | 62.9 | 11.2 | 18.3 | 11.9 | 19.9 | 14.6 |
| JACKSON | KY | 10005 | −6.3 | 0.0 | 61.8 | 12.1 | 17.9 | 9.4 | 23.6 | 9.4 |
| JOHNSON | KY | 17539 | −11.2 | 0.0 | 66.8 | 12.8 | 17.3 | 11.9 | 15.5 | 11.1 |
| KNOTT | KY | 14698 | −15.3 | 0.8 | 59.4 | 9.8 | 16.2 | 7.9 | 22.8 | 11.5 |
| KNOX | KY | 23689 | −6.2 | 1.5 | 63.2 | 12.1 | 17.1 | 9.4 | 20.1 | 12.7 |
| LAUREL | KY | 27386 | 10.0 | 1.0 | 63.2 | 11.6 | 17.5 | 10.8 | 13.6 | 9.7 |
| LEE | KY | 6587 | −11.2 | 0.9 | 63.3 | 14.0 | 18.5 | 11.1 | 19.4 | 14.7 |
| LESLIE | KY | 11623 | 6.2 | 0.0 | 55.6 | 7.8 | 21.9 | 9.5 | 23.3 | 11.4 |
| LETCHER | KY | 23165 | 23.0 | 1.9 | 61.6 | 10.5 | 19.4 | 9.5 | 18.8 | 11.3 |
| MC CREARY | KY | 12548 | 0.7 | 1.6 | 58.2 | 10.8 | 20.6 | 10.8 | 23.7 | 13.9 |
| MAGOFFIN | KY | 10443 | −6.4 | 0.0 | 58.2 | 10.8 | 19.6 | 7.7 | 14.5 | 10.3 |
| MARTIN | KY | 9377 | −8.1 | 0.0 | 56.6 | 9.3 | 17.7 | 8.6 | 27.3 | 10.0 |
| OWSLEY | KY | 5023 | −6.4 | 0.0 | 61.5 | 14.3 | 17.0 | 11.5 | 25.1 | 9.4 |
| PERRY | KY | 25714 | −24.9 | 2.9 | 60.0 | 10.2 | 23.0 | 10.2 | 19.4 | 10.9 |
| PIKE | KY | 61059 | −10.6 | 0.7 | 61.3 | 8.9 | 18.6 | 9.8 | 18.8 | 9.5 |
| PULASKI | KY | 35234 | 2.4 | 1.7 | 66.0 | 12.8 | 14.4 | 10.6 | 13.6 | 9.9 |
| ROCKCASTLE | KY | 12245 | −0.2 | 0.1 | 62.8 | 11.7 | 23.8 | 11.0 | 19.8 | 8.8 |
| WAYNE | KY | 14268 | −2.9 | 2.6 | 63.8 | 12.5 | 15.1 | 12.0 | 25.9 | 8.9 |
| WHITLEY | KY | 24145 | −6.5 | 0.6 | 66.8 | 14.1 | 15.0 | 12.4 | 13.7 | 13.7 |
| WOLFE | KY | 5669 | −13.2 | 0.0 | 60.6 | 13.5 | 14.5 | 13.8 | 25.2 | 11.7 |
| ANDERSON | TN | 60300 | 0.4 | 3.7 | 64.9 | 7.4 | 16.0 | 8.6 | 8.2 | 9.5 |
| CAMPBELL | TN | 26045 | −6.8 | 0.8 | 65.1 | 12.1 | 20.8 | 12.9 | 20.2 | 14.3 |
| CLAIBORNE | TN | 19420 | 1.9 | 0.8 | 66.3 | 11.7 | 16.6 | 10.9 | 18.2 | 9.5 |
| CLAY | TN | 6624 | −9.1 | 1.9 | 67.6 | 12.2 | 14.3 | 10.0 | 20.3 | 11.4 |
| CUMBERLAND | TN | 20733 | 8.4 | 0.0 | 63.6 | 11.0 | 17.7 | 10.8 | 14.1 | 10.0 |
| DE KALB | TN | 11151 | 3.5 | 2.1 | 69.5 | 13.2 | 18.1 | 11.4 | 11.0 | 8.0 |
| FENTRESS | TN | 12593 | −5.2 | 0.0 | 62.2 | 10.4 | 18.4 | 10.4 | 22.3 | 13.9 |
| HANCOCK | TN | 6719 | −13.4 | 1.4 | 65.8 | 11.0 | 13.1 | 10.3 | 23.5 | 15.3 |
| JACKSON | TN | 8141 | −11.8 | 0.6 | 69.0 | 14.2 | 14.7 | 11.7 | 16.6 | 9.7 |
| MACON | TN | 12315 | 1.0 | 0.4 | 69.5 | 14.3 | 15.1 | 12.1 | 18.6 | 7.7 |
| MORGAN | TN | 13619 | −4.8 | 1.5 | 63.0 | 10.0 | 15.0 | 9.1 | 14.2 | 9.9 |
| OVERTON | TN | 14866 | 1.4 | 0.5 | 67.6 | 12.5 | 16.8 | 10.4 | 15.9 | 10.1 |
| PICKETT | TN | 3774 | −14.8 | 0.2 | 67.5 | 12.5 | 13.5 | 9.7 | 18.1 | 10.5 |
| PUTNAM | TN | 35487 | 21.4 | 1.5 | 71.0 | 10.7 | 17.4 | 9.1 | 12.9 | 9.5 |
| SCOTT | TN | 14762 | −4.2 | 0.0 | 61.1 | 10.2 | 23.5 | 10.0 | 21.8 | 13.7 |
| SMITH | TN | 12509 | 3.7 | 5.0 | 69.3 | 14.1 | 14.3 | 13.1 | 12.1 | 7.7 |
| UNION | TN | 9072 | 6.8 | 0.0 | 64.0 | 10.3 | 13.6 | 9.5 | 17.5 | 7.6 |
| WHITE | TN | 16355 | 4.8 | 2.2 | 67.7 | 11.6 | 19.8 | 12.1 | 14.4 | 10.2 |
| BUCHANAN | VA | 32071 | −12.7 | 0.2 | 57.5 | 5.6 | 18.3 | 6.5 | 24.8 | 9.0 |
| DICKENSON | VA | 16077 | −20.5 | 0.7 | 61.1 | 8.5 | 15.8 | 10.4 | 18.6 | 9.3 |
| LEE | VA | 20321 | −21.3 | 0.5 | 68.0 | 14.4 | 14.3 | 12.5 | 24.8 | 13.5 |
| RUSSELL | VA | 24533 | −6.7 | 1.2 | 63.9 | 9.4 | 14.5 | 9.8 | 15.0 | 8.7 |
| SCOTT | VA | 24376 | −5.6 | 0.8 | 67.9 | 11.1 | 15.8 | 9.4 | 17.9 | 9.0 |
| TAZEWELL | VA | 39816 | −11.1 | 3.3 | 65.6 | 9.4 | 18.2 | 10.6 | 14.6 | 10.5 |
| WISE | VA | 35947 | −17.5 | 2.2 | 64.4 | 10.5 | 18.3 | 11.6 | 17.1 | 12.3 |
| FAYETTE | WV | 49332 | −20.1 | 10.9 | 65.9 | 12.5 | 14.6 | 14.2 | 10.2 | 13.2 |
| LOGAN | WV | 46269 | −24.9 | 6.1 | 61.3 | 9.1 | 19.3 | 10.9 | 14.8 | 12.2 |
| MCDOWELL | WV | 50666 | 29.0 | 18.1 | 60.1 | 9.0 | 18.8 | 12.3 | 16.9 | 13.0 |
| MERCER | WV | 63206 | −7.3 | 8.3 | 67.8 | 11.7 | 17.6 | 13.1 | 8.3 | 12.8 |
| MINGO | WV | 32780 | −17.5 | 4.1 | 59.0 | 9.8 | 20.3 | 11.8 | 19.5 | 13.6 |
| MONROE | WV | 11272 | −2.7 | 4.4 | 69.5 | 14.6 | 14.6 | 10.5 | 6.6 | 9.2 |
| RALEIGH | WV | 70080 | 10.0 | 9.9 | 66.0 | 11.5 | 16.1 | 12.2 | 9.3 | 12.3 |
| SUMMERS | WV | 13213 | −15.5 | 4.1 | 67.7 | 15.6 | 13.0 | 13.1 | 8.9 | 13.3 |
| WYOMING | WV | 30095 | −13.6 | 1.7 | 59.7 | 6.7 | 19.6 | 7.8 | 11.4 | 8.2 |

| Variable number | | | | | | | | | | | | |
|---|---|---|---|---|---|---|---|---|---|---|---|---|
| 10 | 11 | 12 | 13 | 14 | 15 | 16 | 17 | 18 | 19 | 20 | 21 | 22 |
| 39.3 | 13.9 | 4.7 | 51 | 39.1 | 122 | 63.5 | 2.7 | 0.1 | 1.2 | 52.1 | 3 | 77 |
| 54.9 | 11.4 | 4.6 | 42 | 56.8 | 118 | 85.7 | 1.4 | 0.0 | 2.2 | 56.2 | 2 | 153 |
| 57.6 | 9.3 | 4.3 | 39 | 62.7 | 124 | 93.5 | 0.8 | 0.1 | 2.2 | 58.9 | 3 | 122 |
| 40.0 | 13.7 | 4.9 | 48 | 47.1 | 123 | 76.9 | 6.9 | 0.6 | 2.9 | 62.1 | 3 | 93 |
| 34.9 | 13.0 | 4.9 | 50 | 34.1 | 115 | 81.6 | 3.2 | 0.1 | 1.7 | 57.6 | 2 | 128 |
| 36.2 | 13.1 | 4.7 | 48 | 36.6 | 138 | 87.2 | 1.2 | 0.0 | 0.5 | 55.6 | 2 | 151 |
| 50.2 | 15.1 | 4.7 | 30 | 63.6 | 144 | 91.1 | 1.8 | 0.0 | 1.8 | 59.6 | 3 | 88 |
| 38.5 | 16.1 | 5.1 | 57 | 35.3 | 125 | 84.8 | 1.2 | 0.1 | 1.0 | 55.8 | 3 | 91 |
| 56.6 | 10.3 | 4.7 | 30 | 56.1 | 124 | 92.7 | 0.9 | 0.0 | 1.8 | 55.7 | 2 | 96 |
| 48.4 | 15.0 | 4.7 | 51 | 47.2 | 121 | 82.9 | 1.3 | 0.0 | 8.9 | 50.7 | 3 | 104 |
| 34.6 | 15.3 | 4.9 | 60 | 36.4 | 117 | 80.1 | 3.7 | 0.1 | 0.9 | 53.4 | 3 | 69 |
| 48.4 | 17.3 | 4.8 | 41 | 58.5 | 135 | 74.6 | 7.3 | 0.3 | 3.7 | 55.1 | 3 | 84 |
| 55.5 | 9.2 | 4.4 | 31 | 70.6 | 142 | 88.4 | 1.2 | 0.0 | 2.0 | 56.9 | 3 | 165 |
| 40.1 | 13.8 | 4.7 | 39 | 48.1 | 103 | 82.6 | 1.8 | 0.1 | 1.9 | 53.7 | 2 | 124 |
| 53.7 | 12.9 | 4.7 | 50 | 53.8 | 117 | 91.2 | 2.1 | 0.0 | 1.8 | 54.1 | 3 | 83 |
| 48.9 | 12.2 | 5.0 | 41 | 51.1 | 97 | 78.5 | 1.7 | 0.3 | 1.6 | 67.8 | 3 | 124 |
| 53.4 | 11.8 | 4.7 | 36 | 55.4 | 189 | 90.9 | 2.2 | 0.1 | 1.6 | 53.5 | 3 | 122 |
| 61.6 | 14.9 | 4.5 | 39 | 70.1 | 129 | 88.4 | 2.9 | 0.0 | 3.3 | 60.8 | 3 | 91 |
| 39.6 | 12.4 | 4.7 | 47 | 44.5 | 138 | 80.6 | 2.4 | 0.0 | 1.5 | 61.8 | 2 | 81 |
| 32.2 | 13.8 | 4.7 | 53 | 35.5 | 95 | 87.9 | 1.3 | 0.3 | 1.5 | 60.2 | 2 | 131 |
| 29.3 | 18.8 | 5.0 | 63 | 31.5 | 146 | 63.9 | 2.8 | 0.2 | 22.7 | 55.5 | 3 | 85 |
| 36.1 | 15.2 | 4.7 | 51 | 47.5 | 104 | 83.4 | 3.7 | 0.3 | 2.4 | 59.7 | 3 | 109 |
| 50.1 | 16.0 | 4.7 | 48 | 46.9 | 128 | 70.7 | 1.5 | 0.1 | 1.6 | 54.9 | 3 | 124 |
| 39.7 | 19.8 | 4.9 | 63 | 36.0 | 133 | 80.9 | 2.4 | 0.1 | 1.7 | 58.5 | 3 | 105 |
| 59.0 | 15.2 | 4.9 | 40 | 63.1 | 157 | 91.4 | 2.1 | 0.1 | 1.9 | 64.2 | 2 | 140 |
| 15.2 | 15.8 | 4.9 | 78 | 11.3 | 191 | 62.5 | 5.1 | 0.9 | 1.2 | 55.6 | 3 | 85 |
| 36.2 | 17.2 | 4.8 | 47 | 35.7 | 164 | 39.1 | 11.1 | 0.2 | 9.9 | 45.2 | 3 | 70 |
| 38.8 | 16.4 | 4.8 | 46 | 42.8 | 166 | 58.2 | 15.0 | 0.7 | 16.3 | 40.3 | 3 | 68 |
| 39.3 | 16.6 | 4.8 | 43 | 43.5 | 134 | 61.1 | 22.7 | 0.5 | 4.7 | 43.1 | 3 | 115 |
| 29.0 | 18.3 | 4.9 | 65 | 27.7 | 125 | 43.0 | 12.0 | 0.3 | 2.4 | 45.6 | 3 | 117 |
| 21.6 | 28.9 | 5.1 | 63 | 26.1 | 112 | 55.1 | 23.2 | 0.1 | 0.1 | 50.3 | 3 | 107 |
| 42.9 | 13.6 | 5.0 | 40 | 47.3 | 145 | 46.8 | 14.3 | 0.8 | 20.3 | 44.7 | 3 | 122 |
| 55.5 | 11.0 | 4.8 | 37 | 60.6 | 126 | 60.2 | 24.4 | 0.0 | 8.8 | 46.2 | 3 | 82 |
| 38.0 | 19.9 | 4.9 | 44 | 44.3 | 139 | 59.5 | 23.9 | 0.0 | 0.0 | 48.1 | 2 | 114 |
| 29.1 | 24.2 | 5.0 | 56 | 39.1 | 135 | 51.9 | 25.7 | 0.3 | 0.0 | 43.7 | 3 | 99 |
| 27.6 | 16.8 | 5.1 | 50 | 33.1 | 182 | 66.2 | 16.4 | 0.3 | 0.3 | 44.3 | 3 | 175 |
| 35.8 | 21.2 | 4.8 | 48 | 37.6 | 96 | 62.9 | 21.4 | 0.3 | 0.1 | 40.1 | 2 | 116 |
| 33.9 | 21.9 | 4.7 | 63 | 43.1 | 139 | 54.1 | 31.6 | 0.6 | 0.0 | 58.4 | 3 | 85 |
| 23.4 | 22.5 | 5.0 | 75 | 17.4 | 152 | 43.0 | 15.0 | 0.3 | 11.4 | 40.9 | 3 | 93 |
| 42.1 | 12.3 | 4.8 | 50 | 44.0 | 162 | 64.8 | 12.2 | 0.5 | 9.8 | 45.8 | 3 | 174 |
| 20.0 | 27.2 | 5.2 | 59 | 32.4 | 119 | 58.8 | 15.8 | 0.4 | 2.8 | 50.3 | 1 | 116 |
| 34.6 | 18.2 | 4.5 | 35 | 54.4 | 101 | 65.1 | 26.2 | 0.4 | 0.3 | 50.5 | 3 | 69 |
| 23.6 | 20.6 | 4.9 | 60 | 26.2 | 122 | 69.9 | 10.4 | 0.2 | 10.7 | 43.0 | 1 | 119 |
| 27.2 | 10.7 | 4.7 | 47 | 40.4 | 95 | 65.2 | 0.8 | 9.8 | 0.0 | 53.2 | 2 | 94 |
| 34.0 | 12.1 | 4.7 | 44 | 42.4 | 159 | 77.7 | 0.1 | 15.7 | 0.0 | 75.5 | 3 | 57 |
| 39.7 | 17.1 | 4.9 | 42 | 46.9 | 132 | 65.9 | 0.2 | 24.8 | 0.0 | 68.0 | 3 | 82 |
| 25.4 | 15.4 | 5.0 | 63 | 37.9 | 148 | 76.4 | 0.5 | 11.7 | 0.4 | 56.6 | 3 | 135 |
| 27.0 | 19.8 | 4.8 | 61 | 40.7 | 104 | 75.0 | 1.7 | 12.4 | 0.0 | 60.3 | 3 | 75 |
| 21.8 | 14.4 | 5.0 | 61 | 26.7 | 145 | 62.3 | 3.5 | 11.1 | 0.0 | 43.4 | 2 | 253 |
| 27.4 | 16.4 | 4.9 | 58 | 31.7 | 138 | 67.7 | 2.9 | 12.3 | 0.0 | 54.5 | 2 | 73 |
| 23.7 | 18.3 | 5.0 | 58 | 21.5 | 132 | 86.6 | 0.7 | 1.4 | 0.4 | 66.8 | 2 | 97 |
| 23.1 | 12.2 | 4.8 | 58 | 21.4 | 125 | 84.4 | 0.2 | 0.5 | 0.6 | 71.6 | 2 | 108 |
| 29.8 | 10.7 | 4.6 | 45 | 38.2 | 129 | 85.0 | 1.4 | 1.0 | 1.5 | 62.2 | 2 | 0 |
| 18.1 | 19.2 | 5.1 | 70 | 15.2 | 135 | 76.1 | 2.3 | 0.7 | 1.2 | 60.9 | 2 | 154 |
| 36.5 | 12.4 | 4.7 | 50 | 31.2 | 152 | 83.0 | 2.2 | 1.2 | 0.6 | 71.3 | 2 | 63 |
| 29.2 | 23.9 | 5.4 | 55 | 32.2 | 104 | 90.4 | 0.2 | 1.1 | 1.3 | 75.2 | 3 | 190 |
| 19.6 | 18.1 | 4.9 | 64 | 17.0 | 114 | 64.4 | 1.3 | 0.8 | 0.6 | 63.8 | 2 | 103 |
| 33.7 | 18.0 | 5.1 | 51 | 31.3 | 121 | 83.3 | 1.6 | 1.0 | 0.6 | 74.6 | 2 | 190 |
| 22.0 | 12.5 | 4.7 | 54 | 28.2 | 180 | 87.2 | 0.8 | 0.8 | 0.6 | 64.5 | 2 | 107 |

## DATA SET 5. RATINGS AND RANKINGS OF GOALS RELATIVE TO HIGHWAY CONSTRUCTION

In 1975, as part of an effort to develop an environmental impact statement for a set of proposed new expressways in the Lynchburg, Virginia, metropolitan area, Wiley and Wilson, Inc., ran an advertisement in the local paper requesting readers to assign weights of importance to 20 prespecified goals toward which highway planners should strive.† Of the over 100 returns, 50 have been selected at random for presentation here. Basically, each person was given a fictional $100 and asked to distribute this over the 20 goals in proportion to the importance of each goal to him or her. We have presented here both the amount of the $100 allocated to each goal by each person (i.e., the rating) and the rank of that goal based on that dollar rating. Ties in ranks are recorded with the lowest-numbered (highest-priority) rank.

The 20 goals were:

1. Providing the straightest, shortest route
2. Maintaining existing neighborhood character
3. Preserving forests and wildlife
4. Improving access to downtown
5. Minimizing noise pollution
6. Preserving historic and architectural landmarks
7. Reducing traffic hazzards
8. Improving nonautomotive transit systems (buses, sidewalks, bicycle paths)
9. Helping people get to work faster
10. Keeping construction costs to a minimum
11. Minimizing housing displacement
12. Improving public facilities and services
13. Minimizing water pollution and soil erosion
14. Promoting commercial and industrial growth
15. Improving park and recreation facilities
16. Speeding up traffic via limited-access highways
17. Keeping community growth in conformance with comprehensive plans
18. Minimizing air pollution
19. Promoting expansion of suburban residential areas
20. Improving community appearance with slower, scenic routes

† For a discussion of this technique, see Chap. 20, method 7.

## Goal ratings ($)

| Person number | Goal 1 | 2 | 3 | 4 | 5 | 6 | 7 | 8 | 9 | 10 | 11 | 12 | 13 | 14 | 15 | 16 | 17 | 18 | 19 | 20 |
|---|---|---|---|---|---|---|---|---|---|---|---|---|---|---|---|---|---|---|---|---|
| 1 | 0 | 0 | 20 | 0 | 10 | 10 | 0 | 10 | 0 | 0 | 5 | 5 | 10 | 0 | 10 | 0 | 0 | 10 | 0 | 10 |
| 2 | 40 | 2 | 3 | 0 | 5 | 2 | 10 | 5 | 5 | 0 | 0 | 0 | 3 | 0 | 2 | 20 | 3 | 0 | 0 | 0 |
| 3 | 0 | 80 | 0 | 0 | 0 | 0 | 0 | 0 | 0 | 0 | 0 | 0 | 0 | 0 | 0 | 20 | 0 | 0 | 0 | 0 |
| 4 | 1 | 10 | 10 | 4 | 1 | 10 | 4 | 10 | 3 | 4 | 10 | 1 | 4 | 1 | 10 | 5 | 3 | 4 | 1 | 4 |
| 5 | 0 | 10 | 10 | 0 | 10 | 3 | 10 | 10 | 0 | 10 | 4 | 0 | 10 | 0 | 3 | 0 | 0 | 10 | 0 | 10 |
| 6 | 0 | 10 | 10 | 0 | 0 | 10 | 10 | 0 | 0 | 0 | 10 | 0 | 10 | 0 | 20 | 0 | 10 | 0 | 0 | 10 |
| 7 | 5 | 5 | 5 | 9 | 7 | 5 | 5 | 3 | 8 | 10 | 6 | 6 | 4 | 5 | 4 | 3 | 2 | 2 | 4 | 2 |
| 8 | 0 | 0 | 5 | 15 | 0 | 5 | 10 | 10 | 0 | 0 | 5 | 0 | 5 | 0 | 10 | 15 | 10 | 10 | 0 | 0 |
| 9 | 0 | 0 | 25 | 0 | 0 | 0 | 0 | 0 | 0 | 25 | 25 | 0 | 0 | 0 | 0 | 0 | 15 | 0 | 10 | 0 |
| 10 | 50 | 25 | 0 | 0 | 0 | 10 | 10 | 0 | 0 | 0 | 0 | 0 | 0 | 0 | 5 | 0 | 0 | 0 | 0 | 0 |
| 11 | 0 | 10 | 10 | 0 | 10 | 10 | 0 | 10 | 0 | 0 | 10 | 0 | 10 | 0 | 10 | 0 | 0 | 10 | 0 | 10 |
| 12 | 75 | 0 | 5 | 0 | 0 | 5 | 10 | 0 | 0 | 0 | 0 | 0 | 0 | 0 | 0 | 5 | 0 | 0 | 0 | 0 |
| 13 | 2 | 6 | 8 | 5 | 5 | 6 | 6 | 5 | 1 | 3 | 6 | 5 | 6 | 4 | 5 | 5 | 8 | 6 | 3 | 5 |
| 14 | 0 | 5 | 5 | 5 | 5 | 10 | 5 | 5 | 5 | 10 | 10 | 5 | 5 | 0 | 5 | 0 | 5 | 5 | 0 | 10 |
| 15 | 0 | 40 | 0 | 0 | 10 | 5 | 10 | 5 | 0 | 0 | 10 | 0 | 5 | 0 | 0 | 0 | 5 | 5 | 0 | 5 |
| 16 | 0 | 20 | 30 | 0 | 10 | 0 | 0 | 20 | 0 | 0 | 0 | 0 | 20 | 0 | 0 | 0 | 0 | 0 | 0 | 0 |
| 17 | 30 | 0 | 0 | 20 | 0 | 0 | 10 | 0 | 20 | 10 | 10 | 0 | 0 | 0 | 0 | 0 | 0 | 0 | 0 | 0 |
| 18 | 10 | 5 | 4 | 4 | 6 | 4 | 9 | 6 | 3 | 4 | 4 | 6 | 7 | 3 | 1 | 9 | 4 | 9 | 1 | 1 |
| 19 | 9 | 1 | 2 | 10 | 1 | 2 | 10 | 1 | 2 | 9 | 1 | 2 | 2 | 10 | 3 | 10 | 2 | 3 | 10 | 10 |
| 20 | 25 | 0 | 0 | 0 | 0 | 0 | 25 | 0 | 0 | 0 | 0 | 0 | 0 | 0 | 0 | 50 | 0 | 0 | 0 | 0 |
| 21 | 0 | 50 | 0 | 0 | 0 | 10 | 10 | 10 | 0 | 10 | 0 | 0 | 0 | 0 | 10 | 0 | 0 | 0 | 0 | 0 |
| 22 | 0 | 8 | 4 | 11 | 8 | 6 | 15 | 5 | 1 | 5 | 8 | 4 | 5 | 4 | 5 | 1 | 4 | 7 | 4 | 5 |
| 23 | 25 | 0 | 0 | 50 | 0 | 0 | 0 | 0 | 0 | 0 | 0 | 0 | 0 | 0 | 0 | 25 | 0 | 0 | 0 | 0 |
| 24 | 5 | 10 | 15 | 0 | 5 | 10 | 5 | 5 | 0 | 0 | 5 | 5 | 10 | 5 | 5 | 0 | 5 | 5 | 0 | 5 |
| 25 | 12 | 1 | 1 | 3 | 1 | 3 | 15 | 3 | 16 | 2 | 2 | 3 | 1 | 15 | 1 | 15 | 3 | 1 | 1 | 1 |
| 26 | 8 | 4 | 4 | 3 | 1 | 5 | 8 | 5 | 8 | 8 | 8 | 3 | 4 | 3 | 3 | 8 | 9 | 1 | 3 | 4 |
| 27 | 0 | 50 | 0 | 0 | 30 | 0 | 0 | 0 | 0 | 0 | 0 | 0 | 0 | 0 | 0 | 0 | 0 | 0 | 0 | 20 |
| 28 | 1 | 5 | 2 | 10 | 10 | 1 | 10 | 2 | 1 | 2 | 3 | 10 | 5 | 10 | 1 | 10 | 10 | 5 | 1 | 1 |
| 29 | 4 | 10 | 4 | 3 | 4 | 5 | 10 | 2 | 0 | 2 | 0 | 3 | 5 | 15 | 3 | 5 | 8 | 2 | 5 | 10 |
| 30 | 20 | 10 | 0 | 0 | 0 | 0 | 20 | 10 | 0 | 0 | 0 | 5 | 10 | 5 | 10 | 5 | 0 | 0 | 5 | 0 |
| 31 | 0 | 20 | 5 | 20 | 5 | 5 | 10 | 5 | 0 | 0 | 10 | 0 | 5 | 0 | 5 | 5 | 0 | 5 | 0 | 0 |
| 32 | 0 | 0 | 20 | 0 | 0 | 20 | 0 | 20 | 0 | 0 | 0 | 0 | 0 | 0 | 20 | 0 | 0 | 0 | 0 | 20 |
| 33 | 0 | 5 | 0 | 10 | 0 | 10 | 0 | 10 | 10 | 5 | 5 | 10 | 0 | 0 | 0 | 20 | 15 | 0 | 0 | 0 |
| 34 | 0 | 20 | 0 | 10 | 0 | 0 | 0 | 20 | 0 | 0 | 10 | 0 | 0 | 0 | 0 | 20 | 0 | 0 | 0 | 20 |
| 35 | 11 | 1 | 4 | 4 | 3 | 3 | 11 | 7 | 0 | 1 | 1 | 10 | 9 | 3 | 4 | 11 | 5 | 10 | 1 | 1 |
| 36 | 0 | 10 | 5 | 10 | 5 | 5 | 5 | 10 | 0 | 0 | 10 | 0 | 5 | 5 | 10 | 0 | 0 | 5 | 0 | 10 |
| 37 | 0 | 4 | 8 | 4 | 4 | 7 | 7 | 10 | 4 | 0 | 8 | 4 | 10 | 0 | 8 | 4 | 10 | 4 | 0 | 4 |
| 38 | 0 | 5 | 10 | 5 | 5 | 5 | 10 | 2 | 0 | 10 | 5 | 2 | 6 | 1 | 15 | 1 | 10 | 10 | 0 | 0 |
| 39 | 5 | 7 | 1 | 7 | 7 | 1 | 9 | 25 | 5 | 3 | 3 | 1 | 1 | 1 | 5 | 8 | 1 | 1 | 0 | 9 |
| 40 | 0 | 5 | 5 | 0 | 5 | 5 | 10 | 5 | 10 | 0 | 0 | 15 | 5 | 20 | 5 | 0 | 5 | 5 | 0 | 0 |
| 41 | 50 | 0 | 5 | 0 | 0 | 0 | 10 | 0 | 10 | 10 | 0 | 0 | 0 | 0 | 5 | 10 | 0 | 0 | 0 | 0 |
| 42 | 0 | 20 | 20 | 0 | 10 | 10 | 0 | 10 | 0 | 10 | 0 | 0 | 10 | 0 | 0 | 0 | 0 | 10 | 0 | 0 |
| 43 | 0 | 5 | 10 | 5 | 5 | 5 | 10 | 0 | 5 | 0 | 5 | 5 | 5 | 5 | 5 | 5 | 0 | 10 | 5 | 10 |
| 44 | 0 | 35 | 5 | 0 | 0 | 0 | 20 | 15 | 0 | 0 | 10 | 0 | 5 | 0 | 0 | 0 | 5 | 0 | 0 | 5 |
| 45 | 1 | 25 | 10 | 1 | 5 | 1 | 10 | 1 | 1 | 2 | 20 | 1 | 3 | 1 | 5 | 5 | 1 | 5 | 1 | 1 |
| 46 | 20 | 0 | 5 | 5 | 5 | 5 | 20 | 0 | 10 | 5 | 5 | 0 | 5 | 0 | 0 | 10 | 5 | 0 | 0 | 0 |
| 47 | 5 | 8 | 5 | 2 | 6 | 2 | 7 | 7 | 6 | 5 | 3 | 3 | 5 | 5 | 5 | 5 | 5 | 8 | 8 | 5 |
| 48 | 0 | 5 | 15 | 3 | 5 | 5 | 5 | 10 | 3 | 0 | 4 | 5 | 10 | 0 | 10 | 0 | 5 | 11 | 0 | 5 |
| 49 | 0 | 5 | 0 | 0 | 0 | 5 | 0 | 10 | 0 | 0 | 10 | 0 | 10 | 0 | 20 | 0 | 20 | 0 | 0 | 20 |
| 50 | 20 | 0 | 0 | 0 | 0 | 0 | 0 | 0 | 0 | 2 | 3 | 5 | 0 | 30 | 0 | 5 | 5 | 0 | 30 | 0 |

## Goal ranks

| Person number | Goal 1 | 2 | 3 | 4 | 5 | 6 | 7 | 8 | 9 | 10 | 11 | 12 | 13 | 14 | 15 | 16 | 17 | 18 | 19 | 20 |
|---|---|---|---|---|---|---|---|---|---|---|---|---|---|---|---|---|---|---|---|---|
| 1 | 11 | 11 | 1 | 11 | 2 | 2 | 11 | 2 | 11 | 11 | 9 | 9 | 2 | 11 | 2 | 11 | 2 | 11 | 11 | 2 |
| 2 | 1 | 10 | 7 | 13 | 4 | 10 | 3 | 4 | 4 | 13 | 13 | 13 | 7 | 13 | 10 | 2 | 7 | 13 | 13 | 13 |
| 3 | 3 | 1 | 3 | 3 | 3 | 3 | 3 | 3 | 3 | 3 | 3 | 3 | 3 | 3 | 3 | 2 | 3 | 3 | 3 | 3 |
| 4 | 16 | 1 | 1 | 8 | 16 | 1 | 8 | 1 | 14 | 8 | 1 | 16 | 8 | 16 | 1 | 7 | 14 | 8 | 16 | 8 |
| 5 | 13 | 1 | 1 | 13 | 1 | 11 | 1 | 1 | 13 | 1 | 10 | 13 | 1 | 13 | 11 | 13 | 13 | 1 | 13 | 1 |
| 6 | 10 | 2 | 2 | 10 | 10 | 10 | 2 | 2 | 10 | 10 | 2 | 10 | 2 | 10 | 1 | 10 | 2 | 10 | 10 | 2 |
| 7 | 7 | 7 | 7 | 2 | 4 | 7 | 7 | 16 | 3 | 1 | 5 | 5 | 13 | 7 | 13 | 16 | 18 | 18 | 13 | 18 |
| 8 | 12 | 12 | 8 | 1 | 12 | 8 | 3 | 3 | 12 | 12 | 8 | 12 | 8 | 12 | 3 | 1 | 3 | 3 | 12 | 12 |
| 9 | 6 | 6 | 1 | 6 | 6 | 6 | 6 | 6 | 6 | 1 | 1 | 6 | 6 | 6 | 6 | 6 | 4 | 6 | 5 | 6 |
| 10 | 1 | 2 | 6 | 0 | 0 | 3 | 3 | 7 | 7 | 7 | 7 | 7 | 7 | 7 | 5 | 7 | 7 | 7 | 7 | 7 |
| 11 | 11 | 1 | 1 | 11 | 1 | 1 | 11 | 1 | 11 | 11 | 1 | 11 | 1 | 11 | 1 | 11 | 11 | 1 | 11 | 1 |
| 12 | 1 | 6 | 3 | 6 | 6 | 3 | 2 | 6 | 6 | 6 | 6 | 6 | 6 | 6 | 6 | 3 | 6 | 6 | 6 | 6 |
| 13 | 19 | 3 | 1 | 9 | 9 | 3 | 3 | 9 | 20 | 17 | 3 | 9 | 3 | 16 | 9 | 9 | 1 | 3 | 17 | 9 |
| 14 | 17 | 5 | 5 | 5 | 5 | 1 | 5 | 5 | 5 | 1 | 1 | 5 | 5 | 17 | 5 | 17 | 5 | 5 | 17 | 1 |
| 15 | 10 | 1 | 10 | 10 | 2 | 5 | 2 | 5 | 10 | 10 | 2 | 10 | 5 | 10 | 10 | 10 | 5 | 5 | 10 | 5 |
| 16 | 6 | 2 | 1 | 6 | 5 | 6 | 6 | 2 | 6 | 6 | 6 | 6 | 2 | 6 | 6 | 6 | 6 | 6 | 6 | 6 |
| 17 | 1 | 7 | 7 | 2 | 7 | 7 | 4 | 7 | 2 | 4 | 4 | 7 | 7 | 7 | 7 | 7 | 7 | 7 | 7 | 7 |
| 18 | 1 | 9 | 10 | 10 | 6 | 10 | 2 | 6 | 16 | 10 | 10 | 6 | 5 | 16 | 18 | 2 | 10 | 2 | 18 | 18 |
| 19 | 7 | 17 | 11 | 1 | 17 | 11 | 1 | 17 | 11 | 7 | 17 | 11 | 11 | 1 | 9 | 1 | 11 | 9 | 1 | 1 |
| 20 | 2 | 4 | 4 | 4 | 4 | 4 | 2 | 4 | 4 | 4 | 4 | 4 | 4 | 4 | 4 | 1 | 4 | 4 | 4 | 4 |
| 21 | 7 | 1 | 7 | 7 | 7 | 2 | 2 | 2 | 7 | 2 | 7 | 7 | 7 | 7 | 2 | 7 | 7 | 7 | 7 | 7 |
| 22 | 20 | 3 | 13 | 2 | 3 | 7 | 1 | 8 | 18 | 8 | 3 | 13 | 8 | 13 | 8 | 18 | 13 | 6 | 13 | 8 |
| 23 | 2 | 4 | 4 | 1 | 4 | 4 | 4 | 4 | 4 | 4 | 4 | 4 | 4 | 4 | 4 | 2 | 4 | 4 | 4 | 4 |
| 24 | 5 | 2 | 1 | 16 | 5 | 2 | 5 | 5 | 16 | 16 | 5 | 5 | 2 | 5 | 5 | 16 | 5 | 5 | 16 | 5 |
| 25 | 5 | 13 | 13 | 6 | 13 | 6 | 2 | 6 | 1 | 11 | 11 | 6 | 13 | 2 | 13 | 2 | 6 | 13 | 13 | 13 |
| 26 | 2 | 10 | 10 | 14 | 19 | 8 | 2 | 8 | 2 | 2 | 2 | 14 | 10 | 14 | 14 | 2 | 1 | 19 | 14 | 10 |
| 27 | 4 | 1 | 4 | 4 | 2 | 4 | 4 | 4 | 4 | 4 | 4 | 4 | 4 | 4 | 4 | 4 | 4 | 4 | 4 | 3 |
| 28 | 15 | 8 | 12 | 1 | 1 | 15 | 1 | 12 | 15 | 12 | 11 | 1 | 8 | 1 | 15 | 1 | 1 | 8 | 15 | 15 |
| 29 | 10 | 2 | 10 | 13 | 10 | 6 | 2 | 16 | 19 | 16 | 19 | 13 | 6 | 1 | 13 | 6 | 5 | 16 | 6 | 2 |
| 30 | 1 | 3 | 11 | 11 | 11 | 11 | 1 | 3 | 11 | 11 | 11 | 7 | 3 | 7 | 3 | 7 | 11 | 11 | 7 | 11 |
| 31 | 13 | 1 | 5 | 1 | 5 | 5 | 3 | 5 | 13 | 13 | 3 | 13 | 5 | 13 | 5 | 5 | 13 | 5 | 13 | 13 |
| 32 | 6 | 6 | 1 | 6 | 6 | 1 | 6 | 1 | 6 | 6 | 6 | 6 | 6 | 6 | 1 | 6 | 6 | 6 | 6 | 1 |
| 33 | 11 | 8 | 11 | 3 | 11 | 3 | 11 | 3 | 3 | 8 | 8 | 3 | 11 | 11 | 11 | 1 | 2 | 11 | 11 | 11 |
| 34 | 7 | 1 | 7 | 5 | 7 | 7 | 7 | 1 | 7 | 7 | 5 | 7 | 7 | 7 | 7 | 1 | 7 | 7 | 7 | 1 |
| 35 | 1 | 15 | 9 | 9 | 12 | 12 | 1 | 7 | 20 | 15 | 15 | 4 | 6 | 12 | 9 | 1 | 8 | 4 | 15 | 15 |
| 36 | 14 | 1 | 7 | 1 | 7 | 7 | 7 | 1 | 14 | 14 | 1 | 14 | 7 | 7 | 1 | 14 | 14 | 7 | 14 | 1 |
| 37 | 17 | 9 | 4 | 9 | 9 | 7 | 7 | 1 | 9 | 17 | 4 | 9 | 1 | 17 | 4 | 9 | 1 | 9 | 17 | 9 |
| 38 | 17 | 8 | 2 | 8 | 8 | 8 | 2 | 13 | 17 | 2 | 8 | 13 | 7 | 15 | 1 | 15 | 2 | 2 | 17 | 17 |
| 39 | 8 | 5 | 13 | 5 | 5 | 13 | 2 | 1 | 8 | 11 | 11 | 13 | 13 | 13 | 8 | 4 | 13 | 13 | 20 | 2 |
| 40 | 14 | 5 | 5 | 14 | 5 | 5 | 3 | 5 | 3 | 14 | 14 | 2 | 5 | 1 | 5 | 14 | 5 | 5 | 14 | 14 |
| 41 | 1 | 8 | 6 | 8 | 8 | 8 | 2 | 8 | 2 | 2 | 8 | 8 | 8 | 8 | 6 | 2 | 8 | 8 | 8 | 8 |
| 42 | 9 | 1 | 1 | 9 | 3 | 3 | 9 | 3 | 9 | 3 | 9 | 9 | 3 | 9 | 9 | 9 | 9 | 3 | 9 | 9 |
| 43 | 17 | 5 | 1 | 5 | 5 | 5 | 1 | 17 | 5 | 17 | 5 | 5 | 5 | 5 | 5 | 5 | 17 | 1 | 5 | 1 |
| 44 | 9 | 1 | 5 | 9 | 9 | 9 | 2 | 3 | 9 | 9 | 4 | 9 | 5 | 9 | 9 | 9 | 5 | 9 | 9 | 5 |
| 45 | 11 | 1 | 3 | 11 | 5 | 11 | 3 | 11 | 11 | 10 | 2 | 11 | 9 | 11 | 5 | 5 | 11 | 5 | 11 | 11 |
| 46 | 1 | 13 | 5 | 5 | 5 | 5 | 1 | 13 | 3 | 5 | 5 | 13 | 5 | 13 | 13 | 3 | 5 | 13 | 13 | 13 |
| 47 | 8 | 1 | 8 | 19 | 6 | 19 | 4 | 4 | 6 | 8 | 17 | 17 | 8 | 8 | 8 | 8 | 8 | 1 | 1 | 8 |
| 48 | 16 | 6 | 1 | 14 | 6 | 6 | 6 | 3 | 14 | 16 | 13 | 6 | 3 | 16 | 3 | 16 | 6 | 2 | 16 | 6 |
| 49 | 9 | 7 | 9 | 9 | 9 | 7 | 9 | 4 | 9 | 9 | 4 | 9 | 4 | 9 | 1 | 9 | 1 | 9 | 9 | 1 |
| 50 | 3 | 7 | 7 | 7 | 7 | 7 | 7 | 7 | 7 | 7 | 7 | 4 | 7 | 1 | 7 | 4 | 4 | 7 | 1 | 7 |

## DATA SET 6. SOCIAL SERVICES INFORMATION AND REFERRAL SURVEY

The data below represent information on the first 100 people in August 1976 requesting social service information and referral services in Montgomery County, Virginia.

| Variable number | Description | Code | Definition |
|---|---|---|---|
| 1 | Day of week of referral | 1 | Monday |
| | | 2 | Tuesday |
| | | 3 | Wednesday |
| | | 4 | Thursday |
| | | 5 | Friday |
| | | 6 | Saturday |
| | | 7 | Sunday |
| 2 | Time of day | | Hour only, 1 corresponds to 1 A.M., 24 to midnight |
| 3 | Type of client | 1 | Individual inquiring for self |
| | | 2 | Individual inquiring for other person |
| | | 3 | Agency inquiring for information |
| | | 4 | Other |
| 4 | Method of client entry | 1 | Walk-in |
| | | 2 | Call-in |
| | | 3 | Write-in |
| | | 4 | Through follow-up |
| 5 | Client's age group | 1 | 0–14 years |
| | | 2 | 15–20 years |
| | | 3 | 21–29 years |
| | | 4 | 30–39 years |
| | | 5 | 40–49 years |
| | | 6 | 50–59 years |
| | | 7 | 60+ years |
| 6 | Problem | 2 | Employment vocational counseling and evaluation |
| | | 5 | Individual counseling |
| | | 25 | Adult basic education |
| | | 39 | Education—other |
| | | 42 | Job placement |
| | | 48 | Child or day care |
| | | 51 | Adoption |
| | | 52 | Companionship programs |
| | | 56 | Emergency financial aid |
| | | 59 | Utility subsidy |
| | | 62 | Pensions and benefits |
| | | 66 | Other financial assistance |
| | | 67 | Medical financial assistance |

| Variable number | Description | Code | Definition |
|---|---|---|---|
| | | 71 | Blindness or sight impairment |
| | | 74 | Deafness or hearing impairment |
| | | 86 | Dental care |
| | | 92 | Visual examination |
| | | 93 | Equipment loan or purchase |
| | | 108 | Live-in for elderly or disabled person |
| | | 120 | Civil liberties or rights |
| | | 121 | Consumer protection |
| | | 123 | General legal information and lawyer referral |
| | | 129 | Other legal information |
| | | 131 | Material assistance—clothing |
| | | 141 | Community education |
| | | 155 | Medically related transportation |
| | | 156 | Transportation |
| | | 160 | Student information for projects |
| | | 162 | Civic information |
| | | 164 | Information on a social service agency |
| | | 165 | Other |
| | | 167 | Senior citizen information and services |
| | | 168 | Unknown |
| 7 | Action taken on problem | 0 | No information or referral possible |
| | | 1 | Information given |
| | | 2 | Referral made |
| 8 | Did our information help client? | 0 | Not applicable |
| | | 1 | No, not at all |
| | | 2 | Somewhat helpful |
| | | 3 | Very helpful |
| | | 4 | Not available |
| 9 | Did client see the agency that we suggested? | 0 | Not applicable |
| | | 1 | Yes |
| | | 2 | No |
| | | 3 | Not available |
| 10 | Is client satisfied with agency services? | 0 | Not applicable |
| | | 1 | No, not at all |
| | | 2 | Somewhat satisfied |
| | | 3 | Very satisfied |
| | | 4 | Not available |
| 11 | Was agency able to help client? | 0 | Not applicable |
| | | 1 | Yes |
| | | 2 | No |
| | | 3 | Not available |
| | | 4 | Continuing/pending |

| Variable number | Description | Code | Definition |
|---|---|---|---|
| 12 | Why did client not go, or not receive help? | 0 | Not applicable |
| | | 1 | Not available |
| | | 2 | Haven't got around to doing it |
| | | 3 | Did something else problem solved itself |
| | | 4 | Had already been to that agency |
| | | 5 | Didn't think that agency could help |
| | | 6 | Transportation problem |
| | | 7 | Babysitting problem |
| | | 8 | Not eligible |
| | | 9 | Had to wait too long/waiting list |
| | | 10 | Agency doesn't offer service I need |
| | | 11 | Agency resources temporarily depleted for this service |
| | | 12 | Couldn't afford to pay |
| | | 13 | The other person needing help wouldn't go |
| | | 14 | Could never make contact with agency |
| | | 15 | Other reason |
| | | 16 | Not hired/no jobs |

| Person number | Variable number 1 | 2 | 3 | 4 | 5 | 6 | 7 | 8 | 9 | 10 | 11 | 12 |
|---|---|---|---|---|---|---|---|---|---|---|---|---|
| 1 | 3 | 14 | 2 | 2 | 7 | 93 | 2 | 2 | 1 | 2 | 2 | 10 |
| 2 | 4 | 13 | 1 | 2 | 5 | 165 | 2 | 0 | 0 | 0 | 0 | 0 |
| 3 | 4 | 12 | 1 | 2 | 3 | 165 | 1 | 0 | 0 | 0 | 0 | 0 |
| 4 | 4 | 14 | 3 | 2 | 7 | 67 | 0 | 0 | 0 | 0 | 0 | 0 |
| 5 | 4 | 14 | 3 | 2 | 3 | 164 | 1 | 0 | 0 | 0 | 0 | 0 |
| 6 | 2 | 16 | 1 | 2 | 7 | 165 | 1 | 3 | 1 | 3 | 1 | 0 |
| 7 | 2 | 10 | 1 | 1 | 4 | 165 | 1 | 0 | 0 | 0 | 0 | 0 |
| 8 | 4 | 11 | 1 | 2 | 3 | 51 | 1 | 0 | 0 | 0 | 0 | 0 |
| 9 | 1 | 14 | 1 | 2 | 3 | 164 | 1 | 0 | 0 | 0 | 0 | 0 |
| 10 | 1 | 14 | 1 | 2 | 4 | 164 | 1 | 0 | 0 | 0 | 0 | 0 |
| 11 | 1 | 13 | 1 | 2 | 4 | 164 | 1 | 0 | 0 | 0 | 0 | 0 |
| 12 | 2 | 9 | 1 | 2 | 3 | 86 | 2 | 0 | 0 | 0 | 0 | 0 |
| 13 | 3 | 13 | 1 | 2 | 3 | 164 | 1 | 0 | 0 | 0 | 0 | 0 |
| 14 | 1 | 16 | 1 | 2 | 3 | 123 | 2 | 0 | 0 | 0 | 0 | 0 |
| 15 | 2 | 11 | 1 | 2 | 3 | 160 | 1 | 0 | 0 | 0 | 0 | 0 |
| 16 | 2 | 13 | 1 | 2 | 3 | 123 | 1 | 0 | 0 | 0 | 0 | 0 |
| 17 | 2 | 11 | 1 | 2 | 5 | 164 | 1 | 0 | 0 | 0 | 0 | 0 |
| 18 | 2 | 14 | 1 | 2 | 3 | 123 | 2 | 2 | 1 | 0 | 2 | 14 |
| 19 | 2 | 14 | 2 | 2 | 1 | 48 | 2 | 3 | 1 | 3 | 1 | 0 |
| 20 | 3 | 8 | 1 | 1 | 2 | 164 | 1 | 0 | 0 | 0 | 0 | 0 |
| 21 | 4 | 10 | 1 | 2 | 3 | 165 | 1 | 0 | 0 | 0 | 0 | 0 |
| 22 | 4 | 12 | 1 | 2 | 4 | 165 | 2 | 0 | 0 | 0 | 0 | 0 |
| 23 | 3 | 12 | 1 | 2 | 3 | 166 | 2 | 2 | 1 | 2 | 2 | 3 |
| 24 | 5 | 9 | 2 | 2 | 7 | 168 | 1 | 3 | 0 | 0 | 0 | 0 |
| 25 | 4 | 15 | 1 | 2 | 3 | 165 | 0 | 0 | 0 | 0 | 0 | 0 |
| 26 | 4 | 13 | 1 | 2 | 3 | 165 | 1 | 0 | 0 | 0 | 0 | 0 |
| 27 | 1 | 12 | 1 | 2 | 4 | 165 | 2 | 3 | 1 | 3 | 1 | 0 |
| 28 | 4 | 9 | 1 | 2 | 4 | 131 | 2 | 3 | 1 | 3 | 1 | 0 |
| 29 | 4 | 14 | 2 | 2 | 2 | 56 | 2 | 3 | 1 | 3 | 1 | 0 |
| 30 | 4 | 13 | 1 | 2 | 4 | 48 | 0 | 0 | 0 | 0 | 0 | 3 |
| 31 | 2 | 11 | 1 | 2 | 4 | 153 | 2 | 0 | 0 | 0 | 0 | 3 |
| 32 | 5 | 15 | 1 | 2 | 3 | 164 | 1 | 0 | 0 | 0 | 0 | 0 |
| 33 | 1 | 9 | 1 | 2 | 3 | 165 | 1 | 0 | 0 | 0 | 0 | 0 |
| 34 | 1 | 9 | 3 | 2 | 0 | 164 | 1 | 0 | 0 | 0 | 0 | 0 |
| 35 | 1 | 10 | 1 | 2 | 4 | 164 | 1 | 0 | 0 | 0 | 0 | 0 |
| 36 | 1 | 10 | 3 | 2 | 0 | 165 | 1 | 0 | 0 | 0 | 0 | 0 |
| 37 | 3 | 11 | 1 | 3 | 7 | 141 | 1 | 0 | 0 | 0 | 0 | 0 |
| 38 | 1 | 13 | 3 | 2 | 0 | 164 | 1 | 0 | 0 | 0 | 0 | 0 |
| 39 | 1 | 12 | 2 | 2 | 2 | 165 | 1 | 0 | 0 | 0 | 0 | 0 |
| 40 | 1 | 12 | 1 | 2 | 3 | 165 | 1 | 0 | 0 | 0 | 0 | 0 |
| 41 | 5 | 16 | 3 | 2 | 0 | 164 | 2 | 0 | 1 | 0 | 1 | 0 |
| 42 | 5 | 9 | 3 | 2 | 3 | 164 | 0 | 0 | 0 | 0 | 0 | 0 |
| 43 | 5 | 10 | 3 | 2 | 3 | 164 | 1 | 2 | 1 | 4 | 4 | 0 |
| 44 | 5 | 11 | 1 | 2 | 3 | 156 | 2 | 1 | 1 | 4 | 2 | 6 |
| 45 | 1 | 15 | 3 | 2 | 0 | 164 | 1 | 0 | 0 | 0 | 0 | 0 |
| 46 | 4 | 11 | 1 | 2 | 3 | 123 | 2 | 0 | 0 | 0 | 0 | 0 |
| 47 | 3 | 14 | 1 | 2 | 3 | 164 | 1 | 0 | 0 | 0 | 0 | 0 |
| 48 | 4 | 12 | 1 | 2 | 7 | 108 | 0 | 0 | 0 | 0 | 0 | 0 |
| 49 | 1 | 16 | 1 | 2 | 5 | 123 | 2 | 0 | 0 | 0 | 0 | 0 |
| 50 | 2 | 14 | 1 | 2 | 4 | 123 | 1 | 3 | 1 | 3 | 1 | 0 |

| Person number | Variable number 1 | 2 | 3 | 4 | 5 | 6 | 7 | 8 | 9 | 10 | 11 | 12 |
|---|---|---|---|---|---|---|---|---|---|---|---|---|
| 51 | 2 | 14 | 1 | 2 | 5 | 164 | 1 | 0 | 0 | 0 | 0 | 0 |
| 52 | 2 | 10 | 3 | 2 | 4 | 165 | 1 | 0 | 0 | 0 | 0 | 0 |
| 53 | 2 | 11 | 3 | 2 | 0 | 164 | 1 | 0 | 0 | 0 | 0 | 0 |
| 54 | 2 | 12 | 1 | 2 | 5 | 164 | 1 | 0 | 0 | 0 | 0 | 0 |
| 55 | 2 | 14 | 1 | 2 | 3 | 42 | 1 | 0 | 0 | 0 | 0 | 0 |
| 56 | 2 | 13 | 2 | 1 | 2 | 164 | 1 | 1 | 1 | 2 | 2 | 11 |
| 57 | 2 | 16 | 1 | 2 | 3 | 166 | 1 | 0 | 0 | 0 | 0 | 0 |
| 58 | 3 | 14 | 1 | 2 | 3 | 71 | 2 | 0 | 2 | 0 | 0 | 14 |
| 59 | 1 | 10 | 1 | 2 | 7 | 39 | 2 | 0 | 0 | 0 | 0 | 0 |
| 60 | 2 | 10 | 1 | 1 | 5 | 155 | 2 | 3 | 1 | 3 | 1 | 0 |
| 61 | 1 | 12 | 1 | 2 | 5 | 67 | 1 | 0 | 0 | 0 | 0 | 0 |
| 62 | 4 | 9 | 1 | 2 | 7 | 165 | 1 | 0 | 0 | 0 | 0 | 0 |
| 63 | 2 | 11 | 1 | 2 | 5 | 131 | 2 | 0 | 2 | 0 | 0 | 2 |
| 64 | 3 | 12 | 1 | 2 | 3 | 164 | 1 | 0 | 0 | 0 | 0 | 0 |
| 65 | 4 | 9 | 1 | 2 | 3 | 123 | 2 | 0 | 0 | 0 | 0 | 0 |
| 66 | 2 | 11 | 2 | 2 | 4 | 164 | 1 | 0 | 0 | 0 | 0 | 0 |
| 67 | 5 | 12 | 1 | 2 | 5 | 121 | 2 | 0 | 0 | 0 | 0 | 0 |
| 68 | 3 | 12 | 1 | 2 | 3 | 123 | 2 | 0 | 0 | 0 | 0 | 0 |
| 69 | 2 | 15 | 1 | 2 | 3 | 59 | 2 | 1 | 1 | 4 | 2 | 8 |
| 70 | 1 | 16 | 1 | 2 | 3 | 164 | 1 | 0 | 0 | 0 | 0 | 0 |
| 71 | 4 | 17 | 1 | 2 | 5 | 165 | 2 | 0 | 0 | 0 | 0 | 0 |
| 72 | 4 | 21 | 2 | 2 | 4 | 164 | 1 | 0 | 0 | 0 | 0 | 0 |
| 73 | 3 | 22 | 1 | 2 | 3 | 164 | 1 | 0 | 0 | 0 | 0 | 0 |
| 74 | 2 | 13 | 1 | 2 | 5 | 164 | 1 | 0 | 2 | 0 | 0 | 14 |
| 75 | 1 | 9 | 2 | 2 | 4 | 67 | 2 | 1 | 1 | 1 | 2 | 8 |
| 76 | 3 | 11 | 2 | 2 | 6 | 66 | 1 | 3 | 1 | 0 | 4 | 0 |
| 77 | 4 | 11 | 2 | 2 | 2 | 2 | 2 | 3 | 1 | 3 | 1 | 0 |
| 78 | 1 | 13 | 2 | 2 | 3 | 42 | 1 | 0 | 0 | 0 | 0 | 0 |
| 79 | 5 | 13 | 1 | 2 | 4 | 164 | 1 | 3 | 1 | 3 | 1 | 0 |
| 80 | 4 | 15 | 1 | 2 | 3 | 129 | 2 | 2 | 2 | 0 | 0 | 5 |
| 81 | 4 | 16 | 2 | 2 | 3 | 167 | 2 | 3 | 1 | 0 | 4 | 0 |
| 82 | 5 | 11 | 2 | 2 | 7 | 108 | 2 | 2 | 2 | 0 | 0 | 5 |
| 83 | 5 | 14 | 1 | 2 | 3 | 5 | 2 | 0 | 0 | 0 | 0 | 0 |
| 84 | 4 | 11 | 2 | 2 | 1 | 92 | 2 | 3 | 1 | 3 | 1 | 0 |
| 85 | 5 | 13 | 2 | 2 | 4 | 71 | 2 | 2 | 1 | 0 | 4 | 0 |
| 86 | 1 | 11 | 2 | 2 | 3 | 120 | 2 | 3 | 3 | 4 | 3 | 0 |
| 87 | 3 | 10 | 2 | 2 | 5 | 62 | 2 | 0 | 0 | 0 | 0 | 0 |
| 88 | 3 | 11 | 2 | 2 | 3 | 121 | 2 | 3 | 1 | 3 | 1 | 0 |
| 89 | 5 | 11 | 2 | 2 | 6 | 74 | 2 | 2 | 2 | 0 | 0 | 2 |
| 90 | 1 | 13 | 1 | 2 | 4 | 123 | 2 | 3 | 1 | 0 | 4 | 0 |
| 91 | 2 | 14 | 1 | 2 | 4 | 165 | 0 | 0 | 0 | 0 | 0 | 0 |
| 92 | 2 | 9 | 1 | 2 | 3 | 164 | 1 | 0 | 0 | 0 | 0 | 0 |
| 93 | 4 | 8 | 1 | 2 | 3 | 166 | 1 | 0 | 0 | 0 | 0 | 0 |
| 94 | 4 | 10 | 3 | 2 | 0 | 164 | 1 | 0 | 0 | 0 | 0 | 0 |
| 95 | 1 | 15 | 1 | 2 | 3 | 162 | 1 | 3 | 1 | 0 | 0 | 0 |
| 96 | 1 | 10 | 1 | 2 | 4 | 162 | 0 | 0 | 0 | 0 | 0 | 0 |
| 97 | 1 | 11 | 1 | 1 | 3 | 67 | 2 | 1 | 1 | 0 | 0 | 14 |
| 98 | 4 | 10 | 1 | 2 | 1 | 52 | 1 | 0 | 1 | 0 | 2 | 10 |
| 99 | 3 | 13 | 1 | 2 | 3 | 25 | 2 | 2 | 1 | 0 | 0 | 15 |
| 100 | 2 | 10 | 1 | 2 | 2 | 42 | 2 | 1 | 1 | 1 | 2 | 15 |

# DATA SET 7. HYPOTHETICAL TOWN OF STRIP MINE

## Town of Strip Mine (for six zones selected randomly)

| Zone ($i$) | $X_1$ | $X_2$ | $Y_1(10^4)$ | $Y_2$ | $Y_3$ | $(X_{i1} - \bar{X}_1)$ | $(X_{i2} - \bar{X}_2)$ | $(Y_{i1} - \bar{Y}_1)$ | $(Y_{i2} - \bar{Y}_2)$ | $(X_{i1} - \bar{X}_1)^2$ | $(X_{i2} - \bar{X}_2)^2$ |
|---|---|---|---|---|---|---|---|---|---|---|---|
| 1 | 25 | 33 | 0.16 | 10 | No | −7 | −2 | −400 | −3 | 49 | 4 |
| 2 | 24 | 34 | 0.17 | 12 | No | −8 | −1 | −300 | −1 | 64 | 1 |
| 3 | 40 | 47 | 0.12 | 20 | Yes | +8 | +12 | −800 | +7 | 64 | 144 |
| 4 | 42 | 43 | 0.15 | 18 | Yes | +10 | +8 | −500 | +5 | 100 | 64 |
| 5 | 29 | 25 | 0.35 | 8 | No | −3 | −10 | +1500 | −5 | 9 | 100 |
| 6 | 32 | 28 | 0.25 | 10 | No | 0 | −7 | +500 | −3 | 0 | 49 |
| Total | 192 | 210 | 1.20 | 78 | | | | | | 286 | 362 |
| Mean | 32 | 35 | 0.20 | 13 | | | | | | | |
| Variance | 57.2 | 72.4 | 0.00728 | 23.6 | | | | | | | |
| Standard deviation | 7.56 | 8.51 | 0.085 | 4.858 | | | | | | | |

| Zone ($i$) | $(Y_{i1} - \bar{Y}_1)^2$ | $(Y_{i2} - \bar{Y}_2)^2$ | $Z_1$ | $Z_2$ | $W_1$ | $W_2$ | $X_1 X_2$ |
|---|---|---|---|---|---|---|---|
| 1 | $16 \times 10^4$ | 9 | −0.926 | −0.235 | −0.469 | −0.825 | $825 \times 10^4$ |
| 2 | 9 | 1 | −1.058 | −0.118 | −0.352 | −0.816 | 816 |
| 3 | 64 | 49 | +1.058 | +1.410 | −0.938 | +1.880 | 1880 |
| 4 | 25 | 25 | +1.323 | +0.940 | −0.586 | +1.806 | 1806 |
| 5 | 225 | 25 | −0.397 | −1.175 | +1.758 | −1.725 | 725 |
| 6 | 25 | 9 | 0.000 | −0.823 | +0.586 | −0.896 | 896 |
| Total | $364 \times 10^4$ | 118 | 0 | 0 | 0 | 0 | $6948 \times 10^4$ |

$X_1$ = mean age of residents (years)
$X_2$ = mean travel time to all employment opportunities (min)
$Y_1$ = median annual per capita income ($ per year)
$Y_2$ = mortality rate (deaths per 1000 people per year)
$Y_3$ = over 20 percent of households with female head? ("yes" or "no")

APPENDIX

# E

# THEORETICAL PROBABILITY DENSITY FUNCTIONS

## Table E-1 The standard normal ($z$) distribution

Each number in the table below is the fraction of the total area under the standard normal distribution which lies between 0 and a positive $z$. In other words, each number is the probability of a value lying in the interval between 0 and $z$. The units and tenths of units of $z$ are read in the left column. The hundredths of units are read in the top row. Probabilities for intervals from 0 to $-z$ are found from symmetry and from $z$ to $\infty$ by subtraction from 0.5000.

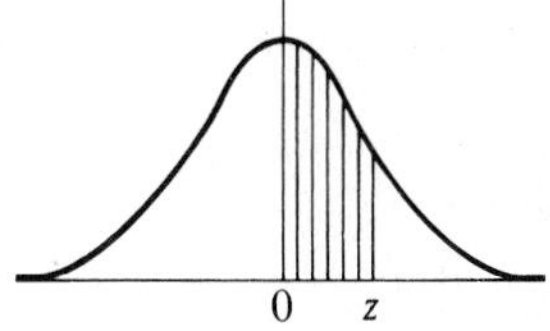


| $z$ | .00 | .01 | .02 | .03 | .04 | .05 | .06 | .07 | .08 | .09 |
|---|---|---|---|---|---|---|---|---|---|---|
| 0.0 | .0000 | .0040 | .0080 | .0120 | .0160 | .0199 | .0239 | .0279 | .0319 | .0359 |
| 0.1 | .0398 | .0438 | .0478 | .0517 | .0557 | .0596 | .0636 | .0675 | .0714 | .0753 |
| 0.2 | .0793 | .0832 | .0871 | .0910 | .0948 | .0987 | .1026 | .1064 | .1103 | .1141 |
| 0.3 | .1179 | .1217 | .1255 | .1293 | .1331 | .1368 | .1406 | .1443 | .1480 | .1517 |
| 0.4 | .1554 | .1591 | .1628 | .1664 | .1700 | .1736 | .1772 | .1808 | .1844 | .1879 |
| 0.5 | .1915 | .1950 | .1985 | .2019 | .2054 | .2088 | .2123 | .2157 | .2190 | .2224 |
| 0.6 | .2257 | .2291 | .2324 | .2357 | .2389 | .2422 | .2454 | .2486 | .2517 | .2549 |
| 0.7 | .2580 | .2611 | .2642 | .2673 | .2703 | .2734 | .2764 | .2794 | .2823 | .2852 |
| 0.8 | .2881 | .2910 | .2939 | .2967 | .2995 | .3023 | .3051 | .3078 | .3106 | .3133 |
| 0.9 | .3159 | .3186 | .3212 | .3238 | .3264 | .3289 | .3315 | .3340 | .3365 | .3389 |

**Table E-1** (*continued*)

| $z$ | .00 | .01 | .02 | .03 | .04 | .05 | .06 | .07 | .08 | .09 |
|---|---|---|---|---|---|---|---|---|---|---|
| 1.0 | .3413 | .3438 | .3461 | .3485 | .3508 | .3531 | .3554 | .3577 | .3599 | .3621 |
| 1.1 | .3643 | .3665 | .3686 | .3708 | .3729 | .3749 | .3770 | .3790 | .3810 | .3830 |
| 1.2 | .3849 | .3869 | .3888 | .3907 | .3925 | .3944 | .3962 | .3980 | .3997 | .4015 |
| 1.3 | .4032 | .4049 | .4066 | .4082 | .4099 | .4115 | .4131 | .4147 | .4162 | .4177 |
| 1.4 | .4192 | .4207 | .4222 | .4236 | .4251 | .4265 | .4279 | .4292 | .4306 | .4319 |
| 1.5 | .4332 | .4345 | .4357 | .4370 | .4382 | .4394 | .4406 | .4418 | .4429 | .4441 |
| 1.6 | .4452 | .4463 | .4474 | .4484 | .4495 | .4505 | .4515 | .4525 | .4535 | .4545 |
| 1.7 | .4554 | .4564 | .4573 | .4582 | .4591 | .4599 | .4608 | .4616 | .4625 | .4633 |
| 1.8 | .4641 | .4649 | .4656 | .4664 | .4671 | .4678 | .4686 | .4693 | .4699 | .4706 |
| 1.9 | .4713 | .4719 | .4726 | .4732 | .4738 | .4744 | .4750 | .4756 | .4761 | .4767 |
| 2.0 | .4772 | .4778 | .4783 | .4788 | .4793 | .4798 | .4803 | .4808 | .4812 | .4817 |
| 2.1 | .4821 | .4826 | .4830 | .4834 | .4838 | .4842 | .4846 | .4850 | .4854 | .4857 |
| 2.2 | .4861 | .4864 | .4868 | .4871 | .4875 | .4878 | .4881 | .4884 | .4887 | .4890 |
| 2.3 | .4893 | .4896 | .4898 | .4901 | .4904 | .4906 | .4909 | .4911 | .4913 | .4916 |
| 2.4 | .4918 | .4920 | .4922 | .4925 | .4927 | .4929 | .4931 | .4932 | .4934 | .4936 |
| 2.5 | .4938 | .4940 | .4941 | .4943 | .4945 | .4946 | .4948 | .4949 | .4951 | .4952 |
| 2.6 | .4953 | .4955 | .4956 | .4957 | .4959 | .4960 | .4961 | .4962 | .4963 | .4964 |
| 2.7 | .4965 | .4966 | .4967 | .4968 | .4969 | .4970 | .4971 | .4972 | .4973 | .4974 |
| 2.8 | .4974 | .4975 | .4976 | .4977 | .4977 | .4978 | .4979 | .4979 | .4980 | .4981 |
| 2.9 | .4981 | .4982 | .4982 | .4983 | .4984 | .4984 | .4985 | .4985 | .4986 | .4986 |
| 3.0 | .4987 | .4987 | .4987 | .4988 | .4988 | .4989 | .4989 | .4989 | .4990 | .4990 |

## Table E-2 The chi-square ($\chi^2$) distribution

Each number in the table below is the chi-square value above which the area (probability) under the chi-square distribution is Pr. The degrees of freedom (df) are shown in the left column. These are calculated in accordance with the particular statistical technique being employed (see examples in the text). When the degrees of freedom exceed 100, use $(2\chi^2)^{1/2} - (2\text{ df} - 1)^{1/2}$ as a standard normal variable.

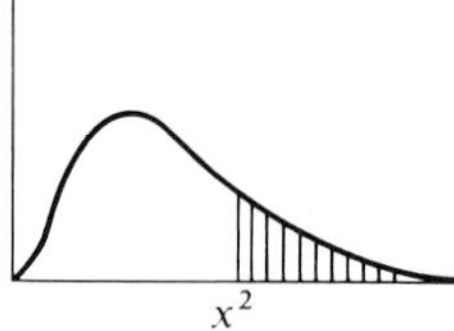


| df \ Pr | 0.995 | 0.975 | 0.050 | 0.025 | 0.010 | 0.005 |
|---|---|---|---|---|---|---|
| 1 | $392704 \times 10^{-10}$ | $982069 \times 10^{-9}$ | 3.84146 | 5.02389 | 6.63490 | 7.87944 |
| 2 | 0.0100251 | 0.0506356 | 5.99146 | 7.37776 | 9.21034 | 10.5966 |
| 3 | 0.0717218 | 0.215795 | 7.81473 | 9.34840 | 11.3449 | 12.8382 |
| 4 | 0.206989 | 0.484419 | 9.48773 | 11.1433 | 13.2767 | 14.8603 |

**Table E-2** *(continued)*

| df \ Pr | 0.995 | 0.975 | 0.050 | 0.025 | 0.010 | 0.005 |
|---|---|---|---|---|---|---|
| 5 | 0.411742 | 0.831212 | 11.0705 | 12.8325 | 15.0863 | 16.7496 |
| 6 | 0.675727 | 1.23734 | 12.5916 | 14.4494 | 16.8119 | 18.5476 |
| 7 | 0.989256 | 1.68987 | 14.0671 | 16.0128 | 18.4753 | 20.2777 |
| 8 | 1.34441 | 2.17973 | 15.5073 | 17.5345 | 20.0902 | 21.9550 |
| 9 | 1.73493 | 2.7003 | 16.9190 | 19.0228 | 21.6660 | 23.5894 |
| 10 | 2.15586 | 3.24697 | 18.3070 | 20.4832 | 23.2093 | 25.1882 |
| 11 | 2.60322 | 3.81575 | 19.6751 | 21.9200 | 24.7250 | 26.7568 |
| 12 | 3.07382 | 4.40379 | 21.0261 | 23.3367 | 26.2170 | 28.2995 |
| 13 | 3.56503 | 5.00875 | 22.3620 | 24.7356 | 27.6882 | 29.8195 |
| 14 | 4.07467 | 5.62873 | 23.6848 | 26.1189 | 29.1412 | 31.3194 |
| 15 | 4.60092 | 6.26214 | 24.9958 | 27.4884 | 30.5779 | 32.8013 |
| 16 | 5.14221 | 6.90766 | 26.2962 | 28.8454 | 31.9999 | 34.2672 |
| 17 | 5.69722 | 7.56419 | 27.5871 | 30.1910 | 33.4087 | 35.7185 |
| 18 | 6.26480 | 8.23075 | 28.8693 | 31.5264 | 34.8053 | 37.1565 |
| 19 | 6.84397 | 8.90652 | 30.1435 | 32.8523 | 36.1909 | 38.5823 |
| 20 | 7.43384 | 9.59078 | 31.4104 | 34.1696 | 37.5662 | 39.9968 |
| 21 | 8.03365 | 10.28293 | 32.6706 | 35.4789 | 38.9322 | 41.4011 |
| 22 | 8.64272 | 10.9823 | 33.9244 | 36.7807 | 40.2894 | 42.7957 |
| 23 | 9.26043 | 11.6886 | 35.1725 | 38.0756 | 41.6384 | 44.1813 |
| 24 | 9.88623 | 12.4012 | 36.4150 | 39.3641 | 42.9798 | 45.5585 |
| 25 | 10.5197 | 13.1197 | 37.6525 | 40.6465 | 44.3141 | 46.9279 |
| 26 | 11.1602 | 13.8439 | 38.8851 | 41.9232 | 45.6417 | 48.2899 |
| 27 | 11.8076 | 14.5734 | 40.1133 | 43.1945 | 46.9629 | 49.6449 |
| 28 | 12.4613 | 15.3079 | 41.3371 | 44.4608 | 48.2782 | 50.9934 |
| 29 | 13.1211 | 16.0471 | 42.5570 | 45.7223 | 49.5879 | 52.3356 |
| 30 | 13.7867 | 16.7908 | 43.7730 | 46.9792 | 50.8922 | 53.6720 |
| 40 | 20.7065 | 24.4330 | 55.7585 | 59.3417 | 63.6907 | 66.7660 |
| 50 | 27.9907 | 32.3574 | 67.5048 | 71.4202 | 76.1539 | 79.4900 |
| 60 | 35.5345 | 40.4817 | 79.0819 | 83.2977 | 88.3794 | 91.9517 |
| 70 | 43.2752 | 48.7576 | 90.5312 | 95.0232 | 100.425 | 104.215 |
| 80 | 51.1719 | 57.1532 | 101.879 | 106.629 | 112.329 | 116.321 |
| 90 | 59.1963 | 65.6466 | 113.145 | 118.136 | 124.116 | 128.299 |
| 100 | 67.3276 | 74.2219 | 124.342 | 129.561 | 135.807 | 140.169 |

## Table E-3 Student's *t* distribution

Each number in the table below is the *t* value above which the area (probability) under the Student's *t* distribution is Pr. This holds for a one-tailed test, with the probabilities shown in the second row. For a two-tailed test, the probabilities shown on the top row are for *t* from $t_p$ to $\infty$ and from $t_n$ to $-\infty$. The degrees of freedom (df) are shown in the left column. These are calculated in accordance with the particular statistical technique being employed (see examples in the text).

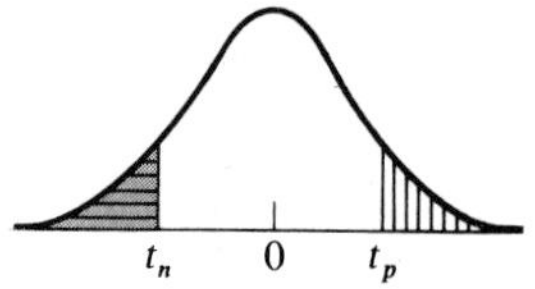


| df \ Pr | 0.20 | 0.10 | 0.05 | 0.02 | 0.010 | Two tail |
|---|---|---|---|---|---|---|
| | 0.10 | 0.05 | 0.025 | 0.01 | 0.005 | One tail |
| 1 | 3.078 | 6.314 | 12.706 | 31.821 | 63.657 | |
| 2 | 1.886 | 2.920 | 4.303 | 6.965 | 9.925 | |
| 3 | 1.638 | 2.353 | 3.182 | 4.541 | 5.841 | |
| 4 | 1.533 | 2.132 | 2.776 | 3.747 | 4.604 | |
| 5 | 1.476 | 2.015 | 2.571 | 3.365 | 4.032 | |
| 6 | 1.440 | 1.943 | 2.447 | 3.143 | 3.707 | |
| 7 | 1.415 | 1.895 | 2.365 | 2.998 | 3.499 | |
| 8 | 1.397 | 1.860 | 2.306 | 2.896 | 3.355 | |
| 9 | 1.383 | 1.833 | 2.262 | 1.821 | 3.250 | |
| 10 | 1.372 | 1.812 | 2.228 | 2.764 | 3.169 | |
| 11 | 1.363 | 1.796 | 2.201 | 2.718 | 3.106 | |
| 12 | 1.356 | 1.782 | 2.179 | 2.681 | 3.055 | |
| 13 | 1.350 | 1.771 | 2.160 | 2.650 | 3.012 | |
| 14 | 1.345 | 1.761 | 2.145 | 2.624 | 2.977 | |
| 15 | 1.341 | 1.753 | 2.131 | 2.602 | 2.947 | |
| 16 | 1.337 | 1.746 | 2.120 | 2.583 | 2.921 | |
| 17 | 1.333 | 1.740 | 2.110 | 2.567 | 2.898 | |
| 18 | 1.330 | 1.734 | 2.101 | 2.552 | 2.878 | |
| 19 | 1.328 | 1.729 | 2.093 | 2.539 | 2.861 | |
| 20 | 1.325 | 1.725 | 2.086 | 2.528 | 2.845 | |
| 21 | 1.323 | 1.721 | 2.080 | 2.518 | 2.831 | |
| 22 | 1.321 | 1.717 | 2.074 | 2.508 | 2.819 | |
| 23 | 1.319 | 1.714 | 2.069 | 2.500 | 2.807 | |
| 24 | 1.318 | 1.711 | 2.064 | 2.492 | 2.797 | |
| 25 | 1.316 | 1.708 | 2.060 | 2.485 | 2.787 | |
| 26 | 1.315 | 1.706 | 2.056 | 2.479 | 2.779 | |
| 27 | 1.314 | 1.703 | 2.052 | 2.473 | 2.771 | |
| 28 | 1.313 | 1.701 | 2.048 | 2.467 | 2.763 | |
| 29 | 1.311 | 1.699 | 2.045 | 2.462 | 2.756 | |
| 30 | 1.310 | 1.697 | 2.042 | 2.457 | 2.750 | |
| 40 | 1.303 | 1.684 | 2.021 | 2.423 | 2.704 | |
| 60 | 1.296 | 1.671 | 2.000 | 2.390 | 2.660 | |
| 120 | 1.289 | 1.658 | 1.980 | 2.358 | 2.617 | |
| $\infty$ | 1.282 | 1.645 | 1.960 | 2.326 | 2.576 | |

## Table E-4 Fisher's $F(f)$ distribution

Each number in the table below is the $f$ value above which the area (probability) under Fisher's $F$ distribution is 0.05. The degrees of freedom ($df_1$ and $df_2$) shown in the left column and top row are calculated in accordance with the particular statistical technique being employed (see examples in the text).

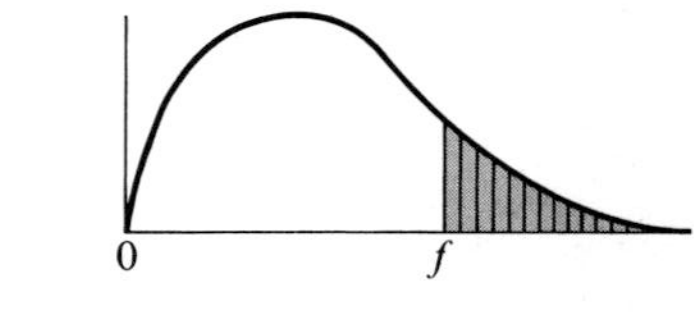


| $df_2$ \ $df_1$ | 1 | 2 | 3 | 4 | 5 | 6 | 7 | 8 | 9 | 10 | 12 | 15 | 20 | 24 | 30 | 40 | 60 | 120 | ∞ |
|---|---|---|---|---|---|---|---|---|---|---|---|---|---|---|---|---|---|---|---|
| 1 | 161.4 | 199.5 | 215.7 | 224.6 | 230.2 | 234.0 | 236.8 | 238.9 | 240.5 | 241.9 | 243.9 | 245.9 | 248.0 | 249.1 | 250.1 | 251.1 | 252.2 | 253.3 | 254.3 |
| 2 | 18.51 | 19.00 | 19.16 | 19.25 | 19.30 | 19.33 | 19.35 | 19.37 | 19.38 | 19.40 | 19.41 | 19.43 | 19.45 | 19.45 | 19.46 | 19.47 | 19.48 | 19.49 | 19.50 |
| 3 | 10.13 | 9.55 | 9.28 | 9.12 | 9.01 | 8.94 | 8.89 | 8.85 | 8.81 | 8.79 | 8.74 | 8.70 | 8.66 | 8.64 | 8.62 | 8.59 | 8.57 | 8.55 | 8.53 |
| 4 | 7.71 | 6.94 | 6.59 | 6.39 | 6.26 | 6.16 | 6.09 | 6.04 | 6.00 | 5.96 | 5.91 | 5.86 | 5.80 | 5.77 | 5.75 | 5.72 | 5.69 | 5.66 | 5.63 |
| 5 | 6.61 | 5.79 | 5.41 | 5.19 | 5.05 | 4.95 | 4.88 | 4.82 | 4.77 | 4.74 | 4.68 | 4.62 | 4.56 | 4.53 | 4.50 | 4.46 | 4.43 | 4.40 | 4.36 |
| 6 | 5.99 | 5.14 | 4.76 | 4.53 | 4.39 | 4.28 | 4.21 | 4.15 | 4.10 | 4.06 | 4.00 | 3.94 | 3.87 | 3.84 | 3.81 | 3.77 | 3.74 | 3.70 | 3.67 |
| 7 | 5.59 | 4.74 | 4.35 | 4.12 | 3.97 | 3.87 | 3.79 | 3.73 | 3.68 | 3.64 | 3.57 | 3.51 | 3.44 | 3.41 | 3.38 | 3.34 | 3.30 | 3.27 | 3.23 |
| 8 | 5.32 | 4.46 | 4.07 | 3.84 | 3.69 | 3.58 | 3.50 | 3.44 | 3.39 | 3.35 | 3.28 | 3.22 | 3.15 | 3.12 | 3.08 | 3.04 | 3.01 | 2.97 | 2.93 |
| 9 | 5.12 | 4.26 | 3.86 | 3.63 | 3.48 | 3.37 | 3.29 | 3.23 | 3.18 | 3.14 | 3.07 | 3.01 | 2.94 | 2.90 | 2.86 | 2.83 | 2.79 | 2.75 | 2.71 |
| 10 | 4.96 | 4.10 | 3.71 | 3.48 | 3.33 | 3.22 | 3.14 | 3.07 | 3.02 | 2.98 | 2.91 | 2.85 | 2.77 | 2.74 | 2.70 | 2.66 | 2.62 | 2.58 | 2.54 |
| 11 | 4.84 | 3.98 | 3.59 | 3.36 | 3.20 | 3.09 | 3.01 | 2.95 | 2.90 | 2.85 | 2.79 | 2.72 | 2.65 | 2.61 | 2.57 | 2.53 | 2.49 | 2.45 | 2.40 |
| 12 | 4.75 | 3.89 | 3.49 | 3.26 | 3.11 | 3.00 | 2.91 | 2.85 | 2.80 | 2.75 | 2.69 | 2.62 | 2.54 | 2.51 | 2.47 | 2.43 | 2.38 | 2.34 | 2.30 |
| 13 | 4.67 | 3.81 | 3.41 | 3.18 | 3.03 | 2.92 | 2.83 | 2.77 | 2.71 | 2.67 | 2.60 | 2.53 | 2.46 | 2.42 | 2.38 | 2.34 | 2.30 | 2.25 | 2.21 |
| 14 | 4.60 | 3.74 | 3.34 | 3.11 | 2.96 | 2.85 | 2.76 | 2.70 | 2.65 | 2.60 | 2.53 | 2.46 | 2.39 | 2.35 | 2.31 | 2.27 | 2.22 | 2.18 | 2.13 |
| 15 | 4.54 | 3.68 | 3.29 | 3.06 | 2.90 | 2.79 | 2.71 | 2.64 | 2.59 | 2.54 | 2.48 | 2.40 | 2.33 | 2.29 | 2.25 | 2.20 | 2.16 | 2.11 | 2.07 |
| 16 | 4.49 | 3.63 | 3.24 | 3.01 | 2.85 | 2.74 | 2.66 | 2.59 | 2.54 | 2.49 | 2.42 | 2.35 | 2.28 | 2.24 | 2.19 | 2.15 | 2.11 | 2.06 | 2.01 |
| 17 | 4.45 | 3.59 | 3.20 | 2.96 | 2.81 | 2.70 | 2.61 | 2.55 | 2.49 | 2.45 | 2.38 | 2.31 | 2.23 | 2.19 | 2.15 | 2.10 | 2.06 | 2.01 | 1.96 |
| 18 | 4.41 | 3.55 | 3.16 | 2.93 | 2.77 | 2.66 | 2.58 | 2.51 | 2.46 | 2.41 | 2.34 | 2.27 | 2.19 | 2.15 | 2.11 | 2.06 | 2.02 | 1.97 | 1.92 |
| 19 | 4.38 | 3.52 | 3.13 | 2.90 | 2.74 | 2.63 | 2.54 | 2.48 | 2.42 | 2.38 | 2.31 | 2.23 | 2.16 | 2.11 | 2.07 | 2.03 | 1.98 | 1.93 | 1.88 |

# Table E-4 (*continued*)

| | | | | | | | | | | | | | | | | | | | |
|---|---|---|---|---|---|---|---|---|---|---|---|---|---|---|---|---|---|---|---|
| 20 | 4.35 | 3.49 | 3.10 | 2.87 | 2.71 | 2.60 | 2.51 | 2.45 | 2.39 | 2.35 | 2.28 | 2.20 | 2.12 | 2.08 | 2.04 | 1.99 | 1.95 | 1.90 | 1.84 |
| 21 | 4.32 | 3.47 | 3.07 | 2.84 | 2.68 | 2.57 | 2.49 | 2.42 | 2.37 | 2.32 | 2.25 | 2.18 | 2.10 | 2.05 | 2.01 | 1.96 | 1.92 | 1.87 | 1.81 |
| 22 | 4.30 | 3.44 | 3.05 | 2.82 | 2.66 | 2.55 | 2.46 | 2.40 | 2.34 | 2.30 | 2.23 | 2.15 | 2.07 | 2.03 | 1.98 | 1.94 | 1.89 | 1.84 | 1.78 |
| 23 | 4.28 | 3.42 | 3.03 | 2.80 | 2.64 | 2.53 | 2.44 | 2.37 | 2.32 | 2.27 | 2.20 | 2.13 | 2.05 | 2.01 | 1.96 | 1.91 | 1.86 | 1.81 | 1.76 |
| 24 | 4.26 | 3.40 | 3.01 | 2.78 | 2.62 | 2.51 | 2.42 | 2.36 | 2.30 | 2.25 | 2.18 | 2.11 | 2.03 | 1.98 | 1.94 | 1.89 | 1.84 | 1.79 | 1.73 |
| 25 | 4.24 | 3.39 | 2.99 | 2.76 | 2.60 | 2.49 | 2.40 | 2.34 | 2.28 | 2.24 | 2.16 | 2.09 | 2.01 | 1.96 | 1.92 | 1.87 | 1.82 | 1.77 | 1.71 |
| 26 | 4.23 | 3.37 | 2.98 | 2.74 | 2.59 | 2.47 | 2.39 | 2.32 | 2.27 | 2.22 | 2.15 | 2.07 | 1.99 | 1.95 | 1.90 | 1.85 | 1.80 | 1.75 | 1.69 |
| 27 | 4.21 | 3.35 | 2.96 | 2.73 | 2.57 | 2.46 | 2.37 | 2.31 | 2.25 | 2.20 | 2.13 | 2.06 | 1.97 | 1.93 | 1.88 | 1.84 | 1.79 | 1.73 | 1.67 |
| 28 | 4.20 | 3.34 | 2.95 | 2.71 | 2.56 | 2.45 | 2.36 | 2.29 | 2.24 | 2.19 | 2.12 | 2.04 | 1.96 | 1.91 | 1.87 | 1.82 | 1.77 | 1.71 | 1.65 |
| 29 | 4.18 | 3.33 | 2.93 | 2.70 | 2.55 | 2.43 | 2.35 | 2.28 | 2.22 | 2.18 | 2.10 | 2.03 | 1.94 | 1.90 | 1.85 | 1.81 | 1.75 | 1.70 | 1.64 |
| 30 | 4.17 | 3.32 | 2.92 | 2.69 | 2.53 | 2.42 | 2.33 | 2.27 | 2.21 | 2.16 | 2.09 | 2.01 | 1.93 | 1.89 | 1.84 | 1.79 | 1.74 | 1.68 | 1.62 |
| 40 | 4.08 | 3.23 | 2.84 | 2.61 | 2.45 | 2.34 | 2.25 | 2.18 | 2.12 | 2.08 | 2.00 | 1.92 | 1.84 | 1.79 | 1.74 | 1.69 | 1.64 | 1.58 | 1.51 |
| 60 | 4.00 | 3.15 | 2.76 | 2.53 | 2.37 | 2.25 | 2.17 | 2.10 | 2.04 | 1.99 | 1.92 | 1.84 | 1.75 | 1.70 | 1.65 | 1.59 | 1.53 | 1.47 | 1.39 |
| 120 | 3.92 | 3.07 | 2.68 | 2.45 | 2.29 | 2.17 | 2.09 | 2.02 | 1.96 | 1.91 | 1.83 | 1.75 | 1.66 | 1.61 | 1.55 | 1.50 | 1.43 | 1.35 | 1.25 |
| $\infty$ | 3.84 | 3.00 | 2.60 | 2.37 | 2.21 | 2.10 | 2.01 | 1.94 | 1.88 | 1.83 | 1.75 | 1.67 | 1.57 | 1.52 | 1.46 | 1.39 | 1.32 | 1.22 | 1.00 |

Pr = 0.05

APPENDIX

# F

# HYPOTHESIS TESTS

The following tests are for commonly asked research questions. The variables used in these tests are assumed to have either a nearly symmetrical distribution or, if this is not the case, the sample sizes are large. These assumptions permit the use of models for which the distributions of variables are not specified (see Sec. 6-4 for a discussion of the central-limit theorem). For all tests, samples are assumed to be simple random samples (see Sec. 5-4).

**F-1** *Research question.* Does the mean of population 1 differ from $\mu_0$, the known mean of population 2 (variance known)?

| | Population 1 | | Population 2 |
|---|---|---|---|
| Mean | Unknown | | Known, $\sigma^2$ |
| Variance | Known | = | Known, $\sigma^2$ |
| Sample size | $n$ | | Not sampled |
| Variable | Interval $X$ | | |

*Model.* $X = \mu_0 + \Delta + E$

$$\mu_X = \mu_0 + \Delta$$
$$\mu_E = 0$$
$$\sigma_X^2 = \sigma_E^2 = \sigma^2$$

*Hypotheses.* $H_0: \mu_X = \mu_0$

$H_1: \mu_X \neq \mu_0$

*Testing functions.* $\bar{X} = \frac{1}{n} \sum X_i$

$$Z = \frac{\bar{X} - \mu_0}{\sigma/n^{1/2}}$$

*Distribution of Z when* $H_0$ *is true.* Approximately standard normal.
*Reference.* Sec. 6-2.

**F-2** *Research question.* Same as Question F-1 but with the population variance not known.

| | Population 1 | Population 2 |
|---|---|---|
| Mean | Unknown | Known, $\mu_0$ |
| Variance | Unknown | Unknown |
| Sample size | $n$ | Not sampled |
| Variable | Interval $X$ | |

*Model.* $X = \mu_0 + \Delta + E$
$\mu_X = \mu_0 + \Delta$
$\mu_E = 0$
$\sigma_X^2 = \sigma_E^2$, unknown

*Hypotheses.* $H_0$: $\mu_X = \mu_0$
$H_1$: $\mu_X \neq \mu_0$

*Testing functions.* $S^2 = \frac{\sum (X_i - \bar{X})^2}{n - 1}$

$$T = \frac{\bar{X} - \mu_0}{S/(n)^{1/2}}$$

*Distribution of T when* $H_0$ *is true.* Approximately $t$ with $(n - 1)$ degrees of freedom.
*Reference.* Sec. 6-3.

**F-3** *Research question.* Does the variance of population 1 differ from $\sigma_0^2$, the known variance of population 2?

| | Population 1 | Population 2 |
|---|---|---|
| Mean | Unknown | Unknown |
| Variance | Unknown | Known, $\sigma_0^2$ |
| Sample size | $n$ | Not sampled |
| Variable | Interval $X$ | |

*Model.* $X = \mu + E$
$\mu_X = \mu$
$\mu_E = 0$

*Hypotheses.* $H_0$: $\sigma_X^2 = \sigma_0^2$
$H_1$: $\sigma_X^2 \neq \sigma_0^2$

*Testing functions.* $S^2 = \dfrac{\sum (X_i - \bar{X})^2}{n - 1}$

$$Z = \frac{S^2 - \sigma_0^2}{\sigma_0^2/n[2(n-1)]^{1/2}}$$

$$\text{CS} = \frac{n^2 S^2}{(n-1)\sigma_0^2}$$

*Distribution when* $\text{H}_0$ *is true.* $Z$ is approximately standard normal. CS is approximately $\chi^2$ with $(n - 1)$ degrees of freedom.
*Reference.* Ref. F-3 (chap. 3).

**F-4** *Research question.* Does the median of population 1 differ from $\theta$, the known median of population 2?

| | Population 1 | Population 2 |
|---|---|---|
| Median | Unknown | $\theta$ |
| Sample size | $n$ | Not sampled |
| Variable | Ordinal $X$ | |

*Model.* $X = \theta + \Delta + E$
$\text{MD}(X) = \theta + \Delta$
$\text{MD}(E) = 0$

*Hypotheses.* $\text{H}_0\colon \text{MD}(X) = \theta$
$\text{H}_1\colon \text{MD}(X) \neq \theta$

*Testing functions.* $B$ = count of all $X_i$ in sample $> \theta$, excluding all cases where $X_i = \theta$ from sample; reduce $n$ accordingly

$$Z = \frac{B - n/2}{n/4}$$

*Distribution when* $\text{H}_0$ *is true.* $B$ is binomial with $p = \frac{1}{2}$. $Z$ is approximately standard normal.
*Reference.* Ref. F-4 (chap. 3).

**F-5** *Research question.* Does the proportion of those with a certain characteristic in population 1 differ from $\pi_0$, the known proportion with the characteristic in population 2?

| | Population 1 | Population 2 |
|---|---|---|
| Proportion | Unknown | $\pi_0$ |
| Sample size | $n$ | Not sampled |
| | Nominal<br>$X_i = 1$ if member $i$ has the characteristic<br>$X_i = 0$ otherwise | |

*Model.* $\Pr(X = 1) = \pi_0 + \Delta$

*Hypotheses.* $H_0$: $\Pr(X) = \pi_0$
$H_1$: $\Pr(X) \neq \pi_0$

*Testing functions.* $B = \sum X_i$ = count in sample with the characteristic

$$P = \frac{B}{n} \qquad Z = \frac{P - \pi_0}{[\pi_0(1 - \pi_0)/n]^{1/2}}$$

*Distributions when* $H_0$ *is true:* $B$ is binomial with parameters $\pi_0$ and $n$. $Z$ is approximately standard normal.
*Reference.* Sec. 6-5.

**F-6** *Research question.* Does the mean of population 1 differ from the mean of population 2 (assuming equal variance)?

| | Population 1 | | Population 2 |
|---|---|---|---|
| Mean | Unknown | | Unknown |
| Variance | Unknown | = | Unknown |
| Sample size | $n_1$ | | $n_2$ |
| Variable | $X_1$ | Interval | $X_2$ |

*Model.* $X_1 = \mu + E$
$\mu_{X_1} = \mu$
$X_2 = \mu + \Delta + E$
$\mu_{X_2} = \mu + \Delta$
$\sigma^2_{X_1} = \sigma^2_{X_2} = \sigma^2_E$, unknown

*Hypotheses.* $H_0$: $\mu_{X_1} = \mu_{X_2}$
$H_1$: $\mu_{X_1} \neq \mu_{X_2}$

*Testing functions.* $S^2 = \dfrac{\sum (X_{i1} - \bar{X}_1)^2 + \sum (X_{i2} - \bar{X}_2)^2}{n_1 + n_2 - 2}$

$$D = \bar{X}_1 - \bar{X}_2$$

$$T = \frac{D - 0}{S[(n_1 + n_2)/n_1 n_2]^{1/2}}$$

*Distribution when* $H_0$ *is true.* Approximately $t$ with $(n_1 + n_2 - 2)$ degrees of freedom.
*Reference.* Sec. 6-8.

**F-7** *Research question.* Same as Question F-6 but not assuming equal variance.

| | Population 1 | Population 2 |
|---|---|---|
| Mean | Unknown | Unknown |
| Variance | Unknown | Unknown |
| Sample size | $n_1$ | $n_2$ |
| Variable | Interval $X_1$ | $X_2$ |

*Model.* $X_1 = \mu + E_1$
$\mu_{X_1} = \mu$
$X_2 = \mu + \Delta + E_2$
$\mu_{X_2} = \mu + \Delta$
$\sigma^2_{X_1} = \sigma^2_{E_1} \neq \sigma^2_{X_2} = \sigma^2_{E_2}$

*Hypotheses.* $H_0: \mu_{X_1} = \mu_{X_2}$
$H_1: \mu_{X_1} \neq \mu_{X_2}$

*Testing functions.* $S_1^2 = \dfrac{\sum (X_{1i} - \bar{X}_1)^2}{n_1 - 1}$

$$S_2^2 = \frac{\sum (X_{2i} - \bar{X}_2)^2}{n_2 - 1}$$

$$D = \bar{X}_1 - \bar{X}_2$$

$$T = \frac{D - 0}{(S_1^2/n_1 + S_2^2/n_2)^{1/2}}$$

*Distribution of T when* $H_0$ *is true.* Approximately $t$ distributed with the degrees of freedom approximated by Eq. (6-23).
*Reference.* Sec. 6-10.

**F-8** *Research question.* Same as Question F-6 but samples are dependent.

| | Population 1 | Population 2 |
|---|---|---|
| Mean | Unknown | Unknown |
| Variance | Unknown | Unknown |
| Sample size | $n_1 = n_2 = n$ | |
| Variable | Interval<br>$X_{1i}$ related to $X_{2i}$ | |

*Model.*
$$X_{1i} = \mu + l_i + E_{1i}$$
$$\mu_{X_{1i}} = \mu$$
$$X_{2i} = \mu + \Delta + l_i + E_{2i}$$
$$\mu_{X_{2i}} = \mu + \Delta$$
$$(i = 1, 2, \ldots, n)$$

*Hypotheses.* $H_0: \mu_{X_1} = \mu_{X_2}$
$H_1: \mu_{X_1} \neq \mu_{X_2}$

*Testing functions.* $D_i = X_{1i} - X_{2i}$

$$\bar{D} = \frac{1}{n} \sum D_i = \bar{X}_1 - \bar{X}_2$$

$$S_D^2 = \frac{\sum (D_i - \bar{D})^2}{n - 1}$$

$$T = \frac{\bar{D} - 0}{S_D/(n)^{1/2}}$$

*Distribution of T when $H_0$ is true.* Approximately $t$ distributed with $(n - 1)$ degrees of freedom.
*Reference.* Ref. F-1 (chap. 13.4).

**F-9** *Research question.* Does the variance of population 1 differ from the variance of population 2?

| | Population 1 | Population 2 |
|---|---|---|
| Mean | Unknown | Unknown |
| Variance | Unknown | Unknown |
| Sample size | $n_1$ | $n_2$ |
| Variable | Interval<br>$X_1$ | $X_2$ |

*Model.*
$$X_1 = \mu_1 + E_1$$
$$\mu_{X_1} = \mu_1$$
$$X_2 = \mu_2 + E_2$$
$$\mu_{X_2} = \mu_2$$

*Hypotheses.* $H_0: \sigma_{X_1}^2 = \sigma_{X_2}^2$
$H_1: \sigma_{X_1}^2 \neq \sigma_{X_2}^2$

*Testing functions.* $S_1^2 = \dfrac{\sum (X_{1i} - \bar{X}_1)^2}{n_1 - 1}$

$$S_2^2 = \frac{\sum (X_{2i} - \bar{X}_2)^2}{n_2 - 1}$$

$$F = \frac{S_L^2}{S_S^2}$$

where $L$ = population number with larger sample variance.
*Distribution of F when* $H_0$ *is true.* Approximately $f$ distributed with $(n_L - 1)$ and $(n_S - 1)$ degrees of freedom.
*Reference.* Sec. 6-9.

**F-10** *Research question.* Does the proportion of those with a certain characteristic in population 1 differ from the proportion with that characteristic in population 2?

| | Population 1 | Population 2 |
|---|---|---|
| Proportion | Unknown | Unknown |
| Sample size | $n_1$ | $n_2$ |
| Variable | Nominal<br>$X_1$ $X_2$<br>$X_{ji} = 1$ if member $i$ of population $j$ has the characteristic<br>$X_{ji} = 0$ otherwise | |

*Model.* $\Pr(X_1 = 1) = \pi$
$\Pr(X_2 = 1) = \pi + \Delta$

*Hypotheses.* $H_0$: $\Pr(X_1 = 1) = \Pr(X_2 = 1)$
$H_1$: $\Pr(X_1 = 1) \neq \Pr(X_2 = 1)$

*Testing functions.* $B_1 = \sum X_{1i}$

$$B_2 = \sum X_{2i}$$

$$P_1 = B_1/n_1$$

$$P_2 = B_2/n_2$$

$$P = \frac{B_1 + B_2}{n_1 + n_2}$$

$$Z = \frac{P_1 - P_2 - 0}{\{P(1 - P)[(n_1 + n_2)/n_1 n_2]\}^{1/2}}$$

*Distribution of Z when* $H_0$ *is true.* $Z$ is approximately standard normal.
*Reference.* Ref. F-1 (chap. 13.2).

**F-11** *Research question.* Do any of the means of $g$ populations differ from the mean of all the populations together?

| | Population 1 | | ... | | Population $g$ |
|---|---|---|---|---|---|
| Mean | Unknown | | ... | | Unknown |
| Variance | Unknown | = | ... | = | Unknown |
| Sample size | $n_1$ | | ... | | $n_g$ |
| Variable | $X_1$ | | ... | | $X_g$ |

*Model.*
$X_k = \mu + \Delta_k + E$
$\mu_X = \mu$
$\mu_{X_k} = \mu + \Delta_k$
$\mu_E = 0$
$\sigma^2_{X_k} = \sigma^2_E$, unknown
$(k = 1, \ldots, g)$

*Hypotheses.*
$H_0$: $\mu_{X_1} = \mu_{X_2} = \cdots = \mu_{X_g} = \mu$
$H_1$: at least one $\mu_{X_k} \neq \mu$

*Testing functions.* $\bar{X}_k = \frac{1}{n_k} \sum_{i=1}^{n_k} X_{ik}$

$$n = \sum_{k=1}^{g} n_k$$

$$\bar{X} = \frac{1}{n} \sum_k \sum_i X_{ik}$$

$$S_B^2 = \sum_{k=1}^{g} n_k \frac{(\bar{X}_k - \bar{X})^2}{g - 1}$$

$$S_W^2 = \sum_{k=1}^{g} \sum_{i=1}^{n_k} \frac{(X_{ik} - \bar{X}_k)^2}{n - g}$$

$$F = \frac{S_B^2}{S_W^2}$$

*Distribution of F when* $H_0$ *is true.* Approximately $f$ with $(g - 1)$ and $(n - g)$ df.
*Reference.* Sec. 6-11.

**F-12** *Research question.* Same as Question F-11 but data are ordinal.
Population means, variances, and sample sizes, model, and hypotheses are same as in Question F-11.
*Variable.* Ordinal $X_k$ for populations $k = 1, \ldots, g$

$R_{ik}$ = rank of $X_{ik}$ in the joint ascending ranking of all $n$ observations

*Testing functions.* $\bar{R}_k = \dfrac{1}{n_k} \sum_{i}^{n_k} R_{ik}$

$$H = \left( \frac{12}{n(n+1)g} \sum_{k=1}^{g} n_k \bar{R}_k^2 \right) - 3(n+1)$$

*Distribution of H when* $H_0$ *is true.* Approximately $\chi^2$ with $(g-1)$ df.
*Reference.* Ref. F-1 (chap. 6).

**F-13** *Research question.* Is $Y$ dependent on $X$ where $Y$ and $X$ are interval-scaled variables?
*Variables.* $X$ and $Y$ are interval bivariate observations $(X_1, Y_1), \ldots, (X_n, Y_n)$ from a sample of size $n$.
*Model.* $Y = \alpha + \beta X + E$, $E$ and $X$ independent, $\mu_E = 0$, $\mu_Y = \alpha + \beta\mu_X$
*Hypotheses.* $H_0$: $\Pr(X \le a \text{ and } Y \le b) = \Pr(X \le a) \Pr(Y \le b)$
$H_1$: $\Pr(X \le a \text{ and } Y \le b) \ne \Pr(X \le a) \Pr(Y \le b)$

*Testing functions.* $R = \dfrac{\sum (X_i - \bar{X})(Y_i - \bar{Y})}{[\sum (X_i - \bar{X})^2 \sum (Y_i - \bar{Y})^2]^{1/2}}$

$$T = \frac{R(n-2)^{1/2}}{(1-R^2)^{1/2}}$$

$$Z = 1.51 \log \frac{1+R}{1-R}$$

*Distributions when* $H_0$ *is true.* $T$ is approximately $t$ with $(n-2)$ df. $Z$ is approximately standard normal.
*Reference.* Sec. 9-1 and Ref. F-2 (chap. 18).

**F-14** *Research question.* Is $Y$ dependent on $X$ where $Y$ and $X$ are ordinal-scaled variables?
*Variables.* $X$ and $Y$ are ordinal bivariate observations $(X_1, Y_1), \ldots, (X_n, Y_n)$ from a sample of size $n$.
*Model.* $\Pr(X \le a \text{ and } Y \le b) = \Pr(X \le a) \Pr(Y \le b) + \Delta$
*Hypotheses.* $H_0$: $\Pr(X \le a \text{ and } Y \le b) = \Pr(X \le a) \Pr(Y \le b)$
$H_1$: $\Pr(X \le a \text{ and } Y \le b) \ne \Pr(X \le a) \Pr(Y \le b)$
*Testing functions.*

$$D_i = \text{rank of } X_i - \text{rank of } Y_i$$

$$\text{RHO} = 1 - \frac{6 \sum D_i^2}{n(n^2-1)}$$

$$T = \frac{\text{RHO}(n-2)^{1/2}}{(1-\text{RHO}^2)^{1/2}}$$

$$P_{ij} = \begin{cases} 1 \text{ if } (X_i - X_j)(Y_i - Y_j) > 0 \\ -1 \text{ if } (X_i - X_j)(Y_i - Y_j) < 0 \end{cases} \quad \text{for } 1 \le i < j \le n$$

$$K = \sum_{i=1}^{n-1} \sum_{j=i+1}^{n} P_{ij}$$

$$Z = \frac{K}{[n(n-1)(2n+5)/18]^{1/2}}$$

*Distributions when* $H_0$ *is true.* $T$ is approximately $t$ with $(n-2)$ df. $Z$ is approximately standard normal.
*Reference.* Sec. 9-3 and Ref. F-1 (chap. 8).

**F-15** *Research question.* Is $Y$ dependent on $X$ where $Y$ and $X$ are nominal-scaled variables?
*Variables.* $Y = c$ if case falls in category $c$, $c = 1, \ldots, g$
$X = k$ if case falls in category $k$, $k = 1, \ldots, r$
$O_{ck}$ = observed number of cases in sample of size $n$ that fall in categories $c$ of $Y$ and $k$ of $X$
*Model.* $\pi_{ck} = \pi_c + \Delta_{ck}$
$\Pr(Y = c \text{ given } X = k) = \pi_{ck}$
$\Pr(Y = c) = \pi_c$
*Hypotheses.* $H_0$: $\pi_{ck} = \pi_c$ for $c = 1, \ldots, g$
$H_1$: $\pi_{ck} \neq \pi_c$ for at least one $c$

*Testing functions.* $n_c = \sum_{k=1}^{r} O_{ck}$

$$n_k = \sum_{c=1}^{g} O_{ck}$$

$$n = \sum_c \sum_k O_{ck}$$

$$E_{ck} = \frac{n_c n_k}{n}$$

$$\text{CS} = \sum_c \sum_k \frac{(O_{ck} - E_{ck})^2}{E_{ck}}$$

*Distribution when* $H_0$ *is true.* CS is approximately $\chi^2$ with $(g-1)(r-1)$ df.
*Reference.* Secs. 9-1 and 9-2.

**F-16** *Research question.* Is $Y$ a linear function of $X$?
*Variables.* $X$ and $Y$ are interval bivariate observations $(X_1, Y_1), \ldots, (X_n, Y_n)$ from a sample of size $n$.
*Model.* $Y = \alpha + \beta X + E$, $E$ and $X$ independent, $\mu_E = 0$, $\mu_Y = \alpha + \beta\mu_X$
*Hypotheses.* $H_0$: $\beta = 0$
$H_1$: $\beta \neq 0$

*Testing functions.* $B = \dfrac{\sum (X_i - \bar{X})(Y_i - \bar{Y})}{\sum (X_i - \bar{X})^2}$

$$A = \bar{Y} - B\bar{X}$$

$$S_B^2 = \frac{\sum (Y_i - A - BX_i)^2}{(n-2) \sum (X_i - \bar{X})^2}$$

$$T = \frac{B - 0}{S_B}$$

$$F = \frac{B^2}{S_B^2}$$

*Distribution when* $H_0$ *is true.* $T$ is approximately $t$ with $(n-2)$ df. $F$ is approximately $f$ with 1 and $(n-2)$ df.
*Reference.* Sec. 8-2.

## REFERENCES


F-1. Blalock, Jr., H. M. B.: *Social Statistics*, 2d ed., McGraw-Hill, New York, 1972.
F-2. Chapman, D. G., and R. A. Scharfele: *Elementary Probability Models and Mathematical Statistics*, 4th ed., Wiley, New York, 1971.
F-3. Hoel, P. G.: *Introduction to Mathematical Statistics*, 4th ed., Wiley, New York, 1971.
F-4. Hollander, M., and D. Wolfe: *Nonparametric Statistical Methods*, Wiley, New York, 1973.
F-5. Lindgren, B. W., and G. W. McElrath: *Probability and Statistics*, 3d ed., Macmillan, 1969.
F-6. Mendenhall, W., L. Ott, and R. F. Larson: *Statistics: A Tool for the Social Sciences*, Duxbury, North Scituate, Mass., 1974.

APPENDIX

# G

# SYNTHESIS PROBLEMS†

While there are many exercise problems throughout the text, they all are associated with individual techniques. Moreover, space does not permit any comprehensive comparison of methods, with indications of the situations under which each, or combinations of each, will be most useful. This appendix thus has been developed to allow the student to undertake perhaps the most important and practical task in relation to the variety of techniques presented—choosing the most relevant for a certain problem and applying them in concert.

The appendix starts with a series of problems aimed at drawing out general verbal comparisons between methods. A set of data then is presented with which it is possible to try a whole series of techniques in sequence. Finally, a scenario is presented so that the student can determine the most appropriate forecasting techniques to make a population projection for a semi-hypothetical city.

**G-1** Consider an organization whose function has been to operate a human blood bank throughout an entire state. It has developed facilities, staff, and the necessary contacts with the medical "industry" to collect, store, and distribute human blood as needed in medical activities. This organization has been told that it will soon be possible to produce synthetic human blood, which can be manufactured cheaply and stored indefinitely without special equipment. What types of forecast now need to be made and what might be the best techniques for making such? Describe each in about one paragraph.

† Problems G-1, G-2, G-5, and G-6 have been adapted from J. P. Martino, *Technological Forecasting for Decisionmakers*, American-Elsevier, New York, 1972.

**G-2** A gas company, which distributes natural gas to residences through underground mains, has a large staff of meter readers who visit each customer periodically to determine the quantity of gas used, so that bills can be prepared. The company is presented with a forecast that it will soon be possible to replace the meters with a device which reports gas consumption, over telephone lines, to a computer at the gas company's office. The computer can then prepare bills automatically. Cost of installation and upkeep of the devices will be far less than the cost of human meter readers. What other forecasts now have to be made? What might be the best techniques for making them? Describe them in about one paragraph each.

**G-3** Present any advantages and disadvantages of the following types of forecasting techniques in two paragraphs each:
(*a*) Delphi
(*b*) Probe
(*c*) Committees
(*d*) "Genius" forecasting
(*e*) Breakthrough analysis (monitoring)
(*f*) Analogy
(*g*) Role playing or gaming
(*h*) Morphological analysis

**G-4** Develop an urban or regional example of each of the following types of model:
(*a*) Poisson
(*b*) Binomial
(*c*) Analogy
(*d*) Systems dynamics

**G-5** Refer to Table G-1 showing total gross consumption of energy resources. Make projections of the historical consumption of each of the energy sources listed (anthracite, bituminous, natural gas, petroleum, hydropower and nuclear power) and of the total gross energy input. Project each to 1980 using several different techniques (possibly including Delphi, Gompertz, and logistic models). Does the total for the component projections add up to the projection of the total? Which component(s) do you think should be adjusted to make the total of the projected components agree with the projected total? Or should the total be adjusted instead? What is the shift in percentage of the total for each component between 1965 and 1980? How do these shifts compare to actual figures (in the years up to 1980)?

**G-6** In the past, city governments have been organized on the basis of functional departments, such as fire, building inspection, sanitation, etc. Each department kept records on those aspects of the city and its residents which pertained to its operations or functions. Thus the records pertaining to any one person could be scattered through many departments. With the use of computers, however, it is now possible to consolidate records so that all of them pertaining to a specific person are combined. What might be the long-term impact of this capability on the structure and organization of city

**Table G-1 U.S. total gross consumption of energy resources by major sources (trillion Btu)**

| Year | Anthracite | Bituminous and lignite | Natural gas, dry† | Petroleum‡ | Total fossil fuels | Hydropower§ | Nuclear power | Total gross energy inputs¶ |
|---|---|---|---|---|---|---|---|---|
| *Historical year* | | | | | | | | |
| 1947 | 1224.2 | 14,599.7 | 4,518.4 | 11,367.0 | 31,709.3 | 1459.0 | — | 33,168.3 |
| 1948 | 1275.1 | 13,621.6 | 5,032.6 | 12,558.0 | 32,487.3 | 1507.0 | — | 33,994.3 |
| 1949 | 957.6 | 11,673.1 | 5,288.5 | 12,120.0 | 30,039.2 | 1565.0 | — | 31,604.2 |
| 1950 | 1013.5 | 11,900.1 | 6,150.0 | 13,489.0 | 32,552.6 | 1601.0 | — | 34,153.6 |
| 1951 | 939.8 | 12,285.3 | 7,247.6 | 14,848.0 | 35,320.7 | 1592.0 | — | 36,912.7 |
| 1952 | 896.6 | 10,971.4 | 7,760.4 | 15,334.0 | 34,962.4 | 1614.0 | — | 36,576.4 |
| 1953 | 711.2 | 11,182.1 | 8,156.0 | 16,098.0 | 36,147.3 | 1550.0 | — | 37,697.3 |
| 1954 | 683.2 | 9,512.2 | 8,547.6 | 16,138.0 | 34,881.0 | 1479.0 | — | 36,360.0 |
| 1955 | 599.4 | 11,104.0 | 9,232.0 | 17,524.0 | 38,459.4 | 1497.0 | — | 39,956.4 |
| 1956 | 609.6 | 11,340.8 | 9,834.4 | 18,624.0 | 40,408.8 | 1598.0 | — | 42,006.8 |
| 1957 | 528.3 | 10,838.1 | 10,416.2 | 18,570.0 | 40,352.6 | 1568.0 | 1.2 | 41,921.8 |
| 1958 | 482.6 | 9,607.6 | 10,995.2 | 19,214.0 | 40,299.4 | 1740.0 | 1.5 | 42,040.9 |
| 1959 | 477.5 | 9,595.9 | 11,990.3 | 19,747.0 | 41,810.7 | 1695.0 | 2.2 | 43,507.9 |

| | | | | | | | | |
|---|---|---|---|---|---|---|---|---|
| 1960 | 447.0 | 9,967.2 | 12,698.7 | 20,067.0 | 43,179.9 | 1775.0 | 5.5 | 44,960.4 |
| 1961 | 403.8 | 9,809.4 | 13,228.0 | 20,487.0 | 43,928.2 | 1628.0 | 17.0 | 45,573.2 |
| 1962 | 381.0 | 10,159.7 | 14,120.8 | 21,267.0 | 45,928.5 | 1780.0 | 23.0 | 47,731.5 |
| 1963 | 361.0 | 10,722.0 | 14,843.0 | 21,950.0 | 47,876.0 | 1740.0 | 33.0 | 49,649.0 |
| 1964 | 365.8 | 11,295.0 | 15,647.5 | 22,385.8 | 49,694.1 | 1873.0 | 34.0 | 51,601.1 |
| 1965 preliminary | 327.7 | 12,030.0 | 16,136.1 | 23,209.3 | 51,703.1 | 2050.0 | 38.0 | 53,791.1 |
| *Projected years* | | | | | | | | |
| 1970 | 309.0 | 14,251.0 | 19,374.0 | 27,275.0 | 61,209.0 | 2193.0 | 874.0 | 64,276.0 |
| 1975 | 280.0 | 16,865.0 | 22,360.0 | 31,875.0 | 71,380.0 | 2422.0 | 1803.0 | 75,605.0 |
| 1980 | 250.0 | 19,290.0 | 25,455.0 | 35,978.0 | 80,973.0 | 3026.0 | 4076.0 | 88,075.0 |

*Source:* Bureau of Mines Information Circular 8384, *An Energy Model for the United States, Featuring Energy Balances for the Years 1947 to 1965 and Projections and Forecasts*, Washington, D.C., 1965.

† Excludes natural gas liquids.

‡ Petroleum products including still gas, liquefied refinery gas, and natural gas liquids.

§ Represents projections of outputs of hydropower and nuclear power converted to theoretical energy inputs at projected rates of pounds of coal per kilowatt hour at central electric stations. Excludes inputs for power generated by nonutility plants, which are included within the other consuming sectors.

¶ Gross energy is that contained in all types of commercial energy at the time it is incorporated in the economy, whether the energy is produced domestically or imported. Gross energy comprises inputs of primary fuels (or their derivatives), and outputs of hydropower and nuclear power converted to theoretical energy inputs. Gross energy includes the energy used for the production, processing, and transportation of energy proper.

government? Use any forecasting technique to make this judgment. Describe the type of survey which may be taken, the types of models employed, and the reasons for using each.

**G-7** Make a matrix with each row being a forecasting technique discussed in this book and each column being a factor (e.g., cost) used to evaluate the different techniques. Try to be exhaustive about your evaluation, but in no case list more than 15 factors. Now rank each technique over each and every factor (e.g., that technique that had the lowest cost would rank 1, the highest would rank last). Be sure to explain the meaning of any factor that may be unclear.

**G-8** For each of the following factors indicate which technique or combination of techniques you would use for forecasting purposes. Give reasons for your choices.

(*a*) World hunger levels in 1980
(*b*) Employment in southwestern Colorado in 1990
(*c*) Crime in a medium-size southern city in 1978
(*d*) Deer population in Virginia in 1986
(*e*) Year (if any) when 20 percent of the housing units in the United States are solar heated

**G-9** Which in your opinion is a better technique for generating new directions for the transportation systems in a medium-sized urban area—a synectics type approach (brainstorming, analogy, etc.) or an optimization technique (similar to that used in the linear programming chapter)? Explain and defend your answer.

**G-10** A set of data is divided into two classes and relationships are developed within each class. If the data are as follows, what is the percentage of sum of squares explained through classification *and* relationships?

| Class 1 | | | Class 2 | | |
|---|---|---|---|---|---|
| $X_i$ | $Y_i$ | $\hat{Y}_i$ | $X_i$ | $Y_i$ | $\hat{Y}_i$ |
| 3 | 3 | 4 | 3 | 7 | 7 |
| 4 | 5 | 5 | 4 | 6 | 5 |
| 7 | 7 | 6 | 7 | 4 | 3 |

Problems G-11 to G-27 are based on the data presented in Table G-2.

**G-11** What probability density function seems to fit the distribution of peak land values across all centers?

**G-12** What is the probability that the peak land value of a center will be greater than or equal to $2000, given that its number of establishments is less than or equal to 150?

**Table G-2 Data on unplanned retail commercial shopping centers in Chicago**

| Center | Variable number | | | | | | | | | |
|---|---|---|---|---|---|---|---|---|---|---|
| (1) | (2) | (3) | (4) | (5) | (6) | (7) | (8) | (9) | (10) | (11) |
| A1 | 7000 | 61 | 253 | 8055 | 799 | 16,133 | 27,095 | 88,326 | 12,119 | 4034 |
| A2 | 4000 | 61 | 185 | 6100 | 554 | 13,845 | 19,166 | 62,936 | 7,902 | 2348 |
| A3 | 5000 | 61 | 208 | 7024 | 580 | 13,600 | 20,583 | 58,548 | 8,457 | 2851 |
| A4 | 2500 | 58 | 176 | 5135 | 398 | 13,472 | 19,878 | 47,829 | 6,012 | 1771 |
| A5 | 2500 | 55 | 137 | 3640 | 333 | 12,340 | 15,438 | 32,173 | 3,617 | 1112 |
| A6 | 2000 | 57 | 178 | 5190 | 438 | 10,537 | 12,976 | 71,806 | 8,088 | 2166 |
| A7 | 2000 | 56 | 156 | 4515 | 430 | 12,281 | 14,095 | 34,308 | 4,163 | 1296 |
| A8 | 2000 | 51 | 94 | 2555 | 244 | 7,968 | 11,100 | 29,909 | 3,279 | 959 |
| A9 | 1250 | 50 | 102 | 2425 | 215 | 10,951 | 13,290 | 48,664 | 5,421 | 1742 |
| A10 | 4000 | 35 | 108 | 3485 | 380 | 13,613 | 21,073 | 44,223 | 6,250 | 2104 |
| A11 | 2500 | 38 | 88 | 2940 | 317 | 6,549 | 10,239 | 32,766 | 4,275 | 1579 |
| A12 | 1750 | 36 | 87 | 2980 | 252 | 9,013 | 13,113 | 27,807 | 3,883 | 1341 |
| A13 | 1700 | 31 | 97 | 2820 | 247 | 9,619 | 14,749 | 46,650 | 6,217 | 1823 |
| A14 | 1600 | 53 | 133 | 3910 | 339 | 7,797 | 10,091 | 25,775 | 3,290 | 1148 |
| A15 | 1200 | 46 | 130 | 3360 | 299 | 8,172 | 17,641 | 27,722 | 3,468 | 1100 |
| A16 | 850 | 38 | 91 | 2450 | 205 | 5,699 | 9,672 | 20,028 | 1,976 | 639 |
| A17 | 2500 | 40 | 119 | 3775 | 414 | 14,184 | 18,037 | 61,884 | 7,659 | 2463 |
| A18 | 1800 | 36 | 90 | 2775 | 296 | 10,236 | 13,070 | 25,007 | 3,270 | 1142 |
| B1 | 2000 | 25 | 41 | 1540 | 187 | 11,765 | 14,409 | 24,547 | 3,057 | 1034 |
| B2 | 1500 | 34 | 73 | 1995 | 171 | 10,132 | 12,245 | 46,834 | 5,107 | 1155 |
| B3 | 1400 | 36 | 62 | 1410 | 99 | 3,701 | 4,685 | 10,034 | 1,556 | 639 |
| B4 | 1400 | 37 | 82 | 2360 | 213 | 8,720 | 10,361 | 35,705 | 3,585 | 1177 |
| B5 | 1200 | 35 | 65 | 1600 | 121 | 10,072 | 11,275 | 25,768 | 2,784 | 770 |
| B6 | 1200 | 34 | 88 | 2075 | 161 | 9,375 | 10,444 | 49,829 | 5,549 | 1625 |
| B7 | 1000 | 31 | 56 | 1755 | 130 | 6,049 | 7,649 | 13,553 | 1,318 | 430 |
| B8 | 1000 | 38 | 93 | 2055 | 149 | 6,355 | 8,729 | 17,286 | 1,791 | 530 |
| B9 | 850 | 32 | 58 | 1620 | 105 | 6,083 | 7,091 | 10,259 | 1,109 | 343 |
| B10 | 750 | 30 | 69 | 1595 | 110 | 8,518 | 9,695 | 13,100 | 1,344 | 487 |
| B11 | 1800 | 36 | 77 | 2305 | 191 | 5,887 | 7,717 | 27,381 | 3,017 | 931 |
| B12 | 1750 | 39 | 93 | 3775 | 319 | 7,823 | 12,167 | 33,285 | 4,410 | 1703 |
| B13 | 750 | 40 | 73 | 1945 | 153 | 1,844 | 1,938 | 9,389 | 1,005 | 286 |
| B14 | 850 | 29 | 52 | 1580 | 117 | 5,894 | 7,041 | 25,199 | 2,220 | 632 |
| B15 | 2750 | 52 | 136 | 3985 | 356 | 7,818 | 11,407 | 24,874 | 3,001 | 1070 |
| B16 | 1200 | 45 | 112 | 2695 | 216 | 6,037 | 7,656 | 36,154 | 3,493 | 1250 |
| B17 | 1700 | 40 | 90 | 2525 | 181 | 7,875 | 9,553 | 32,225 | 3,359 | 1068 |
| B18 | 1200 | 40 | 87 | 2135 | 148 | 7,374 | 9,327 | 21,443 | 2,163 | 750 |
| B19 | 1000 | 42 | 98 | 2540 | 169 | 8,859 | 10,369 | 37,899 | 4,513 | 1393 |
| B20 | 1000 | 41 | 73 | 2425 | 188 | 8,321 | 10,267 | 31,757 | 3,219 | 994 |
| B21 | 800 | 38 | 64 | 1830 | 147 | 7,807 | 9,559 | 22,667 | 2,668 | 885 |
| B22 | 900 | 35 | 60 | 2205 | 119 | 3,561 | 4,549 | 17,211 | 1,712 | 556 |
| B23 | 1750 | 40 | 94 | 2725 | 206 | 10,698 | 16,725 | 36,080 | 4,076 | 1132 |
| B24 | 1200 | 36 | 68 | 2340 | 172 | 8,806 | 12,910 | 25,380 | 3,148 | 1110 |
| B25 | | | | | | 8,237 | 12,690 | 16,651 | 2,030 | 633 |
| C1 | 800 | 24 | 40 | 1095 | 90 | ... | ... | 18,663 | 2,111 | 676 |
| C2 | 750 | 21 | 30 | 900 | 48 | ... | ... | 22,958 | 1,845 | 567 |
| C3 | 1000 | 22 | 39 | 1020 | 73 | ... | ... | 31,517 | 3,954 | 1181 |
| C4 | 800 | 23 | 40 | 1497 | 88 | ... | ... | 15,958 | 1,637 | 613 |

**Table G-2 (*continued*)**

| Center | Variable number | | | | | | | | | |
|---|---|---|---|---|---|---|---|---|---|---|
| (1) | (2) | (3) | (4) | (5) | (6) | (7) | (8) | (9) | (10) | (11) |
| C5 | 800 | 27 | 57 | 1505 | 99 | ... | ... | 10,031 | 1,011 | 353 |
| C6 | 750 | 8 | 10 | 445 | 38 | ... | ... | 7,754 | 1,290 | 385 |
| C7 | 750 | 25 | 34 | 1375 | 78 | ... | ... | 8,444 | 854 | 368 |
| C8 | 2000 | 24 | 70 | 1877 | 112 | ... | ... | 28,051 | 3,557 | 1080 |
| C9 | 2000 | 22 | 56 | 1305 | 118 | ... | ... | 42,292 | 8,428 | 2620 |
| C10 | 1250 | 31 | 45 | 1350 | 126 | ... | ... | 12,238 | 1,329 | 461 |
| C11 | 1250 | 28 | 51 | 1160 | 87 | ... | ... | 15,747 | 1,635 | 600 |
| C12 | 1250 | 19 | 28 | 825 | 49 | ... | ... | 45,512 | 4,921 | 1246 |
| C13 | 1200 | 26 | 43 | 1100 | 79 | ... | ... | 6,234 | 774 | 248 |
| C14 | 1200 | 25 | 49 | 1650 | 149 | ... | ... | 19,923 | 1,980 | 621 |
| C15 | 1100 | 32 | 58 | 1975 | 165 | ... | ... | 15,535 | 1,526 | 581 |
| C16 | 1000 | 25 | 31 | ... | ... | ... | ... | | | |
| C17 | 800 | 27 | 45 | 990 | 111 | ... | ... | 5,923 | 699 | 272 |
| C18 | 800 | 28 | 64 | 1675 | 98 | ... | ... | 36,156 | 4,575 | 1284 |
| C19 | 750 | 25 | 40 | 1340 | 105 | ... | ... | 16,561 | 2,136 | 590 |
| C20 | 750 | 19 | 35 | 1010 | 49 | ... | ... | 5,053 | 559 | 198 |
| C21 | 750 | 25 | 41 | 1200 | 92 | ... | ... | 15,207 | 1,534 | 537 |

*Source:* B. J. L. Berry, *Commercial Structure and Commercial Blight*, University of Chicago, Department of Geography Research Paper No. 85, Chicago, Ill., 1963.

*Column*

(1) Center identification
(2) Peak front foot dollar value of most valuable lot (1961) ($)
(3) Number of different types (standard industrial classification) of businesses in center (1961–1962)
(4) Number of different establishments on ground floor in center (1961–1962)
(5) Total front feet of all buildings in center (1961–1962) (ft)
(6) Total ground floor area of all establishments (1961–1962) (1000 $ft^2$)
(7) Average daily weekday auto driver and passenger shopping trips to center (1956)
(8) Total average daily weekday shopping trips to center (1956)
(9) Total retail sales (1958) ($1000)
(10) Total retail payroll (1958) ($1000)
(11) Number of retail employees (1958)

**G-13** A random sample of the 64 centers gave the eight: B13, B12, A7, B15, B11, B20, A3, B2.

(*a*) What is the standard error of the mean of peak land value?

(*b*) What is the range of the mean within which 95 percent of the sample values are likely to fall?

**G-14** Assuming greater interest in the peak land value of the C-level centers, a stratified random sample was taken: in the A centers, A13, A6, and A15; in the B centers, B12, B13, and B20; and in the C centers, C15, C12, C14, C10, C7, C20, and C5.

(*a*) What is the standard error of the overall population mean?
(*b*) What is the standard error of the mean of the C-level centers?

**G-15** Adding centers B6, B14, B9, and B19 to the sample of those in Prob. G-14, is there a significant difference between mean peak land values in the B and C centers (two-tailed test, $\alpha = 0.05$)? Show the hypothesis-testing procedure.

**G-16** If the centers A16, A8, A5, and A18 were added to the samples in Probs. G-14 and G-15, is there a significant difference between peak land values in the A-, B-, and C-level centers ($\alpha = 0.05$)? Show the hypothesis-testing procedure.

**G-17** Run a regression between peak land value (dependent variable) and ground floor area (independent variable) using the random sample centers A13, A6, A15, A16, A8, A5, and A18. Find:
(*a*) $R^2$, MAPD, MAPE, standard deviation, standard error of regression
(*b*) Estimated slope and intercept
(*c*) Standard error of the slope

**G-18** Run a log-linear regression using the sample data in Prob. G-17. Find:
(*a*) As in Prob. G-17(*a*) for peak land value (not its log)
(*b*) Estimated coefficient (constant) and exponent in $\text{PLV} = \alpha(\text{GFA})^{\beta}E$

**G-19** You are asked to forecast the *mean* 1970 level of sales (in 1970 dollars) for the shopping centers.

**G-20** Assuming that the weights of importance attached to $x_2$, $x_8$, and $x_9$ are 0.5, 0.2, and 0.3, respectively, develop an objective function for these variables (as per method 6 in Chap. 20).

**G-21** Assume you are a zoning administrator being approached by a new shopping center developer. The developer wants to maximize the objective function in Prob. G-20. If you restrict $x_3$ to no more than 70, $x_4$ to no more than 250, and $x_6$ between 300 and 700, and if $x_{11} = 2500$:
(*a*) What values of $x_3$, $x_4$, and $x_6$ will the developer select to maximize $z$?
(*b*) What will be the value of $z$?
(*c*) What will be the resultant values of $x_2$, $x_8$, and $x_9$?

**G-22** Assume now that you as zoning administrator want to have $x_2$ as close to 10,000 as possible, $x_8$ as close to 15,000 as possible, and $x_9$ as close to 100,000 as possible. Assume also the same weights of importance as in Prob. G-20 and the same constraints as in Prob. G-21:
(*a*) What values of $x_3$, $x_4$, and $x_6$ should you require to get as close to these goals (standards) as possible?
(*b*) What will be the value of $z$?
(*c*) What will be the resultant values of $x_2$, $x_8$, and $x_9$?

**G-23** Develop a systems dynamics program (DYNAMO) to simulate the time-varying changes in $x_2$, $x_8$, and $x_9$. With this, forecast the 1980 level of each.

**G-24**† Following is a scenario showing the development of a semi-hypothetical city known as Rurbania. The scenario covers 1744 to 1960, with Census data from 1900 on. You are asked to make a forecast of the 1975 population in Rurbania. Feel free to use any techniques discussed in this text. You can utilize any knowledge of events between 1960 to 1975 (e.g., national legislation, economic conditions, etc.).

## SCENARIO

### Development of the City of Rurbania (1744 to 1960)

Rurbania is an emerging metropolitan center (having reached the 50,000 level of population in 1950) in the South, with a fairly diverse economic base (light manufacturing and fabrication, regional retailing and wholesaling, services), serving as a regional center for various insurance companies and as the site of a major four-year university with significant law and medical schools. Its population is largely middle to upper-middle income families, whose heads of households work in the white-collar industries or are associated with the university. Rurbania is located beyond the immediate influence of other metropolitan centers and serves as a regional trade center for the surrounding rural areas. Most suburban residential areas have been annexed to the city as they emerged, although there are some scattered residential areas in the surrounding rural hinterland. In short, Rurbania is a "free-standing" metropolitan center (albeit relatively small). Yet there still is considerable undeveloped (mainly agricultural) land within the city limits.

Looking briefly at its past history, we find that Rurbania was established close to a beautifully mountainous area in 1744. The university came into existence in 1817, with an emphasis on the arts, law, and medicine. In the years before the Civil War the railroad came to Rurbania, and the city increasingly became a major center for transport of locally grown agricultural products like apples, peaches, and livestock. This process continued after the war.

The development of the streetcar in the early 1900s quickly altered the pattern of Rurbania's growth. For the first time it made suburban development possible and in addition served to tie the university to the city. Real estate values in areas served by the streetcars quickly increased and development soon followed.

† This problem is taken from J. W. Dickey, *Student Manual, Technological Forecasting Module*, Center for Urban and Regional Studies, Virginia Tech., Blacksburg, Va. (for the National Training and Development Service, Washington, D.C.), 1977.

At a broader scale, the train was the vital means of communications with the outside world and served as the artery for both commerce and industry. However, in 1897 the main rail company moved its shops to another city and thus the local economy suffered greatly. Yet this setback was soon to be overcome.

Although a lot could be said for the area's streets, roads, and highways in the early 1900s, they actually were in a terrible condition. Within the next 20 years this situation was to improve somewhat—at least in the central part of the city. The rural areas, on the other hand, were still to experience the inadequacies of these services. Gradually, however, improvements in this area would take place—largely as a result of the automobile. More and more real estate development, agriculture, commerce, and even the tourist trade of the area were dependent upon the auto and therefore good streets and roads. People realized that without these improvements progress would pass them by.

As the city became eager to adopt city ways, real estate developers increased their efforts to attract heavy industry into the area. Yet, the fact was that Rurbania could not really compete with her larger rivals in the deeper south. The area simply had no single staple waiting to be processed, nor did it have a ready supply of cheap labor. By the early 1920s, despite the growth of service companies, agricultural product processing firms, and a lawbook publisher, the largest employers were a woolen mill and two firms producing lumber products. The only local "industry" (if you can call it that) experiencing growth was real estate. Development companies flourished as the farmland on the outskirts of Rurbania was purchased, parceled into lots, and sold at great profits. At first this speculation was concentrated largely to the eastern and southeastern sections of the city. However, after 1900, thanks to the streetcar, the expansion of the university, and the street system, development was focused upon the northern and western fringes. By 1920 most of the choice property within or near the center city had been converted to business or residential purposes and therefore real estate interests turned even more attention to outlying areas.

It can be said that at the beginning of the 1920s Rurbania was a growing business, financial, and distribution center. The area was able to boast a relatively stable economy, a good streetcar system, adequate rail service, and substantial urban growth. The university also was growing, and in 1919 women were admitted to the graduate and professional schools. In addition, the amenities of city life attracted many from the more rural county as was the national trend at that time.

Surprisingly, the Great Depression was relatively kind to Rurbania. During this period the university enrollment actually increased slightly. Enough construction was available to provide for many jobs, and it was during this time that the stadium, the art museum, new engineering school, dormitories, additions to the university hospital, and a nearby national park and scenic drive, and various other school and highway projects were undertaken.

Probably the most unexpected result of the Depression was the change in attitude of bankers and local businessmen with respect to industrial development. Suddenly they were against having heavy manufacturing. They saw what had happened to localities dependent upon large industrial complexes for their economic well-being. As a result, they concluded that a well-balanced economy, dependent upon no single enterprise, was preferable. Also, during this period a great statesman's home was dedicated as a public shrine. This aroused a considerable interest in tourism and the economic potential of the area's historical past.

In 1940 nearly half of Rurbania's labor force was still involved in some form of agricultural production, and within the city center, business and professional services along with retail and wholesale activities provided the bulk of employment. Yet, despite the growth of the university and an improving economic situation, international concerns obviously were becoming increasingly important.

The community's most vital contribution to the war effort, aside from manpower, came from its textiles, lumbering and quarrying, welding, rubber processing, and frozen food activities. Retail businesses were concentrated in the

**Table G-3 Other pertinent events and facts and associated dates for Rurbania (1922 to 1960)**

| Date | Event or fact description |
|---|---|
| 1922 | First radio station in area |
| 1924 | Rebuilt home of one of America's most prominent forefather's opened to tourists |
| 1926 | High school for Negroes opened; no need to go elsewhere for this level of education |
| | Opening of major historical tourist site only 150 miles away |
| 1927 | Major country club opens |
| 1928 | City almost chosen as site for Democratic National Convention |
| | Only 60 percent of eligible school-aged children enrolled |
| | One of largest bequests ever made to a university: $5 million |
| | Switch to city manager form of government |
| 1930 | First air flights to/from city |
| | 1000 "free lodgers" in jail |
| 1933 | End of prohibition; many bars open downtown |
| 1936 | Opening of nearby national park and scenic drive |
| 1938 | Annexation of 2200 county residents |
| 1940 | Labor force divided as: 3500, business and professional services; 1778, manufacturing; 2302, wholesale and retail trade; 957, construction; 618, transportation, communication, and utilities; 92, mining; 3839, agriculture |
| 1942 | Tremendous labor shortage during World War II |
| | Lumber and rubber production big industries as well as food processing |
| 1946 | Temporary rent controls because of housing shortage |
| 1949 | Large city–county high school completed for Negroes |
| 1950 | Fraternal groups are important |
| | First Negro admitted to university law school |
| 1954 | New airport; 3540 outboarding per year |
| 1954–1959 | Integration of schools |
| 1956 | Segregation of buses/trains ceases |
| | Six-story department store opens downtown |
| 1959– | Some private schools established; gerrymandering of public school districts |
| 1959 | Major shopping center opens in county on edge of city |

**Table G-4 Relevant data on Rurbania (1900 to 1960)**

| Factor | Year | | | | | | |
|---|---|---|---|---|---|---|---|
| | 1900 | 1910 | 1920 | 1930 | 1940 | 1950 | 1960 |
| *Population* | | | | | | | |
| Total | 34,922 | 36,636 | 36,693 | 42,226 | 44,052 | 52,631 | 60,396 |
| Male | 16,980 | 17,814 | 18,056 | 20,941 | 21,603 | 26,997 | 30,485 |
| Female | 17,942 | 18,822 | 18,637 | 21,285 | 22,449 | 25,634 | 29,901 |
| White | 21,969 | 24,434 | 26,177 | 31,905 | 34,236 | 42,962 | 50,193 |
| Negro | 12,950 | 12,197 | 10,516 | 10,315 | 9,812 | 9,658 | 10,106 |
| *Dwellings* | 6,510 | 7,155 | 7,456 | 9,105 | 11,461 | 13,427 | 17,380 |
| *Farms* | | | | | | | |
| Number | 2,649 | 2,743 | 3,174 | 2,537 | 2,591 | 1,957 | 1,272 |
| Size (acres) | 151 | 141 | 123 | 137 | 130 | 164 | 217 |
| Value ($ per acre of land only) | 10.52 | 21.82 | 40.19 | 38.84 | 26.98 | 98.86 | 182.84 |
| *Manufacturing* | | | | | | | |
| Number of establishments | 151 | | 99 | 61 | 48 | 62 | 78 |
| Number of wager earners | 917 | | 1,440 | 2,297 | 2,709 | 2,853 | 4,278 |
| Value of products ($ millions) | 1.3 | | 3.8 | 5.4 | 5.3 | 16.3 | 48.3 |
| *University* | | | | | | | |
| Total students | | | | | 3,062 | 4,964 | 4,761 |
| Undergraduate | | | | | 2,061 | 3,621 | 3,062 |
| Graduate | | | | | 1,001 | 1,343 | 1,699 |

center city area. Because of labor shortages and good wages, submarginal farm operations were abandoned. Nevertheless, the area remained closely tied to its rural, service-oriented heritage. Neither large defense installations nor sprawling factories were left after the war's end.

Following the war the community, which was an outlet for agricultural produce and a trading center, would become an urban industrial-technical complex. Field after field was to become either residential property or pastureland and the people were to become commuters. During the 1950s one issue tended to dominate local life: segregation. Until August, 1955, only limited token integration, especially in the schools, had been achieved. However, defeats in the Federal Courts, and President Johnson's Civil Rights Act, eventually paved the way for integration.

In conclusion, the growth of Rurbania appears to be the result of its natural beauty, early history, and the university and activities associated with it. Tables G-3 and G-4 summarize relevant events, facts, and statistics on Rurbania in the period from 1900 to 1960.

# INDEX